Readings on the Sociology of the Family

READINGS ON THE SOCIOLOGY OF THE FAMILY

BERT N. ADAMS

University of Wisconsin

THOMAS WEIRATH

Wisconsin State University, Whitewater

Markham Publishing Company / Chicago

MARKHAM SOCIOLOGY SERIES
Robert W. Hodge, Editor

Adams, *Kinship in an Urban Setting*
Adams, *The American Family: A Sociological Interpretation*
Adams and Weirath, eds., *Readings on the Sociology of the Family*
Appelbaum, *Theories of Social Change*
Farley, *Growth of the Black Population: A Study of Demographic Trends*
Filstead, ed., *Qualitative Methodology: Firsthand Involvement with the Social World*
Karp and Kelly, *Toward an Ecological Analysis of Intermetropolitan Migration*
Laumann, Siegel and Hodge, eds., *The Logic of Social Hierarchies*
Zeitlin, ed., *American Society, Inc.: Studies of the Social Structure and Political Economy of the United States*

Introduction

The study of the family is only gradually coming into its own as a sub-area of sociology. For many years the family area has had two major foci: the practical orientation of the social worker and family counsellor and the descriptive emphasis of the sociologist. There has been little theory to answer the questions "how" and "why" about the family's history and current forms in the Western world. An important development during the 1960's, however, has been the several attempts at theory building which have been produced by family sociologists. Not only have general treatises on the family and industrialization appeared, but efforts have been made to understand and explain such subcategories of family experience as identification with parents, family disorganization, and the power relations between spouses. Some of these explanatory beginnings are found in books and monographs, while others are contained in journal articles and commentaries.

Several books of readings on the family are already available, ranging from extensive compilations of sixty or more readings to intensive collections of ten to fifteen major articles. Some of these volumes are excellent, and valuable for use in general courses on the family. Many of the extant volumes, however, still try to straddle the fence between the practitioner and the sociologist, and herein lies the major justification for the present volume. This book of readings seeks by means of three types of materials to introduce the reader to the American family from a sociological perspective. First, it includes conceptualizing and theoretical articles, often leading to the clarification of a sub-area of family life. Second, think-pieces on such subjects as the black family in America, love, women's family roles, and family reaction to death may aid the reader in grasping the significance of these issues. Third, a considerable number of research articles and notes are reprinted, covering Hutterite marriage, dating, premarital sex, family businesses, husband-wife social participation, and other subjects.

The editors determined at the outset that the guiding principle should be to include the minimum number of articles or excerpts necessary to introduce the most vital issues in the study of the American family. Sometimes, as in Section Two, American Family Varieties, this meant publishing pieces on the middle-class, lower-class, black, and religious minority family. At other times this principle led to the inclusion of two or more pieces on the same subject, either for the sake of difference of opinion (as in the case of Eckland's and Bolton's discussions of mate selection), or in order to include both a think-piece and one based on hard data (as is true of Rubin and Bell and Chaskes on premarital sex). It is our hope that student and instructor alike will find this book useful for factual information, but more importantly for discussion and debate—without overburdening the reader with papers on any one subject. Furthermore, it is our belief that those with a practical orientation to the family will likewise find this volume stimulating, perhaps even providing bases for decisions regarding how problems arising within the family might be resolved. Whatever else is accomplished, we are convinced that many of the readings that follow will help the reader to *think sociologically* about the American family.

Contents

The Family in Western History

Despite the fact that an understanding of the past is vital to comprehending the present, the perspective and techniques of the historian have seldom been adequately exploited by the sociologist. In fact, it has only been with increasing concern about contemporary social changes that sociologists have begun to realize the value of historical insight.

Nowhere in sociology is the dearth of historical information more evident than in the study of the family. Historians themselves have generally investigated political, legal, economic, and medical currents, the assumption being that these are the arenas where important events take place. As a result, the number of sources that deal directly with various historical aspects of the family is quite small, though growing. In the present section we present four of the better recent analyses of family features in Western history, including discussions of childhood and the family, marital roles, adolescence, and divorce.

The first selection contains three excerpts from Philippe Ariès' book *Centuries of Childhood*. Originally published in French, this book describes the development of the concepts of "child" and "family" in France between the Middle Ages and the Victorian era (ca. 1500–1850). Of special note is Ariès' historical methodology; he uses art works such as sculpture and painting as the basis for his generalizations. He finds the family of the earlier period very much embedded in the larger community, there being "no professional premises" for judge, merchant, or banker. In fact, all the major activities which comprised the life of the earlier period took place within the household. The basic change which Ariès finds is toward the "ascendancy of the family" in the Victorian era, with great concern for its sanctity and privacy from community milieu.

Several questions should arise as one reads Ariès' discussion. How valid are conclusions based upon art forms, and if they are valid are they so only for understanding the upper class or high status family or for understanding the average or typical family of that time? Is the family still ascendant today, or has it begun—since Victorian times—to give way to individualistic currents? In attempting to answer this latter question, the reader should compare Ariès' analysis with O'Néill's conclusions, later in this section, regarding *Divorce in the Progressive Era* (1880–1920).

The second selection concerns the important subject of the relation between industrialization and the family. William J. Goode is one of the most serious students of this relationship, and in the present paper he not only discusses marital role changes during the 19th and 20th centuries, but makes several comments regarding the historical study of the family. Pointing out the unknown as well as the known, Goode acknowledges his lack of historical sources. One way, he feels, to avoid endless debate about whether the family did or did not change with industrialization is to isolate specific family features or variables and note their stability or change. Among his conclusions are that the conjugal or nuclear family, rather than the socially embedded family unit of which Ariès speaks, has characterized low status groups for many centuries. Nor, he says, should one view the changes that have occurred merely as functions of external influences such as the development of the factory system. Rather, strains within the traditional family system itself often give rise to change when an alternative structural form is available. The reader should at some point in his study compare Goode's discussion with that of Dennis Wrong (Part VIII) regarding the breakup or reorganization of the contemporary family.

John and Virginia Demos' article is primarily an historical account of the rise, during the nineteenth and early twentieth centuries, of the concept of adolescence as a definable period of human growth. They show convincingly that the theory of adolescence is itself a product of the social and economic changes that removed young people from a productive role in the industrial economy. The reader should note their conclusions and use them to give an historical orientation to Farber's discussion (Part III) of independence seeking. In addition, he should evaluate the methodological technique of content analysis these authors and other historians have recently employed in order to quantify historical data.

The fourth selection is an excerpt from William O'Neill's interesting book on *Divorce in the Progressive Era*. Showing how progressive and conservative thinkers from 1880 to 1920 debated the virtues and evils of divorce, O'Neill concludes that the progressives had legal and public opinion on their side, while the conservatives were defending an outmoded Victorian morality. He notes that many progressive radicals were opposed to the family system itself, and that they agreed with the conservatives that the freedom to divorce would further the family's disintegration. Yet both groups were incorrect; instead of destroying the family, divorce was the safety valve the nuclear family needed to entrench itself even more in the social system of the industrial world. Not only should the reader compare Ariès, Goode, and O'Neill of this section and Wrong in Part VIII regarding the family's ascendancy, re-organization, or breakup; he should also refer back to O'Neill while reading the materials on divorce in Section Seven. What, one might ask, is the significance of contemporary divorce for the family?

In reading the selections of Part I four key questions should be kept in mind: (1) What key issues are being dealt with by the writer? (2) What "loose ends" or unanswered questions are left dangling? (3) What methodologies are employed and how valid do they seem to be? and (4) What is the time period with which the author is concerned?

The Family

PHILIPPE J. ARIÈS

The big house fulfilled a public function. In that society without a café or a 'public house', it was the only place where friends, clients, relatives and protégés could meet and talk. To the servants, clerics and clerks who lived there permanently, one must add the constant flow of visitors. The latter apparently gave little thought to the hour and were never shown the door, for the seventeenth-century pedagogues considered that the frequency and the time of these visits made a regular time-table, especially for meals, quite impossible. They regarded this irregularity as sufficiently harmful for children's education to justify sending them to college, in spite of the moral dangers of school life. The constant coming and going of visitors distracted children from their work. In short, visits gave the impression of being a positive occupation, which governed the life of the household and even dictated its mealtimes.

These visits were not simply friendly or social: they were also professional; but little or no distinction was made between these categories. A lawyer's clients were also his friends and both were his debtors. There were no professional premises, either for the judge or the merchant or the banker or the business man. Everything was done in the same rooms where he lived with his family.

Now these rooms were no more equipped for domestic work than they were for professional purposes. They communicated with one another, and the richest houses had galleries on the floor where the family lived. On the other floors the rooms were smaller, but just as dependent on one another. None had a special function, except the kitchen, and even then the cooking was often done in the hearth of the biggest room. Kitchen facilities in the towns did not allow of many refinements, and when there were guests, dishes were bought ready-cooked from the nearest caterer. When Hortensius, Francion's master, wanted to entertain some friends, he told his servant: 'Go and ask my neighbour the tavern-keeper to send me some of his best wine together with a roast. Now he said this because as it was already very late, and seeing that the latest to arrive had brought a hurdy-gurdy, he realized that he would have to offer supper to all the people in his room.' Francion went out with the servant. At the tavern-keeper's, 'we found nothing to suit us and we just bought some wine. We decided to go to the cook-shop on the Petit Pont. The servant bought a capon, and as he also wanted a sirloin of beef, went into all the cook-shops to see if he could find a good one.'

People lived in general-purpose rooms. They ate in them, but not at special tables: the 'dining-table' did not exist, and at mealtimes people set up folding trestle-tables, covering them with a cloth, as can be seen from Abraham Bosse's engravings. In the middle of the fifteenth century the humanist architect Alberti,[1] very much a *laudator temporis acti*, recalled the manners of his childhood: 'When we were young . . . the wife would send her husband a little jug of wine and something to eat with his bread; she dined at home and the men in the workshop.' He must not be taken literally, for this custom was still common in many artisan and peasants homes at the time he was writing. But he contrasted this simple custom with urban usage at the time: 'the table put up twice a day as for a solemn banquet'. In other words, it was a collapsible table, like so many pieces of furniture in the early seventeenth century.[2]

In the same rooms where they ate, people slept, danced, worked and received visitors. Engravings show the bed next to a dumb-waiter loaded with silverware, or in the corner of a room in which people are eating. A picture by P. Codde (1636) shows a dance: at the far end of the room in which the mummers are dancing, one can make out a bed with the curtains around it drawn.[3] For a long time the beds too were collapsible. It fell to the apprentices or pages to put them up when company was expected. The author of *Le Chastel de joyeuse destinée* congratulates the youths 'dressed in the livery of France' on their agility at setting up beds.[4] As late as the early seventeenth century Heroard wrote in his diary on March 12th, 1606: 'Once he [the future Louis XIII] had dressed, he helped to undo his bed.' March 14th, 1606: 'Taken to the Queen's apartments, he was lodged in the King's bedchamber [the King was away fighting] and helped to take his wooden bed round to the Queen: Mme de Montglat installed her bed there to sleep there.' On September 8th, 1608, just before setting out for Saint-Germain, 'he amused himself by undoing his bed himself, impatient to leave.'[5] Already, however, beds had become less mobile. Alberti, in his regrets for the good old days, wrote: 'I remember . . . seeing our most notable citizens, when they went off to the country, taking their beds and their kitchen utensils with them, and bringing them back on their return. Now the furniture of a single room is bigger and more expensive than that of a whole house used to be on a wedding-day.'[6] This transformation of the collapsible bed into a permanent piece of furniture undoubtedly marks an advance in domesticity. The ornamental bed, surrounded by curtains, was promptly seized upon by artists to illustrate the themes of private life: the room in which husband and wife came together, in which mothers gave birth, in which old men died, and also in which the lonely meditated. But the room containing the bed was not a bedroom because of that. It remained a public place. Consequently the bed had to be fitted with curtains which could be opened or drawn at will, so as to defend its occupants' privacy. For one rarely slept alone, but either with one's husband or wife or else with other people of one's own sex.

Since the bed was independent of the room in which it stood, there could be several in the same room, often one in each corner. Bussy-Rabutin tells how one day, in the course of a campaign, a girl frightened by the troops asked him for protection and hospitality: 'I finally told my servants to give her one of the four beds in my room.'[7]

It is easy to imagine the promiscuity which reigned in these rooms where nobody could be alone, which one had to cross to reach any of the communicating rooms, where several couples and several groups of boys or girls slept together (not to speak of the servants, of whom at least some must have slept beside their masters, setting up beds which were still collapsible in the room or just outside the door), in which people forgathered to have their meals, to receive their friends or clients, and sometimes to give alms to beggars. One can understand why, whenever a census was taken, the houses of notabilities were always more crowded than the little one-room or two-room apartments of ordinary folk. One has to regard these families, for all that they were giving birth to the modern concept of the family, not as refuges from the invasion of the world but as the centres of a populous society, the focal points of a crowded social life. Around them were established concentric circles of relations, increasingly loose towards the periphery: circles of relatives, friends, clients, protégés, debtors, etc.

THE FAMILY AND SOCIABILITY

The historian who studies inconographic documents in the hope of discovering the tremor of life which he can feel in his own existence, is surprised at the scarcity, at least until the sixteenth century, of interior and family scenes. He has to hunt for them with a magnifying-glass and interpret them with the aid of hypotheses. On the other hand he promptly makes the acquaintance of the principal character in this iconography, a character as essential as the chorus in the classical the-atre: the crowd—not the massive, anonymous crowd of our overpopulated cities, but the assembly of neighbours, women and children, numerous but not unknown to one another (a familiar throng rather similar to that which can be seen today in the *souks* of Arab towns or the *cours* of Mediterranean towns in the evening). It is as if everyone had come out instead of staying at home: there are scenes depicting streets and markets, games and crafts, soldiers and courtiers, churches and tortures. In the street, in the fields, outside, in public, in the midst of a collective society—that is where the artist chooses to set the events or people he wishes to depict.

The idea of isolating individual or family portraits gradually emerged. But the importance which we have given to these early attempts should not blind us to the fact that they were rare and timid to begin with. For a long time—until the seventeenth century, when the iconography of the family became extremely rich—the important thing was the representation of public life. This representation doubtless corresponds to a profound reality. Life in the past, until the seventeenth century, was lived in public. We have given a good many examples of the ascendancy of society. The traditional ceremonies which accompanied marriage and which were regarded as more important than the religious ceremonies (which for a long time were entirely lacking in solemnity), the blessing of the marriage bed; the visit paid by the guests to the newly-married pair when they were already in bed; the rowdyism during the wedding night, and so on—afford further proof of society's rights over the privacy of the couple. What objection could there be when in fact privacy scarcely ever existed, when people lived on top of one another, masters and servants, children and adults, in houses open at all hours to the indiscretions of callers? The density of society left no room for the family. Not that the family did not exist as a reality: it would be paradoxical to deny that it did. But it did not exist as a concept.

We have studied the birth and development of this concept of the family from the fifteenth century to the eighteenth. We have seen how, until the eighteenth century, it failed to destroy the old sociability; admittedly it was limited to the well-to-do classes, those of the notabilities, rural or urban, aristocratic or middle-class, artisans or merchants. Starting in the eighteenth century, it spread to all classes and imposed itself tyrannically on people's consciousness. The evolution of the last few centuries has often been presented as the triumph of individualism over social constraints, with the family counted among the latter. But where is the individualism in these modern lives, in which all the energy of the couple is directed to serving the interests of a deliberately restricted posterity? Was there not greater individualism in the gay indifference of the prolific fathers of the ancien regime? Admittedly the modern family no longer has the same material reality as under the ancien regime, when it was identified with an estate and a reputation. Except in cases whose importance is constantly diminishing, the problem of the transmission of property takes second place to that of the children's welfare, and that welfare is no longer necessarily seen in loyalty to a professional tradition. The family has become an exclusive society in which its members are happy to stay and which they enjoy evoking, as General de Martange did in his letters as early as the end of the eighteenth century. The whole evolution of our contemporary manners is unintelligible if one neglects this astonishing growth of the concept of the family. It is not individualism which has triumphed, but the family.

But this family has advanced in proportion as sociability has retreated. It is as if the modern family had sought to take the place of the old social relationships (as these gradually defaulted), in order to preserve mankind from an unbearable moral solitude. Starting in the eighteenth century, people began defending themselves against a society whose constant intercourse had hitherto been the source of education, reputation and wealth. Henceforth a fundamental movement would destroy the old connections between masters and servants, great and small, friends or clients. It was a movement which was sometimes retarded by the inertia of geographical or social isolation. It would be quicker in Paris than in other towns, quicker in the middle classes than in the lower classes. Everywhere it reinforced private life at the expense of neighbourly relationships, friendships, and traditional contacts. The history of modern manners can be reduced in part to this long effort to break away from others, to escape from a society whose pressure had become unbearable. The house lost the public character which it had in certain cases in the seventeenth century, in favour of the club and the café, which in their turn have become less crowded. Professional and family life have stifled that other activity which once invaded the whole of life: the activity of social relations.

One is tempted to conclude that sociability and the concept of the family were incompatible, and could develop only at each other's expense.

> He was free, infinitely free, so free that he was no longer conscious of pressing on the ground. He was free of that weight of human relationships which impedes movement, those tears, those farewells, those reproaches, those joys, all that a man caresses or tears every time he sketches out a gesture, those countless bonds which tie him to others and make him heavy.
> (Saint-Exupéry)

CONCLUSION

In the Middle Ages, at the beginning of modern times, and for a long time after that in the lower classes, children were mixed with adults as soon as they were considered capable of doing without their mothers or nannies, not long after a tardy weaning (in other words, at about the age of seven). They immediately went straight into the great community of men, sharing in the work and play of their companions, old and young alike. The movement of collective life carried along in a single torrent all ages and classes, leaving nobody any time for solitude and privacy. In these crowded, collective existences there was no room for a private sector. The family fulfilled a function; it ensured the transmission of life, property and names; but it did not penetrate very far into human sensibility. Myths such as courtly and precious love denigrated marriage, while realities such as the apprenticeship of children loosened the emotional bond between parents and children. Medieval civilization had forgotten the *paideia* of the ancients and knew nothing as yet of modern education. That is the main point: it had no idea of education. Nowadays our society depends, and knows that it depends, on the success of its educational system. It has a system of education, a concept of education, an awareness of its importance. New sciences such as psycho-analysis, pediatrics and psychology devote themselves to the problems of childhood, and their findings are transmitted to parents by way of a mass of popular literature. Our world is obsessed by the physical, moral and sexual problems of childhood.

This preoccupation was unknown to medieval civilization, because there was no problem for the Middle Ages: as soon as he had been weaned, or soon after, the child became the natural companion of the adult. The age groups of Neolithic times, the Hellenistic *paideia*, presupposed a difference and a transition between the world of children and that of adults, a transition made by means of an initiation or an education. Medieval civilization failed to perceive this difference and therefore lacked this concept of transition.

The great event was therefore the revival, at the beginning of modern times, of an interest in education. This affected a certain number of churchmen, lawyers and scholars, few in number in the fifteenth century, but increasingly numerous and influential in the sixteenth and seventeenth centuries when they merged with the advocates of religious reform. For they were primarily moralists rather than humanists: the humanists remained attached to the idea of a general culture spread over the whole of life and showed scant interest in an education confined to children. These reformers, these moralists, whose influence on school and family we have observed in this study, fought passionately against the anarchy (or what henceforth struck them as the anarchy) of medieval society, where the Church, despite its repugnance, had long ago resigned itself to it and urged the faithful to seek salvation far from this pagan world, in some monastic retreat. A positive moralization of society was taking place: the moral aspect of religion was gradually triumphing in practice over the sacred or eschatological aspect. This was how these champions of a moral order were led to recognize the importance of education. We have noted their influence on the history of the school, and the transformation of the free school into the strictly disciplined college. Their writings extended from Gerson to Port-Royal, becoming increasingly frequent in the sixteenth and seventeenth centuries. The religious orders founded at that time, such as the Jesuits or the Oratorians, became teaching orders, and their teaching was no longer addressed to adults like that of the preachers or mendicants of the Middle Ages, but was essentially meant for children and young people. This literature, this propaganda, taught parents that they were spiritual guardians, that they were responsible before God for the souls, and indeed the bodies too, of their children.

Henceforth it was recognized that the child was not ready for life, and that he had to be subjected to a special treatment, a sort of quarantine, before he was allowed to join the adults.

This new concern about education would gradually install itself in the heart of society and transform it from top to bottom. The family ceased to be simply an institution for the transmission of a name and an estate—it assumed a moral and spiritual function, it moulded bodies and souls. The care expended on children inspired new feelings, a new emotional attitude, to which the iconography of the seventeenth century gave brilliant and insistent expression: the modern concept of the family. Parents were no longer content with setting up only a few of their children and neglecting the others. The ethics of the time ordered them to give all their children, and not just the eldest—and in the late seventeenth century even the girls—a training for life. It was understood that this training would be provided by the school. Traditional apprenticeship was replaced by the school, an utterly transformed school, an instrument of strict discipline, protected by the law-courts and the police-courts. The extraordinary development of the school in the seventeenth century was a consequence of the new interest taken by parents in their children's education. The moralists taught them that it was their duty to send their children to school very early in life: 'Those parents', states a text of 1602, 'who take an interest in their children's education [*liberos erudiendos*] are more worthy of respect than those who just bring them into the world. They give them not only life but a good and holy life. That is why those parents are right to send their children at the tenderest age to the market of true wisdom [in other words to college] where they will become the architects of their own fortune, the ornaments of their native land, their family and their friends.'[8]

Family and school together removed the child from adult society. The school shut up a childhood which had hitherto been free within an increasingly severe disciplinary system, which culminated in the eighteenth and nineteenth centuries in the total claustration of the boarding-school. The solicitude of family, Church, moralists and administrators deprived the child of the freedom he had hitherto enjoyed among adults. It inflicted on him the birch, the prison cell—in a word, the punishments usually reserved for convicts from the lowest strata of society. But this severity was the expression of a very different feeling from the old indifference: an obsessive love which was to dominate society from the eighteenth century on. It is easy to see why this invasion of the public's sensibility by childhood should have resulted in the now better-known phenomenon of Malthusianism or birth-control. The latter made its appearance in the eighteenth century just when the family had finished organizing itself around the child, and raised the wall of private life between the family and society.

The modern family satisfied a desire for privacy and also a craving for identity: the members of the family were united by feeling, habit and their way of life. They shrank from the promiscuity imposed by the old sociability. It is easy to understand why this moral ascendancy of the family was originally a middle-class phenomenon: the nobility and the lower class, at the two extremities of the social ladder, retained the old idea of etiquette much longer and remained more indifferent to outside pressures. The lower classes retained almost down to the present day the liking for crowds. There is therefore a connection between the concept of the family and the concept of class. Several times in the course of this study we have seen them intersect. For centuries the same games were common to the different classes; but at the beginning of modern times a choice was made among them: some were reserved for people of quality, the others were abandoned to the children and the lower classes. The seventeenth-century charity schools, founded for the poor, attracted the children of the well-to-do just as much; but after the eighteenth century the middle-class families ceased to accept this mixing and withdrew their children from what was to become a primary-school system, to place them in the *pensions* and the lower classes of the colleges, over which they established a monopoly. Games and schools, originally common to the whole of society, henceforth formed part of a class system. It was all as if a rigid, polymorphous social body had broken up and had been replaced by a host of little societies, the families, and by a few massive groups, the classes; families and classes brought together individuals related to one another by their moral resemblance and by the identity of their way of life, whereas the old unique social body embraced the greatest possible variety of ages and classes. For these classes were all the more clearly distinguished and graded for being close together in space. Moral distances took the place of physical distances. The strictness of external signs of respect and of differences in dress counterbalanced the familiarity of communal life. The valet never left his master, whose friend and accomplice he was, in accordance with an emotional code to which we have lost the key today, once we have left adolescence behind; the haughtiness of the master matched the insolence of the servant and restored, for better or for worse, a hierarchy which excessive familiarity was perpetually calling in question.

People lived in a state of contrast; high birth or great wealth rubbed shoulders with poverty, vice with virtue, scandal with devotion. Despite its shrill contrasts, this medley of colours caused no surprise. A man or woman of quality felt no embarrassment at visiting in rich clothes the poor wretches in the prisons, the hospitals or the streets, nearly naked beneath their rags. The juxtaposition of these extremes no more embarrassed the rich than it humiliated the poor. Something of this moral atmosphere still exists today in southern Italy. But there came a time when the middle class could no longer bear the pressure of the multitude or the contact of the lower class. It seceded: it withdrew from the vast polymorphous society to organize itself separately, in a homogeneous environment, among its families, in homes designed for privacy, in new districts kept free from all lower-class contamination. The juxtaposition of inequalities, hitherto something perfectly natural, became intolerable to it: the revulsion of the rich preceded the shame of the poor. The quest for privacy and the new desires for comfort which it aroused (for there is a close connection between comfort and privacy) emphasized even further the contrast between the material ways of life of the lower and middle classes. The old society concentrated the maximum number of ways of life into the minimum of space and accepted, if it did not impose, the bizarre juxtaposition of the most widely different classes. The new society, on the contrary, provided each way of life with a confined space in which it was understood that the dominant features should be respected, and that each person had to resemble a conventional model, an ideal type, and never depart from it under pain of excommunication.

The concept of the family, the concept of class, and perhaps elsewhere the concept of race, appear as manifestations of the same intolerance towards variety, the same insistence on uniformity.

NOTES

[1] P. H. Michel, *La Pensée de L. B. Alberti,* 1930.

[2] Pere du Colombieri, *Style Henri IV ct Louis XIII,* 1941, p. 49.

[3] P. Codde, reproduced in Berndt no. 187.

[4] Droz and Piaget, *Jardin de Plaisance,* p. 93.

[5] Héroard, *Journal sur l'enfance et la jeunesse de Louis XIII,* edited by E. Soulie and E. de Barthelemy, 2 vols. 1968.

[6] P. H. Michel, *op. cit.*

[7] Bussy-Rabatim, *Mémoires,* 3 vols., 1704.

[8] *Academia sive speculum vitaie scholasticae,* Arnheim, 1602.

The Process of Role Bargaining in the Impact of Urbanization and Industrialization on Family Systems

WILLIAM J. GOODE

The study of urbanization and industrialization is only one part of the study of social change, but in our time it has become the main focus of this field because they are the major social processes going on in all parts of the world. Unfortunately, the massive and dramatic character of both processes tempts us into supposing that by merely labelling them "urbanization and industrialization" we have in fact explained everything that happens today, including family changes. Moreover, this constricted focus tempts us to ignore great periods of change which have occurred in the past. For example, had we wished to study social change between the fifth and seventh centuries A.D. in Western Europe, we would have focused on *de*-urbanization and the *lowering* degree of technological achievement. Another weakness is that our contemporary analysis is rooted in only a shallow manner in any body of theory; social change remains perhaps the least rigorously developed of all the fields of social science. On the other hand, in our present pursuit of these matters, we are gathering many empirical data, so that perhaps eventually some adequate generalizations may emerge. Certainly our studies will not soon lead to "laws of sequence", which must be the aim of a general theory of social change. However, because these processes are occurring under so many conditions and in so many different social structures, perhaps we may at least eventually discover more rigorous causal relationships. That is, there are enough variations to permit much combination and re-combination of factors, and perhaps by statistical analysis we can factor out some relationships between one variable and another in spite of the complexity of the empirical phenomena.

In spite of our proper optimism about long-term results, we continue to fall victim to several confusions, and are harried by a number of difficulties. Notable among these difficulties is the simple lack of information about the past history of family systems under varying conditions of urbanization or industrialization. As far as I have been able

Reprinted from *Current Sociology*, Vol. 12, with permission of Basil Blackwell, Publisher, Oxford, England. Footnotes have been renumbered.

to ascertain, there is no good general history of the family in any language. Historians do not often choose the topic of the family, but are rather interested in political and economic events. On the other hand, sociologists and psychologists almost never are competent historians. In addition, there is no adequate history of the family even in the two cultures that are best known to us in the distant past, that is, Rome and Greece. Third, if we instead confine ourselves to only the last half-century, I think it is fair to say that there are almost no histories which document and demonstrate with any precision exactly what changes have taken place even in European countries. One could perhaps put together a fair contrast between the past and the present family systems for a tiny handful of primitive societies to which anthropologists have gone recently and in the past. This might be done, for example, for a few American Indian tribes. Over a short generation, Margaret Mead has made some comparisons of this kind for a Melanesian group, the Manus. Next, we should not underrate the difficulty of measuring with precision the changes which have taken place under the impact of urbanization or industrialization, even in the cultures which we do know well. Our best data about the family have been gathered in the present period, but we have no base-line data from half a century ago with which to compare them. We can sometimes compare a few vital statistics indexes such as fertility, divorce, illegitimacy, or age at marriage, but these are relatively small bits of data with which to reconstruct past family relationships.[1]

We are also handicapped greatly by the fact that *myths* about even the recent past of the family are very common. Indeed, it is safe to say that almost every reader of this paper accepts some of these myths about his own family system. I need not describe them in detail, but may comment that within the United States the myth takes the form that half a century ago the typical family lived in a self-sufficient manner, and in great harmony, with all of the extended family under one roof. The elders controlled marriages to a considerable degree, and marriages were very early. However, in fact we know little about the family patterns of half a century ago, for they have not been studied in any detail, and we do know enough to suspect that the picture often presented in text-books is a legend or myth.[2]

RELATIONSHIPS BETWEEN URBANIZATION AND INDUSTRIALIZATION

Especially during the 1920's and 1930's, when American sociologists studied the disorganization of American cities, the effects of urbanization and industrialization were widely confused with each other. I believe this confusion is common in European social thought as well. Here again, we not only lack historical perspective, but we do not have adequate control over quantitive data. Very likely this is inherent in the problem itself. Urbanization probably never occurs without some advance in technological level, beginning with those first important technological advances which permitted agricultural families to feed more than themselves, and thus to have something to trade to others. On the other hand, cities have existed for centuries in a relatively stable way, without cumulative changes in technology. In our own time, by contrast, industrialization probably never takes place without urbanization. Since, however, we do not have good data about urban life under relatively static conditions, we cannot as yet say just what is the impact of the city on the family or indeed other institutions as well.

We must not only distinguish urbanization and industrialization; we must also distinguish urban life from the processes of *urbanization*. In a culture that is *becoming* urban, of course, the breakdown of many institutions will occur. However, a *re*-stabilization may take place as well, so that over time the family life within cities may come to be guided normatively as fully as that in rural areas.[3] When families *come* to the city, changes in their social patterns may occur, and indeed from Plato's time onward, comments about the differences between urban and rural life have been made. What breaks down may be only the older rural virtues, perhaps a delight in war, and the control by the elders over family patterns. Since this kind of comment is nearly always a political and ideological one, by which the commentator exhorts his listeners to return to ancient virtues, we have little way of knowing how many elements in all social relationships are changed, or whether we moderns would approve some of those changes which a given commentator thought bad.

The distinction may be illustrated in one way by referring to the United States. Here the so-called urban disorganization was evident in the late nineteenth century and it continued through the 1920's at least, attracting the attention of many social analysts, who deplored the passing of the frontier and of rural virtues. However, in the last two decades, American sociology has paid little attention to urban disorganization, for two reasons. One is that it soon became evident that the term "urbanization" covered far too many variables to be usable in quantitative and precise research. Thus, "urbanization" is not the *cause* of changes; it *is* those changes.

Second, and perhaps more important, is that the United States has moved into a new stage of urbanism, one which is perhaps unique in world history, in which the differences between rural and urban social patterns have decreased considerably. The rural areas have also become "urban" and the populations in the cities and suburbs do not exhibit to the same degree the anomic rootlessness of a generation or so ago. The anomie of modern times does not seem to be due to the city as such, but to the total impact of industrial life.

Nor do we have as yet an adequate statement of the variables which make up industrialization or industrialism. We can define these in role terms, using a common terminology (T. Parsons) which emphasizes the functional specificity of role relationships, their universalism, and their basis in occupational achievement. This complex seems to be relatively uncommon in the history of the world, and seems to have developed initially out of the capitalistic ethos with its roots in ascetic Protestantism. Certainly the complex is not directly due to the machine as such. We are most aware of this in the United States, where far from "worshipping the machine" as the European often supposes, we are enough the masters of it to be able to treat it quite casually. Instead, it is a civilization based upon technical knowledge and on a widespread system of education, which emphasizes the pursuit by the individual of a high occupational achievement if that is possible.

Nevertheless, among the various arguments which have been developed to indicate the relationships between industrialism and the family, none of them has been able to show precisely *where* the impact occurs. It can be shown, as I and others have done, that the ideal-typical nuclear or conjugal family is relatively well "fitted" to the open-class industrial system, whether capitalist or not, but precisely how these two *interact* with one another is not at all clear even in theory. Specifically, we do not distinguish three separate sets of family complexes: the ideal, the ideal-typical, and the real. All are important, but how do they interact?

It has been argued, for example, that the industrial system requires geographical mobility in order for the individual to find the job that is suited to him. Thus the family is reduced to the conjugal unit. On the other hand, industrialism equally permits communication and rapid transportation (the real) so that the individual can maintain an extended kin network if he *wishes* to do so (the ideal). (Granted, it costs time and money.) The high degree of class mobility in an industrial system means that siblings may move to very different class positions, so that kin relationships might be somewhat awkward for them, with their different tastes and values. On the other hand, these class differences are not likely to be great, and the interaction may be only intermittent and on festive occasions, so that the awkwardness is not a serious matter. As a consequence it does not seem likely that this is a *major* factor in undermining kin networks in industrialized social systems.

Certainly some impact occurs through the industrial system offering employment to the young and to wives, so that both can support themselves without being dependent upon a set of family elders or (in the case of the wife) the husband. To this extent, the power of the male and of the elders is somewhat reduced. A further factor which I believe to be of very great importance in the countries now undergoing industrialization and urbanization is the spread of what I would call the "ideology of the conjugal family", an ideology which seems as potent as that of freedom and democracy. It offers to the disadvantaged, the young, and to women a set of arguments for greater freedom of choice and decision, and denies the validity of many customs in each culture. However, there seems to be at present no way of assessing the power of this ideological component in industrialization.

Without question the definiteness of role obligations of the old extended family system does weaken under urbanization and industrialization. This does not necessarily mean "disorganization" because the new patterns may be able to cope as well with the problems of modern society as the old ones coped with their problems. At present, I do not see that anyone has been able to show even in theoretical terms precisely why this weakening of role obligations takes place. One is almost forced to say that if everything changes, then so does the family. Or possibly under older systems the various activities of the society, such as political and economic action, utilized the kin framework as a way of allocating energies and making decisions relative to these various activities. However, family and kin as such were not crucial to this process. With the emergence of new agencies and facilities, the extended kin network is simply supplanted. It was a skeleton based upon a number of reciprocities, which failed as soon as other agencies arose, which facilitated those same payments or counter-payments. Offering alternative pay-offs, they are at least able to weaken the social controls of kin over kin. It is not so much that the new system is incompatible, as that it offers an alternative pattern of payments.

Nevertheless, even in this conception, the theoretical relations among these factors seem vague and not at all rigorous.

CONJUGAL FAMILY UNDER INDUSTRIALIZATION

But though we are safe in asserting that the extended kin network breaks down under industrialization in every country for which we have data, we must not fall into the common error of supposing that the ideal-typical conjugal family actually occurs as a real system in *any* society— if by that we mean that the nuclear family exists without any extended kinship ties. There are only a few places in which such a relatively complete breakdown has moved far, without specific political pressures in that direction. These are all areas in which there has been a considerable amount of cultural and social destruction, a state of anomie. They may be found in the populations of many of the Caribbean countries, such as Jamaica, the Dominican Republic, Haiti, and so on.[4] The same breakdown may be found in several industrializing and urbanizing areas of sub-Saharan Africa. In these areas the illegitimacy rate is high, marriage is greatly delayed, concubinage is common, and unions between men and women are highly unstable. However, I believe that in *no* society is the conjugal system in this sense to be found throughout all classes. In two countries, a reduction of the strength of kinship ties *within* the nuclear family—to this extent, a step *beyond* the conjugal system—has been attempted, in the Chinese communes and in the Israeli kibbutzim. Note, however, that in neither case did the system develop without external ideological and political pressures, and in neither case has this pattern become statistically normal for the entire population. It is entirely possible that such a system fits better the demands of industrialization than even the hypothetical conjugal family, though again its costs may be eventually very high.

With respect to Western countries, none has developed such a system. Very few studies have attempted to trace out the kinship network of individual families by empirical means, but all of them show that families in at least the United States and England recognize a considerable number of kin—about a hundred—with whom the family members have some continuing relations.[5]

Moreover, it is very likely theoretically impossible for the conjugal system in this sense to exist. At a minimum, a *second* layer of kinfolk will always be included, by virtue of their relationship to members of the nuclear family itself. Thus, for example, children cannot ignore their grandparents without angering or hurting their own parents. They cannot repudiate easily their siblings-in-law without annoying their own siblings. They cannot refuse contact with uncles and aunts without hurting or angering their own parents. Thus, at a minimum, some network of kin continues to exist beyond the nuclear family, and though empirically it is evident that one cannot describe a typical network for all families, all of them do recognize many kin.

On the other hand, just how strong or emotionally intense these ties are, how frequently they are reasserted, and how much flow of payments and counter-payments of services, resources, or even affection takes place, we do not know as yet.

What is certain, however, is that this kin network is not at all a "holdover" or "an outmoded inheritance from the past". It is fed by the continuing demands of the present system. Finally, we do not know at present how much this system has been modified, at least in the United States, from the family system of two or three generations ago. Change is always more dramatic and perhaps more easily visible than stability, and it may be that in many crucial respects the system has changed only slightly over this period.

I should like, however, to follow two brief lines of inquiry with respect to the impact of industrialization and urbanization on the family. One of these might be called macro-structural, since it deals with the differential impact of industrialization and urbanization on different classes. Specifically, I should like to ask, *where* is the impact strongest, and how does it operate? Secondly, I should like to pursue briefly an inquiry which might well occupy a lengthy analysis, and which is essentially micro-structural. I should like to ask, what are some of the specific strains in certain family systems of the world, and thus which ones are more likely to give way when alternative arrangements or role-patterns are altered by the new form of society. In my own terminology, which of these role-relationships is likely to give way because under the new industrial or urban system one or the other individual can now obtain a better "role-bargain"?[6]

THE CLASS DIFFERENTIAL IMPACT OF INDUSTRIALIZATION AND URBANIZATION

Scanty and scattered, but persuasive, data suggest that in the most industrialized of countries there are substantial class differentials in family patterns. In some countries the divorce rate, and in most the illegitimacy rate, are lower as one moves up the social scale. Marriages occur later, a higher proportion of the men eventually get married, and a somewhat lower proportion of the women. It seems likely that fertility is higher, at least at the very top of the class pyramid. Certainly at the top there is more control over the courtship and dating behaviour of the young, through private schools, choice of neighbourhoods, the debut, and so on. Apparently the dominance of the male is greater than in the lower strata. Of course, the upper strata enjoy longer lives. They engage in more family rituals and get-togethers, and through their command over the facilities of transportation and communication they maintain larger networks than do the lower strata.

Here we seem to have a small paradox. The families that by definition are most "adjusted" to industralization and urbanization, since they are most successful in it and enjoy more of its fruits, seem at the same time to exhibit family patterns that are farthest removed from the "conjugal family" that has been so widely described as characteristic of and harmonious with the new era of industrialization and urbanization. Whence come these differences? How can the paradox be resolved?

Let us examine, then, the impact of these processes on the extremes of class position so as to see more clearly just how it is that the Western upper strata even now, after several hundred years of industrialization, have maintained a more active kinship network. Perhaps it is best to begin by noting the obvious points that *given* such an extended upper class kin network, the older generation has a greater amount of facilities with which to reward or punish those who conform or fail to conform. In terms of role-bargaining, it is to the interest of the younger to conform to the goals and persuasions of their elders. Moreover, it is not possible to maintain an upper stratum in any strength unless the network is extensive enough to interlock in the same fabric nearly all of the relevant families. If there are gaps, if parts of the network are excluded to some extent, these may then establish marital relationships with families still lower down, and thus create a bridge by which the lower families can rise.

By contrast, among lower class strata the other family units of the network are of no great utility to any given family because they are without facilities. There can be little collective action, and there is no family leader, simply because no leader is able to muster sufficient sanctions or resources with which to press for conformity. Moreover, because there is little sense of the significance or worth of their own family line, the motivation to do so will be low.

Considering for a moment the initial situation in industrialization, we must keep in mind that a primary point or focus of impact is in the opportunities for new jobs, new areas of achievement, and thus at least to some extent an opening of class barriers. The fully industrialized system must be classified as "open class", though, of course, in all systems the sons of upper-stratum families obtain a disproportionate share of the rewards.

When, then, a movement towards industrialization begins and thus opportunities open, necessarily these are at least potentially threatening to established family patterns because they do offer alternative opportunities, new bases on which the younger members may establish an independent existence.

The opportunities may be found in several directions. One, there are alternative ways of life now open, different from those of the individual's family of orientation. That is, there are new ways of thinking, of choosing, of furnishing one's home, in short, an increasingly wide gamut of styles of life become available. Moreover, one *can* make this choice because one can obtain support from new colleagues, from a new stratum, or from new cliques, with which to resist the pressures of one's family of orientation. Secondly, and perhaps more important, an alternative socio-economic base is offered, which by definition is not fully under the control of one's family elders (because this opportunity will be based to some extent on achievement) so that the individual can obtain some independence from his family. In short, he does not have to reciprocate support and subsistence by submission to the judgments of his elders.

Let us consider this large factor in detail for just a moment. First of all, such an alternative economic base rarely develops in a static, land-based economy. The land is taken up already. There is only so much to go around, and one's livelihood depends upon one's relationship to that land. Failure to conform may mean that the individual no longer has a basis for his livelihood. Next, however, there *is* expansion when a people begins to move beyond the frontier. Thus, the frontier opportunities in the United States certainly undermined the older kinship networks there, precisely because some part of the younger generation always had the alternative of moving to the frontier and thus establishing themselves independently and being freed thereby of having to conform to the family judgments of their elders.

Third, a similar expansion can occur when the industrial economy begins to grow. Here the family typically does not own the jobs and they are not handed down from father to son.

An expansion can occur through war and conquest. This is the equivalent of the land frontier. A country may establish colonies and new governments, or by conquest take over governmental systems. This especially occurred in the New World during the sixteenth century, when so many Portuguese and Spanish men of relatively low origins achieved high positions. Of course, most of the important jobs are given to the upper strata, but those from lower positions do have some chance, and are thereby freed of having to conform to the family customs of their stratum. Their kin network has no way of paying them or punishing them enough to counter these great opportunities.

We also should keep in mind that such an expansion may occur in the area of religion. Much of the general economic expansion that began to gather momentum in the eleventh century took the form of an extensive development of the enterprise of the Church. Monasteries, nunneries, and convents were founded, and numerous churches were built during this period. One may call this the functional equivalent of war in a different institution, religion. New job opportunities were thus opened. Again the highest positions were typically given to the aristocracy, but once again some were given to those of lower origins, especially when they had talent.

For all of these reasons, the open class pattern does at least threaten to undermine a given family system. To the extent that the individual can work out a role bargain to his advantage, while rejecting some of the conformity and submission characteristic of all families, to that extent the old kinship system is undermined, no matter what form its extension took, whether matrilineal or patrilineal, a four- or eight-class marriage system, whether Crow or Dakota systems.

However, such a theoretical comment merely suggests that industrialization might undermine *any* extended family system. Why would there be a *class* difference? The answer seems to lie in the fact that in all of these patterns of expansion and opening of the class system to which we refer, the upper class families do in fact control those opportunities, and far more than the lower class controls the new opportunities given to some of its members. Fundamentally, we can see that for the lowest stratum, the new opportunities come by virtue of actions taken by those *outside* their own family patterns. These are decisions made by a foreign elite (such as conquerors) or by the native elite who are opening some new frontier. Note that even in a land frontier situation, some upper-stratum family has typically been given large land grants. If there are new governments and colonies, it is the existing elite families who have founded them. If there are wars, these were organized by the elite. The monasteries and churches were typically built by the elite, and often they furnished much of the funds. In the emerging countries of today, with their beginnings of capitalism, the new industries and factories are often founded by elite families, sometimes with pooled family funds.

In short, the differential impact may be seen in the basic elements of the process, that in these new opportunities which create an open-class system, the upper-stratum families control these opportunities because they made them. In addition, aside from the economic advantages which the upper strata can offer to their own sons, they offer social position. The sons must maintain their ties if they are to keep their status. The families in somewhat lower strata, however, did not create them and do not control them. Often, too, the new opportunities move these people geographically distant, and there are no strong motivations to maintain family relations. Consequently they cannot refuse them these new opportunities, to their own younger members who desire to utilize and thus to become somewhat more independent of their family ties. To that extent, then, we would expect what seems in fact to take place, that the upper stratum, both initially and for a considerable period afterwards, is in fact less affected in its family structure than the lower strata. Thus we have the apparent paradox resolved, that the families that are most successful in the industrialized and urbanized system are precisely those families which are farthest removed in pattern from the conjugal family which is thought to be so harmoniously adjusted to industrialization.

The foregoing discussion assumes that family members, especially the elders, will keep control over the younger members if they can, and will maintain the system if they can, and that the younger members are typically subordinate, but at various junctures they do feel strained in adjusting to the demands of the elders. At certain points they would like to have their own way. This does not seem a far-fetched assumption, since it is a widespread observation in all cultures. The older members do benefit in power and prestige if they keep this control, since typically the system emphasizes the importance of the elders. The elders in addition want to keep the old values intact because they have been living by them throughout their lives, and to deny them now is to deny essentially the value and worth of their own lives. Finally, the elders do not have to face the same decisions, for many of the decisions faced by the young were settled long ago by the elders, such as whom to marry, where to settle, whether to obey most of the family rules, and so on.

But there is still a question as to the class differential *value* of this maintenance, that is, assuming that the upper strata *can* maintain their family systems better, are they more strongly *motivated* to do so?

It seems likely, first of all, that the kin network is not generally so valuable, even in a pre-industralizing phase, to the family members of the lower strata, as the network of the upper-class families is to their members, so that one would not expect the motivation to be as deeply embedded in each individual through the socialization process.

Secondly, among lower-class networks, the individual has mainly to keep on good terms with his own father and his father's immediate ruler or lord, but the rest of his kin are not so important, simply because the rest of the network cannot pay off or punish the young man very much.

Thirdly, the differential mortality and perhaps the differential fertility as well have probably favoured the upper class in most countries where the mortality has been high. They have been better fed and somewhat better protected against most natural elements and marauders.

Moreover, the upper strata have had the advantage that they could command what transportation and communication facilities existed, so that entirely aside from whether the *values* or ideals of an extended network were stronger or weaker in the two extreme class positions, very likely the upper-class network probably had a higher number of members actively moving and shaping each other in the same social space than did lower-class family members. Consequently any given generation of the upper class will have greater expectations and thus greater motivations relative to maintaining the system.

Indeed, I am inclined to guess now that in most peasant societies, and this includes Western societies until the industrial revolution, whatever the ideal family patterns were, universally some form of conjugal family system was the modal form among the lowest strata. That is to say, the extended kin network had some emotional meaning but little effectiveness in practice, and the primary influences and cohesions were centred within the nuclear family, with the extended kin somewhat excluded from serious concern. One of the consequences of this is that in spite of the considerable discussion about the problem of motivating workers in underdeveloped countries to work in industrial enterprises, it seems apparent that wherever the alternative opportunities being offered are substantial, there has never been a labour shortage.[7] Workers have always been willing to leave their family-centred villages in order to work in factories. This does not mean that they laid no stress on the family customs or even that they were primarily escaping from arbitrary elders. In part they were escaping from the general poverty and powerlessness of their lives. Nevertheless, the result is the same, that thereby they do escape these continuing family controls, and thus weaken and dissolve the continuity of the kinship network.

IMPACT ON SPECIFIC ROLE RELATIONSHIPS

Ideally, we should continue with an elaborate discussion of the specific role-relationships in industrializing and urbanizing societies, in evaluating the differential impact of industrialization and urbanization on each. Clearly, however, this would entail a volume in itself. We think it perhaps useful, however, to select a few such nexuses, where we believe the strain in the existing families is relatively high, and the alternative opportunities offered by industrialization and urbanization will weaken these relationships, or perhaps has already begun to do so.

I should like to emphasize one theoretical point of some importance here. The existence of strain does not mean that the individual necessarily rejects the traditional definitions of appropriate role behaviour. The daughter-in-law in classical China may well have accepted as morally proper the power of her mother-in-law to impose heavy burdens on her. On the other hand, we do assert that for many major values and even for many specific values in most role-relationships, the individual also accepts what we would call "latent values" by which we mean that in the contemporary value scheme of the society, there are alternative value justifications for a quite different behaviour. Thus, though the Chinese daughter-in-law might accept the behaviour of her overbearing mother-in-law as proper, an equally important value in classical China was the *noblesse oblige* which was the duty of the elder to the younger. In fact, the mother-in-law was not supposed to be overbearing though the daughter-in-law was supposed to accept such behaviour. Consequently, when the structural situation of the family changed, so that the daughter-in-law could now obtain support from the outside for different behaviour, she had a basis for resistance, since she could always assert that it was not right for the elder person to be domineering or overbearing.

It is because in most of our role-relationships we do accept such latent values, that a change in our structural position may cause these latent values to become dominant and thus our behaviour to change substantially. Notably among these latent values is the notion that the individual should be free to choose and that there should be fairness and justice in social relations. When external changes occur that change the relative bargaining power of either, or different role demands are made on one or other (because one assumes a different status, e.g. chief) these latent values may become powerful.

Let us consider a few of these role relations that are changing under the impact of industrializing and urbanizing forces.

Uncle-Nephew in Matrilineal Societies

This is an especially vulnerable set of role obligations. As Schneider has brilliantly shown, a matrilineal system is not simply a patrilineal system reversed.[8] Its peculiar structure creates a number of interesting strains, only one of which need detain us here, the fact that typically the mother's brother is responsible for the moral development and economic welfare of his sister's son, not his own son. As a sociologist I do not assume any mystic biological tie between father and son, but note that father and son do live together in the most important formative and emotional years of the latter's growth, and that the father's paternal attachment to his son is as great as in other family systems. It is even possible that this emotional tie is more intense than in others—because the father need not curb his feelings in order to impose the moral sanctions typical of patriarchal relations. In addition, socialization in a matrilineal society seems not to destroy or eliminate the nearly universal wish of fathers to procreate sons, to live yet another generation through their children. When new jobs become available that are not in control of the lineage, so that the failure or refusal of mother's brother to turn over his skills, magic, and possessions to sister's son cannot be effectively met by counter-sanctions, the father is increasingly inclined to help sister's son (or sons) only minimally, and rather to demand control over his own sons, and to give them his resources. Note that he does not seek to repudiate his sister (this may occur as an unintended consequence). He is supported, of course, by the wishes of his own son or sons: his new income may be larger, and they are emotionally closer to him. In addition, wherever urbanization and industrialization have made any headway in a colonial situation (as in Africa), European laws and customs, as transmitted through missionary and court influence, typically back him in this move. The change is gradual, naturally, but it is definite, and has already been commented on in various reports.

Mother-in-Law—Daughter-in-Law in China and Japan

In both Ch'ing China and Tokugawa as well as early Meiji Japan, the young bride had to submit to the demands of her husband's parents, especially those of her mother-in-law. The many similarities between the two family systems have been noted, but there were at least two important structural differences: (1) Primogeniture was the rule in Japan, and only one son was expected to bring his bride home, whereas in China sons inherited equally (except for a small difference in favour of the eldest son who had to assume certain ritual obligations) and all were ideally expected to bring their wives home. Aside from other consequences, this meant that the mother-in-law's authority was greater, having more subordinates to control. (2) Especially in rural Japan, which constituted most of the population, easy divorce was used as a mechanism by which brides were sent back who did not please the mother-in-law or elders. This mechanism thus reduced the total amount of strain between the two statuses in a marriage that continued.

Although one might expect change in this relationship under industrialization, the pattern was altered but little in the early stages of Meiji industrialization, which took place primarily in rural areas, where extended kin could exercise control both directly and by their power over available factory jobs.[9] However, both industrialization and urbanization eventually affected this pattern of mother-in-law domination. Urban housing is not dependent on the decisions of elder kin, and there is no room for the mother-in-law. Her services in turn are less useful to the young household, than in agricultural regions. She has fewer of her own kin in her generation who live close enough to support her domination. Next, in both China and Japan, the young husband sometimes became attached emotionally to his bride, but was not permitted to protect her—a strain that had no real outlet. Now, however, he can protect her better, since he is somewhat less dependent on his own elder kin for his livelihood, and is less likely to be living with them.

Next, though the Western courtship patterns have not been accepted by the Japanese, there are more so-called "love matches" now than formerly, which means that the husband-wife coalition is more likely to form, if the mother-in-law should become unreasonable. The lesser power of the Japanese mother-in-law and of the paternal kin generally may be seen in the steady decline of the divorce rate over the past half century. A further index of this change is the lower percentage of parents who want or expect the young generation to take care of them in their old age.

The spectacular political attempts in China to change the family system have overshadowed the considerable alterations in it during the generation after the 1911 Revolution. Precise quantitative data on these shifts are not available, but the control by the elders over the young has been an important focus of ideological and legal attack. The establishment of the communes, the approval of marriages made independently by the young, and the granting of jobs on a non-family basis have all undermined the domination of the daughter-in-law by the mother-in-law.

Decline in Marriages between Kin

The previous two relationships were buttressed by many payments and counter-payments in the social structure, and were given much social attention. A group of weaker relationships has begun to be undermined in many societies, including Western societies—marriages between kin, especially between cross or parallel cousins. It would not be possible to analyse all these forms in this brief space, but two elements are important for our immediate comment. (1) They serve to maintain property in a given kin line, and to maintain the corporate character of the line itself. (2) Such marriage forms are vulnerable to the impact of industrialization and urbanization because they all depend on the control by elders over marriages of the younger generation, and on geographical stability.

Industrialization lessens the importance of the lineage, because each individual can make his own career more independently than in other systems. Moreover, formal agencies emerge which carry out many social tasks formerly executed by the lineage. Consequently, the motivation to maintain it through kin marriages diminishes. In addition, as kin lines lose their definiteness and clarity, a wider range of nonkin spouses are viewed as eligible. Here again ideological factors play a role: the ideology of free choice in marriages makes it appeal most strongly to the young, who will only by accident wish to marry a kinsman.

We should not close this brief discussion without taking note of one or two role relationships which we predict will *not* become weakened greatly by urbanization and industrialization.

mother-son in India
male Siblings

Mother-Son in India

Many commentators have noted the very strong mother-son tie in India, and the speculation has even been made that the Indian male is psychologically hampered for industrial initiative because of the mother's failure to temper her love-support with performance-demands. I have not as yet understood precisely what are the institutional supports in the Indian family system for this closeness, though, of course, the general psychodynamics of the mother-son tie have been analysed extensively for the Western family system. However, I see no obvious point at which industrialization will undermine this tie to any great degree over the next generation. The mother remains a refuge from the strains and perils of both industrial life and other external social difficulties. Moreover, nothing in the ideology of the conjugal family in India attacks that tie.

Male Siblings

The tie between male siblings seems to be especially hardy, not only surviving the various transitional phases away from the older family systems, but perhaps in a few instances becoming emotionally stronger. In many patrilineal polygynous societies the problem of succession to rulership or to the land generated many conflicts among siblings. In China the eldest son was given ritual and family authority, but the property was divided equally. In India, inheritance was equal, but the property was ideally held jointly. In both systems, when young males were close in age the ideal of working together was often difficult to achieve, and the problem of authority was equally hard to solve in practice.

The decline in the importance of clans and lineages, of personal responsibility for corporate kinship property and religious activities, and of problems of succession, mean a decline in strains between male siblings when they were common. Thus, the sociologically expected closeness of those of the same sex and status, who have been reared together, comes to the fore. Here again, the ideology of conjugal freedom contains no attacks on this relationship, so that it does not weaken much from this impact. Thus, the male sibling-sibling relationship does not weaken under the massive forces of industrialization and urbanization.

CONCLUSION

The critic of contemporary sociology frequently objects to the lack of "historical dimensions", but in the field of the family even the data necessary for such analyses are missing, aside from the very complex problems of social change theory. Typically, family analysts discussing the past rely upon myths and legends of the European family—of half a century or more ago. These problems are intensified by the conceptual and empirical confusion of urbanization and industrialization. *Urbanization* never occurs without some development of technology, but urban life may continue for generations with little cumulative change in technology. We do not know what were typically "urban" patterns in the past, during epochs of little change in the industrial or economic sphere. Moreover, in current analysis the total "grab-bag" of industrialization and urbanization as a congeries of processes cannot be used as a set of *causes* in research, for they *are* the very things they are thought to "cause".

The "conjugal family system" is thought to be harmonious with the industrial system, but we have not specified the points of impact between industrialization and the family system. Paradoxically, upper-class families—by definition, those who have been living most in harmony with the new system, since they own it—are least conjugal. Lower-class families seem to be freer of one another's kin network, to have less control over each other's behaviour. This was so under older systems, and continues to remain so to a considerable extent, because the new job opportunities permitting the younger generation to make new "role bargains" against the demands of their elder relatives, remained in the hands of the *elite*, who could thus control *their* sons. But the new opportunities were outside the control of the lower strata who could not control their sons. It is hypothesized that universally in the major civilizations, most of the population lives in fact under a conjugal pattern, but that in no social system as a whole is the conjugal pattern either the ideal or the reality—except for systems such as China or Israel, where experimental systems have gone *beyond* the conjugal system. Even in these latter, great ideological and political pressures have been used, and the evidence so far is that the family patterns have not yet yielded, that families have not yet gone beyond the conjugal system.

Finally, by investigating the points of strain within certain family systems, a few relationships have been noted which yield easily under the impact of industrialization and some which remain firm under such attack. Kin ties in all family systems weaken somewhat under industrialization, but some weaken quickly because they were under strain under the traditional system, or the new era puts them under special strains. Others, such as the mother-son tie in India, were not and are not under such strains. It is thus suggested that the theory of role bargaining may profitably be used in understanding many changes in the family system under urbanization and industrialization.

NOTES

[1] The most recent attempt is my *World Revolution and Family Patterns*, Glencoe, Ill.: The Free Press, 1963.

[2] Ernest W. Burgess and Harvey J. Locke, *The Family*, 2nd ed. (New York: American, 1953), ch. 3.

[3] For an account of the family in a "static" situation see Gideon Sjoberg, *The Preindustrial City* (Glencoe, Ill.: The Free Press, 1960), ch. 6.

[4] See William J. Goode, "Illegitimacy in the Caribbean Social Structure", *American Sociological Review*, 25 (February, 1960), pp. 21–30 and also William J. Goode, "Illegitimacy, Anomie, and Cultural Penetration", *American Sociological Review*, 26 (December, 1961), pp. 910–925.

[5] See, for example, Elaine Cumming and David M. Schneider, "Sibling Solidarity: A Property of American Kinship", *American Anthropologist*, 63 (June, 1961), pp. 498–507. Raymond Firth, ed., *Two Studies of Kinship in London* (London School of Economics Monographs on Social Anthropology, No. 15), University of London, The Athlone Press, 1956. Eugene Litwak, "Geographic Mobility and Extended Family Cohesion", *American Sociological Review*, 25 (June, 1960), pp. 385–394. Eugene Litwak, "Occupational Mobility and Extended Family Cohesion", *American Sociological Review*, 25 (February, 1960), pp. 9–20.

[6] For a more extended discussion of the concept "role-bargain" see William J. Goode, "A Theory of Role Strain", *American Sociological Review*, 25 (August, 1960), pp. 483–496. William J. Goode, "Norm Commitment and Conformity to Role-Status Obligations", *American Journal of Sociology*, LXVI (November, 1960), pp. 246–258.

[7] See Neil J. Smelser, *Social Change in the Industrial Revolution* (Chicago: University of Chicago Press, 1959), Chs. IX, X, and XI, and also Wilbert E. Moore and Arnold J. Feldman (eds.), *Labor Commitment and Social Change in Developing Areas* (New York: Social Science Research Council, 1960), pp. 366–368.

[8] See David M. Schneider and Kathleen Gough (eds.), *Matrilineal Kinship* (Berkeley: University of California Press, 1961).

[9] In the 1880's the number of reported divorces in Japan was over 300 per 1,000 marriages. See *Marriage and Divorce*, 1867–1906, Part 1, U.S. Bureau of the Census, Washington, 1909, p. 386.

Adolescence in Historical Perspective

JOHN DEMOS AND VIRGINIA DEMOS

The idea of adolescence is today one of our most widely held and deeply imbedded assumptions about the process of human development. Indeed most of us treat it not as an idea but as a *fact*. Its impact is clear in countless areas of everyday life—in newspapers, magazines, and books; in various forms of popular entertainment; in styles of dress and of language. Its causes and meaning have been repeatedly analyzed in the work of psychologists and sociologists. Its effects are endlessly discussed by teachers, social workers, officers of the law, and parents everywhere.

Yet all of this has a relatively short history. The concept of adolescence, as generally understood and applied, did not exist before the last two decades of the nineteenth century. One could almost call it an invention of that period; though it did incorporate, in quite a central way, certain older attitudes and modes of thinking. It will be our purpose in this paper to describe the roots and the growth of the concept, to the point in the early twentieth century when it had become well established in the public consciousness. We shall limit our attention to developments in the United States, since adolescence was on the whole an American discovery.

We shall begin with a sketch of some common ideas about childhood and "youth" during the period 1800–1875, as revealed in two kinds of sources: (1) a rapidly developing literature of child-rearing advice, and (2) a large body of books and pamphlets directed to the young people of the country and bearing especially on their "moral problems." Then we shall summarize the activities of the "child-study movement" (beginning in about 1890) and in particular the work of the psychologist G. Stanley Hall, for there the concept of adolescence can be examined at its source. And finally we shall propose a hypothesis for drawing together these various types of material and above all for explaining the relationship between the *idea* of adolescence and the social phenomena to which it was a response. It is here that questions of family life will come most fully into view, since adolescence was, we believe, profoundly related to certain fundamental changes affecting the internal structure of many American homes. But this matter of the connection between "ideas" and "facts," between major cultural assumptions like

Reprinted from *Journal of Marriage and the Family*, November 1969, 632–38.

adolescence and the social realities in which they develop, presents extremely tricky problems. It lurks as an uncomfortable presence behind most serious study that bears in one way or another on the history of the family. The difficulty lies in the nature of the evidence available to historians, which comprises for the most part a variety of written materials. It is much easier, therefore, to construct a history of ideas *about* the family than of the family as such.

The present paper cannot pretend to resolve such problems; indeed it may serve chiefly to illustrate them. But it is at least our intention to keep sight of the important distinctions. And if the bulk of our efforts are directed toward the realm of "ideas," it is only because this seems the logical way to begin.

The literature of child-rearing advice is one of the most revealing, and least exploited,[1] sources for the history of the American family. Its beginnings can be located in the early part of the nineteenth century; and it has been growing steadily, and changing in character, ever since. Before about 1825 relatively few books on child-rearing could be found in this country, and those that were available came chiefly from England.[2] In general, they were mild in tone and full of simple moral homilies strung endlessly together. They do not, in short, seem to have been directed to any very pressing needs or problems in the lives of their readers.

After 1825 the situation, for this country at least, changed rapidly. Child-rearing books by American authors began to appear, some of which went through numerous editions and sold many thousands of copies.[3] This development was owing to several different factors. In the first place it was related to a deepening interest in the fact of childhood itself as a distinct period of life and one which was little comparable to the years of maturity. Secondly, it expressed the broad impulse of nationalism that engulfed the country at this time. English books on child-rearing could no longer be regarded as suitable to American conditions. Finally, the new and authentically "native" literature on this subject reflected deep anxieties about the quality of American family life.[4]

Most of the concern which was evident in these books related to problems of authority. In one form or another they all imparted the same message: the authority of parents must be established early in a child's life and firmly maintained throughout the years of growth. Even the smallest infant reveals a "willfulness" that "springs from a depraved nature and is intensely selfish."[5] This must be suppressed by strict training in obedience, or it will rapidly develop beyond the possibility of control with dire implications for the later (adult) personality.

These injunctions seemed all the more necessary because—so many people thought—parental authority was steadily on the wane. In describing the average home, the writers of the child-rearing books repeatedly used words like "disorder," "disobedience," "licentiousness," and above all "indulgence" (i.e., of the children). Statements such as the following were typical:

> It must be confessed that an irreverent, unruly spirit has come to be a prevalent, an outrageous evil among the young people of our land. . . . Some of the good old people make facetious complaint on this. . . . "There is as much family government now as there used to be in our young days," they say, "only it has changed hands."[6]

This seeming change in the traditional family pattern had other dimensions as well. Thus many authors noted the growth of a kind of "child-centered" attitude and condemned it out of hand. More and more parents, for example, appeared to feel compelled to show off their children before any and all guests. Similarly, there was in many households far too much concern with efforts to amuse and entertain the young.[7] Children who were often made the center of attention in this manner would inevitably become conceited and selfish. Another alarming development was the increasing tendency of children to seek social satisfactions outside of the family, among groups of their own peers. Mrs. Lydia Child, whose *Mother's Book* went through many editions, returned again and again to the theme that "youth and age are too much separated."[8] She and many of her contemporaries decried the "new custom" of holding parties exclusively for young people[9] and urged that parents should always be the closest friends and confidants of their children.

Lest it be imagined that Americans of the nineteenth century had no special concern whatsoever for the period which we now call adolescence (and which in their day was simply termed "youth"),[10] we must turn to another category of books that were written specifically *for* the "youth" of the time and about their particular problems. The general nature of these writings is implicit in their titles: *A Voice to Youth; How to Be a Man; Papers for Thoughtful Girls; The Young Lady's Companion; On the Threshold; Lectures to Young Men.*

From all of these works there emerges quite clearly a sense of "youth" as a critical transition period in the life of nearly everyone. It is a time, first of all, when people are extremely impressionable, extremely open to a wide range of outside influences. It is—to quote from Joel Hawes's *Lectures to Young Men* (1832)—

> pre-eminently . . . the forming, fixing period. . . . It is during this season, more than any other, that the character assumes its permanent shape and color.[11]

Words such as "pliant," "plastic," and "formative" appear again and again in the discussions of youth.

Because of this characteristic openness, young people are vulnerable to many kinds of "danger." To begin with, boys and girls entering their teens experience a sudden and sharp upsurge of the "passions." They become highly emotional; their mood fluctuates unpredictably from exuberance to melancholy. Henry Ward Beecher, whose *Lectures to Young Men* were among the best known examples of the genre, declared:

> A young man knows little of life; less of himself. He feels in his bosom the various impulses, wild desires, restless cravings he can hardly tell for what, a sombre melancholy when all is gay, a violent exhilaration when others are sober.[12]

In keeping with their Victorian conventions, these writers never directly mentioned the physiological changes that occur at puberty, in particular the strong new charge of sexual energy and tension. Occasionally one finds an allusion to "internal revolutions" and "occult causes, probably of a physical kind"[13]; but for the most part people were content to define youth in the above terms, that is, as a vast outpouring of the emotions.

As if to complement these disruptive changes within the personality, the world at large was full of "seductive temptations," of inducements to all manner of wicked and ruinous behavior. As Beecher said,

> These wild gushes of feeling, peculiar to youth, the sagacious tempter has felt, has studied, has practiced upon, until he can sit before that most capacious organ, the human mind, knowing every step and all the combinations.[14]

Here, then, was the wider, social dimension of the problems which confront the young person. The world lies in wait for him, and "ardent, volatile, inexperienced, and thirsting for happiness," he is

> exceedingly liable to be seduced into the wrong paths—into those fascinating but fatal ways, which lead to degradation and wretchedness.[15]

There are, at this stage of life, dangers both within and without.

Most of the material considered so far has been drawn from the period 1825–1850. As the years passed and the century neared its end, the picture of youth that we have been describing was embellished somewhat in certain important respects. Thus, for example, the sexual factor began to receive some attention.[16] And some writers were struck by a kind of aimlessness and indecision that seemed increasingly common among American young people. Theodore T. Munger, whose book *On the Threshold* was published in 1881, declared that:

> Young men of the present years . . . are not facing life
> with that resolute and definite purpose that is essential both to
> manhood and to external success. . . . [They] hear no voice
> summoning them to the appointed field, but drift into this or
> that, as happens.[17]

Moreover, towards the end of the century, many writers identified the
"dangers" and "temptations" which threatened youth directly with
urban life. Something of this had been implicit from the beginning, but
now it came clearly into the open.[18] The city loomed as the prime source
of corrupting influences for the young. Its chaotic social and economic
life, its varied population, its frenzied commercial spirit, and its dazzling
entertainments were all sharply antagonistic to proper growth towards
adulthood.

At roughly the same time, meanwhile, the formal concept of
adolescence was receiving its first public expression. The immediate
context of this development was a new movement for systematic "child
study," inspired and guided by G. Stanley Hall. Hall was, of course,
one of the major figures in the early history of American psychology.
After a lengthy period of study in Germany, he became in 1881 a
professor at Johns Hopkins, and six years later he accepted the presidency of Clark University. There he remained for the rest of his life,
presiding over a wide range of research and teaching activities.

The aim of the child-study movement was to enlist large numbers
of ordinary citizens in a broad effort to deepen both public and scientific
understanding of human development. The mothers who belonged to
the various local organizations were encouraged to keep detailed
records of the behavior of their children and to participate in regular
discussions about such records. They were also exposed to, and themselves reflected back, the major themes in Stanley Hall's own work—
not least, his theory of adolescence.

The essentials of Hall's view of adolescence appeared in one of his
earliest papers on psychology: "The Moral and Religious Training of
Children," published in 1882 in the *Princeton Review*. The great point
of departure, then as later, was the idea of "storm and stress," of severe
crisis characterized by

> lack of emotional steadiness, violent impulses, unreasonable
> conduct, lack of enthusiasm and sympathy. . . . The previ-
> ous selfhood is broken up . . . and a new individual is in
> process of being born. All is solvent, plastic, peculiarly sus-
> ceptible to external influences.[19]

The suggestions contained in this article were subsequently elaborated in much greater detail by some of Hall's students at Clark. Efforts
were made to link the adolescent "crisis" with a wide range of personal

and social phenomena—with religious conversion, for example,[20] and with the rising rate of juvenile delinquency.[21] Hall himself provided the capstone to this whole sequence of activity, with the publication in 1904 of his encyclopedic work *Adolescence: Its Psychology, and Its Relations to Physiology, Anthropology, Sociology, Sex, Crime, Religion, and Education.* It is impossible to summarize here the many ideas and vast assortment of data embraced therein, but certain underlying themes can at least be singled out. From the very start Hall's thinking had been profoundly influenced by Darwinism, and the psychology he proposed was explicitly bound to an evolutionary, or "genetic," model. He urged a kind of "archaeology of the mind," in which all the various stages in the development of human consciousness would be rediscovered and understood in their proper order.[22] A key link here was the theory known as "recapitulation," which affirmed that every individual "lives through" each of the major steps in the evolution of the race as a whole. Adolescence assumed a special importance in this scheme, for it represented (and "recapitulated") the most recent of man's great developmental leaps. The adolescent, Hall believed, reveals truly enormous possibilities of growth and "is carried for a time beyond the point of the present stage of civilization."[23] This is not, however, an easy situation, for it encompasses a variety of contradictions and "antithetic impulses." Among the impulses which Hall paired in this context were hyperactivity and lassitude, happiness and depression, egotism and self-abasement, selfishness and altruism, gregariousness and shyness, sensitivity and cruelty, radicalism and conservatism. Caught in the midst of so much change and conflict, the adolescent was bound to experience "storm and stress" more or less continuously.

Hall's work on adolescence quickly exerted a considerable influence in many different directions. Its impact was clear in general texts on psychology,[24] studies of education,[25] the new literature, on child-rearing,[26] and a variety of books on child labor, religious training, vocational guidance, and the like.[27] Even critical comments showed the extent to which the idea of adolescence had captured the public imagination: there were those who complained that "we are today under the tyranny of the special cult of adolescence."[28]

Hall's reputation was, however, relatively short-lived. From the very beginning his theories of adolescence aroused at least some criticism. Men like E. L. Thorndike (himself an important figure in the history of American psychology), Charles H. Judd, and Irving King charged him with many forms of exaggeration and overstatement.[29] And after 1925 his work went rapidly into eclipse. Many scholars came to feel that it was unreasonable to view growth in terms of set "stages" of any kind whatsoever. Margaret Mead, in her famous study of Samoan children, tried to show that adolescent "storm and stress" are a function of certain *cultural* determinants.[30] By contrast, Hall was seen as the representative of an outmoded, wholly physiological orientation.[31]

Moreover, his fervent, almost missionary approach to his subject, his florid writing, his long-range goal of race improvement—all this came to seem irrelevant, or even offensive, to later generations of psychologists.

Thus G. Stanley Hall has been largely forgotten, if not rejected outright. Yet, we suggest, he has left his mark all the same. Hall's critics denied the validity of considering personal growth in terms of "stages"; but we still regard adolescence in just such a context. His critics accused him of having greatly exaggerated "storm and stress" phenomena, and yet today more than ever we view adolescence in exactly those terms. In fact, the "special cult of adolescence" seems to have lost no strength at all. And it was Hall, more than anyone else, who fixed it in our imagination.

It would be easy to overstate the element of innovation in Hall's thinking. If we compare the kind of adolescence that he was describing with some of the ideas that were current just before his time,[32] we find a considerable degree of continuity. His achievement lay in reshaping certain aspects of popular belief about youth, combining them with some of the most exciting new ideas in science (i.e., evolution), gathering data on a large scale, and presenting the whole in a persuasive and meaningful fashion.

Yet certain questions about the rise of the concept of adolescence remain. What larger developments in American society did it reflect? To what popular attitudes, or needs, or anxieties, did it minister? We offer, in conclusion, the following very tentative suggestions—some of which we have simply lifted from contemporary thinking about adolescence in the fields of psychology and sociology.[33]

We propose, as a starting point, the longterm transformation of the United States from an agricultural into an urban and industrial society; for this change—which has, of course, been basic to so much of our history during the last 150 years—has exerted a profound influence on the structure of American families. Consider that most farm families are characterized by a high degree of internal unity. Children and adults share the same tasks, the same entertainments, the same friends, the same expectations. There is a continuum between the generations. The child appears not so much as a child per se but as himself a potential farmer; he is, then, a miniature model of his father. Such, we would argue, was the prevalent situation in nearly *all* the families of this country before the nineteenth century.

But when Americans began to move to the city, all this changed. City children, for example, do not often have a significant economic function within the family as a whole. (Or alternatively—as in the case of poor children employed as factory hands—their work is likely to be quite different from that of their parents.) Moreover, they are thrust into close proximity with other families and have the opportunity to form numerous contacts among their own peers. Thus there develops in the urban setting an important "discontinuity of age-groups."[34] Children and adults are much more obviously separated from each other than is ever the case in a rural environment.

This second configuration was starting to show itself in some American families during the early part of the nineteenth century, and perhaps it helps to explain the material presented in our opening section. Now—i.e., with the new, typically urban family structure— childhood as such is "discovered"; it is no longer feasible to regard children simply as miniature adults. Now, too, "child-centered" families become possible. The behavior of the young is increasingly seen as bizarre and also as appropriate to their particular time of life. A new tolerance for such behavior develops, and parental authority appears to weaken.[35] Finally, there is an obvious place for a literature on child-rearing.

Most cultures with sharp discontinuities of this kind possess a system of "age-grading," which defines the various steps in the transition from childhood to adulthood.[36] In many cases there are elaborate initiation rites to dramatize this change. But our society lacks such rites; ceremonies like confirmation and graduation exercises are losing whatever significance in this regard they once had. It is in such situations, as Kenneth Keniston has suggested, that a "youth culture" is likely to develop. "Youth culture" may be defined, somewhat carelessly, as institutionalized adolescence. It refers, of course, to the special way of life characteristic of large groups of young people of approximately the same age. It is more than a simple substitute for formal age-grading and initiation rites. It is not, Keniston writes,

> so obviously transitional . . . [but is] . . . more like a waiting period . . . a temporary stopover in which one can muster strength for the next harrowing stage of the trip.

Its pattern is "not always or explicitly anti-adult, but it is belligerently non-adult."[37] In many respects adulthood looks rather forbidding when compared with the life of a child, and youth culture reflects some reluctance to bridge this gap.

It is pertinent to recall at this point the deep concern of many nineteenth-century Americans about the growth of peer-group contacts. We suggest that these people were witnessing the rudimentary beginnings of a youth culture. Of course, there were none of the artifacts so prominent in our own modern-day youth culture (e.g., "rock 'n roll," "teen magazines," special kinds of dress, and so forth). But the very fact of "wanting to be with and for [their own] kind"[38] was significant. By about 1900 the situation had become more clear. The many and varied writings on "gangs," on juvenile delinquency, and on vocational guidance all show some feeling for the special characteristics of a youth culture.

Keniston argues that a second kind of discontinuity—that between specific generations—is also important in the formation of youth culture.

By this he means a clear separation between the parents and the children within an individual family. In such cases the situation of the parents offers no viable goal at which their children may aim. Intrafamily conflict is likely to become chronic, and the adolescent is on his own in the formation of an identity. This pattern is characteristic of societies with a high rate of social change and a plurality of alternatives in regard to careers, moral codes, and life styles. The young person shrinks from such a bewildering array of choices and becomes part of the youth culture, where a clear-cut, if temporary, identity comes ready-made.

All of this seems to describe nineteenth-century America fairly well, especially the new life of the cities. Social and economic change was everywhere apparent; ambitions were high; there was an astonishing diversity of people, ideologies, occupations. The disparity between generations was assumed; it became, indeed, a part of the national mythology. Immigrant families presented an especially dramatic case in point; likewise those families in which the children of uneducated parents had the chance to go to school. Thus, once again, there was the youth culture.

The growth of the concept of adolescence was the final step in this long and somewhat devious process. It was the response to an observable *fact*—the fact of a youth culture, of many young people seemingly in distress (or at least behaving in ways that distressed their elders). Americans needed some means of understanding the problems of, and the problems created by, these young people. We have tried to show them groping toward such an understanding through much of the nineteenth century. And we have located, chiefly in the work of G. Stanley Hall, a kind of culmination of these efforts: the first comprehensive theory of adolescence in modern history.

NOTES

[1] We know of only three attempts to confront this material directly: Bernard Wishy, *The Child and the Republic,* Philadelphia: University of Pennsylvania Press, 1968; Robert Sunley, "Early Nineteenth-Century American Literature on Child-Rearing," in *Childhood in Contemporary Cultures,* ed. by Margaret Mead and Martha Wolfenstein, Chicago: University of Chicago Press, 1955, pp. 150–167; and Elaine V. Damis, *The History of Child-Rearing Advice in America from 1800–1940,* unpublished honor's thesis, Radcliffe College, 1960.

[2] See, for instance, Juliana Seymour, *On the Management and Education of Children,* London, 1754; and Miss Appleton, *Early Education,* London, 1821.

[3] Parallel to this increase in books on child-rearing, there developed at this time a new kind of magazine directed specifically to "mothers." *Mother's Magazine* and the *Mother's Assistant* were prominent examples. Both seem to have achieved a wide circulation within a very few years. The magazines, in turn, were closely related to

the movement for "maternal associations." These societies, operating at the local level and devoting their energies largely to the discussion of child-rearing problems, became quite a vogue in the 1820s and 1830s. All of this demonstrates further the heightened interest in motherhood—and thus childhood—that characterized the period.

⁴ These anxieties were a matter of great complexity and wide ramifications. Indeed they must be understood as relating not only to conditions internal to the family but also to the wider social climate of the time. For some useful discussion of all this, see Bernard Wishy, The Child and the Republic.

⁵ H. W. Bulkeley, A Word to Parents, Philadelphia: Presbyterian Board of Publication, 1858, p. 12.

⁶ Warren Burton, Helps to Education, Boston: Crosby and Nichols, 1863, pp. 38–39. Similar observations can be found in the writings of foreign visitors to this country. See Arthur W. Calhoun, A Social History of the American Family, New York: Barnes and Noble, 1945, pp. 17–19, for some extensive discussion of this travel literature. See also Max Berger, The British Traveller in America, New York: Columbia University Press, 1943.

⁷ On this matter see, for example, Lydia M. Child, The Mother's Book, Boston: Carter, Hendee and Babcock, 1835, p. 94; and Burton, op. cit., pp. 74–75, 92.

⁸ Child, op. cit., p. 95.

⁹ See ibid., p. 138; also Mother's Magazine, 1, pp. 42–45.

¹⁰ The word "adolescence" was known in the nineteenth century, but we have found only a very few cases of its use in the literature on child-rearing and "youth."

¹¹ Joel Hawes, Lectures to Young Men, Hartford, Connecticut: Cooke & Co., 1832, p. 35. See also Child, op. cit., p. 125.

¹² Henry Ward Beecher, Lectures to Young Men, Boston: J. P. Jewett & Co., 1844, p. 21. Beecher actually delivered these lectures to an audience of young people in Boston before publishing them. Such was the pattern for many of the other works of this kind. For a similar comment on the turmoil characteristic of youth, see Henrietta Keddie, Papers for Thoughtful Girls, Boston: Crosby and Nichols, 1860, p. 1.

¹³ Isaac Taylor, Home Education, New York: D. Appleton & Co., 1838, p. 131.

¹⁴ Beecher, op. cit., p. 21.

¹⁵ John M. Austin, A Voice to Youth, New York: J. Bolles, 1838, p. 1.

¹⁶ See, for example, Elizabeth Blackwell, Counsel to Parents on the Moral Education of Their Children, New York: Brentano's Literary Emporium, 1879.

¹⁷ Theodore T. Munger, On the Threshold, Boston: Houghton Mifflin & Co., 1881, p. 5. See also William A. Mowry, Talks with My Boys, Boston: New England Publishing Company, 1885, pp. 30ff.; and Philip S. Moxon, The Aim of Life, Boston: Roberts Brothers, 1894, pp. 11–29.

¹⁸ See, for example, George H. Hepworth, Rocks and Shoals, Boston: American Unitarian Association, 1870; and Mowry, op. cit.

¹⁹ G. Stanley Hall, "The Moral and Religious Training of Children," in Princeton Review (January, 1882), pp. 26–48. This essay was later republished in a slightly revised form in Pedagogical Seminary, 1, pp. 196–210.

²⁰ See E. D. Starbuck, The Psychology of Religion, New York: Ginn & Co., 1899; and an essay by the same author, "A Study of Conversion," in American Journal of Psychology, 8, pp. 268–308.

²¹ See Edgar J. Swift, "Some Criminal Tendencies of Boyhood: A Study in Adolescence," in Pedagogical Seminary, 7.

²² See G. Stanley Hall, Adolescence, New York: D. Appleton & Co., 1904, Vol. 2, pp. 61, 69.

²³ See the "epitome" of Hall's theories by G. E. Partridge, The Genetic Philosophy of Education, Boston: Sturgis & Walton Co., 1912, p. 31.

²⁴ For example, James R. Angell, Psychology, New York: H. Holt & Co., 1904. See especially p. 358.

²⁵ See George H. Betts, The Mind and Its Education, New York: D. Appleton

& Co., 1906; P. M. Magnusson, *Psychology as Applied to Education,* New York: Silver, Burdett and Company, 1913; and Arthur Holmes, *Principles of Character-Making,* Philadelphia: J. B. Lippincott Company, 1913.

[26] See William McKeever, *Training the Boy,* New York: Macmillan Company, 1913; and *Training the Girl,* New York: Macmillan Company, 1914; also W. B. Forbush and Catherine M. Burrell, *The Mother's Book,* New York: The University Society, Inc., 1919.

[27] See George B. Mangold, *Child Problems,* New York: The Macmillan Company, 1910; George A. Coe, *Education in Religion and Morals,* New York: F. H. Revell Company, 1904; and Meyer Bloomfield, *The Vocational Guidance of Youth,* Boston: Houghton Mifflin Company, 1911.

[28] Frank O. Beck, *Marching Manward,* New York: Eaton & Mains, 1913, p. 38.

[29] See E. L. Thorndike, *Notes on Child-Study,* in *Columbia University Contributions to Philosophy, Psychology, and Education,* 8:3–4, p. 143; also Thorndike's article, "Magnitude and Rate of Alleged Changes at Adolescence," in *Educational Review,* 54, pp. 140–147. See too Charles H. Judd, *The Psychology of High School Subjects,* Boston: Ginn & Company, 1915; and Irving King, *The Psychology of Child Development,* Chicago: University of Chicago Press, 1903, pp. 222ff.

[30] Margaret Mead, *Coming of Age in Samoa,* New York: W. Morrow and Company, 1928.

[31] On this point Hall was somewhat misrepresented. It is true that he regarded the critical changes of adolescence as proceeding from within; but he also spent much effort in analyzing various factors in our *environment*—which, he felt, greatly accentuated adolescent distress. See Hall, *Adolescence, op. cit.,* Vol. 1, pp. xv, 321ff., 348ff., 376ff.; and Vol. 2, pp. 59–60.

[32] *Ibid.,* pp. 5–8.

[33] We have tried to draw together ideas from several different sources, chief among them: Kenneth Keniston, "Social Change and Youth in America," *Daedalus* (Winter, 1962), pp. 145–171; Erik H. Erikson, "Youth: Fidelity and Diversity," *Daedalus* (Winter, 1962), pp. 5–27; Ruth Benedict, "Continuities and Discontinuities in Cultural Conditioning," in *Psychiatry,* 1, pp. 161–167; Kingsley Davis, "The Sociology of Parent-Youth Conflict," *American Sociological Review,* 5, pp. 523–535.

[34] The phrase is Kenneth Keniston's. See his article cited above.

[35] This may have been *only* a matter of appearance. The reality may have been quite different; indeed parental authority seems, if anything, stronger in the nineteenth century than in the eighteenth. But the fact that children were now more visible and more often approached on their own terms was interpreted by many observers as a symptom of decadence and loosened family bonds.

[36] Ruth Benedict, "Continuities and Discontinuities in Cultural Conditioning," *Psychiatry,* 1, p. 165.

[37] Keniston, *op. cit.,* p. 161.

[38] William B. Forbush, *The Boy Problem,* Chicago: The Pilgrim Press, 1901, p. 20.

Divorce in the Progressive Era

WILLIAM J. O'NEILL

. . . It is hardly a coincidence that the shift in American attitudes toward divorce took place during the period Henry F. May has identified as "the end of American innocence." The whole of American society and culture was undergoing a change in the years immediately before American entry into the Great War: the Victorian synthesis was fragmenting, and new modes of thought and behavior which we recognize as distinctively our own were coming into being. We would not expect divorce to evolve independently of its social context, and in fact it was very much a part of the cultural revolution discussed by May. Divorce, therefore, has implications that deserve mention even though they go beyond the limits of this study.

We saw at the outset that divorces began to increase as America came to grips with the machine age. The dynamics of an industrialism that regarded human beings not as members of families or even as individuals but simply as "hands" inevitably affected traditional relationships. Great social energies were released in the process and, as science and technology were making old assumptions untenable, prophets arose to establish new ones. Few subjects escaped re-examination, and the people I have called New Moralists stepped forth to do for divorce in particular and sex in general what the social scientists were doing for the other areas of human experience.

As society became ever more dense and intricate, new professions developed, and divorce became the province of sociologists who were themselves far more under the influence of the new morality than was the general public. The combination of sociology and the new ideas about morality proved to be both potent and crucial to the evolution of the divorce controversy. The tradition-minded opponents of divorce were compelled to fight on ground not of their own choosing. Orthodox Christianity had once seemed an impregnable bastion in which moral conservatives could hold out forever. But by the turn of the century sociologists were simply bypassing Christianity, and if the conservatives proposed to fight they had to attack divorce on the basis of its social inutility. But by engaging the enemy on his own terms conservatives made a fatal, if inescapable, mistake, for they were in no position to challenge the professional credentials and equipment of the sociologists.

Conservatives were disarmed by their obligatory shift from moral to practical grounds, dismayed by their inability to retard the divorce rate, and more than a little disillusioned with the culture responsible for their plight. One can see, therefore, the beginnings of the great attitude change which was to occur after the First World War taking shape well before American entry. One of the major features of nineteenth-century American thought had been what Professor May calls "inveterate optimism." But by the turn of the century, only moral liberals could be optimistic about the family. Thus we find liberals making sanguine prophecies about marriage and the family that conservatives simply could not accept, even though most of them had always been squarely in the mainstream of American thought—optimism included.

Moreover, since the relaxation of the prohibitions against divorce was billed as a "reform," conservatives had even more reason for distrusting the liberal, reformist values of the Progressive era. In their worst moments conservatives reacted to the dilemma by witch-hunting and scapegoating. But more importantly, their disenchantment over the movement for divorce prepared them for the greater disappointments to come. In this manner the discontent which is so prominent a feature of modern conservatism and the conservatives' disposition to see America's moral fiber as badly in need of stiffening probably owe something to the pre-World War I experience.

Another aspect of contemporary conservatism, its emphasis on individualism, may also be related to the struggle over divorce. As we have seen, the critics of divorce consistently accused those who obtained divorces, and those who defended the practice, of espousing a dangerously antisocial individualism. Indeed, their major objection to socialist doctrines was that they believed socialism put the rights of individuals ahead of the needs of society. They distrusted big government not because it suppressed individualism but because it exalted the individual by breaking down the local and familial associations that had previously checked his antisocial impulses. Today, of course, conservatives argue just the opposite. Senator Goldwater's presidential campaign in 1964 was proclaimed as an effort to obtain greater rights for the individual. At the same time, however, Goldwater was obviously the champion of moral as well as political conservatism, and his candidacy illustrates what has happened to moral conservatism in the past fifty years.

A moral conservative in 1904 would certainly have been opposed to divorce, prostitution, erotic literature, and unwed motherhood, but he would have been just as likely to favor unemployment insurance, the Social Gospel, and generous immigration policies. He would not have thought these inconsistent beliefs, because all of them could be justified on the grounds that they promoted social order and advanced the general welfare. Conservatives continue to insist upon social order and to demand the suppression of direct action and civil disobedience programs because, like crimes of violence, they are thought to be subversive of public harmony. However, conservatives have soured on the general welfare and no longer recognize it as an important object of good government.

To explain the contemporary emphasis on individualism would require an examination of the political history of the past half century. The adoption of individualistic values foreign in spirit to traditional conservative doctrines was in part a matter of expediency. A concern with individual rights is deeply embedded in the American experience, and its enduring popularity made it helpful in the defense of property rights threatened by zoning laws, fair housing ordinances, taxes, regulatory commissions, and the whole apparatus of public control that has evolved in recent years. Moreover, the failure of the Communist bloc to protect individual rights gave political conservatives another valuable argument and a further reason for using it.

But if individualism has been useful to political conservatism, it remains a problem for moral conservatives faced with a continuing sexual evolution that derives its strength from the very American belief in the pursuit of happiness. One cannot easily proclaim the rights of every man to dispose of his property as he sees fit while denying him the right to use his body in the same manner. The dilemma confronting moral conservatives in 1904 has, therefore, become much more acute in our time. The older divorce critics were in most respects sympathetic with the progressive, optimistic assumptions of their age. But to the degree that they believed that divorce was destroying the moral and social underpinnings of the national life, their confidence and faith in American culture was being undermined. One sees in them the beginnings of that alienation which is so marked a feature of modern conservatism. In 1904 or 1914 moral conservatives, however frustrated by their inability to retard divorce, could still believe that most Americans maintained the same moral standards as themselves. By 1924, much less 1964, this was obviously no longer true. Divorce, which once seemed so flagrantly immoral, is now obscured by things like pornography and promiscuity, which have become, not the vices of a few, but the pleasures of the many. The commercialized exploitation of sex is no longer a furtive, underground business, but a mainstay of American capitalism. One can understand, then, why moral conservatives have become so profoundly disaffected, so estranged from the mainstream of American culture, that it has become possible to run for president by indicting the moral character of the nation.

However, by abandoning their traditional anti-individualism, conservatives have only compounded their difficulties. Whatever they may have gained politically by adopting individualistic arguments, they have lost emotionally and intellectually by having to use one set of standards for economic problems and another for social and sexual ones. We have already seen how the relatively mild conflict between a progressive, optimistic view of American history and society on the one hand, and a pessimistic view of marriage and the family on the other made moral conservatives cranky and irritable at the turn of the century. How much more reason there is for the conservatives of our time, torn between moral authoritarianism and economic liberalism while at the same time experiencing a much more profound sense of isolation and alienation, to be peevish and intemperate.

The position of the moral liberals seems to have been in some ways less difficult. Not only was their optimistic, progressive view of divorce in keeping with the spirit of their age, but they were in the enviable position of those who win without effort. Throughout these years divorces increased, and conservatives were driven back without liberals having to lift a finger. Since history was working with them, they could afford to be relatively even-tempered. Perhaps for these reasons liberals were less prepared for the shocking denouement of the Wilson era and the plunge into normalcy. Certainly the future proved very different from what they had imagined it would be. Many of those who had urged divorce as a way of freeing women from sex lived to see the open adoration of sexuality in the jazz age, while most of the sociologists who believed that the divorce rate would level off and family cohesion increase had to wait a long time for their hopes to be realized.

Yet despite their predictive failures, liberals very well may have had the best of it. If divorce failed to live up to their expectations, neither did it produce the disasters anticipated by conservatives. We know today that divorce has not grown at the expense of marriage and the family. Not only do Americans now marry more often than in the recent past, but they marry earlier and have larger families. The institution of marriage has changed somewhat in the past half century, yet the changes do not seem to have noticeably decreased the sum total of human happiness or imperiled the structure of society. In the long run those who defended divorce for libertarian reasons found themselves on the safest ground. For one thing, since civil liberties are primarily a matter of principle, they are not subject to revision on the basis of experience. For another, there is no question that easier divorce has strengthened women's rights, even if it has not improved their social position, and from a libertarian point of view such a result is self-justifying.

However, while many did support the right to divorce for libertarian reasons, their case was far from free of the manipulative and authoritarian undercurrents which marred the advanced thought of their age. As Christopher Lasch has recently pointed out, progressive intellectuals like Jane Addams and Randolph Bourne (whom he somewhat misleadingly calls new radicals) had a definite bias against the family, which they regarded as oppressive and tyrannical.[1] Their attitude helped inspire a certain distrust of the family on the part of sociologists like George Howard, who, while certainly not overtly antifamilial, rejoiced in the modern tendency of the state to view its citizens as individuals rather than as members of family units.

One clear advantage of this proposition was that it made social control much easier to accomplish. The patriarchal family seemed balky, awkward, and resistant to change. The streamlined contemporary family, on the other hand, was considered to be susceptible of intelligent handling and consequently far less of a problem to aspiring social engineers. Thus it was possible for a radical sociologist like Arthur W. Calhoun to call in one breath for a more democratic society and in another for tighter controls over marriage and the suppression of newspaper stories about divorce, ending with a crude appeal to the self-interest of capitalists and managers:

> The spread of the "scientific management" movement for economic efficiency should have a large bearing on the problem of divorce. Employers are coming to recognize the importance of family troubles as an element in inefficiency. The influence of divorce upon the productivity of adults and the development of children and thus upon the interests of property must be very considerable. In general the burden and expense of divorce and its consequences is a noteworthy reduction of social efficiency that should direct the attention of administrators to the economics of the problem.[2]

The intellectual gulf between conservatives and liberals was not, therefore, quite as wide as their emotional differences might suggest. Liberals did not commonly regard individual rights as inviolable, although they attached more weight to them than conservatives did, and both sides unhesitatingly advanced coercive solutions to problems which did not easily lend themselves to permissive alternatives. Since both factions were committed to many of the same principles and were composed in many cases of individuals from similar social backgrounds, the precise differences between them were sometimes far from obvious. The essence of the ideological conflict was, after all, that while they started from essentially the same position, their understanding of what was at stake and their moral reference points came in the end to be very different.

Of crucial importance was their reaction to the feminist thrust. The critics of divorce were almost all antifeminists; its defenders invariably sympathized with the woman movement. It is surely no accident that Richard Hofstadter, in his brilliant and influential analysis of the Progressive era, *The Age of Reform*, pay virtually no attention to feminism. If one wishes to prove, as Hofstadter does, that the Progressives were conservative counterrevolutionaries motivated by status anxieties, then obviously one cannot spend much time on the feminists, for they are not so easily fitted into this pattern as some of the other people we have examined.

But the feminists and liberals are interesting precisely because they do reflect the moral fervor in Progressive thought that Hofstadter feels has been overemphasized. While some Progressives, such as Felix Adler and Margaret Deland, called for a return to the patriarchal family and the old social order, others hoped for newer and more flexible arrangements. The feminist vision of a free and equal marriage prepared for by sex education and based on equal employment opportunities commanded impressive support among advanced progressives. Even the modest statements by social scientists that a substantial divorce rate was no danger to society indicated an outlook on social change that was more forward-looking than reactionary.

Divorce was a moral and ideological issue which cut across class and interest lines. It might be said that the campaign for free divorce reflected the status anxieties of the new middle-class business and professional women, but it was believed that free divorce accelerated the breakdown of the traditional family system, and its proponents hardly can be described, therefore, as conservative counterrevolutionaries. The liberal ideologists of the feminist movement—Schreiner, Gilman, Dorr—were deeply committed to many aspects of the changing morality, of which divorce was only the most conspicuous part. Those who defended or advanced the new sexual norms did so for reasons that cannot be explained in terms of the social groups to which they belonged. Feminists wished to see mores changed to conform to the position of educated women in an industrial society, and some attorneys may have supported them because divorces were good business. But the reasons that impelled the professoriat and the liberal clergy to defend the new morality would seem to owe more to ideology than to status or interest.

It could be argued also that divorce as an issue was peripheral to the mainstream of Progressivism. No party platform called for divorce reforms, although leading politicians sometimes did. In this respect the relationship of divorce to politics in the Progressive era was something like the relationship of juvenile delinquency to politics today. To the extent that there is a difference between liberals and conservatives on juvenile delinquency, the tendency of liberals is to argue that delinquency can be dealt with best by eliminating the conditions that breed it. Conservatives, on the other hand, are more likely to call for direct action against delinquency itself. The contemporary liberal sees the delinquent as a social casualty; the conservative sees him as a criminal. The same pattern of responses marked the progressives' approach to divorce. Liberals like E. A. Ross and moderates like Samuel Dike insisted that divorce was symptomatic of more serious problems, which could only be solved by changes in the social order. Conservatives demanded legal action against divorce. Liberals saw the divorcee as a helpless victim of circumstance bravely facing a difficult future; conservatives saw her as a wilful hedonist, selfishly and irresponsibly warping the structure of society.

The divorce controversy illustrates the difficulties in trying to interpret the social reforms of this century in terms of status politics. Ideology is not just a rationalization of the needs of particular groups but an expression of values that are themselves motivating forces. The divorce controversy was not waged between two sets of groups with contradictory status anxieties, for most of the protagonists on both sides of the issue belonged to the same social groups. The real conflict was between those who wished to maintain the traditional family structure and those who supported the newer, more egalitarian family that they believed was coming into existence. The difference was between those who argued that the needs of society took precedence over those of the individual, and those who believed the reverse—that marriage was made for man. The traditional conservative insistence on order was set against the historic liberal appeal for freedom.

The moral transformation which was getting under way in the Progressive era owed relatively little to previous American experience. It was this radical expectancy in advanced Progressivism that distinguished it from most earlier reform movements. The feeling that the old moral and cultural order was being overthrown was not confined to the urban avant-garde. Kenneth Rexroth has remarked that society today bears little resemblance to the world which his parents' generation assumed was coming:

> People like my parents had a moral confidence in the future that is incomprehensible today. They and everyone like them believed soon all life from clothing design to a game of chess was going to change for the better. It wasn't a political attitude as we understand the word today; in fact, nobody I knew until after my minority was over thought politically in the present meaning of the word.[3]

The misty notion of a time when art, culture, and a frank, healthy (though moral) relationship between the sexes would transform the style of middle-class life obtained in Elkhart, Indiana, and Davenport, Iowa, as it did in New York and Chicago.

Any interpretation which ignores the changing moral climate of the Progressive era does less than justice to the period. Certainly these moral alterations and Progressivism were not identical developments. This became clear in the 1920s, when one withered and the other flourished. But the two were bound together by more than their temporal coexistence. What united them was their utopian quality, and this is exactly what was missing from the new sexual standards of the 1920s and the political reforms of the 1930s. The hard-boiled, pragmatic, not to say opportunistic, reformism of the New Deal was as remote from the airy hopefulness of Progressivism as the careless sexuality of the Lost Generation was from the high-minded innocence of the prewar rebellion. Both the political reforms and the moral changes of the Progressive years were sustained by a belief in the relative perfectibility of society. The death of this vision in the trenches of France and the conference halls of Versailles, did not mean the end of political reform and moral change. But reforms and reformers were never quite the same again.

This is not to say that confidence and optimism were unique to the Progressive era. The whole difficulty in dealing with recent historical periods is that they share many of our own attributes. The progressives were not so greatly different from ourselves that we cannot understand them. Quite the contrary, the problem is that because they were much like us we tend to ignore the subtle distinctions that, taken as a whole, made the feel and texture of their life and the flavor of their thought unlike our own. That the future will be better than the present has been an article of faith in America since before we were a nation. But the intensity with which this was believed, the sense of what the present was like and the future ought to be, and the areas where progress was expected have changed repeatedly. Thus, in the 1830s and 40s the Transcendentalists and Utopians dreamed of a radically different future that had little connection with their own day, while the Jacksonians visualized a society very much like the one they lived in except that opportunity would be broader and the corrupt institutions of privilege contained or destroyed.

In our time we are inclined to see the future as a direct extension of the present. Winning the war on poverty means that everyone will live in tract houses or high-rise apartments. Tomorrow will be like today, except more so. We can understand why high school graduates who are sending their children to college believe in progress, but once we go beyond this limited perspective, if we find anything at all, it is a kind of forced, nightmarish, technological futurism. Buckminster Fuller proposes to solve the Harlem problem by erecting gigantic hive cities atop the existing slums.[4] The future development of San Francisco is to be effected apparently by leveling the hills and filling in the bay. Lewis Mumford is almost alone in calling for a city that meets man's spiritual and aesthetic needs.

But Mumford is a living reminder of a way of viewing the human condition that was once quite common. It is not that his ideas are in any way dated or old-fashioned. They are, in fact, tougher, tighter, and more sophisticated than anyone could fashion who had not experienced the continuing crisis of these past fifty years. It is the contour, not the content, of his social thought that is suggestive. At the turn of the century technical improvements were welcomed by the visionary, but they were understood to be instruments of progress and not progress itself. People like Ellis and Carpenter and Mrs. Gilman were concerned principally with human beings rather than the physical environment. They were vague about the mechanics of the good society, but they had a fairly clear idea of the kind of people they wanted to live in it. As the twentieth century wore on, however, it became harder and harder to sustain the simple faith in human nature that had animated the prophets and reformers of the prewar era, and so we have come to rely upon techniques and technologies that are constant and reliable in ways that fractious humanity can never be.

History has operated in America, and most other developed countries as well, to diminish our faith in man and to preserve the least agreeable aspects of late nineteenth-century social thought. The technocratic elitism of Wells marches on, while the hopes of his colleagues for a new man and woman in a new world have long since been forgotten. As with everything else, sex and marriage have become objects of investigation and manipulation. We do not concern ourselves with the broad social context in which these things function, but rather view sexual inadequacy, marital breakups, and the like as discrete problems to be studied, experimented with, and prescribed for as if they were simply mechanical breakdowns. We are in consequence deluged with handbooks on sexual intercourse, proposals for divorce bureaus and marital counseling services, endless studies of behavioral patterns, and the whole varied output of the sex and marriage industry.

By this I do not mean to suggest that there is something inherently wrong with explicit directions and scientific studies, but rather that our preoccupation with style and technique at the expense of a large concern for the future of society is, as much as any other single thing, what makes us different from the Progressives. Many of them were technicians and manipulators, and the whole idea of the reformer as expert, for example, dates from this period, but the new moralists' great interest in the quality of life, the meaning of human relationships, and the social atmosphere in which people function is alien to us.

The failure of divorce to justify either the expectations of liberals or the fears of conservatives is, therefore, part of the whole process by which their system of attitudes and ideas has been replaced by our own. What was once a moral issue has become increasingly a clinical problem. That we have not solved it any more than the Progressives did is probably less important than our abandonment of their utopian stance. We are different from them because we have become more sophisticated about the mechanics of social change, and less hopeful of its possibilities.

NOTES

[1] Christopher Lasch, *The New Radicalism in America* (New York: Knopf, 1965).

[2] Arthur W. Calhoun, *A Social History of the American Family*, 3, New York: Barnes and Noble, 1945, p. 281.

[3] Kenneth Rexroth, *An Autobiographical Novel* (Garden City, 1966), p. viii.

[4] J. Meyer, "Instant Slum Clearance," *Esquire, 63* (1965), 108–11.

II

American Family Varieties

There is no such thing as "*the* American family." American families vary greatly in their behaviors, motivations, residential locations, number of members, child rearing practices, marital roles, and ability to cope with crises. Some of these differences are clustered within various subcategories of the American population, making it possible to speak of the family characteristics which typify a religious, racial, ethnic, or socioeconomic subgroup. While an entire volume might be devoted to describing family varieties, we have chosen in this section to review four types: the middle-class family, the economically deprived family, the black family, and the family in a religious subsociety. As you read these selections you should watch for the ways in which your family experience fits and diverges from the model with which you most closely identify.

The first paper in this part, which is entitled by Talcott Parsons "The Normal American Family," describes middle-class families in the United States. At least three questions are raised by this article, and the first concerns the title itself. In what way or to what extent can the middle-class family be considered "normal" in the United States? Is this nuclear family, little involved in the kin group, typical numerically? Billingsley, in selection three of this section, notes that Glick found the nuclear family *not* to be the typical household unit. Perhaps, then, the middle-class family described by Parsons is normal in the sense of embodying the major motivations and goals of "official" American morality. But one cannot help wondering whether the author's use of the term "normal" implies that other forms of American family life are considered abnormal in some way. Regardless of how the reader decides this question in the process of reading the paper, he should be cautious about adopting a value-laden term such as "normal" to describe any one of the family varieties found in American society.

Crucial to understanding Parsons' article is the economic analogy which he employs. Is this analogy appropriate and accurate as a description of the middle-class family system? If it is not entirely accurate, at what points does it fall short? The third issue raised by Parsons' paper involves neither title nor economic analogy, but his use, in the latter portion of the paper, of the term "social acceptance." By this he is elliptically referring to prejudice and discrimination as the beginning points for understanding the situation of the black lower classes in the United States. Some authors have argued that the disorganized aspects of black family life are a result of differing values or irresponsibility on the part of blacks. Parsons and Billingsley agree that whatever deviant forms the black family demonstrates are a result of treatment by the larger society.

Arthur Besner's piece on economically deprived families deals briefly with the characteristics of families that are suffering from lack of an adequate income. Accurate and insightful at most points, it also raises important questions. First, Besner begins by referring to families on public assistance, yet throughout the paper he discusses two-parent families—few of whom are receiving public assistance—as well as those with a parent missing. Thus, it is never clear whether he is concerned only with welfare families, or with low income, poor, economically deprived, or lower-class families. Are these terms synonymous, we might ask, or do they symbolize valid distinctions? A second issue which Besner raises concerns the tendency of those who work with economically deprived families to implant their values and expectations upon them. Besner warns against this, and asserts that even the one-parent family should not be dealt with as a unit which needs "patching up," but as a mechanism used by some persons to cope with a particular set of life circumstances. We do well to keep this admonition in mind as we review the varieties of American family life.

Billingsley's book on *Black Families in White America* is an attempt to give an alternative perspective to the one fostered by the works of E. F. Frazier and Daniel Moynihan on the black family. The disorganized, matricentric model of these latter authors simply does not fit the facts, says Billingsley. Not only is disorganization in the black community a product of white treatment (as Parsons admits), but disorganization itself is *not* characteristic of the black family. The nuclear family is the typical black family unit, and Billingsley does an excellent job of pointing out statistically the variety of domestic units that are present among American blacks. There is not, he is saying, one model of the black family, but many. The greatest difficulty is that the lower class black family has been treated as typical, and black families in general have been dealt with as problems and white middle-class families as typical. One way to change this is by asking, with Billingsley, how black families have been as viable as they have in a society which has never really allowed them in and has held them down in numerous ways. Thus, the reader is presented with an alternative to the older notion of the black family as a problem; rather it may be seen as the chief buffer between the black individual and a discriminatory society.

The final selection in Part II describes the marriage practices of a religious subsociety—the Hutterites. A key question the reader should keep in mind throughout is how long it may take for American society to destroy the culture of such a group and "swallow it up." The authors note that the family is still embedded in the larger kin-community unit among the Hutterites, and as long as this continues, Hutterite society is likely to survive. Is it true, as the authors indicate in the closing paragraph, that the rise of the nuclear-conjugal family is the beginning of individualism? If so, then the changes described by Ariès in Part I were bound to give rise to the individualism of the progressive and postprogressive eras of which O'Neill speaks. This issue merits discussion.

The sorts of categorical distinctions found in these readings, especially those between middle-class and lower-class families, will appear from time to time in the succeeding sections. Particularly in the sections on socialization, marital relationships, the family and other systems, and crises, the reader will again find himself confronted with ethnic and socioeconomic differences in American life.

The Normal American Family

TALCOTT PARSONS

It is of course a commonplace that the American family is predominantly and, in a sense, increasingly an urban middle-class family. There has indeed been, if not a very great equalization of income (though there has been some in the present century), a very substantial homogenization of patterns of life in the population with reference to a number of things. Basic to this are the employment of one or more family members outside the home; the nuclear family household without domestic service except for cleaning and baby-sitting; and the basic constituents of the standard of living, including in particular the familiar catalogue of consumer durable goods, which constitute the basic capital equipment of the household [1].

It can then be said that, in a sense that has probably never existed before, in a society that in most respects has undergone a process of very extensive structural differentiation, there has emerged a remarkably uniform, basic type of family. It is uniform in its kinship and household composition in the sense of confinement of its composition to members of the nuclear family, which is effective at any given stage of the family cycle, and in the outside activities of its members, e.g., jobs for adult men, some participation in the labor force for women, school for children, and various other types of community participation. Indeed it is also highly uniform in the basic components of the standard of living, e.g., the private dwelling, the merchanical aids, the impingement of communications from the outside through the mass media, etc. There is one increasingly conspicuous and distressing exception to the general pattern, namely, the situation of the lowest groups by most of the socioeconomic indices, such as income, education, occupational level, etc. This problem will have to be taken up again later.

The author has, perhaps more than anyone else, been responsible for defining the phrase "isolated nuclear family" to describe one aspect of this unit. This concept has recently been challenged notably by two groups of sociologists, Eugene Litwack and Melvin Seeman and their associates, in the name of the importance of the network of extended kinship relations beyond the nuclear family. To my mind the two views are not contradictory but complementary. The concept of isolation applies in the first instance to kinship structure as seen in the perspective of anthropological studies in that field. In this context our system represents an extreme type, which is well described by that term. It does not, however, follow that all relations to kin outside the nuclear family are broken. Indeed the very psychological importance for the individual of the nuclear family in which he was born and brought up would make any such conception impossible.

By and large, however, as our population elements are further removed from peasant or other similar backgrounds, these extended kinship elements do not form firmly structured units of the social system. They are not residential or economic units—in the consuming, to say nothing of the producing, sense—nor are they "corporate groups" in the sense that clans and lineages in so many societies have been. There are above all two significant features of their relations to the nuclear family. First, in the maintenance of going relations, though there seems to be clear precedence of members of the families of orientation of both spouses—parents so long as they live, and siblings, even among siblings as between the two families, and much more so beyond that—there is a marked optional quality of the expectation system. There certainly are some structured preferences on kinship bases, and others on those of geographical propinquity, but still there is a strong tendency for kinship to shade into friendship in the sense of absence from the latter of ascriptive components of membership. Hence, the amount of visiting, of common activity, of telephone and written communication, etc., is highly variable within formal categories of relationship. This suggests that extended kin constitute a resource which may be selectively taken advantage of within considerable limits.

This supposition is greatly strengthened by the second consideration. This is the extent to which extended kin, especially members of the family of orientation but not only they, serve as a "reserve" of expectations of solidarity and willingness to implement them which can be mobilized in case of need. To take one primary context, there is a clear expectation that adult siblings, children, and, increasingly, parents of adults will be economically independent and should not need to be the recipients of direct financial aid from relatives. The extended family is, in this sense, normally not a solitary-operating economic unit. In case of special need, however, the first obligation to help, if there is no organized community provision and sometimes when there is, falls on close relatives who are financially able to bear the burden. Such obligations are not likely to be unlimited, but they are none the less real—in cases of sickness, of the dependency of old age, and similar cases.

An interesting case is the one mentioned above. The tendency is for earlier marriage, which, in the most highly educated groups, very frequently occurs before completion of higher education. Not only does this situation give rise to an important part of the employment of younger married women—who thereby earn the fictional degree of

P.H.T. ("put hubby through"). There is also a substantial amount of aid from parents and some from older siblings which helps fill the gap. Often this is partially concealed in the form of "gifts," e.g., of a car or a vacation trip, testifying to the importance of the need for "independence." Ritual solidarity on the occasion of weddings, but even more especially funerals, fits in with this pattern.

On this background I may now turn to a few functional and analytical considerations. More than any other influence, psychoanalytic psychology has, during the last generation, made us aware of two crucial things. The first is the fundamental importance for the individual personality of the process of growing up in the intimacies of the family. Not only is mental illness to a large, though by no means exclusive, extent generated in the relations of a child to members of his family [2], but normal personality development is highly contingent on the proper combination of influences operating in the family situation. Of course the family stands by no means alone, and as the child grows older, influences from the neighborhood, then the school and beyond become increasingly important. The family, however, lays the essential foundations and continues always to be important.

There has been a good deal of discussion of the importance of psychological "security" in this whole context. An individual's sense of security naturally depends on his experience in his family of orientation. It remains, however, an essential problem throughout life [3]. We have become increasingly aware that for the adult, in psychologically very complex ways, his family of procreation is dynamically most intimately linked with his family of orientation. The experience of parenthood is of course a recapitulation in reverse of that of the child in relation to his parents, and in important ways reactivates the psychological structures belonging to that period. Just as much, marriage is a complex organization of components in the personality which are derived from childhood experience—the common involvement of eroticism in both is the surest clue to the relationship.

For the normal adult, then, his marriage and his role as parent constitute the primary going reinforcement of his psychological security. The family can thus be seen to have two primary functions, not one. On the one hand it is the primary agent of socialization of the child, while on the other it is the primary basis of security for the normal adult. Moreover, the linkage of these two functions is very close. The point may be put by saying that their common responsibility as parents is the most important focus of the solidarity of marriage partners, and that the desire for children is the natural outcome of a solid "romantic" attraction between two persons of opposite sex. The primary link between these two functions in terms of agency is clearly the feminine role in its dual capacity as mother and as wife.

I think it reasonable to suggest that the broad pattern of the contemporary American family fits this functional analysis. It seems to be a case of a process of differentiation through which the central functions of early socialization and giving individuals a psychological security base have become separated out from others to which they have been ascribed in less differentiated societies. The sharing of the common household as the place to "live" with all its implications is the fundamental phenomenon—it is this sharing which makes the normal nuclear family a distinctive unit which cannot be confused with *any* others, based either on kinship or on other criteria. The home, its furnishings, equipment, and the rest constitute the "logistic" base for the performance of this dual set of primary functions.

The family, however, is not only a setting into which individuals escape from the pressures of the outside society; it also has profoundly important functions in that society. The keynotes to what I have in mind may be stated with reference to two concepts mentioned above, namely that of "reserves" of solidarity and that of basic trust as discussed by Erickson. Following Durkheim, I should say that one of, to me the four, essential conditions of the adequate functioning of a social system is the solidarity among its members. This may be conceived as their motivational readiness to accept their common belongingness as members of a collective system and to *trust* each other to fulfill mutual expectations attached to membership in their respective roles.

The more differentiated and the larger the scale of the social system which depends on solidarity, however, the less can solidarity be dependent on common membership in groups where norms are highly particularistic and the relations rigidly ascribed, and where loyalties are highly diffuse and grounded in immediate affective motivational interests. Thus national community and a highly generalized system of legal norms are foci of organization highly dependent on solidarity, but clearly not meeting the above criteria. The problem is, how is it possible to develop solidarity and the attendant mutuality of trust where these conditions do not obtain—or is it possible at all?

As a first approach to an answer it may be said that the family is the "primordial" solitary unit of all human societies. Indeed, in the most primitive, kinship, which includes much more than the nuclear family, is the mode of organization of *all* solidarity. Furthermore, it is within these units that all the principal human needs are met. In a modern society this can be true only for the small child. For him "dependency" in the most diffuse sense is more highly concentrated in his relations within this small unit than in any other previous social conditions—a unit which we have seen is more sharply distinguished from others, both of kinship and of nonkinship constitution. As the child matures he develops a variety of roles outside his family. First, perhaps, come neighborhood play groups, then participation in formal education in the school with, concurrently, a new order of relation to age-peers—in the elementary school period virtually confined to the same sex, later increasingly involving the opposite sex. Then more or less well coordinated in time comes emergence into the adult responsibilities of occupational roles and of marriage. The latter usually eventuates in parenthood.

One aspect of the process is that from total and intense dependency on the family of orientation the child becomes increasingly independent from *that* nuclear family, and he continues to play a wide range of nonfamilial roles in his later life. Indeed his capacity to do so successfully is one of the two principal indices of the success of the socialization function in the family of orientation. But the other dramatic aspect is the switchover from family of orientation to the new family of procreation through marriage. The intensity of its emotional significance is attested by the pattern of romantic love on the one hand and the deep concern for having children on the other—both of which are in important part motivated by residues of childhood socialization experience.

Finally, let me emphasize again that the modern family has been deprived of a whole range of its historic functions, particularly those of economic production, but also others. It has become not only a structurally differentiated but a functionally specialized agency. What then can be said about the significance of these remaining specialized functions, not only for the personalities of the individual members but for the wider society?

I suggested above that solidarity was one of four principal conditions of the functioning of a social system. The other three may be said to be economic productivity; political effectiveness, not only for the society as a whole but also for its important collectively organized subsystems; and the integrity of institutionalization of its value commitments. Comparison with one or more of these three may yield suggestions of the significance of what is gained by individuals in their families of orientation and, as it were, "stored" in those of procreation.

The comparison may seem farfetched, but I suggest quite seriously that the grounding of the value of money in "real assets" and its most elementary form in metal coinage are the "primordial" bases of productivity in a sense parallel to that in which family solidarity is the primordial basis of social solidarity generally, "guaranteed" by the personal security of the individual. It is the groundwork on which the possibility of mutual trust in ramified systems of associative relationships—and hence openness to mutual influence—is built in a complex society. Furthermore, because of the irreducible element of ascription on the parent-child relationship, this significance of family solidarity comes to focus in that of the marriage relationship. One of the striking features of modern marriage is, of course, its increasingly voluntary character, This is the product of a long evolution from maximally prescriptive marriages in kinship terms, through marriages arranged by parents and other kin. It is the prototypical, fully unfettered personal commitment to a merging of interests, fortunes, and responsibilities. It is, however, not a simple contract for the mutual furtherance of specific interests, but a diffuse merging, with understood differentiation of function, "for better, for worse, for richer, for poorer," etc. This establishes a certain presumption, that persons capable of honestly undertaking such a commitment of mutual loyalty, including the attendant responsibilities of parenthood, may be regarded as generally trustworthy persons.

It is this generalization of the presumption of trustworthiness which seems to me to be the most crucial societal asset grounded in the solidarity of the family. To help in understanding how this can work it may be recalled that in the parallel context the value of money is grounded in the economic utility, first of real assets generally, then of its metal "base." I suggest that the solidarity of marriage is parallel to the utility of gold—perhaps a not unfamiliar figure of speech. But money as medium of exchange is not a real asset in the present sense: it has no "commodity value." It is a means of acquiring real assets and in turn can itself be acquired by selling them, but as the medium it cannot be consumed. Its significance lies in the possibility of a kind of pooling of the resources of the exchanging system. This involves increased risk for units who put some of their resources into monetary form—as they must if such a system is to operate. But if the value of the medium is secure, the units taken severally and the system as a whole gain enormously in productive potential, especially when not only finished goods and services but the factors of production become marketable.

The indispensable condition of security of the value of the monetary medium cannot, however, rest only on the intrinsic commodity value of its metallic base. It must rest just as much on confidence in exchangeability for real assets, including the availability of such assets in the system—hence the general level of productivity of the system.

The analogue of money as a measure of utility and medium of economic exchange in the field of social solidarity is what, in a technical sense, I have called influence [4]. By this I mean generalized capacity to persuade, through giving "good reasons" why the object of influence should believe or do something in "his own interest." The outcome of successful use of influence in this sense is an increased level of consensus or solidarity in the system to which both belong—though of course the relation to third parties remains problematical.

Persuasion may be carried out by "intrinsic means," e.g., direct information of commitment of intentions to specific action. This is analogous to the exchange of real assets through barter. What I mean by influence goes beyond this to persuade and thereby mobilize commitments, power of control of resources, through a generalized symbolic medium. This consists essentially in the "reputation" of the user of influence for a combination of integrity in commitment to the values presumptively shared with the object of influence, ability to help mobilize the necessary resources, and competence in implementing any action implications of the achieved consensus. Thus, to take an example which is very familiar, physicians very generally use influence to get the consent of patients or their families to recommended regimes of treatment. Information alone would not do because so frequently the layman is not competent to evaluate technical information even if it is given to him. He must *trust* both the physician's competence and his integrity. Without the institutionalization of this truth, the presumption that a physician is *trustworthy*, the effectiveness of health care in our complex society would be very much lower than it is. This, however, is only one of many examples which could be adduced. The necessity for influence to bridge the gap between the responsibilities taken by political leadership and the competence of their constituents to evaluate the issues by themselves is certainly one of the most striking instances. The assassination of President Kennedy brought out with special vividness the extent to which not only Americans but much of the world depended on his leadership and was in fact accessible to his influence—however severe the limits to which it was subject, e.g., to Congress. This influence is, in turn, a function on the one hand of the great office of the American Presidency and on the other of the personality of the incumbent.

If, then, influence can be considered to be a generalized medium parallel to money—and to political power—it would be reasonable to believe that on the one hand its value is grounded in the "gold" of family solidarity, while on the other hand it depends on the capacity of the relevant social system or systems to achieve, maintain, and extend its solidarity, expressed above all in its capacity to achieve consensus in matters involving actual and potential conflict of interest. Clearly, trusting others, especially those with whom one does not have a prior diffuse relation of solidarity, involves risk, just as leaving one's economic assets in banks rather than in gold involves risk. The prevalence of anxiety over the risks of trust is eloquent testimony to this. Thus there is a vocal minority who consider all medical practitioners to be no better, than pious frauds who simply exploit the helplessness and gullibility of their patients. Others, or many of the same people, consider all politicians to be simple parasites, who are promoting their personal interests at the expense of the public. Finally, the seriousness of basic mistrust in international affairs, especially where ideological conflicts are involved, scarcely needs further comment.

Furthermore, there are many different levels of differentiation of influence systems, which can be analyzed as parallel to that of monetary systems extending from simple market exchange, through the marketability as noted of the factors of production, notably labor and capital, to complex systems involving elaborate forms of banking and credit. The parallel to simple markets for consumers' goods lies in the use of influence to persuade people to make decisions and commitments which are immediately within their capacities or spheres of freedom of action to make. Thus a physician may use his influence to persuade a patient to accept a recommended course of treatment though at the sacrifice of time, money, and other things, including the assumption of risks.

It is a much further step in differentiation to establish systems where the factors involved in enhancing the solidarity of a system are themselves mobilized by the use of influence. A major type of example would seem to be those elements of educational processes which are essentially optional in the system in question. Thus in order to be influential, the physician must have been properly trained. We tend, in evaluating professional training, to emphasize the factor of competence, but it would seem that reputation for integrity is no less important, and indeed access to facilities—i.e., through membership in the staff of a first-rate hospital—would not be neglected. Hence from this point of view medical education may be regarded in part as an "influence-producing industry," in that it produces a class of professional people who have a far higher capacity than would otherwise be the case to persuade people to accept good health care. The ubiquitous resistances to such acceptance should make it clear that this is by no means to be taken for granted.

The analogy to credit in influence systems raises problems of sufficient complexity so that within the limits of this brief paper, it is probably best not to enter into them. One more general point about such systems does, however, need to be made. This is that the basic organizational form of influence systems is the voluntary association. This is not, however, a matter of presence or absence, but of a component in all relational systems with a collective significance. Influence, however, is a medium of persuasion and a person is not in the relevant sense genuinely persuaded unless he is entirely free to reject the influence. Intermixture with economic inducements, with explicit or implied coercive threats, or even appeal to prior commitments is not "pure" persuasion. Generally speaking, the voluntary association is the relational nexus within which there can be said to be a presumption of the achievability of consensus. It will be limited on the one hand by boundaries of membership, which may be more or less formalized, and on the other by boundaries of relevant content—thus consensus with one's physician is relevant within the sphere of health, but not, for example, within the sphere of political opinion.

In the light of these considerations, which may seem to digress a long way from the traditional interest of family sociology, let us now come back to the contemporary family. First this functional context may throw some light on the significance of some of the trends of development of that family. My suggestion here is that it is to be expected that the family would, as the foundation of the solidarity-influence system, itself develop progressively in the direction of the voluntary association. In the aspect of marriage this is very clear indeed —namely, the trend to make marriage as nearly as possible a purely personal and voluntary relationship. This has gone to the point where the depth of commitment is considered to a high degree to be a function of its voluntary character. More problematical, but highly significant, is the tendency to bring children into the status of members of a voluntary association much earlier and more extensively than before. Of course there is an inherent limitation to this trend in that infants cannot rationally "choose" their parents, but this is clearly a major trend in the American family.· Like other such trends it has undoubtedly had its excesses, and surely its limits are not yet clearly defined, but that it is a fundamental trend can scarcely be doubted. Perhaps the most important keynote is that by the isolation of the marriage pair from "structural supports" of more or less ascribed character, children are put in a position of having to trust their parents to an extremely high degree. The corollary is that parents will be expected to reciprocate this trust to an increasing degree, hence to trust children as far as possible as responsible members of the family association.

In this connection it is particularly important to note that what I call trust is *not* to be identified with moral commitment. Common values are certainly essential to the solidarity of any social system, but as *one* factor, not as its totality. Most problems of trust in the present sense arise at a different level where, presuming common values, the questions concern action within the sphere of autonomous personal responsibility. On the part of many parents, and more generally the "view-with-alarm" school of thought on the problems of contemporary youth, the tendency is to confuse the two, and to treat as essentially a moral problem what should be one of trust in the present sense. On the part of young people trained in independence, defining problems as moral tends to activate anxiety about the basic consensus—the complaint is, "Don't you trust me?"

A second major set of considerations emerges. This is that while the family is the primary locus of most elementary instrumental learning for children, e.g., walking and talking, and is for both children and adults an essential agency for meeting their biological and other needs, e.g., food, sleep, relaxation, etc., its most crucial functions lie in the area of solidarity. In socialization it is above all the agency for establishing cathexes and identification, for integration into the series of *social* systems in which the child will function as an adult. Above all, perhaps, it is the primary agency for developing his capacity to integrate with others, to trust and be trusted, to exercise influence, and to accept legitimate influence. Here, of course, two axes are essential. One is the balance of trust over distrust, the "intensity" component. The other is the component of generalization. This is the capacity to enter into solitary relations over a *range*, both of associative partners and of subject-matter areas. In view of the increasing pluralism of our type of society, this is a particularly critical factor. It has become essential for the responsible citizen to be able to balance a variety of complex contexts of obligation and expectation, to be ready to enter into many, but not arbitrarily to sacrifice the interests of some to others. My suggestion would be that the family type which approaches the pattern of voluntary association is the best instrument for laying the foundations of this capacity—though it must be supplemented by other agencies. For the adult the combination of marriage and parenthood in such a family type provides a more or less optimal basis for maintaining the motivational foundations of this more generalized capacity. In this connection socialization and adult participation are above all related in that the capacity to become a good spouse and parent is the underlying capacity for effective participation generally in solitary relations.

Finally, a third inference may be drawn. The "intrinsic utility" of gold is connected with certain features of its sheer physical stability. Its problematical feature is not this but its scarcity. The "gold" of solidarity, however, seems to be an intrinsically unstable entity. Its value depends on its being scarce in the sense that persons who disperse their deepest interpersonal loyalties too widely, e.g., through incapacity to commit them adequately to their marriages and their own children, thereby on the whole lessen their capacity for trust in more generalized and impersonal contexts. But the balances in the personality system, and the meshing of the several commitments in the family, seem to be inherently complex and precarious. This seems to be the most fundamental reason why, once socialized, the typical individual is not finished with family problems, but positively *needs* to marry and to have children.

It would seem to follow that in so far as families are placed under strain, their tendencies to breakdown and various social pathologies should be expected to be conspicuous. Hence I have long felt that what underlay the high divorce rates of our society was not, as so commonly alleged, the decline in the importance of marriage, people's "indifference" to it, but exactly the reverse [5]. Divorce is an index of the severity of the burden placed on the marriage relationship in modern society, and back of that, of the importance of its functions. It is not correct to treat it in any simple sense as a symptom of "decline," except the decline of older patterns of social organization which in any case could not be fitted in with the other principal features of modern society. Essentially the same can be said of failures in the socialization of children, which, of course, are many. Modern child training is far more difficult and demanding on the parents but also on the children themselves than before. In this matter one should not be misled by economic affluence and the like. The hard physical work of a traditional farm boy is not nearly as difficult psychologically as the demands of secondary and higher education and adjustment to peers where the relationship patterns are freely responsible and not ascribed. Whether there is a larger proportion of serious breakdowns than in earlier times is exceedingly difficult to judge—the very anxiety generated by the present difficulties certainly predisposes to the expectation of failure.

But that a substantial proportion should be expected is almost in the nature of the relation of the family to the general society of which it is such an essential part.

I was asked to write about the normal American family. In doing so, however, one is eventually led to some consideration of its strains and pathologies. In conclusion, especially since this is a group predominantly of social workers, it seems appropriate to say a few words about that group in which the strains and difficulties of the modern family situation, as in other respects, are most highly concentrated, namely, those who stand lowest on the familiar scales of socioeconomic status, as by family income, education, job level, housing, and type of neighborhood.

Both with respect to the family and in other respects the trends of development of modern society have led to a concentration of certain problems in this lowest group, and by differentiation to a removal or weakening of the structural supports of the kind which, for example, have been more characteristic of the lower statuses in peasant societies —though the tendency to romanticize rural life should not lead one to overlook the reality of many noxious "rural slums." From a middle-class perspective absolute levels of deprivation stand out very prominently, but sociologically it seems more important to emphasize *relative* deprivation. By this I mean that the general trend of development in our society has included a massive upgrading of standards in many respects and the inclusion of much higher proportions of the population in the groups enjoying the higher standards. Education and the general standard of living are perhaps the most conspicuous contexts, but it is also important that the proportion of the labor force in unskilled occupations has declined greatly.

The great source of difficulty is, of course, that in spite of many improved welfare arrangements, in a society where mobility and hence competition for preferment are so conspicuous, it has not yet proved possible to prevent a very substantial residual group from failing to meet what, however vaguely, must be defined as the minimum generally acceptable standards. To a degree and in certain respects it is legitimate to treat these cases as "failures" at the individual level, but it is surely much more a failure of the society in that though some persons brought up in the lowest conditions succeed in lifting themselves out of them, those set in them by and large are certainly severely handicapped in a wide variety of ways.

It is well known what a wide variety of "social problems" is concentrated in this group: poverty itself; substandard housing; educational retardation and early "dropout"; juvenile delinquency; alcoholism; illness, both physical and mental; broken families; and others. It is clearly a vicious circle which, like the high divorce rates more generally, is in important part a consequence of the generally rapid process of upgrading. Thus, to take one example, the very rise in general educational standards makes the position of the relatively handicapped—whether by low IQ, lack of family support, or other factors—relatively *more* difficult. I suggest that this is a major factor in juvenile delinquency.

It is a healthy sign that there are recent indications of increased concern over this situation as a national problem, a concern apparently brought to focus primarily by two interconnected developments, namely, the new phase of the struggle of the Negro for equality and the chronic unemployment connected with automation, even in an economy which is developing at a relatively normal rate.

Whatever the residue of a genuine "caste" system in the South, which is certainly rapidly breaking up, on the national level it has long been clear that basically the race problem is a *class* problem, but in a dual respect. The more obvious one is that the Negro, especially in urban society, has in fact been predominantly in lower-class status, and that in so far as there is any empirical truth in his imputed character-istics, these have been the characteristics shared with other lower-class groups. Indeed in study after study, for example, of such "pathological" behavior as delinquency, it has turned out that if class is controlled sufficiently rigorously the differences by race are negligible.

The second primary aspect, however, is that the Negro has become a, if not the, primary *symbol* of lower-class status. The new phase of the protest movement testifies that he himself is coming to be much less willing to accept this imputation, but it is this symbolic status which is at the core of the whole resistance to granting equal status. Furthermore the resistance centers in the white groups who feel insecure in their own status. The nonrational "reasoning," which must be interpreted in psychoanalytic terms, is to the effect that "if to be lower class is to be black, since I am white there is no danger of *my* falling into that status." Acceptance of the Negro is basically equal status, thus, would remove an important symbolic support to the security of the least secure white elements. The latter are presumably concentrated near the margin of lower-class status, but need not be found only there [6].

It has recently been much publicized that the Negro has double the rate of unemployment of the white labor force, which is a dramatic confirmation of this status since it is in these lower groups generally that unemployment is concentrated.

There is no space to discuss this general situation further. I would like only to point out the relevance of my main analysis to this context. It may, that is, be reasonably supposed that a major factor in the vicious circle to which the lower class, white and Negro alike, is subject lies in the field of the relations between the family and the solidarity and in-fluence systems with which it articulates. My essential point is that this is a two-way and not a one-way relation. By nearly every criterion "family disorganization" is particularly prevalent in the lower class. Not only is this one principal source of the other social problems in that group, but in another sense it is not an isolated phenomenon. It is in part a consequence of the low input to lower-class families of influence in the special form of "social acceptance": from the point of view of the higher groups they are "the wrong kind of people."

Though it is not possible to mobilize the relevant evidence here, I think it is adequate to support the proposition that broadly the lower class, including its Negro component, is not characterized by basically different value commitments from those of the higher groups. It is true that members of the lower class are economically disadvantaged. Perhaps their least serious handicap lies in the field of political power since both the ballot and power through trade unions is available to them, though very incompletely mobilized.

My own view, however, is that the critical problem of the status of the lower class is social acceptance. From any points of view accessible to social policy, it seems to me that in particular it is futile to expect that by exhortation lower-class families will be motivated to pull themselves together. Indeed, I am of the opinion that economic subsidies will not be effective unless they are accompanied by social support on a sufficient scale. The cure for the ills of the lower-class family is a massive input of the very social medium for which the higher-class (not upper-class) family is the primary base in our society in one major set of respects—influence in the form of social acceptance.

The essential goal of any such policies would be to break down group identifications which are interpreted directly, or indirectly as by the criterion of race, as lower class in the invidious residual sense. The neighborhood, the school, and the church are probably the crucial empirical areas for the important reason that the more limited the social participation, the more it is confined to the more immediately personal concerns of the family. Thus increased income would be likely to be important only so far as it enables families to break away from lower-class identifications, e.g., by neighborhood.

It would be expected that improvement in the solidarity of families at the lowest socioeconomic levels would be perhaps the most sensitive index to the success of such social policies. There must always be a bottom of any social scale with a hierarchical aspect, and an achievement-oriented society must be partly hierarchical. But this does not mean that the "outside" status of the present lower class is inevitable. I regard this as perhaps the most important single internal challenge to American society today.

NOTES

[1] Another important set of facts concerns the very large proportion of single-family dwellings in this country, and within this, the high proportion of owner occupancy.

[2] The psychoanalytic tendency has been to "individualize" these relations by treating a child's relation to each of the other members one at a time—his mother, his father, his rivalry with a particular sibling, etc. More recently, however, there has emerged, particularly in the work of Theodore Lidz and his associates, a tendency to treat the family as a system in such a way that both illness and normality are conceived to be a function of the impact of the system as a whole—not of particular members in isolation—on the individual.

[3] Erik Erikson has, in his *Childhood and Society*, given an especially clear formulation of this point in his discussion of the importance of what he calls "basic trust" and its relation to personality development.

[4] Cf. Talcott Parsons, "On the Concept of Influence," *Public Opinion Quarterly*, Spring, 1963.

[5] To take an analogy which I think is appropriate, the distressing toll of highway accidents is an index of the positive importance, and even, to a degree, of the successful ordering, of vehicular traffic. There is one way to abolish such accidents, namely, to eliminate motor vehicles. Similarly, modern divorce could be quite certainly eliminated if we went back to a primitive kinship system. But we are not, in either case, ready to pay the cost.

[6] It is important to note that I do not identify lower and "working" class here. The solid upper-working-class groups, especially in the more skilled trades, seem to be pretty definitely included in the main national community in a sense in which the lower are not.

Economic Deprivation and Family Patterns

ARTHUR BESNER

The elemental place of the family in every person's life and the primacy of its influence make it a factor to be reckoned with in any effort at long-term change, either in society or in the individual. If, for example, we are to intervene successfully in the lives of the several million children in families receiving public assistance, we must at least know the outlines of their home environments. Otherwise, we are likely to miss the most vital points of leverage for our efforts.

Since family patterns are responsive to basic life conditions, the relative prevalence of different types of families varies between societies and between segments of a single society. Research to date seems to show that in the United States economic deprivation is associated with relatively more frequent occurrence of some family types and with characteristic differences in the internal functioning of the classic two-parent nuclear family.

Some of the most significant of these features are revealed in the typical lower class courtship, adjustment to marriage, division of marital responsibilities, marital values, peculiarities of the single-parent family, and child-rearing patterns.

COURTSHIP

In the very selection of a spouse, lower class men and women manifest several of the attitudes highlighted in the preceding paper.* For instance, there is some evidence that they do not regard themselves as active choosers of mates.[1] This fatalism on sense of powerlessness may be responsible, in part, for the relative lack of initiative displayed during courtship.

In comparison with other social classes, the American poor are influenced more by residential proximity in selection of marriage partners.[2] This appears consistent with the lower class reluctance to contract primary social relationships outside the immediate environment.[3]

Reprinted from *Low-Income Life Styles,* by Lola Irelan, ed., U.S. Department of Health, Education, and Welfare, Publication No. 14 (1966), pp. 15–29.

Another contrast is the relative absence of strong feelings about the decision to marry. This is not surprising in view of the lower class inclination to fatalism and the consequent belief that one cannot control even the selection of a marriage partner.

Courtship is frequently of short duration. In one study of the marriage patterns of the poor, the typical responses to a question about the decision to marry were—"We just did it"; "It was just time"; "Somehow it was settled."[4] What is also to be expected is a lack of elaboration in planning marriage (possibly related to the shortened time perspective of the class), and corroborating findings are beginning to emerge.

ASPECTS OF EARLY ADJUSTMENT TO MARRIAGE

Discernible from the very beginning of the typical lower class marriage is a pattern that seems to permeate the entire family organization. This is the relative emotional isolation of spouses from each other. In contrast to the typical newly married couple in the middle class, lower class partners cling to old friendship and kinship ties rather than reorganize ties to make each partner comfortable in moving within one network. For example, the middle-class couple typically will drop from their circle of close friends those persons who are unacceptable to either spouse. This is not generally true for the lower-class couple.[5] Individual choice is not the only or even the most important motivation operating to produce this pattern. Poverty lends itself to it, for each partner must cling to time-tested ties as insurance against the future.

Needs which are not satisfied through the conjugal family may be supplied through friends and relatives. In a comprehensive west coast study of social class, it was reported that lower class persons interact more with their kin, absolutely as well as relatively to their interaction with others.[6] The individual quality of these relationships may make them valued, particularly when they provide means of avoiding potentially painful encounters with institutional sources of support. Analysis of data collected by the Bureau of Social Science Research, in connection with a project supported by the Welfare Administration,[7] showed that the poor, in comparison with the non-poor, receive substantially more help from relatives (see table, page 69).

DIVISION OF MARITAL RESPONSIBILITIES

That the lower class family is a relatively loose structure rather than a tightly unified social entity becomes more apparent as one analyzes the roles of the marriage partners. The division of their responsibilities is formal. Each partner is something of a specialist who relates to the other as a specialist.[8] For example, in many of the homes of the poor there is a sharp demarcation of roles according to whether the jobs are inside or outside the house.[9] This is in contrast to the more flexible pattern in the middle-class home, where the needs of the family are usually satisfied through joint planning and sharing of domestic and social functions. To illustrate, child-rearing is usually within the domain of the wife in the lower class while both parents in the middle class usually expect to be involved in the socialization of children. There is division of labor in the middle-class home, but it is relatively fluid; an interest in doing things together allows interchangeability in roles.[10] The firmer lines of authority drawn in the lower class home serve to reinforce the pattern of psychological isolation and to maintain the emotional distance between spouses by limiting permissible channels for communication.[11]

Extent of Aid Received from Kin, by Economic Level

Economic Level	Percent Receiving Different Levels of Aid	
	Moderate or Less	More than Moderate
Poor (N = 169)	76	24
Not Poor (N = 160)	87	13
Percent difference*	11	11

* Significant at less than the .02 confidence level.

More research is needed on the distribution of responsibility in families, but available information suggests an inverse relationship between social status and the degree of responsibility assumed by the wife.[12] That is, the lower class wife has relatively more duties than either the middle or upper status wife or the lower class husband. There are several studies which show that the lower class wife has more influence in family decision-making than housewives on other socioeconomic levels.

This is especially noticeable in the area of family financial management. As socioeconomic status decreases, there is more tendency to feel that "earning the money is the man's responsibility; spending it wisely is the woman's duty."[13] The husband's role in finances thus ends after delivery of his paycheck. In contrast, the middle-class couple most commonly share decisions over major purchases and reach some measure of agreement over the portion of the budget allotted to the wife for daily purchases. The middle-class husband has a definite role. In fact, it has been said that he serves as "architect of the family's fiscal policy," determining the proportion which should be saved, designing the insurance program, and planning how to invest any extra money.[14] Economic conditions may have much to do with these contrasting patterns. When a large proportion of income is consigned to routine necessities, there is less need for joint functioning.

Even in those areas in which sharing is culturally prescribed, lower class husbands have a low rate of performance. For example, compared with upper and middle-class husbands, they are less likely to share in the supervision of the children's school work, to decide on family insurance, or plan vacations.[15]

The great differential in the distribution of responsibilities between the husband and wife suggests that the husband plays a minimal role in the low-income home. He seems to conceive of his responsibility as being the simple provision of money to meet material needs.[16] Nevertheless; he does seem to expect a periodic reassurance of at least a titular authority,[17] while at the same time demanding freedom to come and go at will. As a result, the lower class wife performs the majority of functions in the home mostly by her husband's default rather than through a usurpation of power.

MARITAL VALUES

The emotional distance between lower class husbands and wives supports, and is in turn reinforced by, a disparity in marital values. Their initial isolation from each other prevents the kind of exchange which could reconcile their opposing needs. Lower class men and women are likely to see themselves as opposed to each other and belonging to quite different worlds.[18] There is little joint social participation either within or outside the home; family members usually go their separate ways in search of diversion.[19] There are comparatively few instances of friends in common, and visiting as a family group seldom extends beyond a narrowly circumscribed kinship circle.[20]

Anthropologists have ascribed a "cult of masculine superiority" to the lower class, and this would seem to be another force producing and maintaining the isolation between husband and wife. Researchers have found from analyses of interviews with low-income men and women that, in relation to one another, the men feel dominant and the women downtrodden.[21] This seems to be the case even in face of the fact that many low-income women, particularly low-income Negro women, can more easily obtain and hold jobs than the men.[22]

Interestingly, it has been found that lower class men and women also tend to view each other much as the class, as a whole, perceives the external world. Thus men are described by the women as unpredictable, difficult to understand, inconsiderate, and overwhelming. Similarly, lower class husbands tend to think on women as temperamental, emotional, demanding, and irrational.[23]

Isolation, as well as a great deal of friction, may arise from the general expectations lower class husbands and wives have of each other. It was implied in the discussion on the division of responsibilities that the husband regards the home simply as a retreat for the satisfaction of physical needs. Accordingly, the husband places primary value on the non-emotional aspects of the wife's role. A "good wife," for him, is one who prepares the meals for the family, keeps his clothing in order, raises the children, and frees him from everyday worries. In short, the husband conceptualizes the wife's role as housekeeper-mother. This is antithetical to the wife's wish for emphasis on the interpersonal aspects of marriage, the friend-lover role. Her wish for open expression of affection is not met by the husband who does not see this as important.[24] It is not that she resists the performance of household and motherly duties, rather she resents the husband's limitation of the marital relationship to them. It has been suggested that much of the tension observed in the families of the poor arises from this basic conflict in role expectation.

Hence, the lower class wife must endure emotional deprivation as well as the ever-present fear of physical-economic deprivation. She is handicapped, however, by her subservient position vis-a-vis her husband and by her view of men, from managing the marital relationship to serve her needs better. What might also be thought of as a handicap is the special significance of marriage to the lower class woman. Women in the lower socioeconomic strata are likely to find it difficult to think of themselves other than in a familial role. They tend to feel somewhat lost after outgrowing the daughter role and look to the wife-mother role to regain a clear-cut familial status. Some family sociologists have suggested this as a reason for the fact that women in the lower socioeconomic classes marry at a younger age than women in higher social classes.[25] Furthermore, from the lower class woman's viewpoint, a husband offers the most tangible opportunity for love and security and represents a defense against the workings of the unpredictable world. The wife is thus wary about asserting herself against the husband lest he should leave her, though the gap between the ideal and the real husband is great.

The special significance of motherhood to the lower class woman may arise from economic deprivation as well as the emotional deprivation in the husband-wife relationship. Being denied most of the tangible and intangible satisfactions of marriage, the lower class woman defines herself mainly as a mother and seeks gratification in life through this function. The limited outside interests of the lower class woman also increase the significance of motherhood. Children may represent compensation for the husband's lack of attention and for the dullness of life. The mother-child relationship is considered by many students to be the strongest and most enduring family tie in the lower class. A recent study of lower class women in Philadelphia illustrates the greater significance attached to the role of mother as opposed to that of a wife. Specifically, the mothers were asked: "If you could only be a wife or mother (but not both) which would you choose?" The majority of these women, in both the single and paired parent groups, chose the mother's role.[26]

The passive role of the father in the home seems to strengthen the dependence of children on the mother. Lower class children, studies report, are reluctant to confide in the father. Those who try may experience rebuffs from the fathers who maintain independence from child-rearing or may be discouraged by mothers.[27]

THE SINGLE–PARENT FAMILY IN THE LOWER CLASS

The characteristics of lower class family life seem to be crystallized most intensely in the single-parent family. The female-based household is a widely prevalent and persisting form among the poor. It has been estimated that between 25 and 40 percent of the child-rearing units in urban "slum" areas are of this type.[28] Usually such a household will consist of one or more women of child-bearing age, often related by blood or through marriage and spanning two or more generations—for example, the "single parent" and her mother and/or aunt. Associated with this household type is a marriage pattern in which the woman has a succession of temporary partners during her procreative years.[28]

Some research suggests that this type of family is not entirely disadvantageous. We have noted the minimal significance of the husband and father in some lower class families and his insistence on being recognized as the family head without making substantial contributions. Frequently it is the husband who is the economic burden—lower class women often realize more success in obtaining and holding a job than the men. It may be a gamble to marry and risk losing control over a low but stable income. In short, middle-class ideals of marriage for economic support, love and companionship simply are not realistic for many lower class women. Need for love and companionship and the desire for children lead some of these women to enter into brief non-legal unions.

The greater bulk of research, however, points out the dysfunctions of single-parent families. For children, the effects of the absence or only sporadic presence of a father are detrimental to emotional and social development. There are detailed studies which report a wide range of negative conditions associated with absence of the father. For example, such children, when compared under clinical observation with children who have fathers present in the home, are discovered to suffer from difficulty in resolving the oedipal conflict, overattachment and dependence on the mother, and lack of a solid basis for the development of both masculine and feminine roles.[29] More than other children, they experience unsatisfactory peer group relations and feel inferior and insecure.[30] Some studies have shown that these children focus more on the immediate than the future, a fact which has consequences for educational achievement and social mobility. Many of these children react as if they feel personally responsible for the father's absence. They often consider themselves unlovable and develop feelings of self-derogation. There is evidence that such children see love relationships between sexes as being capricious.[31]

As noted earlier, lower class women develop great emotional attachment to children as compensation for the emotional distance and lack of communication with their husbands. With absence of the adult male, this pattern sometimes intensifies.

A peer relationship often develops between the mother and her children of either sex. A son is sometimes expected to contribute economically and become the man of the house before he is really able.[32] This may also propel him to marriage before he has the training and background necessary to cope with its economic demands. Sometimes, older daughters are seen as rivals, competing with the mother for the attention of male acquaintances.[33] The prematurely adult role of a daughter is augmented when she has to become a housekeeper and part-time mother.

For the mother, however less painful it may be not to have to tolerate an unsatisfying marital relationship, the absence of a permanent adult male presents practical problems. She must usually take a job to support the family. Other functions discharged by the husband, however few these are in the lower class two-parent setting, also must be assumed. In short, she must engage in activities and to some degree manifest attributes generally associated with the adult male. There is also the problem of housing. In some jurisdictions, the policy of public housing discriminates against the female-based household.[34] This offers a strange dilemma since public housing is primarily for the poor and the female-headed household is a frequent family type among the poor.[35]

CHILD–REARING

Research on American child-rearing patterns has suffered from hazily defined concepts and from failure to explore the meaning as well as the pattern of behavior. Recent studies have moved toward correcting these lacks. However, it is still necessary to be cautious in using reported findings.

With this caveat in mind, it is nevertheless possible to list some of the effects of lower class status on the way children are reared.

Much of the earlier work concerned itself with techniques involved in child-rearing. Attention was paid to comparing the practices of different social classes on factors like weaning and feeding, cleanliness training, thumbsucking, techniques of discipline, aggression control,[36] etc. But even in the employment of this simple conceptual framework there were many inconsistencies in the findings. In some of the studies, middle-class parents were generally reported to be more exacting in their expectations. Training was reported to begin earlier than in the lower class home, with more emphasis on early training for responsibility and close supervision of children's activities. On the other hand, there were studies in which these trends went in the opposite direction.[37]

Recent studies have begun to probe the background of child-rearing techniques—the purpose for which parents do what they do in relation to their children.[38] Lower class parents appear more concerned with the development of "respectable" behavior in children—obedience, neatness, and cleanliness. Emphasis on discipline is particularly strict. Incidental findings of a recent study in Baltimore (see footnote 7) reveal a significant 9 per cent difference between poor and non-poor parents in emphasis on obedience:

Economic Level and Agreement With the Statement, "Obedience is the most important thing for parents to teach their children."

Economic Level	Percent Indicating Agreement
Poor (N = 169)	26
Not Poor (N = 166)	17
Percent difference*	9

* Significant at the .05 confidence level.

Middle-class parents can take respectability for granted. Child-rearing can center on developing self-reliance and independence in children and on encouraging their full realization of potentialities. These values, it should be noted, are voiced also by low-income parents. At this level, however, respectability is a more urgent need and is, therefore, more strongly emphasized in the training of children.

Most current research and a large part of the older data can be summarized in the statement that lower classes tend to be more "traditional" in raising their children, while the more affluent are able to emphasize "developmental" principles.[39] The traditional attitude values the physical duties performed by parents. The attention of parents is to maintenance functions—providing food for the children, making sure that they are clean and get sufficient rest, etc. The goal is to steer children to conformity with patterns of being neat and clean, obedient and respectful of parents, polite and socially acceptable. Here roles and parent-child interaction patterns are rigid and oriented toward maintaining order and discipline.[40]

Middle-class parents are more concerned with psychological growth and development than with specific behavioral conformities. Permissive guidance, with parents training children for self-reliance, encouraging independence, and providing intellectual stimulation, is the keynote. Roles and patterns of interaction between parent and child are dynamic and flexible. The child has wide latitude in which to develop and express himself.

Several explanations have been advanced and explored for this class differential. Traditional child-rearing can be considered natural to a milieu of economic deprivation where the focus must be on the physical, rather than the introspective, aspect of life. Income stability, on the other hand, allows parents to concentrate on the inner dynamics of children—their motivations and feelings.[41] Such consideration of inner development would be especially difficult for the poor because of their usually low educational backgrounds and relative inability to deal with the abstract.

Occupational experiences probably have great effects on the behavior of parents and on their expectations of children. The occupations of the poor involve manipulation of physical objects at a comparatively unskilled level under routine and direct supervision. In contrast, members of the middle and higher strata manipulate ideas and symbols in their occupations. When they do manipulate physical objects, it is at a more skilled level. They also enjoy more independence and self-direction in their work. The rigid and ordered behavior of lower class homes is understandable as a carry-over from their occupational setting. The middle-class parents' attention to the internal dynamics of the child and their more flexible attitudes toward his behavior are natural extensions of their occupational climate. Traits esteemed in children follow the same pattern. Traits encouraged by lower class parents—obedience, politeness, etc.—are those which are functional to low occupational jobs. On the other hand, traits that middle-class parents value in children—responsibility, initiative, independence, etc.—are themselves traits [which are] functional to success in the middle-class occupational life.[42]

SUMMARY AND IMPLICATIONS

The low-income American family is a qualitative variant of the national family type. Differences are of degree rather than of type. The nuclear lower class family is generally less closeknit. Husbands and wives have fewer overlapping responsibilities, with the wife having more responsibility allotted to her than is true in the middle class. Greater possibility for husband-wife conflict exists due to lack of agreement on what is expected from marriage. The single-parent family, headed by a woman, is more frequent. Child-rearing patterns concentrate more on discipline and conformity training than on psychological development of the child.

Poverty and dependency, which this generation of Americans has committed itself to destroying, must be grappled with in its nuclear setting—the family life of the poor. More research will increase and make more useful the knowledge which has been summarized here. Meanwhile, on the basis of the information that we have, we can be very hopeful. We know that low-income parents do value better material lives for their children. We know that they are concerned for their children's psychological health and development but lack both knowledge and opportunity to implement their concern.

Any attempt to reach these parents with help, through information, training, material aid, or indigenous action programs, must be planned to allow for:

1. The possible lack of understanding or consensus between husbands and wives. From what we now know, women appear to have a greater investment in family life than do their husbands. They are probably better targets for educational programs and for any attempt to bring the lower class in from society's perimeter. Their own present needs would be served by efforts to help them help their children. Lower class husbands, on the other hand, may feel threatened by attempts to upgrade the family or its children. Intervention programs must be planned so as to serve the needs of the entire family and to allow for the emotional and communicative isolation within it. This would be particularly true in the area of education for family planning.

2. The material and economic limitations of lower class family living. The permissive, psychological techniques of child-rearing, so touted by middle-class intellectuals, are often impossible in a low-income setting. A middle-class child with a temper tantrum can be sent to his own room until the storm is over. When an entire family lives in two rooms, however, a screaming child cannot be isolated and must be silenced. When a husbandless woman works all day to support her family, it is next to impossible for her to avoid making more than ordinary demands on her older children. Material and financial help can do much to alleviate these conditions and enable parents to participate in programs for change. Such programs should be supplemented by research into the means for improving lives within the limitations which do exist.

3. The efficiency, limited though it may be, of lower class family patterns. We should be careful, when trying to discourage seemingly pernicious forms, to see that alternate means are available to serve their purposes. The single-parent family, for example, despite its discomforts and negative aspects for children, is economically advantageous for some women at a poverty level. Such paradoxes must give pause to advocates of programs for the arbitrary elimination of apparently deviant life patterns.

NOTES

* Editor's Note: The paper is not included in this volume.

1 Rainwater, Lee. *And the Poor Get Children*. Quadrangle Books, Chicago, 1960, pp. 61–63.

2 Knupfer, Genevieve. "Portrait of the Underdog," *Public Opinion Quarterly*, Spring 1947, p. 107.

3 Reissman, Leonard. "Class, Leisure, and Social Participation," *American Sociological Review*, vol. 19. February 1954, pp. 76–84.

4 Rainwater, *op. cit.*, p. 63.

5 Cohen, Albert K., and Harold M. Hodges, Jr. "Characteristics of the Lower-Blue-Collar Class," *Social Problems*, vol. 10, no. 4, Spring 1963, pp. 303–334.

6 Cohen and Hodges, *op. cit.*, p. 310.

7 Derived from unpublished data made available by the Bureau of Social Science Research Inc., Washington, D.C., in connection with a project supported under the Cooperative Research and Demonstration Grants Program of the Welfare Administration and the Social Security Administration (Project No. 125, Leonard Goodman, principal investigator).

8 Komarovsky, Mirra. "Class Differences in Family Decision-Making on Expenditures," in Marvin B. Sussman, ed. *Sourcebook In Marriage and The Family*. 2nd ed. Houghton Mifflin Co., Boston, 1963, pp. 261–266. Keos, Earl L. "Class Differences in Family Reactions to Crisis," *Marriage and Family Living*, vol. 12, Summer 1950, p. 77. Rainwater, Lee, *et al. Workingman's Wife*. Oceana Publications, Inc., New York, 1959, pp. 80–87.

9 *Ibid.*, p. 80.

10 *Ibid.*, p. 81.

11 Rainwater, *And the Poor Get Children*, p. 69.

12 Olsen, Marvin E. "Distribution of Family Responsibilities and Social Stratification," *Marriage and Family Living*, vol. 22, February 1960, pp. 60–65: Blood, Robert O., Jr., and Donald M. Wolfe. *Husbands and Wives: The Dynamics of Married Living*. The Free Press, Glencoe, Ill., 1960, p. 61: Heer, David M. "Dominance and the Working Wife," *Social Forces*, vol. 36, May 1958, pp. 341–347.

13 Rainwater. *Workingman's Wife*, p. 82.

14 *Ibid.*, pp. 83–84.

15 Olsen, *op. cit.*, pp. 64–65.

16 Kohn, Melvin L., and Eleanor E. Carroll, "Social Class and the Allocation of Parental Responsibilities," *Sociometry*, December 1960, p. 389.

17 Cohen and Hodges, *op. cit.*, p. 327.

18 Herzog, Elizabeth. "Some Assumptions About the Poor," *Social Service Review*, vol. 37, no. 4, December 1963, p. 399.

19 Roberts, Robert E. T. "The Urban Lower Class in the United States of America." Prepared for Training Center, National Federation of Settlements and Neighborhood Centers. Mimeographed. August 1963.

20 *Ibid.*, p. 14.

21 Herzog, *op. cit.*, p. 400.

22 King, Charles E. "The Negro Maternal Family: A Product of an Economic and a Cultural System," *Social Forces*, vol. 24, October 1945, pp. 100–104.

23 Rainwater. *And the Poor Get Children*, pp. 72–77.

24 *Ibid.*, pp. 66–69.

25 *Ibid.*, pp. 71–72.

26 Bell, Robert R. "The One-Parent Mother in the Negro Lower Class." Paper read at the meetings of the Eastern Sociological Society, New York, 1965.

[27] Kohn and Carroll, *op. cit.*, p. 391.

[28] Miller, Walter B. "Implications of Urban Lower-Class Culture for Social Work." *Social Service Review*, vol. 33, September 1959, p. 225.

[29] Steigman, Joseph E. "The Deserted Family," *Social Casework*, vol. 38, April 1957, pp. 161–171: McCord, Joan, *et al.* "Some Effects of Paternal Absence on Male Children," *Journal of Abnormal and Social Psychology*, vol. 64, May 1962, pp. 361–367: Lerner, Samuel H. Effects of Desertion on Family Life, *Social Casework*, vol. 35, January 1954, pp. 3–8: Bartemeier, Leo. "The Contribution of the Father to the Mental Health of the Family," *American Journal of Psychiatry*, vol. 110, October 1953, pp. 277–280.

[30] Green, Morris, and Patricia Beall. "Paternal Deprivation: A Disturbance in Fathering," *Pediatrics*, vol. 30, July 1962, pp. 91–99; Lynn, David B., and William L. Sawrey, "The Effects of Father-Absence on Norwegian Boys and Girls," *Journal of Abnormal and Social Psychology*, vol. 59, September 1959, pp. 258–262.

[31] Gardner, George E. "Separation of the Parents and the Emotional Life of the Child," *Mental Hygiene*, vol. 40, January 1956, pp. 53–64.

[32] Wylie, Howard L., and Rafael A. Delgado. "A Pattern of Mother-Son Relationship Involving the Absence of the Father," *American Journal of Orthopsychiatry*, vol. 29, July 1959, pp. 644–649: Despert, J. Louise, "The Fatherless Family," *Child Study*, vol. 34, Summer 1957, pp. 24–28.

[33] Miller, *op. cit.*, p. 226.

[34] Willie, Charles V., and Janet Weinandy. "The Structure and Composition of 'Problem' and 'Stable' Families in a Low-Income Population," *Marriage and Family Living*, vol. 25, November 1963, p. 440.

[35] For a recent discussion of some problems specific to the single-parent family, see Paul Glasser and Elizabeth Navarre. "Structural Problems of the One-Parent Family," *Journal of Social Issues*, vol. 21, January 1965, pp. 98–109.

[36] Examples of some of the studies: Ericson, Martha C. "Child-Rearing and Social Status," *American Journal of Sociology*, vol. 52, November 1946, pp. 190–192; Havighurst, Robert J., and Allison Davis. "A Comparison of the Chicago and Harvard Studies of Social Class Differences in Child-Rearing," *American Sociological Review*, vol. 20, August 1955, pp. 438–442; Litman, Richard A., *et al.*, "Social Class Differences in Child Rearing: A Third Community for Comparison with Chicago and Newton," *American Sociological Review*, vol. 22, December 1957, pp. 694–704.

[37] An attempt to reconcile these contradictory findings was made by Urie Bronfenbrenner, "Socialization and Social Class through Time and Space," in Eleanor E. Maccoby, Theodore M. Newcomb, and Eugene L. Hartley, eds. *Readings in Social Psychology*. 3d ed. Henry Holt and Co., New York, 1958.

[38] Kohn, Melvin L. "Social Class and Parental Values," *American Journal of Sociology*, vol. 64, January 1959, pp. 337–351.

[39] Duvall, Evelyn Millis. "Conceptions of Parenthood," *American Journal of Sociology*, vol. 52, November 1946, pp. 193–203.

[40] Maas, Henry S. "Some Social Class Differences in the Family Systems and Group Relations of Pre- and Early Adolescents," *Child Development*, vol. 22, June 1951, pp. 145–152.

[41] Kohn, Melvin L. "Social Class and Parent-Child Relationships: An Interpretation," *American Journal of Sociology*, vol. 68, January 1963, p. 477.

[42] Aberle, David F., and Kaspar D. Naegele. "Middle Class Fathers' Occupational Role and Attitudes Toward Children," *American Journal of Orthopsychiatry*, vol. 22, April 1952, pp. 368–378.

The Structure and Functions of Negro Family Life

ANDREW BILLINGSLEY

THE STRUCTURE OF NEGRO FAMILY LIFE

It is very common to observe that there are two types of family structure in America: male-headed families and female-headed families.
Such characterization is almost always followed by the assertion or assumption that male-headed families are stable whereas female-headed
families are unstable, and that the latter are more than twice as common among Negroes as among whites.

This manner of characterizing the structure of Negro family life
has a number of inadequacies. First, it underestimates the variations
among Negro families living under different basic conditions.

On the basis of such conditions, three general categories of families
may be identified: primary families, extended families, and augmented
families. A family is commonly defined as a group of persons related by
marriage or ancestry, who live together in the same household. Nuclear
families arc confined to husband and wife and their own children, with
no other members present. Extended families include other relatives or
in-laws of the family head, sharing the same household with the nuclear
family members. Augmented families include members not related to the
family head who share the same household living arrangements with
the nuclear family. Each of these three categories of families will be
considered in some detail. Roughly two thirds of all Negro families are
nuclear families, a quarter are extended families and a tenth are augmented families.

Further, within the framework of these three categories, twelve
different types of family structure may be specified. In addition, this
typology allows for the elaboration of subtypes within several of these
twelve types of family structure. The basic typology of Negro family
structures appears in Table 1.

Among nuclear families, three specific types of family structure may
be observed. Type I, the *incipient nuclear family,* is composed of

Andrew Billingsley, *Black Families in White America.* © 1968. Reprinted by
permission of Prentice-Hall, Inc., Englewood Cliffs, New Jersey. Footnotes, figure,
and tables have been renumbered.

TABLE 1

Negro Family Structure

Types of Family	Household Head		Other Household Members		
	Husband and Wife	Single Parent	Children	Other Relatives	Non-relatives
Nuclear Families					
I. Incipient Nuclear Family	X				
II. Simple Nuclear Family	X		X		
III. Attenuated Nuclear Family		X	X		
Extended Families					
IV. Incipient Extended Family	X			X	
V. Simple Extended Family	X		X	X	
VI. Attenuated Extended Family		X	X	X	
Augmented Families					
VII. Incipient Augmented Family	X				X
VIII. Incipient Extended Augmented Family	X			X	X
IX. Nuclear Augmented Family	X		X		X
X. Nuclear Extended Augmented Family	X		X	X	X
XI. Attenuated Augmented Family		X	X		X
XII. Attenuated Extended Augmented Family		X	X	X	X

husband and wife living together in their own household with no children. Nearly a fifth of all Negro families, or roughly a million families, are of this type. They are young married couples who have not yet had time or economic security to start their family, older couples who have not been able or willing either to have their own children or to adopt others, and still older couples whose children have grown up and left the home. This type also includes a few families whose minor children have been placed in foster homes or institutions because of illness or other incapacity of one or both parents. The largest single subgroup in this category consists of those husbands and wives who do not have children of their own for a variety of reasons. These families are generally economically viable because both partners work, except during illness, old age, or widespread unemployment. Incipient nuclear families, then, are a large, important, and complex aspect of the structure of Negro family life. Yet they are almost completely ignored in studies of Negro families. They offer an important potential for the care of children in the Negro community, though there is some indication that among many Negro families those with some children already may be more willing to take in other children than those without children of their own.

A second type of family is the *simple nuclear family*. This family type consists of husband and wife and their own or adopted children living together in their own household with no other members present. This is the traditional type of family structure in America and Europe. Among students of the family, it is considered the ideal and most universal family form.

It might be instructive to note, however, that while this nuclear family arrangement is the ideal and the model against which all other families, particularly Negro families, are compared, it does not encompass the majority—even among white families. A study by Paul C. Glick found that in 1953 only 28.6 per cent of household units consisted of a husband and wife and their own minor children.[1] And a study in 1965 in Richmond, California, by Alan Wilson found that 45 per cent of white families and 49 per cent of Negro families consisted of husband, wife, and their own children.[2] Thus the "ideal" family pattern, the simple nuclear family, may not be any more common among whites than it is among Negroes. Nationally, about 36 per cent of all Negro families, or more than 1½ million families, are of the simple nuclear type.[3]

A third type of family structure is the *attenuated nuclear family*. This type of family structure has either a father or a mother—but not both—living together with minor children in the parent's own household with no other persons present. Commonly referred to as a broken family, this is an important type of family structure in the United States. Its most frequent form is mother and children living together.

Of the more than 2½ million attenuated nuclear families in the United States in 1965, 733,000 were Negro families, constituting about 6 per cent of all Negro families. The vast majority of these families

(689,000) were headed by females, while 44,000 were headed by males who were not married and not living with other relatives.[4] A wide variety of families are encompassed within this type. The specific sub-types may be derived, depending on whether the single parent is male or female and whether he or she is (a) single, (b) married with an absent spouse, (c) legally separated, (d) divorced, or (e) widowed.

When we speak of attenuated families, then, and when others speak of one-parent families or broken families, we are not referring to a unified entity, for the attenuated family encompasses a wide variety of subtypes, with different meanings, different causes, and different consequences for its members. The concept of attenuated families is designed to minimize some of the invidiousness associated with other terms and to be simply descriptive, suggesting as it does that somebody important to the family constellation is missing.

Extended Families

In all three types of nuclear families described above, the members live together in their own house, every member being related to the head of the household either by marriage or by birth. In the second major category of family structures, other relatives are introduced into this nuclear household, making of it an extended family.

The types of extended families include: (a) the *incipient extended family,* consisting of a married couple with no children of their own who take in other relatives; (b) the *simple extended family,* consisting of a married couple with their own children, who take in other relatives; and (c) the *attenuated extended family,* consisting of a single, abandoned, legally separated, divorced, or widowed mother or father living with his or her own children, who takes into the household other relatives. Each of these patterns exists in appreciable numbers among Negro families. To know which of the subtypes of extended family is under consideration would help to clarify the generalizations which can be made, for these subtypes differ greatly in their causes and their conse-quences for their members and for society.

It is also possible to distinguish extended families by examining who is being taken into the primary family. Thus it may make a great deal of difference whether the relative coming to live with a nuclear family is a six-year-old nephew, or an 87-year-old aunt.

There are, then, four classes of relatives who can and often do come to live with Negro families. These are (a) minor relatives, including grandchildren, nieces, nephews, cousins, and young siblings under eighteen; (b) peers of the primary parents, including, particularly, siblings, cousins, and other adult relatives; (c) elders of the primary parents, including, particularly, aunts and uncles; and finally, (d) parents of the primary family heads. The structure of authority, to mention only one aspect of family life, may shift considerably, de-pending on the status of the relative coming to live in the family.

In 1965 nearly 15 per cent of all Negro families had one or more minor relatives living with them who was not their own child, and better than a quarter of all Negro families had a relative living with them who was eighteen or over.[5] Many of these families had more than one relative living with them, and some had more than one level or status of relative living with them. Among the husband and wife families with children of their own, for example, fully 26.7 per cent had one or more additional relatives living with them in their house. A majority of the female-headed attenuated families and a third of the male-headed attenuated families also had another relative living in the home.

There is a further basis for differentiating subtypes of extended families. Some relatives who come to live with a family come alone. They become, then, *secondary members* of the family. Other relatives come with their spouse or their children. These become *subfamilies*. There are, then, *incipient subfamilies,* or husband and wife pairs who come to live in the household of their relatives; *simple nuclear subfamilies,* consisting of husband, wife, and their small children, who live with another family; and *attenuated subfamilies,* consisting of one parent and his or her children, living in a relative's household. Furthermore, it is very common for two families of siblings or other relatives to share the same household.

Among the 4.4 million Negro families in 1965, there lived a total of 248,000 subfamilies. Altogether, 210,000 of these subfamilies had their own children under eighteen. (The average number of children in each subfamily was 2.6) The heads of these subfamilies were relatively young, with 34.7 per cent under twenty-five years of age and 67.3 per cent being under thirty-five. But many were obviously peers, elders, and parents. Fully 22.6 per cent were thirty-five to forty-four years old and 10.1 per cent were forty-five years old or over.

The subfamilies seem to consist mostly of young families living with relatives before they are able to make it on their own. The median age of heads of these subfamilies was 29.2, compared with a median age of 43.3 for primary family heads. Altogether, among the 248,000 subfamilies in 1965, 43 per cent were married couples—the majority with children of their own; roughly 15 per cent were incipient subfamilies with no children of their own; 30 per cent were simple nuclear subfamilies; and another 57 per cent were attenuated subfamilies, the majority headed by females.

Augmented Families

It would not be appropriate to conclude this discussion of structures and substructures of Negro family life without adding a third major category of families. These are families which have unrelated individuals living with them as roomers, boarders, lodgers, or other relatively long-term guests. Since these unrelated persons often exert major influence in the organization of Negro families, this group of families is referred to as "augmented families." While the number of augmented families is unknown, it is obviously substantial. In 1965 there were nearly a half million Negro persons living with family groups with whom they were not related by marriage, ancestry, or adoption. Of these, 326,000 were men and 173,000 were women. They were mostly adults; 80 per cent of the men and 70 per cent of the women were eighteen years of age and over, and nearly a third were fifty-five years of age and over.

In every Negro neighborhood of any size in the country, a wide variety of family structures will be represented. This range and variety does not suggest, as some commentaries hold, that the Negro family is falling apart, but rather that these families are fully capable of surviving by adapting to the historical and contemporary social and economic conditions facing the Negro people. How does a people survive in the face of oppression and sharply restricted economic and social support? There are, of course, numerous ways. But surely one of them is to adapt the most basic of its institutions, the family, to meet the often conflicting demands placed on it. In this context, then, the Negro family has proved to be an amazingly resilient institution.

FUNCTIONS OF NEGRO FAMILY LIFE

All families are expected to meet certain responsibilities placed on them by the wider society and to provide for the basic needs of their members. The degree to which the family is able to meet these responsibilities and needs is a measure of family functioning. There is a general tendency in discussions of Negro families to focus on a very limited number of family functions—specifically, on the manner in which families are *not* functioning adequately. While this limitation is both understandable and necessary for specific studies, it often contributes to the distortions and excessively negative characterizations of Negro family life. In a general work such as this, then, it seems desirable to approach the discussion of family functioning in the broadest possible framework.

Some family functions are essentially instrumental in character, serving to maintain the basic physical and social integrity of the family unit—e.g., the provision of food, clothing, shelter, and health care. Other functions are more expressive in character, designed to maintain and enhance the socio-emotional relationships and feelings among family members. Still other functions involve an inextricable mixture of instrumental and expressive qualities.

These functions are highly interrelated with each other, and their effective execution depends not only on the structure of the family, but also on the structure of the society and the place of the family in that social structure. The place of Negro families in the wider society, and in the Negro community viewed as an ethnic subsociety, varies greatly; consequently, the ability of Negro families to meet the requirements of society and the needs of their members also varies across a wide spectrum.

According to Talcott Parsons, the distinction between instrumental and expressive functions is relative rather than absolute.

> These distinctions are . . . defined in terms of amount and mode of influence on the functioning of the family as a social system. . . . The instrumental-expressive distinction we interpret as essentially the differentiation of function, and hence of relative influence, in terms of "external" vs. "internal" functions of the system. The area of instrumental function concerns relations of the system to its situation outside the system, to meeting the adaptive conditions of its maintenance of equilibrium, and "instrumentally" establishing the desired relations to desired goal objects. The expressive area concerns the "internal" affairs of the system, the maintenance of integrative relations between the members, and regulation of the patterns and tension levels of its component units.[6]

Figure 1 shows a conceptual view of the functions of Negro families.

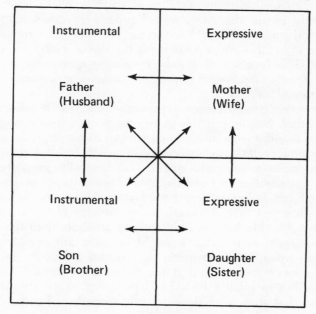

FIGURE 1

Functions of the Negro Family

Adapted from Parsons and Bales, *Family, Socialization and Interaction Process* [Free Press, 1955], p. 46. Reprinted [in the original] by permission of the Macmillan Company. The arrows are designed to stress the interchange of roles so common among Negro families of both high and low status.

Instrumental Functions

Chief among the instrumental functions of families is the economic function. Society expects families to sustain themselves economically through the efforts of their own members. This requirement is also consistent with the needs of family members for food, clothing, and shelter. Another important demand society places on families is that they maintain their physical and social boundaries. Families are expected to be stable, which implies that no member should leave the family prematurely, except for a good cause. For the senior members of the family, death is the only recognized good cause. The junior members are often expected to stay with the family until they get married.

These two very important instrumental functions of the family are highly interrelated in ways that are both complimentary and conflicting. Social workers have known for a long time that there is nothing like a good steady job with adequate and dependable income to make a man get married, stay married, remain with his family, and support it, while the absence of such economic viability is highly correlated with the refusal of men to insure the stability of their families. Attorneys who have recently begun the long-avoided process of developing and expanding legal protections for low income Negroes have reported vivid illustrations of family break-up following the loss of a job by the husband and father. The function of family stability required by society and desired by family members is impossible unless the economic functions of the family are fulfilled.

Under some circumstances, however, these two functions conflict with each other. Nowhere is this more conspicuous than among low income Negro families who must rely on various forms of public assistance. As late as January 1968, the only way in which stable families victimized by unemployment could qualify for federally supported public assistance payments in the overwhelming majority of states was for the husband and father to desert his family. Many low income Negro men have done just that. Although many students of the Negro family consider this a highly irresponsible act and attribute it to the historical tendencies toward matriarchy, it might be more appropriately viewed as a highly responsible, innovative, and painful act in the face of two impossible demands. Eighteen states do make it possible for simple nuclear families to qualify for AFDC payments when the husband is unemployed, but they have done so only recently, and many of them are very restrictive. (They are all among the richest states, with not a single southern state among them.)

Some students of the family hold that the responsibilities of economic well-being, education, and health have passed from the family to larger societal institutions. The family, however, must still mediate the relations between its members and these institutions and prepare its members to understand and manipulate these institutions if they are to function effectively. The family cannot, of course, perform its instrumental functions effectively unless these major economic, education, and health institutions function adequately and with respect to the needs of families. This is a particular problem for low income Negro families, for most of these institutional arrangements have been developed according to the needs and response patterns of middle class white families. Only in recent years have we come to see the essential cultural rigidities and dysfunctions built into our institutional framework. Although many families, including low income Negro families, function amazingly well in the face of the most intransigent institutional obstacles, in general the family will not be able to meet the instrumental needs of its members or its responsibilities to the larger society until this institutional framework is reconstructed. Even then, however, some families will be better able to do so than others.

It is sometimes said by students of the family that husbands and fathers play a preeminent role in the meeting of instrumental functions, while women are assigned the more expressive functions. This view, however, provides far too simplistic a framework for examining the functioning of Negro families. As we have just seen, the dramatically increased economic hazards faced by the Negro ethnic subsociety, and the consequences of the caste system have a direct bearing on the difficulty and complexity of carrying out the major instrumental functions of the Negro family. The white breadwinner's security of employment and his reliance upon community systems in fulfilling the functions of providing stability and basic needs to family members are denied the Negro breadwinner. Thus the simple model which allocates instrumental functions to the father cannot be expected to describe all of the adaptations required for the Negro family in its struggle for survival. Indeed, as we shall see later, even in the area of economic functioning, as well as in other instrumental areas, Negro women play a very active role, and Negro families vary across a wide spectrum on the nature of male-female role relationships in family life.

It is not at all uncommon for Negro men to engage in expressive functions with respect to the maintenance of family solidarity and to help with child rearing and household tasks.[7] Researchers have found Negro men to be more helpful around the house than a sample of white men, but they have chosen to give this fact a negative reading. These men are considered to be henpecked or under the domination of their strongly matriarchal wives. In the absence of a theoretical framework to provide interpretation of such findings, one is hard put to substantiate such reasoning. According to our view, this behavior may be more appropriately interpreted as another example of the strong tendency toward mutual aid and a reflection of the pragmatic qualities in Negro family life. The reverse situations, in which Negro wives and mothers often play a predominant role in the execution of instrumental functions, are better known. Older children often play the role of the principal adult members, and boys and girls often take on role behavior generally considered, in the larger society, to be proscribed because of their sex. In some low income Negro families of the attenuated variety, older daughters sometimes take on aspects of the role of husband and father.

Expressive Functions

Prominent among the expressive functions of the family is the provision of what Robert Winch calls "psychic security,"[8] and what Robert Blood calls "the mental health function of the family."[9] This is the kind of atmosphere which generates a sense of belonging, of self-worth, self-awareness, and dignity. Another important function of the family is the provision of companionship. Still a third is the generation and propagation of the various forms of love.

Students of the American family traditionally have been concerned more with expressive functions than instrumental ones. But students of the Negro family have focused almost exclusively on instrumental functioning. The general family literature, for example, is replete with studies of marital adjustment, happiness, and parent-child relationships. Negro family studies, on the other hand, tend to focus on the ability of the families—or more specifically, the inabilities of families—to provide their members with the more basic necessities of life. It is an understandable difference of focus, for instrumental functions are a precondition for the proper execution of expressive ones, and the difficulties for Negro families in the first area have been legion and are the subject of a great deal of social concern. However, a general understanding of family life demands a more systematic consideration of the wide rage of functions required of families, and the differentiation which exists *among* Negro families make such studies both possible and necessary.

Instrumental and expressive functions, even when distinct, are highly interrelated. The middle class Negro man who goes off to work every day is meeting the instrumental needs of his family. Failure to do this will threaten their economic and fiscal integrity. When he kisses his wife and children before he leaves and when he returns, he is meeting their expressive needs. Failure to do these, or to provide some functional equivalent, may also have similar consequences. Furthermore, if he loses his job, or if he has to have two jobs because he cannot earn enough on one, which is quite common among middle class Negro families, the strain developing from the impairment in the instrumental functions may have adverse effects on the more expressive functional relationships in the family.

A graphic illustration of the interrelatedness of instrumental and expressive functions for a low income family is provided by Lee Rainwater:

When the field worker first came to know them, the Wilsons seemed to be working hard to establish a stable family life. The couple had been married about three years and had a two-year-old son. Their apartment was very sparsely furnished, but also very clean. Within six weeks, the couple had acquired several rooms of inexpensive furniture and obviously had gone to a great deal of effort to make a livable home. Husband and wife worked on different shifts so that the husband could care for the child while the wife worked. They looked forward to saving enough money to move out of the housing project into a more desirable neighborhood. Six weeks later, however, the husband had lost his job. He and his wife were in great conflict. She made him feel unwelcome at home and he strongly suspected her of going out with other men. A short time later, they had separated.[10]

In this case, the family situation was too complex and the data too limited to establish simple cause and effect relationships. It is clear, however, that both father-mother roles and instrumental-expressive functions were at variance with more traditional expectations.

Instrumental–Expressive Functions

By far the most important set of family functions in America center around the trilogy of sex, reproduction, and child rearing. These are both instrumental and expressive in quality. They are also highly interrelated, although the ability to separate these three functions from one another is a mark of achievement which varies appreciably with the position of the family in the ethnic subsociety. Middle and upper class Negro families, for example, make a greater distinction between sex and reproduction than do families in the lowest socioeconomic classes. Sex among Negroes has not been systematically studied, though some observers think that for the lower class, sex, like religion, is an island of freedom, one of the few areas of life not thoroughly dominated by the white society.

The socialization of children remains, perhaps, the most exclusive domain of the family. It is within the intimate circle of the family that the child develops his personality, intelligence, aspirations, and, indeed, his moral character. Even here, however, the family does not act alone, but as a subsystem of the wider society. Parsons has made this point rather explicitly:

. . . we must never forget that the nuclear family is *never*, most certainly not in the American case, an independent society, but a small and highly differentiated subsystem of a society. This fact is crucially relevant to our interests at two points. First, the parents, as socializing agents, occupy not merely their familial roles, but these articulate, i.e., interpenetrate, with their roles in other structures of the society, and this fact is a necessary condition . . . of their functioning effectively as socializing agents, i.e., as parents, at all. Secondly, the child is never socialized only for and into his family of orientation, but into structures which extend beyond this family, though interpenetrating with it. These include the school and peer group in later childhood and the family of procreation which the child will help to form by his marriage, as well as occupational roles in adulthood.[11]

It is often assumed, particularly by liberal intellectuals and sometimes by social scientists and social workers, that what is required of Negro families in our society is essentially the same as what is required of white families. According to this view, it is not the demands made on the family, but the ability of the family to meet these demands which distinguishes Negro family life. If, however, the Negro people are viewed as an ethnic subsociety, it can be appreciated that while there are basic similarities in the requirements of all families in America, there are particular requirements for Negro families, which grow out of three factors: (a) the peculiar historical development, (b) the caste-like qualities in the American stratification system which relegates all Negroes to inferior status, and (c) the social class and economic systems which keep most Negroes in the lower social classes.

For the Negro family, socialization is doubly challenging, for the family must teach its young members not only how to be human, but also how to be black in a white society. The requirements are not the same.

Negro families must teach their children very early in life, sometimes as early as two years of age, the meaning of being black. "Every Negro child I know," says Robert Coles, "has had to take notice in some way of what skin color signifies in our society."[12] A Negro mother in Jackson, Mississippi, put it this way:

> When they asks all the questions, they ask about their color too. They more than not will see a white boy or girl and it makes them stop and think. They gets to wondering, and then first thing you know, they want to know this and that about it, and I never have known what to say, except that the Lord likes everyone because He makes everyone. . . . I tell them that no matter what it's like around us, it may make us feel bad, but it's not the whole picture, because we don't make ourselves. . . . When they ask me why colored people aren't as good as whites, I tell them its not that they're not as good; it's that they're not as rich. Then I tell them that they should separate being poor and being bad, and not get them mixed up.[13]

She also needs to teach them to separate being *black* and being bad, which is the real problem and much harder to separate.

In many respects, high income Negro families who live in white suburbs in the North are at the other socioeconomic extreme from low income Negro families who live in the rural South. They often must face the same kinds of problems, however, in teaching their children how to grow up black in a white society. Some face it with resignation. "All you can do is make your children understand that some people are just not going to like them," one middle class suburban Negro mother told Mel Watkins of *The New York Times*.[14]

> You can tell them that some people are ignorant or something like that, but they still have to get used to it. You can't hide them from reality. We've had the same experience. We had to learn to live with it—they will too.

Another mother takes a similar approach. Her daughter came home from school one day crying because a white boy had refused to hold her hand during a school game because she was "colored." The daughter wanted to know what that meant.

> I sat down and tried to explain that sometimes Negroes are called colored. You see, I wanted her to know that often that kind of thing happens. It's a handicap being a Negro in America and you have to learn to live with a handicap. If the child doesn't know this, she'll get hurt. What else can you tell them?

Still other middle class Negro families take a laissez-faire approach to the problem. An attorney observed:

> We've found it best to more or less leave our children to themselves. Left alone—given enough security—they'll determine where the lines are drawn and how to react to them. We've never really talked to our children about racial problems.

Another father spoke in the same vein:

> There's no need to tell your children how some people feel about the Negro, they know it, man. It seems a parent should try to minimize the child's concern over it. I wouldn't advise my children unless they got into serious trouble.

It does not take much sophistication to imagine that children with parents who hold these laissez-faire attitudes seldom, if ever, talk with their parents about the dilemmas they encounter growing up black. They learn this silence at a very early age.

Still other black suburbanites take a more activist role in dealing with the problem. "Of course my son has had difficulties," said another father, himself a school teacher, and each time we've tried talking with him afterwards. Let's face it, there is an undercurrent of bigotry here, and it's not that far from the surface. We've tried to show our son the difference between his value as a person and the distorted view people may have of him. He was eight when we moved here. We were the first Negroes in any of these buildings. A lot of times he'd come in crying from school or from playing in the courtyard outside. Someone would have told him something like—"we don't play with niggers" or "coons stink." I'd tell him children often use bad names or say things that aren't true, but he'd have to understand that they needed to do this. It really had nothing to do with him. I think this helped. He's been able to cope with it. I'm not sure, but I think the well-adjusted Negro has to have a clearer picture of himself. The society, too. There aren't any dreams he can rely on.

Hopefully the dreams may be only deferred. It is a constant challenge for Negro parents, at all levels of the ethnic subsociety, to teach their children how to be human and American and black and proud. Even educated middle class parents who read avidly do not find much help with this problem from psychology books or treatises on child rearing. The books have been written for white parents, to deal with other problems. "The best advice I've had," said one mother, "has been passed along by word of mouth, talking with other Negro parents."

Negro children must be taught not only to distinguish themselves from whites and to accept themselves, but, even more crucial to their survival, they must be taught to deal with white people. There are, of course, a number of ways both of teaching and doing this; but hatred and fear are the basic mechanisms of survival which go into the socialization of lower class Negro children. Another Negro mother expressed this problem vividly:

> I guess we all don't like white people too much, deep inside. You could hardly expect us to after what's happened all these years. It's in our bones to be afraid of them, and bones have a way of staying around even when everything else is gone. . . . So if you want your kids to live long they have to grow up scared of whites; and the way they get scared is through us; and that's why I don't let my kids get fresh about the white man even in their own house. . . . So I make them store it in the bones, way inside, and then no one sees it.[15]

It is becoming increasingly difficult for Negro parents to teach their children to hide the hate and fear "way inside." For, in addition to the tremendous toll it takes of the personality of these young people as they grow older and as times change swiftly, the hatred and fear are beginning more and more to explode in patterns of behavior which are no less healthy, though perhaps more immediately destructive than the more gradual effects of self-hatred.

The dilemmas facing the Negro parent in rearing their children in the face of these conflicting demands are deep and intricate. How, indeed, are the ravages of self-hatred to be avoided when a parent may state to a child "It is not you who are bad," but when, for the child's own physical and psychic safety, the obvious corollary, "It is *they* who are bad," cannot be taught? How does a parent impart a moral code to a child when they are surrounded by a socio-legal system which also upholds much of this same code, while violating at every turn their basic human rights?

How Negro parents have resolved these dilemmas is a virtually untouched field of study. While Negro parents have informally shared their experiences with one another, the startling neglect of such important areas of expressive functioning in Negro family life finds us without information which is vital to understanding not only the Negro family, but also a very rich part of the human experience.

NOTES

[1] Paul C. Glick, *American Families* (New York: John Wiley & Sons, Inc., 1957), p. 2.

[2] Alan Wilson, "Western Contra Costa County Population, 1965: Demographic Characteristics" (unpublished paper, 1966, Survey Research Center, University of California, Berkeley), p. 16.

[3] This typology is based on data taken from the U.S. Bureau of the Census, U.S. Census of Population, 1960, *Families,* PC(2)-4A-P-1, Table 1 (Washington, D.C.: U.S. Government Printing Office, 1965).

[4] U.S. Bureau of the Census, U.S. Census of Population, 1960, *The Negro Population* (Washington, D.C.: U.S. Government Printing Office, 1965).

[5] *Ibid.*

[6] Reprinted with permission of the Macmillan Company, *Family, Socialization, and Interaction Process,* by Talcott Parsons and Robert F. Bales, p. 46. Copyright, © Free Press of Glencoe, a division of the Macmillan Company, 1955.

[7] Robert C. Stone and F. T. Schlamp, "Family Life Styles Below the Poverty Line: A Report to the State Social Welfare Board from the Institute for Social Science Research" (San Francisco State College, 1966).

[8] Robert F. Winch, *The Modern Family,* rev. ed. (New York: Holt, Rinehart & Winston, Inc., 1963), p. 295.

[9] Robert O. Blood and Donald M. Wolfe, *Husbands and Wives: The Dynamics of Married Living* (New York: The Free Press, 1960), p. 175.

[10] Lee Rainwater, "Crucible of Identity: The Negro Lower-Class Family," *Daedalus* (Winter 1966), 193.

[11] Parsons and Bales, p. 35. Reprinted with permission of the Macmillan Company.

[12] Robert Coles, *Children of Crisis* (Boston: Little, Brown & Co., 1964), p. 62.

[13] *Ibid.,* pp. 63–64.

[14] The following quotations are from Mel Watkins, "White Skins, Dark Skins, Thin Skins," *The New York Times Magazine* (December 3, 1967), pp. 126–39. © 1967 by The New York Times Company. Reprinted by permission.

[15] Coles, p. 66.

Marriage Under a Monastic Mode of Life: A Preliminary Report on the Hutterite Family in South Dakota*

S. C. LEE AND AUDREY BRATTRUD

Is it possible to enter any American home and not find a kitchen and a dining area? These are certainly assumed to be an integral part of family living. In fact, the old saying that "the kitchen is the heart of the home" is widely accepted by American people. However, in our recent study of the Hutterite colonies of eastern South Dakota,[1] we witnessed many homes devoid of these physical aspects. In these colonies, when the word "kitchen" is used, it is in reference to the public or community kitchen, in which all the families of the colony do their cooking jointly. The food is prepared and served in the dining hall by the women, most of whom work there on a rotating basis.

In the communal dining hall, the men eat on one side of the room, the women on another. The children, up to age 15, eat in an entirely separate dining room under the supervision of the adults in charge of them. The only time a married couple enjoys the privilege of sitting and eating together in public is on the occasion of their wedding day.

This pattern of disjunction of the family unit is observed not only in the colonies' manner of preparing, serving, and eating meals, but also in many other aspects of life. Each colony forms a little world, or "cosmos," of its own, with a great degree of internal consistency and cohesion. A cosmos, as such, has been varyingly referred to as a utopian organization,[2] a true *gemeinschaft*,[3] a folk culture,[4] a little community,[5] a communal society,[6] or a total institution,[7] and many others. In spite of their morphological similarity, each type of cosmos has its own mechanisms for achieving its unity or wholeness. As a general rule, this internal cohesion is established through molding and adjusting the values and norms cherished by various institutions to form a closely knit, integrated whole, based on one set of principles. The organization known as Hutterian *Bruderhof* or Brotherhood is integrated by the Anabaptist Christian faith, the essence of which is "worldly asceticism"[8] or "theocratic communism."[9] Colony life is accurately and graphically described

Reprinted from *Journal of Marriage and the Family*, August 1967, 512–20.

in the Hutterite Chronicle: "Such a *Bruderhof* is somewhat like a big beehive where all the busy bees work together to a common end, the one doing this and the other that, not for their own needs but for the good of all."[10]

Since the Hutterite colony attains its unity as a cosmos through a religious faith, it is expected that the family, as generally defined in socio-anthropological literature,[11] cannot possibly function as an *independent, full-fledged unit* in the community. In contrast to American society, in which the conjugal family is the basic social agency aside from the individual, the Hutterite family becomes a "cog" of the colony and serves in an auxiliary capacity to strengthen the effective performance of the church. Life in any colony is marked by simplicity, orderliness, and austerity. With reference to Hutterite marriage, Robert Friedmann aptly remarks: "In general the Hutterites had an ascetic outlook on life; in fact, were it not for their acceptance of marriage their way of life could best be characterized as 'monastic.' "[12]

In the analysis of the Hutterite family, we find that it assumes a form which defies classification. It fits neither the pattern of a patriarchal family, as in the instance of the Amish,[13] nor can it be described as the conjugal family of American society. One principal characteristic of the conjugal family is present, however, i.e., the practice of regarding each marriage as the formation of a new unit for which a neolocal residence is to be established. In all other aspects, such as child training, economic support, emotional attachment, group loyalty, etc., it is not the individual family, but rather the colony, which operates as an integral entity. Viewed from this standpoint, the colony closely resembles an extended family, and this was, indeed, the ideal of its founder, Jacob Hutter.[14] In fact, the Hutterite family is so embedded in a religious commune that it does not even function as a primary group per se. It ceases to be *the* major agency in bringing about socialization of the young. The feeling of a psychological unity is engendered toward the colony as a whole.[15] Because of this peculiarity, the Hutterite family deserves special attention. The findings obtained through empirical field studies should be of interest to the student of human society.

This investigation was primarily exploratory. In October, 1964, we began visiting the Hutterite colonies located nearby, carrying on conversations with any person or persons who came out to meet us. We were generally directed to the minister or the deacon (second minister). With his consent, we then continued our contact with members, using the method of interview. We used an interview guide so that the same areas in life would be covered in depth with each subject and so that comparable information would be ensured.

At the last stage of the procedure, we formulated a lengthy questionnaire and distributed it in all of the colonies in South Dakota. By August, 1965, we had visited all but one of the 26 colonies in South Dakota. Since quantitative data obtained through the questionnaire are still being collected and analyzed, this paper is primarily based on the information gathered through field observations, conversations, and interviews, particularly the latter.

When we arrived in a colony at lunch hour, we were often entertained in the communal kitchen. It was the communal kitchen and the physical arrangement of the residential dwellings which first aroused our interest and led us to the study of the family. Each of the residential dwellings, an elongated, bungalow-like house, is usually divided into four or six separate units. Each unit is divided into a series of bedrooms, enough to accommodate a large family, and is separated from all other units by a solid wall. In this respect, the lodging place may be regarded as the family's private domain. However, one would be woefully mistaken if he should think of the Hutterite home in terms of the old English adage, "Every man's home is his castle." The custom, "knocking before entering," which is so strictly observed in American society, is simply *not* practiced in the Hutterite colony. Any member of the same colony, or even a visitor, can go freely into any home without intruding.

In our early visits, we were struck by their practice of entering the house and their eating together in public dining halls. Only much later were we able to fit together all the pieces of Hutterian life as an integral whole or cosmos and then to see the meaning and significance of these practices. Both are the devices used by the Brethren to deny privacy to the family and prevent it from becoming an independent agency competing with the community for the loyalty and emotional attachment of the individual.

In describing the Amish family, William Kephart maintains that,

> An Amishman's life, almost literally, revolves about his home. He seldom leaves it, and when he does, he doesn't stay away very long. He traditionally is born at home; he works at home, and the chances are that he will die at home.[16]

This description can be applied only superficially to a Hutterite man, though both the Hutterites and the Amish share the same faith in Anabaptism. True, people engaged in agriculture tend to be earthbound, but the life of a Hutterite revolved *not about his home but about his colony*.

A married Hutterite man depends upon the colony to provide lodging, food, and clothing materials. Since hard work is looked upon as man's fulfillment of God's will and since hiring out of the colony for pay is regarded as incompatible with the practice of communal living, the Hutterite man is busy from morning to evening in his job assignment, whether it is being a "steward" (business manager), a teacher, or a "chicken man" (a Hutterite term referring to the man who tends the chickens). He works to advance the interests of the whole colony. Unless disabled by physical conditions such as sickness, pregnancy, childbirth, or old age, the Hutterite woman contributes her part to the same end. She may be working in the kitchen one week and the bakery another before she can do her own family chores, such as sewing and clothes-making.

In a number of ways, particularly in the case of a "binary fission,"[17] each family is considered as a unit either to stay on in the old colony or to branch out to a newly organized one. It otherwise lacks the essentials of an entity. In comparison with the Amish,[18] the Hutterite family does not form the center of production and consumption activities. With the family stripped of all these economic functions, its domicile is reduced to a lodging place where a married couple enjoys its evenings and holidays together with the children and preferably reads to them some episodes and anecdotes from the Gospel to supplement the religious teachings of their church.

To say that the family is enervated in favor of the church does not necessarily imply that adjustments between the individual family members are unsatisfactory or that their ties become weakened. On the contrary, both may be strengthened if a system of role-relationships is well defined and integrated on the basis of some source of authority, such as the Bible. The relationships are sanctioned much more stably by religious faith than by the sole ground of love and affection.

In the Hutterite household, the biblical mode of husband and wife relationships is observed. The husband is the head of the household, and the wife is his assisting partner. Concerning domestic decisions, the husband's voice carries more weight than the wife's. He is the one who takes disciplinary measures. The patterns of behavior in a colony have been well established through the ages, and the husband and wife perform roles which are well established and strongly reinforced by the community and are bolstered by religious faith. It is marvelous to note that marital adjustments are evidently made exceedingly easy and satisfactory. Domestic quarrels are seldom heard and divorce is unknown. Concerning this aspect of life, one of our informants, a teacher and a deacon, offers the following exposition:

> Our life is so well imbued with the ideas and ideals of the Gospel that when two Hutterites get married, they know they have committed themselves for a life time. The situation of discord may not arise and the idea of a divorce would never occur in their mind.

The responsibility of child training in the colony does not rest primarily on the parents at home but rather on the woman taking charge of the kindergarten, the teacher of the German school, and also, to a lesser extent, on the minister(s). In this respect, the practice of the Hutterite colony comes close to that of the kibbutz system tried in Israel, although they are diametrically different in purpose.

The kibbutz was originally founded by a small group of youthful Zionist pioneers with the intention of replacing the Jewish culture of the *shtetl* and setting up a community of comrades.[19] "The Kibbutz views itself," maintains Melford E. Spiro, "as an attempt to revolutionize the structure of human society and its basic social relations." In order to achieve this end, children are separated from their parents to live in "children's houses" and are supervised by the nurse and the teacher.[20] On the other hand, the major concern of the Hutterian Brotherhood is the preservation of the language, folkways, customs, costume, and even the physiognomy of their founders, who lived in Central Europe during the early sixteenth century. If the kibbutz is characterized as a "child-centered society," the Hutterian Brotherhood is one approaching gerontocracy.[21]

In comparison with its Israeli counterpart, the Hutterite family plays a relatively more significant role in the socialization process of the young and in the molding and development of a child's personality, though the influence of the whole colony is much stronger than that of the family as a component unit.[22] In Hutterite colonies, infants below the age of three and a half stay at home with their parents. From three and a half to five, children go to kindergarten, under the supervision of a woman. At the age of five, they begin attending the German school and studying the Bible, the Hutterite history, hymnal songs, and their native language of Tyrolean German. The following year, young boys and girls go to the regular grade school in the colony and have two 45-minute periods of biblical study added at the beginning and end of their school hours. They also attend the German school until noon on Saturdays, and on Sundays they go to church in the morning and Sunday school in the afternoon. In addition, all members attend the regular religious services every evening. It must also be remembered that during the period when the children are in school (up to age 15), they eat their meals together in the juvenile dining hall.

As is apparent, much of the day of a child older than three and a half years is spent away from home, though still in close physical proximity to it. The matter of discipline is necessarily undertaken by persons other than the parents. A German school teacher explains his duties in the following terms:

> When a child does wrong at home, the father is the one who is to punish him. When a child behaves badly outside, then it is my responsibility, as the German teacher, to rectify him, regardless of whose child it is. I shall try my best to convince him how and why his behavior is punishable with the hope that he will not repeat it.

A further point that may be raised is the way in which child discipline is meted out. Not unlike the practice of the patriarchal family found in traditional China (where the senior author was born and brought up), child discipline is primarily based on the principle, "Spare the rod, spoil the child."[23] The father and, for that matter, the German teacher say in no equivocal terms that they mean to observe the inherited customs and traditions of the sect and to enforce conformity to them. In an interview, a housewife gave an answer which was frequently stated by others later: "We were put in the corner for punishment. Also we had to kneel down on other occasions. We got spanked, too." Another informant, a turkey man, puts the matter of child discipline in the following words:

> How do we punish our children? It depends on what mischief a child has committed. He may be scolded, or spanked, and also we use the strap. We have to make the punishment compatible with the offense.

By American standards, the practice of discipline in the colony is restrictive and rigorous. In spite of this, we have found very little which can be described as feelings of ambivalence or the Oedipus complex on the part of the young. Neither have we found any complaint or hatred against the person or persons who dispense the punishment. What we did find were intimate relationships between father and son and cordial relationships between teacher and pupil. Our tentative, a priori interpretation of this situation, which directly contradicts a basic assumption of Freudianism and the revised version of this assumption advanced by Malinowski, is that resentment or hatred is aroused only when the individual feels that his self image or pride is hurt through his subjugation to an authority, particularly if he is humiliated by punishment. The Hutterites train their young in self-denial, as manifested in *gelassenheit* (self-surrender to the guidance of God) and brotherly love. This leaves no room for individual pride.

The fifteenth year is the threshold to adulthood in the Hutterian way of life. During this year, the youths, having completed their eighth grade of education (the last year of schooling) begin to participate in community activities. The girl is privileged to add the polka-dotted scarf to her hat, which she has worn since the age of five. She takes turns working as a baby-sitter, a housecleaner, a cloth-maker, a seamstress, and the like. A boy may be given a tractor to practice driving, or he may become an apprentice in one of the various jobs of the colony. Another change signifying the attainment of adulthood is that the youngster begins to have his (or her) meals in the adult's dining hall upon his (or her) fifteenth birthday.

The Hutterite youth is now ready to proceed, in two more steps, namely, baptism and marriage, to assume his full-fledged status of membership in the colony. In Hutterian practices, religion takes precedence over marriage, and no wedding can be arranged without a formal commitment to the Hutterian faith through baptism. Individually one may achieve this status earlier or later, baptism generally being given to a youth upon his request between the ages of 18 and 21, slightly preceeding the ages for marriage. These ages, as it may be emphasized, fall in the period of what social psychologists designate "adolescent awakening," corresponding with sexual maturity. If a youth, at this stage of development, is induced into adopting a way of life, especially through a solemnly conducted religious ceremony with the sanction of the whole community, the effect, comparable to the initiation rites practiced in many folk cultures, is a "blossoming of religious faith" or regeneration.[24] It would be very unlikely for him to renounce his commitment later. Commenting on this Anabaptists' practice elsewhere, the senior author of this paper makes the following remark:

> Thus, the lion of adolescence which is still roaring in American society today is tamed once and for all through the channel of conventional norms (baptism) by a bait of nothing other than granting satisfaction to one of the juvenile's own primary needs and to his craving for personality integration.[25]

Having gained eligibility for marriage through baptism, many Hutterite youths follow the latter ceremony with the former. One may wonder how this basic need of sex is satisfied in a community which so strongly stresses spiritual devotion and asceticism. In the early development of this sect, courtship and romantic love between young boys and girls were considered pernicious with their consecrated monastic mode of life. Thus, marriage was strictly arranged by the elders and ministers. A typical statement concerning the principle of marriage was that "one should not ask his flesh but the elders that God might show through them what He has appointed for him. This, then one should take with gratitude as a gift from God."[26] Though it was unpopular, this practice continued until the middle of the last century, when an episode in a colony in Russia brought about changes in the age-old custom. A Hutterite girl refused to marry the person chosen for her by the elders and escaped from home to seek protection of the Mennonite trustee of the government. The trustee persuaded the Brethren to modify the custom, and the changes have been in effect ever since.[27]

Living in mid-twentieth century America, the Brethren realized that youth outside the colony select their own mates. They now allow adolescents to engage in dating activities. This loosening of restrictions in one particular area of life, such as dating, is a technique once referred to by Eaton as "controlled acculturation."[28] It is a concession made to preserve, not to undermine, their basic, religion-centered mode of life.

In courtship, if both partners are living in the same colony, it is always the boy who goes to visit his girl friend in her parents' house. Sunday evenings usually are the time for such a visit, which may not last any longer than 11 o'clock. On a pleasant day, they may, during their leisure hours, go out together to take a walk in the garden or yard. Since very little privacy can be kept in a colony, young people, although they appear to be shy to outsiders, often tease one another on their courtship activities. Once the girl has consented to marry the boy suitor, they are considered to have "gone steady." In our study we found that several adolescent boys and girls had "paired up" in this fashion and were awaiting the occasion to get baptized and married.

However, if an eligible candidate in dating is to be sought in a distant colony for one reason or another,[29] the story is a different one. Through the "grapevine" of kin, most potential mates in other colonies are known. Still there is the handicap of transportation to overcome. The chance of an initial contact must be provided for the young people to get acquainted with one another. Thus, it is not uncommon for the minister or some other official of a colony to bring, by a panel truck, a number of youths of marriageable ages on visits to other colonies. Other opportunities, such as summer work, mutual assistance programs, business consultations, or simply visiting relatives, can be used by young people to find their dates. After the initial contact is made, they carry on their courtship through correspondence.

Although courtship is practiced today among the Hutterite youths, it would be wrong to assume that dating activities are similar to those in American society. A hog man, about 20 years old, points out this difference:

> The practice of dating in the colonies is different from outside. A boy outside may bring a girl a gift of some kind after one or two visits. We do not do that in the colonies. No present would be accepted by a girl unless she had already accepted him. In your terms, the relationship would be one of "going steady."

Despite the Hutterite's belief that marriage is guided by divine will, love has become an important consideration in choosing a marriage partner. The same youth who advanced the information above has the following to say concerning his idea of marriage:

> How about love? That should come to be the very first. I would never marry a person without love. The three or four girls I am going with, I could get married to any one of them [he snapped his fingers] just like that. But I am in love with a different person.
> How do I know I am in love with her? My senses told me.

Oh, no! One could not possibly miss it. When I was with her, there seemed to be only the two of us in the whole world.

Strong parental supervision in dating may account for another departure from the prevailing pattern of courtship in American society. Without the approval of the parents, no suitor can visit his girl friend in her home. Since all activities are carried on within the colony, any attempts at a rendezvous would likely fail. In an interview, the wife of a chicken man provided this information concerning parental supervision:

In the colony parents never go ahead to arrange marriage for their children, but they help them by making their views available to them. They would like their sons or daughter to pick a marriage partner with a solid religious background.

As compared with the practice outside, the period known as dating or courtship in the colony is often relatively brief. Many couples get married after only a few visits. If the beloved one is a member of a distant colony and the youngsters are expressing love through correspondence, the period of courtship may be prolonged. When a boy and a girl have "gone steady," they are expected to become engaged if both have been baptized. They bring the matter to the minister and congregation for approval. Generally, the request is readily granted, since their relationship has been allowed to be carried on up to this point.

If two colonies are involved, the engagement ceremony is conducted in the bride's colony by her minister, and the ceremony for the wedding is performed by the minister of the groom in his colony. Both, particularly the latter, are regarded as great and merry occasions. They are celebrated in the air of a festival, with relatives of both families and members of both colonies participating. On the wedding day, the bride takes whatever are regarded as her personal belongings and whatever is given her by her mother as a "dowry" to her husband's colony. She then joins this colony. A room or a small unit in one of the dwelling buildings is furnished and ready to accommodate the newlyweds.

The interval between engagement and marriage is, as a rule, only a week. The engagement is short for the same reason it was short in the kibbutz. As observed by one author:

The kibbutz member about to marry is not influenced by income or career or prospects of employment, neither does he have to consider whether he can afford to set up home. All that is of importance is the personal relationship and the desire of the couple to live their lives together. Long engagements become unnecessary; and marriage *has an opportunity of being based on love* [italics added].[30]

However, marriages in the early stage of the kibbutz movement were not very stable, and many divorces ensued.[31] This raises a serious question as to whether love *alone* is a solid base upon which a happy and everlasting marital relationship can be built. Though love has been increasingly emphasized by the young members, the foundation of the Hutterite marriage rests not so much upon the couple's interpersonal affection as on their faithful commitment to the Anabaptist religion. "Love and sex," emphatically pointed out a German biblical teacher, "are kept in the sidelines in Hutterite life." These needs are recognized, of course, but they are not allowed to be brought to the surface so as to contaminate the practice of religious spiritualism. Thus, to be a faithful Hutterite, one must be a good husband or a loyal wife; and consequently, he *cannot* forfeit his church membership and yet retain his marriage. Normally there has been no divorce, although there were several cases of separation, one minister admitted. He explained that these cases had not resulted from maladjustment of the couples, but rather from the defection of the husbands whose families refused to follow them. Because of this separation, the marriage vow was considered breached and the marriage relationship terminated. In view of this and other similar practices, one can see with assurance the extent to which the endogamous rule of marriage is enforced and, more significantly, the degree to which the conjugal family is made to subserve the interest of the colony.

The advancement from adolescence to adulthood has, behaviorally, more bearing on the boy than on the girl. This is so, because the Hutterian Brotherhood, modeled after the primitive church of the Bible, is strictly a man's society. Only men can be elected officials of the colony, and only men are present in the congregation in making decisions. A girl, at a very young age, has been inculcated to be obedient and to accept man as the superior. After marriage, she recognizes her husband as the head of the household and assists him in living a faithful Hutterian life. Her assignments usually are what she has been doing ever since age 15. On the other hand, the status of maturity of the Hutterite man is manifested in more than one way. First of all, he begins to grow a beard. He is also qualified to assume some responsibility and to take charge of certain work in the business corporation (each colony is organized as a church and a business corporation) such as the tending of hogs or turkeys (consequently, he is called a "hog man" or a "turkey man"). After he has demonstrated his competence in handling the assigned task, he may be elected an official of the colony.

Although the ethos of life in the Hutterite colony is ascetic and monastic, marriage, paradoxically, serves the major function of group perpetuation and growth. Since most members are married—and married at relatively young ages—and no artificial birth control is practiced, the result of marriage is procreation. "Unlike monastic orders," maintains Victor Peters, "the colonies are not dependent on recruiting outsiders for membership in order to survive; they have one of the highest birth rates in the world."[32] During the period of 1945–1950, the Hutterites had a birth rate of 45.9 and a death rate of 4.4, yielding a rate of natural increase of 41.5 for every 1,000 persons, or 4.15 percent a year.[33] According to our own survey, carried out during 1964–1965, the total population of the 27 colonies (one in Minnesota) was 2,656 persons, and the total number of families 375. This means that there are, on the average, 13.88 families per colony and 7.08 persons per family. The average number of children born to each married couple is 9.08, with a range from 4 to 20 children.[34] In this regard, "the Hutterite," as aptly pointed out by Theodore Caplow, "comes closest to a conventional domestic arrangement" of the utopian ruling goals.[35]

Reproduction is regarded as a family function; discontinuance of it, however, even due to the wife's physical conditions, requires the approval of the minister and the congregation. In our interview files, one woman, with the approval of the colony, underwent surgery to terminate pregnancy after the birth of her eighth child. In conversations (note: not formal interviews) with nonofficial intellectuals in the colony, the idea of birth control did come up a few times. Allegedly, it was first suggested by the lawyer who fills out the income tax returns for the various colonies in South Dakota. However, insofar as can be ascertained, no artificial contraception of any sort is practiced. According to one informant, a couple were brought to confession before the congregation when their secret application of the rhythm method became known. The informant believed that this is still the observed rule.

If viewed as a "population policy," the practice of natural fertility fits rather neatly with other aspects of the Hutterian life. Ideologically, one cannot adopt a program of family planning and still insist upon adherence to a way of life completely in accordance with the Bible, which teaches to "be fruitful and multiply, and fill the earth and subdue it." Furthermore, the burden of child support is not on the individual parents, so there is little incentive for birth control aside from consideration of the wife's health. As a result, increasing numbers of children firmly anchor the family in the colony. The disadvantage of large families outside the colony accounts in part for the fact that the few who have defected from colonies have overwhelmingly been unmarried youths of adolescent ages.

The rapid growth in population does, however, create some thorny problems for the Hutterian Brotherhood. One of them is that farmland and machinery have become increasingly expensive, and a farm large enough to be considered by the Hutterites is hard to find on the market. (Each colony in South Dakota today owns and operates 4,000 acres of land, on the average.) This means that a binary fission in the future will become more difficult. Furthermore, when the population of a colony has grown beyond the optimum size,[36] not only are there not enough assignments to keep every member busy, but the nature of relations between members can no longer be maintained on the primary basis. Under such circumstances, the colony is operating on a low efficiency as a business corporation and, more significant, is losing its quality of cohesiveness as a primary group. Thus, a division must take place. The colony may then find that it has not accumulated sufficient capital to finance the branching out of a new unit. It was estimated by Hutterites that to establish a new colony today requires a capital somewhere from a quarter to half a million dollars.

The biggest challenge which the Hutterian Brotherhood faces, and, perhaps, which all other forms of cosmos face, is the cultivation of a strong esprit de corps among members so that group cohesion and solidarity can be achieved at the expense of the individual. In the Hutterite colony, this spirit is called *gelassenheit*, which means self-surrender to the guidance of God. The key issue here seems to be the control of the individual family.

In referring to the nuclear family of early kibbutzim in Israel, Yonina Talmon maintains that "there is a certain fundamental incompatibility between commitment to a radical revolutionary ideology and intense collective identification on the one hand and family solidarity on the other."[37] Lee Emerson Deets, who pioneered empirical research studies of South Dakota colonies some 30 years ago, speaks of the internal conflict of the Hutterite colony as "the natural enmity" and a "sociological battle" between the two basic institutions, the (conjugal) family and the community, "with the community at present holding the upper hand."[38] Theodore Caplow, in his analysis of real utopias, took as examples the Oneida community, the Catholic convent of cloistered nuns, the Israel kibbutz, and the Hutterian Brotherhood. He found that despite wide differences in other practices, one feature was shared by all: "The nuclear family is effectively replaced in all four utopian organizations."[39]

One further piece of evidence may be added to the above observations. The same enmity or antagonism between the larger organization and its conjugal units exists even if the organization is familial, such as the patriarchal family. For instance, as practiced in traditional China, the commitment to intense, collective identification of the patriarchal family is made *on the basis of family solidarity,* i.e., the kinship group as a whole; this same basic conflict frequently is the underlying cause for the breaking up of many a big house.[40] Evidence of this nature seems to suggest that even under the familistic mode of collectivism, group solidarity and cohesion are contingent upon the "effective replacement" of the conjugal family.

In the light of all the evidence presented above, we are forced to reach the conclusion that no matter how a cosmos is achieved, the degradation and suppression of the conjugal family are a necessary measure. It is so, because the rise of the conjugal family is tantamount to the rise of individualism, and the result will be the eclipse and finally the disintegration of the once closely knit cosmos. Hence, an ascending influence of the conjugal family can be taken as a sign of a corresponding weakening of the integral organization of the community. Such a change has happened to bring about decline of China's patriarchal family and, perhaps, is also happening in the kibbutz system, but it is not found to have taken place in the Hutterite colony.

NOTES

* Revised version of a paper presented at the annual meeting of the Midwest Sociological Society in Minneapolis, Minnesota, April 23, 1965. This paper is part of a broader research study concerning life of the Hutterite colonies in South Dakota. It was supported by a research grant, No. MH 10586–01, from the National Institute of Mental Health, U.S. Department of Health, Education and Welfare.

[1] According to the *Sioux City Journal,* Section C, Sunday, November 7, 1965, there are between 15,000 and 16,000 Hutterites in 163 colonies in the United States and Canada. The colonies are divided into three groups: the Schmiedenleut, the Dariusleut, and the Lehrerleut. The 27 colonies included in this study belong to the Schmiedenleut group. All but one are located in the East River region of South Dakota.

[2] Theodore Caplow, *Principles of Organization,* chap. 8, "The Utopian Formula," New York: Harcourt, Brace & World, Inc., 1964, pp. 291–316.

[3] The reference to the Hutterian Brotherhood as a "true *gemeinschaft*" is found in Robert Friedmann's excellent, scholarly work, *Hutterite Studies,* Goshen, Indiana: Mennonite Historical Society, 1961, p. 83.

[4] Robert Redfield, "The Folk Society," *American Journal of Sociology,* 52 (January, 1947), pp. 293–308.

[5] Robert Redfield, *The Little Community,* Chicago, University of Chicago Press, 1955. The four qualities Redfield uses to define a small community include (A) distinctiveness, (B) smallness, (C) homogeneity, and (D) all-providing self-sufficiency. These are the characteristics of the Hutterite colony.

[6] In his discussion of the types of societies, Ely Chinoy dichotomized them into the communal and the associational. The Hutterite colony fits well into his description of the communal society. See Chinoy, *Society, An Introduction to Sociology,* New York: Random House, 1963, p. 88.

[7] The concept of a total institution, according to Erving Goffman, includes "all the organizations which constitute a complete world for their members, involving them with their fellows day and night and segregating them from the outside world." Though it was developed with quite a different perspective in view, the Hutterian Brotherhood's practices come very close to the above. See Goffman, "On the Characteristics of Total Institutions," in *The Prison: Studies in Institutional Organization and Change,* ed. by Donald R. Cressey, New York: Holt, Rinehart & Winston, 1961, pp. 15–106. Also, the concept of total institution is adopted by Theodore Caplow in his discussion and analysis of the nature of utopian organizations. Cf. Caplow, *op. cit.,* p. 292.

[8] Max Weber, in his authoritative analysis of Protestant ethics, concluded that the practice of "worldly asceticism" was a common feature in many sects of Protestantism, for instance, in Puritanism and later in Pietism. Obviously, the Hutterian Brotherhood is one of them. See Max Weber, *Protestant Ethics and the Spirit of Capitalism,* trans. by Talcott Parsons, New York: Charles Scribner's Sons, 1930, pp. 95–154.

[9] The Hutterian Brotherhood differs from other Protestant denominations only in its practice of "the Christian community of goods." This can be translated into "theocratic communism." See Friedmann, op. cit., pp. 76–85; and John Horsch, The Hutterian Brethren, 1528–1931, Goshen, Indiana: The Mennonite Historical Society, Goshen College, 1931, pp. 131–133.

[10] This translation of the Chronicle's description is taken from Friedmann, op. cit., pp. 115–116.

[11] The family may be defined thus: "As a social group characterized by a common residence, economic cooperation and reproduction, it includes adults of both sexes, at least two of whom maintain a socially approved sexual relationship, and one or more children, own or adopted, of the sexually cohabiting adults" (by George Murdock, an anthropologist, in Social Structure).

It could also be defined as "a group of persons united by ties of marriage, blood, or adoption; constituting a single household; interacting and communicating with each other in their respective social roles of husband and wife, mother and father, son and daughter, brother and sister; and creating and maintaining a common culture" (by Ernest W. Burgess, a sociologist, in The Family).

Regardless of the definition, anthropological or sociological, it is evident that the family in the Hutterite colony is reduced to something less than an independent entity and a full-fledged unit.

[12] Quoted from Robert Friedmann, "Marriage, Hutterite Practices," in The Mennonite Encyclopedia, Vol. III, pp. 510–511.

[13] Such an account is given by John A. Hostetler, Amish Society, Baltimore: Johns Hopkins Press, 1963, pp. 148–170; William Schreiber, Our Amish Neighbors, Chicago: University of Chicago Press, 1962, pp. 52–60.

[14] According to Friedmann, "the idea of love—brotherly togetherness and mutual giving and sharing—was the very center of Jacob Hutter's work. He visualized the brotherhood as a great family." Friedmann, Hutterite Studies, op. cit., p. 83.

[15] When the personal pronoun "we" is used by a Hutterite, it is invariably addressed not to the immediate relatives in a nuclear family but to the members of the whole colony. In regard to what makes a group primary, see S. C. Lee, "The Primary Group as Cooley Defines It," Sociological Quarterly, 5 (Winter, 1964), pp. 23–34.

[16] William Kephart, The Family, Society and the Individual, Boston: Houghton, Mifflin Co., 1966, p. 185.

[17] According to Joseph W. Eaton, "binary fission" is the term preferred by Hutterites in reference to a division in which a daughter colony is separated from or branched off a mother colony. See Joseph W. Eaton and Robert J. Weil, Culture and Mental Disorder, New York: The Free Press, a division of the Macmillan Co., 1955, p. 30.

[18] For an account of this aspect of Amish life, see William I. Schreiber, op. cit., pp. 55–60; John Gillin, The Ways of Men, New York: Appleton-Century-Crofts, 1948, pp. 209–220.

[19] Stanley Diamond, "Kibbutz and Shtetl: The History of An Idea," Social Problems, 5 (1957–1958), pp. 68–99; Henrick F. Infield, Cooperative Living in Palestine, New York: The Dryden Press, 1944, pp. 17–34; and Y. Talmon Garber, "Social Change and Family Structure," International Social Science Journal, 14 (1962), pp. 468–487.

[20] Quoted from Melford E. Spiro, "Is the Family Universal?" American Anthropologist, 56 (October, 1954), p. 843; also see his book, Kibbutz: Venture in Utopia, New York: Schorken Books, 1953, p. 127.

[21] The original revolutionary radicalism adopted in the early kibbutz movement has been modified in recent developments. In some 15 kibbutzim, children of a wide range of ages now sleep in rooms adjoining their parents', no longer in their own separate living quarters. See Moche Kerem, "The Kibbutz," (a report published by Israel Digest) in Israel Today, No. 27, Jerusalem, October, 1963.

[22] A typical Hutterite colony is governed by a board of elders. This group consists of from four to six members, with the minister serving as its chairman. As a general rule, elders are married males who are elected to this position after they have made contributions to the colony in one way or another. The minister—the spiritual leader of the colony—is, almost without exception, an older man, generally in his fifties or sixties. One minister we interviewed was in his seventies. A minister is not supposed to retire until his health does not permit him to serve the colony in full capacity.

[23] Cf., S. C. Lee, "China's Traditional Family, Its Characteristics and Disintegration," *American Sociological Review,* 18 (June, 1953), pp. 272–280.

[24] Cf. Kurt Lang and Gladys E. Lang, *Collective Dynamics,* New York: Thomas Y. Crowell Co., 1961, pp. 157–169.

[25] S. C. Lee, *Social Cohesion in a Utopian Community: A Pilot Study of the Hutterite Colonies in South Dakota,* the final progress report submitted to the National Institute of Mental Health, April 1, 1966, p. 35.

[26] Robert Friedmann, "Marriage, Hutterite Practices," *op. cit.,* pp. 510–511.

[27] *Ibid.*

[28] Joseph W. Eaton, "Controlled Acculturation: A Survival Technique of the Hutterites," *American Sociological Review,* 17 (June, 1952), pp. 331–340.

[29] Age, consanguinity, and personal preference are usually the reasons that some Hutterites must find dating partners in other colonies. For instance, one boy we interviewed remarked, "The girls around here (in his colony) are just a bunch of silly geese. I could have any one of them to marry, except they are either too young or too old." Responding to the interviewer's question, "Why should you go to a distant colony to find a girl friend?" another boy said with a twinkle in his eye, "As people say, the grass is always greener on the other side of the fence."

[30] Esther Lucas, "Family Life in the Kibbutz," in Gideon Baratz *et al., A New Way of Life, The Collective Settlements of Israel,* London: Shindler & Golomb, 1949, p. 62.

[31] Spiro, *Kibbutz—Venture in Utopia, op. cit.,* pp. 112–114.

[32] Quoted from Victor Peters, *All Things Common,* Minneapolis: University of Minnesota Press, 1965, p. 4.

[33] These rates were originally established by Joseph W. Eaton and A. J. Mayer in *Man's Capacity to Reproduce,* New York: The Free Press, a division of the Macmillan Co., 1953, and adapted by Robert C. Cook in his "The North American Hutterites," *Population Bulletin,* 10 (December, 1954), pp. 97–107.

[34] Lee, *Social Cohesion in a Utopian Community, op. cit.,* particularly Table IX in the Appendix of this report.

[35] Caplow, *op. cit.,* p. 304.

[36] The point of an optimum population, in connection, with the effective operation of a primary group, was first raised by Melford E. Spiro in his paper, "Is the Family Universal?" *op. cit.,* p. 846. If the average of each of the Hutterite colonies in North America is taken as a rough estimate of the optimum population, it is 90–100 persons. If the 27 colonies we surveyed are tabulated separately, using figures obtained from responsible officials (usually the minister), the average number of persons per colony is 98.34.

[37] Yonina Talmon, "The Family in a Revolutionary Movement—The Case of the Kibbutz in Israel," in M. F. Nimkoff, *Comparative Family Systems,* New York: Houghton, Mifflin Co., 1965, pp. 260–261.

[38] Lee Emerson Deets, "The Origins of Conflict in the Hutterische Communities," *Publications of the Sociological Society of America,* 25 (May, 1931), pp. 131–132. For further reference, see his doctoral dissertation titled, *The Hutterites: A Study In Social Cohesion,* submitted to Columbia University and published by Times and News Publishing Co., Gettysburg, Pa., 1939.

[39] Caplow, *op. cit.,* p. 304.

[40] See Footnote 23.

III

Socialization in the United States

At this point we turn to the family life cycle, beginning in this part with socialization or child rearing, and concluding in Part Seven with old age and death. Numerous studies of the family's influence upon the social and psychological development of the child have appeared over the past forty years. The first article in this part, by Urie Bronfenbrenner, is a summarizing and interpretive piece comparing working-class and middle-class socialization between 1930 and 1955. We have reprinted most of this important paper, but have omitted the early portion in which he notes the difficulties in comparing the various studies. Because studies were carried out at different times and places, some employed seven social classes, others only two or three. Bronfenbrenner decided to use only the white collar/blue collar, or middle class/working class, distinction.

After surveying the results of the studies, Bronfenbrenner draws these conclusions: The middle classes have been more democratic in their treatment of children throughout the twenty-five year period. In expression of affection, the working-classes were more expressive in the 1930's, but the middle-classes are more expressive in the mid-1950's. Child-rearing practices apparently fluctuate more in the middle class than the working class, the former using the mass media more to keep in touch with the latest fads in advice. Finally, the two social classes appear to be approaching each other in socialization behavior. This last conclusion leads to a question: if the social classes were in fact becoming increasingly similar in the 1950's, what has happened by the 1970's? Does Besner's brief discussion of lower-class socialization (Part II) give any hints? It may be necessary to distinguish further the stable, affluent working classes from the economically deprived working classes, with the former now closely approaching the socialization methods of the middle class and the latter still resembling Bronfenbrenner's "working classes" of the 1930's.

The second article on socialization concerns the identification of offspring with their parents. In the first excerpt from Winch's book the concept, *identification*, is distinguished from six other related and frequently used terms in social psychology. He then proceeds to a functional analysis of the relation between societal differentiation or specialization, the loss of family functions, and the identification of off-spring with their parents. The fewer functions the family performs, the less likely it is that the individual will find his major identifications within the family. What about Winch's analysis when applied to Ariès' and O'Neil's discussions in Section One? Would identification with parents have been at a high point during the Victorian era? And in contemporary society would a son or a daughter be more likely to identify with his same-sex parent? This last question should also be raised after reading Farber's discussion of independence in this section.

Goode's intriguing think-piece and summary of information about authoritarianism and democracy makes a valuable addition to the discussion of socialization. What kind of socialization, Goode asks, results in a democratic or tolerant stance regarding differences? After reviewing the findings of many studies, Goode presents several suggestions as to the way parents might socialize tolerance into their offspring. Are any of his findings contradictory? According to Bronfenbrenner's conclusion regarding socialization, is Goode's assertion that high-status families are more likely to produce tolerant offspring correct? Do we, after all, *want* human freedom and human rights, or are we actually afraid of freedom and differences? This last question should be raised simultaneously regarding Goode's article and Wrong's piece in Part VIII on family "breakup."

The final selection of Part III is a brief excerpt from Bernard Farber's book on *Family: Organization and Interaction.* Noting that some persons tend, during their socialization, to remain passive and unquestioning, Farber focusses upon two types of independence: sponsored and unsponsored. Sponsored independence is achieved within the value system of one's parents, while unsponsored independence is based upon true rebellion and a rejection of parental ways. These two types of independence are, of course, related to Winch's conceptualization of identification, and one should ask whether passive dependence, sponsored independence, or unsponsored independence is more likely to characterize American girls or boys, working classes or middle classes, urbanites or ruralites. Is there any relation between Farber's view of independence in American society and Goode's conclusions regarding the development of concern with human rights in the growing individual?

A massive literature exists concerning socialization in other countries besides the United States. The interested reader may want to branch out to such works as Beatrice Whiting's *Child Rearing in Six Cultures* in order to place U.S. socialization in its proper perspective—only one approach among many.

Socialization and Social Class Through Time and Space

URIE BRONFENBRENNER

SOCIAL CLASS DIFFERENCES IN INFANT CARE, 1930–1955

In interpreting reports of child-rearing practices it is essential to distinguish between the date at which the information was obtained and the actual period to which the information refers. This caution is particularly relevant in dealing with descriptions of infant care for children who (as in the Eugene or Detroit studies) may be as old as 12, 14, or 18 at the time of the interview. In such instances it is possible only to guess at the probable time at which the practice occurred by making due allowances for the age of the child. The problem is further complicated by the fact that none of the studies reports SES differences by age. The best one can do, therefore, is to estimate the median age of the group and from this approximate the period at which the practice may have taken place. For example, the second Detroit sample, which ranged in age from birth to 18 years, would have a median age of about nine. Since the field work was done in 1953, we estimate the date of feeding and weaning practices as about 1944.[1] It should be recognized, however, that the practices reported range over a considerable period extending from as far back as 1935 to the time of the interview in 1953. Any marked variation in child-rearing practices over this period could produce an average figure which would in point of fact be atypical for the middle year 1944. We shall have occasion to point to the possible operation of this effect in some of the data to follow.

If dates of practices are estimated by the method outlined above, we find that the available data describe social-class differences in feeding, weaning, and toilet training for a period from about 1930 to 1955. The relevant information appears in Tables 1 through 3.

It is reasonable to suppose that a mother's reports of whether or not

TABLE 1

Frequency of Breast Feeding

1.	2.	No. of cases reporting			Percentage breast fed			9.
	3.	4.	5.	6.	7.	8.	
Sample	Approx. date of practice	Total sample	Middle class	Working class	Total sample	Middle class	Working class	Difference*
National I	1930	1856	842	1014	80	78	82	−4†
National II	1932	445	201	244	40	29	49	−20†
Chicago I	1939	100	48	52	83	83	83	0
Detroit I	1941	112	59	53	62	54	70	−16
Detroit II	1944	200	70	130	Percentages not given			+
Eugene	1946–47	206	84	122	46	40	50	−10
Boston	1947–48	372	198	174	40	43	37	+6
New Haven I	1949–50	222	114	108	80	85	74	+11†
Palo Alto	1950	74	36	38	66	70	63	+7
Upstate New York	1955	1432	594	838	24	27	21	+6†

* Minus sign denotes lower incidence for middle class than for working class.
† Denotes difference significant at 5-percent level of confidence or better.

TABLE 2

Scheduled versus Self-demand Feeding

1. Sample	2. Approx. date of practice	No. of cases reporting			Percentage fed on demand			Difference*
		3. Total sample	4. Middle class	5. Working class	6. Total sample	7. Middle class	8. Working class	
National I	1932	470	208	262	16	7	23	−16†
Chicago I	1939	100	48	52	25	4	44	−40†
Detroit I	1941	297	52	45	21	12	53	−41†
Detroit II	1944	205	73	132	55	51	58	−7
Boston	1947–48	372	198	174	Percentages not given			−
New Haven I	1949–50	191	117	74	65	71	54	+17
Palo Alto	1950	74	36	38	59	64	55	+9

* Minus sign denotes lower incidence of self-demand feeding in middle class.
† Denotes difference significant at 5-percent level of confidence or better.

she employed a particular practice would be somewhat more reliable than her estimate of when she began or discontinued that practice. This expectation is borne out by the larger number of statistically significant differences in tables presenting data on prevalence (Tables 1 and 2) rather than on the timing of a particular practice (Tables 3–5). On the plausible assumption that the former data are more reliable, we shall begin our discussion by considering the results on frequency of breast feeding and scheduled feeding, which appear in Tables 1 and 2.

General Trends

We may begin by looking at general trends over time irrespective of social-class level. These appear in column 6 of Tables 1 and 2. The data for breast feeding are highly irregular, but there is some suggestion of decrease in this practice over the years.[2] In contrast, self-demand feeding is becoming more common. In both instances the trend is more marked (column 8) in the middle class; in other words, it is they especially who are doing the changing. This fact is reflected even more sharply in column 9 which highlights a noteworthy shift. Here we see that in the earlier period—roughly before the end of World War II—both breast feeding and demand feeding were less common among the middle class than among the working class. In the later period, however, the direction is reversed; it is now the middle-class mother who more often gives her child the breast and feeds him on demand.

The data on duration of breast feeding (Table 3) and on the timing of weaning and bowel training (Tables 4 and 5) simply confirm, somewhat less reliably, all of the above trends. There is a general tendency in both social classes to wean the child earlier from the breast but, apparently, to allow him to suck from a bottle till a somewhat later age. Since no uniform reference points were used for securing information on toilet training in the several studies (i.e., some investigators report percentage training at six months, others at ten months, still others at 12 or 18 months), Table 5 shows only the direction of the difference between the two social classes. All these figures on timing point to the same generalization. In the earlier period, middle-class mothers were exerting more pressure; they weaned their children from the breast and bottle and carried out bowel and bladder training before their working-class counterparts. But in the last ten years the trend has been reversed—it is now the middle-class mother who trains later.

These consistent trends take on richer significance in the light of Wolfenstein's impressive analysis[3] of the content of successive editions of the United States Children's Bureau bulletin on *Infant Care*. She describes the period 1929–38 (which corresponds to the earlier time span covered by our data) as characterized by:

> . . . a pervasive emphasis on regularity, doing everything by the clock. Weaning and introduction of solid foods are to be

TABLE 3

Duration of Breast Feeding
(for those breast fed)

Sample	Approx. date of practice	No. of cases††			Median duration in months			
		Total sample	Middle class	Working class	Total sample	Middle class	Working class	Difference**
National II*	1930	1488	654	834	6.6	6.2	7.5	−1.3†
Chicago I	1939	83	40	43	3.5	3.4	3.5	−.1
Detroit I*	1941	69	32	37	3.3	2.8	5.3	−2.5
Eugene	1946–47	95	34	61	3.4	3.2	3.5	−.3
Boston	1947–48	149	85	64	2.3	2.4	2.1	+.3
New Haven I*	1949–50	177	97	80	3.6	4.3	3.0	+1.3
Upstate New York	1955	299	145	154	1.2	1.3	1.2	+.1

* Medians not given in original report but estimated from data cited.

† Denotes difference significant at 5-percent level if confidence or better.

** Minus sign denotes shorter duration for middle class than for working class.

†† Number of cases for Chicago, Eugene, Boston, and Upstate New York estimated from percentages cited.

TABLE 4

Age at Completion of Weaning
(either breast or bottle)

Sample	Approx. date of practice	No. of cases			Median age in months			Difference*
		Total sample	Middle class	Working class	Total group	Middle class	Working class	
Chicago I	1940	100	48	52	11.3	10.3	12.3	−2.0†
Detroit I	1942	69	32	37	11.2	10.6	12.0	−1.4†
Detroit II	1945	190	62	128	— Under 12 months —			—
Eugene	1947–48	206	85	121	13.6	13.2	14.1	−.9
Boston	1948–49	372	198	174	12.3	12.0	12.6	−.6
New Haven I	1949–50	222	114	108	— Over 12 months —			—
Palo Alto	1951	68	32	36	13.1	14.4	12.6	+1.8

* Minus sign denotes earlier weaning for middle than for working class.
† Denotes difference significant at 5-percent level of confidence or better.

TABLE 5

Toilet Training

Sample	Approximate date practice begun	No. of cases		Direction of relationship			
		Bowel training	Bladder training	Beginning bowel training	End bowel training	Beginning bladder training	End bladder training
National II	1931	2375	2375		−†		−*
National I	1932	494	494		−	−	
Chicago I	1940	100	220†	−†	−	−†**	+†
Detroit I	1942	110	102	−	−	+	−
Detroit II	1945	216	200	+†			
Eugene	1947–48	206	206	+	−	+	+
Boston	1948–49	372		−	+†		
New Haven I	1950–51	214		+†			
Palo Alto	1951	73		+†			

* Minus sign indicates that middle class began or completed training earlier than lower class.

† Denotes difference significant at 5-percent level of confidence or better.

** Based on data from 1946 report.

accomplished with great firmness, never yielding for a moment
to the baby's resistance . . . . bowel training . . . must be
carried out with great determination as early as possible . . .
The main danger which the baby presented at this time was
that of dominating the parents. Successful child training meant
winning out against the child in the struggle for domination.

In the succeeding period, however,

> . . . all this was changed. The child became remarkably harm-
> less . . . . His main active aim was to explore his world . . . .
> When not engaged in exploratory undertakings, the baby
> needs care and attention; and giving these when he demands
> them, far from making him a tyrant, will make him less de-
> manding later on. At this time mildness is advocated in all
> areas: thumbsucking and masturbation are not to be inter-
> fered with; weaning and toilet training are to be accomplished
> later and more gently.[4]

The parallelism between preachment and practice is apparent also
in the use of breast feeding. Up until 1945, "breast feeding was emphatically recommended," with "warnings against early weaning." By
1951, "the long-term intransigence about breast feeding is relaxed."
States the bulletin edition of that year: "Mothers who find bottle feeding
easier should feel comfortable about doing it that way."

One more link in the chain of information completes the story.
There is ample evidence that, both in the early and the later period,
middle-class mothers were much more likely than working-class mothers
to be exposed to current information on child care. Thus Anderson cites
table after table showing that parents from higher SES levels read
more books, pamphlets, and magazines, and listen to more radio talks
on child care and related subjects. This in 1932. Similarly, in the last five
years, White, in California, and Boek, in New York, report that middle-
class mothers are much more likely than those in the working class to
read Spock's best-seller, *Baby and Child Care*[5] and similar publications.

Our analysis suggests that the mothers not only read these books
but take them seriously, and that their treatment of the child is affected
accordingly. Moreover, middle-class mothers not only read more but
are also more responsive; they alter their behavior earlier and faster
than their working-class counterparts.

In view of the remarkably close parallelism in changes over time
revealed by Wolfenstein's analysis and our own, we should perhaps not
overlook a more recent trend clearly indicated in Wolfenstein's report
and vaguely discernible as well in the data we have assembled.
Wolfenstein asserts that, since 1950, a conservative note has crept into
the child-training literature; "there is an attempt to continue . . . mild-
ness, but not without some conflicts and misgivings . . . . May not con-

tinued gratification lead to addiction and increasingly intensified demands?"[6] In this connection it is perhaps no mere coincidence that the differences in the last column of Tables 1 to 3 show a slight drop after about 1950; the middle class is still more "relaxed" than the working class, but the differences are not so large as earlier. Once again, practice may be following preachment—now in the direction of introducing more limits and demands—still within a permissive framework. We shall return to a consideration of this possibility in our discussion of class differences in the training of children beyond two years of age.

Taken as a whole, the correspondence between Wolfenstein's data and our own suggests a general hypothesis extending beyond the confines of social class as such: *child-rearing practices are likely to change most quickly in those segments of society which have closest access and are most receptive to the agencies or agents of change (e.g., public media, clinics, physicians, and counselors)*. From this point of view, one additional trend suggested by the available data is worthy of note: rural families appear to "lag behind the times" somewhat in their practices of infant care. For example, in Anderson's beautifully detailed report, there is evidence that in 1932 farm families (Class IV in his sample) were still breast feeding their children more frequently but being less flexible in scheduling and toilet training that nonfarm families of roughly comparable socioeconomic status. Similarly, there are indications from Miller and Swanson's second Detroit study that, with SES held constant, mothers with parents of rural background adhere to more rigid techniques of socialization than their urban counterparts. Finally, the two samples in our data most likely to contain a relatively high proportion of rural families—Eugene, Oregon and Upstate New York— are also the ones which are slightly out of line in showing smaller differences in favor of middle-class permissiveness.

The above observations call attention to the fact that the major time trends discerned in our data, while impressive, are by no means uniform. There are several marked exceptions to the rule. True, some of these can be "explained" in terms of special features of the samples employed. A case in point is the New Haven study, which—in keeping with the rooming-in ideology and all that this implies—shows the highest frequency and duration of breast feeding for the postwar period, as well as the greatest prevalence of feeding on demand reported in all the surveys examined. Other discrepancies may be accounted for, at least in part, by variations in time span encompassed by the data (National 1930 *vs.* 1932), the demonstrated differential rate in breast feeding for first *vs.* later children (Palo Alto *vs.* National 1930 or Boston), ethnic differences (Boston *vs.* Chicago), contrasting ages of mothers in middle- *vs.* working-class samples (Chicago), etc. All of these explanations, however, are "after the fact" and must therefore be viewed with suspicion.

Summary

Despite our inability to account with any confidence for all departures from the general trend, we feel reasonably secure in our inferences about the nature of this trend. To recapitulate, over the last 25 years, even though breast feeding appears to have become less popular, American mothers—especially in the middle class—are becoming increasingly permissive in their feeding and toilet-training practices during the first two years of the child's life. The question remains whether this tendency is equally apparent in the training of the child as he becomes older. We turn next to a consideration of this issue.

CLASS DIFFERENCES IN THE TRAINING OF CHILDREN BEYOND THE AGE OF TWO

Once we have the stage of infancy, data from different studies of child training become even more difficult to compare. There are still greater variations in the questions asked from one research to the next, and results are reported in different types of units (e.g., relating scales with varying numbers of steps diversely defined). In some instances (as in the Chicago, Detroit II, and, apparently, Eugene surveys) the questions referred not to past or current practices but to the mother's judgment about what she would do at some later period when her child would be older. Also, when the samples include children of widely varying ages, it is often difficult to determine at what period the behavior described by the mother actually took place. Sometimes a particular age was specified in the interviewer's question and when this occurred, we have made use of that fact in estimating the approximate date of the practice. More often, however, such information was lacking. Accordingly, our time estimates must be regarded as subject to considerable error. Finally, even though we deal with substantially the same researches considered in the analysis of infant care, the total period encompassed by the data is appreciably shorter. This is so because the mothers are no longer being asked to recall how they handled their child in infancy; instead they are reporting behavior which is contemporary, or at least not far removed, from the time of the interview.

All of these considerations combine to restrict severely our ability to identify changes in practices over time. Accordingly, the absence of evidence for such changes in some of the data is perhaps more properly attributed to the limitations of our measures than to the actual course of events.

Permissiveness and Restriction on Freedom of Movement

The areas of impulse expression documented in Table 6 reflect a continuity in treatment from babyhood into early childhood. With only one minor, statistically insignificant exception, the results depict the middle-class parent as more permissive in all four spheres of activity: oral behavior, toilet accidents, sex, and aggression. There is no suggestion of a shift over the somewhat truncated time span. The now-familiar trend reappears, however, in the data on restriction of freedom of movement shown in Table 7.

In Table 7 we see a gradual shift over time with the middle class being more restrictive in the 1930's and early 1940's but becoming more permissive during the last decade.

Techniques of Discipline

The most consistent finding documented in Table 8 is the more frequent use of physical punishment by working-class parents. The middle class, in contrast, resort to reasoning, isolation, and what Sears and his colleagues have referred to as "love-oriented" discipline techniques.[7] These are methods which rely for their effect on the child's fear of loss of love. Miller and Swanson referred to substantially the same class of phenomena by the term "psychological discipline," which for them covers such parental behaviors as appeals to guilt, expressions of disappointment, and the use of symbolic rather than direct rewards and punishments. Table 8 shows all available data on class differences in the use of corporal punishment, reasoning, isolation, and "love-oriented" techniques. Also, in order to avoid the risks, however small, involved in wearing theoretical blinders, we have listed in the last column of the table all other significant class differences in techniques of discipline reported in the studies we have examined.

From one point of view, these results highlight once again the more lenient policies and practices of middle-class families. Such parents are, in the first place, more likely to overlook offenses, and when they do punish, they are less likely to ridicule or inflict physical pain. Instead, they reason with the youngster, isolate him, appeal to guilt, show disappointment—in short, convey in a variety of ways, on the one hand, the kind of behavior that is expected of the child; on the other, the realization that transgression means the interruption of a mutually valued relationship.

These consistent class differences take on added significance in the light of the finding, arrived at independently both by the Boston and Detroit investigators, that "love-oriented" or "psychological" techniques are more effective than other methods for bringing about desired behavior. Indeed, both groups of researchers concluded on the basis of

TABLE 6

Permissiveness toward Impulse Expression

Sample	Approx. date of practice	No. of cases reported	Direction of trend for middle class			
			Oral behavior	Toilet accidents	Sex	Aggression
National I	1932	470			More infants allowed to play on bed unclothed.*	
Chicago	1943	100		Treated by ignoring,* reasoning or talking,* rather than slapping,* scolding, or showing disgust.*		More children allowed to "fight so long as they don't hurt each other badly."*
Detroit II	1946	70–88	Less often disciplined for thumb sucking.		Less often disciplined for touching sex organs.	
New Haven	1949–50	216	Less often disapproved for thumb sucking, eating habits, mannerisms, etc.*			
Eugene	1950	206		Less often treated by spanking or scolding	More permissive toward child's sexual behavior.*	Fewer children allowed "to fight so long as they don't hurt each other badly." More permissiveness toward general aggression.

Sample	Approx. date of practice	No. of cases reported	Direction of trend for middle class			
			Oral behavior	Toilet accidents	Sex	Aggression
Boston	1951–52	372	Less restriction on use of fingers for eating.*	Less severe toilet training.*	Higher sex permissiveness (general index).*	More permissive of aggression toward parents,* children† and siblings. Less punishment of aggression toward parents.*
Palo Alto	1953	73		Less severe toilet training.*		More permissive of aggression toward parents.* Less severe punishment of aggression toward parents.

* Indicates difference between classes significant at the 5-percent level or better.
† The difference between percentages is not significant but the difference between ratings is significant at the 5-percent level or better.

TABLE 7

Restriction on Freedom of Movement

Sample	Approx. date of practice	No. of cases reported	Age	Item	Direction of relationship*
National II	1932	2289	1–5	Play restricted to home yard	—
				Play restricted to block	+
				Play restricted to neighborhood	++†
				No restriction on place of play	++†
National III	1932	669	6–12	Child goes to movie with parents	+++
				Child goes to movie with other children	++
National IV	1932	2414	1–12	Child goes to bed earlier	++†
Chicago	1943	100	5	Age at which child is allowed to go to movie alone or with other children	—†
				Age at which child is allowed to go downtown	++†
				Time at which children are expected in at night	—†
New Haven I	1949–50	211	1	Definite bed time	—†
Boston	1951–52	372	5	Restriction on how far child may go from home	—
				Frequency of checking on child's whereabouts	—**
				Strictness about bed time	—†
				Amount of care taken by persons other than parents	
Detroit II	1953	136	0–18	Child supervised closely after 12 years of age	—†
Palo Alto	1953	74	2½–5½	Extent of keeping track of child	0

* Plus sign denotes greater restriction for middle class.

† Denotes difference significant at 5-percent level or better.

** The difference between percentages is not significant but the difference between mean ratings is significant at the 5-percent level or better.

TABLE 8

Techniques of Discipline

Sample	Approx. date of practice	No. of cases reporting	Age	Direction of relationship*				Nature of Love-oriented technique	Other significant trends for middle class
				Physical punishment	Reasoning	Isolation	Love-oriented technique		
National II	1932	1947	1–5	–†					
National III	1932	839	6–12			+†			
National IV	1932	3130	1–12		+†				Infractions more often ignored† More children deprived of pleasure as punishment
Chicago I	1943	100	5	+		–	+†	Praise for good behavior.	Soiling child more often ignored,† rather than spanked† or shown disgust
Detroit I	1950	115	12–14	–†			+†	Mother expresses disappointment or appeals to guilt	
Detroit II	1950	222	0–19	–			+	Mother uses symbolic rather than direct rewards and punishments	
Eugene	1950	206	0–18	–	0	+†			
Boston	1951–52	372	5	–†	+	+	0	No difference in overall use of praise or withdrawal of love	Less use of ridicule,† deprivation of privileges** or praise for no trouble at the table†

* Plus sign indicates practice was more common in middle class than in working class.

† Denotes difference between classes significant at 5-percent level or better.

** The difference between percentages is not significant but the difference between mean ratings is significant at the 5-percent level or better.

their data that physical punishment for aggression tends to increase rather than decrease aggressive behavior. From the point of view of our interest, these findings mean that middle-class parents, though in one sense more lenient in their discipline techniques, are using methods that are actually more compelling. Moreover, the compelling power of these practices, rather than being reduced, is probably enhanced by the more permissive treatment accorded to middle-class children in the early years of life. The successful use of withdrawal of love as a discipline technique implies the prior existence of a gratifying relationship; the more love present in the first instance, the greater the threat implied in its withdrawal.

In sum, to return to the issue posed in the preceding section, our analysis suggests that middle-class parents are in fact using techniques of discipline which are likely to be effective in evoking the behavior desired in the child. Whether the high levels of expectation held by such parents are actually achieved is another matter. At least, there would seem to be some measure of functional continuity in the way in which middle-class parents currently treat their children from infancy through childhood.

Before we leave consideration of the data of Table 8, one additional feature of the results deserves comment. In the most recent study reported, the Boston research, there were three departures from the earlier general trend. First, no class difference was found in the over-all use of praise. Second, working-class parents actually exceeded those of the middle class in praising good behavior at the table. Third, in contrast to earlier findings, the working-class mother more frequently punished by withdrawing privileges. Although Sears et al. did not classify "withdrawal of privileges" as a love-oriented technique, the shift does represent a change in the direction of what was previously a method characteristic of the middle-class parent. Finally, there is no clear trend in the differential use of love-oriented techniques by the two social classes. If we view the Boston study as reflecting the most recent trends in methods of discipline, then either middle-class mothers are beginning to make less use of techniques they previously relied upon, or the working class is starting to adopt them. We are inclined toward the latter hypothesis in the belief that the working class, as a function of increasing income and education, is gradually reducing its "cultural lag." Evidence from subsequent studies, of course, would be necessary to confirm this speculative interpretation, since the results cited may merely be a function of features peculiar to the Boston study and not typical of the general trend.

Over–All Character of the Parent–Child Relationship

The material considered so far has focused on specific practices employed by the parent. A number of researches document class differences as well in variables of a more molar sort—for example, the emotional quality of the parent-child relationship as a whole. These investigations have the additional advantage of reaching somewhat further back in time, but they also have their shortcomings. First of all, the results are not usually reported in the conventional form of percentages or means for specific social-class levels. In some studies the findings are given in terms of correlation coefficients. In others, social status can only be estimated from educational level. In others still, the data are presented in the form of graphs from which no significance tests can be computed. Partly to compensate for this lack of precision and comparability, partly to complete the picture of available data on class differences in child rearing, we cite in Table 9 not only the results from these additional studies of molar variables but also all other statistically significant findings from researches considered previously which might have bearing on the problem at hand. In this way, we hope as well to avoid the bias which occasionally arises from looking only at those variables in which one has a direct theoretical interest.

The data of Table 9 are noteworthy in a number of respects. First, we have clear confirmation that, over the entire 25-year period, middle-class parents have had a more acceptant, equalitarian relationship with their children. In many ways, the contrast is epitomized in Duvall's distinction between the "developmental" and "traditional" conceptions of mother and child. Duvall asked the mothers in her sample to list the "five things that a good mother does" and the "five things that a good child does." Middle-class mothers tended to emphasize such themes as "guiding and understanding," "relating herself lovingly to the child," and making sure that he "is happy and contented," "shares and cooperates with others," and "is eager to learn." In contrast, working-class mothers stressed the importance of keeping house and child "neat and clean," "training the child to regularity," and getting the child "to obey and respect adults."

What is more, this polarity in the value orientation of the two social classes appears to have endured. In data secured as recently as 1957, Kohn[8] reports that working-class mothers differ from those of the middle class in their choice of characteristics most desired in a child; the former emphasize "neatness, cleanliness, and obedience," while the latter stress "happiness, considerateness, and self-control."

Yet, once again, it would be a mistake to conclude that the middle-class parent is exerting less pressure on his children. As the data of Table 9 also show, a higher percentage of middle-class children are punished in some manner, and there is more "necessary" discipline to prevent injury or danger. In addition, though the middle-class father typically has a warmer relationship with the child, he is also likely to have more authority and status in family affairs.

Although shifts over time are difficult to appraise when the data are so variable in specific content, one trend is sufficiently salient to deserve comment. In the early Berkeley data the working-class parent is more expressive of affection than his middle-class counterpart. But in the

TABLE 9

Overall Character of Parent–child Relationship

Sample	Approx. date of practice	No. of cases reported	Age	Middle-class trend	Working-class trend
Berkeley I	1928–32	31	1–3	Grants autonomy Cooperative Equalitarian	Expresses affection Excessive contact Intrusive Irritable Punitive Ignores child
National I	1932	494	0–1		Baby picked up when cries†
National IV	1932	3239	1–12	Higher percentage of children punished†	Nothing done to allay child's fears†
Yellow Springs, Ohio	1940	124	3–12	Acceptant-democratic	Indulgent Active-rejectant
Berkeley II	1939–42	31	9–11	Grants autonomy Cooperative Equalitarian Expresses affection	Excessive contact Intrusive Irritable Punitive Ignores child
Chicago I	1943	100	5		Father plays with child more†
Chicago II	1943–44	433	1–5	"Developmental" conception of "good mother" and "good child."†	"Traditional" conception of "good mother" and "good child."†

New Haven I	1949–50	219	1	More necessary discipline to prevent injury or danger.†	More prohibitive discipline beyond risk of danger or injury.
Boston	1951–52	372	5	Mother warmer toward child† Father warmer toward child* Father exercises more authority* Mother has higher esteem for father† Mother delighted about pregnancy† Both parents more often share authority*	Father demands instant obedience† Child ridiculed† Greater rejection of child† Emphasis on neatness, cleanliness, and order† Parents disagree more on child-rearing policy*
New Haven II	1951–53	48	14–17	Fathers have more power in family decisions† Parents agree in value orientations†	
Palo Alto	1953	73	2½–5½	Baby picked up when cries†	Mother carries through demands rather than dropping the subject†
Eugene	1955–56	206	0–18	Better relationship between father and child†	
Washington, D.C.,	1956–57	400	10–11	Desirable qualities are happiness,* considerateness,* curiosity,* self-control*	Desirable qualities are neatness-cleanliness,* obedience*

* Trend significant at 5-percent level or better.
† The difference between percentages is not significant but the difference between mean ratings is significant at the 5-percent level or better.

follow-up study of the same children eight years later the trend is reversed. Perhaps the same mothers behave differently toward younger and older children. Still, the item "Baby picked up when cries" yields a significant difference in favor of the working-class mother in 1932 and a reliable shift in the opposite direction in 1953. *Sic transit gloria Watsoniensis!*

Especially with terms as heavily value laden as those which appear in Table 9, one must be concerned with the possibility that the data in the studies examined document primarily not actual behavior but the middle-class mother's superior knowledge of the socially acceptable response. Undoubtedly, this factor operates to inflate the reported relationships. But there are several reassuring considerations. First, although the items investigated vary widely in the intensity of their value connotations, all show substantially the same trends. Second, four of the studies reported in Table 9 (Berkeley I and II, Yellow Springs, and New Haven II) are based not on the mother's responses to an interview but on observation of actual interaction among family members. It seems highly unlikely, therefore, that the conclusions we have reached apply only to professed opinions and not to real behavior as well.

RETROSPECT AND PROSPECT

It is interesting to compare the results of our analysis with the traditional view of the differences between the middle- and lower-class styles of life, as documented in the classic descriptions of Warner,[9] Davis,[10] Dollard,[11] and the more recent accounts of Spinley,[12] Clausen,[13] and Miller and Swanson.[14] In all these sources the working class is typically characterized as impulsive and uninhibited, the middle class as more rational, controlled, and guided by a broader perspective in time. Thus Clausen writes:

> The lower class pattern of life . . . puts a high premium on physical gratification, on free expression of aggression, on spending and sharing. Cleanliness, respect for property, sexual control, educational achievement—all are highly valued by middle class Americans—are of less importance to the lower class family or are phrased differently.[15]

To the extent that our data even approach this picture, it is for the period before World War II rather than for the present day. The modern middle class has, if anything, extended its time perspective so that the tasks of child training are now accomplished on a more leisurely schedule. As for the lower class the fit is far better for the actual behavior of parents rather than for the values they seek to instill in their children. As reflected in the data of Table 8 and 9, the lower-class parent —though he demands compliance and control in his child—is himself more aggressive, expressive, and impulsive than his middle-class counterpart. Even so, the picture is a far cry from the traditional image of the casual and carefree lower class. Perhaps the classic portrait is yet to be seen along the skid rows and Tobacco Roads of the nation, but these do not lie along the well-trodden paths of the survey researcher. He is busy ringing doorbells, no less, in the main section of the lower-class district, where most of the husbands have steady jobs and, what is more important, the wife is willing to answer the door and the interviewer's questions. In this modern working-class world there may be greater freedom of emotional expression, but there is no laxity or vagueness with respect to goals of child training. Consistently over the past 25 years, the parent in this group has emphasized what are usually regarded as the traditional middle-class virtues of cleanliness, conformity, and control, and although his methods are not so effective as those of his middle-class neighbors, they are perhaps more desperate.

Perhaps this very desperation, enhanced by early exposure to impulse and aggression, leads working-class parents to pursue new goals with old techniques of discipline. While accepting middle-class levels of aspiration he has not yet internalized sufficiently the modes of response which make these standards readily achievable for himself or his children. He has still to learn to wait, to explain, and to give and withhold his affection as the reward and price of performance.

As of 1957, there are suggestions that the cultural gap may be narrowing. Spock has joined the Bible on the working-class shelf. If we wish to see the shape of the future, we can perhaps do no better than to look at the pages of the newly revised edition of this ubiquitous guidebook. Here is a typical example of the new look—a passage not found in the earlier version:

> If the parent can determine in which respects she may be too permissive and can firm up her discipline, she may, if she is on the right track, be delighted to find that her child becomes not only better behaved but much happier. Then she can really love him better, and he in turn responds to this.[16]

Apparently "love" and "limits" are both watchwords for the coming generation of parents. As Mrs. Johnson, down in the flats, puts away the hairbrush and decides to have a talk with her unruly youngster "like the book says," Mrs. Thomas, on the hill, is dutifully striving to overcome her guilt at the thought of giving John the punishment she now admits he deserves. If both ladies are successful, the social scientist may eventually have to look elsewhere in his search for ever larger F's and t's.

Such speculations carry us beyond the territory yet surveyed by the social scientist. Perhaps the most important implication for the future from our present analysis lies in the sphere of method rather than substance. Our attempt to compare the work of a score of investigators over a score of years will have been worth the labor if it but convinces future researchers of the wastefulness of such uncoordinated efforts. Our best hope for an understanding of the differences in child rearing in various segments of our society and the effects of these differences on personality formation lies in the development of a systematic long-range plan for gathering comparable data at regular intervals on large samples of families at different positions in the social structure. We now have survey organizations with the scientific competence and adequate technical facilities to perform the task. With such hopes in mind, the author looks ahead to the day when the present analysis becomes obsolete, in method as well as substance.

NOTES

[1] It is true that because of the rising birth rate after World War II the sample probably included more younger than older children, but without knowledge of the actual distribution by age we have hesitated to make further speculative adjustments.

[2] As indicated below, we believe that these irregularities are largely attributable to the highly selective character of a number of the samples (notably, New Haven I and Palo Alto) and that the downward trend in frequency and duration of breast feeding is probably more reliable than is reflected in the data of Tables 1 and 3.

[3] M. Wolfenstein, "Trends in Infant Care," *Am. J. Orthopsychiat.*, 1953, XXIII, 120–130. Similar conclusions were drawn in an earlier report by Stendler surveying 60 years of child-training practices as advocated in three popular women's magazines. *Cf.* C. B. Stendler, "Sixty Years of Child Training Practices," *J. Pediatrics*, 1950, XXXVI, 122–134.

[4] Wolfenstein, *op. cit.*, p. 121.

[5] Benjamin Spock, *Baby and Child Care* (New York: Pocket Books, Inc., 1957).

[6] Wolfenstein, *op. cit.*, p. 121.

[7] These investigators also classify "isolation" as a love-oriented technique, but since this specific method is reported on in several other studies as well, we have tabulated the results separately to facilitate comparison.

[8] Melvin Kohn, Social Class and Parental Values. Paper read at the annual meeting of the American Sociological Association, Washington, D.C., August 27–29, 1957.

[9] W. L. Warner and P. S. Lunt, *The Social Life of a Modern Community* (New Haven: Yale University Press, 1942); Warner, Meeker, and others, *Social Class in America* (Chicago: Science Research Associates, 1949).

[10] A. Davis, B. Gardner, and M. R. Gardner, *Deep South* (Chicago: University of Chicago Press, 1941).

[11] J. Dollard, *Caste and Class in a Southern Town* (New Haven: Yale University Press, 1937).

[12] B. M. Spinley, *The Deprived and the Privileged: Personality Development in English Society* (London: Routledge & Kegan Paul, Ltd., 1953).

[13] J. A. Clausen, "Social and Psychological Factors in Narcotics Addiction," *Law and Contemporary Problems*, 1957, XXII, 34–51.

[14] Donald Miller and Guy Swanson, *The Changing American Parent* (New York: Wiley and Son, 1958).

[15] Clausen, *op. cit.*, p. 42.

[16] Spock, *op. cit.*, p. 326.

Identification and Its Familial Determinants

ROBERT F. WINCH

IDENTIFICATION AND SOCIALIZATION

To further our attempts at conceptual clarification, it is important to take note of certain terms whose meanings seem close to that of identification. In particular, let us consider socialization, symbiosis, love, introjection, internalization, imitation, and empathy.

Since the acquisition of socially approved (and also of socially condemned) behavior is said to occur both through identification and through socialization, it is advisable to distinguish between these two terms. In customary parlance, "socialization" refers to the acquisition of skills, attitudes, values, norms, and the disposition to conform by a person who is usually but not necessarily young. There is emphasis on the specific behaviors which the socializer(s) are trying to induce in the socializee—e.g. bowel control in the young child, surgical skills in the young intern. The terminus of the period of learning and the completion of the acquisition of the desired skills are frequently marked by licensing, a graduation ceremony, or other *rite de passage*.

In customary parlance, "identification" means that *I* admires and wishes to model himself after *M*. There is emphasis on *I*'s feeling toward *M* and on his drive to simulate that part of *M*'s behavior which is visible to *I*. Because of the relevance of *I*'s feelings about *M* and because the simulation is thought to be global rather than segmental, it makes a difference who *M* is. The behavior and the identity of the socializer, on the other hand, are merely incidental; the socializee may be subjected to a sequence of more or less interchangeable socializers (as in the educational system) or the role of socializer may even become automated (as in teaching machines).

A somewhat different emphasis concerning the difference between identification and socialization seems to emerge from the peripheralist-centralist distinction. Peripheralists view a person in terms of his overt

Summary and Comparison of Winch's and Slater's Views on Positional and Personal Identification

Properties of Identification	Winch		Slater	
	Positional	Personal	Positional	Personal
1. Relationship between M's behavior and I's	Initially reciprocal; may become similar or opposite	Similar or opposite	Apparently similar	Similar
2. Interaction governed by norms	Yes	Not necessarily	....	....
3. Segment of behavior involved	Small	Large	Small	Large
4. Duration of relationship	Any duration	Long	Any duration (implied)	Long
5. Control over resources by M?	Yes, at present	Yes, sometime, not necessarily at present	....	....
6. Feelings of I for M.	Admiration, respect; possibly love through halo and/or hate through envy	Love; possibly admiration, respect through halo	Wish to be in shoes of; hostility	Wish to be like; love
7. Irreplaceability of other	Not necessarily	Yes	Not necessarily (implied)	Yes (implied)
8. Process by which developed	Consequences of I's being put in role relationship with M.	Tentatively, Slater's formulation	M does not supply I with warmth; I reacts defensively	Consequences of M's warmth and support: similar identification, internalization of values

behavior and frequently speak of the acquired pattern of overt behavior as socialization (product). Centralists, on the other hand, see
the "real" person as delineated through his intrapsychic processes.
With this outlook, identification (as product) refers to acquired attitudes, feelings, and emotions, which, like the iceberg in the familiar
psychoanalytic metaphor, are largely below the level of consciousness.

A difference in the kind of learning is implied in the distinction between the socializer, who is viewed as some sort of teacher or tutor,
and *M*, who may not even know of *I*'s existence, as in the case of the
small boy's athletic hero. It would seem, then, that socialization typically involves direct tuition with direct reinforcement whereas identification typically involves observation and vicarious reinforcement.

One other possible distinction between socialization and identification, as those terms are generally used, is in the breadth of the behavior
acquired. It would seem that "socialization" is frequently used with
reference to a more or less segmental or situation-specific behavior,
whereas "identification" is frequently used to refer to a response or set
of responses which permeates most or all of a person's behavior. Thus
we tend to say that a person is "socialized into a role" whereas he
acquires a "personality trait" through identification. A social position
generally embraces a number of roles. For example, a position as district sales manager of the XYZ Corporation includes the roles of subordinate to the vice-president in charge of sales, supervisor to the salesmen in the district, and perhaps special sales representative to the district's most important accounts. Learning the behavior appropriate to a
social position involves learning the corresponding roles. Learning a
role involves learning the norms which specify behaviors appropriate to
an integrated part of a social position, and it also involves the capacity
to produce those behaviors. A person knows a role if, given the appropriate situation, he responds with the appropriate behaviors. Personality, on the other hand, may be conceptualized as more or less stable
tendencies of the person irrespective of the situation. If a man is
gruffly decisive only when coaching a football team and off the field appears quite diffident, we may think of the former behavior as part of a
role performance. If he is gruffly decisive in most or all situations, we
may speak of this as a personality trait. Indeed, we might characterize
his personality in terms of a disposition to enact one of the roles of his
position as coach—that of coach *vis-à-vis* player—wherever he is.

How does identification as conceived in the present book conform
to the distinctions which have just been noted? In the present formulation no specification has been made as to the nature of *I*'s feelings about
M or the awareness of intensity of a drive to simulate *M*'s behavior. It
seems at the moment that it would be fruitful to think of *I*'s perception
of and feeling toward *M* as a topic for investigation. Since *M*'s behavior
is the functional antecedent of behavior subsumable as identification-
as-product, the identity and behavior of *M* are emphasized. With re-

spect to the personality-*vs.*-role problem the present formulation is open, and the choice of course (if choice should seem desirable) should be determined by considerations of research strategy and design. And with respect to the kind of learning involved, the present formulation of identification is open and thus permits the inclusion of direct tuition as well as of other kinds of learning. It seems possible, however, that the behaviors acquired through direct tuition can be quite easily explained without reference to the more or less difficult concept of identification, and therefore the strategy of investigation will probably call for the exclusion of learning through direct tuition.

IDENTIFICATION AND SIX OTHER SOMEWHAT RELATED TERMS

At this point it is desirable to consider six other terms which are usually used with a meaning more or less akin to that of Freud's view of identification.

As it is usually used, "symbiosis" denotes the reciprocality (or complementariness and mutuality) of gratification in a relationship of which that between mother and infant is prototypical—i.e., a nurturant-providing person in relation to a dependent-receptive individual. A common connotation of the symbiotic relationship is that the relationship involves one-sided or two-sided exploitation (Winch, 1958). In the language of the present formulation, symbiosis may be regarded as reciprocal identification along the dimension of nurturance.

Freud (1922) emphasizes the distinction between identification with the father and love of father (or, in Freud's terms, "the choice of the father as an object"): "In the first case one's father is what one would like to *be,* and in the second he is what one would like to *have.* The distinction . . . depends upon whether the tie attaches to the subject or to the object of the ego" (p. 62). Redl and Wineman (1951) make love of *M* a necessary precondition for identification. In their phrasing, identification becomes possible only when "the child renounces some of the intensive demands for counterlove from the adult and replaces those exuberant love demands by a readiness to incorporate part of the personality of the adult into the ego ideal and finally into the superego" (p. 191). Thus love seems to denote one person's positive affect toward and desire to possess another, and not necessarily a desire to be like the other. When completely worked out, the concept of love probably implies both similar and reciprocal (or complementary) identification (Winch, 1958, Chaps. 1, 3, 4).

It has been observed that even Freud was not consistent in distinguishing "introjection" from identification. Healy, Bronner, and Bowers (1930) suggest that in the Freudian context identification refers to a desire to be the object (or model) whereas introjection "seems to arise out of the desire to have or retain (incorporate) an object which has been lost, or is in danger of being lost" (p. 241; see also Sanford, 1955). Thus introjection sounds like love as described above, except for the added condition that the object is thought to be lost or imminently losable. This condition seems to suggest the romantic love of the adolescent (Winch, 1952, Chap. 14). Some writers use introject as a transitive verb whose customary object is "values." In this sense introject seems equivalent to internalize (see below). Howe (1955, p. 67) says that some psychoanalytic writers use introjection to refer to less mature relationships in contrast to the more mature relationships they denote with identification; but she then goes on to say that other psychoanalytic writers reverse this distinction. Thus, contingent upon the writer, introjection seems to be an approximate synonym for either love or identification. In any case the term seems unnecessary, and we advocate its abandonment.

"Internalization" may be defined as "adopting as one's own the ideas, practices, standards, or values of another person or of society" (English and English, 1958, p. 272). Thus internalization is a special case of similar identification.

"Empathy" may be defined as the process of imagining oneself in the role of another and responding as one thinks the other would to the situation in which the other is perceived or imagined to be. To Sullivan (1953) empathy appeared to be a process of communication occurring in infancy whereby the anxiety of the mother induces anxiety in the infant. The concept of empathy appears often in discussion of role-taking skill (e.g., Sarbin, 1954, pp. 236–38, 246–48) and of skill in judging the responses of others (Dymond, 1949; Bruner and Tagiuri, 1954, pp. 640–46; Lindzey and Borgatta, 1954, p. 427). Another frequent connotation of the term is that the affect which accompanies the empathic response is regarded as positive. Evidence suggests that positive feelings toward the other do increase the extent to which the judge regards the judged as similar to himself (Knight, 1923; Shen, 1925; Ferguson, 1949; Fiedler, Blaisdell, and Warrington, 1952; Lundy, 1956). We may recall that Sears has built role-taking into his paradigm of the process of identification (cf. pp. 7–8 above).

"All role-taking is imitation," posits Maccoby (1959, p. 241), "but not all imitation is role-taking." Lazowick (1955) distinguishes between imitation and identification. Imitaton occurs, he says, when I copies or approximates the reaction patterns of M "without, at first, having any understanding of their significance, meaning, or purpose." He defines identification in terms of the relation between I's set of meanings and M's set of meanings (p. 176). Miller and Dollard (1941) suggest that "different types of imitation [may] form a continuum ranging from pure matched-dependent behavior at one extreme to copying at the other" (pp. 159–60). Usage suggests that imitation has a more behavioral connotation, with emphasis on cognition, whereas identification (especially through its development in Freudian psychology) has a more psychodynamic connotation, with emphasis on emotion. (It will be recalled that a parallel distinction was drawn above between socialization and identification.) It seems, moreover, that imitation—including the Miller-Dollard notion of matched-independent behavior—refers to *I*'s observing *M*'s behavior and being directly rewarded for simulating it. Thus it appears that according to usage imitation refers to the more overt aspects of identification-as-product plus a specific method of learning that behavior.[1]

Now let us draw some conclusions concerning the utility of these six terms for the present investigation. *Love* may refer to *A*'s feeling of warmth and positive affect for *B*, or it may additionally refer to a "wish to possess" *B*, or it may carry other surplus meaning. Because of its ambiguity, "love" does not seem a useful term for such discourse; terms of more limited denotation and connotation would seem preferable. Because of contradictory usage, it seems desirable also to discard *introjection*. *Symbiosis* and *internalization* refer to special cases of identification (reciprocal and similar, respectively). Since for some these terms carry moral connotations, it would seem sensible to discard them in favor of identification plus the appropriate qualifiers. *Imitation* seems a useful term to denote a particular way of acquiring a particular class of behaviors, and *empathy* appears to be a suitable synonym for attitudinal role-taking.

There are numerous other terms which might be considered here; identity, ego-identity, ego, superego, self, etc. We shall not pause to consider them, however, because we are restricting our attention to the more or less lasting influence of one person, *M*, on another, *I*, and because none of the latter terms pertains precisely to such a dyadic relationship.

The semantic morass sketched in the foregoing paragraphs has caused some students to conclude that the term "identification" should be discarded in the interests of better communication. Opposed to this view is a school of psychologists who "know" what identification means and aver that whatever confusion exists merely attests to the psychological heresy or ignorance of those who profess the confusion. To the writer there is a third and more acceptable position. There can be no dispute as to the confusion surrounding the term when the user is trying to be precise in his denotation, but if the term is used without qualifiers, it can serve very well to denote not a single variable but a whole area of inquiry. That is the sense in which the term seems useful and in which it is being used in the present context. It follows, then, that when an attempt is made to refer to identification as a variable, one or more qualifying words or phrases are required to communicate with precision.

In the present context identification in general refers to the more or less lasting influence of one *M* on the behavior (including attitudes) of

I. Where precision is called for, qualifications will be made in terms of:

1. Whether the reference is to identification as *product* or as *process*
2. The type of identification (i.e., the nature of the relationship between the behavior, including attitudes, of M and I)—whether *similar, reciprocal,* or *opposite*
3. The level of I's conciousness involved: *overt, covert but conscious,* or *unconscious*
4. The kind of identification—whether *positional* or *personal*—and, if possible, a more precise specification—e.g., the role-relationship of foreman-worker or the personality trait of dominance.

IDENTIFICATION AND DEGREE OF FUNCTIONALITY IN THE FAMILY[2]

To the extent that the nuclear family is the social group within which the basic societal functions are performed, we may speak of it as a task-oriented group. We shall assume that members of task-oriented groups tend to be aware of the significance and importance of their task-oriented behaviors. Depending upon the level of need and the organization of the society, however, a specific behavior may be conceived as functional and task-oriented or as nonfunctional and recreational. With respect to the behaviors which the society and the family conceive as useful, significant, and important (task-oriented and functional), it follows that their importance is generally recognized by the fully participating adult members of the society.

We shall assume that the child gradually develops the ability to discriminate between task-relevant and task-irrelevant behaviors—i.e., to strip away conceptually the nonfunctional aspects of the parent's behavior and to identify with those aspects which are functional, or important. The general recognition of the importance of these activities implies that norms exist whereby the fully participating members of the family are expected to perform the related activities in accordance with certain standards. Learning the society's norms is a part of the process of becoming socialized. Thus it should follow that the extent that the nuclear family performs basic societal functions, the child learns to assess his parents (him M's) in terms of their task-oriented skills.[3]

Let us consider an example of two. The hunter who is a good marksman, the housewife who bakes a delectable cake—these are persons performing activities with creditable skill. When these activities are regarded as sufficiently important to warrant esteem, the child learns to value the parent because of the latter's skills. Perhaps the converse is more important for our purposes. When the corner butcher provides better meat at lower cost than the father can provide by his hunting and when the bakery sells a better and cheaper cake than the mother can make, then hunting and baking on the part of the parents are regarded as recreational rather than task-oriented activities, and the child is given no task-performance test in terms of which to assess his parents.

To the degree that the nuclear family does not perform basic societal functions, our postulates imply that other societal structures must be performing these functions. Functional analysis leads us to ask which structures are performing which functions. Two answers may be ventured—one pertaining directly to the father-husband as breadwinner, and the other to the children.

It may be argued that the modern corporation has in a sense superseded the medieval church as a sort of all-purpose structure. More and more, the corporation is becoming a highly functional organization with political, socializing-educational, and religious functions as well as economic. W. H. Whyte, Jr. (1956) sees the corporation as demanding an ever-greater degree of commitment from employees in the administrative hierarchy. Here we can observe the usefulness of thinking of basic societal functions as individual-serving in addition to society-serving. Our functional interpretation of Whyte's observation would be that as functions shift from family to corporation, the consequent shift in rewards (individual-serving aspect) brings about a shift in the loyalties of men in management from wife and family to boss and company. The shift in functions can be seen in the increase in roles and role prescriptions which have been subsumed under Whyte's apt rubrics, "the organization man" and "the company wife."[4]

There has been a proliferation of groups whose functions bear more or less directly on children. As this implies, the roles whose occupants become the more or less obvious models for the child are those like the scoutmaster at the First Methodist Church and the football coach at Jonesville High rather than—or in addition to—the members of the nuclear family.

To the degree that the nuclear family does *not* perform basic societal functions, what happens to the child's orientation to his parents? Let us begin our answer by asking another question: What will be the nature of the activities which comprise the context of parent-child interaction to the extent that the family is functionless? To the extent that the family is functionless (nontask-oriented), it appears that family members assess each other (and thus children assess parents) on the basis of congeniality, affability, and other characteristics of personality rather than on the basis of task-oriented competence. To a considerable degree this statement is a deduction from the premises of functional analysis, but Riecken and Homans (1954, pp. 789–90, 800, and the studies referred to there by Jennings, Homans, Gilchrist, and Schachter) cite evidence to support it. It would seem to follow that where core relationships are relatively absent, there must be much more reliance on affection to bind parent and child, as well, of course, as husband and wife. It would seem that most of the functionless interaction would be oriented to recreation and the expression of cogeniality (including what Parsons [1955, pp. 16–17] calls the stabilization of personalities and what Thibaut and Kelley [1959] refer to as group-maintenance functions).

The foregoing suggests two other functional consequences for social groups in general and for families in particular:

1. Function is integrating; lack of it is disintegrating.
2. Function guides socialization; lack of it leaves socialization without direction.

"Integration" here denotes the cohesiveness of the group—i.e., "the extent to which structure and operations are capable of being maintained under stress" (Stogdill, 1959, p. 198). The reasoning is that when the group's activity is functional, the activity is perceived by the members as rewarding and important. This perception reinforces the continuing participation of the members and gives orientation to the way in which they train their young. Let us examine these points.

We have assumed that members of task-oriented groups tend to be aware of the significance and importance of their task-oriented behaviors. And by postulate the basic societal functions have benefits for individuals as well as for the society. In the context of the family, it is reasoned that the recognition that the maintenance of familial relationships is beneficial to the individual as well as to the group persuades parent and child to maintain their relationship even though they may dislike each other heartily. Thus the situation rewards the submergence of feelings of hostility and the creation of emotional distance between parent and child and even of an authoritarian familial structure as a safeguard against overt conflict and rupture of the relationship. In the functionless situation, on the other hand, no delay is imposed on the response to frustration and no basis is provided for awe and reverence of child toward parent. With the elimination of the basis for awe and reverence, the parent-child relationship would seem to have to be one of love and intimacy, if the feelings are positive, or else of hatred and rejection, if they are negative. Thus function provides incentive for the members of a group to maintain the integrity of the group and for conflicts to be controlled and contained.

Since the relatively functionless family is characterized by few roles and core relationships, it follows that there are few norms on the basis of which members of such a family can interact. Hence they must improvise patterns of interaction. (We can rephrase this idea in terms of the values of democratic equalitarianism: in the relatively functionless family, the members are freed from having to carry out traditionally determined behaviors and are allowed freer expression of their personalities.) Of course, this development has had profound implications for marital relationships, but perhaps the most significant implication for the study of identification is that there is a lack of normatively supported roles for parents to teach their children.

It seems plausible that in a society with well-defined familial roles parents should know what kind of children their infants should develop into and also the "correct" method of infant and child care to effect this end. Our analysis suggests that the relative absence of functions and associated roles deprives the family of a definite objective with respect to child-rearing. It is consistent with this state of affairs that American middle-class parents should be amenable to all sorts of "expert" advice, from the aloof, antiseptic view of John B. Watson (1928) to the cloying maternalism of Margaret Ribble (1943) and back again. (On such swings see Brim, 1959; Escalona, 1949; Stendler, 1950; Sunley, 1955; Vincent, 1951; Wolfenstein, 1953.)

When productive activities, such as farming, are carried on by the family, the child may be expected to assume adultlike responsibilities at an early age. But as the productive function has been relinquished by the middle-class American family, childhood has come to be regarded as a period of carefree play, and the phrase "child labor" has taken on connotations of an exploitatively cruel and unenlightened past. Since a relatively functionless family has few roles, it follows that such a family has little in the way of roles to teach its young. It is consistent with this formulation, then, that we find the modern American middle-class family not training its young for any occupations (since occupations are no longer "hereditary")—indeed, scarcely feeling free to *suggest* suitable occupations, and conversely struggling to encourage in their children "skills" of adjustment, self-expression, and integration with their peers. We find them not even venturing to train their girls for the roles of wife and mother, and we encounter the cultural anomaly of college and high-school courses in marriage and family life.

This state of affairs probably contributes to a feeling on the part of the child that he is roleless. Of course, the fact that the family is relatively functionless makes the child feel that he is useless. This may be some of the background of the adolescent's struggle for identification which Erikson (1950) believes he can see. Perhaps this is related to the American practice of shielding youngsters from their parents' problems. For this reason, Francis Hsu (1953) believes, American school children are quite naive and insecure while their Chinese counterparts are "already little old rogues with a fairly realistic view of men and things" (p. 83).

We can now summarize and extend the implication of functional analysis for the study of identification. Core relationships, it will be recalled, tend to be cast in superordinate-subordinate terms. One implication of being a superordinate in a relationship is that one has some power over the subordinate. In a core relationship the superordinate can presumably permit or deny the subordinate the enjoyment of some portion of the reward involved in the corresponding function. If we denote the superordinate as A and the subordinate as B, we have the following paradigm:

1. The core relationship involves a function which eventuates in resources which, if made accessible to the individual, can become importantly rewarding for approved behavior.

2. The presence of the resources constitutes an incentive to members of a social group to participate and to continue their participation. Hence functionality is an integrating factor (Thibaut and Kelley, 1959).

3. In part the degree of A's superordination over B is determined by A's power to permit B to obtain or to deny B the resources; A's power over B is mitigated to the extent that B has the opportunity to escape from A's field and to obtain the resources elsewhere.

4. In part the degree of A's superordination over B is determined by the degree to which A exercises his power.

5. The presence of function(s) bears on the nature of the interaction between A and B and increases the probability that A will exercise his power over B. Hence the presence of function increases the intensity and structure of A's influence over B.

6. It is possible for a group to be relatively nonfunctional and still have resources which can be used as rewards. Here both the intensity and structure of A's influence on B are problematic.

The concept of the "idle rich" illustrates the idea in statement 6, which has not been introduced previously. Let us assume a family presided over by a wealthy dowager whose fortune was built by a long-dead ancestor. The dowager has the resources to influence the behavior of her heirs, but in the present the family may not be highly functional. What, then, is the distinction between the functional and the non-functional relationship when in each A has control over some resource desired by B? A functional relationship is task-oriented, and there is a presumption that A's control over B will be task-related, as, for example, the control of the foreman over the worker. A nonfunctional relationship implies the absence of a task-orientation, with the further implication that the control of A over the behavior of B can be capricious. Let us invoke the image of the expectant heir dancing to the quaintly eccentric tense called by the doddering dowager.

Statement 4 presents the prospect of translating this paradigm of a functional sociology into psychological behavior theory and five possible schedules of reinforcement, as follows:

a. A always (unconditionally) makes resources available to B.

b. A uses resources for total or nearly total reinforcement—i.e., A gives B resources when A approves B's behavior and withholds when he disapproves.

    c. *A* uses partial reinforcement.

    d. *A* allows *B* random access to resources (and thus confuses rather than reinforces).

    e. *A* always denies *B* access to the resources.

From the functional analysis it would appear that procedure *a, d,* or *e* might be followed in a minimally functional situation (cf. Ribble, 1943), whereas *b* or *c* would appear to be more likely for a highly functional situation.

    Now that the paradigm has related our major concepts to one another—function, reward, use of reward (or control of resources), and influence (including identification)—we are able to formulate some additional hypotheses:[5]

H_5

The more functional the family, the greater will be the identification of the child with each parent.[6]

H_6

The more functional the parent, the greater will be the identification of the offspring with that parent.

H_7

To the extent that one parent is more functional than the other, the offspring will tend to identify with the more functional parent.

H_8

The more functional the family, the more formal will be the relationships between parents and children.

H_9

The more functional the family, the more children will be socialized into occupational roles within the family; conversely, the less functional the family, relatively speaking, the more children will be socialized into recreational roles within the family.[7]

The foregoing analysis has suggested a host of other hypotheses. For example, with level of function held constant, identification should be positively correlated with level of resources, with level of resources constant, identification should be positively correlated with degree of functionality. The elucidation of statement 4 of the paradigm into schedules of reinforcement may be regarded as another set of hypotheses. Other hypotheses could be developed relating size of structure to degree of functionality, degree of functionality to role differentiation, role differentiation to authoritarianism, etc.

QUALIFICATIONS ON THE UTILITY OF BASIC SOCIETAL FUNCTIONS FOR THE STUDY OF IDENTIFICATION

The utility of the concept of basic societal function, we have maintained, is that it directs our attention to important activities which eventuate in some resource and that *I*, realizing the importance of the resource, will modify his behavior so as to acquire the resource, which thereby becomes a reward. Thus functions, by this reasoning, lead us to rewards. Deductively this is true, but practically it must be qualified in two important respects:

1. Within a simple society and within each stratum of a complex society, conditions of life tend to be homogeneous; hence families tend to be like one another with respect to the level of need involved in each of the basic societal functions and also with respect to the manner of meeting that need. To the extent that this is so, it follows that within simple societies and the strata of complex societies there will be little variation with respect to the basic societal functions and hence that within such relatively homogeneous social groupings this concept will have relatively little explanatory power with respect to any phenomenon, including identification.

2. To the extent that societies are efficient and affluent, it appears that their economic, political, and other structures operate inconspicuously and are taken more or less for granted. Again let us recall that we tend to become aware of the air we breathe only when someone calls it to our attention or when it is scarce. To push the matter further, a child would presumably be highly sensitive to the economic function in a situation where goods were in short supply, either absolutely (e.g., if he should be constantly hungry) or relatively (e.g., if he should be aware that other children had more luxurious toys than did he). Similarly, he would be expected to become sensitive to political or religious need under conditions of absolute or relative deprivation with respect to their respective resources—freedom from chaos and from anxiety.

Finally, it seems that the individual-serving aspect of the replacement (familial) function—a sense of intergenerational continuity—is much more likely to be experienced as a reward by adults than by children. To the extent that the above two qualifications apply in any given research problem, they imply that the concept of basic societal function has utility for the study of identification mainly when used intersocietally or among strata of a complex society. These qualifications do not necessarily apply to other functions, and we now turn our attention to the parental functions—nurturance and control.

NOTES

[1] Professor Donald Campbell asserts that for an approach goal, matched-dependent and observational formulations lead to the same behavior. The crucial distinction, he insists, arises in the case of punishment: if *I* inhibits his response on seeing *M* punished, then the behavior is observational and not matched-dependent.

[2] "Degree of functionality" refers to the degree to which a group or an individual carries out functions, whether basic societal or other functions.

[3] This analysis does not imply that the child will avoid identifying—consciously or unconsciously—with task-irrelevant behaviors of the parent, but merely that such identification is not a consequence of the process under consideration here.

[4] This discussion parallels somewhat the formulation that American society is shifting from an entrepreneurial to a bureaucratic emphasis (cf. Miller and Swanson, 1958, Chap. 2). Large corporations and "big" government constitute multipurpose structures of this type.

[5] Earlier hypotheses have not been reprinted here.

[6] Again, this is an orienting rather than a research hypothesis.

[7] The functions referred to in the antecedent condition of this hypothesis exclude the socializing-educational function, for to include it makes the hypothesis tautological to the extent that the terms "socialization" and "identification" are equivalent. On this point see pp. 22–25 above.

REFERENCES

BRIM, O. G., JR., 1959. *Education for child rearing.* New York: Russell Sage Foundation.

BRUNER, J. S., and R. TAGIURI, 1954. The perception of people. In G. LINDZEY (ed.), *Handbook of social psychology.* Cambridge: Addison-Wesley. Vol. 2, pp. 634–54.

DYMOND, ROSALIND F., 1949. A scale for the measurement of empathic ability. *J. consult. Psychol., 13,* 127–33.

ENGLISH, H. B., and AVA C. ENGLISH, 1958. *A comprehensive dictionary of psychological and psychoanalytical terms: a guide to usage.* New York: Longmans, Green.

ERIKSON, E. H., 1950. *Childhood and society.* New York: Norton.

ESCALONA, SIBYLLE, 1949. A commentary upon some recent changes in child-rearing practices. *Child Develpm., 20,* 157–62.

FERGUSON, L. W., 1949. The value of acquaintance ratings in criteria research. *Personal Psychol., 2,* 93–102.

FIEDLER, F. E., F. J. BLAISDELL, and W. G. WARRINGTON, 1952. Unconscious attitudes as correlates of sociometric choice in a social group. *J. abnorm. soc. Psychol.,*

FREUD, S., 1922. *Group psychology and the analysis of the ego.* London: Hogarth. *47,* 790–96.

HEALY, W., AUGUSTA F. BRONNER, and ANNA M. BOWERS, 1930. *The structure and meaning of psychoanalysis: as related to personality and behavior.* New York: Knopf.

HSU, F. L. K., 1953. *Americans and Chinese: two ways of life.* New York: Schuman.

KNIGHT, F. B., 1923. The effect of the "acquaintance factor" upon personal judgments. *J. educ. Psychol., 14,* 129–42.

LAZOWICK, L. M., 1955. On the nature of identification. *J. abnorm. soc. Psychol., 51,* 175–83

LINDZEY, G., and E. F. BORGATTA, 1954. Sociometric measurement. In G. LINDZEY (ed.), *Handbook of social psychology*. Cambridge: Addison-Wesley. Vol. I, pp. 405–48.

LUNDY, R. M., 1956. Self-perceptions and descriptions of opposite-sex sociometric choices. *Sociometry, 19*, 272–77.

MACCOBY, ELEANOR, 1959. Role taking in childhood and its consequences for social learning. *Child Develpm., 30*, 239–52.

MILLER, N. E., and J. DOLLARD, 1941. *Social learning and imitation.* New Haven: Yale University Press.

PARSONS, T., and R. F. BALES, 1955. *Family, socialization, and interaction process.* Glencoe, Ill.: Free Press.

REDL, F., and D. WINEMAN, 1951. *Children who hate: the disorganization and break-down of behavior controls.* Glencoe, Ill.: Free Press.

RIBBLE, MARGARET, 1943. *The rights of infants.* New York: Columbia University Press.

RIECKEN, H. W., and G. C. HOMANS, 1954. Psychological aspects of social structure. In G. LINDZEY (ed.), *Handbook of social psychology*. Cambridge: Addison-Wesley, 1954. Vol. II, pp. 786–832.

SARBIN, T. R., 1954. Role theory. In G. LINDZEY (ed.), *Handbook of social psychology*, Cambridge: Addison-Wesley, 1954. Vol. I, pp. 223–58.

SHEN, E., 1925. The influence of friendship upon personal ratings. *J. app. Psychol., 9*, 66–68.

STENDLER, CELIA B., 1950. Sixty years of child-training practices. *J. Pediatrics, 36*, 122–34.

STOGDILL, R. M., 1959. *Individual behavior and group achievement.* New York: Oxford University Press.

SULLIVAN, H. S., 1953. *The interpersonal theory of psychiatry.* New York: Norton.

SUNLEY, R., 1955. Early nineteenth-century American literature on child rearing. In MARGARET MEAD and MARTHA WOLFENSTEIN (eds.), *Childhood in contemporary cultures.* Chicago: University of Chicago Press.

THIBAUT, J. W., and H. H. KELLEY, 1959. *The social psychology of groups.* New York: Wiley.

VINCENT, C., 1951. Trends in infant care. *Child Develpm., 22*, 199–209.

WATSON, J. B., 1928. *The psychological care of infant and child.* New York: Norton.

WHYTE, W. H., JR., 1956. *The organization man.* New York: Simon and Schuster.

WINCH, R. F., 1952. *The modern family.* New York: Holt.

———, 1958. *Mate-selection: a study of conplementary needs.* New York: Harper.

WOLFENSTEIN, MARTHA, 1953. Trends in infant care. *Amer. J. Orthopsychiat., 33*, 120–30.

Family Patterns and Human Rights[1]

WILLIAM J. GOODE

The fight for human rights is fraught with perils, not the least of which is that those to whom we wish to grant these freedoms may reject the gift, since they enjoy their chains.

The central psychological problem in extending human rights to disadvantaged groups is that what is one man's right must be another man's obligation. If I am an authoritarian father, my wife and children gain some freedom only if I give up what I now consider my rights. To urge *others* to grant freedom to their slaves, to share the right of decision with their subordinates is of course easy if we ourselves are not scheduled to give up any of our own privileges, but our ethical position becomes thereby somewhat dubious.

The central sociological problem is to ascertain empirically just what are the social systems or social patterns which will maximize the protection of human rights. This is an almost completely neglected area of research, so that the question cannot really be answered from the data now available. When we do have the answer, we must be prepared to face the harsh possibility, so often the result of precise scientific inquiry, that we shall then consider the costs of achieving or maintaining such a system to be excessive.

Meanwhile, however, it costs little to explore the problem, to clarify it by descriptive and analytic steps. Perhaps thereby we can ascertain at least the dimensions of the task. My ultimate set of questions, which guide this exploration but which must remain unanswered until we have more adequate data, are these:

1. What kinds of family patterns are most likely to support a full implementation of human rights?

2. What kinds of family patterns would the full implementation of a human rights programme create?
More technically formulated, we are asking whether the family patterns of a society, and the extent to which it protects human rights, vary at random with reference to one another; or whether they correlate in any way.

I should like to ignore the thorny task of defining human rights here, to prevent the tedious detours and fruitless debates about social philosophy that will very likely ensue, but my central empirical problem is

From *International Social Science Journal*, Vol. XVIIII, No. 1, 1966. Reproduced with the permission of UNESCO.

partially defined by my conception of human rights as a specific part of the social structure, as indeed a social sub-system itself. Therefore, I shall briefly address the problem. I hope, however, that the reader will not stop long to argue with me about what are the basic human rights— and of course on this matter the basic charter of Human Rights offers an excellent guide—but will instead focus on the social structural patterns that support those rights.

The cultural heritage of every civilization contains such kernels of moral wisdom, such all-encompassing definitions of human rights, usually phrased as a moral injunction. One of these, which has its counterpart in perhaps all major civilizations—and, I hasten to remind you, is actually applied in none—will serve my analytic purposes here as the core meaning of civic rights. (It has obvious limitations as a definition of family rights.) This injunction tells us to treat the stranger as our brother.

Such exhortations are necessarily cryptic. The prophet does not mean, of course, that we should treat the stranger as we in fact treat our brother, but rather as we ought to treat our brother. Presumably, in the realm of civic rights this would mean that we ought to protect and even cherish those (the strangers) whose opinions are different from our own, who might be in our economic power or under our political rule. Economic exploitation, arbitrary political condemnation or conquest, repression of artistic, political, or religious expression, prohibitions against geographical or social mobility—all these would appear to be forbidden by such an injunction.

I am here less concerned with whether such a moral preachment contains an adequate programme of human rights, than with (a) the clear fact that some central planks in any defensible human rights programme *are* to be found in such a capsule statement; and (b) any such programme requires a vast expenditure of human energy to implement it. At the microstructural level of the family, for example, the inculcation of such moral sentiments as a set of role obligations, and not simply a set of empty sentiments to be mouthed on appropriate ritual occasions, requires a special kind of child rearing. It is so difficult that even in countries where these rights are relatively well established, such as the United States of America, (a) only a modest majority or a large minority will uphold them, and (b) violations of these rights occur every day.

The difficulty of transforming such 'rights on paper' into role obligations which parents successfully persuade the child to accept may be seen dramatically in the contrast between national constitutions and the respect for human rights in most countries. The egalitarian social philosophies that were expressed by the American and French Revolutions had such an impact on the Western nations that almost all the hundreds of constitutions and civil codes promulgated since the beginning of the nineteenth century have contained guarantees of free elections, free speech, freedom of religious practice, and freedom from arbitrary arrest or seizure of property, but in only a few countries have these rights been generally secure, and in none have they been absolutely secure.

This difficulty may be sensed, if not clearly understood, by commenting that most of the freedoms that are called 'human rights' in fact violate the common sense of the average person in most countries. It seems as irrational to the man in the street as it does to the despot to permit a group to publish wrong-headed opinions, to organize political opposition to the party in power, or to utter blasphemies. Doubtless, most employers throughout history have felt that their employees 'ought' to support them politically. Justice has meant even-handed impartiality in the legal ideals of all nations, but common sense has always urged that only a cold or foolish man would betray his friends or family by judging against their cause. It seems to run counter to common sense for a man in power to step down merely because he has lost an election. The right of base-born men to rise to high position through merit is an ideal proclaimed in many societies and epochs, but upper-class families have felt it was simple common sense to protect the ineptitude of their own members against such rivals.

Yet it is a tragic irony that common sense is wrong. The force that is used to uphold it is misplaced and, especially in the modern era, futile. Slavery and colonialism have corrupted both the exploiter and the exploited, and the removal of these evils has profited both. Secure freedom of speech and religion, far from creating turmoil and instability, develops an adaptable, resilient social structure, which survives long after the highly controlled totalitarian or despotic régimes have crashed.

When the élite families protect their inept sons by denying entrance to the able from other social strata they guarantee their own downfall, often by revolution. In a most fundamental sense, the idealism of human rights is practical, and the common sense of repression and exploitation is unwise, but the family experiences in most societies do not persuade children that this is true.

I should like to add, parenthetically, that neither political science nor sociology has as yet been able to state how a nation can transform its old authoritarian régime into one of liberty.[2] There may well be particular social structural requirements, especially in the short run, before such freedoms can be guaranteed. One might argue, for example, that complete freedom of speech in Ghana might at this time create political chaos, or that England can afford this freedom while Indonesia cannot.

Just what those social-structural conditions are, however, is a separate problem which we cannot investigate here.

I noted earlier the kernel of the psychological problem of extending human rights to a given group, i.e., that each right is someone else's obligation, that to grant a right requires that someone loses what he had formerly considered his right. This problem has an obvious political form as well, that those who are to yield or grant a right are now in possession of that privilege precisely because of their political power, and thus can and usually do resist. Classical China, for example, gave to the eldest male the legal prerogative of making most decisions regarding any member of his family, from mate choice to divorce. The exploitation of any group is never based solely on custom or habit, but is always backed by force, defined as legitimate by the ruling group.

Indeed, it is precisely this resistance that so frequently makes a revolution necessary. Those who rule will not yield, and they have not sufficient wisdom to see that superior force will be arrayed against them. Traditional wisdom is a poor guide in a time of revolution.

And this is an era of revolution, unprecedented in world history. Its aims, and the great social forces that have swept over government throughout the world, have largely centered on human rights. Whether they will turn out to be genuine revolutions, or only transfers of power from one group to another, cannot be known at present, but I predict that the rest of the century will witness the consolidation and establishment of human rights at a rate that no other historical epoch has ever experienced.

In country after country the old stratification system is being rejected. Men demand, as never before, the right to a voice in their governments, the right to have their children educated, the right to be heard. They will not accept a slave or colonial status. They have raised their aspirations beyond any standard in the past, except that of a few industrialized countries and the élite of classical Western republics, such as Athens, Rome, or Florence.

It cannot be a surprise to the sociological theorist, then, that so much of this revolutionary wave has attempted to change family patterns. From at least the time of Plato two and a half millenniums ago, wise men have suggested that if human rights are to be guaranteed, if each human being is to be granted an adequate opportunity for the full development of his talents, the family system must be altered.

Every rigid stratification system, erecting barriers against the able poor, has relied on a highly controlled family system as its base, whether we look in the past at Tokugawa Japan, or in the present at India. The family system is the keystone of every stratification system. Very likely, every utopia conceived by man has an imagination changed the existing family system. Every wise man has also said that to transform a society it is necessary to rear the children differently, to socialize them for a new set of role obligations.

Since those who are concerned with human rights are not likely to be in positions of power, and therefore are more likely to view with alarm than to point with pride to accomplishments, it is perhaps useful to assert that at least in this one crucial area of human rights a considerable revolution is taking place. Though the facts noted here are well known to students of social change, and have been documented in great detail elsewhere, it is worth while to summarize some of the areas in which human rights relative to family patterns have been extended over the past half century.[3] Let me simply list the main points of change here.

Mate choice. Prior to the Chinese Revolution of 1911, it is safe to say, most marriages in the world were arranged by the parents of the couple. A high but unknown proportion of the girls who married were given little or no choice because they were married in their early 'teens. Since that time, and at an increasing tempo since the Second World War, young people in every major area of the world have gradually come to have a voice in this important decision.

Bride price or dowry. Linked with parental arrangement of marriages in most societies was some type of dowry or bride price. These were not typically purchases, of course, but merely reflected the economic stake of the elders in the alliance between families. As young people have come to make their own choices, they have also begun to reject such exchanges, thereby achieving a greater freedom of choice in their own lives.

Inter-caste and inter-class marriage. Barriers to inter-caste and inter-class marriages have been rooted in custom as well as law. In almost all parts of the world the legal barriers have been eliminated, and custom has been eroded, too, under the impact of the freedom of choice given to young people. That most marriages will continue to be intra-caste and intra-class goes without saying, but the individual has a wider range of alternatives open than a half century ago.

Control by elders and other kin. Most social systems, including those of great nations such as China, India, Japan and the Arab countries, permitted by law and custom a rather wide control by elders over the young. These areas included geographical mobility, occupational choice, the level of education to be achieved, the allocation of income, and the participation in religious rituals, not to mention more trivial matters. Of course, even in the most industrialized of nations the network of kin plays an important role in the lives of married couples, but in most countries the adult now has a greater freedom in choosing which relatives he will support or listen to. In these respects, India remains perhaps most laggard among the great nations. In perhaps no country can young adults ignore their elders without personal cost, but in most they can obtain jobs without the blessing of their elders, and need not remain in tutelage until their elders die.

Inheritance. Although it may be asserted that any inheritance system which permits much property to pass from one generation to the next within the same family gives an advantage to one set of people and thereby restricts the freedom of another set, some steps toward freedom in this area may be noted. In traditional societies, there is little testamentary freedom, since the direction of inheritance is clear and fixed: e.g., equal inheritance among sons in China, primogeniture among *samurai* in Tokugawa Japan, inheritance by brothers from the brothers of the previous generation in India, and so on. However, the modern civil codes have increasingly granted testamentary freedom. In addition, most of these great societies omitted the female almost altogether. Islam did not, of course, but the girl received a half-share. The newer civil codes have moved steadily toward granting equal inheritance to all children, and widows have come to be recognized even in societies that were once only patrilineal.

Contraception. The right to choose whether one will bear children, or how many, has until recently been granted to only a minority of the world's population. That some will wish to bear many children in order to obey a religious injunction need not be questioned, but equally no advocate of human rights would wish to condemn a couple to having more children than they wish. The threat of over-population has stimulated many campaigns which are gradually opening this area of choice to the peoples of the world. It is also worth mentioning here that this is especially an area in which women have not been permitted any choice, although the burden of children was theirs. Numerous studies have shown that even in areas of high birth rates most women are generally willing, and more than men are, to limit their families.

Abortion. Most countries continue to deny the right of the woman, in the event of an unwanted pregnancy, to end it. This freedom has been most widely granted in the Communist countries and in Japan, with somewhat less tolerance in the Scandinavian nations. Various arguments are currently used to support the prohibition against free choice in this area, although without question open debate about the issue is much more acceptable than a generation ago.

Divorce. It is surely a denial of choice if individuals are forced to remain in a marriage they dislike, and at the present time almost all of the world's population is permitted by law to divorce. In India, brahmins were not permitted to divorce, though some divorce did occur, and lower castes did have that permission. Of course, in India as in other nations permitting no divorce the husband typically had or has other alternatives open to him, such as concubines, second wives, and so on. The Westerner should keep in mind, however, that some nations and cultures did permit divorce before the modern era. Islam traditionally gave the husband great freedom to divorce, and divorce rates were very high among the farmers in Tokugawa and Meiji Japan. Both of these were patrilineal societies. Matrilineal societies have ordinarily been relatively permissive regarding divorce.

Egalitarianism within the family. Although there is little quantitative evidence on this point, almost all observers seem to agree that in almost all nations the woman has been given greater authority, respect and freedom within the family, and this relaxing of a patriarchal tradition has also improved the position of children. As will be noted later, the ideology of familial egalitarianism has its source in a broader stream of radical thought, and its impact can be observed in most countries. One of the most striking consequences of this change has been that women have come to be permitted to occupy responsible positions outside the family. Again it is difficult to quantify such matters, but it seems likely that egalitarianism in the occupational sphere has spread most rapidly in the Socialist countries. It must be emphasized that I am not referring to 'women in the labour force'. After all, women have borne heavy burdens in all epochs and countries. Rather, I am pointing to a radically different phenomenon, the right of a woman to obtain a job (and the training necessary for it) and to be promoted within it, on the basis of her own merits without the permission of her husband or father. Needless to say, this factor supports egalitarianism within the family, since it reduces the dependence of women on the males, but it also creates a new respect for the woman as an individual.

Of course, with reference to all of these, the new civil codes are more advanced than the actual behaviour and attitudes of the populations concerned. The codes and new administrative rules are written by a new elite who intend to lead these populations toward new types of family relations, but the process is relatively slow.

Moreover, it is not clear just how far such changes can go, whatever the ideological campaigns or the economic pressures. All such moves are purchased at some costs, and these may rise too high to be tolerated. It seems unlikely, for example, that any society can completely eliminate the parent-child bond as a way of creating the new civic man without particularistic ties to hamper the political programme. I doubt, too, that any society will in our lifetime be able to create genuine egalitarian relations between men and women.

In addition, we must keep in mind that each of these freedoms is a loss to someone, and most of them reduce the individual's emotional and even financial security. For the former, there may be no structural substitute. For the latter, various types of social welfare and pension programmes may suffice.

Even after taking note of these qualifications, we must concede, nevertheless, that the trends noted are steps toward the securing of human rights. Granted, they do not at first glance seem to be as dramatic or spectacular as the freeing of slaves or the abolition of a feudal system. On the other hand, those liberations may in fact have consequences similar to those of such grander political acts. If one could construct a numerical index, I would predict that the extensions of human rights to women and children in their domestic and occupational roles would loom as large as any other single step in the contemporary fight for human rights—certainly, far more real progress than has occurred in the areas of freedom of speech, religion, and publication, or the right of free elections or assembly. That step added as much or more to the economic production of the nations in which it has taken place and, very likely, at levels which we cannot easily explore here, helped to lay a firmer foundation for human rights in still other areas.

One of these levels does deserve brief attention here, which is that most of these extensions of human rights in the family area have not occurred only passively, but have been impelled by a positive and radical ideology of the family, which grows from but feeds back into a radical ideology of human relations in society.

The ideology of the conjugal family, as it is expressed in debates about family trends over much of the world, asserts the worth of the individual against the claims of caste, clan, or social stratum. It proclaims egalitarianism and the right to take part in important decisions. It urges new rights for women and children, and for adult males against the traditional claims of their elder kin. It demands the right to change exploitative relations among people.

In the West, its roots lie in the philosophic tradition that accompanied and interpreted the ascetic segment of the Protestant Revolution, and that runs counter to central philosophic elements of the Lutheran sects. Its fundamental human roots are still more universal, in that it radically asserts the rights of all to enjoy human freedom, i.e., choices among real alternatives. That no society and no family system wholly lives up to these principles goes without saying, but the contemporary pressures toward those goals are hardly to be denied.

However, we cannot evade the more problematic questions which I raised at the beginning of this paper. Even if most family systems of the world are moving toward granting more human rights to their members, can we assert that any particular kinds of family patterns or relations will produce a higher percentage of adults who will support the claims of their fellow citizens to the full enjoyment of human rights in the broader civic realm? Or, in a less cautious formulation, is it likely that the early experiences of the child in the family have *no* relationship with the willingness of the later adult to grant tolerance, freedom, and protection to others? Or, in a more utopian query, what type of family pattern would be most likely to produce adults who could live up to the really difficult role obligations that are demanded by the full extension of human rights to all?

The difficult task of socialization is not the inculcation of a love for one's personal freedom, which may be an easy goal: after all, any animal prefers at the outset to be free. But training children to support others' freedom and rights requires a more complex psychological and social pattern. Does any type of family pattern do that? Perhaps we might begin by taking note of a speculation often made by social philosophers and sociologists, essentially that extreme familism denies human rights to others. That is, when individuals are reared largely within the family and derive almost all of their satisfactions there, they are likely to over-value the ingroup—the ethnic group, the tribe, the region. Consequently, they feel free to treat outsiders as of little value, not deserving of any protection. An extreme form of this unwillingness to grant human rights to others may be found in many peasant regions. A well-analysed example is to be found in Edward C. Banfield's perceptive analysis of a southern Italian village.[4]

This suggestion, which we may explore at a later point, that immersion in the family unit fosters intense ethnocentric attitudes that run counter to the role obligations of human rights, also receives some slight support from the finding that children are more likely to be democratic in their social behaviour if they spend more of their time with peers (who have roughly equal power) than with parents, who have superior power (we shall, however, consider this point).

This general hypothesis seems to be roughly correct, if not precisely stated, and of course many essays in the Western world have called on this and prior generations to abjure their loyalties to family and clan, in order to embrace a loyalty to all humanity.

However, the renunciation of extreme familism is hardly sufficient as a directive for rearing children who will support human rights. Speculatively, one would suppose that a high degree of permissiveness and egalitarianism within the family would be more likely to produce individuals who could not adjust easily to a repressive political system, or who would not create such a system. Much evidence on this point has accumulated since the publication of Horkheimer's collection of investigations entitled *Studien uber Autorität und Familie* in 1936.[5]

Without attempting to summarize a considerable mass of data and critiques,[6] well known to the student of human rights, let me simply remind you of the central suggestions in those studies. By and large, they have asked the question, what kinds of socialization experiences create the type of personality that is most prone to deny human rights to Jews, Negroes and other ethnic groups? However, the answers suggest parallel hypotheses about the denial of human rights generally.

Authoritarian control of the family by the father is correlated with such traits as those: deification of the parent, high evaluation of the father role, the child's passive adjustment to the present situation, the suppression of the child's aggression, suppression of sexual impulses in the child, and the fostering of dependency in the child. "Democratic" attitudes of fathers correlate with egalitarian treatment of children, encouragement of their independence, and affection as a means of control.[7]

Adults who exhibit intolerance of others' rights are more likely than other adults to have grown up under authoritarian parental control and, of course, to continue that tradition with their own children. The stereotyping that is so characteristic of those who consider people who differ from themselves as having few redeeming traits is emphasized by parental efforts to ascribe fixed, clearly distinct, traits to the two sexes; indeed, the more authoritarian the mother's attitudes, the greater the children's imitation of the like-sex parent.[8]

Additional suggestions as to the kinds of family relations that might maximize the support of human rights can be derived from Allport's description of the 'tolerant' personality,[9] which summarizes the findings of many studies. Perhaps central is the necessity of family interaction based on security and love, rather than threat, and that concedes the right of individuals to have pleasure without guilt. Under a régime of threat, the child—and later, the adult—feels the need to have precise instructions, for fear of making errors and being punished for it. There is, then, an intolerance of ambiguity, whereas in a society that guarantees human rights the individual must be able to interact with others without at all knowing exactly what they will do in turn; more important and more specific, the individual does not have to interact with them as members of neat categories, such as "Communist", "deviationist", "bourgeois formalist", "decadent imperialist", "Jew", "Moslem", and so on. Similarly, in such families, individuals are conceded to have their own unique traits, and not to be forced rigidly into the categories of "male" and "female"—for example, chores might be shared on the basis of need and capacity, rather than sex.

Given greater security in affection, and the right to have pleasure without guilt, the individual's tolerance of frustration is greater, and his need to attack others when things go wrong will be less. Thus, he is less likely to approve any denial of human rights to those who differ in political or other beliefs. In more technical terms he will have less repressed aggression, and less need to displace it against people who have not directly harmed him.

Certain family experiences do seem to correlate with some of the attitudes necessary for democratic participation in civic life.[10] Generally, a higher percentage of the people in countries granting more secure human rights feel that they were free as children to participate in family decisions. This finding parallels Allport's suggestion that in the family which fosters tolerance in a child the junior members are permitted to be critical. They need not dread the superior power of the parents.[11]

In addition, Almond and Verba report that a higher percentage also felt that they actually had some influence on these decisions, and were free to complain about matters if they did not like them. Correspondingly, a higher percentage actually did complain.

These findings also parallel the findings of several studies in the United States of America, showing that there is a higher tolerance of deviance and a greater willingness to give civic rights to people with radical opinions, toward the upper social strata, whether this is defined by education or by holding positions of leadership. For it is also in such strata that the ideology and practice of sharing family decisions is more widely found.[12] Toward the upper strata, a higher percentage of adults felt that as children they were able to complain, and did so.

Those who participated in family decisions also feel more competent as adults to influence their own government.[13] It is worth noting that this correlation is weaker within the higher educational levels, where other types of experiences may supplement any lack of participation within the family itself.

Bearing in mind that we are not searching for the most effective ways of developing the superego in the child, but a particular superego content, let us further suggest (on the basis of research outside the family, but supported by investigations carried out by Kurt Lewin, Ronald Lippitt and many others over the past ten years in a wide range of organizational settings) that a collaborative style of rearing is more likely to create adults who respect the wishes and contributions of others. By contrast, the autocracy that a Luther rejects in his father and his Church simply re-emerges in his own pattern of repression as well as in his notion of fixed statuses and duties imposed by fiat.

One of the likely consequences of the collaborative style, in which parents and children co-operate to solve problems, is the development of faith or trust in other people. This, in turn, as most readers know, is negatively correlated with authoritarianism. Faith in people, it is interesting to note here, appears to be highest in countries in which human rights are more secure.[14]

A complex relationship exists between these factors and love. The manipulation of love is one of the most effective techniques for developing a strong superego, but there is some evidence that the threat of love withdrawal creates many psychological problems. Among these is a distrust of others. If love is dependent, for example, on performance, performance may be high but regression is also a possible outcome. It seems likely that the security of parental love must be great enough to permit the child to face aggression by parent or outsider without great anxiety. The ability to face hostility without any inner compulsion to aggress against those who oppose; or without any inner compulsion to bow to the opposition when it is powerful (seeking love by compliance) can be most effectively based on security in parental love.

This security would appear to be based, in turn, on conveying to the child that he is loved as a unique person, not because of his status as elder or younger, male or female. The recognition that each member of the family is unique, with his or her own needs and demands, rather than merely a set of ascribed statuses, should contribute to the generalized feeling that other individuals are also unique: they need not be manipulated to serve one's own needs, or rejected as outcasts.

Such a security has an added by-product of some consequence in the broader area of human rights. When adults or children fail to live up to the norms they themselves claim to accept, it is unlikely that they can face that fact, or improve their behaviour, if they can develop some kind of legitimation or rationalization for the discrepancy. As has been widely demonstrated, those who discriminate against others often assert non-discriminatory norms, and avoid confronting the divergence between their behaviour and their norms. Thus they protect themselves against the strain of actually living up to those standards in the civic realm. It is unlikely that many individuals can achieve such a confrontation unless they have been given a considerable internal security, specifically a feeling that they are loved in spite of moral lapses.

This last point is linked, in turn, with a widely held psychodynamic notion that self-acceptance is the strongest foundation for the acceptance of others. The child whose parents hammer into him a sense of his pervasive and continual moral failure is much less likely to accept himself as well as others. Reciprocally, those who as adults are authoritarian are more likely than others to express low evaluations of their own parents.[15] With reference to an hypothesis stated earlier, that intense familism is likely to be associated with an unwillingness to grant human rights to strangers, it should be noted that the personal autonomy arising from security permits the individual to be able to leave the family, to feel secure outside it, to trust even the stranger.

Finally, a collaborative style of family relations requires that youngsters take into account the needs and feelings of others. They become, therefore, more skilled at empathy. The authoritarian is less able to intuit correctly the attitudes and emotions of others. Correspondingly, it is not surprising that children from more democratic homes tend to be more popular among their peers than are children from authoritarian homes.[16]

But though such suggestions may be correct, and certainly deserve to be tested and made more precise by cross-cultural research, to persuade parents in many countries to change their ways is a difficult task. It is easier to push a highway through a jungle, or to purify a water supply, than to alter the details of family relations, as we know already from the repeated failures of birth control campaigns. Traditional parents are not more willing to share their authority with their children than are husbands to yield control over their wives. It is likely that the contemporary transformations in the political, economic, and social macrostructures of most nations will ultimately have more impact on the microstructure of the family than will any particular programme aimed at changing those internal relations of the family.

Equally ambiguous are the relations between personality variables and those of the larger social structure. No one has as yet succeeded in showing that personalities of particular types will create particular kinds of societies. Although adults who were reared under the ideal conditions sketched above would probably be more inclined to support human rights, it is not clear that traditional patriarchal, even authoritarian, family relations necessarily create authoritarian political and social structures. Perhaps the German family system contributed, as so many analysts claimed, to Nazism, but the Swiss, Dutch, French, Swedish and Belgian families were hardly less patriarchal or authoritarian.[17]

Nor can we cite as evidence the efforts of totalitarian régimes to control their family systems in order to gain support for their political system. Specifically, systems of high political control often do try to subordinate the individual directly to the State, by-passing the family where possible; and they also try to enlist the family members in campaigns to bring the apathetic or dissident members in line.

Such events prove, however, no more than that revolutionary leaders will use whatever instrumentalities they can command. Whether their hypotheses were correct is a separate matter for study. At present we do not know that these particular family experiences helped to produce adults who would wish to impose a repressive political control over others.

I think that these qualifications and doubts need not arouse pessimism as to the future of human rights in the world. For though the revolutions in many countries have merely substituted a tight political control in place of the old-fashioned, looser despotism, almost all of these new programmes have promised freedom, and derive much of their support from an ideology of human rights. Ultimately, they will have to fulfil the terms of that implicit contract.

Perhaps, at a still more fundamental level, the family patterns that are being preached in these countries and the trends that are now visible are precisely those most likely to produce a next generation which would rebel still more strongly against political repression, and would support more firmly a programme of human rights. Thus, the revolutionary ideologies of egalitarianism do more than accentuate those trends toward human rights in the limited area of family relations, but reciprocally, the new patterns of family relations will also produce individuals who are more likely to put into effect and uphold a broad programme of human rights. It is possible, then, that the changes in family patterns over the past half century are not only important in themselves; they may also act as a catalyst that will eventually transform the massive flux of modern revolution into a clear movement toward greater human freedom.

NOTES

[1] In writing this paper, I have had the benefit of talks with Orville G. Drim, Paul F. Lazarsfeld, Herbert Hyman, Ronald Lippitt, Margaret McClure, Matthew B. Miles, Stanley Schachter and Stanton Wheeler, and wish to thank them for their help.

[2] In this connexion, see the illuminating essay by S. M. Lipset, 'Establishing National Authority', in his *The First New Nation* (New York, Basic Books, 1963, p. 15–60).

[3] William J. Goode, *World Revolution and Family Patterns* (New York, Free Press, 1964).

[4] Edward C. Banfield, *The Moral Basis of a Backward Society* (New York, Free Press, 1958), especially Chapters 5 and 6.

[5] *Forschungsberichie aus dem Institute für Sozialforschung,* Paris, Félix Alcan, 1936.

[6] The best-known study in English is T. W. Adorno, E. Frenkel-Brunswik, D. J. Levinson and R. N. Sanford, *The Authoritarian Personality* (New York, Harper, 1950). See the critiques in Richard Christie and Marie Jahoda (eds.), *Studies in the Scope and Method of the Authoritarian Personality* (Glencoe, Ill., Free Press, 1953).

[7] R. Nichols, 'A Factor Analysis of Parental Attitudes of Fathers', *Child Development,* 33, 1962, p. 797–8.

[8] W. Hartup, 'Some Correlates of Parental Imitation in Young Children', *Child Development,* 33, 1962, p. 94.

[9] Needless to say, Allport himself objects to the pale qualities of the term 'tolerant' but no good English word exists which conveys the meaning of 'supporting human rights'. Perhaps there is no such word in other Western languages, either. See Gordon W. Allport, *The Nature of Prejudice* (New York, Doubleday, 1958), especially Chapter 27. See also Chapters 10 and 25.

[10] Gabriel A. Almond and Sidney Verba, *The Civic Culture* (Boston, Little, Brown, and Co., 1965), p. 274–284, 286–7.

[11] Allport, op. cit., p. 399–400.

[12] On the class differences in the support of civil liberties, see Samuel A. Stouffer, *Communism, Conformty and Civil Liberties* (Gloucester, Mass., Peter Smith, 1963), especially Chapter 2 and Appendix E.

[13] Almond and Verba, op. cit., p. 284.

[14] Almond and Verba, op. cit., p. 212–4.

[15] J. Cooper and J. Lewis, 'Parent Evaluation as Related to Social Ideology and Academic Achievement', *Journal of Genetic Psychology,* 101, 1962, p. 135.

[16] J. Howard Kauffman, 'Interpersonal Relations in the Traditional and Emergent Families Among Midwest Mennonites', *Marriage and Family Living,* 23, August 1961, p. 251.

[17] In this connexion, see the complexities suggested by comparisons among British, German and American child-rearing patterns, in Lipset, op. cit., p. 277–81, especially his suggestion that perhaps a different type of personality is needed for stable democracy in different kinds of societies.

Sponsored and Unsponsored Independence

BERNARD FARBER

SPONSORED INDEPENDENCE

Generally, research on sponsored independence is performed with middle-class samples in comparison with lower-class samples and emphasizes the maturation of the child to a responsible, respected adult who strives for prestige or for material wealth or for both in conventional society. The studies dealing with sponsored independence indicate that:

1. Although both the adolescent peer group and parents are influential in stimulating boys to pursue a professional career (rather than a blue-collar career), the parental pressure is more effective than the peer-group pressure.[1]

2. Children of working mothers are more highly motivated to achieve goals presumably associated with occupational success than are children of mothers who are not gainfully employed.[2] Apparently, parental values related to economic and social mobility are more effectively transmitted to the child when both parents act as models.

3. Children of employed mothers perform more household chores than do children whose mothers are not employed.[3] With boys performing household tasks and children seeing *both* parents working, children would find little sex differentiation in family roles. There would be an implicit expectation that each family member be responsible for maintaining the family as a domestic unit and as an economic cooperative group.

4. McClelland and his associates found that Catholic parents expect their children to achieve sponsored activities of independence at a later age than do Protestant and Jewish parents.[4] The sponsored activities investigated include the child's knowing his way around the city, trying new things for himself, doing well in competition, and making his own

Reprinted from *Family: Organization and Interaction,* with permission of Chandler Publishing Company, and Science Research Associates. Copyright © 1964. Footnotes have been renumbered.

friends. Since Protestant and Catholic American families have generally originated in different countries, it is difficult to determine the effect of religion separately from effects of national culture. There are differences in age of expected independence even within the Catholic group. On the whole, Catholic parents of Italian descent expect their children to achieve independence in the mentioned sponsored activities at a later age than do Catholic parents of Irish descent. McClelland and his associates suggest that parent sponsorship of activities related to the child's independence from the nuclear family promotes the child's achievement of economic and occupational success. On the basis of these findings as well as similar ones by Miller and Swanson, one would expect that children in Protestant and Jewish families are more pressured into independence in sponsored activities than are children in Catholic (especially Italian) families. Catholic parents may give greater attention to the prevention of unsponsored independence.

5. In their study of gifted children, Getzels and Jackson distinguished between parents who were vigilant about their children's behavior and academic performance and those parents who focused on their children's development of interests, new experiences, and "enthusiasm for life."[5] They found that the children of vigilant, pressuring parents tended to have high general intellectual ability but little creativity whereas the children of less vigilant parents were more highly creative. This finding suggests that the kinds of activities sponsored by parents may be highly individuated.

6. Miller and Swanson have suggested that, with the spread of large-scale organizations in our society, parents may give less attention to sponsoring independent activities in children and more attention to maintaining stable social relations.[6] Miller and Swanson argue that fostering independence and responsibility in children was appropriate to training children to be individualistic entrepreneurs. However, with the decline in independent enterprises, child raising must be oriented toward developing adults who will not be highly individualistic. The trend in child raising will probably be toward increased sociability and mental health and away from responsible independence. Viewed in combination with the Getzels and Jackson findings, the Miller and Swanson study suggests that sponsored independence in the future may take on recreational and mental-health purposes rather than occupational training.

In summary: the various studies of sponsored independence of youth take the stance of "conventional" society and regard the performance of sponsored activities as training for adulthood—*parents* are more influential than adolescent peers in stimulating boys to pursue a professional career, families in which both parents work stimulate children to achieve occupational and financial success and require the children to perform family maintenance tasks, parents sponsor children's activities in conformity with their own considerations of "the important things in life," and the independence-inducing activities sponsored by parents reflect the parents' work setting and religious and ethnic background.

UNSPONSORED INDEPENDENCE

Problems relating to unsponsored independence appear in lower socio-economic families and in families without close ties binding the parents and children together. Various investigators have found that problems in the home are related to delinquent behavior in children, to alcoholism, and to other deviant behavior.[7] Moreover, when children center their activities around the home, they tend to view their parents as satisfied with their behavior even when the parents are dissatisfied; however, children who spend much time away from home tend to underestimate their parents' satisfaction with them.[8] Unsponsored independence then not only entails actual deviance from parental expectations but also magnifies this deviance in the eyes of the children. This magnification in turn probably stimulates further deviance.

Unsponsored independence includes not only delinquent acts but also other acts which might meet with parental disapproval. These acts are related to the loss of parental supervision and control of children's conduct. Findings related to unsponsored independence in courtship behavior reveal that:

1. Parents are more ignorant of their sons' love life than their daughters'. Various studies have indicated that girls are more closely bound to their parents and discuss courtship problems with them (especially with the mother).[9] Perhaps cross-sex inhibitions associated with the incest taboo operate to diminish son-mother communication; possibly the sons have more than the daughters to hide; or boys may merely be less communicative about their affective life. In any case, sex differences in independence are reflected in parental knowledge about the child's love life as well as about other activities of the child.

2. The separation of mother and daughter when the girl goes to college affects the girl's attitude toward love behavior that is deviant from parental expectation.[10] Until college, the girl and her mother are similar in their attitude toward virginity prior to marriage. However, after the girl enters college, she frequently becomes more liberal in her attitude toward premarital intercourse. The more liberal attitude does not necessarily mean that the girl herself is participating in pre-marital erotic activity, only that she revises her views concerning the conditions under which intercourse is permissible before marriage. Going away to college is a special instance of the loosening of family ties that increases the probability of unsponsored independent behavior.

TYPES OF ADULT–YOUTH RELATIONSHIPS

This discussion has distinguished between two kinds of independence achieved by youth in their development—sponsored and unsponsored. It has not, however, related these modes of independent behavior to each other. Pairing modes of independent behavior establishes four extreme types of youth-adult relations:

The *emancipated youth* (high sponsored independence, high unsponsored independence) is one who, in the process of achieving a successful position in accordance with parental wishes, deviates from many of the norms held by his parents. The individual who is highly socially mobile (as through sports, dating popularity, academic achievement) and who is assimilated into a different segment of society is typical of the youth emancipated from the family.

The *All-American boy* or *girl* (high sponsored independence, low unsponsored independence) is one who achieves success in the areas in which the parents promote achievement while, at the same time, he avoids behavior which deviates from parental wishes. The individual who is a star in sports, very popular in dating, or achieves academic success (if these are the activities promoted by the parents) and who stays out of trouble with adults typifies the All-American boy or girl.

The *deviant* (low sponsored independence, high unsponsored independence) is one who achieves little in the activities promoted by his (or her) parents, but deviates considerably from parental expectations by performing unsponsored acts (for example, truancy, premarital sex activity, brawls, belonging to a gang). In middle-class segments of society, the hipster and the beatnik are characterized by low sponsored independence and high unsponsored independence.

The *passive individual* (low sponsored independence, low unsponsored independence) is one who is highly dependent upon his parents for the performance of many activities which are ordinarily done by the child himself. The passive individual does not get into trouble, yet neither does he (or she) achieve independence in sponsored activities ordinarily associated with his age-sex role.

An evaluation of the usefulness of this typology must await its application to particular problems. Getzels and Jackson studied social factors in high intelligence and creativity in children. The vigilant and nonvigilant families in their study appear to reflect family relations associated with the All-American child (high-IQ child) and the deviant (high creative child) respectively. The vigilant family applies pressure for achievement to the child while giving him close supervision to prevent deviant behavior. The nonvigilant family offers little pressure and permits the child to develop as he will, thereby risking much deviance and nonachievement in school. The Getzels and Jackson formulation, however, does not take into account family relations associated with the emancipated youth. Similarly, the Miller and Swanson entrepreneurial family appears to be associated with the All-American child whereas their bureaucratic family seems an appropriate environment for developing a sociable, affable, passive individual. Possibly, the other two parent-child relationship types can also be incorporated into the Miller and Swanson scheme. In any case, the distinction between sponsored and unsponsored independence of youth may provide various insights into the development of family relations.

NOTES

[1] Richard L. Simpson, "Parental Influence, Anticipatory Socialization, and Social Mobility," *American Sociological Review*, 27 (1962), pp. 517–522.

[2] Kathryn S. Powell, "Maternal Employment in Relation to Family Life," *Marriage and Family Living*, 23 (1961), pp. 350–355. See also Marian Radke Yarrow, Phyllis Scott, Louise de Leeuw, and Christine Heinig, "Child-Rearing in Families of Working and Nonworking Mothers," *Sociometry*, 25 (1962), pp. 122–140.

[3] Prodipto Roy, "Maternal Employment and Adolescent Roles: Rural-Urban Differentials," *Marriage and Family Living*, 23 (1961), pp, 340–349.

[4] David C. McClelland, A. Rindlisbacher, and Richard de Charms, "Religious and Other Sources of Parental Attitudes toward Independence Training," in David C. McClelland, ed., *Studies in Motivation,* New York: Appleton-Century-Crofts, 1955, pp. 389–397.

[5] Jacob W. Getzels and Philip W. Jackson, *Creativity and Intelligence: Explorations with Gifted Students,* New York: Wiley, 1962.

[6] Daniel R. Miller and Guy E. Swanson, *The Changing American Parent,* New York: Wiley, 1958.

[7] For example, F. Ivan Nye, *Family Relationships and Delinquent Behavior,* New York: Wiley, 1958.

[8] Bernard Farber and William C. Jenné, "Family Organization and Parent-Child Communication," *Monographs of the Society for Research in Child Development,* 28 (1963), No. 7 (Serial No. 91).

[9] For example, Carlfred B. Broderick and Stanley E. Fowler, "New Patterns of Relationships between the Sexes among Preadolescents," *Marriage and Family Living*, 23 (1961), p. 29 (Table 4).

[10] Robert R. Bell and Jack V. Buerkle, "Mother and Daughter Attitudes to Premarital Sexual Behavior," *Marriage and Family Living,* 23 (1961), pp. 390–392.

IV

Dating and Mate Selection

A crucial aspect of the young person's move toward independence from his family in American society involves his dating relationships and eventual choice of a mate. Love, dating, premarital sex, and mate selection are issues which are ordinarily of considerable interest to the student of the family, and these are the subjects of Part IV.

In many societies the individual has not been free to choose his own mate, love has been a by-product of marriage rather than its basis, and dating has been nonexistent. American society, however, has seen the development of a system which includes experimenting in relations with members of the opposite sex, deciding whether or not to engage in sexual intercourse prior to marriage, and choosing one's own mate on the basis of the emotional attachment called "love." The first article in this section is an excerpt from Peter Blau's book, *Exchange and Power in Social Life*. In this "Excursus on Love," he shows the difficulties that may confront the dating individual as he struggles with physical and emotional commitment to another person. As Willard Waller stated many years earlier, the individual least committed to a relationship tends to control it, and this can make for heartache for the more serious couple member. Blau shows how difficult it is, especially for the female in the United States, to walk the tightrope between dispensing sexual favors to keep the male from looking elsewhere, and avoiding over-indulgence, which may cause the male to lose interest. Written primarily from the perspective of male dominance, this excerpt raises many of the issues which are discussed at length in the subsequent papers of this section.

The other six papers should be read in pairs, beginning with McDaniel's and Bayer's empirical investigations of dating. McDaniel finds that the woman in U.S. society must cease to be aggressive and learn to be receptive, or passive, in the process of dating, or she may never marry. She must learn to bolster the male ego, play up his achievements, and under no circumstances compete openly with him. One of the many issues raised by McDaniel's analysis concerns whether his conclusion indicates that the woman is as bound to a subordinate position and passive role today as in the past. What, then, of all the talk of the depolarization of sex roles in today's world; is it just talk? And

167

what of marriage itself? Is it not likely that the female who has played a receptive role in order to gain a husband may begin to be assertive following marriage, the result being marital difficulties? This article should be related to Stuckert's paper on conjugal roles in Part V, especially to his assertion that the wife must do more adjusting of expectations in marriage than the husband. Finally, the antithesis between McDaniel's arguments and conclusions and those of the women's liberation movement deserve the reader's serious attention.

The longer one dates, says Alan Bayer, the more likely it is that he will make an adequate choice of a mate, Not the age at which one starts to date but his number of years of dating experience is directly related to his later marital adjustment. On the assumption that the more dating the individual engages in the more he knows about the opposite sex and the better choice he can make, Bayer's conclusions seem correct. It should, however, cause the reader to wonder whether the relation between length of dating experience and marital satisfaction might instead be curvilinear. Is it not possible that the individual who fails to marry at the typical age in American society, perhaps between ages 20 and 25, might become increasingly desperate, thus making a poorer or less reasoned choice, despite long experience? Bayer's data do not provide an answer to this question.

Another pair of articles which should be read in tandem are Isadore Rubin's think-piece and Bell and Chaskes' research paper on premarital sex. Rubin notes the multiplicity of sexual values in contemporary American society. With the efficacy of moral absolutes against premarital sex diminished, Rubin advocates critical thinking and individual choice on the part of the young person—a "democratic value stance." He does not, unfortunately, include data which might show the distribution of these six value approaches among American adults and young people. However, at this point Bell and Chaskes' brief research note becomes valuable. Applying Rubin's framework, we might conclude from Bell and Chaskes' paper that the movement among young people is away from the two forms of asceticism and toward humanistic liberalism and even the fun morality. This, of course, agrees with Ira Reiss in *The Social Context of Premarital Sexual Permissiveness,* where he concludes that permissiveness with affection, or Rubin's humanistic liberalism, is most typical of American young people today. Premarital intercourse should not be considered normative at present any more than abstinence should. Rather, according to Bell and Chaskes, choice and amoralism, that is, defining the issue outside the realm of morality, are becoming normative. Beside the issues already raised, two others should be mentioned. First, do Bell and Chaskes' samples lack representativeness, and, if so, what does this say of their conclusions? Secondly, is there no longer a place for discussion of how the young person *should* behave in this area?

The culmination of the dating process is the choice of a marriage partner, and the last two articles of this section concern mate selection. When I choose a mate, is it true that "opposites attract," or that "birds of a feather flock together," or that I select "a girl just like the girl that married dear old Dad?" Bruce Eckland's article summarizes well the many variables which have been employed to try to predict who will marry whom. He freely admits their inadequacies as well as their value. In fact, Eckland's summary should demonstrate to the reader why there have been few recent attempts at large-scale marriage prediction studies. At present, there is much stock-taking and concern with the theoretical basis for any variables that might be employed. Charles Bolton indicates another aspect of the inadequacy of variables predicting mate choice. Mate selection is not an occurrence but a process. It is the end result not only of the social and psychological backgrounds which the individual brings to his dating experience, but of the internal dynamics of specific dating relationships. There are "escalators," such as the engagement, which move a couple toward marriage despite their individual characteristics and backgrounds.

These two papers make clear the uncharted territory in the study of mate selection in a system based upon personal choice. Some marriages are a result of a premarital pregnancy, others of the effort to escape from an unhappy home; how could these be incorporated into the frameworks of Eckland and Bolton? Is it not possible, furthermore, that a different theory is needed for males and females, or for the different ages at which the individual might marry, as we hinted above in the introduction of Bayer's article? The reader will at least have become aware that much remains to be done in understanding the factors which are basic to the choice of a mate in the United States.

Excursus on Love

PETER BLAU

Love is the polar case of intrinsic attraction. Whereas it finds undoubtedly its purest expression in the relation between mother and child, its development as the result of the increasing attraction of two independent individuals to one another can best be examined in a romantic relationship. Love appears to make human beings unselfish, since they themselves enjoy giving pleasure to those they love, but this selfless devotion generally rests on an interest in maintaining the other's love. Even a mother's devotion to her children is rarely entirely devoid of the desire to maintain their attachment to her. Exchange processes occur in love relations as well as in social associations of only extrinsic significance. Their dynamics, however, are different, because the specific rewards exchanged are merely means to produce the ultimate reward of intrinsic attraction in love relations, while the exchange of specific rewards is the very objective of the association in purely instrumental social relations. In intrinsic love attachments, as noted earlier, each individual furnishes rewards to the other not to receive proportionate extrinsic benefits in return but to express and confirm his own commitment and to promote the other's growing commitment to the association. An analysis of love reveals the element of exchange entailed even in intrinsically significant associations as well as their distinctive nature.

A man falls in love if the attractiveness of a woman has become unique in his eyes. "All that is necessary is that our taste for her should become exclusive." This happens, Proust continues, when we start to experience an "insensate, agonising desire to possess her."[1] The woman who impresses a man as a most desirable love possession that cannot be easily won and who simultaneously indicates sufficient interest to make ultimate conquest not completely beyond reach is likely to kindle his love. His attraction to her makes him dependent on her for important rewards and anxious to impress and please her to arouse a reciprocal affection that would assure him these rewards.

In the early stages of falling in love, the fears of rejection and dependence engendered by the growing attraction motivate each lover to conceal the full extent of his or her affection from the other and possibly

Reprinted from *Exchange and Power in Social Life,* by Peter Blau with permission of John Wiley & Sons, Inc. Copyright © 1964. Footnotes have been renumbered.

also from himself or herself. Flirting involves largely the expression of attraction in a semi-serious or stereotyped fashion that is designed to elicit some commitment from the other in advance of making a serious commitment oneself. The joking and ambiguous commitments implied by flirting can be laughed off if they fail to evoke a responsive cord or made firm if they do.[2] But as long as both continue to conceal the strength of their affection for the other while both become increasingly dependent on the other's affection, they frustrate one another. In the lovers' quarrels that typically ensue, as Thibaut and Kelley have pointed out, "each partner, by means of temporary withdrawal or separation, tests the other's dependence on the relationship."[3] As both are threatened by these quarrels with the possible end of their relationship, they are constrained to express sufficient commitment for it to continue. Of course, one may not be ready to do so, and the conflict may terminate their relationship.

Human beings evidently derive pleasure from doing things for those they love and sometimes make great sacrifices for them. This tendency results partly from the identification with the other produced by love, from the desire to give symbolic expression to one's devotion, from the function providing rewards has for strengthening a loved one's attachment to oneself, and perhaps partly from the process previously termed reverse secondary reinforcement. The repeated experience of being rewarded by the increased attachment of a loved one after having done a variety of things to please him may have the effect that giving pleasure to loved ones becomes intrinsically gratifying. Further feedback effects may occur. Since doing favors and giving presents are signs of love, a man's gifts and efforts for a woman may stimulate his own affection for her as well as hers for him, and a woman may encourage a man to give her things and do things for her not primarily out of interest in the material benefits but in order to foster his love for her. "Benefactors seem to love those whom they benefit more than those who have received benefits love those who have conferred them," said Aristotle.[4]

The more an individual is in love with another, the more anxious he or she is likely to be to please the other.[5] The individual who is less deeply involved in a love relationship, therefore, is in an advantageous position, since the other's greater concern with continuing the relationship makes him or her dependent and gives the less involved individual power. Waller called this "the principle of least interest."[6] This power can be used to exploit the other; the woman who exploits a man's affection for economic gain and the boy who sexually exploits a girl who is in love with him are obvious examples.[7] Probably the most prevalent manifestation of the principle of least interest, however, is that the individual whose spontaneous affection for the other is stronger must accede to the other's wishes and make special efforts to please the other. Such an imbalance of power and extrinsic rewards is often the source and remains the basis of lasting reciprocal love attachments.

Hence, the lover who does not express unconditional affection early gains advantages in the established interpersonal relationship. Indeed, the more restrained lover also seems to have a better chance of inspiring another's love for himself or herself.

Costly possessions are most precious, in love as elsewhere. A man's intrinsic attraction to a woman (and hers to him) rests on the rewards he expects to experience in a love relationship with her.[8] An analytical distinction can be made between his actual experiences—resulting from her supportiveness, her charming talk, her kisses, and so forth—and the value he places upon these experiences with her compared to similar experiences with other women. His gratifications are the product of the experiences themselves and the value he places on them. The ease with which he obtains the rewards of her love, however, tend to depreciate their value for him. This is the dilemma of love, which parallels the previously discussed dilemma of approval. Just as a person is expected to give approval to his associates, but his doing so too freely will depreciate the value of his approval, so is a woman under pressure to give evidence of her love to her admirer, but if she does so too readily the value of her affection to him will suffer.

How valuable a woman is as a love object to a man depends to a considerable extent on her apparent popularity with other men. It is difficult to evaluate anything in the absence of clear standards for doing so, and individuals who find themselves in such an ambiguous situation tend to be strongly influenced by any indication of a social norm for making judgments.[9] Evaluating the intrinsic desirability of a woman is an ambiguous case of this kind, in which any particular man is strongly influenced by her general popularity among men that socially validates her value as a love object. Of course, a girl can only become generally popular by being attractive to many particular boys, but her attractiveness to any one depends in part on evidence that others find her attractive too. Good looks constitute such evidence, and so does her behavior on dates.

A woman whose love is in great demand among men is not likely to make firm commitments quickly, because she has so many attractive alternatives to weigh before she does. The one who is not popular is more dependent on a man who takes her out and has more reason to become committed to him. A woman who readily gives proof of her affection to a man, therefore, provides presumptive evidence of her lack of popularity and thus tends to depreciate the value of her affection for him. Her resistance to his attempts to conquer her, in contrast, implies that she is in great demand and has many alternatives to choose from, which is likely to enhance her desirability in his eyes. Her reluctance to become committed helps to establish the value of her affection, partly because he takes it as an indication of her general desirability, notably in the absence of any direct knowledge of how desirable she appears to other men. To be sure, men sometimes discuss women among themselves, their desirability and even their behavior on dates, the social taboo on doing so notwithstanding, but these discussions only increase the importance a woman's restraint has for protecting the value of her affection. If a woman has the reputation of readily engaging in sexual affairs, the value of this expression of her affection greatly declines, largely because her sexual favors entail less commitment to, and ego support for, a man than those of a woman who very rarely bestows them.

To safeguard the value of her affection, a woman must be ungenerous in expressing it and make any evidence of her growing love a cherished prize that cannot be easily won. Ultimately, to be sure, a man's love for a woman depends on her willingness and ability to furnish him unique rewards in the form of sexual satisfaction and other manifestations of her affection. The point made here is *not* that a woman who fails to provide a man with sexual and emotional gratifications is more likely to win his love than one who does. The opposite undoubtedly is the case, since such gratifications are the major source of a lasting love attachment. The point made is rather that a man's profound love for a woman depends not only on these rewarding experiences themselves but also on the value he places upon them and that a woman who refrains from bestowing expressions of her affection freely increases the value of these expressions *when she does bestow them.* Of course, unless she finally *does* bestow these rewards, she does not profit from their increased value. This is precisely the reason for the dilemma. A woman promotes a man's love by granting him sexual and other favors, as demonstrations of her affection and as means for making associating with her outstandingly rewarding for him, yet if she dispenses such favors readily—to many men or to a given man too soon—she depreciates their value and thus their power to arouse an enduring attachment.

Social pressures reinforce the tendency to withhold early evidence of great affection. If most girls in a community were to kiss boys on their first dates and grant sexual favors soon afterwards, before the boys have become deeply committed, it would depreciate the price of these rewards in the community, making it difficult for a girl to use the promise of sexual intercourse to elicit a firm commitment from a boy, since sexual gratifications are available at a lesser price. The interest of girls in protecting the value of sexual favors against depreciation gives rise to social pressures among girls not to grant these favors readily. Coleman's study of high schools shows that these pressures tend to take the form of making a girl's social standing contingent on her reputation in regard to her sexual behavior with boys.[10] This social pressure, which helps to maintain the sexual favors of girls worthy of permanent commitments of boys, strengthens the position of girls in their exchange relations with boys in the courtship market.[11] The situation among boys is complementary, which means that the social pressures here discourage early commitment. The aim of both sexes in courtship is to furnish sufficient rewards to seduce the other but not enough to deflate their value, yet the line defined by these two conditions is often imperceptible.

The challenge of conquest is an important element in the formative stages of a love relationship, and its significance as a catalyst for the development of a lasting attachment is dissipated by making conquest too easy. A basic function of the casual dating among young people is to provide opportunities for them to ascertain their own attractiveness as lovers and their chances in the competition for desirable mates. In dating—and to some extent in intimate sociable intercourse generally—an individual places the attractiveness of his own self on the market, so to speak, which makes success of extreme importance for his self-conception. The girls or boys who are successful in making many conquests of the other sex validate their attractiveness in their own eyes as well as those of others. In casual dating, therefore, girls and boys use each other to test their own attractiveness through conquests. A girl's resistance to being easily conquered constitutes a refusal to let herself be used as such a test object and a demand for a minimum commitment as a condition of her affection. By prolonging the challenge of the chase until a boy has become intrinsically attracted to her, a girl exploits the significance of conquest to promote a more fundamental attachment that makes this incentive for dating her superfluous. Since an interest in conquest may be a boy's primary initial reason for courting a girl, an easy conquest robs him prematurely of this inducement for continuing the relationship.

A girl's demonstrations of affection for a boy, moreover, imply a commitment by her and a demand for a countercommitment from him. If he was satisfied with the previous level of involvement and is not yet ready to commit himself further, such a demand for greater commitment may alienate his affection for her. Love is a spontaneous emotion that cannot be commanded, and the command to love her more implicit in the girl's expressions of increasing affection for him may act as an external restraint that withers the boy's existing affection for her. A boy's growing love for a girl he pursues is typically accompanied and spurred by an anxiety lest he lose his love object, but the fear of becoming too deeply involved that her great involvement arouses in him is incompatible with and corrodes the anxiety of losing her and the affection associated with it. Although he can take advantage of her greater commitment to obtain sexual favors from her, his exploitative orientation in doing so is not likely to stimulate an intrinsic attachment; and if his superego prevents him from exploiting her, he is likely to terminate the relationship under these circumstances. The jealousy characteristic of the more deeply involved lover constitutes an explicit demand for a more exclusive commitment on the part of the other, and it frequently provides the final stimulus for the less involved lover to withdraw from the relationship. The growth of love is often stifled by the pressure put on it by the other lover's too great affection.

Whereas the processes just considered discourage the free expression of affection in early courtship, lovers also experience pressures to express their feelings. If an individual is in love, he or she obtains gratification from declaring his love to the beloved and even "to shout it from the treetops." Identification with the person one loves makes rewarding him enjoyable, and rewarding him tends to involve some expressions of love for him. Besides, many actions of a girl that reward a boy and express her feelings for him are simultaneously rewarding for her, such as her willingness to kiss him. Flirting, moreover, gives rise to expectations that must later be fulfilled to maintain the love relationship. The conduct of the flirtatious girl implies that, although she may not yet be ready to let the boy hold her hand, continued association with her would ultimately bring these and much greater rewards. The implicit promises made in the course of flirting put subsequent pressure on lovers to live up to the expectations they have created and begin to provide at least some of the rewards promised. The result is a dynamic force of increasing rewards and commitments, since each new commitment creates further expectations, lest frustrated expectations lead to the termination of the relationship. The girl lets the boy kiss her, he takes her to the "prom," she permits some sex play, he ceases to date others, so does she, and he ultimately gives her the ring that formalizes their relation—unless, of course, these pressures toward stepped-up rewards and increasing commitments induce one of the lovers to discontinue the affair.

Finally, the gratifications a woman experiences as the result of being loved by a man are greatly enhanced if she loves him too, and this may unconsciously incline her to return his love. The love of a man animates a woman and makes her a more fascinating and attractive person. Going out with a man who is in love with her enhances her self-image as a captivating woman and thus probably affects her behavior to make her actually more charming and appealing. For a man's loving admiration to have pronounced effects on her self-image and conduct, however, his estimation of her must be of great significance for a woman, and the more she loves him the greater is its significance for her. A woman's love for a man who loves her, therefore, helps to make her a more charming and self-confident person, because it magnifies, as it were, the mirror that reflects and partly shapes her personality as a lover. Although a woman cannot will herself to love a man who loves her, the advantages she gains from reciprocating his love may unconsciously motivate her to do so.

Lovers, then, are under pressure to express affection for one another as well as under pressure to withhold expressions of affection. The basic dilemma is that a woman who freely provides evidence of her affection for a man in order to make associating with her more attractive to him thereby depreciates the value of her affection. The generic processes are the same for both sexes, although cultural sex role differences determine their specific forms. The willingness to enter into sex relations, for example, entails less of a commitment for a boy than for a girl in our culture, and he can more easily declare his love first, since this too tends to imply less of a commitment for a boy than for a girl. But those acts of a boy that signify his commitment to a girl, such as his introducing her to his parents or his giving her his fraternity pin, have essentially the same implications as her acts of commitment. If both lovers are interested in continuing the relationship, both are also interested in having the other commit himself or herself first and more deeply. Hence, there is an element of "brinkmanship" in courtship, with both partners seeking to withhold their own commitment up to the point where it would endanger the relationship, because courtship is a mixed game with some common and some conflicting interests, just as is the establishment of other social relations discussed in chapter two.[12]

One lover's apparent affection and increasing commitment sometimes stimulate the growth of the other's love for him, while they sometimes inhibit the other's love and cause the other to lose interest in the relation. What determines which is the case? The personality structure of the lovers is unquestionably the most important factor,[13] but the social condition in the developing love relation also exerts an influence. Since lovers tend to suppress the strength of their growing affection for one another, a lover's own deepening involvement produces a state of tension. This state makes him anxious to receive evidence of the other's increasing affection for him, which would avert the danger of rejection and of one-sided dependence and permit him to cease suppressing his strong feelings of attraction. In this situation the eagerly anticipated expressions of affection of a woman tend to relieve a man's distress and intensify his love for her. If, on the other hand, there is no such reservoir of suppressed feeling and a lover is no more involved than is manifest, a woman's demonstrations of great affection for him are likely to alienate his affection for her, because they depreciate the value of her love, undermine the challenge of pursuing her, and make demands for stronger commitments than he is ready to undertake. In parallel fashion, a man's expressions of affection that meet a woman's suppressed desires tend to intensify her love for him, but if his affection far exceeds her feelings and desires it is likely to alienate her.

In brief, it seems that commitments must keep abreast for a love relationship to develop into a lasting mutual attachment. If one lover is considerably more involved than the other, his greater commitment invites exploitation or provokes feelings of entrapment, both of which obliterate love. Whereas rewards experienced in the relationship may lead to its continuation for a while, the weak interest of the less committed or the frustrations of the more committed probably will sooner or later prompt one or the other to terminate it. Only when two lovers'

~~affection for and commitment to one another expand~~ at roughly the same
pace do they tend mutually to reinforce their love.

NOTES

[1] Marcel Proust, *Remembrance of Things Past,* New York: Random House, 1934, Vol 1, p. 177.

[2] For the analysis of a special case of this strategy, see James D. Thompson and William J. McEwen, "Organization Goals and Environment," *American Sociological Review,* 23 (1958), 29–30.

[3] John W. Thibaut and Harold H. Kelley, *Social Psychology of Groups,* New York: Wiley, 1959, p. 66.

[4] Aristotle, *The Nicomachean Ethics,* London: William Heinemann, 1926, p. 545 (Book IX, vii, 1).

[5] Providing extrinsic benefits may be a substitute for proving oneself intrinsically attractive, as Proust has noted (*op. cit.*, p. 205): "For the moment, while he lavished presents upon her, and performed all manner of services, he could rely on advantages not contained in his person, or in his intellect, could forego the endless, killing effort to make himself attractive."

[6] Willard Waller and Reuben Hill, *The Family,* New York: Dryden, 1951, pp. 190–192.

[7] For a discussion of exploitation in courtship, see *ibid.,* pp. 159–173. See also the fictional account of the game of making another dependent in order to derive pleasure from exercising power over him or her, played actually as a game and in real life, in Roger Vailland, *The Law,* New York: Knopf, 1958, esp. pp. 42–52, 196–198.

[8] To make the following discussion less burdensome, it will refer largely to men's orientations to women, but it is assumed to apply, in principle, also to women's orientations to men, although there are, of course, sex role differences in specific practices, as will be noted.

[9] See Muzafer Sherif, "Group Influences upon the Formation of Norms and Attitudes," in Eleanor E. Maccoby, Theodore M. Newcomb, and Eugene L. Hartley, *Readings in Social Psychology* (3d ed.), New York: Holt, 1958, pp. 219–232.

[10] James S. Coleman, *The Adolescent Society,* Glencoe: Free Press, 1961, pp. 118–123.

[11] See Waller and Hill, *loc. cit.*

[12] Another dilemma posed by this mixed game is that the lover who expresses his eagerness to spend time with his beloved enables her to enjoy dates with him without revealing how eager she is to do so and without making the commitment implicit in such revelations.

[13] Generally, this discussion has not attempted to deal with the psychological forces and motivational structures underlying the socio-psychological processes analyzed. Waller and Hill's comment concerning their analysis is also appropriate for the one presented here (*ibid.,* pp. 172–173): "It happens that we have directed our own analysis at the interaction process in courtship; we recognize the necessity of supplementing this analysis by pointing out how these processes are related to the inner nature and developmental history of the participants. Here the psychoanalytic contributions are much in point." Special attention should be called to the neglect of emotional conflicts and the resulting irrational tendencies of individuals, that is, tendencies produced by unconscious drives that defeat the individual's own objectives.

Dating Roles and Reasons for Dating*

CLYDE O. McDANIEL, JR.

There is a large inconsistency within the literature on female dating behavior. On the one hand, the female is characterized as assertive and unmindful of the marriage-oriented reasons for dating.[1] Bowman declares that

> The woman plays a role and has a vital part in making choices and in developing the [dating] relationship. . . . There are indications that women are losing their traditional reserve and are more direct and aggressive in their approach to men.[2]

Herman's 1955 study shows that dating represents, for many girls, merely doing as others do and a means for lessening competition.[3] He labels this type of dating "dalliance."

On the other hand, the female is characterized as receptive and very much aware of the marriage-oriented reasons for dating.[4] Tyler declares that

> [While dating] women assume the role of the pursued. Women respond favorably to pursuit by men. . . . It is worth keeping in mind that there is a feminine as well as a masculine role in dating. We have not yet reached the stage where both sexes widely accept the principle of 'dutch dating'. An open display of aggression or initiative on the part of a woman makes men avoid her.[5]

Cameron and Kenkel's 1960 study shows that 70 percent of the students in their sample were thinking of marriage,[6] and Hewitt's 1958 study shows that most of the traits his sample desired in a date were also desired in a marriage partner.[7]

One of the reasons for such inconsistence is the failure, on the part of current dating theorists, to specify which stage of courtship is being used as a reference point. While studies have been done to assert that courtship is a progressive phenomenon and that girls do assume different roles for different reasons, no one has related stages and reasons for dating, or stages and dating role. This study was aimed at answering a set of questions which inquire about some of the relationships between

Reprinted from *Journal of Marriage and the Family*, February 1969, 97–107.

the female's role in dating and her reasons for dating (in each stage of courtship). Since these questions also inquire about the conditions under which the relationships obtain, their answers aid in placing dating-courtship firmly within the boundaries of socialization.

This study was designed essentially to discover what impact stages of courtship have on the relationship between female dating role and reasons for dating by answering the following specific questions:

1. In what sequence do stages of courtship occur?[8]
2. What is the relationship between stages of courtship and dating roles?[9]
3. What other factors influence dating roles?[10]
4. What is the relationship between stages of courtship and reasons for dating?[11]
5. What is the relationship between dating roles and reasons for dating?
6. Is a penalty paid by girls if their dating roles do not change as they move through the stages of courtship?
7. What impact do the perceptions of males have on facilitating change in female dating behavior?

METHODOLOGY

Survey methodology was employed to execute the study. Of the 600 questionnaires which were distributed to undergraduate students at the University of Pittsburgh, 396 were returned from single females while 181 were returned from single males.

Determining adequate sample sizes and selecting respondents were not done arbitrarily. In order to determine the sample size for single females, the author used the following criterion as a guideline: select a sample size which is practical and manageable and yet which is large enough to allow for subgroup analyses. This criterion was buffered by the awareness that the aim of the study was not to generalize to any particular population, but to test relationships. The author consequently decided on a sample size of 400. Since the major intent of the study was to discover the impact of stages of courtship (a trichotomized variable) on the relationships between two sets of dichotomized variables—role behavior (assertiveness and receptivity) and reasons for dating (recreation, mate selection, and anticipatory socialization)—a sample size of 400 allowed the possibility of simultaneously analyzing these relationships. Such a cross-tabulation scheme would result in forty-eight subgroups with a chance possibility of eight to nine cases in each.

In order to place female "subjects" on a sample list, simple random sampling was employed: random sampling, not for the purpose of facilitating accurate generalization to the parent population, but for the purpose of making sure all categories in the antecedent and independent variables would be substantially represented. Since there were about 5,000 single dormitory females in the population from which the sample of 400 was to be drawn, from a list of all the single females in the population, every eighth one was designated as a respondent for the study.

A sample size of 200 for single males was arrived at in much the same way. Since there were 9,000 single male students at the University from which a sample of 200 was to be drawn, from a list of all the single male students, every forty-fifth one was designated as a respondent. The reason for using the smaller sample was to make simple comparative analyses of females who were actually dating (and had not completed progress through the courtship system) with males' perceptions of how females should act while dating. The smaller sample facilitated the testing of implicit hypotheses such as the following: "dating males, at certain stages of courtship, expect their girl friends to be assertive (or receptive)."

Summarily, the entire sample can be described in a few statements. It was composed predominantly of young single female students. Further, being undergraduates, they were principally freshmen and sophomores. They were overwhelmingly democratic, upper middle-class, and white. Most of them began dating at or around junior-high-school age. The girls, in a typical middle-class fashion, were somewhat sensitive about revealing their ages or anything connected with age. Most of them had had the experience of the first two stages of courtship—random dating and going steady—but few had been pinned or engaged. Finally, most of the sample presently were either random dating or going steady.

It was impractical to observe directly the behavior which constituted the data for this study. However, indirect observation was practical. Among the many methods available which would facilitate indirect observation, the self-administered questionnaire seemed most appropriate. The foregoing was especially true because the self-administered questionnaire lent itself to simultaneously questioning members of the respondent group with a minimum of interaction among them. The method, which did not require an interviewer because each respondent read the questions herself (himself) and filled in her (his) own answers, took the following form: After each of the potential respondents had been identified and placed on a sample list, each of them was contacted via campus mail. Upon such contact, they were notified that they had been selected and were asked to be available on a specified date in order to fill in the questionnaires. Then, with the aid of the Dean of Men, the Dean of Women, and relevant dormitory heads, the questionnaires were distributed and promptly returned via campus mail.

The contents of the questionnaire were based on a list of items which are characteristic of dating behavior. These were categorized and judiciously assigned to each variable (see the next section for conceptual and operational definitions of each variable). Where feasible, the items were incorporated in the critical-incident technique form.[12] Furthermore, most of the questions incorporating the items were either phrased normatively or hypothetically in order to allow the respondents to answer the questions freely and nonthreateningly.[13] The items came from published results of research and from observations of the author and referred to both attitudinal sets and to behavior, such as engaging in sex. In assigning items to variables, the author employed the Guttman Scalogram model. Adherence to this measurement model made it possible to construe each variable along a unidimensional scale and to make no measurement assumptions which exceeded ordinality.

The questionnaire was pretested with small samples of graduate and undergraduate students at the New Kensington branch of the University of Pennsylvania, at Carnegie Institute of Technology, and at Chatham College. In analyzing the data, all zero-order relationships were assessed through the use of Spearman's Rho along with a conservative level of significance (.05). All higher-than-zero-order relationships were assessed through the use of elaboration and percentaging with no level of significance being chosen. That is, where it was necessary to tease out subgroup relationships, percents were employed with modal differences being indications of the patterns of relationships. One essential feature of elaboration is that it allows no single hypothesis to be viewed independently of others. Instead, there is a series of hypotheses which must be looked at in combination. Consequently, the tactic here was to capitalize on *patterns* of percentage differences.

DATA ANALYSIS AND DISCUSSION

1. Stages of Courtship

Since it was postulated that significant changes take place among females within certain stages of courtship, it was necessary to hypothesize the sequence in which the changes were expected to occur. Dating is known to manifest itself in at least three stages: random dating, going steady, and pinned/engaged. Random dating occurs when the female is dating but not with any special person; going steady occurs when she is dating a special person but has not made any commitment to marry; and being pinned/engaged occurs when she is dating a special person and has made a commitment to marry.

Hypothesis I: It was expected that these three stages were progressive, i.e., that girls randomly date before they go steady, and randomly date and go steady before they become pinned/engaged.

The rationale for the progression is based on the assumption that girls must scout around a bit before they learn that society expects them to choose special persons who are suitable for marriage mates. When they find such persons, they must test their compatibility by dating them steadily. If compatibility cannot be attained, the girls revert back to random dating, and the process starts again. If and when compatibility is attained, the girls commit themselves to marriage and become engaged.

In order to discover whether or not occupancy in one stage of courtship presupposes occupancy in other stages, the three stages were incorporated as items in the questionnaire. Table 1 shows that among

TABLE 1

Stages of Courtship Participated in

		Single Females	
Scale Scores		F	%
Random Dating Going Steady, Engaged	1	103	26
Random Dating, Going Steady	2	186	47
Random Dating	3	107	27
Total		396	100

Coefficient of Reproducibility = .972; Minimal Marginal Reproducibility = .820; no non-scalable questions.

single females, all the items scaled and yielded a very high Coefficient of Reproducibility (.972) and Minimal Marginal Reproducibility (.820). In the order of their decreasing attractiveness, the stages arranged themselves in the following manner: (1) random dating, (2) going steady, and (3) pinned/engaged. One can be sure, with such a high Coefficient of Reproducibility, that if a girl is going steady, she has random dated; and if she is pinned/engaged, she has random dated and gone steady; and any variable which correlates fairly well with stages of courtship participated in can, to that extent, be used in the same manner in which the latter can be used. While it must be remembered that stage of courtship participated in is not synonymous with present stage of courtship, it appears that Hypothesis I was not disconfirmed.

2. Role Behavior

Robert Winch, et al., while empirically elaborating the Winch theory of the complementarity of needs in mate selection, suggested an excellent analytical role scheme which was used in assessing role behavior in this study.[14] The scheme was suggested when, through cluster analysis, Winch and his associates arrived at the general hypothesis that "an important dimension of dating for both sexes is the assertive-receptive dimension."[15] They found, on the one hand, that the *assertive* dater was achievement-oriented, autonomous, dominant, hostile, a status aspirant, and a status striver; they found, on the other hand, that the *receptive* dater was abasive, deferential, succorous, prone to vicariousness, an approacher, and anxious.[16] The behavioral indicants of these were used in this study as assertive and receptive roles respectively.[17] The assertive-receptive role was a combination.

Although eighteen items were included in the questionnaire to measure assertiveness, only nine scaled such that an acceptable Coefficient of Reproducibility (.90) and Minimal Marginal Reproducibility (.76) were produced. The items which scaled acceptably—in the order of their decreasing attractiveness—were the ones dealing with a girl's (1) always being in control on dates, (2) wishing to marry only a potential success, (3) not being dependent on her date, (4) reprimanding her date for misbehavior, (5) being cautious on dates, (6) staying at least one step ahead of her date, (7) wishing to stay at least one step ahead of her date, (8) subtly manipulating her date, and (9) making all the decisions on dates.

As was the case in measuring assertiveness, eighteen items were used to measure receptivity. Again, in order to achieve an acceptable Coefficient of Reproducibility (.90) and an acceptable Minimal Marginal Reproducibility (.819), nine of the items had to be discarded. The items which conformed to an acceptable scale—in the order of their decreasing attractiveness—were those dealing with a girl's (1) rejoicing when her date rejoices, (2) enjoying being near her date, (3) admiring her date, (4) wanting to be tenderly cared for by her date, (5) dressing to suit her date, (6) being disturbed if her date is disturbed with her, (7) allowing her date to make the decisions on dates, (8) accepting her date's criticisms, and (9) never going stag to a party.

Hypothesis II: It was expected that the girls in this study would be assertive in the first stage of courtship, assertive-receptive in the second stage, and receptive in the last stage.

The rationale for such a progression is as follows: Girls, in the early stage of courtship, are inexperienced and unsophisticated with regard to appropriate role behavior. They are assertive initially because they view their right to act as aggressors in social interaction as identical with boys' right to act as aggressors. In heterosexual interaction on dates, however, they are made aware of their inappropriate role behavior through negative reinforcement from boys. In this way, they learn that receptivity is more frequently approved than assertiveness. At the same time, they are beginning to place a premium on attaining a mate. Both of these are seen as significant features in the definition of their adult status. They resort to receptivity, then, because it enables them to obtain a mate, and because it is consistent with their adult status definition.

To test Hypothesis II, present stage of courtship was related to assertiveness and to receptivity. The first stage, of course, is random dating and was assigned a lower weight than the later stages—going steady and pinned/engaged.

The first column in Table 2 shows that (1) *there is a tendency for girls in the early stage of courtship to be assertive*, and (2) *there is a tendency for girls in the later stage of the courtship to be receptive.* Although the correlations are small, they are significant, indicating that a fairly high degree of confidence can be placed in them. Since stages of courtship scale, there is reason to believe that girls in the early stage of courtship approach heterosexual relationships with the belief that they have just as much right, power, and authority as boys. Their immediate goal is to initiate cross-sexual relationships, and the data indicate that they do so with straightforwardness. However, something happens between early dating and later dating, because female role behavior tends to shift toward receptivity. Whatever the influence is, it is difficult to say, but an attempt is made in the succeeding sections to tease out much of it.

It is interesting to note that the two correlations in the first column of Table 2 differ not only in direction (or sign) but also in magnitude. This seems to imply that there is a stronger tendency for girls to be assertive in the first stage than there is for them to be receptive in the last stage, or that fewer girls have changed to receptivity in the later stages. The differences in the sizes of the correlations are probably due to the fact that those girls who have not changed cluster in the second, or transitional, stage of courtship—going steady—wherein they are becoming receptive while not actually relinquishing assertiveness. If this is true, it can be said that the girls in the second stage of courtship are assertive-receptive. Furthermore, it means that a certain amount of credence is accorded to Hypothesis II.

3. The Influence of Reference Systems, Degree of Dissatisfaction, Commitment, and Complementarity on Role Behavior[18]

Many other factors can be hypothesized to account for the girls' being assertive in the first stage of courtship and receptive in the last stage. The author thought that if some of these other factors related significantly with role behavior, then confidence could be placed in the assumption that they influence assertiveness initially and receptivity later. The last seven columns in Table 2 show the relationships among some of the other factors and role behavior.

A number of facts become apparent when these columns are per-

TABLE 2

The Relationships Among Other Factors and Assertiveness Receptivity Among Single Females

Role Behavior	Stages of Courtship	Original Family Orientation	Peer-Group Orientation	Personal Orientation	Degree of Dissatisfaction	Commitment to Date	Traits Desired in a Date	Actual Traits of Date
				Other Factors				
Assertive	−.35	.13	.18	−.12	—	.20	−.16	.14
Receptive	.24	.26	.12	.12	.23	.29	−.13	.17

N = 396, P ≤ .05.

used. It seems that as the girls make the shift from assertiveness to receptivity, they simultaneously become: (1) more original-family oriented, (2) less peer-group oriented, (3) much more personally oriented, (4) much more dissatisfied with their dating role, (5) more committed to their dates, and (6) relatively unchanged in terms of complementarity (both assertive and receptive girls desire fewer traits in their dates than they actually get).

In view of the foregoing, it is believed that a series of events occur in the process of girls' changing from assertiveness in the first stage of courtship to receptivity in the last stage. Some of the events cause assertiveness, some of them result from assertiveness and cause receptivity, and some of them result from receptivity.

It is believed that achievement as prescribed by the peer group and the original family dominates the first stage of courtship. The girls are much more aware of peer-group norms than they are of original-family norms, but they are unaware of their own ability to prescribe the content of their dating behavior. First, the peer group demands that they initiate cross-sexual relationships; and later the original family demands that they select particular dates and exclude others. Concurrently, the girls in the first stage have not learned that they have less power than the males in initiating cross-sexual relationships, since they were socialized, in the past, on the same generational plane as the males.[19] As a result, they feel that they have just as much right and power to act as aggressors in attaining their goals—heterosexual though they may be—as the males. This causes them to be assertive in their dating behavior and to be fairly satisfied with their dating role, since it conforms with the expectations of their most important reference groups (at that time) and is consistent with their past socialization.[20]

Continuing, the early daters are not nearly as much "in love" with their dates as are their "sisters" in the later stages of courtship. But it appears that many of them are sometimes inclined to indicate that they are committed to their dates. They have a fairly high evaluation of their dates (even though they do not necessarily desire many traits in their dates). It is quite likely that some of the early daters are "falling in love" with their dates. If this is true, it means that their reference source is shifting to themselves and their boyfriends. When these two phenomena occur, the girls move into the later stages of courtship wherein their boyfriends more seriously reject assertiveness among girls. With emotional investment in boyfriends, the girls are forced to become receptive, because now it conforms to the expectations of their new reference source.

Receptivity, however, is not consistent with past socialization,[21] and one of the interesting findings in this study is that the receptive girls are dissatisfied with having to play their receptive role. The girls in the later stages play the receptive role, but this does not mean that they have accepted the role. This, indeed, seems to provide a built-in conflict for newlyweds, especially since it is known from a separate finding that married females are more avant-garde than single females and that they advocate assertiveness in some of the more crucial areas of dating behavior much more strongly than single females.[22]

As a summary, it may be well to speculate on the order in which the dating roles are probably subscribed to by the girls in this study. It appears that the girls are assertive first; that is, they enter the courtship process feeling themselves equal to boys in rights, power, and authority, and they express themselves accordingly while random dating. At a second stage—going steady—the girls are assertive-receptive; that is, receptivity is gradually being learned and is gradually supplanting assertiveness. And finally, at the third stage—pinned/engaged—when the girls are ready to be married, they are receptive.

4. Reasons for Dating

The findings from a study done by Lowrie in 1951 were applicable here.[23] Lowrie's study was designed to discover why students date. Four reasons were identified: (1) mate selection, (2) recreation, (3) anticipatory socialization, and (4) adult role clarification. Because of ambiguity of definition, adult role clarification was not used in this study. Mate selection is the conscious searching for compatible dating and/or marriage partners. Recreation is dating solely for the purpose of enjoying heterosexual interaction. Anticipatory socialization is learning, through dating, the knowledges and skills which are prerequisite to assuming specific marital roles.

In the present study, ten items were incorporated in the questionnaire to measure the extent to which mate selection was used as a reason for dating. All ten items scaled and yielded a Coefficient of Reproducibility of .911 and a Minimal Marginal Reproducibility of .818. In the order of their decreasing attractiveness, the ten items were concerned with a girl's (1) making herself as attractive as possible to attract the boy of her choice, (2) *incidentally* dating to choose the right husband, (3) dating, prior to engagement, enough boys to make a choice from a wide range of potential husbands, (4) being provided, through dating, with opportunities to refine her standards for good husbands, (5) not thinking of incompatible dates as good husbands, (6) comparing, in the dating situation, her ideal mate choice with reality, (7) *not just incidentally* considering mate selection while dating, (8) considering "romantic love" as secondary to her other standards for a good husband, (9) dating only those boys whom she considers potentially good husbands, and (10) *primarily* dating to choose the right husband.

Again, ten items were used to measure the extent to which recreation was used as a reason for dating. Only one of these proved nonscalable. With a Coefficient of Reproducibility of .916 and a Minimal Marginal Reproducibility of .820, the remaining nine scalable items—in the order of their decreasing attractiveness—were those concerning a girl's (1) *incidentally* dating to have lots of fun, (2) considering dating as a pleasant opportunity for companionship with the opposite sex without the responsibility of marriage, (3) having fun while dating in order not to miss a large portion of the beauty of youth, (4) considering enjoying herself as a major issue when contemplating going out on a date, (5) dating only those boys with whom she feels most comfortable, (6) obtaining sexual enjoyment while dating, (7) not worrying about marriage while on dates, (8) *primarily* dating to have lots of fun, and (9) not worrying about pleasing her date, just herself.

From among the ten items used to measure anticipatory socialization, only one proved nonscalable. The Coefficient of Reproducibility and the Minimal Marginal Reproducibility were quite satisfactory, being .917 and .800, respectively. In the order of their decreasing attractiveness, the remaining nine scalable items are those concerning a girl's (1) not being marriageable to a particular boy until he has seen her assuming a variety of different roles, (2) learning, through dating, the general attitudes and behaviors of boys in order to facilitate initial marital adjustment, (3) *incidentally* dating in order to learn what behavior is necessary for being a good wife, (4) learning how to please a date in order to learn how to please a husband, (5) testing sexual compatibility with a potential mate while dating, (6) allowing engagement to serve as a trial marriage, (7) not seeing anything "wrong" with trial marriages, (8) *primarily* dating in order to learn what behavior is necessary for being a good wife, and (9) dating only those boys who can teach her something about marital roles.

Hypothesis III: It was expected that the girls in this study date for the purpose of recreation in the early stage of courtship, mate selection in the second stage, and anticipatory socialization in the last stage.

The rationale for the progression is based on the assumption that girls are either not aware of or not interested in the maritally oriented functions of dating in the early stage. They learn soon that, women, to be socially acceptable, must be married. As a result, a conscious mate selection process ensues; this is done in a sequence of tests while going steady. Once a mate has been selected and tested, girls' emphases shift to the more immediate future wherein they begin actively to anticipate some of their perceptions of their roles as wives.

While these three reasons for dating are isomorphic with the implicit deductions of each of three theoretical schools of thought (see next section), Lowrie failed to cash in on a major theoretical contribution by not relating them with certain types of dating roles, stages of courtship, or with any of the variables involved in courtship. However, Lowrie's study does indicate that young people do not date solely for the purpose of having fun. Many are seriously concerned with other functions, particularly the marital and socialization functions.

TABLE 3

Some of the Relationships Among Stages of Courtship, Female Reasons for Dating, Female Role Behavior, and Male Attitudes Toward Female Assertiveness and Receptivity

	Present Stage of Courtship			Female Role Behavior	
	Random Dating	Going Steady	Engagement	Assertive-ness	Receptivity
Female Reasons for Dating					
Anticipatory Socialization	−.28**	−.15**	.30**	− **	.16**
Recreation	.24**	−.17**	−.30**	.23**	− **
Mate Selection	.15**	.32**	.12**	.29**	.32**
Male Attitudes Toward Female Assertiveness	.10*	−.12*	−.24*		
Toward Female Receptivity	.16*	.20*	.30*		

* N = 181 (Number of Males).
** N = 396 (Number of Females).
P ≤ .05.

The first three cells in the first three columns of Table 3 show the relationships among present stage of courtship and the three reasons for dating among single females. The data indicate that anticipatory socialization is positively correlated with the engagement stage of courtship; recreation is positively correlated with the random dating stage of courtship; and mate selection is positively correlated with all three stages of courtship, but the highest correlation obtains with the going-steady stage of courtship. This makes it highly probable that the following relational pattern obtains: (1) in the early stage of courtship, there is a tendency for the girls to justify their dating on the basis of mate selection and recreation (however, recreation dominates); (2) in the interim stage of courtship, there is a tendency for them to justify their dating on the basis of mate selection; and (3) in the last stage of courtship, there is a tendency for the girls to justify their dating on the basis of mate selection and anticipatory socialization (however, anticipatory socialization dominates). If such a pattern obtains, a certain amount of credibility is accorded to Hypothesis III and to the assumptions underlying it.

5. Relationships Among Role Behavior and Reasons for Dating

From the foregoing it follows that role behavior and reasons for dating among single females are related to each other in the following manner:

Hypothesis IV: The females who date primarily for the purpose of recreation are very likely to be assertive.

Hypothesis V: The females who date primarily for the purpose of mate selection are very likely to be assertive-receptive.

Hypothesis VI: The females who date primarily for the purpose of anticipatory socialization are very likely to be receptive.

The main focus of Hypotheses IV, V, and VI is: "Exactly what do assertive and/or receptive girls get out of courtship?" As seen in the last two columns of Table 3, this question was answered by relating types of role behavior to reasons for dating. The data indicate that (1) *the assertive girls date for the purposes of mate selection and recreation;* (2) *the receptive girls date for the purposes of mate selection and anticipatory socialization;* and, since both assertive and receptive girls justify their dating on the basis of mate selection, (3) *the assertive-receptive girls date for the purpose of mate selection.*

It seems that if girls were continually assertive throughout courtship, two of the functions uncovered by Lowrie would go lacking, but if they were continually receptive, they would get no fun out of dating. If they were sometimes assertive and sometimes receptive, they would be continually searching for mates. Assertiveness does not undermine the functions of courtship; it merely contributes to specialized aspects of them. Since it is known that the girls shift from assertiveness to receptivity as they move through courtship and that their dating emphases also shift, the findings in the last two columns of Table 3 were expected. However, the findings indicate that Hypotheses IV, V, and VI are not disconfirmed.

The data show that at least three schools of thought can be used to summarize the role behavior of modern-day females.[24] Waller and Gorer's school (an Assertive school) seems to present a neat characterization of early female daters as assertive and motivated by hedonistic considerations.[25] Burgess and Locke's school (an Assertive-Receptive school) seems to give a fairly accurate presentation of females who are in transit from the early stage (random dating) to the last stage (pinned/engaged).[26] Their girls are pictured as sometimes assertive and sometimes receptive and motivated by desires to select mates. The stage of courtship which best describes this school is going steady. Lowrie's school (a Receptive school) more properly portrays later daters, wherein the girls are receptive and motivated by desires to attain anticipatory socialization benefits.[27] The stage of courtship which best describes this school is pinned/engaged.

Each of the schools is valuable as far as it goes. Each characterizes a part of the dating process. When the three schools are combined, however, a much clearer picture of dating roles and functions is presented, wherein one can see that dating roles and functions change as the girls move through courtship. The question immediately arises as to what would happen if the roles and functions do not change. Apparently, some penalty is paid by the girls if they do not change their role behavior from one stage to another. The next section presents insight into the nature of this penalty.

6. Assertiveness, Receptivity, and Socialization

If the girls do not change from assertiveness to receptivity while moving through courtship, one wonders what happens. The data, in this study, show that two things happen: (1) society imposes negative sanctions, and (2) the girls do not progress to later stages of courtship, or if they do progress, they soon regress to earlier stages. The first finding is presented in the last two cells of the first three columns of Table 3. These six cells show that "society" (in the form of the male) does not, in fact, like females who are assertive. And more significantly, they dislike them most in the last stages of courtship.[28] The more advanced the men are in the stages of courtship, the more they de-emphasize female assertiveness and the more they emphasize female receptivity. It can be assumed, then, that with such an attitude toward the female role in dating, the males impose serious negative sanctions on the expression of female assertiveness during the later stages of courtship. Credibility is added to this statement when one remembers (from Table 2) that girls become, during the later stages, more personally and boyfriend oriented. This means that they are, indeed, aware of the types of sanctions imposed by their boyfriends and that they are more concerned with learning the proper role behavior for an adult woman and wife.

TABLE 4

The Relationship Between Present Stage of Courtship and Stage of Courtship Participated in

Present Stage of Courtship		Stage of Courtship Participated in	
	%		%
Random Dating	55	Random Dated	26
Going Steady	30	Random Dated, Gone Steady	47
Pinned/Engaged	15	Random Dated, Gone Steady, Pinned/Engaged	27
Total	100 (396)		100 (396)

$r_8 = -.60, P \leq .05$

The second finding is presented in Table 4 which shows that a significant number of girls do, in fact, regress or fail to progress to further stages of courtship. This is evidenced by the fact that the correlation between present stage of courtship and stage of courtship participated in in is −.60, indicating that (1) most of the girls who presently reside in later stages of courtship are quite likely to have participated in earlier stages, and (2) *many of those who have participated in later stages are quite likely to be presently residing in earlier stages*. The negative exchange which is implied by the second statement seems to take place between random dating and going steady, pinned/engaged. More girls are presently random dating than have *only* random dated in the past. And fewer girls are presently going steady or are pinned/engaged than have gone steady or have been pinned/engaged in the past. The residue of present random daters is accounted for in the two succeeding categories under "Stages of Courtship Participated In" (Random Dated, Gone Steady" and "Random Dated, Gone Steady, Pinned/Engaged"). This means that some of the girls who are presently random dating were once going steady and were once pinned/engaged.

Since it is known that the early daters (random daters) are assertive and the later daters (pinned/engaged) are receptive, one would guess that one of the main reasons for the negative exchange is the failure, on the part of some later daters, to shift from assertiveness to receptivity. One can visualize a learning cycle wherein girls learn through trial and error to become receptive. If they do not become receptive, they never get married. Admittedly, the foregoing is a very strong statement, but the evidence in Table 2 shows that most of the later daters are not assertive, and most of the early daters are not receptive in spite of the fact that many of them were once residents of later stages of courtship. Presumably, the later daters who are still assertive will repeat the cycle until they become receptive.

SUMMARY

In order to provide a picture of the foregoing findings, elaborate cross-tabulation procedures (contingency analyses) were performed, the results of which are reported in Table 5. The cross-tabulation involved: (1) dichotomizing each of the variables in the paradigm (except stages of courtship and commitment which were trichotomized); (2) cross-tabulating role behavior with reasons for dating among single females (modal categories were pulled out and placed in column 2); and (3) sequentially cross-tabulating the results in column 2 with present stage of courtship, reference groups, complementarity, commitment, and degree of dissatisfaction. The modal categories were pulled out and placed in column 1, 3, 4, 5, and 6.

Such a picture makes it quite clear that the six hypotheses raised at the outset are credible. Now it is possible to summarize the major findings of this study. The findings are as follows:

1. There is a tendency for the girls in this study to random date first, to go steady second, and to become pinned/engaged third or last.

TABLE 5

Summary

Socialization Sequence: Stages of Courtship	Relationship Between Role Behavior—Reasons for Dating	Reference-Group Orientation	Degree of Complementarity	Degree of Commitment	Degree of Satisfaction with Dating Role
1. Random Dating	Assertive—Recreation	Original Family, Peer Group	Complementary Plus	Low/ Medium	Satisfied
2. Going Steady	Assertive Receptive— Mate Selection	Original Family, Peer Group	Complementary Plus	Medium	Satisfied/ Dissatisfied
3. Pinned/Engaged	Receptive—Anticipatory Socialization	Self and Boyfriend	Complementary Plus	Medium/ High	Dissatisfied

2. There is a tendency for girls in this study to be assertive in the first stage (random dating) and receptive in the last stage (pinned/engaged). They are assertive-receptive in the second stage (going steady).

3. There is a tendency for girls in this study who are assertive to be original-family and peer-group oriented, complementary plus, low-medium in commitment, and mostly satisfied-dissatisfied with their dating roles.

4. There is a tendency for girls in this study who and receptive to be original-family and personally and boyfriend oriented, complementary plus, medium-high in commitment, and mostly dissatisfied with their dating roles.

It is believed that some of the intervening variables cause assertiveness, some result from assertiveness and cause receptivity, and some result from receptivity. However, further research is needed to assess the exact causal status of the intervening variable set.

5. There is a tendency for girls in this study who are in the first, second, and third stages of courtship to give recreation, mate selection, and anticipatory socialization, respectively, as their primary reasons for dating.

6. There is a tendency for the girls in this study who give recreation as their primary reason for dating to be assertive. They are probably participating in the first stage of the courtship socialization sequence (random dating). This is consistent with Waller and Gorer's Assertive school with regard to reason for dating and role behavior.

7. There is a tendency for the girls in this study who give mate selection as their primary reason for dating to be assertive-receptive. They are probably participating in the second stage of the courtship socialization sequence (going steady). This is consistent with Burgess and Locke's Assertive-Receptive school with regard to reason for dating and role behavior.

8. There is a tendency for the girls in this study who give anticipatory socialization as their primary reasons for dating to be receptive. They are probably participating in the third stage of the courtship socialization sequence (pinned/engaged). This is consistent with Lowrie's Receptive school with regard to reason for dating and role behavior.

Assertive dating behavior does not undermine the functions of courtship, but contributes to specialized aspects of them, i.e., recreation and mate selection.

9. Tentatively, evidence is offered to the effect that girls in this study do learn to be receptive. If they are not receptive in the early stages, they probably have a lot of fun while dating. If they are not receptive in the later stages, they either regress to earlier stages, or at least they fail to progress to more advanced stages. Such a phenomenon is enhanced by the males' strong dislike for girls who are assertive in the later stages.

A single testing of a theory is never definitive. Each hypothesis included in a theory is always threatened by the possibility of its rejection. Such a possibility is allowable only through an appeal to more research. A single testing only heightens the awareness that further research, to be useful, should be conducted with different and more sophisticated methods. In the present study, a college population, the use of the questionnaire technique, the use of percentages, and the use of ordinal statistics may have presented impediments to the validity of the findings. Further testing of the theory in this study must attempt to avoid these limitations.

NOTES

* This paper is based on the author's doctoral dissertation, "Relationships between Female Dating Roles and Reasons for Dating" (unpublished Ph.D. dissertation, University of Pittsburgh, 1967). The author is grateful for the advice of Robert W. Avery, Jiri Nehnevajsa, Morris Berkowitz, Ray Elling, Howard Rowland, and Jacquelyn A. Alford in preparing the dissertation. Data for the study were gathered from December, 1966, through February, 1967.

[1] An assertive girl is one who takes the initiative or acts as aggressor in most dating activities.

[2] Henry A. Bowman, *Marriage for Moderns* (New York: McGraw Hill Book Company, Inc., 1960), pp. 9 and 128.

[3] Robert D. Herman, "The Going Steady Complex: A Re-Examination," *Marriage and Family Living*, 17 (1955), pp. 92–98.

[4] A receptive girl is one who is responsive in most dating activities to male initiative.

[5] Leona E. Tyler, *The Psychology of Human Differences* (2nd ed.; New York: Appleton-Century-Crofts, Inc., 1956), p. 310.

[6] William J. Cameron and William F. Kenkel, "High School Dating: A Study in Variation," *Marriage and Family Living*, 22 (1960), pp. 74–76.

[7] Lester Hewitt, "Student Perceptions of Traits Desired," *Marriage and Family Living*, 20 (1958), pp. 344–349.

[8] Only three stages of courtship were used in this study: random dating, going steady, and pinned/engaged.

[9] Three types of dating roles were used in this study: assertive, assertive-receptive, and receptive. The assertive-receptive role type is manifest when the girl alternates about evenly between assertiveness and receptivity.

[10] Other factors used in this study were three types of reference sources (original family, peer group, and personal-boyfriend), degree of dissatisfaction with dating role, commitment to boyfriend, and complementarity of girl's and boyfriend's personality traits.

[11] Three reasons for dating were used in this study: recreation, mate selection, and anticipatory socialization (training to become good marriage mates).

[12] John C. Flanagan, *The Critical Incident Technique* (Pittsburgh: The American Institutes for Research, July, 1954).

[13] There is clear evidence that expressed value positions do provide insight into behavior. See, for example, Winston Ehrmann, *Premarital Dating Behavior* (New

York: Henry Holt and Co., 1959), pp. 213–276. In this section of his book, Ehrmann provides convincing evidence that girls' most intimate courtship behavior correlates quite well their expressed personal codes about intimate courtship behavior.

[14] Robert F. Winch, Thomas Ktsanes, and Virginia Ktsanes, "Empirical Elaboration of the Theory of Complementary Needs in Mate Selection," *Journal of Abnormal and Social Psychology,* 51 (1955), pp. 508–518.

[15] *Ibid.,* p. 513.

[16] *Ibid.,* pp. 509–513. Winch and his associates defined each need (n) and each trait (t) behaviorally as follows: a. *achievement* (n)—to work diligently to create something and/or to emulate others; b. *autonomy* (n)—to get rid of constraint of other persons or to be unattached and independent; c. *dominance* (n)—to influence and control the behavior of others; d. *hostility* (n)—to fight, injure, or kill others; e. *status aspiration* (n)—to desire a socioeconomic status considerably higher than one has; f. *status striving* (n)—to work diligently to alter one's socioeconomic status; g. *abasement* (n)—to accept or invite blame, criticism, or punishment or to blame or harm the self; h. *deference* (n)—to admire and praise another; i. *succorance* (n) —to help sympathetically; to nurse, to love, to protect, to indulge; j. *vicariousness* (t)—the gratification of a need derived from the perception that another person is deriving gratification; k. *approach* (n)—to draw near and enjoy interaction with another person or persons; and l. *anxiety* (n)—fear, conscious or unconscious, of harm or misfortune arising from the hostility of others and/or social reactions to one's behavior.

[17] From a strict role standpoint, these two concepts may appear to be polar extremes of a single continuum and thus analytically inseparable. From a behavioral and empirical standpoint, however, the two concepts comprise two separate continua, because a given act can only be either assertive or receptive. Since a role is manifest by acts, by modal definition it may be either of the three role types.

[18] *Original-family orientation*—From among the ten items used to measure the extent of orientation to the original family, only one proved non-scalable. The ten items were hypothetical activities wherein the respondents were asked to indicate how they would be affected if their parents (or parent substitutes) disapproved of their participation in the activities. The nine remaining items yielded a Coefficient of Reproducibility of .911 and a Minimal Marginal Reproducibility of .699. The nine items—arranged in the order of their decreasing attractiveness—were the ones concerning the respondents' (1) bcoming engaged, (2) dating a particular person, (3) dating, (4) petting on dates, (5) going to the movies with a date, (6) attending a football or basketball game with a date, (7) talking to strange boys, (8) studying along with a boy, and (9) having lunch with a boy.

Peer Orientation—The extent of peer-group orientation was measured by asking respondents to indicate how they would be affected if their age-association sex group (peer group) disapproved of their participation in the same ten hypothetical activities used in measuring the extent of original-family orientation. Again, only one item proved non-scalable. In this case, the Coefficient of Reproducibility was .925 and the Minimal Marginal Reproducibility was .753. The nine scalable items—in the order of their decreasing impact on the respondents assuming their peer groups' disapproval —were the ones concerning their (1) becoming engaged, (2) dating a particular person, (3) dating, (4) petting on dates, (5) talking to strange boys, (6) going to the movies with a date, (7) attending a football or basketball game with a date, (8) having lunch with a boy, and (9) studying alone with a boy.

Personal Orientation—Ten items were used to measure the extent to which the respondents evaluate and determine their own dating behavior. All of the items scaled except two. With a Coefficient of Reproducibility of .915 and a Minimal Marginal Reproducibility of .832, the eight scalable items—in the order of their decreasing attractiveness—were concerned with whether the respondent (1) would prefer to be the sole determiner of whether or not to pet on dates, (2) would enjoy having interesting experiences on dates in spite of whether or not they could be related to friends, (3) would prefer not to discuss with friends the fact of their having sexual intercourse on dates, (4) would disregard her friends' opinions if she wished to hold hands on dates, (5) would prefer to be the sole determiner of whether her dating conduct was rewarding to her, (6) would prefer not to have her friends around when she is with her date, (7) would rather go to the movies alone with her date, and (8) would prefer going to games alone with her date.

The Extent of Satisfaction with Dating Role—Ten items were used to measure the extent of satisfaction-dissatisfaction with the dating situation. Only five of them did not scale.Those which did scale yielded a Coefficient of Reproducibility of .900 and a Minimal Marginal Reproducibility of .666. The five items included in the scale —in the order of their decreasing attractiveness—concerned whether the respondent would be disturbed if she found it necessary to (1) ask her date to talk to her when he is obviously preoccupied in conversation with someone else, (2) ask her date for another date, (3) "pay the tab" for her and her date's dinners, (4) tell her date where the two of them are to go on a date, and (5) straighten her date's tie, hat, hair, etc.

Commitment to Dating Partner—Twenty-one items were used to measure the extent of commitment to dating partner. Ten of these did not scale. With a Coefficient of Reproducibility of .918 and a Minimal Marginal Reproducibility of .774, the eleven items which did scale—in the order of their decreasing attractiveness—were those concerned with whether the respondent would comply, if her dating partner wished her to (1) run an errand for him, (2) correct her general, apparently disorderly conduct, (3) raise her scholastic average, (4) travel a long distance to visit his parents, (5) help him pass a test, (6) "pay the tab" for their dinners, (7) give him expensive presents, (8) defy her parents, (9) change her religious preference, (10) change her political preference, and (11) ostracize a long-time friend.

Complementarity of Traits—Complementarity of traits was measured by combining a scale of traits desired in a date with a scale of perceived traits of respondent's date. *Traits Desired in a Date*—Ten items were used to measure traits desired in a date. These were incorporated in the questionnaire as a list of traits, and respondents were asked to indicate whether or not they desired each one in an ideal date. Five of them did not scale. Yielding a Coefficient of Reproducibility of .900 and a Minimal Marginal Reproducibility of .690, the five traits which did scale—in the order of their decreasing attractiveness—were: (1) emotional maturity, (2) stability and dependability, (3) affection, (4) industriousness, and (5) family-mindedness. *Perceived Traits of Respondent's Date*—The same ten traits used in measuring traits desired in a date were used to measure perceived traits of date. The only difference is that this time the respondents were asked to indicate whether or not they thought their dates actually possessed the traits. None of the traits proved non-scalable, and at the outset a Coefficient of Reproducibility of .900 and a Minimal Marginal Reproducibility of .730 were obtained. In the order of their decreasing attractiveness, the traits were as follows: (1) neat appearance and good manners, (2) pleasantness of disposition, (3) physical attractiveness, (4) considerateness, (5) affection, (6) industriousness, (7) poise and confidence, (8) stability and dependability, (9) emotional maturity, and (10) family-mindedness.

[19] See Talcott Parsons and Robert F. Bales, *The Family, Socialization, and the Interaction Process* (Glencoe, Illinois: The Free Press, 1955).

[20] *Ibid.*

[21] *Ibid.*

[22] Clyde O. McDaniel, Jr., "Relationships among Female Dating Roles and Reasons for Dating" (unpublished Ph.D. dissertation, University of Pittsburgh, 1967), p. 135.

[23] Robert H. Lowrie, "Dating Theories and Student Responses," *American Sociological Review*, 16 (1951), pp. 334–340.

[24] These three schools can be abstracted from a careful reading of the following sources: Willard Waller, *The Family: A Dynamic Interpretation* (New York: Holt,

Rinehart, and Winston, 1938); Geoffrey Gorer, *The American People* (New York: W. W. Norton and Company, 1948); Ernest Burgess and Harvey Locke, *The Family: From Institution to Companionship* (New York: American Book Company, 1945); and Samuel H. Lowrie, "Dating Theories and Student Responses," *American Sociological Review*, 16 (1951), pp. 334–340.

[25] Waller, *The Family;* and Gorer, *The American People.*

[26] Burgess and Locke, *The Family.*

[27] Lowrie, "Dating Theories and Student Responses."

[28] The attitudes of males toward female assertiveness and female receptivity were assessed by asking the 181 single males in the study to respond to the same items which were used to measure assertiveness and receptivity among females. For both attitudes toward female assertiveness and attitude toward female receptivity, about half of the items had to be discarded in order to obtain Coefficients of Reproducibility of .90. The items which were retained were identical with those included in the scales of assertive and receptive dating behavior among females.

Early Dating and Early Marriage*

ALAN E. BAYER

The dating process has often been viewed as an "educational experience" which aids the individual in developing sound criteria for future mate selection. Dating is viewed as providing the individual with additional maturity in heterosexual relationships as well as greater acquaintance with his own motives and needs and those of others. The anticipated result is acquired sophistication in sorting the field of eligible mates and in selecting a future spouse. Those who maintain this position may often promote early dating as an important means to avoid later personal and social handicaps.

Others have taken a contrasting view, maintaining that early dating among American young people has "robbed them of their childhood" and forced them to "grow up too soon." Early dating is also assumed to lead to early marriage and subsequent increased probability of marital discord.[1] The conclusions derived from the available research evidence have generally supported this contention, but the documentation has usually been based on small samples drawn from relatively homogeneous populations of a local school district or an academic institution. Moreover, retrospective data, acquired at only one point in time, have often been employed in place of a longitudinal design to assess antecedent conditions.[2]

The present paper partially overcomes these limitations of earlier research and focuses on the relationship between early dating and age at marriage.[3] The study employs data from a large national sample and incorporates a longitudinal design.

THE DATA

In 1960 the American Institutes for Research, with support from the Cooperative Research Program of the United States Office of Education, initiated "Project TALENT," a nationwide study of American youth.[4] Approximately 73,000 twelfth-grade students in a stratified random sample of schools throughout the United States completed the two-day battery of tests and inventories in the spring of 1960. One-year and five-year follow-ups of this sample have been undertaken, and ten- and

Reprinted from *Journal of Marriage and the Family,* November 1968, 628–32.

20-year follow-ups are planned. This paper is based primarily on the data from the five-year follow-up, to which approximately 39,000 individuals responded. Of these, 32,833 had usable questionnaires with complete information on the variables employed in the current analysis (sex, date of birth, socioeconomic status, age at first date, marital status, and date of marriage if married).[5]

The socioeconomic index is constructed from nine separate items reported by the students in 1960. The index is composed of items on family income, father's occupation, educational level of the parents, and the number of specified family possessions.[6] In this report the respondents are classified into one of five relatively evenly distributed groups.

Age at First Date

The age at first date is also derived from the 1960 survey data. While these data are thus also post hoc, thereby introducing the obvious restrictions of retrospective information, the information is collected *prior* to marriage and in closer proximity to the actual event than is the case in most previous research. It can, therefore, be assumed that these event data are relatively accurate reports of the age of actual occurrence. For the total sample, 9,287 (57.0 percent) of the 16,299 males and 9,633 (58.3 percent) of the 16,534 females reported first dating before the age of 15. These distributions closely approximate those of the total population of 1960 high-school seniors from which the sample was drawn. In the total population, an estimated 55.9 percent of the boys and 56.2 percent of the girls reported first dating before age 15.[7]

The age at which dating begins has been shown to be related to socioeconomic status. Early dating is particularly prevalent among higher socioeconomic groups.[8] In the present sample, while substantially more than one-half of both the boys and the girls in the lowest socioeconomic quintile had not begun to date by age 15, only about 30 percent of the boys and one-fourth of the girls from the highest socioeconomic quintile had not dated before reaching age 15 (Table 1). With increasing socioeconomic level there is a consistent concomitant *decrease* in the proportion of young people delaying dating ($C_{adj.} = (-) .26$ for males; $C_{adj.} = (-) .29$ for females).[9]

Age at Marriage

The current age at first marriage in the United States averages 22.7 years for males and 20.3 years for females.[10] For the present sample, age at marriage is determined from the five-year follow-up items requesting marital status and date of marriage. If married, the age at marriage is derived by computing the difference between the birth date and the reported date of marriage. This computation indicates that the median age at marriage for those in the sample is higher than that for the general population, being more than 23 years of age for the men and 22.4 years of age for the women. This relatively high average age at marriage is primarily a function of the exclusion of most high-school dropouts from the sampling frame.

TABLE 1

Age at Commencement of Dating and Socioeconomic Status, by Sex: 1960 High-School Seniors

Sex and Socioeconomic Status	Age at First Date							
	≤ 12		13–14		≥ 15		Total	
	N	%	N	%	N	%	N	%
Male[1]								
Low SES	313	9.1	1,157	33.6	1,972	57.3	3,442	100.0
Low Middle SES	341	11.4	1,218	40.8	1,423	47.7	2,982	100.0
Middle SES	484	14.1	1,443	42.1	1,504	43.8	3,431	100.0
High Middle SES	375	16.1	1,055	45.4	893	38.4	2,323	100.0
High SES	976	23.7	1,925	46.7	1,200	29.6	4,121	100.0
Total	2,489	15.3	6,798	41.7	7,012	43.0	16,299	100.0
Female[2]								
Low SES	177	4.8	1,377	37.3	2,137	57.9	3,691	100.0
Low Middle SES	250	8.0	1,367	43.8	1,505	48.2	3,122	100.0
Middle SES	392	11.0	1,751	49.2	1,414	39.8	3,557	100.0
High Middle SES	345	14.5	1,207	50.6	831	34.9	2,383	100.0
High SES	718	19.0	2,049	54.2	1,014	26.8	3,781	100.0
Total	1,882	11.4	7,751	46.9	6,901	41.7	16,534	100.0

[1] df = 8; Chi-square = 759.6; p < .001; C = .21; $C_{adj.}$ = (−).26
[2] df = 8; Chi-square = 1,011.8; p < .001; C = .24; $C_{adj.}$ = (−).29
Note: See textual footnote 9 for Specification of $C_{adj.}$

The age at marriage is also highly related to socioeconomic status, with early marriage particularly prevalent among the lower socio-economic groups.[11] If early marriage is defined as below the median age at first marriage for the total population (*before* age 23 for men and *before* age 21 for women), in the current sample 5,571 (34.2 percent) of the boys and 5,282 (31.9 percent) of the girls have married early. By socioeconomic status, approximately two-fifths of both the boys and the girls from the lowest socioeconomic homes married early. In contrast, only about one-fourth of the boys and one-fifth of the girls from the highest socioeconomic quintile married early (Table 2).[12] With in-creasing socioeconomic level, there is a consistent concomitant *increase*

TABLE 2

Age at Marriage and Socioeconomic Status, by Sex

Sex and Socioeconomic Status	Age at First Marriage								Not Married Before Age 23		Total	
	≤19		20		21		22					
	N	%	N	%	N	%	N	%	N	%	N	%
Male[1]												
Low SES	269	7.8%	300	8.7%	405	11.8%	389	11.3%	2,079	60.4%	3,442	100.0
Low Middle SES	182	6.1	207	6.9	311	10.4	367	12.3	1,915	64.2	2,982	100.0
Middle SES	176	5.1	250	7.3	375	10.9	423	12.3	2,207	64.3	3,431	100.0
High Middle SES	84	3.6	134	5.8	234	10.1	323	13.9	1,548	66.6	2,323	100.0
High SES	129	3.1	156	3.8	325	7.9	532	12.9	2,979	72.3	4,121	100.0
Total	840	5.2	1,047	6.4	1,650	10.1	2,034	12.5	10,728	65.8	16,299	100.0
Female[2]												
Low SES	986	26.7	460	12.5	473	12.8	359	9.7	1,413	38.3	3,691	100.0
Low Middle SES	681	21.8	433	13.9	386	12.4	356	11.4	1,266	40.6	3,122	100.0
Middle SES	744	20.9	493	13.9	466	13.1	425	11.9	1,429	40.2	3,557	100.0
High Middle SES	375	15.7	334	14.0	340	14.3	330	13.8	1,004	42.1	2,383	100.0
High SES	383	10.1	393	10.4	483	12.8	661	17.5	1,861	49.2	3,781	100.0
Total	3,169	19.2	2,113	12.8	2,148	13.0	2,131	12.9	6,973	42.2	16,534	100.0

[1] df = 16; Chi-square = 260.0; p < .001; C = .13; $C_{adj.}$ = (+).14
[2] df = 16; Chi-square = 504.3; p < .001; C = .17; $C_{adj.}$ = (+).19
Note: See textual footnote 9 for specification of $C_{adj.}$.

in the proportion of people delaying marriage ($C_{adj.} = (+)$ .14 for males; $C_{adj.} = (+)$ .19 for females).

FINDINGS

Inasmuch as it has been shown above that (a) age at initiating dating tends to become earlier as socioeconomic level rises, and (b) age at marriage tends to become later as socioeconomic level rises, it may be expected that as a sample becomes more heterogeneous with respect to socioeconomic background (i.e., more representative of the total population) the strength of the relationship between age at beginning to date and age at marriage will diminish. This result is shown in Table 3 for the present sample. While early dating is related to early marriage, the relationship is a fairly weak one for this specified age cohort which approximates a representative sample of the population ($C_{ajd.} = (+)$ .09 for males; $C_{ajd.} = (+)$ .16 for females).

The consideration of socioeconomic level is, therefore, crucial to any generalized statement of relationships between early dating and early marriage. Moreover, what is now known of the relationship between these two variables has been based almost exclusively on small homogeneous samples of middle-class adults. "In principal, we know nothing at all about this important relationship in the balance of the society."[13] Indeed, a central concern of this paper is the question: "Does the relationship between early dating and early marriage hold within all socioeconomic strata of the society?"

The results from this nationwide sample of American youth are indicative of an affirmative answer to this question. In all of the socioeconomic strata, for both sexes, those who began dating early (prior to age 15) had a higher rate of early marriage (prior to age 23 for men and prior to age 21 for women) than did those who began dating at a later age (Table 4).

DISCUSSION

One of the most consistently demonstrated findings in family research has been that of a strong relationship between early marriage and poor adjustment to marriage. Those who have experienced early marriage are considerably more likely to experience greater marital discord, including less marital satisfaction and more marital dissolution, than are those who marry at a later age.[14] It is also those in the lower socioeconomic strata who experience the greatest marital disruption.[15]

In light of these findings, the results of this present study yield questionable conclusions with regard to the ultimate relationship between early dating and marital outcomes. Early dating is related to

TABLE 3

Age at Marriage and Age at Commencement of Dating, by Sex

Sex and Age at First Date	Age at First Marriage									Not Married Before Age 23		Total	
	≤19		20		21		22						
	N	%	N	%	N	%	N	%	N	%	N	%	
Male[1]													
≤12	155	6.2	179	7.2	278	11.2	354	14.2	1,523	61.2	2,489	100.0	
13–14	403	5.9	465	6.8	720	10.6	894	13.2	4,316	63.5	6,798	100.0	
≥15	282	4.0	403	5.7	652	9.3	786	11.2	4,889	69.7	7,012	100.0	
Total	840	5.2	1,047	6.4	1,650	10.1	2,034	12.5	10,728	65.8	16,299	100.0	
Female[2]													
≤12	410	21.8	257	13.6	266	14.1	272	14.4	677	36.0	1,882	100.0	
13–14	1,673	21.6	1,093	14.1	1,088	14.0	1,007	13.0	2,890	37.3	7,751	100.0	
≥15	1,086	15.7	763	11.1	794	11.5	852	12.3	3,406	49.4	6,901	100.0	
Total	3,169	19.2	2,113	12.8	2,148	13.0	2,131	12.9	6,973	42.2	16,534	100.0	

Note columns: N, % under each "Age at First Marriage" subcategory and "Not Married Before Age 23" and "Total".

[1] df = 8; Chi-square = 96.4; p < .001; C = .08; $C_{adj.}$ = (+).09
[2] df = 8; Chi-square = 271.3; p < .001; C = .13; $C_{adj.}$ = (+).16
Note: See textual footnote 9 for the specification of $C_{adj.}$.

TABLE 4
Age at Commencement of Dating and Early Marriage,[1] by Socioeconomic Status and Sex

Sex and Socioeconomic Status	Age at First Date											
	≤12			13–14			≥15			Total		
	Total N	N Married Early	% Married Early	Total N	N Married Early	% Married Early	Total N	N Married Early	% Married Early	Total N	N Married Early	% Married Early
Male												
Low SES	313	144	46.0%	1,157	520	44.9%	1,972	699	35.4%	3,442	1,363	39.6%
Low Middle SES	341	155	45.4	1,218	485	39.8	1,423	427	30.0	2,982	1,067	35.8
Middle SES	484	210	43.4	1,443	551	38.2	1,504	463	30.8	3,431	1,224	35.7
High Middle SES	375	146	38.9	1,055	375	35.5	893	254	28.4	2,323	775	33.4
High SES	976	311	31.9	1,925	551	28.6	1,220	280	22.9	4,121	1,142	27.7
Total	2,489	966	38.8	6,798	2,482	36.5	7,012	2,123	30.3	16,299	5,571	34.2
Female												
Low SES	177	85	48.0	1,377	672	48.8	2,137	689	32.2	3,691	1,446	39.2
Low Middle SES	250	114	45.6	1,367	565	41.3	1,505	435	28.9	3,122	1,114	35.7
Middle SES	392	168	42.9	1,751	684	39.1	1,414	385	27.2	3,557	1,237	34.8
High Middle SES	345	124	35.9	1,207	396	32.8	831	189	22.7	2,383	709	29.8
High SES	718	176	24.5	2,049	449	21.9	1,014	151	14.9	3,781	776	20.5
Total	1,882	667	35.4%	7,751	2,766	35.7%	6,901	1,849	26.8%	16,534	5,282	31.9%

[1] Early marriage is defined as marriage before age 23 for men and before age 21 for women.

early marriage, which implies greater marital instability; but early dating is also more prevalent among those from higher socioeconomic backgrounds, where subsequent marital instability is generally less frequent.

These apparent contradictions imply that family life educators and practitioners should possibly hold in abeyance any conclusion regarding the relationship between early dating and any long-range criterion of marital success. Indeed, any such conclusion may prove as fallacious as may be one which suggests that early marriage *causes* marital failure, when it may actually be that those with the poorest chance of achieving a satisfying marriage are more likely to marry early.

A more compelling conclusion from the current data is that the age at commencement of dating is largely *unrelated* to any particular future marital outcome. Rather, it is the *length* of the dating experience prior to marriage which may have a crucial impact on subsequent outcome. Such a hypothesis is consistent with the fact that those in the lower socioeconomic strata begin dating later, but have a shorter hiatus from commencement of dating to marriage, and experience greater marital instability than do those from higher socioeconomic groups. This hypothesis is also consistent with the prevalent theory of dating; viz., dating is an educational experience through which the skills required for valid mate selection and the personal growth necessary for sufficient "marriage readiness" are cumulatively acquired over time.

NOTES

* The research reported here was partially supported by grants from the Carnegie Corporation and the Russell Sage Foundation to the Commission on Human Resources and Advanced Education. Additional support was derived from Project TALENT, a cooperative effort of the United States Office of Education, the University of Pittsburgh, and the American Institutes for Research. The author is grateful to Al Carp, Karl King, and Ivan Nye for several suggested revisions of an earlier draft of this paper. The data employed in this paper were collected in 1960 and 1965. Analyses for this paper were completed in October, 1967.

[1] For a further discussion of these contrasting opinions, see Samuel H. Lowrie, "Early and Late Dating: Some Conditions Associated with Them," Chapter 16 in *Kinship and Family Organization*, ed. by Bernard Farber, New York: John Wiley, 1966, pp. 181–189.

[2] A fairly complete recent bibliography of studies relating dating experience to marital outcomes is presented by Karen Winch Bartz and F. Ivan Nye, "Age at Marriage—A Formulation from Axiomatic Theory," paper presented at the annual meeting of the American Sociological Association, Miami Beach, Florida, August, 1966. An extended critique of these studies and family research in general is presented in F. Ivan Nye and Alan E. Bayer, "Some Recent Trends in Family Research," *Social Forces*, 41 (March, 1963), pp. 290–301.

[3] Additional analysis of the relationship between age at marriage and dating

practices, including dating frequency and "steady" dating experiences, is the subject of another paper currently in progress. Another follow-up of this sample is also scheduled in 1970, after which a report is planned on how age at marriage and these dating practices are related to marital instability.

[4] An extensive discussion of the development of Project TALENT, sampling design, and the testing instruments is presented in John C. Flanagan *et al., Design for a Study of American Youth,* Boston: Houghton-Mifflin, 1962.

[5] While these cases yield a cross-section of this age cohort, it is not a completely representative sample of this group in the population. The sampling frame (twelfth grade high-school students), the varying sampling ratios for the various high-school strata and the non-respondent biases yield an unweighted sample which is slightly skewed toward the higher socioeconomic groups, those who begin dating somewhat earlier than the general population and marry somewhat later than the United States population (see text for a further discussion of these differences). Nevertheless, while these data must be interpreted with caution if population parameters are to be estimated, they appear sufficiently representative for assessing the relationship between variables.

[6] A detailed description of this socioeconomic index is presented in Marion F. Shaycoft, *The High School Years: Growth in Cognitive Skills,* Cooperative Research Project No. 3051, Pittsburgh: American Institutes for Research and the University of Pittsburgh, 1967, Appendix E.

[7] John C. Flanagan *et al., The American High School Student,* Cooperative Research Project No. 635, Pittsburgh: American Institutes for Research and the University of Pittsburgh, 1964, pp. 5–9.

[8] See, for example, Lowrie, *op. cit.*

[9] While the variables employed may be conceptualized as continuous, the classification system employed and the open-ended nature of some of the items required treating them as discrete variables. As a consequence, Pearson's coefficient of contingency (C) is employed as an approximation of the actual correlation coefficients. As C has a lower limit of 0 when there is complete lack of association and may approach but not equal unity when variables show complete dependence, with $C_{max.}$ dependent upon the number of rows and columns, the attained value of C is divided by $C_{max.}$ to yield $C_{adj.}$ which has a range of 0 to 1 and yields generally comparable statistics. Signs of the direction of the relationships are added by the author. The formula for computing the upper limit of C for any r by k table is presented in Maurice G. Kendall and Alan Stuart, *The Advanced Theory of Statistics,* Vol. 2, New York: Hafner, 1961, pp. 556–559. A discussion of $C_{adj.}$ is also presented in Sidney Siegel, *Nonparametric Statistics for the Behavioral Sciences,* New York: McGraw-Hill, 1956, pp. 196–202; and Hubert M. Blalock, Jr., *Social Statistics,* New York: McGraw-Hill, 1960, pp. 230–231.

[10] The reported figures are medians for 1962, based on Current Population Survey data supplemented by data from the Department of Defense for men. See U.S. Bureau of the Census, "Marital Status and Family Status: March, 1962," *Current Population Reports—Population Characteristics,* Series P-20, No. 105, Washington, D.C.: U.S. Government Printing Office, March 22, 1963, p. 2. Somewhat lower estimates of median ages at first marriage are reported by J. R. Rele, "Trends and Differentials in the American Age at Marriage," *Milbank Memorial Fund Quarterly,* 43 (April, 1965), pp. 219–234.

[11] See, for example, Lee G. Burchinal, "Research on Young Marriage: Implications for Family Life Education," *Family Life Coordinator,* 9 (September, 1960), pp. 6–24; Robert J. Havighurst *et al., Growing Up in River City,* New York: John Wiley, 1962, pp. 120–121; and Lee G. Burchinal and Loren E. Chancellor, "Social Status, Religious Affiliation, and Ages at Marriage," *Marriage and Family Living,* 25 (May, 1963), pp. 219–221.

[12] In table 2 and the subsequent tables, those not married by the time of the five-year follow-up are assumed in this analysis to marry "late." In actuality, some of

those in this group will never marry, and thus the reported relationships may partially reflect differences between those who marry and those who do not ever marry. However, an analysis analogous to that herein reported, but restricted to only those in the sample who had reported being married by the time of the five-year follow-up, yields similar outcomes and conclusions to those discussed in this paper based on the full sample.

[13] Nye and Bayer, op. cit., p. 298. The implication of this statement in the present context is that socioeconomic status may act as a *moderator* variable, with the relationship between age at marriage and age at commencement of dating varying, or actually *reversing*, among different socioeconomic strata. See the discussion of possible moderator effects in David R. Saunders, "Moderator Variables in Prediction," *Educational and Psychological Measurement*, 16 (Summer, 1956), pp. 209–222; and Marilyn C. Lee, "Interactions, Configurations, and Nonadditive Models," *Educational and Psychological Measurement*, 21 (Winter, 1961), pp. 797–805.

[14] For reviews of these various studies, see Burchinal, op. cit.; Rachel M. Inselberg, "Social and Psychological Factors Associated with High School Marriages," *Journal of Home Economics*, 43 (November, 1961), pp. 766–772; and J. Richard Udry, *The Social Context of Marriage* (Philadelphia: Lippincott, 1966), pp. 317–321. See also Paul C. Glick, *American Families*, New York: Wiley, 1957; and Karl E. Bauman, "The Relationship Between Age at First Marriage, School Dropout, and Marital Instability: An Analysis of the Glick Effect," *Journal of Marriage and the Family*, 29:4 (November, 1967), pp. 672–680.

[15] August B. Hollingshead, "Class Differences in Family Stability," in *Class, Status, and Power*, ed. by Reinhard Bendix and Seymour Martin Lipset (New York: Free Press, 1953), pp. 284–292; J. Richard Udry, "Marital Instability by Race, Sex, Education, and Occupation Using 1960 Census Data," *American Journal of Sociology*, 72 (September, 1966), pp. 203–209; Jessie Bernard, "Marital Stability and Patterns of Status Variables," *Journal of Marriage and the Family*, 28:4 (November, 1966), pp. 421–439; and J. Richard Udry, "Marital Instability by Race and Income Based on 1960 Census Data," *American Journal of Sociology*, 72 (May, 1967), pp. 673–674.

Transition in Sex Values—Implications for the Education of Adolescents*

ISADORE RUBIN

This paper concerns the kind of education which the United States as a pluralistic society can give to adolescents and young adults in its various educational institutions. The concern is *not* with our private set of values either as individuals or parents, but rather with a philosophy of sex education for a democratic society.

THE CONFUSION OF TRANSITION

Family professionals may not agree on the causes of the change, the extent, or the direction, but they do agree that there has been a great transition in sex values in the 20th century. Evelyn Duvall has characterized this transition as "a basic shift from sex denial to sex affirmation throughout our culture."[1]

This transition from sex denial to sex affirmation has not been an easy or smooth one. American culture historically has been rooted in the ideal of asceticism, and only slowly and with a good deal of rear-guard opposition is this philosophy being relinquished. Most official attitudes today still constitute what a distinguished British jurist called "a legacy of the ascetic ideal, persisting in the modern world after the ideal has decreased."[2] As a result of the conflict and confusion inherent in the transition of sex values, there exists today an interregnum of sex values which are accepted in theory and in practice by the great majority of Americans.

The confusion is especially great among those who are responsible for the guidance of youth. Last year Teachers' College together with the National Association of Women Deans and Counselors decided to hold a two-week "Work Conference on Current Sex Mores." Esther Lloyd-Jones, Head of the Department of Guidance and Student Personnel Administration at Teachers' College explained why:

"The reason that made me determine to hold that conference was the repeated statement by deans and counselors—as well as by parents

Reprinted from *Journal of Marriage and the Family*, May 1965, 185–89. Footnotes have been renumbered.

—that the kids were certainly confused in the area of sex mores, but that they thought they were just as confused as the kids. They just plain felt they did not know. They were clearly in no position to give valuational leadership."[3]

It is unnecessary to state that this conference—like many others held before it—did not reach agreement on what the sex mores should be.

THE IMPOSSIBILITY OF CONSENSUS

At the present time, there seems no possibility for our pluralistic society as a whole to reach a consensus about many aspects of sex values. We cannot do it today even on so comparatively simple a problem as the moral right of persons who are married to have free access to contraceptive information, or the right of married couples to engage in any kind of sex play that they desire in the privacy of the marriage bedroom, or even the right of individuals to engage in the private act of masturbation. Certainly we cannot expect to do so on so emotionally laden a problem as premarital sex relations.

Even in NCFR, made up the most sophisticated students of this problem, no consensus has been reached after more than 25 years of debate and dialogue, although, as Jessie Bernard pointed out to NCFR last year, there has been a change. "There was a time," she said, "when those arguing for premarital virginity could be assured of a comfortable margin of support in the group. This is no longer always true. Especially the younger members no longer accept this code."[4]

This change in NCFR thinking reflects the great debate that is taking place on a national and an international scale. This debate reflects the fact that—whether we like it or not—we do not today possess a code of sex beliefs about which we can agree. Significantly, it is not only those who refuse to look to religion for their answers who seek a new value framework for sex. A growing body of religious leaders recognize that our modern sex morality can no longer consist of laws which give a flat yes-or-no answer to every problem of sex. These leaders concede that there are many moral decisions which persons must make for themselves.[5]

THE MAJOR COMPETING VALUE SYSTEMS

This writer has found it of value to define six major conflicting value systems of sex existing side by side in this transitional period of morality.[6] These value systems extend along a broad continuum ranging from extreme asceticism to a completely permissive anarchy. The major ones are characterized as follows: (1) traditional repressive asceticism; (2) enlightened asceticism; (3) humanistic liberalism; (4) humanistic radicalism; (5) fun morality; and (6) sexual anarchy. To discuss each of these very briefly:

1. Traditional repressive asceticism—which is still embodied in most of our official codes and laws—proscribes any kind of sexual activity outside of the marriage relationship and accepts sex in marriage grudgingly, insisting upon the linkage of sex with procreation.[7] This value system is intolerant of all deviations from restrictive patterns of heterosexual behavior, it places a taboo on public and scientific discussion and study of sex, and it conceives of sex morality solely in absolute terms of "Thou shalt" and "Thou shalt not."

2. Enlightened asceticism—as exemplified in the views of such spokesmen as David Mace[8]—begins with a basic acceptance of the ascetic point of view. Mace sees asceticism as a safeguard against the "softness" to which we so easily fall prey in an age when opportunities for self-indulgence are so abundant. He sees youth as the time when invaluable lessons of self-control and discipline must be learned, with sex as one of the supreme areas in which self-mastery may be demonstrated, and he opposes any slackening of the sexual code. However, he takes neither a negative nor a dogmatic attitude toward sex and has been an ardent exponent of the "open forum" in which issues can be stated and weighed.

3. Humanistic liberalism has been best exemplified by the views of Lester Kirkendall.[9] Kirkendall opposes inflexible absolutes and makes his prime concern the concept of interpersonal relationship. He sees the criterion of morality as not the commission or omission of a particular act, but the consequences of the act upon the interrelationships of people, not only the immediate people concerned but broader relationships.

Kirkendall thus is searching for a value system which will help supply internalized controls for the individual in a period when older social and religious controls are collapsing.

4. Humanistic radicalism—exemplified best by the views of Walter Stokes[10]—accepts the humanistic position of Kirkendall and goes further in proposing that society should make it possible for young people to have relatively complete sex freedom. He makes it clear that society must create certain preconditions before this goal may be achieved. He envisions "a cultural engineering project" which may take generations to achieve.

5. Fun morality has as its most consistent spokesman Albert Ellis.[11] Without compromise, he upholds the viewpoint that sex is fun and that the more sex fun a human being has, the better and psychologically sounder he or she is likely to be. He believes that, despite the risk of pregnancy, premarital intercourse should be freely permitted, and at times encouraged, for well-informed and reasonably well-adjusted persons.

6. Sexual anarchy has as its philosopher the late French jurist René Guyon.[12] Guyon attacks chastity, virginity, and monogamy and calls for

the suppression of all anti-sexual taboos and the disappearance of all anti-sexual taboos and the disappearance of the notions of sexual immorality and shame. The only restriction he would apply is the general social principle that no one may injure or do violence to his fellows.

Can educators resolve these competing philosophies of sex? Judging by present disagreements, it is hardly conceivable that a consensus will be possible for a long time to come, even by our best social theorists. In fact, it would be dangerous—on the basis of the fragmentary information we now have—to come to a conclusion too quickly.

EDUCATION VERSUS INDOCTRINATION

What then are the educational implications of the confusion and conflict which exist in this transitional period?

The beginning of wisdom for educators is the recognition of the fact that the old absolutes have gone; that there exists a vacuum of many moral beliefs about sex; and that we cannot ignore the conflicting value systems which are openly contending for the minds not only of adults but particularly of youths.

Our key task—if we are to have a dialogue with youths—is to win and hold their trust. This means that we cannot fob them off with easy, ready-made replies; that we cannot give dishonest answers to their honest questions; that we cannot serve up information tainted with our bias.

If we tell them, for example, that there is only one view concerning the need for sexual chastity, they will quickly learn that there are many views. If we give them false information about any area of sex, they will sooner or later learn that we have lied. If we withhold the available data and merely give them moral preachments, they will nod their heads . . . and seek their answers elsewhere.

Our major educational problem is this: How can we help young people (and ourselves) to find some formula for coping with our dilemmas? How can we help them keep their bearings in a period of rapid and unending change, and help them make intelligent choices among the conflicting value systems?

If we indoctrinate young people with an elaborate set of rigid rules and ready-made formulas, we are only insuring the early obsolescence of these tools. If, on the other hand, we give them the skills and attitudes, the knowledge and understanding that enable them to make their own intelligent choice among competing moral codes, we have given them the only possible equipment to face their future. This type of guidance does not deny that a dilemma exists whenever choices must be made. Each choice commands a price, and the individual must weigh the price to be paid against the advantages to be gained.[13]

There are some adults who would try to hide the obvious from adolescents—that we adults ourselves have no agreement about sex values, that we too are searching. To do this, however, is to forfeit our chance to engage in a dialogue with our youngsters. It is far wiser to admit our own dilemmas and to enlist them frankly in the task of striking a balance in this interim of confusion.

When it comes to sex education, most parents and educators have overlooked a rather simple lesson. The fact of the matter is that we do have a time-tested set of basic principles of democratic guidance that serve us well in many fields, but which are unfortunately laid aside the moment we enter the taboo-laden area of sex.[14]

In teaching politics and government, we do not feel the need to indoctrinate all students into being members of one or another political party. Rather we try to teach them the skills and attitudes which they require to make intelligent choices as adults when faced with a changing world and an array of alternative.

In science and industry, we do not equip them with a set of tools that will be outmoded in a rapidly evolving technology, but try to equip them with skills which can adjust to a changing field.

Certainly indoctrination of moral values is an ineffective educational procedure in a democratic and pluralistic society where a bewildering array of alternatives and conflicting choices confront the individual—particularly in a period of transition.[15]

A DEMOCRATIC VALUE FRAMEWORK

At this point, the writer hastens to say that he is not advocating that we jettison all the moral values that we have developed over the centuries. He would be very loath to abandon anything that has been tested by time, particularly those institutions that have been found to be almost universal. But there have been virtually no universals in sex values, with only the prohibition of incest coming close to being one.[16] And as the anthropologist Murdock pointed out, as a society we have been deviant—not typical—in our past attitudes toward sex and pre-marital chastity.[17]

We do have need for a value framework for sex guidance. Value commitments are necessary for any person who forms part of a social group, and no society can survive without a set of core values which the majority of its members really believe in and act upon.[18] However, it is clear that most of the values represented in the official sex code have left the core of our culture and entered the arena of competing alternatives.

We must then seek our core values for sex education in the core values of a democratic society. These values have been defined as (1) faith in the free play of critical intelligence and respect for truth as a definable moral value; (2) respect for the basic worth, equality, and dignity of each individual; (3) the right of self-determination of each human being; and (4) the recognition of the need for cooperative effort for common good.[19]

The acceptance of a scientific point of view in our thinking about sex ethics would be of inestimable importance in the education of youth. Since a great deal of thinking about sex has been based either on religious values, prejudice, or irrational fears, the consistent application of this point of view would be of tremendous significance in bringing about a re-evaluation of our thinking about sex.

It would imply, first of all, that the effect of practices which are not sanctioned in our official codes would be described objectively and scientifically rather than in terms of special pleading for the official code. Reiss has shown that treatment by leading marriage and family texts of the consequences of premarital intercourse "neglects or misinterprets much of the available empirical evidence.[20] Studies by Gebhard *et al.*[21] (on abortion), Kirkendall[22] (on premarital intercourse), Vincent[23] (on unwed mothers), and other investigators, for example, have shown that behavior contrary to the accepted codes cannot be described solely in terms of negative consequences for individuals engaging in it, even in our present culture.

The application of critical intelligence also implies that moral behavior would be viewed not in terms of obedience to fixed laws, but on the basis of insights from various disciplines "that add to the picture of the world in which man lives and acts, that throw light upon the nature of man and his capacities, social relations, and experiences." It would also mean that adolescent sex activities would be limited for the actual protection of their health and well-being rather than for the protection of adult moral prejudice.[24]

There is no doubt that there is an extremely difficult problem for social control when the individual is allowed a choice in moral behavior. Landis asserts: "In moral codes taboo acts must be condemned regardless of advantages gained by certain individuals or groups who violate them. . . . When acts are no longer forbidden to all, when the individual is authorized to decide whether or not violation will be advantageous, the moral code vanishes."[25]

This is indeed a dilemma for society. Unfortunately, at the present time many of the taboos still present in our official codes are no longer accepted either in precept or in practice by the vast majority of our people. We can take as an obvious example the proscription against birth control. A great debate has been opened on many other aspects of our sexual codes. If we do not equip our adolescents to participate intelligently in this debate, we do not ensure the protection of our moral codes. What we do ensure is that youngsters will have no rationale to enable them to make intelligent decisions.

To advocate autonomy is not necessarily to encourage the flouting of conventional mores or to encourage libertarian behavior. In the absence of fixed and rigorously enforced codes, a great deal of adolescent sexual behavior is determined by the mores of the teen-age subculture. The advocacy of self-determination, therefore, may foster resistance to teen-age pressures rather than to conventional norms.[26]

In short, what the educator must do is not provide ready-made formulas and prepackaged values, but provide knowledge, insight, and values on the basis of which the adolescent may choose for himself with some measure of rationality among competing codes of conduct.[27] In a changing world, we must develop "a frame of mind which can bear the burden of skepticism and does not panic when many of the habits are doomed to vanish."[28]

SEX EDUCATION AND SOCIAL POLICY

In our thinking about sex education and the adolescent, we almost always think solely in functional terms of helping the adolescent cope with his problems and of preparing him for courtship and marriage. We tend to overlook completely the aspect of social policy—the fact that increasing knowledge of all areas of sex is being required of all individuals as citizens.

Issues dealing with all aspects of sex are more and more entering the arena of national and international debate and decision. On an international scale, problems of birth control, venereal disease, and prostitution have been subject to wide-scale discussion and decision. In legislative and legal arenas, with the concomitant aspects of public discussion, there have been sharp conflicts about public policy concerning censorship, pornography, birth control, abortion, illegitimacy, changes in sex laws, homosexuality, and emergent problems like artificial insemination.

All of these require for their solution an informed citizenry sufficiently open-minded to make required decisions on the basis of rational consideration rather than prejudice and irrationality.

SUMMARY

In summarizing the major tasks of sex guidance of the adolescent, the writer would like to repeat the proposals which he made to the Deans' Workshop on Changing Sexual Mores at Teachers' College last year:

1. Create the "open forum" that Mace has emphasized in the family life field. Do not attempt to hide the obvious from college students—that major value conflicts exist in our society and that no consensus exists among adults. Enlist students to take responsibility for helping resolve the confusion inherent in the transition of values. Re-evaluate texts and curricula so that in this field, as in others, the principles of scientific objectivity will hold.

2. Apply the time-tested and traditionally accepted principles of education in a democracy—give guidance by education rather than

indoctrination; deal with all the known facts and results of research; teach critical judgment in dealing with ethical controversy.

3. Adopt as the main goal in regulating adolescent conduct measures that will equip students for intelligent self-determination rather than conformity to procedures which will have no educative effect on their real choices of conduct.

4. Help identify and destroy those outmoded aspects of the ascetic ideal which no longer represent the ideals of the vast majority of American ethical leaders or of the American people, and which no longer contribute either to individual happiness and growth or to family and social welfare.

All of this in no way denies that teachers should have strong ethical convictions of their own, or that they should feel it necessary to conceal these convictions from the adolescents with whom they deal. What they should *not* do is play the role of the apologist for the status quo, devising a "new rationale for an established policy when it has become clear that the old arguments in its favor are no longer adequate."[29]

NOTES

* This paper was originally presented at the annual meeting of the National Council on Family Relations, Miami, Fla., October 1964.

[1] *Sex Ways—In Fact and Faith: Bases for Christian Family Policy,* ed. by E. M. Duvall and S. M. Duvall, New York: Association Press, 1961.

[2] G. Williams, *The Sanctity of Life and the Criminal Law,* New York: Alfred A. Knopf, 1957.

[3] E. Lloyd-Jones, "The New Mortality," unpublished paper presented at the New York State Deans and Guidance Counselors Conference, November 3, 1963.

[4] J. Bernard, "Developmental Tasks of the NCFR, 1963–1988," address delivered at the annual meeting of the National Council on Family Relations, Denver, August 1963, published in *Journal of Marriage and the Family,* 26:1 (February 1964), pp. 29–38.

[5] See, for example, A. T. Robinson, *Christian Morals Today,* Philadelphia: Westminster Press, 1964; and J. M. Krumm, "The Heart and the Mind and the New Morality," unpublished baccalaureate sermon, Columbia University, June 2, 1963.

[6] I. Rubin, *Conflict of Sex Values, in Theory and Research,* unpublished paper, Workshop on Changing Sexual Mores, Teachers' College, August 2, 1963.

[7] See A. C. Kinsey *et al., Sexual Behavior in the Human Male,* Philadelphia: W. B. Saunders, 1948; and A. Ellis, *The American Sexual Tragedy,* New York: Grove Press, 1963.

[8] D. A. Mace and R. Guyon, "Chastity and Virginity: The Case For and the Case Against," in *The Encyclopedia of Sexual Behavior,* ed. by A. Ellis and A. Abarbanel, New York: Hawthorn Books, 1961, pp. 247–257; D. A. Mace and W. R. Stokes, "Sex Ethics, Sex Acts and Human Needs—A Dialogue," *Pastoral Psychology,* 12 (October–November 1961), pp. 34–43, 15–22; and W. R. Stokes and D. A. Mace,

"Premarital Sexual Behavior," *Marriage and Family Living*, 15 (August 1953), pp. 235–249.

[9] L. A. Kirkendall, *Premarital Intercourse and Interpersonal Relations*, New York: Julian Press, 1961; L. A. Kirkendall, "A Suggested Approach to the Teaching of Sexual Morality," *Journal of Family Welfare* (Bombay, India), 5 (June 1959), pp. 26–30; and T. Poffenberger et al., "Premarital Sexual Behavior: A Symposium," *Marriage and Family Living*, 24 (August 1962), pp. 254–278.

[10] W. R. Stokes, "Guilt and Conflict in Relation to Sex," *The Encyclopedia of Sexual Behavior, op. cit.*, pp. 466–471; W. R. Stokes, "Sex Education of Children," in *Recent Advances in Sex Research*, ed. by H. G. Beigel, New York: Hoeber-Harper, 1963, pp. 48–60; Mace and Stokes, *op. cit.*; and Stokes and Mace, *op. cit.*

[11] A. Ellis, *If This Be Sexual Heresy*, New York: Lyle Stuart, 1963.

[12] R. Guyon, *The Ethics of Sexual Acts*, New York: Alfred A. Knopf, 1934; and Mace and Guyon, *op. cit.*

[13] C. Kirkpatrick, *The Family: As Process and Institution*, New York: Ronald Press, 1954.

[14] W. H. Kilpatrick, *Philosophy of Education*, New York: Macmillan, 1951.

[15] J. F. Cuber, R. A. Harper, and W. F. Kenkel, *Problems of American Society: Values in Conflict*, New York: Henry Holt, 1956.

[16] M. Edel and A. Edel, *Anthropology and Ethics*, Illinois: Charles C. Thomas, 1959.

[17] G. P. Murdock, *Social Structure*, New York: Macmillan, 1949.

[18] A. Kardiner, *Sex and Morality*, New York: Bobbs-Merrill, 1954.

[19] Kilpatrick, *op. cit.*; and E. Nagel, "Liberalism and Intelligence," Fourth John Dewey Memorial Lecture, Bennington, Vt.: Bennington College, 1957.

[20] I. L. Reiss, "The Treatment of Pre-Marital Coitus in 'Marriage and the Family' Texts," *Social Problems*, 4 (April 1957), pp. 334–338.

[21] P. H. Gebhard et al., *Pregnancy, Birth, and Abortion*, New York: Hoeber-Harper, 1958.

[22] See footnote 9.

[23] C. E. Vincent, *Unwed Mothers*, Glencoe, Ill.: Free Press, 1961.

[24] R. A. Harper, "Marriage Counseling and Mores: A Critique," *Marriage and Family Living*, 21 (February 1959), pp. 13–19.

[25] P. H. Landis, book review in *Marriage and Family Living*, 24 (February 1962), pp. 96–97.

[26] D. Riesman, "Permissiveness and Sex Roles," *Marriage and Family Living*, 21 (August 1959), pp. 211–217.

[27] D. P. Ausubel, "Problems of Adolescent Adjustment," *The Bulletin of the National Association of Secondary-School Principals*, 34 (January 1950), pp. 1–84, and I. Rubin, *A Critical Evaluation of Certain Selected Operational Principles of Sex Education for the Adolescent*, unpublished Ph.D. dissertation, New York University School of Education, 1962.

[28] K. Mannheim, *Diagnosis of Our Time*, New York: Oxford U. Press, 1944.

[29] D. Callahan, "Authority and The Theologian," *The Commonweal*, 80 (June 5, 1964), pp. 319–323.

Premarital Sexual Experience Among Coeds, 1958 and 1968

ROBERT R. BELL and JAY B. CHASKES

Over the past twenty-five years it has been generally assumed in the mass media that the premarital sexual experiences of American girls have been steadily increasing. Furthermore, it is frequently assumed that the college girl has been at the forefront in attaining greater sexual experience. However in the past the assumption as to increasing sexual experience among college girls has not been supported by research findings. In general, the studies have shown that the significant increase in premarital coital experience for unmarried girls occurred in the 1920's and since that time there have been no striking changes in their probabilities of having premarital coitus (Bell, 1966). One of the authors, after an extensive look at past studies, came to the conclusion that "there is no evidence to suggest that when women born after 1900 are compared by decades of birth, there are any significant differences in their rates of premarital coitus (Bell, 1966:58).

The writers believed that a change *has* been occurring in the sexual experiences of college girls since the mid 1960's. In recent years, even more so than ever, the group primarily responsible for rebellion among the young has been the college student. While there has always been rebellion by the younger generation toward their elders, it probably never has been as great in the United States as it has been since the mid 1960's. In recent years youths have not only rebelled, but have also rejected many aspects of the major institutions in American society. The mid 1960's have produced an action generation and their *modus vivendi* has been to experience, to confront, to participate and sometimes to destroy. Since the mid 1960's a small but highly influential proportion of college students has been deeply involved in the civil rights movement and then in the protest over the Vietnam War. What may be most important about this generation of college students is that many are not just alienated as others have been in the past, but are *actively* alienated.

Many college students now believe that a number of the norms of adult institutions are not only wrong but also immoral. This is the view held by many college students toward the treatment of the Black,

Reprinted from *Journal of Marriage and the Family*, February 1970, 81–84.

toward the war in Vietnam, toward American political procedures, and so forth. It therefore seems logical that if many of the norms of these institutions are viewed as wrong and immoral by large numbers of the younger generation, they are also going to be suspicious and critical about other norms in other adult controlled institutions. Certainly a social institution that one would expect the younger generation to view with skepticism would be that concerned with marriage and sexual behavior. This increasingly negative view of adult institutions plus other factors led to the hypothesis that significant changes have been occurring in the premarital sexual experiences of college students since the mid 1960's. Before examining some research data as to whether or not there have been changes in sexual experience, we may briefly examine some other social factors that might be related to change in premarital sexual experiences.

One important factor of the 1960's has been the development, distribution and general acceptance of the birth control pill. On most large university campuses the pill is available to the coed or it is easy for her to find out where to get it in the local community. While studies have shown that fear of pregnancy has not been a very important deterrent to premarital coitus for a number of years, it now seems to have been largely removed for most college girls.

A second influence since the mid 1960's has been the legitimization of sexual candor. In part the new sexual candor has been legitimized by one of the most venerable of American institutions—the Supreme Court. In recent years the young person has had access to a level of sexual expression far greater than just ten years ago. In the past year, even the most conservative of the mass media, that of television, has begun to show it. This new sexual candor, whatever its original cause, is often seen by the rebelling younger generation as "theirs" in that it too, critically subverts the traditional institutions. As a result the sexual candor of the late 1960s is often both a manifesto and a guidebook for many in the younger generation.

Finally, it must also be recognized that the rebellion of the younger generation has been given both implicit and explicit approval by many in the older generation. Many adults want to think of themselves as part of the younger generation and its youth culture. For example, this is seen in the music and fashion of the youth culture which has had a tremendous impact on adults. It would seem that if many adults take on the values of the youth culture, this would raise questions as to the significance of many of their adult values for the youth world. In other words, the very identification of many adults with youth culture contributes to adult values having less impact on college youths.

In brief, it was assumed that the social forces developing in the mid 1960's led to a rapid increase in the rejection of many adult values, and the development of increasingly important patterns of behavior common to a general youth culture. For the reasons already suggested, one change would be an increased rate of premarital coitus among college girls along with less feelings of guilt about these experiences.

METHOD

In 1958, the senior author did a study of premarital sexual behavior and attitudes among a sample of coeds in a large urban university (Bell and Blumberg, 1959, 1960). In 1968 it was decided to use the same questionnaire with a sample of coeds in the same university. A careful effort was made to match the 1968 population with that of 1958 according to a number of variables. It was possible to match the two samples by age and by the class standings of the coeds. The two time groups were alike in social class background as measured by the education and occupations of their fathers. The distribution of the two samples by religious backgrounds was also the same. The 1958 sample included 250 coeds and that of 1968 included 205 coeds.

There had been no change in the ten-year period as to the mean age of first date for the two samples; in 1958 it was 13.3 and in 1968 it was 13.2 years of age. There was a significant difference in the number of different individuals ever dated by the coeds in the two time samples. In 1958 the mean number of different individuals dated was 53, while in 1968 it was only 25. In 1968 the coeds went out on dates just as often but went out more often with the same individuals in a dating relationship than did the coeds in 1958.

There was no significant difference in the two time samples as to whether the coeds had ever gone steady. In 1958, 68 percent of the coeds had gone steady at least once, while in 1968 this had been the experience for 77 percent. Furthermore, there was no significant difference as to age at first going steady. In 1958 the mean age was 17.0 years and in 1968 it was 16.7 years of age. There were some slight differences as to engagement experience. Somewhat more girls in 1968 had ever been engaged; 37 percent as compared to 22 percent in 1958. However, coeds in 1968 were somewhat older when they first became engaged (20.5 years) than were the coeds in 1958 (19.1 years).

In the discussion that follows there will first be a presentation of some comparative data about the two coed populations of 1958 and 1968. Secondly there will be a discussion with further analysis of the 1968 population of coeds.

COMPARISONS OF 1958 AND 1968 COED POPULATIONS

The data to be discussed refers to the highest level of intimacy ever reached by the coed in a specific relationship of dating, going steady, and engagement. Table 1 shows the number and percent of girls in 1958

TABLE 1

Females, Number and Percent Having Intercourse, by Dating Relationship and Religion, 1958 and 1968

	Jew				Protestant				Catholic				Totals			
	1958		1968		1958		1968		1958		1968		1958		1968	
	%	No.	%	No.	%	No.	%	No.	%	No.	%	No.	%	No.	%	No.
Dating	11	(15)	20	(25)	10	(6)	35	(17)	8	(4)	15	(6)	10	(25)	23	(48)
Going Steady	14	(13)	26	(26)	20	(8)	41	(16)	14	(4)	17	(4)	15	(25)	28	(46)
Engaged	20	(7)	40	(19)	38	(6)	67	(8)	56	(7)	18	(3)	31	(20)	39	(30)

and 1968, by religion, who had intercourse while dating, going steady, or engaged. An examination of the totals indicate some significant changes from 1958 to 1968. The number of girls having premarital coitus while in a dating relationship went from 10 percent in 1958 to 23 percent in 1968, and the coitus rates while going steady went from 15 percent in 1958 to 28 percent in 1968. While there was some increase in the rates of premarital coitus during engagement, from 31 percent in 1958 to 39 percent in 1968, the change was not as striking as for the dating and going steady stages. Further examination of the data suggests that in 1958, the relationship of engagement was very often the prerequisite to a girl having premarital sexual intercourse. Engagement often provided her with a high level of emotional and future commitment which she often felt justified having coitus. However, in 1968 it appeared that the need to be engaged and all it implied was much less a condition the coed thought necessary before sexual intercourse. Therefore, the data suggests that the decision to have intercourse in 1968 was much less dependent on the commitment of engagement and more a question of individual decision regardless of the level of the relationship. To put it another way, if, in 1958, the coed had premarital coitus, it most often occurred while she was engaged. But in 1968, girls were more apt to have their first sexual experience while dating or going steady.

Table 1 also shows the changes that have occurred in rates of premarital coitus at the three stages of dating involvement by religious background. Both the Protestant and Jewish girls show a consistent increase in rates of premarital coitus at dating, going steady, and engaged levels from 1958 to 1968. (The number of Catholic coeds is too

TABLE 2

Females, Percent Having Intercourse, by Dating
Relationship Who Felt They "Went too Far," in 1958
and 1968

	1958 Percent (N = 250)	1968 Percent (N = 205)
While dating	65	36
While going steady	61	30
While engaged	41	20

small for analysis.) In general, the pattern by religious background in 1968 was the same as 1958. Protestant girls had the highest rates of premarital coitus, next came the Jewish coeds, and the lowest rates were for Catholic girls. It would appear that both the Protestant and Jewish girls have been susceptible to the patterns of change, although the rates are greater for Protestant coeds.

The respondents were also asked at each stage of the dating relationship if they had ever felt they had gone "too far" in their level of intimacy. Table 2 shows the percentage of coeds by dating relationship, who said they had at some time, felt they had gone "too far." Table 2 reveals that the percentage of coeds feeling guilty about coitus was reduced by approximately half at all three dating levels from 1958 to 1968. It may also be seen that there were significantly less feelings of guilt about coitus during engagement, while in 1968 variations in feelings of guilt were less differentiated at the three stages of dating involvement. In general, when the data of 1958 is compared with 1968 the indication is that in 1968 the coeds were more apt to have had intercourse at all levels of the dating relationship and at the same time felt less guilty than did their counterparts in 1958.

SOME FURTHER ANALYSIS OF THE 1968 SAMPLE

Given the indication of change in the sexual behavior and attitudes of coeds from 1958 to 1968, it is useful to look a little more in detail at the 1968 sample. The sample was analyzed by a number of variables to see if there were any significant differences. No significant differences were found by father's occupation, father's education, marital status of parents, mother working, or number of siblings. One variable that did show statistically significant differences was that of religious attendance. Those coeds, regardless of religious background, who had the highest rates of religious attendance had the lowest rates of premarital coitus and the greatest feelings of guilt when they did have coitus.

In the 1968 population of coeds it was found that there was a relationship between age at first date and the probability of having premarital coitus. Coeds who had their first date at 14 years of age and younger (as compared to 15 years of age and older) had overall higher rates of coitus (31 percent vs. 12 percent). However, there were no significant differences as related to age at first going steady or first engagement. One explanation for the higher frequencies of coitus among those who start dating younger is that they have been dating relatively longer and therefore have had more opportunity. It may also be that girls who start dating younger are more sexually mature, both physically and socially.

It was found that girls who dated more different boys (21 or more vs. 20 or less) had higher rates of premarital coitus (36 percent vs. 14 percent). This difference is in part a reflection of the fact that some girls who have few dates are extremely conservative in their sexual behavior. On the other hand the coeds who dated a large number of different boys often had a wide variety of experiences and a greater probability of sexual intimacy. There was also some indication of a relationship between the number of times a girl went steady and her probability of having premarital coitus. When coeds who had gone steady three or more times were compared with those who had gone steady one or two times, the intercourse rates were 46 percent vs. 22 percent. It may be that some girls who have intercourse are inclined to define that relationship as going steady whether in actual fact it may or may not have been.

As pointed out, studies in the past have consistently shown that for the coed who has premarital coitus, it has usually been limited to one partner and then during engagement. "The studies indicate that being nonvirgin at the time of marriage is not an indication of extensive premarital experiences with a variety of partners" (Bell, 1966:58). If the assumption earlier suggested is true, it would be expected that a number of the coeds in the 1968 sample would have had their first premarital sexual experiences while dating and going steady, rather than waiting until engagement.

When all girls in the 1968 sample, who were ever engaged and who had ever had premarital coitus, were analyzed it was found that only 19 percent had limited their coital experience just to the period of engagement. Expressing it another way, of all girls who were ever engaged and ever had premarital coital experience, 75 percent had their first experience while dating, 6 percent while going steady and 19 percent during engagement. For all coeds with premarital coital experience at each stage, 60 percent had coitus while dating, going steady, and engagement.

These data suggest important changes in the premarital coital experience of coeds. No longer is the girl so apt to have her degree of sexual intimacy influenced by the level of the dating relationship. There is also some evidence that girls having premarital coitus are having this experience with more different individuals. For example, of all those girls who had premarital coitus while in a dating relationship 56 percent had more than one partner—in fact, 22 percent had coitus in a dating relationship with five or more partners.

SUMMARY

If one were to construct a continuum of sexual experience and attitudes by which coeds in various colleges and universities in the United States might be measured, it seems that the sample studied would fall somewhere in the middle. In fact, there is some reason to argue that the sample may be somewhat conservative in that most of the coeds lived at home and a disproportionate number of them were Jewish. Yet, in dealing with the same general population over a ten year period the factor of change can be noted. The most important finding of this study appears to be that the commitment of engagement has become a less important condition for many coeds engaging in premarital coitus as well as whether or not they will have guilt feelings about that experience. If these findings are reasonably accurate, they could indicate the first significant change in premarital sexual behavior patterns since the 1920's. The findings indicate, furthermore, a widening slit between the conventional morality of the adult world and the real behavior common to many groups of young people. However, it should be kept in mind that this study was with small samples at one university and must be seen only as an indication of sexual behavior change and not as an argument that a national change has occurred. Further research with larger and better samples is needed before any broad generalizations may be made.

REFERENCES

BELL, ROBERT R.
   1966 Premarital sex in a changing society. Englewood Cliffs: Prentice-Hall, Inc.
BELL, ROBERT R. and LEONARD BLUMBERG.
   1959 "Courtship intimacy and religious background," Marriage and Family Living XXXI (4) (November):356–360.
   1960 "Courtship stages and intimacy attitudes," The Family Life Coordinator, VIII (3) (March):61–63.

Theories of Mate Selection

BRUCE K. ECKLAND

This paper is devoted to a review and clarification of questions which both social and biological scientists might regard as crucial to an understanding of nonrandom mate selection. Owing to the numerous facets of the topic, the diverse nature of the criteria by which selection occurs, and the sharp differences in the scientific orientations of students who have directed their attention to the problem, it does not seem possible at this time to shape the apparent chaos into perfect, or even near-perfect, order and, out of this, develop a generalized theory of mate selection. Nevertheless, it is one of our objectives to systematize some of our thinking on the topic and consider certain gaps and weaknesses in our present theories and research.

Before embarking on this task, it would be proper to ask why the problem is worth investigating, a question which other speakers no doubt also will raise during the course of this conference. If the social and biological scientists had a better understanding of mate selection, what would happen to other parts of our knowledge or practice as a result? Despite the fact that our questions arise from quite different perspectives, there is at least one obvious point at which they cut across the various fields. This point is our common interest in the evolution of human societies, and assortative mating in this context is one of the important links between the physical and cultural components of man's evolution.

Looking first from the geneticists' side, at the core of the problem lies the whole issue of natural selection. Any divergence from perfect panmixia, i.e., random mating, splits the genetic composition of the human population into complex systems of subordinate populations. These may range from geographically isolated "races" to socially isolated caste, ethnic, or economic groups. Regardless of the nature of the boundaries, each group is viewed as a biological entity, differing statistically from other groups with respect to certain genes. To the extent that different mating groups produce more or fewer children, "natural" selection takes place.

In the absence of differential fertility, assortative mating alone does not alter the gene frequencies of the total population. Nevertheless, it *does* change the distribution and population variance of genes (Stern,

1960) and this, itself, is of considerable importance. Hirsch (1967), for example, has stated:

> As the social, ethnic, and economic barriers to education are removed throughout the world, and as the quality of education approaches a more uniformly high level of effectiveness, heredity may be expected to make an ever larger contribution to individual differences in intellectual functioning and consequently to success in our increasingly complex civilization. Universally compulsory education, improved methods of ability assessment and career counseling, and prolongation of the years of schooling further into the reproductive period of life can only increase the degree of positive assortative mating in our population. From a geneticist's point of view our attempt to create the great society might prove to be the greatest selective breeding experiment ever undertaken. (p. 128)

Long-term mate selection for educability or intelligence increases the proportion of relevant homozygous genotypes which over successive generations *tends* to produce a biotic model of class structure in which a child's educability and, therefore, future social status are genetically determined. Since these propositions hold whether or not everyone has the same number of children with exact replacement, assortative mating would seem to have consequences just as relevant as any other mechanisms involving the genetic character of human societies.[1]

Also from the biological point of view, it is probable that assortative mating is becoming an increasingly important factor relative to others affecting the character of the gene pool. Infant mortality, for instance, does not appear to exert the same kind of selection pressure on the populations of Western societies today that it did a hundred, or even fifty, years ago. Likewise, accompanying the rise of mass education and spread of birth control information, fertility differentials appear to have narrowed markedly, especially in this country (Kirk, 1966). For example, the spread is not nearly as great as it once was between the number of children in lower and upper socio-economic families. It is not altogether clear, of course, just how the relaxation of selection pressures of this kind would, in the long run, affect future generations. Yet, assuming, as some have suggested, that these trends will continue, then a broader understanding of the nature and causes of mate selection may eventually become one of the outstanding objectives of population geneticists. One reason is that the more the assortative mating, the greater the rate of genetic selection. If nearly all members of a society produce and most reproduce about the same number of children, and these in turn live to reproduce, it might then be just as important to know who mates with whom as to know who reproduces and how much.

The interest of social scientists in mate selection has been more uneven and much more diffuse. Some anthropologists undoubtedly come closest to sharing the evolutionary perspective of geneticists, as indicated by their work in a variety of overlapping areas which deal in one way or another with mating, e.g., genetic drift, hybridization, and kinship systems. In contrast, sociologists have been less sensitive to genetic theories. We share with others an evolutionary approach, but one that rests almost wholly on social and cultural rather than physical processes. Nonetheless, mate selection lies at the core of a number of sociological problems. These range, for example, from studies of the manner in which class endogamy is perpetuated from one generation to the next to studies in which endogamy is conceived as a function of marital stability. While sociologists have helped to ascertain many facts as well as having developed a few quasi-theories about assortative mating, it is rather difficult when reviewing our literature on the subject to distinguish between that which is scientifically consequential and that which is scientifically trivial. The general orientation of social scientists, in any case, is far from trivial and can be used instructively in the region of mate selection and in ways heretofore neglected by population geneticists. Some of their "theories" will be reviewed later in this paper.

EVOLUTION IN PARALLEL AND INTERACTION

Differences in the basic theoretical orientations of the social and biological sciences with respect to human evolution and assortative mating perhaps can best be understood in terms of the set of diagrams that follow. Figure 1 illustrates the usual manner in which investigators in

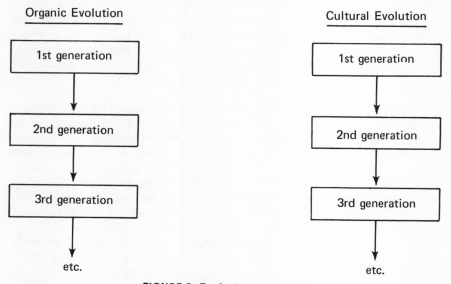

FIGURE 1. Evolution in parallel

either field approach their subject matter. The course of human development is traced on separate but parallel tracks. Some textbooks and elementary courses in sociology begin with a brief treatment of genetics, but it is soon forgotten. In a like manner, students in a course in genetics are told that the expression of the genetic character of an individual depends largely on environmental influences, after which no further reference to environment seems to be necessary (Caspari, 1967).

Evolution viewed in parallel has allowed each field to articulate its own theories and perspectives. Mate selection is only one case in point, but a good one. The anthropologist or sociologist typically begins with some universal statement to the effect that in no society is mate selection unregulated and then he may proceed to analyze the cultural controls that regulate the selection process. As he has defined his problem, there perhaps has been no need to consider physiological processes. The geneticist, on the other hand, typically introduces the topic with some statement about how mate selection alters the proportion of heterozygotes in the population (as we have done) and then proceeds to a discussion of allele frequencies or consanguinity. Because he is concerned almost exclusively with the nature of the genetic material, he does not care, for example, why tall people seem to prefer to marry tall people. I doubt that sociologists especially care either. There are, however, traits far more relevant than these, like education, which serve as a basis of assortative mating and to which sociologists have given considerable attention and the geneticists relatively little.

The gap about which I am speaking also can be illustrated by the manner in which some geneticists define assortative mating. To repeat a definition which appeared recently in the *Eugenics Quarterly*, assortative mating is "the tendency of marriage partners to resemble one another as a result of preference or choice" (Post, 1965). The reference to individual "preference or choice" illustrates one of the major weaknesses in the geneticist's understanding of the nature of culture and society. (It is not just this particular statement that is troublesome, but many others like it throughout the literature.)

Mate selection is *not* simply a matter of preference or choice. Despite the increased freedom and opportunities that young people have to select what they believe is the "ideal" mate, there are a host of factors, many *well* beyond the control of the individual, which severely limit the number of eligible persons from which to choose. As unpalatable as this proposition may be, it rests on a rather large volume of data which suggests that the regulatory system of society enforces in predictable ways a variety of norms and sometimes specific rules about who may marry whom. Perhaps the most important point I will have to make in this paper is that geneticists must begin to recast their assumptions about the nature of culture and society, just as sociologists must recast their thinking about genetics (Eckland, 1967).

Assuming that both geneticists and sociologists do reconsider their positions and assuming, too, that each discipline has a hold on some part of the truth, there still remains the unfilled gap in the kinds of knowledge needed to develop a set of interlocking theories between the social and biological sciences with regard to mate selection. I do not question that organic and cultural evolution can and, in many ways, must be studied as separate phenomena. The point is, however, that they do interact and this, too, should be studied; and to do so will require a much broader historical perspective than most geneticists and social scientists have exhibited up to now.

An interaction model of organic and cultural evolution must specify the precise nature of the relationships between the hereditary factors and environmental influences. Although certainly a very old idea, the notion of *interaction* has lain relatively dormant until recent years, probably largely due to the nature-nurture controversy and the racist arguments that covered most of the first half of the twentieth century. The expanded model in Figure 2 suggests a more elaborate system of

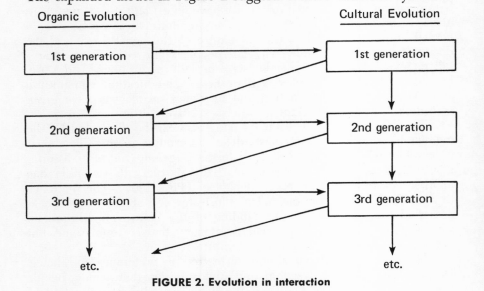

FIGURE 2. Evolution in interaction

causal paths along which there is continuous feedback between the genetic and cultural tracks from one generation to the next. As before, we are dealing with the processes by which generational replacement and change occur. However, in addition to the duplication of most genes and most cultural traits in each succeeding generation, new patterns invariably emerge through the interaction of heredity and environment. Briefly, and with no intent on my part to intimate either purpose or consciousness, (*a*) genes restrict the possible range of man's development and (*b*) within these limits he alters his environment or cultural arrangements in such ways as to change the frequencies or distribution of genes in the next generation which (c) enables him to carry out further changes.

It is important to note here that the interaction of heredity and environment does not occur within the duration of a single generation, a point that social scientists, in particular, need to recognize. Holding for inspection a very short segment of the life span of a single cohort, as so often we do, it is not possible to observe, even to logically think about, heredity and environment in interaction. Within the span of one generation, the relationship appears only as a one-way process, with the genetic makeup of individuals determining the norms of reaction to the environment. The path from environment *back* to genetics which actually allows us to speak in terms of *inter*action appears only *between* generations, as in the above model. In other words, models of the sort abbreviated in Figure 3 do not fit reality. The cultural environment,

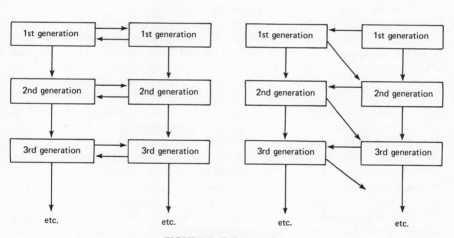

FIGURE 3. False models

of course, may have an immediate and direct effect upon an individual's endocrine system, as well as other physiological and morphological structures, but it cannot, as far as we know, alter his genes. Environment can only alter their phenotypic expression and, owing to selective mating, the genes of one's progeny in the next generation.

We have now moved into a position whereby we might raise two rather crucial questions regarding the search for significant variables in mate selection, that is, significant in the context of an interaction model. The first is: What genotypes have social definitions attached to their behavioral manifestations or, conversely, what physical, personality, and social traits depend on our genes? The answer requires determining how much, if any, of the variance of a particular trait is due to heredity (and how much to environment). For example, taking the operational definition of intelligence we now employ, if none of the variance can be attributed to genetic sources, then no matter how intense assortative mating is for intelligence, we most certainly would exclude it from any further consideration in our model. Objections sometimes have been raised against partitioning the variance on the grounds that there is a strong interaction component in the development of most traits. It will be recalled, however, that our general model permits no interaction of this form between heredity and environment in the development of the intelligence or any other phenotype of an *individual*. Every character is determined during the lifetime of that individual, with genotypes determining part of the course of development and not the other way around. There are other problems to be encountered in any analysis of variance which attempts to sort out the hereditary component, but this is not one of them.

The second question is: What criteria for mate selection are *functionally* relevant within a particular population at a particular time? This question, of course, raises some long-standing issues in genetics regarding the "adaptive" quality of characteristics which are genetically variable. It appears, for example, that some traits like the O, A, B, and AB blood types for the most part are adaptively neutral or, at least, it is not known how they affect the biological or social fitness of their possessors in any significant way. Likewise, there are traits like eye color which apparently have no clear functional value and yet seem to be involved in the sorting which unites one mate with another. By this, I do not mean that the search for socially relevant traits in mate selection should be directed toward putting the science of genetics to the service of human welfare. Rather, it is my belief that the discovery of socially relevant biological dimensions of human variation is likely to be of the sort, such as intelligence, which may be treated simultaneously as Mendelian mechanisms in the reproductive process and as sorting and selecting mechanisms in the allocation of social status and in the maintenance of boundaries between social groups, the discovery of which may serve to further our general understanding of human evolution. Any delimiting, therefore, of the class of mate selection variables we eventually must take into account should deal, on the one hand, with traits which are understood in terms of genetic processes and partly in terms of social and other environmental processes and, on the other hand, with traits whose survival or social value is at least partly understood.

NOTES ON TERMINOLOGY

Two basic forms of nonrandom mate selection are *assortative* mating and *inbreeding*. Assortative mating usually encompasses all character-specific mate selection which would not be expected to occur by chance. Inbreeding, on the other hand, encompasses all mating where departures from perfect panmixia involve the relatedness or ancestry of individuals. While some authors have used the terms in essentially this manner (e.g., Spuhler, 1962; Post, 1965), others have not (e.g., Allen, 1965; Warren, 1966). The latter have not restricted assortative mating to refer only to character-specific situations but have included inbreeding as one of its forms. Another variation is that some authors have used the labels *genotypic* assortative mating to refer to inbreeding and *phenotypic* assortative mating to refer to the nonrandom, character-specific form (e.g., Fuller and Thompson, 1960). Also, the terms *consanguine* and *conjugal* sometimes are used to make the same distinction.

Attention to the rules governing the selection of a spouse has led to another set of terms: the first, representing conformity to the norms, called *agathogamy;* the second, involving prohibited deviations from the norms, called *cacogamy* (Merton, 1964). *Incest,* a special case of inbreeding, involves prohibited deviations from the rules controlling matings between closely related persons and is also a special case of cacogamy since the latter includes other forms of socially disapproved matings as well, such as *mesalliance,* a marriage with one of an inferior position. Special cases of mesalliance are *hypergamy* to denote the pattern wherein the female marries upward into a higher social stratum (the male marries the one in the inferior position) and *hypogamy* wherein the female marries downward into a lower social stratum.

In common use are the more general terms *endogamy* and *exogamy* which refer to in-group marriages of almost any kind. Inbreeding is a special case of endogamy; *hybridization* and *admixture* are special cases of exogamy in which "racial" features are the implied criteria. *Interbreeding* and *intermarriage* also have about the same meaning as above, except the latter term is more frequently used in reference to traits dealing with categories other than race, such as *interfaith* marriages. Miscegenation, another form of exogamy, is the term usually applied to interbreeding between white and Negro or other intergroup matings (legitimate and illegitimate) wherein the contractants have violated cultural proscriptions; and, in this respect, miscegenation is also a form of cacogamy, as well as a form of mesalliance.

Still another term commonly employed to describe assortative mating is *homogamy* which denotes something about the likeness or similarity of the married couples, with or without specific reference to any particular set of characteristics. Thus, one may speak in terms of racial homogamy or social homogamy or, simply, homogamous marriages. The antonym, *heterogamy,* is not widely used but could logically refer to mixed matings, the tendency toward random mating, or selection for "dissimilar" traits. The latter, however, is more often called *negative* assortative mating; all other forms are called *positive* assortative mating.

The above discussion probably comes close to exhausting the arsenal of terms we employ. However, with few exceptions, the concepts which arise from their meaning do not appear to be especially useful for classifying mating patterns in such a manner as to provide a sound basis for bridging the gap between the organic and social models presented earlier. It is quite probable that not only do we need more knowledge of assortative mating upon which to base more generalized theories, but we very well might find it necessary either to develop a new set of concepts (and terms) or to undertake a major revision of those now used. At present, they are confusing and often redundant, many do not appear particularly relevant to our problem, and few perhaps mean the same thing to both the geneticist and social scientist.

In the remainder of this paper, I shall review briefly some of the current theories of mate selection. By no means a complete review, I have neglected, for example, the very large body of work of anthropologists and population geneticists dealing with inbreeding. Studies of consanguineous marriages provide important information about genetic processes, such as the mutation load which is especially sensitive to inbreeding. Also reported in this literature, but not here, are a number of theories that attempt to explain the cultural development of kinship systems in which inbreeding is permitted or prescribed. However, most, although not all, of this work tends to deal with small populations which have been isolated for many generations. It is not convenient for explaining assortative mating in large, relatively open, and highly mobile cultures. The following discussion, therefore, involves a search for those psychological and structural features which best show how assortative mating operates in contemporary societies.

INDIVIDUALISTIC THEORIES

The disappearance of unilineal kinship systems in Western societies has led to a decline of kinship control over mate selection. The resulting freedom which young people now enjoy has brought about an enormously complex system. No doubt, the selection process actually begins long before the adolescent's first "date." Moreover, under conditions of serial monogamy where it is possible to have many wives but only one at a time, the process for some probably never ends. Determining the "choice" are a myriad of emotional experiences and it is these experiences, along with a variety of subconscious drives and needs, upon which most psychological and other "individualistic" theories are based.

THE UNCONSCIOUS ARCHETYPE

Some of the earliest and perhaps most radical theories of mate selection suggested that what guides a man to choose a woman (it was seldom thought to be the other way around) is instinct. Scholars believed that there must be for each particular man a particular woman who, for reasons involving the survival of the species, corresponded most perfectly with him. A modern rendition of the same idea is Carl Jung's belief that falling in love is being caught by one's "anima." That is, every man inherits an anima which is an "archetypal form" expressing a particular female image he carries within his genes. When the right woman comes along, the one who corresponds to the archetype, he instantly is "seized" (Evans, 1964). However, no one, as far as we know, has actually discovered any pure biologically determined tendencies to assortative mating.

THE PARENT IMAGE

A psychoanalytic view, based on the Oedipus configuration, has been that in terms of temperament and physical appearance one's ideal mate is a parent substitute. The boy, thus, seeks someone like his mother and the girl seeks someone like her father. While it admittedly would seem reasonable to expect parent images to either encourage or discourage a person marrying someone like his parent, no clear evidence has been produced to support the hypothesis. Sometimes striking resemblances between a man's wife and his mother, or a woman's husband and her father, have been noted. Apparently, however, these are only "accidents," occurring hardly more frequently than expected by chance.

LIKE ATTRACTS LIKE

Another generally unproven assumption, at least with respect to any well-known personality traits, involves the notion that "likes attract." Cattell and Nesselroade (1967) recently found significant correlations between husband and wife on a number of personality traits among both stably and unstably married couples. The correlations, moreover, were substantially higher (and more often in the predicted direction) among the "normal" than among the unstably married couples. As the authors admit, however, it was not possible to determine whether the tendency of these couples to resemble each other was the basis for their initial attraction ("birds of a feather flock together") or whether the correlations were simply an outgrowth of the marital experience. Although the ordering of the variables is not clear, the evidence does tend to suggest that the stability of marriage and, thus the number of progeny of any particular set of parents, may depend to some extent on degrees of likeness.

THE PRINCIPLE OF COMPLEMENTARY NEEDS

Probably as old as any other is the notion that "opposites attract"; for example, little men love big women, or a masochistic male desiring punishment seeks out a sadistic female who hungers to give it. Only in the past 20 years has a definitive theory along these lines been formulated and put to empirical test. This is Winch's theory of complementary needs which hypothesizes that each individual seeks that person who will provide him with maximum need gratification. The specific need pattern and personality of each partner will be "complementary" (Winch, 1958). Accordingly, dominant women, for example, would tend to choose submissive men as mates rather than similarly dominant or aggressive ones. The results of a dozen or so investigations, however, are inconclusive, at best. More often than not, researchers have been unable to find a pattern of complementary differences. No less significant than other difficulties inherent in the problem is the discouraging fact that the correlation between what an individual thinks is the personality of his mate and the actual personality of his mate is quite small (Udry, 1966). Nevertheless, the theory that either mate selection or marital stability involves an exchange of interdependent behaviors resulting from complementary rather than similar needs and personalities is a compelling idea and perhaps deserves more attention.

No firm conclusions can yet be reached about the reasons for similarity (or complementariness) or personality and physical traits in assortative mating. (Even the degree of association or disassociation on most personality characteristics is largely unknown.) To state that "like attracts like" or "opposites attract," we know are oversimplifications. Moreover, few attempts to provide the kinds of explanations we seek have thus far stood up to empirical tests.

SOCIOLOGICAL THEORIES

In a very general way, social homogamy is a critical point in the integration or continuity of the family and other social institutions. It is a mechanism which serves to maintain the status quo and conserve traditional values and beliefs. And, because marriage itself is such a vital institution, it is not too difficult to understand why so many of the social characteristics which are important variables generally in society, such as race, religion, or class, are also the important variables in mate selection. Thus, most studies in the United States report a very high rate, over 99 percent, for racial endogamy, an overall rate perhaps as high as 90 percent for religious homogamy, and moderately high rates, 50 percent to 80 percent for class homogamy, the exact figures depending on the nature of the index used and the methods employed to calculate the rate.

One possible way of illustrating the conserving or maintenance function of social homogamy in mate selection is to try to visualize momentarily how a contemporary society would operate under conditions of *random* mating. Considering their proportions in the population, Negroes actually would be more likely to marry whites than other Negroes, Catholics more often than not would marry Protestants, and a college graduate would be more apt to marry a high school drop-out than to marry another college graduate. In a like manner, about as often as not, dull would marry bright, old would marry young, Democrats would marry Republicans, and teetotalers would marry drinkers. What would be the end result of this kind of social heterogamy? A new melting pot, or chaos?

It seems that, in the absence of "arranged marriages," a variety of controls governs mate selection and, in the process, substantially reduces the availability of certain individuals as potential mates. Many structures in society undoubtedly carry out these functions, sometimes in quite indirect ways, such as, the subtle manner in which the promotion of an "organization man" may be based, in part, on how well his mate's characteristics meet the qualifications of a "company wife." Thus, despite the "liberation" of mate selection and the romantic ideals of lovers who are convinced that social differences must not be allowed to stand in their way, probably one of the most important functions of both the elaborate "rating and dating" complex and the ceremonial "engagement" is to allow a society to make apparent who may "marry upward" and under what conditions exogamy is permitted. We are referring here, then, not merely to a society's control over the orderly replacement of personnel, but to its integration and the transmission of culture as well.

Rather than reviewing any very well-formulated theories (since there may be none) in the remaining discussion, I have attempted to touch upon a fairly broad range of conditions under which homogamy, as a social fact, relates to other aspects of contemporary societies.

PROPINQUITY AND INTERACTION

Whether we are speaking about place of residence, school, work, or such abstruse features of human ecology as the bus or streetcar routes along which people travel, propinquity obviously plays a major part in mate selection since, in nearly all cases, it is a precondition for engaging in interaction. (The mail-order bride, for instance, is one of several exceptions.) A person usually "selects" a mate from the group of people he knows. Findings which illustrate the function of distance have been duplicated in dozens of studies. In Columbus, Ohio, it was once found that more than half of the adults who had been married in that city had actually lived within 16 blocks of one another at the time of their first date (Clarke, 1952). Cherished notions about romantic love notwithstanding, the chances are about 50–50 that the "one and only" lives within walking distance (Kephart, 1961).

As many authors have pointed out, people are not distributed through space in a random fashion. In fact, where people live, or work and play, corresponds so closely with one's social class (and race) that it is not quite clear whether propinquity, as a factor in mate selection, is simply a function of class endogamy or, the other way around, class endogamy is a function of propinquity. Ramsøy's (1966) recent attempt to resolve this issue, I want to note, misses the mark almost completely. Investigating over 5000 couples living in Oslo, Norway, she concludes that propinquity and social homogamy are "totally independent of one another" and, therefore, rejects the long-standing argument that "residential segregation of socioeconomic and cultural groups in cities represents a kind of structural underpinning both to propinquity in mate selection and to homogamy." More specifically, the author shows that "couples who lived very near one another before marriage were no more likely to be of the same occupational status than couples who lived at opposite sides of the city." This is astonishing, but misleading. The author equated the social status of the bride and, implicitly, her social class origin with *her* occupation at the time of marriage. No socioeconomic index other than the bride's occupation unfortunately was known to the investigator and, thus, it was a convenient although poorly considered jump to make. To most sociologists, it should be a great surprise to find in any Western society, including Norway, that the occupations young women hold before marriage give a very clear indication of their social status, relative either to the occupational status of men they marry or to their own places of residence.

EXCHANGE THEORY

An explanation often cited in the literature on mate selection, as well as in that on the more general topic of interpersonal attraction, deals in one form or another with the principle of exchange. A Marxian view, marriage is an exchange involving both the assets and liabilities which each partner brings to the relationship. Thus, a college-educated woman seldom brings any special earning power to the marriage, but rather she typically enters into contract with a male college graduate for whom her diploma is a social asset which may benefit his own career and possibly those of his children. In exchange, he offers her, with a fair degree of confidence, middle-class respectability. Norms of reciprocity might also help to explain the finding that most borderline mentally retarded women successfully marry and even, in some cases, marry upward, if they are physically attractive. This particular theory, however, has not been well-developed in regard to mate selection, despite its repeated usage. Also, it may be a more appropriate explanation of deviations from assortative mating or instances of negative mate selection than of positive selection.

VALUES AND BELIEF PATTERNS

In contrast to the inconclusive evidence regarding assortative mating in terms of personality characteristics, numerous studies do indicate that married couples (and engaged couples) show far more consensus on various matters than do randomly matched couples. Even on some rather generalized values, as in the area of aesthetics or economics, social homogamy occurs. Apparently, our perception that other persons share with us the same or similar value orientations and beliefs facilitates considerably our attraction to them (Burgess and Wallin, 1943).

The importance of norms and values in mate selection, part of the social fabric of every society, also can be illustrated in a more direct way by looking at some of the specific sanctions that we pass along from generation to generation. Without really asking why, children quite routinely are brought up to believe that gentlemen prefer blondes (which may be only a myth perpetuated by the cosmetic industry), that girls should marry someone older rather than younger than themselves (which leaves most of them widows later on), and that a man should be at least a little taller than the woman whom he marries (which places the conspicuously tall girl at an enormous disadvantage). Simple folkways as such beliefs presently are, they nevertheless influence in predictable ways the "choice" of many individuals.

SOCIAL STRATIFICATION AND CLASS ENDOGAMY

We have already noted that the field of eligible mates is largely confined to the same social stratum to which an individual's family of orientation belongs. Social-class endogamy not only plays a significant part in the process of mate selection, it may also help to explain other forms of assortative mating. For example, part of the reason why marriage partners or engaged couples share many of the same values and beliefs no doubt is because they come from the same social backgrounds.

There are at least five explanations which can be offered for the persistence of class endogamy, each of which sounds reasonable enough and probably has a hold on some part of the truth.

First, simply to turn the next to last statement around, persons from the same class tend to marry *because* they share the same values (which reflect class differences) and not because they are otherwise aware or especially concerned about each other's background.

Second, during the period of dating and courtship most young people reside at the home of their parents. (Excluded here, of course, are the large minority in residential colleges and those who have left both school and home to take an apartment near their place of work.) The location of parental homes reflects the socioeconomic status of the family and is the general basis for residential segregation. With respect to both within and between communities, the pattern of segregation places potential mates with different backgrounds at greater distances than those with similar backgrounds. Thus, to the extent that the function of distance (or propinquity) limits the field of eligibles, it also encourages class endogamy by restricting class exogamy.

Third, class endogamy in some cases is simply a function of the interlocking nature of class and ethnicity. A middle-class Negro, for example, probably is prevented from an exogamous marriage with a member of the upper-class not so much because class barriers block it but because he (or she) is Negro. The majority of the eligible mates in the class above are whites and, in this instance, what appears to be class endogamy is really racial endogamy.

Fourth, ascriptive norms of the family exert a great deal of pressure on persons, especially in the higher strata, to marry someone of their "own kind," meaning the same social level. The pressures that parents exert in this regard sometimes are thought to have more than anything else to do with the process and certainly are visible at nearly every point at which young people come into meaningful contact with one another. Norms of kinship regarding the future status of a child may be involved, for example, in the parent's move to the right community, sending a child to a prep school, or seeing that he gets into the proper college.

Fifth, and an increasingly convincing argument, even as the structure of opportunities for social mobility open through direct competition within the educational system, class endogamy persists owing to the educational advantages (or disadvantages) accrued from one's family of orientation. Most colleges, whether commuter or residential, are matrimonial agencies. As suggested earlier, despite whatever else a woman may gain from her (or, more often, her parents') investment in higher education, the most important thing she can get out of college is the proper husband or at least the credentials that would increase her bargaining power in an exchange later on. Given the fact that men generally confer their status (whether achieved or ascribed) upon women and not the other way around (female proclamations to the contrary notwithstanding), marriage as a product of higher education has far more functional value for women than vocational or other more intrinsic rewards.

To carry this argument a bit further, access to college depends in large measure on the academic aptitude (or intelligence) of the applicants. Moreover, the hierarchical ordering of colleges which is based on this selectivity has led to a system of higher education which, in many ways, replicates the essential elements of the class structure. Differentiating those who go to college from those who do not, as well as where one goes to college, are *both* aptitude and social class. These two variables correspond so closely that despite the most stringent policies at some universities where academic aptitude and performance are the central criteria for admissions and where economic aid is no longer a major factor, students still come predominately from the higher socio-economic classes. For whatever the reason, genetic and environmental, this correspondence facilitates the intermarriage of individuals with similar social backgrounds, especially on American campuses where the sex ratio has been declining. It is interesting to note in this context that Warren's recent study of a representative sample of adults showed that roughly half of the similarity in class backgrounds of mates was due to assortative mating by education (Warren, 1966).

ETHNIC SOLIDARITIES

While intermarriage is both a cause and consequence in the assimilation of the descendants of different ethnic origin, various writers claim that the American "melting pot" has failed to materialize. Religious and racial lines in particular, are far from being obliterated. In fact, the very low frequency of exogamous marriages across these lines itself underscores the strength of the cleavages. Most authors also agree that nationality is not as binding as either race or religion as a factor in mate selection. Nation-type solidarities are still found among some urban groups (Italians and Poles) and rural groups (Swedes and Finns), but our public school system and open class structure have softened considerably what were once rather rigid boundaries. There is some evidence, too, that religious cleavages have been softening somewhat, and perhaps are continuing to soften as the functions of this institution become increasingly secular and social-problem oriented. On the other hand, racial boundaries, from the view of mate selection, appear to be as binding today as at any previous point in history; at least I have found no evidence to the contrary. The gains that Negroes have made in the schools and at the polls during the past ten years apparently have not softened the color line with respect to intermarriage.

Explanations of racial endogamy in America, some of which would take us back several centuries in time, are too varied to discuss here. It might be well to point out, however, that cultural and even legal prohibitions probably have relatively little to do with the present low rate of interracial marriage. As one author has stated, "the whole structure of social relationships between white and Negroes in the United States has been organized in such a way as to prevent whites and Negroes from meeting, especially under circumstances which would lead to identifying each other as eligible partners. . . . Under these circumstances, the few interracial marriages which do occur are the ones which need explaining" (Udry, 1966).

For the population geneticist, too, it would seem that the deviant cases are the ones which require attention. Elsewhere I have suggested, for example, that genes associated with intelligence may simply drift across the white and Negro populations since it appears that only certain morphological features, like skin color, actually operate to maintain the color line (Eckland, 1967). In other words, if the skin of an individual with Negro ancestry is sufficiently light, he may "pass" (with no strings attached) into the white population. Even just a lighter-than-average complexion "for a Negro" probably enhances his chances of consummating what we socially define as an "interracial" marriage. In neither the first or second case, however, is intelligence necessarily involved.

If intelligence *were* associated in any predictable way with racial exogamy, the drift would not be random and we would then have a number of interesting questions to raise. For instance, do only the lighter *and* brighter pass, and, if so, what effect, if any, would this be likely to have on the character of the Negro gene pool? What, too, is the character of the inflow of genes from the white population? We do know that the great majority of legally consummated interracial marriages involve Negro men and white women. Does this information provide any clues? And, what about the illegitimate progeny of white males and Negro prostitutes? How often are they placed for adoption in white households and with what consequences? Before taking any of these questions too seriously, we would want to have many more facts. For obvious reasons, our knowledge is extremely meager.

PRECAUTIONARY NOTES

In conclusion, five brief comments may be made upon the present state of research and theories of mate selection as revealed in the foregoing discussion.

First, there is a great deal of evidence of homogamous or assortative mating but relatively few theories to explain it and no satisfactory way of classifying its many forms.

Second, nearly all facts and theories regarding mate selection deal with engaged or married couples and hardly any attention has been given to illegitimacy (including adultery) and its relationship to assortative mating. It may be, such as in the case of miscegenation, that some of the most important aspects of mate selection occur outside the bonds of matrimony.

Third, our heavy emphasis upon courtship and marriage has obscured the fact that people often separate, divorce, and remarry. Mate selection may be a more or less continuous process for some individuals, affecting the character of the progeny of each new set of partners.

Fourth, the relationships between fertility and assortative mating still must be specified. Are there, for example, any patterns of assortative mating on certain traits, like education, which affect the number of children a couple will have?

Fifth, most of the factors in mate selection appear to covary. We discussed some of the more obvious problems in this regard, such as the relationship between residential segregation (propinquity) and class endogamy. It would appear that much more work of this sort will need to be done.

In regard to the last point, it would also appear that it is precisely here that social scientists, and sociologists in particular, may best serve the needs of population geneticists. Through the application of causal (chain) models and multivariate techniques, it may eventually be possible to sort out the relevant from the irrelevant and to specify in fairly precise terms not only the distribution of assortative mating in the social structure with regard to any particular trait, but also the ordering of variables and processes which restrict the field of eligibles.

NOTE

[1] I have attempted in the early part of this paper to place mate selection in an evolutionary perspective. The discussion later will focus on explanatory theories, treating assortative mating as the dependent variable. In another paper, I shall discuss in much greater depth than outlined here the social-evolutionary consequences of mate selection. See Bruce K. Eckland, "Evolutionary Consequences of Assortative Mating and Differential Fertility in Man," in Theodosius Dobzhansky (ed.), *Evolutionary Biology,* vol. IV (New York: Appleton-Century, [in press]).

REFERENCES

ALLEN, GORDON. Random and nonrandom inbreeding. *Eugenics Quarterly,* 1965, 12:181–198.

BURGESS, ERNEST W., and PAUL WALLIN. Homogamy in social characteristics. *American Journal of Sociology,* 1943, 49:109–124.

CASPARI, ERNST. Genetic endowment and environment in the determination of human behavior: Biological viewpoint. Paper read at the annual meeting of the American Educational Research Association, February 17, 1967.

CATTELL, RAYMOND B., and JOHN R. NESSELROADE. "Likeness" and "completeness" theories examined by 16 personality factor measures on stably and unstably married couples. (Advanced Publication No. 7.) 1967, The Laboratory of Personality and Group Analysis, University of Illinois.

CLARKE, ALFRED C. An examination of the operation of residential propinquity as a factor in mate selection. *American Sociological Review*, 1952, *17*:17–22.

ECKLAND, BRUCE K. Genetics and sociology: A reconsideration. *American Sociological Review*, 1967, *32*:173–194.

EVANS, RICHARD I. *Conversations with Carl Jung*. Princeton: Van Nostrand, 1964.

FULLER, J., and W. THOMPSON. *Behavior genetics*. New York: John Wiley & Sons, Inc., 1960.

HIRSCH, JERRY. Behavior-genetic, or "experimental," analysis: The challenge of science versus the lure of technology. *American Psychology*, 1967, *22*:118–130.

KEPHART, WILLIAM M. *The family, society and the individual*. Boston: Houghton Mifflin Company, 1961.

KIRK, DUDLEY. Demographic factors affecting the opportunity for natural selection in the United States. *Eugenics Quarterly*, 1966, *13*:270–273.

MERTON, ROBERT. Intermarriage and the social structure: Fact and theory. In Rose L. Coser (ed.), *The Family: Its Structure and Functions*. New York: St. Martin's, 1964, 128–152.

POST, R. H. (ed.). Genetics and demography. *Eugenics Quarterly*, 1965, *12*:41–71.

RAMSØY, NATALIE ROGOFF. Assortative mating and the structure of cities. *American Sociological Review*, 1966, *51*:773–786.

SPUHLER, J. N. Empirical studies on quantitative human genetics. In the use of vital and health statistics for genetics and radiation studies. United Nations and World Health Organization, 1962, New York, 241–252.

STERN, CURT. *Principles of human genetics*. San Francisco: W. H. Freeman, 1960.

UDRY, J. RICHARD. *The social context of marriage*. Philadelphia: J. P. Lippincott, 1966.

WARREN, BRUCE L. A multiple variable approach to the assortative mating phenomenon. *Eugenics Quarterly*, 1966, *13*:285–290.

WINCH, ROBERT. *Mate selection*. New York: Harper and Row, Publishers, 1958.

Mate Selection as the Development of a Relationship*

CHARLES D. BOLTON

The scientific study of mate selection has, with few exceptions, concentrated upon the statistical relating of demographic and personality variables presumed to characterize the marriageable individuals and to channel their selection of mate. In view of the history of the family area this procedure is not surprising. The field of the family, including mate selection, has developed as a semi-autonomous area of study in the interstices of sociology, psychology, anthropology, social psychiatry, medicine, and home economics. Students of the family have borrowed piecemeal from the theories of the disciplines which serve as the wings for the stage of family study. The almost inevitable result is a concentration upon the scattered variables suggested as possibly significant by the theories of the surrounding disciplines, but with little or no consideration of the precise functions of these variables in the mate selection process nor of the modification of these factors in the process by which a mating relationship is built up.

The conceptualization of the problem, not as the development of a love relationship, but as one of "mate selection," involves an imagery which compresses into a unitary non-processual, psychological act of choice what is actually a process of building over time a human relationship. In addition, the mate selection rhetoric—in the context of viewing the family as a texture of institutional roles—creates a hiatus between the premarital and postmarital relationships of the couple, since the learning of marital roles is assumed to be largely culturally transmitted through models available during childhood. As a result, we know very little, scientifically, about mate selection either as a process or as a relationship as such—that is, as a love or intimate relationship.

The dominance of the "variables" conception is seen in the fact that the one consistent thread of theoretical dispute in the area is that between the theories of homogamy and heterogamy (or its more recent version, the theory of complementary needs). Yet after decades of correlation studies, this dispute remains unresolved. While, on the surface, homogamy appears to have the stronger case, the evidence actually is

Reprinted from *Marriage and Family Living*, August 1961, 234–40, by permission of the National Council on Family Relations.

indecisive. Except for factors such as propinquity, race, religion, education, and class, in which selectivity is largely a reflection of differential contact—and, at any rate, limiting only within extremely broad ranges—the correlations of mates found for socio-psychological variables have been of a low order. If sociological theories of socialization are valid, the selective contact should also be reflected in fairly high correlations on a variety of personality, attitudinal, and social practice items since individuals from the same demographic categories have presumably been subject to similar patterns of socialization. Yet, when instead of simple correlations, the ratio of actual to expected similarity of couples in a sample is computed, as the Burgess-Wallin study,[1] the homogamous ratios for socio-psychological variables are very much lower than for demographic type variables. And even then, since the expected distributions must be calculated from the distribution of the characteristic in the sample, the more diversified the sample the less homogeneous the distribution of the characteristic in the sample will be relative to the distribution of the characteristics in what Winch calls the "field of eligibles"[2] of any of its individual members—hence producing the appearance of greater personality homogamy in the sample than would be the case if the ratio of actual to expected similarity were computed using the field of eligibles of each individual. It is perhaps significant that the large and diversified Burgess-Wallin sample produced, for personality traits, a very small ratio in the homogamous direction, while Winch's sample, drawn entirely from Northwestern University undergraduates and therefore likely to have a more homogeneous set of fields of eligibles, exhibited a generally complementary relation in personality characteristics.[3]

It can be argued that, if the psychological aspects of mate selection "naturally" operate on a principle of complementariness in a truly free marriage market, the homogamy of traits resulting from common socialization within demographic entering into differential association may partially or wholly cancel out statistical evidence of complementary selectivity in a high pressure marriage market. That over 90% of Americans marry indicates that social and personal pressures to marry are extremely heavy and that these pressures operate to limit the "free market" character of mating by pushing the individual toward a choice of mate within the categories of persons available to him in his selective contacts during youth. The younger the person the more selective his differential association in terms of propinquity, ethnicity, religion, education, and class, and hence the greater the socio-psychological homogeneity of the market within which he chooses, thus cancelling out tendencies toward complementarity.

However, the complementary needs theory fares no better under careful scrutiny. The psychiatric evidence is almost wholly drawn from patently neurotic cases in which only one member is studied. Winch's somewhat more systematic study,[4] though widely acclaimed, can hardly be said to offer convincing evidence for complementary needs as a sufficient explanation of mate selection. In view of the facts (1) that Winch uses Murray's set of personal needs and (2) that the TAT was devised for getting at just these needs, the fact that the TAT ratings were not only the least favorable of three sources of data used by Winch to test his complementarity hypotheses but were actually more often than chance contrary to his hypotheses casts considerable doubt on the findings.[5] Barely half the correlations based on case-history data were in the hypothesized direction. Only when Winch made what he calls a "global or molar or clinical or projective or holistic analysis" were a respectable number of permutations found in the hypothesized direction. Even then the number of significant correlations out of 388 is only 71.

Martinson's study of girls graduating from high school in 1945–49 and identified as married or unmarried in 1950 indicates that people with feelings of ego deficiency marry before those who feel more adequate.[6] Since Winch's sample consists completely of couples in which at least one, and presumably usually both, members married as undergraduates, it precisely fits the "married" category in Martinson's study, thus probably containing a disproportionate number of persons with ego deficiency, hence tending to over-represent complementariness if, as seems likely, marriages with a significant neurotic component are especially apt to involve complementarity. But the greatest weakness of Winch's study is that it really indicates almost nothing about how or whether the inferred need structure of the two individuals, considered separately, constituted a basic factor in their selection of one another as mates during the period of premarital interaction.

These comments are not, of course, intended to indicate that either the homogamy or the complementarity theory is without merit. Both approaches have been successful in sensitizing us to a number of factors that narrow the range of choice which must be explained by a complete theory of mate selection. The two theories are not, in fact, in any necessary conflict but may, as Winch points out, be thought of as complementing one another.[7] Yet the fact remains that, even taking the contributions of both the homogamy and complementarity theories, much if not most of the variance in mate selection continues to be unexplained. Is it not possible that the set of presuppositions surrounding the mate selection rhetoric is inadequate? Perhaps mate selection must be studied not only in terms of variables brought into the interaction situation but also as a process in which a relationship is built up, a process in which the *transactions between individuals* in certain societal contexts are determinants of turning points and commitments out of which marriage emerges. Seen from this viewpoint, the development of a mate selection relation is a problematic process. By "problematic" is meant that the outcome of the contacts of the two individuals is not mechanically predetermined either by the relation of their personality characteristics or the institutional patterns providing the context for the development of the relation—though these are both certainly to be taken into account—but that the outcome is an end-product of the sequence of interactions characterized by advances and retreats along the paths of available alternatives, by definitions of the situation which crystallize tentative commitments and bar withdrawals from certain positions, by the sometimes tolerance and sometimes resolution of ambiguity, by reassessments of self and other, and by the tension between open-endedness and closure that characterizes all human relations which have not been reduced to ritual. In short, the development of love relations is problematic because the product bears the stamp of what goes on between the couple as well as of what they are as individuals.

The viewpoint implied in this approach is the symbolic inter-actionist frame of reference, especially as recently represented in the writings of Blumer, Strauss, and Foote.[8] As an initial step toward assessing the fruitfulness of this approach, the development processes in the love relationships of a sample of twenty recently married couples were investigated intensively. These couples resided in Chicago, and as individuals may be characterized as white Americans, almost all in their twenties, not previously married, college educated, of diverse but predominantly Protestant religions, from a number of academic fields, from urban, middle-class backgrounds, somewhat upwardly mobile, and of dating, peer, and family backgrounds not significantly different from those typical of their demographic categories. Data on backgrounds and self-conceptions were gathered largely by a questionnaire, while material on the development of the love relation was obtained in a series of interviews, with each member of the couple being interviewed independently.

The analysis of the data involves two major phases: (1) the development of a process language for handling the development of intimate relationships, and (2) a consideration of the kinds of generalizations which are supported by the data. (The limitations of the sample made it desirable to present the generalization in a typological form). The development of the process language—which cannot be spelled out in detail here—suggests that it is profitable to view social interaction as operating in three modes as a determinant of the course of development of a relationship. The first mode takes "episodes of interaction" as the unit of analysis and seeks to establish the manner in which *one episode conditions the character of subsequent episodes.*[9] For example, in several cases, at the outset of the development of the relation, personal difficulties of the two individuals in their separate episodes environing, that is, preceding and paralleling, their mutual episode directed the couple's early interaction away from taking on an amorous cast and permitted the couple a non-amorous episode, out of which later arose a love involvement. Especially where one or both members are strongly inhibited or fearful of lasting involvement, it may be crucial that, prior to amorous episodes, there be a phase in which a *gemütlich* atmosphere is established or in which a dependency and trust growing out of handling other problems develops as a condition for the later episode of love involvement.

The second mode of process analysis was to break down the episodes of interaction into a variety of *forms of interaction* which, as units of interaction *per se*, have a determinant function on the direction of action in an episode. This form of analysis sensitizes us to interpersonal forms of interaction such as didactic, therapeutic, coaching, and supportive processes. There are also tactical processes such as pressuring for commitment, isolating of problem areas from the relation, testing oneself or the partner, retreating to some solid core of the relation under stress, and shifting cognitive level from abstract to particular and from impersonal to personal topics and finally to the relationship itself. Interpersonal exchange may be examined in terms of empathy in communication and exchange of personality currency. (That is, exchange of information about the personal makeup or symbolic clothing of the two parties.) In many cases it was not the currency itself that was crucial but the process aspect: the timing of exchange, the confidentialness of communication, the order in which material is revealed, etc.

The third mode of process analysis was in terms of turning points. From the viewpoint of this study, interpersonal and personal change is conceived of as a series of related transformations in actors' definition of themselves and their relations to others. A transformation is not simply an addition or an unfolding of an existing theme, but a reformulation, an employing of a new vocabulary, a shift from one perspective to another (as may be seen in the case of a psychoanalytic patient as he comes to see himself in a new way from the perspectives of unconscious motivation and mental economics with the Freudian vocabulary of defense mechanisms). The concept of "turning points" is used to denote these points of transformation. Turning points are not necessarily dramatic or even made into conceptual objects by the actors; a major transformation is ordinarily the product of a sequence of small turning points. Consider the following remark by a person for whom acceptance of commitment was very difficult:

> It is hard for both of us to say when we privately got engaged. The subject would come up time after time, and each time we would be more seriously attached afterwards, until it was just "there." I'm not sure when it occurred exactly. There was no time it exactly occurred—it was a gradual transition.

Clearly this development was not really gradual in the sense of a continuous stream filling up a channel but was a series of small turning points which eventually piled up to an acceptance that they were really engaged, and, as the informant put it, they "cemented it with an engagement ring." Of course, some turning points are more dramatic: breakthrough points at which some ambiguous matter "jells," [sic.] jump points where there is a sudden surge in affective involvement, points of decommitment from past relations or identities, etc.

The remainder of the report focuses upon certain typological conclusions and upon some of the general implications of the process approach to mate selection. A basic difficulty of almost all mate selection studies is the attempt to treat as a homogeneous class all relations culminating in marriage. There is a confounding of a legal category, marriage, with sociological categories of relationships. When analyzed in terms of development process, the heterogeneity of relations is apparent. Five types of development processes crystallized out in the analysis of even the present small sample of twenty cases. The great difference in these types makes clear the necessity of having multiple rather than monolithic explanations for mate selection.

TYPE I: *Personality meshing developmental processes.* (Four cases in the sample most nearly approximated this type.) The predominant characteristic of this type is the mutual perception of personality "fit," with the chief functions of interaction being those of bringing into meshing the existing personality orientations of the two parties and providing the qualities of experience which serve as indexes of a marriageable relation. Couples tend to be homogamous in background and values but complementary in personality needs and organization. Attraction is felt early, the developmental tempos of the pair are in close rhythm, and interactions increase in frequency to the saturation point, with erotic interaction, empathy, and idealization important. These relations, then, correspond fairly closely to romantic expectations.

TYPE II: *Identity clarification developmental processes.* (Four cases in the sample most nearly approximated this type.) The central theme is the focus of interaction upon the clarification or change of one or both individuals' identities.[10] Though the two individuals may initially differ about values, interaction brings about increasing agreement along with a role pattern tending to be equalitarian. The assumption of compatibility either is made early or emerges implicitly out of interaction about identity problems. In the early stages identity problems are not yet in the foreground or are not yet defined as part of the relationship, but are precipitated in manifest form by interactions in the relationship— such as through generation of conflict with parents or threat to defenses against intimate involvement. The relation cannot progress to marriage until the identity problems are resolved. The importance of interpersonal strategies is great; turning points are frequent; and a texture of shared understandings of considerable depth is built up. More than in any other type there is a withdrawal into the relationship and away from outside influences.

TYPE III: *Relation centered developmental processes.* (Five cases in the sample most nearly approximated this type.) The central theme is the building up of images of the other, amorous identifications and bonds which lead the couple to the decision that theirs is a viable relationship for marriage. Personalities do not spontaneously mesh; their "fit" remains in doubt through a large portion of the premarital period. Adjustments, shared understandings, and commitments are consciously built up, though they may not have much depth. There is an initial superficial commitment, and then one or both parties begin having questions, and the central theme becomes the viability of the relation. There are more ups and downs, breaks, rivals, incongruities of definition, and outside pressures to maintain the relation than in any other type.

TYPE IV: *Pressure and intrapersonal centered developmental processes.* (Four cases in the sample most nearly approximated this type.) The two parties are rather similar and traditional in background, and both dislike conflict. But their personalities decidedly do not mesh. One party uses direct, frontal pressure while the other depends upon subtle manipulation, with one being relatively free of blocks while the other has personality barriers to forming intimate involvements. Several themes emerge: (1) one member, being under an expediency pressure to marry, falls in love quickly and pressures the other for marriage, but the resisting or apathetic member blocks; (2) a concentration directly upon questions of indexes of marriageability and upon securing commitments; (3) a dependence of one or both members more upon the relationship *per se* than upon one another; and (4) a great importance of fantasy for one or both members. Identity problems are avoided except at crisis points—and then interaction halts short of efforts at resolution—and even amorous identifications tend to be built up primarily in intrapersonal processes. The marked lack of congruity of definitions is met by fantasy and tactical maneuvering. There is an emphasis upon formality, romanticism, and role playing, with an avoidance of the directly erotic. Often crucial developments come by correspondence, where the inhibited member feels freer and ambiguity is harder to maintain.

TYPE V: *Expediency centered developmental processes.* (Three cases in the sample most nearly approximated this type.) The relation centers around a strongly felt pressure to marry on the part of one or both members, this need occurring in the context of a basic personality problem or identity crisis. Where this pressure characterizes only one partner, the other is inexperienced in heterosexual relationships, highly suggestible, or apathetic toward his interpersonal fate. If expediency exists at the outset, the process is short; if it emerges after a casual relation is in progress, there are a series of sharp turning points and tactical maneuvers through which the relation quickly moves toward marriage. Personality "fit" and mutuality of values are only superficially considered, though some fantasy is important for providing the trappings of a romantic atmosphere.

As would be expected from the finding of different developmental patterns, the study revealed a number of different patterns by which commitment to a marital relationship occurs. Several of these patterns ordinarily occur in any given relationship, often for the same individual and often different for the two partners. Analysis indicated the following four major classes of process patterns by which persons become committed to a relationship.

1. *Escalators.* I use the term escalator to indicate the fact that certain types of action sequences seem to have a built-in momentum such that, once the individual takes the first step, he is carried along toward a final commitment to marriage. Such things as the romantic fantasy pattern and the "dating—going steady—pinned—engaged—marriage" pattern, often reinforced by the sanctions of the couple's immediate associates, exemplify institutionalized escalators. Equally important are intra- and inter-personal escalators such as the inter-contingencies of the individual's definitions of his situation and the contingencies emerging within the interaction episodes over time. It seems profitable to think of five types of escalators. The first is the *involvement escalator,* which comes into operation as the individual finds that his educational and career plans, his religious and moral identity, his daily schedule of going to and fro, and so on, become involved in the relation with a particular person. Second is the *commitment escalator,* which operates mainly through the sequence of formal, publicly announced commitments, but also through the fact that an informal or even implicit commitment is not only a pledge to another but a commitment to a definition of self and of one's broader situation. The commitment escalator is not only binding but propellent, for one commitment contains the seeds of propulsion to another—for example, a commitment to love in our culture implies one is thinking about a commitment to marry. Third is the *addiction escalator,* extending Lindesmith's conceptions about drug addiction to love relations insofar as the individual seeks to perpetuate a relationship in order to avoid the psychological withdrawal symptoms accompanying cessation of sexual, affectional, or prestigeful relations.[11] Fourth is the *fantasy escalator* in which there is a compulsive propulsion to maintain the relation as a symbol of some fantasy, whether the institutionally provided romantic fantasy or some more individual one. Finally, there is the *idealization escalator,* which comes into play as a result of the involvement of the individual's self-esteem in his indications to others of his choice of mate, creating in some cases a tendency to idealize the image of the partner in order to maintain self-esteem.[12]

2. *Commitment as a by-product of the interaction process by which a structure is built up in the relationship.* As a sequence of dating interaction continues, the couple gradually come to identify their pattern of interaction as being an objective relationship. That is, the relationship is perceived as having an objective, public existence, not merely an imputed or subjective existence.[13] ("It's relation without which my whole world would go smash," "His proposal didn't really change anything, it just confirmed what was already there," "We felt married already.")

When the relationship has reached this point of objectification, the individual sees his own and his fiance(e)'s identities and the relational qualities of the pairing as no longer problematic. One does not "direct love toward the other person"; one is "in love." Such questions as one has about marrying are then apt to be questions of timing rather than of choice of mate. Objectification occurs through three kinds of processes: (1) differentiation of the couple from the general dating complex of their milieu by the recognition of special bonds and structural characteristics of the relation, (2) public buttressing of the relation both by respecting the exclusiveness of the relation and by positive actions treating the couple as a unit, and (3) formalization, or the procedures by which the couple give their relationship a position in the larger socio-cultural framework of society (such as by engagement).

3. *Commitment through the movement of interaction processes toward the individual's definition of what constitutes a marriageable relationship.* In our culture definitions of a marriageable relationship include both a certain kind of image of the partner and the perception of certain qualities in experience in the relation. While this committing pattern is closest to conventional conceptions, the process data indicate two qualifications. First, it is crucial to distinguish between the image of the other held by the lover and the actual personality of the other. The high per cent of respondents who said, "I've found out a lot I didn't know about him since we got married," is indicative of this distinction. The image of the other is not merely what one "finds out" about the other but contains many elements which are built up in inter- and intra-personal transactions. Idealization, focusing on the absence of negatively valued traits, efforts to change the other, and taking some single act as symbolic of a complex process ("That letter showed me that she had just suddenly grown up") suggest the manner in which the image of the other is built up over time. Second, the perception of certain qualities of experience in the relation seem fully as significant as the image of the partner in rendering the relation acceptable for marriage. Among the qualities most often perceived as indexing a marriageable relation were a relaxed, *gemütlich* feeling, mutual responsiveness, feeling able to express normally suppressed behaviors, a minimum of quarreling, not getting on each other's nerves, perceiving the role adjustment as that of a "good team," and proved ability of the relation to survive crises. While the image of the partner is nominally held to be most important, the images offered are almost always conventional pictures painted in clichés and lacking in richness. Emphasis is rarely upon the partner's ethical attitudes toward others outside the relation but almost always on the performance of the other within the relation, suggesting a focusing upon qualities of experience with the other rather than traits of the other as a personality.

4. *The involvement of the relation in the resolution of identity crises.* Persons often bring—in latent or recognized form—identity problems to their love relationship and employ this relationship as a

vehicle for the clarification and/or resolution of these problems. In many cases—as when sex relations crystallize a struggle for emancipation from parental controls—a latent identity difficulty may be precipitated as a crisis by the relationship itself. Since expediency factors are ordinarily closely tied up with identity problems, expediency may be viewed as a special case of the involvement of the relation in the resolution of identity crises. As the importance of expediency build up for the individual or as the resolution of his identity crisis becomes dependent upon the relation, he becomes by that much committed to the relation. In a number of cases the amorous phases of the relation were preceded by or interlarded with essentially nonamorous phases which dealt with extra-relational identity problems. Whether the relation offers a vehicle for escape from parental controls, a means of downgrading unattainable career aspirations, or a sheltered world within which an insecure identity finds moorings, the person feels impelled to complete the objectification of the relation by marriage and directs his tactics to bringing his partner to the same commitment.

IMPLICATIONS

The work reported here is only exploratory, but what are some of its implications? It suggests, I think, the need for a new way of conceptualizing certain sociological propositions. In addition to propositions stating the probability of occurrences on the basis of atemporal, static variables, we need propositions about the probabilities of interaction processes taking certain alternative career-lines through specified sequences of turning points. Along with correlations between variables presumed to represent characteristics of non-situated social and psychological units we need propositions about, as Foote puts it, the manner in which one episode of interaction conditions another.[14] Instead of focusing on variables connected either to individual organisms or to abstract systems in equilibrium, perhaps we need more concentration upon the forms of interaction processes as processes and as interactional units.

In the field of mate selection itself a knowledge of processes can be of considerable value. Certainly the unexpected frequency with which expediency was significant may—if borne out in a larger sample—call for modification of conceptions about "free" marital choice in our society. While expediency was the *major* factor in only a small portion of cases, for 26 individuals in 15 of the 20 cases there appears to have been a perception of a pressure to marry at that particular stage in their lives which was over and above the culturally constant pressure to which all people are subject in our society. Moreover, for 21 of these persons the perception of this pressure was the product of one or more specific interpersonal episodes environing their mate selection episode rather than simply of such factors as reaching the age when chances of marriage diminish. A somewhat comparable finding was the considerable significance of sanctions applied by associates to ensure the continuation of a relation which has achieved at least informal public acknowledgment.

The considerable extent to which young people appear to use their love relations as vehicles for dealing with identity problems is a finding of relevance for the student of individual development. It is important to note that the development process of a love relation may at least precipitate a latent identity problem and in some cases create such a problem. Since the identity problems dealt with in love relations concern not only psychosexual identity but such areas as occupation, moral orientation, religious orientation, and relations to parents, the process approach permits a closer articulation of mate selection activities with the individual's general social development.

For the applied student of the family, it is a reasonable hypothesis that the character of the texture of shared understandings and techniques of consensus built up in the premarital period may be a significant determinant of the mode of adjustment in the crucial early marital period. Sketchy data collected in the present study on the immediate postmarital period suggest that this hypothesis has some validity. A corollary area of examination is the problem posed for couples during the marital period by differences in the degree of sharedness of conceptions about the relationship and its process of development.

For the sociologist, the process approach to mate selection affords an opportunity to study mating as a relationship rather than as the behaviors of two individuals. Since the process approach focuses upon interpersonal transactions, often from multiple status bases, upon the elaboration of a culture and role structure within the relationship, upon intercontingencies in episodes of interaction, and upon transformations in definitions of the situation, the analysis of the process in mate selection has distinctive promise as a procedure for reaching a genuinely sociological understanding of this aspect of the family field.

If it is true that the heart of the process approach is the view that the transactions between human subjects are determinants in the outcome of social encounters, then it becomes imperative to gather information on what actually transpires between people in building up their social acts as well as information on what initially composes the situation.

NOTES

* A fuller elaboration of the material in this paper may be found in Charles D. Bolton, *The Development Process in Love Relationships,* unpublished doctoral dissertation, University of Chicago Library, 1959.

[1] Ernest W. Burgess and Paul Wallin, *Engagement and Marriage.* Chicago: J. B. Lippincott, 1953.

[2] Winch suggests that demographic categories such as race, religion, class, etc., "determine with whom we associate [and that] they define for each of us a field of eligible spouse-candidates within which it is likely that we shall choose our spouses." Robert F. Winch, *Mate Selection: A Study of Complementary Needs.* New York: Harper and Bros., 1958, p. 14.

[3] *Ibid.* This same study was somewhat earlier reported on in Robert F. Winch, "The Theory of Complementary Needs in Mate-Selection: Final Results on the Test of the General Hypothesis," *American Sociological Review,* 20 (1955), pp. 552–55.

[4] *Ibid.*

[5] See the journal report of the study. *Ibid.*

[6] Floyd M. Martinson, "Ego Deficiency as a Factor in Marriage," *American Sociological Review,* 20 (1955), pp. 161–64.

[7] Winch, *Mate Selection, op. cit.,* pp. 9–15.

[8] See especially Herbert Blumer, "The Psychological Import of the Human Group," in Muzafer Sherif and M. O. Wilson, *Group Relations at the Crossroads,* New York: Harpers, 1953; Anselm Strauss, *Mirrors and Masks,* Glencoe, Ill.: The Free Press, 1959; and Nelson N. Foote, "Concept and Method in the Study of Human Development," in Muzafer Sherif and M. O. Wilson, *Emerging Problems in Social Psychology,* Norman, Oklahoma: The University Book Exchange Duplicating Service, 1957, pp. 29–53. The symbolic interactionist point of view of course descends from the work of George Herbert Mead and Charles Horton Cooley. The first systematic application of this viewpoint to mate selection appears to be in the work of Willard Waller. See Willard Waller, *The Family, A Dynamic Interpretation.* New York: The Cordon Co., 1938, especially pp. 263–75.

[9] For the conception of episodic conditioning see Foote, *ibid.*

[10] Though widely used, "identity" does not seem to be clearly defined in the literature. In the present context "identity" is used to refer to an individual's definition of the articulation of his sense of personal integrity with the selves he perceives himself as presenting to others in his major spheres of participation in the social process.

[11] Lindesmith briefly discusses the possibility of such an extension of his theory of drug addiction in Alfred R. Lindesmith, "Problems and Implications of Drug Addiction and Related Behavior," in Muzafer Sherif and M. O. Wilson, *Emerging Problems in Social Psychology,* Norman, Oklahoma: University Book Exchange Duplicating Service, University of Oklahoma, 1957.

[12] See a discussion of idealization in somewhat comparable terms by Paul Wallin, "Two Conceptions of the Relation of Love and Idealization," *Research Studies of the State College of Washington,* 20, No. 2 (1952), pp. 21–35.

[13] The conception of "objectification" used here is parallel to Durkeim's conception of the collective representations as being social facts which are external and coercive to the actor, and also similar to Simmel's view that actors experience the existence of the group as supra-individual.

[14] Nelson N. Foote, "Concept and Method in the Study of Human Development," *op. cit.,* pp. 29–53.

V

Marriage

The heart of the American family is the marital relationship itself, and this is the focus of Part V. Husbands and wives play the roles of provider and household manager, make decisions, have and raise children, and engage in social activities together. All these issues and others are considered by the writers of the six selections which follow.

The first two, by Joan Aldous and Hilda Krech, present marriage and family responsibilities from the husband's and the wife's perspectives, respectively. Aldous introduces the reader to several of the critical issues confronting the husband in the contemporary American family. To what extent does the husband's work or economic role behavior carry over into his marriage? Does he treat his family the same way that he does his work associates, or is his family a place of escape, where he can "be himself" and leave his work role behind? How does he balance his work and family responsibilities; how much of his time and energy does he give to each, and with what result? How important is communication between him and his wife for *his* marital satisfaction? Once again, the reader must be on guard against the stereotypic picture, in Aldous' article, of the matriarchal black family, and should recall Billingsley's presentation in Part II. Krech's discussion of the contemporary woman's position in the family raises as many issues as does Aldous' for the male. Does the woman today have the "best of both worlds"—the domestic and the occupational—or the worst? According to Krech, the role of housewife is deprecated by many educated middle-class women, but if she works she is still stigmatized, regardless of her motive for working. Nor should the decisions facing the American woman be restricted to holding a job or staying home; she may also involve herself in various community affairs of a voluntary nature. This, however, brands her as an aggressive or assertive woman, and you will recall McDaniel's view of the difficulties encountered by the assertive female. What, after all, is Krech's view of woman's status today, and what does she think it should be? Do you agree or disagree?

Phyllis Hallenbeck's analysis divides the bases for power into five, and shows how these must be distinguished in order to understand the power and decision-making processes that occur in marriage. She shows how economic resources, attractiveness, role playing, and personality all may go into determining the balance of power within the family. In addition, her thought-provoking discussion of roles and role choices provide an excellent introduction to Robert Stuckert's piece on roles and marital satisfaction. According to Stuckert, satisfaction is related to the individual's perception that he and his spouse are playing the roles which they desire to, or "should," play. Recalling McDaniel's argument once again, does the reader agree with Stuckert's assertion that the wife must do more adapting of her role expectations in marriage than the husband?

In the 1950's, E. E. Lemasters published a piece entitled "Parenthood as Crisis." Since that time, Everett Dyer, Daniel Hobbs, Alice Rossi, and others have debated whether the coming of the first child causes a crisis for the married couple or not, and Arthur Jacoby's paper is the latest in this series. Of course, a part of the disagreement rests upon whether one defines a crisis as the readjustment necessary following an event for which current role behaviors are inadequate, or whether a crisis involves an unanticipated event and a major role disorganization. Introducing many important variables to the discussion of parenthood as crisis, Jacoby asks the reader to ponder whether there may be more of a crisis for new parents in the middle class than in the working class, and whether, in fact, many of the disagreements between Lemasters, Hobbs, and others may not be traced to their methodologies and samples. Parenthood does require a readjustment, but is it likely to be a crisis event?

The final reading in Part V is an empirical study of the social participation of married couples. Beginning with seven social categories based upon occupational type, Adams and Butler observe the engagement of couples in commercial recreations, home entertaining, religious attendance, kin visiting, and shopping together. Upper-middle-class couples almost all engage in the first three activities together with substantial frequency, thereby epitomizing the "togetherness" which is frequently called for in the popular family magazines. Blue-collar couples to a great extent replace commercial recreation and churchgoing with visits to kin, thereby filling their social lives with a meaningful, but less expensive, form of activity. Several questions are left unanswered by these data. Is it not possible that when blue-collar individuals engage in commercial recreation they do it separately, instead of with their spouses? Unfortunately, the data concern couples only. Also, these couples average 34 years of age; how might their activity patterns change over the entire span of their married lives? Surely the patterns of parents with young children and of the aged whose children have left home should diverge greatly.

Consideration in Adams and Butler's paper of kinship visiting prepares us for the consideration in Part VI of relations between the family and other societal systems, such as kin, business, and religion.

Occupational Characteristics and Males' Role Performance in the Family*

JOAN ALDOUS

A great deal has been written on the differentiation of work from family roles in modern industrial societies. The general separation in time and space of family and occupational role performance is readily apparent. In addition, the formal requirements of the work group are often at variance with those of the family. Increasingly men, and women too, are playing their occupational roles in settings with bureaucratic characteristics. Here there are a number of supervisory levels. Obtaining a job and job advancement are determined by rules defining universalistic, specific standards of merit. Rules define the duties and privileges constituting the job, and the jobs are highly specialized. Unlike the highly formal bureaucratic organization, the family as a primary group is characterized by highly charged affective relations rather than impersonal contacts, and the vagaries of conception that may or may not follow intercourse rather than specific qualifications determine family membership. There is only one supervisory level, though parents may dispute this. Family members interact with each other while playing many roles as opposed to the segmented relationships of the factory and office. Family members for better or worse are involved in relatively lasting arrangements, while on the job their associates change because of merit promotions or seniority options. Finally, family interaction patterns develop over time in conformity to the family's version of the culture transmitted by important reference groups. This routinization of group activities is quite in contrast to the formal rule specification that provides the framework for interaction on the job.[1]

However, it can be argued that the supposed contrast between family and occupational roles is overdrawn. The whole "human relations" approach in industrial management grew out of the recognition that there existed an informal structure of communication and friendship networks that often circumvented the regimen of rules of the formal job structure.[2] Merit may be one of the requirements for getting a job or advancement, but personal impressions and contacts influence selection from those qualified, even in the most regulation-conscious bureaucracy. Sponsorship and social networks are particularly important for

Reprinted from *Journal of Marriage and the Family*, November 1969, 707–12.

obtaining a position when job requirements are unclear and there is no simple measure of who qualifies, or job requirements are not too demanding so that many qualify. Once on the job, the incumbent rarely is able to remain affectively neutral toward his close associates whether behind the counter or on the assembly line. As a result, the "highly charged affective relations" found in the family are also present in the occupational world and influence what goes on there from job selection to job performance.[3]

Regardless of the extent of difference between family and work roles, they do articulate if for no other reason than that the male is an actor in both spheres. And there are other reasons. Formal organizations are eager to lessen the distance between family and job and to enlist the support of other family members as well as the husband-father. They hope thereby to encourage the family role set to push the man toward the same goals his job supervisor is sanctioning. In this paper, however, the main focus is on the influence of the workman's role on family functioning rather than on the reciprocal effect of parental and marital functions on occupation. Structural characteristics of the occupation that affect the man's parental and marital functioning regardless of the personality of the job incumbent provide the major independent variables to be discussed. Because of the dearth of research, however, it is not possible to maintain a rigid separation between characteristics unique to a particular occupation or related occupations that affect parental and marital role functioning, and characteristics specific to a particular work setting such as a bureaucracy where persons in a number of occupations are active.

To begin with, the male's participation in the job market is essential for providing him the means for participating in the family. In our society the man's adult status depends upon his holding some kind of job. The research on unemployed men and their families in the thirties demonstrated the importance of the breadwinner role to the man's family status. Loss of a job meant his loss of power and influence on the actions of wife and children, as one of them or an outside agency succeeded him as economic support of the family.

Much the same phenomenon occurs in lower-class Negro and white families today. These families have a segregated conjugal role organization where there is a rigid division of labor in household tasks. The husband-father supplies the money for physical maintenance of the family, and the wife-mother performs housekeeping and child-care functions. When the husband is supplying an adequate income, the wife caters to his wants, overlooks his shortcomings, and is prepared to reward him for any household task or decision in which he engages. A positive reinforcement cycle of participation, reward, and further participation is set up, drawing the man into ever deepening involvement in family activities. Insufficient and unstable earnings on the other hand are associated with the man's lack of involvement in the family. The wife has less to reward him for and so provides little incentive for him to involve himself in family affairs. Thus within one working-class sample the higher the amount of income per family member, the more the husband performed household tasks and helped make family decisions.[4] Among lower-class Negro families where the matriarchal tradition is strong, unemployed men withdraw from the family not only because of their own feelings of inadequacy but at their wives' insistence. If the man is not supplying the family income, his wife often refuses to perform her wifely duties and drives him from the household.[5] Even when the man is employed, having a wife who is also employed appears to constitute a threat to his position as household head. He is less active in household affairs than his compeers whose wives are not competitors in the breadwinner role.[6] The opportunity to practice an occupation, therefore, is one community tie that enables the male to perform the role of provider, a role that for most men appears a prerequisite for their performing other family roles.

But once one goes beyond the simple dichotomy of employment and unemployment, the characteristics of the job the man holds in the occupational structure can have profound effects on his marital and parental role performance. First, there is the matter of how compatible occupational characteristics are with family participation. The *relative salience* of the job in comparison with family roles is important in this connection. If the occupation is of intrinsic interest to the man, it often competes with or even supplants the family as his major concern. Occupations that engage the man's attention at the expense of his family usually have some or all of the following qualities. The job incumbent has some autonomy in structuring its pace and schedule as well as the methods used. The occupation encompasses a variety of activities and provides a stable career line. It often requires special training, and there are sustained contacts with fellow workers, clients, or customers. Professions and positions in the higher echelons of business, highly skilled blue-collar occupations such as printing, or dangerous jobs such as mining are examples of high salience occupations.

The effect of such occupations on the man's family varies. Often the wife-mother has to assume virtually sole responsibility for the family, as the husband-father is too busy or too disinterested to supply much assistance. Particularly among the men of management as Whyte discovered, the man may co-opt the family and use it as a means of career advancement.[7] The man eliminates the autonomy of the family sphere and makes it an adjunct to his central occupational concern. He uses the family's consumption patterns and the wife's interpersonal skills in the service of his mobility strivings. Moreover, family concerns can mask occupational concerns and also permit him to escape from awkward professional commitments. The academician, for example, who finds his colleagues unexciting and his position at a dead end can suddenly discover his family's unhappiness with the climate and begin looking openly for a more satisfactory appointment. A strategic retreat into family roles disarms critics while permitting continued occupational striving.

Unfortunate, indeed, are those families where the wife's development after marriage has not kept pace with the husband's so that his family though co-opted is not useful to him. In such cases he often seeks a more compatible partner.[8] Many of the intrinsically interesting white-collar occupations encourage change in their incumbents—change that may threaten the interpersonal "fit" of the couple. The young man preparing to enter a profession, for example, may not wish to face the long years of training in a state of celibacy. But while he is being socialized into a demanding occupational role, his wife—busy in her daily round of supporting him or attempting to cope with unplanned offspring—may not be changing as much as he. The result can be the post-Ph.D. or post-M.D. divorce. Organization man and wife may also fail to match in phase of development when the husband, at his company's behest, moves in a variety of social milieus and comes into contact with different roles, life styles, and perspectives while the wife keeps the family together. Failure of husband and wife to remain "in phase" so that their development is comparable and compatible is a constant threat to the stability of the marriages of men in management or the professions.

A dimension of the man's occupation other than its salience that affects marital and parental functioning is the *synchronization of occupational and family responsibilities*. This dimension encompasses such aspects of the job as its hours, the amount of geographical mobility it requires, and at what stage of the family life cycle the occupation makes its peak demands. Occupations having irregular hours or requiring night work, as well as those taking the man away from home for days at a time, all limit his opportunity to assist with family decisions and tasks as well as to become acquainted with his children. Afternoon shift workers, one study showed, have particular difficulty with father roles, night shift workers with marital roles.[9] Since the marital role difficulties center on such sensitive areas as sexual relationships and companionship, it is no wonder the friction between husband and wife is greater for night than day workers, though it is more pronounced for all non-day workers. Night workers develop crony cliques to supply the sociability and emotional support their families, geared to a daytime existence, are literally too asleep to provide. The man on the road may seek a compliant woman to supply the sexual comforts he is not at home to receive. It is no wonder then that Lang as far back as 1932 reported that wives of traveling salesmen and musicians were most unhappy in their marriages. Wives of bankers, physicians, corporation officials, and the owners of large businesses were less unhappy but more so than wives of teachers and accountants. Presumably the former group of husbands found their jobs more salient than their families.[10]

Where spatial synchronization and time complementarity between family and work setting seem necessary for parental and marital role performance, synchronization of family and occupational demands can create difficulty. The peak years for child-bearing and child-rearing responsibilities for the man tend to be in the 22- to 35-year age range, but this is the same period when occupational demands are highest and most worrying. The white-collar man is trying to climb the hierarchial ladder of the bureaucracy while learning the requirements of his changing responsibilities. The blue-collar worker too may be trying out a number of different jobs because of choice or the exigencies of the job market. Young men, as a result, no matter how devoted to home and family may face difficulties in coping adequately with both job and parental responsibilities.

Wilensky has also noted the squeeze the husband-father experiences at this time between family economic needs and income rewards from the job—a squeeze that can exacerbate the marital disenchantment of the child-rearing years. Medical expenses and demands for consumer goods are high at this time, but the income peaks for white-collar men come later as does job security because of seniority for manual workers. Wives cannot eliminate the squeeze through joining the labor force because of small children at home. Job satisfaction parallels the marital satisfaction trend, recalling to our attention the reciprocal nature of the occupation-family relation. The larger the family, understandably, the longer and lower job satisfaction dips from the high of the bachelor and young married without children periods. Just as with the departure of the children there is some increase in marital satisfaction, so too does job satisfaction show some recovery in the age years of 45–54 as family economic demands diminish, job aspirations lower, and income and occupational security increase.[11]

In addition to the synchronization or the lack thereof in family and occupation careers, an additional characteristic of the job affects the men's fulfilling family responsibilities. This has to do with *overlap*—the degree of overlap in family and work settings and, often associated with the latter, overlap in the personnel of work group and family. In this country aside from the family farm and the neighborhood grocery stores where the family lives in the back or upstairs, there are few examples of this phenomenon; but in Europe even the professional has his office in a portion of his home. When this is the case, the differentiation between family and work roles that occurred because of the Industrial Revolution breaks down. Although family concerns may take second place to business matters when the family is the economic unit, at the very least the husband-father is close at hand ready to respond to family emergencies. At most, the members of his family role set also constitute the members of his occupational role set and can sanction behavior that threatens his performing essential family functions.

To this point the discussion has covered the occupational characteristics of (1) relative salience as compared with the family, (2) the degree of synchronization of family and occupational responsibilities, and (3) the degree of overlap in family and work setting and their effect on husband-father's family role functioning. Now it will cover the intra-family dynamics affected by the husband-father's occupation. The Rapoports speak of the *isomorphism* or *similarity* of behavior patternings between occupation and family.[12] As an example, they report a finding that science-oriented technologists make more conjugal decisions on an equalitarian basis than is true among technologists concerned with equipment. They interpret the difference partly in terms of the carry-over from occupation to home of the universalistic norms underlying science.[13] Another example of isomorphism is that professionals, organization men, and others heavily concerned with interpersonal relations on the job hold high expectations of the companionship aspects of marriage. They appear to be demanding professionalization of the marital roles, perhaps in order partially to redress the balance between occupation and family. They expect high levels of competence in the performance of marital and parental roles. But the variety of roles they see as constituting the parent-spouse positions—lover, companion, housekeeper, breadwinner, teacher, and disciplinarian, to name only a few—with their contradictory requirements call for systematic training that is lacking. Therefore, though the expectations are for family roles meeting professional standards, the socialization that would enable these standards to be met is largely nonexistent. This may help explain the marriages Cuber and Harroff in their study of individuals in decision-making, policy-setting occupations designate as "conflict-habituated," "devitalized," or "passive-congenial"—terms that indicate the negative qualities of the marriage.[14]

It is in the upper middle-class group where professionals and men who manage predominate that Rainwater found husbands and wives usually have a joint conjugal role relationship. These are patterns where the couple shares activities, or either partner is willing to perform various household activities. True, these couples see themselves as concerned with activities outside the home—often separate concerns—but they expect the partner to be willing to listen and to provide support for the separate activities.[15] These are the kinds of marriages Cuber and Harroff dub "vital" as opposed to the couples with "total" relationships where each spouse is involved in the complete activity range including occupational performance of the other.[16] Husbands in such vital marriages, with their very high standards of role performance, fear the isomorphism that may exist between their occupational and family behavior. They worry that they may be too aggressive or assertive in their families, personal qualities required on the job but apt to create tense relationships in the home.[17]

For most professional and managerial couples though, the power relationship between husband and wife is such as to make the marriage a "colleague" rather than a companionship type to use Gold and Slater's terminology.[18] Despite the heavy emphasis on companionship, the spouses are not equals in decision-making. There is isomorphism between occupation and family role performance. The family's status clearly rests on the husband-father's achievements and though the wife as a good colleague mobilizes special skills to aid his advancement, she makes fewer family decisions alone.[19] Husbands accustomed to having decision-making responsibilities in the office continue to make them at home. They, also, because of occupational demands engage in fewer household activities.[20]

The occupation also affects the paternal roles of professionals and executives. Aberle and Naegele found that men in these occupations have clear perceptions of the kind of sons they want and evaluate sons in terms of occupational role demands. Men expect their sons to be responsible, aggressive, show initiative, and be competent—all indicators that the boys will succeed in the middle-class occupations their fathers hold and envision for their sons. Fathers are anxious if the sons are passive, irresponsible, and overly excitable—qualities than do not augur well for the boys' future occupational accomplishments. The fathers show less concern and have fewer expectations of their daughters, who presumably will be less involved in the job market.[21]

Isomorphism also exists between the occupational and family roles of men who are in occupational roles other than those of professionals or managers. Small entrepreneurs are an example. They, of necessity, have to plan as well as to participate in the organization of their economic activity. Gold and Slater found in their sample of self-employed and workers in small businesses that white-collar wives, when they work outside the home, most often assist their husbands in the family business. Even so, the husbands retain more power in family decision-making, a power position consistent with their position in the occupational world and also consistent with their position as primary determiners of the family's social status.[22] Interestingly enough, however, the farmer-entrepreneur, several recent studies have shown, seems not to set policy for the family as he does for the land.[23] In household task performance too he is much less active than urban men, which suggests the pressure of ever present occupational duties caused by the spacial overlap of occupational and family settings.[24]

The haven of the companionship family where husband and wife interact as equals is in the lower middle class. The situation here is in direct contrast to that of men in high job saliency occupations. Husbands tend to be in lower-level bureaucratic and quasi-professional jobs or in blue-collar supervisory and craftsmen level jobs of little intrinsic interest. Men, far from seeking to carry over job-related behaviors to the family, often look to their homes as havens from job monotonies and as sources of the satisfactions lacking in the occupational sphere. Husband and wife are apt to have an intermediate conjugal role organization in which both participate in child-rearing but maintain a traditional division of labor in other areas. Social activities outside the family constitute a threat to the family-centered relation, so men worry about their tendencies to withdraw from family activities in favor of personal interests. Wives, in turn, fear their own egocentricity and also that they will be their aggressiveness deny their family-centered husbands a voice in family affairs.[25]

Yet heightened domesticity is not always associated with work alienation. Kin and cronies can provide alternate sources of emotional support and in the lower class often do. Even in the working class where men in operative type occupations have some job security and are more active in family roles than laborers and service workers in the lower-lower class, moves to the suburb that destroy social networks with relatives and peers result in increased household activity.[26]

Laborers and service workers are least involved in family tasks or decisions.[27] It is not only that these men experience enough unemployment that their wives, as noted earlier, may give them scant encouragement to participate. On their jobs they have little opportunity to associate with men in other occupations or specialties, holding different values and possessing different skills that would sharpen the role-taking abilities of these lower-class men. Many lower-class men interact with others on the basis of routinized reactions and projections of their own views.[28] Because women play different roles, lower-class men find their projecting strategy in interpersonal relations ineffective. As a consequence marital communication is limited. The job, therefore, through its limitations on security, pay, and provision of opportunities for exercising interpersonal skills offers little encouragement to the lower-class male to perform his marital and parental functions.

Thus the paper has come full cycle. The discussion began with an analysis of the economic resources which employment in some occupations gives a man—resources that supply the minimum essentials for his functioning in the family. It concludes with an analysis of how the right kind of occupation can facilitate communication skills needed for marital interaction. In both instances as in the rest of the paper's analysis, the separation of the occupation and family spheres has been demonstrated to be more myth than reality. They affect each other in many ways, and not all of them are harmful—the nepotism literature to the contrary. And this conclusion should really come as no surprise, since occupational and family roles for the overwhelming majority of men constitute first- and second-ranking life interests. The roles may not always coexist in harmony, but the dynamics arising from their conflicting as well as similar requirements provide a fruitful research area for persons in their working roles of family or occupational specialist.

NOTES

* The author would like to thank Judith D. Bennett and William S. Silverman for their comments on the original of this paper, which was prepared for the 1967 Groves Conference.

[1] This discussion owes much to Eugene Litwak, *Technological Innovation and Ideal Forms of Family Structure in an Industrial Democratic Society,* paper presented before the International Seminar on Family Research, Tokyo, 1965, pp. 2–3.

[2] There is a voluminous literature on the informal structure in work groups. See among others, George C. Homans, *The Human Group,* New York: Harcourt, Brace and Co., 1950, pp. 40–88; Hans Zetterberg, "The Secret Ranking," *Journal of Marriage and the Family,* 28 (May, 1966), pp. 134–142; and Edward Gross, *Work and Society,* New York: Thomas Y. Crowell, 1958, pp. 222–260.

[3] It is even questionable whether family members see each other play so many more roles than do job associates. Perhaps it is the backstage, undress quality of family life that makes it appear that individuals reveal so much more of themselves in the family than they do when playing occupational roles.

[4] Joan Aldous, "Lower Class Males' Integration into Community and Family," paper presented before the Sixth World Congress of Sociology, 1966, p. 144. "The provision of needed income even enables women to overlook such unfortunate husbandly behaviors as incestuous activities. A concern about the family livelihood leads women to blame their husbands less for incestuous activities than the daughter-victims for reporting the activities to the police." The same situation occurs in brother-sister incest. "When the brother is the aggressor he usually is condemned, unless the family wholly or partly depends upon him for support." S. Kirsten Weinberg, *Incest Behavior,* New York: Citadel Press, 1955, pp. 182 and 255.

[5] Lee Rainwater, "Crucible of Identity: The Negro Lower-Class Family," *Daedalus,* 95 (Winter, 1966), p. 192.

[6] Joan Aldous, "The Restoration of the Lower-Class Male as Household Head: Support for the Moynihan Thesis," paper presented before the American Sociological Association, 1967, p. 6.

[7] William H. Whyte, Jr., "The Wives of Management," *Fortune,* 44 (October, 1951), pp. 86–88; and William H. Whyte, Jr., "Corporation and the Wife," *Fortune,* 44 (November, 1951), pp. 109–111.

[8] Nelson N. Foote, "Matching of Husband and Wife in Phases of Development," in *Sourcebook in Marriage and the Family,* ed. by Marvin B. Sussman, Boston: Houghton Mifflin, 1963, pp. 15–21.

[9] Paul E. Mott *et al., Shift Work: The Social, Psychological and Physical Consequences,* Ann Arbor: University of Michigan Press, 1965, pp. 111 and 146.

[10] R. O. Lang, *The Rating of Happiness in Marriage,* unpublished M.A. thesis, University of Chicago, 1932, quoted by J. Richard Udry, in *The Social Context of Marriage,* New York: J. B. Lippincott, 1966, p. 388.

[11] Harold L. Wilensky, "Work Situation and Participation in Formal Associations," in *Aging and Leisure,* ed. by Robert W. Kleemeier, New York: Oxford University Press, 1961, p. 228.

[12] Robert Rapoport and Rhona Rapoport, "Work and Family in Contemporary Society," *American Sociological Review,* 30 (June, 1965), p. 385.

[13] Robert Rapoport and Edward O. Laumann, "Technologists in Mid-Career: Factors Affecting Patterns of Ten-Year Out Engineers and Scientists from Three Universities," in *The Impact of Space Efforts on Communities and Selected Groups,* ed. by Robert Rapoport, American Academy of Arts and Sciences, Committee on Space, cited in *ibid.*

[14] John F. Cuber and Peggy B. Harroff, *The Significant Americans: A Study of Sexual Behavior among the Affluent,* New York: Appleton Century, 1965, pp. 44–54.

[15] Lee Rainwater, *Family Design: Marital Sexuality, Family Size and Contraception,* Chicago: Aldine Publishing Company, 1965, pp. 314–317.

[16] Cuber and Harroff, *op. cit.*, pp. 55–60.

[17] Rainwater, *Family Design, op. cit.*, p. 317.

[18] Martin Gold and Carol Slater, "Office, Factory, Store—and Family: A Study of Integration Settings," *American Sociological Review*, 23 (February, 1958), pp. 65–66.

[19] Robert O. Blood, Jr. and Donald M. Wolfe, *Husbands and Wives: The Dynamics of Married Living*, Glencoe, Illinois: Free Press, p. 31. For a further discussion of how the comparative resources of husbands and wives affect decision-making power, see David M. Heer, "The Measurement and Bases of Family Powers: An Overview," *Journal of Marriage and the Family*, 25 (May, 1963), pp. 133–139; also Blood's "Rejoinder" and Heer's "Reply" in *Journal of Marriage and the Family* (November, 1963), pp. 475–478.

[20] Blood and Wolfe, *op. cit.*, pp. 60–61.

[21] David F. Aberle and Kaspar D. Naegele, "Middle-Class Fathers' Occupational Role and Attitudes toward Children," *American Journal of Orthopsychiatry*, 22 (April, 1952), pp. 366–378.

[22] Gold and Slater, *op. cit.*, p. 67.

[23] Blood and Wolfe, *op. cit.*, p. 24; and Lee G. Burchinal and Ward A. Bauder, *Family Decision-Making and Role Patterns among Iowa Farm and Non-Farm Families*, Ames, Iowa: Agricultural and Home Economics Experiment Station Bulletin 528, June, 1964, p. 167.

[24] Blood and Wolfe, *op. cit.*, pp. 58–59. It should be noted that Burchinal and Bauder did not find this segregated task performance among their rural couples. Burchinal and Bauder, *op. cit.*, p. 168.

[25] Rainwater, *Family Design, op. cit.*, p. 315. As with the discussion of the marital and parental relations of the top-level professional or organization man, it is difficult to separate occupational and class influences on the husband-father roles.

[26] Lee Rainwater and Gerald Handel, "Changing Family Roles in the Working Class," paper presented before the Annual Meeting of the American Sociological Association, 1963.

[27] Aldous, "Lower Class Males' Integration into Community and Family," *op. cit.*, p. 188; Rainwater, *Family Design, op. cit.*, pp. 318–321; and Blood and Wolfe, *op. cit.*, pp. 30 and 62.

[28] Herbert J. Gans, *The Urban Villagers: Group and Class in the Life of Italian-Americans*, New York: Free Press of Glencoe, 1962, p. 98.

Housewife and Woman? The Best of Both Worlds?

HILDA SIDNEY KRECH

Scoldings, dissections, and revolutionary proposals—all about modern woman—have been filling the air for ten or fifteen years. They've also been filling newspaper columns, books, TV programs, learned journals, not-so-learned journals, and symposia from the Vassar campus to the University of California Medical School. Surprisingly, words about modern woman have been flowing and symposia have been gathering at an increasing rather than a decreasing rate. More surprising still, a lot of people seem to be willing (sometimes even eager) to hear about her once again. I find myself challenged to say something new about her before the subject (and the discussers of the subject) are exhausted.

When I considered the concern—the serious, frivolous, scientific, sympathetic, and sometimes furious concern—that's been lavished on modern woman, and most especially modern American woman, I started wondering why she remains bewildered and bewildering, why her dilemma remains unsolved. And I was struck by the fact that we haven't all been talking about the same American woman.

Most of the talk and most of the criticism has been lavished on the more or less privileged, more or less educated, presumably intelligent woman. She is the one who has encouraged the word "discontented" to be linked with the words "American woman." She has been forced to add the feeling of guilt to her feelings of frustration because so many people for so many years have been telling her how lucky she is. And she is. And she knows it. But still—but still what? Her dissatisfaction is about equally divided between what she *does* do and what she *does not* do.

Speaking with women who are quite happily married, one often gets the feeling that housework and child care are both too much and too little for each one of them; too much because they take all her time, energy, and thought during the period when her children need constantly to be fed, clothed in clean clothes, fetched and carried, and tended to in one way or another; too little in that she'd somehow been led to believe that she would be using her time and her talents and her energy quite differently—at least for a portion of each day. All through school and, for many, through college as well, these talents—whether artistic, intellectual, practical, or human—have been respected and encouraged.

Though, deep inside, there is nothing she would rather do than be a mother, she often feels, while her children are young, like a drudge. When they are grown, she is a has-been—sometimes feeling that she's a *has*-been without ever really having *been*. She is no longer needed as a full-time mother, yet no longer able to be whatever it was she set out to be all those long years ago. For, contrary to polite and gallant statements which suggest that simply "being a woman" is a vocation, this is not the case.

To make such a woman's discontent stronger still, the truly lucky woman is married to a man who does interesting, challenging, perhaps useful, and sometimes lucrative work which often gets more challenging and useful as the years go by, while her work gets less challenging, less useful. Growing up, she didn't wish she were a boy. She doesn't wish now that she were a man. Yet something is wrong with this picture of the luckiest woman in the world.

In answer to the countless articles, speeches, and books which have painted just such a picture, *The Saturday Evening Post* recently ran an article defending the American woman, refuting the countless statements which accuse her of being "lonely, bored, lazy, sexually inept, frigid, superficial, harried, militant, overworked." The adjectives are those of the authors, Dr. George Gallup and Evan Hill, who made a survey and then described what they call the "typical" American woman.

(Though one-third of the married women in America are employed outside the home, and though nearly 15 per cent of women over forty-five are widowed or divorced, the authors specifically state that these women are not "typical," and, therefore, they are neither discussed nor included in the composite picture. Getting ahead of my story for a moment, I'd like to point out, also, that Gallup and Hill's typical American woman is forever young, forever surrounded by young children.)

The charges against the American woman are untrue, say Dr. Gallup and Mr. Hill. She is happy; she is content; she wants only "the simple pleasures"; her family is "her whole life." Their typical wife sums up her situation by saying: "If I don't want to do the dishes or laundry right now, I can do them later. My only deadline is when my husband comes home. I'm much more free than when I was single and working. A married woman has it made."

Her house may be cluttered, but her mind is not. Only half of the women interviewed read books at all; only 13 per cent consider "intelligence as a prerequisite in husbands." The only reference to the life of the mind in this article quotes the typical wife as saying: "I spend my spare time broadening my interests so I won't bore Jim." So I won't bore Jim! Apparently she doesn't mind boring herself. She may be free, she may be content, but if she is indeed typical, I can't help considering the possibility that modern woman, for all her modern appliances, isn't modern any more.

The *Saturday Evening Post*'s typical woman, at any rate, knows neither the nagging worry of poverty nor the nagging pull to be part of the activity and thought of a world that extends beyond her eventually made bed, her eventually cleaned house. But, of course, *she* is not the woman that commentators have in mind when they talk about "frustration" or when they describe the Radcliffe diploma mildewing over the kitchen sink.

And when we read the *Report of the President's Commission on the Status of Women,* the emphasis is on a still different woman, a woman who works because she has to or because she wants to give her children a better life. She cannot be called a career woman, for she is likely to do clerical work or saleswork, service work, factory work or agricultural work, and only a small percentage of the women working in our country today are in professional or managerial jobs.

Clearly, it is impossible to speak in the same breath about all these kinds of women, at least in any meaningful way. Even within these groups, of course, there are enormous differences between individual women—differences in ability, in intellect, in preferences, in temperament, in values. But about these differences remarkably little is ever said. This tendency to speak of women as though they were interchangeable units like the parts of a Ford is one reason why (for all the talk) woman's dilemma remains unsolved.

A second reason is that while we've been talking, the picture has been changing. For women have not turned a deaf ear to this talk. If anything fascinates them, it's the topic of themselves—a fact which suggests a close relation to the rest of the human race—and they have tried to follow the suggestions, heed the warnings. While reflecting the feminine condition, therefore, some of the commentators have, at the same time, helped to shape that condition.

"Womanpower"—the word and the commodity—was discovered during World War II. When the war was over and womanpower was no longer needed in factories and hospitals and schools (or so they thought), many voices started urging women to go home, stay home, and like it. In 1947 Marnya Farnham and Ferdinand Lundberg wrote *Modern Woman: The Lost Sex,* in which they predicted: "Close down the commercial bakeries and canning factories today and women will start being happier tomorrow."

They were talking to the young women of my generation who had started out to do great things—not only the privileged and the educated; all kinds of girls were going to have "careers" in those days. Then, as each girl married (always to her great surprise, for she never dreamed she was going to meet George or Bill or Frederick, or if she did, she kept her dreams to herself), she would "throw over her career," as she liked to put it. Sometimes she did so cheerfully, for she knew there really was no career in the making, sometimes reluctantly because it was nearly impossible to keep on after her first or second child arrived. She became a housewife or, as she tended to put it, "just a housewife."

Dorothy Thompson created a new cliché or, at the very least, gave new life to an old one, when she pointed out in 1949 that a wife and mother should never feel apologetic for being "just a housewife" because that homely word means that she is a professional "business manager, cook, nurse, chauffeur, dressmaker, interior decorator, accountant, caterer, teacher, private secretary" all rolled into one. "I simply refuse to share your self-pity," Miss Thompson told the American housewife in the *Ladies' Home Journal*. "You are one of the most successful women I know."

The following year, in *The Atlantic Monthly*, another woman journalist wrote an even angrier article. Agnes E. Meyer not only tried to reassure those women who spent their entire time being mothers; she fiercely denounced those who made some effort to be something in addition to being mothers. She wrote:

> Women must boldly announce "that no job is more exacting, more necessary, or more rewarding than that of housewife and mother. . . . There have never been so many women who are unnecessarily torn between marriage and a career. There have never been so many mothers who neglect their children because they find some trivial job more interesting. . . . The poor child whose mother has to work has some inner security because he knows in his little heart that his mother is sacrificing herself for his well-being. But the neglected child from a well-to-do-home, who realizes instinctively that his mother prefers her job to him, often hates her with a passionate intensity."[1]

Each time such a statement was made, and they were made often, it was a shot in the arm for those who had felt aimless and demoralized, who had, to quote one of them, "begun to feel stupid with nothing to contribute to an evening's discussion after a solitary morning of housecleaning and an afternoon of keeping peace between the children." Now they were able to face themselves with more self-respect, for they were doing the most important job of all. What's more, they were able to look with *less* respect at their friends who had outside work or interests.

As for these women, the ones involved outside the home as well as within, many of them were intimidated by the strong voices. It was confusing to them, even frightening, to be told they weren't good mothers, to be accused of preferring their outside activities to their children. Increasingly, therefore, many turned their full attention, their full energies upon their little families and shut the door on the world.

And so, while the canneries and bakeries did not literally close down, the spirit of this advice was taken; and many highly educated or trained women have been making their own bread, putting up endless little jellies. But according to the latest attack on the subject, *The Feminine Mystique* by Bettey Friedan, these women aren't happy at all but are slowly going mad and battering their children's heads!

Nobody's happy about them either. The consensus at the Vassar symposium held in the spring of 1962 was that: "If the performance of college women from 1920 through World War II has been somewhat disappointing, the mental attitudes of young women since World War II are alarming."

This kind of criticism came from looking inside woman's head and heart. Looking at her from the outside came another kind of criticism— first, the accusation that having no other interest in her life, she latched fiercely onto her children, ruining them, being a "Mom." More recently, still another kind of criticism has been coming: that she hasn't been pulling her weight. "A Huge Waste: Educated Womanpower" is the title of a typical *New York Times* article, this one published in May, 1961. Two years later, under the heading "Tapping a U.S. National Resource," came another *Times* article concerning itself with "the educated woman."

This past summer Max Lerner wrote an article called "Let's Draft Our Girls," and he meant all kinds of girls. Four years earlier *Harper's* had published an article in which Marion Sanders discussed the possibility of drafting not only girls before they become mothers, but also strong, able women after they have finished their full-time mothering, unless they are already engaged in work that has some value. Though her style is gay, almost frivolous, and I don't think Mrs. Sanders seriously wants a draft for women, she does want us to pull our socks up and is quite serious both about the need for teachers, nurses, and social welfare workers and about her scorn for what she calls Non-Work or Sub-Work or Redundant Housewifery—the pointless tasks with which so many middle-aged women fill their lives.

As an example of women she would *not* exempt, she tells about a hospital ladies' auxiliary in Long Island which "boasted that its 900 Pink Pinafore Volunteers last year spent 51,280 hours reading to sick children, giving patients alcohol rubs, and running a gift shop. This averages out to a little more than an hour a week per volunteer— scarcely time to don and doff the pinafores."

In addition, then, to the great differences between different women (about which too little is said), and in addition to the changes constantly taking place in our attitudes and in our ways of living, there is a third reason we've been progressing so slowly in gaining insight into modern woman—her role, her function, her old dilemma. Many true things have been said, but since they aren't all said at the same time, we get part of the picture in one strong statement, another part in another (seemingly contradictory) statement. We never get a full, accurate picture in one glance, but a blurred and confused impression. And while I can't say everything all at once either (not even the things I do know, let alone the things I don't), I'd like to give an example of what I mean.

One often hears that too much is expected of the American woman. "How can she be wife, lover, confidante, companion, hostess, cook, seamstress, floor scrubber, purchasing agent, teacher, chauffeur, child analyst?" ask her defenders.

But in Mrs. Sanders's "Proposition for Women" she speaks of middle-aged and older women with "time for leisurely jaunts to the lonely housewife's dream world of 'shopping'—so different from 'marketing.'" And she describes clubs with many meetings which "did not contribute to anyone's enlightenment since their programs revealed no coherent purpose. (January: Flower Arrangement. February: The Bright Side of Menopause. March: Whither the UN?)" Women caught up in such activities spend an enormous amount of time telephoning to arrange similar meetings which, in Mrs. Sanders's terms, is "Circular (or self-perpetuating) Puttering, a form of Sub-Work."

Both kinds of descriptions are valid, although it's obvious that both apply more accurately to middle-class and upper-class women. What people *don't* always recognize, however, is that the demanding description applies only to a woman's early years when her children are young and she is in constant demand, that the idleness comes later and, worse, it comes gradually, imperceptibly. Most of us have heard a great deal about this bonus of twenty, thirty, or even forty years women now have because they stop bearing children at an earlier age and they live—with health and vigor—much longer than people have ever lived before. And though we're still floundering, are not yet sure exactly what we want to do with this bonus and how to plan for it, many girls and young women are completely unaware of it. This may be hard to believe; but the one sour note in the otherwise sweet *Saturday Evening Post* article is that Dr. Gallup and Mrs. Hill report the women they interviewed could not imagine having their children grown and out of the house, leaving them jobless. They had simply never given a thought to this eventuality.

And so women were scolded for going out of the home and then, more recently, they've been scolded for staying in. The next logical step is to urge women out of the house and into high-powered careers on a par with men's, thus bringing us full circle, back to the feminist days. I'm afraid this step is coming. Whether advertisements follow public opinion or make it I don't quite know, but I've noticed a small straw blowing in the wind which may be significant, the beginning of a trend. After years of picturing lovely ladies who beam with joy while cleaning their toilet bowls or waltzing around the living room with a roll of Alcoa Wrap, some advertisers are taking a new tack. One blouse manufacturer has announced a new advertising campaign addressed to the 24,584,000 "Wonderful Women Who Work." Going even further, a different shirt company recently ran an ad picturing a girl as a naval architect and running a caption which said: "Man's world? Bah! Women are in everything."

The girl is extremely pretty and looks about eighteen and is totally unconvincing as an architect, naval or otherwise. But when I think of the other kind of ad, I realize it's not the unconvincingness that's new, and I wonder if, after pushing housewifery to the limits, they're now going to push for "a career for every girl." Look out for that swinging pendulum; here we go again.

What really alarms me is the strident voice, the strong note of resentment in Betty Friedan's *The Feminine Mystique* when she asks why women are always supposed to be satisfied with second-string careers and second-level positions. Having said that, I suppose I've put myself on the spot and had better explain why *I'm* satisfied. Am I being wishy-washy? Or have I boldly taken the position of defending "the radical middle"? I'll say what I believe and you can decide.

I believe that only the rare, truly exceptional woman with way-above-average ability, energy, and drive can—while maintaining a home and being a real mother to several children—achieve a full-fledged career. It takes enormous flexibility and ingenuity, for the children *do* come first, and women *do* move when the husbands are transferred on their jobs, and they don't have their mothers living nearby or maiden aunts or maids to lend a hand when the unpredictable but inevitable complications arise. In our society, husbands carry the main financial burden of supporting the family, whether or not their wives have salaries. And in the same spirit, whether it's a matter of tradition or instinct, wives are usually the ones who carry the main responsibility for keeping things running smoothly at home, for being emotionally supportive to their husbands as well as to their children.

We have to face the fact that for all these same reasons, it is extremely difficult to work out even a half-time job or profession or avocation. Why, then, should anyone bother? And why should I believe this to be a sound and satisfying course for a great many women in our time? If someone has strong, specific interests, proven ability, or a shining talent, it may be worthwhile; but why should other young women go out of their way to seek goals, to seek spheres of interest and activity? Aren't they just looking for trouble? In a sense, yes; it may seem that they're deliberately choosing the hard way and that I'm egging them on.

By not making a deliberate choice, however, by drifting along as so many have been doing, being buffeted by the changing winds of social pressure, present-day women who are in a position to choose haven't found their lives hard, exactly, but too many have found them empty, purposeless. Deliberately making their lives hard by adding all sorts of do-it-yourself chores—from paper hanging and upholstery to weaving and preserving—has been tried by many but has turned out to be the answer for relatively few. Not only is it artificial, but it puts something of a strain on the marriage relationship to ask a woman to live in a homespun, horse-and-buggy age while her husband continues to forge ahead in a Dacron, Acrilan, jet age.

However, since so many traditional functions have gradually been taken away from mothers—not only the weaving, canning, and baking which many of us would cheerfully forego, but even teaching children about sex and sewing and social problems (whatever happened to mother's knee, by the way, and all the things a child used to learn there?)—it's obvious that unless she and her life are to become empty, something must be substituted.

As long ago as 1950, Lynn White, Jr., former president of Mills College, recognized this problem clearly. In his book *Educating Our Daughters,* he said:

> If the housewife no longer pumps water from the well, she must be sure that the city water supply is pure. She no longer wrings the necks of barnyard hens for dinner, but an honest meat inspection in the interests of public health affects the health of her family. Her children learn their letters at school rather than at her knee, but in return she must work for the P.T.A.

Mr. White saw the question and he gave us one answer. But I believe that in considering it the *only* answer, we may have lost as much as we gained. By calling "homemaking plus volunteer community work" *the* ideal pattern for modern woman we are threatened with a new kind of standardization. During the years that girls have been educated much as their brothers and their future husbands, they have come to be appreciated as individuals. Parents and teachers, too, have recognized and have even emphasized individual differences, drumming home the idea that there are all kinds of ways of being a valuable person, that "different" doesn't necessarily mean "better or worse." When a girl marries, is she supposed to forget all this and learn, just as girls learned in the past: *this* is the kind of life a good wife and mother leads; this and no other?

There is a second fallacy in the "homemaking-plus volunteer-community-work" formula—at least when it is recommended as a suitable formula for most women. In the old days each mother had (using Lynn White's own example) to haul each pail of water into the house and had to wring the neck of each chicken. But the way things are now, we don't need *all* mothers working for pure food and drug laws, for fluoridation or antifluoridation, or even for the PTA. Women going into these volunteer efforts soon find out that not all of them are needed. It soon becomes clear that the purpose of much of their work is occupational therapy—not for others but for themselves. Wanting to be useful, many flit from one volunteer or creative activity to another—one year marching for diseases, the next year making mosaics out of broken bottles, the next year being crazy about mental health.

Since the family itself has shrunk, it's true that certain community concerns have taken the place of certain family concerns. We might say that today's extended family has, reasonably and legitimately, been extended to include the community. But different women can make different contributions to the community—both because different women are different and because all sorts of things are needed and duplication of effort is tremendously wasteful. Nor are all contributions measurable by the same standards. Some, such as pure research or pure art, cannot be evaluated at all by most of us. And I wish we could just accept that, as we do with much of man's work, not making a woman feel guilty about or accountable for any work she does which is not clearly contributing to her family—or her extended family, the community.

Now that I'm nearing the end of my paper, I'll make three more wishes. I would like to see less distinction made between the woman who must work for financial reasons and the one who has decided to work. The borderline is so hazy, so vague that only in cases of extreme poverty or where no husband is present and employed can one say that this woman simply must work in order for her family to survive. Beyond that who can say whether women are working for necessities or luxuries? Is a washing machine a necessity or a luxury? Is a college education for her children a necessity or a luxury? I maintain that this is for each couple to decide.

Making a sharp distinction between women who must work and these who have decided to work leaves out of account the powerful but often ignored phenomenon of "mixed motivation." Certainly, in most cases, the second income is needed or at least warmly welcomed; but there are other satisfactions, too, whether it's a feeling of usefulness, of accomplishment or simply the human contact to be found in any store or office.

In the eyes of many people, saying that a woman *must* work for financial gain casts a reflection on her husband. The question is raised: "Can't he support her?" Ironically, reflections are also cast on the woman who has chosen to work. The question is raised: "Does she really love her children? Is she a good mother?" For all these reasons, then, I think the question of whether a woman is working through choice or necessity is often meaningless and destructive.

My second wish for women is that a less sharp distinction be made between the paid and the volunteer worker. I would like to see a climate of opinion in which the paid woman worker is neither apolo-

getic about needing the money nor arrogant about being "a professional."
Were it taken for granted that everyone works to capacity, the professional would become less defensive and the volunteer would become
more professional—that is, she would feel a strong and continuing sense
of responsibility toward her work and her colleagues, a sense of commitment which would keep her from quitting whenever the going got
rough (or boring).

My third wish, then, is just that: a climate of opinion in which it's
taken for granted that women will do something with their training,
their abilities, their energy once their children are half-grown and they
have free time at their disposal. First of all, there is the obvious waste
of "womanpower" which was first noticed during the war, but was then
forgotten until relatively recently—perhaps because of Sputnik and our
"educational lag," as the shortage of first-rate teachers was called. People
can understand that, just as they understand a shortage of nurses. But,
again, we have to appreciate that there are all sorts of less obvious
needs, and women can make contributions in various and quite varied
ways.

I latch onto the economic and social waste, putting it first, because
it's respectable, it's measurable, and lately all sorts of people out there in
the real world have been noticing that women haven't been pulling
their weight. But long before this happened I used to think about the
waste from the point of view of the individual women—not so much
in terms of what they could do for society, but what a waste it is for
themselves and how much they would gain by being participating
members of society. If it were taken for granted that once a woman's
children were grown and no longer needed her full time, she would
find a specific place for herself (whether through a job, volunteer work,
or in some other way), she would put to better use the little scraps of
time available during her busiest years.

As it is now, the short stretches of time she can find for herself are
usually frittered away. It's true that during the peak of her motherhood,
before the children go to school, when all of them need her almost
every hour of the night and day, she has neither time nor energy to
spend. The hour here, the half-hour there are needed simply for "relief"
—a stolen nap, a few snatched moments of window-shopping, a story
read while wheeling a carriage or stirring a pot. I remember a friend
who said it was a treat to go to the dentist because she got to sit down.

But this period passes. It passes so gradually, it's true, that there
isn't a precise day when a woman can say she has free time to spend
and ask herself how to spend it. And just as expenses rise imperceptibly
to meet rising income (Parkinson's second law), so chores and errands
and what Marion Sanders calls self-perpetuating puttering, what Veblen
called ceremonial futility increase as women grow older and their home
duties lighter. If a young mother knew, however, that at some future
time she would be allowed, encouraged, and expected to use her time,

training, and abilities for some purpose, she would have something specific to do with her scraps of time as soon as they started to become just a little bigger and more dependable. Having a goal, a realistic yet flexible goal, would also add zest to a woman's life while she is still young, with time only for a course here, a volunteered hour there, or an hour in the library now and then.

Of course, while she is completely tied down, it's hard for a girl to believe she'll ever have time on her hands, that her house and her days will be empty, and she herself will be unneeded. Reaching the age of forty is like having triplets or winning the Irish Sweepstakes, the unlikely kind of thing that happens only to other people. Yet word could get through to her, somehow, that this might just possibly happen to her.

Another thing that's likely to happen—and this is something that has not been generally recognized—is that a lot of girls who now foresee only marriage and motherhood for themselves will, at some period in their lives, be looking for jobs. The Women's Bureau estimates that of the girls now in high school 8 out of 10—whether because of widowhood, divorce, economic need, emotional need, or psychological need—will at some period be employed. If girls and women could accept this while young, they'd have motivation to keep their skills from rusting, their minds from shrinking, and their work habits from deteriorating.

Perhaps a representative of the Women's Bureau should be invited to confront girls in high school and in college (the majority of whom want and see only motherhood ahead) and say to them: "I have news for you! You will be looking for a job some day, so give it a thought now, so that you'll be qualified for the best, most interesting kind of work of which you are capable." If someone could say it so that the girls would really believe it, this would be helpful—just as it would have been helpful if someone had brought news to the academic and career-minded girls of my generation that, chances were, we would not be pleading at the bar, saving humanity, or running a corporation in ten or fifteen years; we'd be marketing and cooking meals, raising our children and cleaning our houses.

As it is now, even the brightest young girl takes any old job that has a salary attached because it is frankly a stopgap until her future husband comes along or (for the lucky, the truly "in" girls) until her present husband finishes college or professional school. After that, she thinks, she'll never have to see the inside of an office or store again.

Worse than that, it seems to me, is what happens to the women who have followed the prescribed course of devoting themselves full-time to being wives, homemakers, and mothers and then find themselves—for one reason or another—looking for a job at the age of forty or fifty. They have to start at the bottom of the ladder. If they find themselves in the position of having to earn a living, it is wasteful and absurd, as well as unsatisfying, to plug away in a job far below one's capacities.

If they don't have to earn money but are looking for worthwhile work, even volunteer organizations will use them in the lowliest assignments if their work habits and self-discipline have atrophied for lack of exercise. This is unsuitable for many and unbearable for some; and so, those who have any choice in the matter soon give up.

If girls could have the foresight to recognize at the beginning of their lives as women that this time will come—not only with hindsight, after a great deal of trial and error, disappointment, and heartbreak—they could try to look ahead, try to plan ahead, try to achieve some sort of balance between their work life and their personal life. My repeated use of the word "try" means I am well aware that one cannot see one's life stretching ahead, clearly and accurately. And as for planning, I realize that it is, in a sense, planning the unplannable. But if Herman Kahn and the Rand Corporation can think about the unthinkable, women should find that they have a lot to gain by planning the unplannable. If they had a general sort of goal, knowing perfectly well that it would be modified and that the road toward it would swerve and curve and, occasionally, backtrack, their journey would still be richer, more interesting, and more meaningful. If, further, they could accept such a life pattern, not as a makeshift, patched-up compromise, but as a complicated, intricate arrangement necessitated by the fact that they have the privilege and responsibility of being *both* mothers at home *and* women who have a place in the world outside the home, they could do the planning, the arranging (*and* the necessary *re*arranging) without resentment.

Last year in Belgium, while I was talking with some women about the problems connected with doing professional work while, at the same time, living a normal family life, one woman said something which I have thought of many times since then. This woman is a scientist, a *docent* at one of the universities, which is equal, approximately, to the rank of associate professor in America. She is the wife of a businessman, the mother of two sons—one at the university and one in medical school.

"When the boys were little," she told me, "my career, which was just beginning, could move along only very slowly since I was home a good deal then and couldn't spend as much time in the laboratory as my men colleagues. Even when my sons were older, but still young boys, and I had a chance to go to congresses and international meetings, for example—well, I just didn't go. I didn't really want to. Probably I didn't do as much research as I would have done had I been a man and concerned chiefly with my career. And so I didn't progress as much as if I'd been a man. I'm a *docent* now; I might perhaps have become a professor." She gave a shrug as if to say: "So what?" And then she spelled it out, quite beautifully I thought, by saying: "But that's all right for a woman because all the time you've had the pleasure of being a mother too."

And so, when I say that I'm content with second-string or second-level positions, I don't mean that women, because they are *women*, should be content with second best. I mean that if a woman is also going to run her home and be a wife to her husband and a mother to her children, it is a rare woman indeed who can hold down a full-time job which is on a par with her husband's, a rarer one still who can have a full-fledged career.

While I am wishing, I would like to get rid of the word "career" entirely. I've always been amused at the way the word "career" seems to go with the word "woman" whenever this general subject is being discussed. Most men (except for movie stars, boxers, and diplomats) have to be content with jobs. The reason the word "career" is so dangerous, I feel, when used freely, as it is, in connection with women is that many are left feeling that if they can't have a real "career," why bother at all?

Why bother? It isn't easy, I admit: this juggling of time, of energy, of one's very emotions. Sometimes you're frustrated in all your endeavors at once so that it's hard not to feel you've been left with the worst of both world. And yet I feel we have no choice. Maurice Chevalier is supposed to have confided to a friend: "Old age isn't so bad—not when you consider the alternative."

In much the same spirit I seriously propose that the alternative to living a full, perhaps overfull life is being half-dead. And things being the way they are, women are more likely to become victims than men. As long ago as the turn of the century Justice Oliver Wendell Holmes' wife remarked that "Washington is full of interesting men; and the women they married when they were young." This remark was sad then, but it is sadder still today, for modern couples expect more of one another in the way of companionship. We do so for a host of reasons, but one of them has to do with sheer numbers. When you look at the picture on the cover of this conference announcement, a photograph of an old-fashioned family, it's hard to tell who's the mother, who's the father, who's the husband, who's the wife. Somewhere in that large and varied group, I can't help feeling, each man and each woman could surely find a congenial soul. Today, with families small and, furthermore, isolated from grandparents, in-laws, uncles, aunts, cousins, and grown brothers and sisters, an extra demand of understanding and companionship is asked of each husband and each wife—a shared growing and deepening far beyond "developing some interests so as not to bore Jim."

Husbands, particularly, are often asked to carry an extra burden when wives expect them to supply, through their work, not only the family's entire financial support but everything that makes life "interesting." Whether they mean friends, colleagues, prestige, or being in the know depends upon each woman and what is important to her, but there are a great many who live vicariously; there are a great many young ones, newly married, who plan and expect to live vicariously, to have their husband's contact with the world make up for the fact that they have none. This, I maintain, is too much to ask of a man. And so, for the sake of the marriage, if for no other reason, each woman should continue to grow with her husband, to enrich their shared life. Mostly, however, for her own sake should she live to the full and savor to the full her "long intense alliance with the world."

NOTE

[1] Agnes E. Meyer, "Women Aren't Men," *The Atlantic Monthly*, 186:32–6, August, 1950. From *Out of These Roots* by Agnes E. Meyer. Copyright 1950 by Agnes E. Meyer. Reprinted [in the original] by permission of Atlantic-Little, Brown and Company, publishers.

An Analysis of Power Dynamics in Marriage

PHYLLIS N. HALLENBECK

The purpose of this paper is to discuss power structure in marriage in terms of its bases and manifestations. The theoretical framework of French and Raven[1] derived from the study of small groups will be related to the findings of marriage-power studies. Suggestions for research stemming from this integration will be made.

Power has been defined by French and Raven[2] as stable potential influence in a dyadic relation between two persons. They delineate five types of power as follows: (1) reward power, based on the ability of the person possessing power to provide rewards for the one influenced; (2) coercive power, based on the powerful one's ability to mediate punishments for the one influenced; (3) legitimate power, based on the influenced one's belief that the powerful one has the right to control his behavior or opinions; (4) referent power, based on the influenced one's identification with the powerful one; and (5) expert power, based on the influenced one's perception of superior knowledge and skill in the powerful one. The range of power refers to the number of areas affected, with the result that interpersonal power structure is relevant to the areas of influence under consideration. It is in marriage and family life that we see the broadest ranges of influence and the greatest likelihood of all types of power coming into use, because in family life there occurs the greatest interaction of cultural, social, and personal factors over the longest periods of time.

Blood and Wolfe[3] advance the theory that the balance of power in marriage belongs to the spouse bringing the most resources to the marriage. Heer[4] lists these resources as economic contributions, personal attractiveness, and ability to fulfill roles adequately. Economic resources, i.e., earning power plus material possessions, appear to fall in the French and Raven "reward" category.[5] Hill brings overtones of coercion into the picture, stating, "Money is a source of power that supports male dominance in the family. . . . Money belongs to him who earns it, not to her who spends it, since he who earns it may withhold it."[6] French and Raven[7] state that while the withholding of a reward may resemble punishment, reward and coercive powers are dynamically

Reprinted from *Journal of Marriage and the Family*, May 1966, 200–3.

different because negative valences set up by coercion tend to cause withdrawal from the field of action.

In the Detroit sample studied by Blood and Wolfe,[8] the power of the husbands as described by their wives varied directly with their socioeconomic status. It was also found that the relative power of the wife was greater if she worked. The authors believe these two findings support their view of a primary importance of economic resources. However, Heer[9] feels that the hypothesis does not explain certain other of their findings, mainly the longitudinal rise and fall of husband's power in the same family. As the husband's power appears to be greatest when the children are of preschool age, Heer proposes that the husband is dominant because it is more difficult at that time for the wife to work outside the home. Heer's theory, a revision of Blood and Wolfe's, states[10] that the power of the husband depends on the difference set by the wife on the value of the resources contributed by her husband as contrasted with the value of those she might earn herself outside the marriage. His proposal implies that wives actually weigh the advantages and disadvantages, giving serious thought to possible separation.

Further study of families having preschool children might clarify the issue. The following questions might be asked in such a study: Do statistics show that more wives having independent means or good earning power leave the marriage while the children are very young? Would comparison of the perceptions of wives who are financially dependent and independent show that the husband's earning power is the important and only factor? Another consideration may be the well-described chronic fatigue which affects young mothers with preschoolers. Does amount of available energy have an effect on marital power structure? Does a man assert his male dominance, as folklore would have it, by keeping his wife more or less continuously pregnant? Is the modern-day wife reversing this trend by limiting the number of children she is willing to have? Or might the predominance of power in the husband at this time in the marriage reflect the Parson and Bales concepts of male "instrumentality" and female "expressivity"? Surely a mother with preschool children is as emotionally supportive as at any time in the marriage; and "executive" functions of decision-making except those concerning the children may be left to the one who has time and energy for them.

Perhaps it is too limiting to define conjugal power in terms of economic resources only. Heer[11] mentions "attractiveness," especially in women, as a resource. Waller[12] observed that dominance in marriage derives from the "relative position of the mates in the scale of courtship desirability." In our glamour-conscious culture, desirability in the woman is often equated with sex appeal, especially at the younger ages. If this attractiveness is somehow overemphasized, as with photographers' models or movie starlets, the "position on the courtship scale" is elevated to a point requiring the offer of great resources on the part of the man seeking marriage. It is apparent and interesting, from a turnabout view, that the man who desires or values the woman as a mate more than she desires or values him will be in the position of wanting to please her. Her enhancement in his eyes may be physical attractiveness, pleasing personality, his perception of her as a "perfect" wife and mother, or an artifact of his own poor self-image. The advantage a woman derives from this power relationship may go a long way to counteract advantages built into the culture for the husband. The woman, however, must be willing to take the dominant position in this respect and retain it, since she can nullify it by voluntarily giving control to her husband.

Blood and Wolfe also speak of decision-making, "The power to make decisions stems primarily from the resources which the individual can provide to meet the needs of his marriage partner and to upgrade his decision-making skill."[13] Competent decision-making, if categorized in the French and Raven framework,[14] appears to lead to the establishment of "expert" power. The basis is purported to be the influenced one's attribution of skill, knowledge, or perception *to* the powerful one; and it is suggested that expert power is limited to cognitive systems and rather narrow areas. This concept partly fits with Blood and Wolfe's findings that in many marriages decisions are "apportioned" according to the areas involved. Thus, husbands decide about their own jobs, selecting cars, buying life insurance; while wives make the decisions concerning the food-buying and choice of doctors. Couples are more likely to make joint decisions about where they are to live and vacation.

If the wife gives power to her husband based on his "expertness" of decision-making, he must demonstrate that he is, indeed, an expert. Hill[15] refers to the "mating-gradient tendency" of men to marry women younger than themselves with less education and, therefore, less qualified to make decisions. The same kind of protective device seems to operate for men whose serious objections to their wives' working are not realistically based, but stem from feelings that their dominance is undermined when they are not the sole or primary breadwinners.

"Legitimate" power, state French and Raven,[16] stems from the internalized values of the influenced one, which in turn come from the culture. The values are often role-expectations and may be perceived as part of the wife's duty to respect and submit to her husband, or the child's duty to be obedient to his parents. The influenced one believes he has an obligation to accept the "rightful" influence of the powerful one; and this believing makes the powerful one a legitimate authority figure. Hill[17] points out several cultural factors contributing to male dominance, namely the cultural definitions of masculinity and femininity, the legal tradition of husband as "family head," and the Judeo-Christian concept of the superiority of the husband. In this century there has been a trend away from the overt demonstration of this power, e.g., removal of "obey" from the marriage vows; it is a moot question whether the indirect pressures delineating the role of the wife as a non-working homemaker tend to counteract this trend. Instances of such pressure are the assumption of many public school systems that mothers are available for teacher conferences and PTA meetings during the day and their refusal to make provisions for children to stay at school during the lunch hour.

The powers to reward and coerce become stronger when associated with legitimate power. The tendencies toward withdrawal generally set up by coercive forces are much lessened. The strength of reward power depends on the influenced one's perception of the actual ability of the powerful one to provide the reward; it is modified by perception of the legitimacy of the rewards.

Coercive power is probably best exemplified in Waller's discussion[18] of how control in marriage may be maintained. The spouse most willing to quarrel before outsiders, threaten to break up the marriage, and shatter rapport and refuse to be the first to make up can maintain dominance by such punitive measures in a middle-class milieu. In the lower classes, physical abuse may also be a decisive factor.

Reward power tends to increase attraction in the dyad, providing for the development of "referent" power. The desire of the person influenced to be like the one possessing power or the group he belongs to may lead him to behavior like that of the powerful one. French and Raven[19] speak of a "feeling of oneness" and "conformity based on identification." The term *identification* in the narrow sense covers the referent power of father over son and mother over daughter; it must be broadened to encompass the influence of father over daughter, mother over son, and husband and wife over each other. "To be like the group the powerful one belongs to," when the powerful one is a parent, teacher, or camp leader must refer to the fact that the group aspired to is an adult group. What group is involved in referent power between spouses? Logically, we can assume that there is such a group and that, in the case of married adults, the group consists of happily married men and women. This implies role concept, a set of behaviors and attitudes which the individual perceives as ideal for marriage. That such ideal or modal role concepts exist has been shown by several authors.[20] It is the contention of this paper that referent power in marriage stems from the desire of the spouses to be like their concepts of the "ideal" husband or wife. It is not the husband who holds referent power over his wife, or vice versa, except indirectly as he reinforces her role concept; it is the role of ideal wife to which she aspires which has the referent power.

This can be understood in terms of the universal human dislike of ambiguity. Roles of married people are not clearly and uniformly defined in our culture; and newly married couples must adjust to this ambiguous situation lacking the elaborately prescribed rituals which characterize more primitive, unchanging societies. The lack of structure in the situation is counteracted by the construct of a reference group; the marshalling of beliefs and attitudes which derive from the reference group follows, and the "ideal" or "modal" role for the wife or husband comes into active being. Spouses hold these concepts for both themselves and their partners; the relationship of agreement about ideal roles to marital success has been shown in several studies.[21]

It appears that the referent power in marriage is most directly used or misused, as Friedan[22] suggests, by women's magazines and advertisers of home products. Rossi[23] recently stated the advantages of careers to women who may also be mothers in an article accepted by one such magazine, which titled it, "The Case Against Full-Time Motherhood," and prefaced it by saying it would make "most women bristle." Important social institutions, such as the school or church, seem able to utilize marital referent power for desired ends much less successfully than commercial or political holders of power.

The French and Raven[24] concept of power involves mainly the willingness of one party to be influenced by the other and his perception of the influencing one. These perceptions may concern ability to mediate rewards or punishment, legitimacy of authority position, expertness in skill or ability, or attractiveness as a basis of identification. Since perception is mediated by cognitive structure, any discussion of power in marriage must take into account factors which influence cognition. For instance, French and Raven's[25] observation that the primary basis of expert power is the attribution of expertness to the powerful one, as distinguished from impersonal acceptance of information, suggests kinship with Rokeach's theory[26] of dogmatism. If a closeminded person cannot differentiate the content of information from information about its source, he is more likely to be influenced by consideration of the source rather than the information itself. That is to say, if he attributes expertness of knowledge to the Communist Party, the Catholic Church, or the Daughters of the American Revolution, he will be easily influenced by any information coming from the source without much consideration of the information itself. It would be interesting to study the effects of the extremes of dogmatism on power balance in marriage, not only from this aspect, but from the viewpoint that extremely open-minded people are not as subject to cultural values or rewards and punishments from the environment. One could hypothesize that an open-minded woman might more or less reject legitimate power and expert power as bases of authority and be more immune than average to reward and coercive power. One could further hypothesize that such a woman would be most likely to find marital happiness with an open-minded husband, with whom she shares similar views about referent power (marriage roles).

In summary, considering marriage as a special case in small group theory, we find that hypotheses about the dynamics of power are most relevant. The couple coming into marriage brings with them various resources, such as earning power, intelligence, skills, physical attractiveness, and personality traits, which they have presumably examined and weighed during the courtship period. They also possess or quickly develop a personal concept of the "ideal" wife and husband. In their behavior and attitudes, they reflect the cultural norms they have internalized. From the interaction of these variables, the balance of power is established and maintained, affecting every other aspect of the marriage—division of labor, amount of adaptation necessary for either spouse, methods used to resolve conflicts, and so forth. The empirical assessment of dominance is usually based on who makes the decisions or who wins the arguments; but it might be elaborated more fruitfully in terms of the theories already discussed. For instance, one might ask, "Is your spouse superior to you in any way? How?" or "What rewards are there for you in the relationship with your spouse?" The variables basis to the delegation of power in marriage are more difficult to analyze but would give a multi-dimensional description of authority structure, rather than the more usual superficial analysis.

NOTES

[1] John R. P. French, Jr. and Bertram Raven, "The Bases of Social Power, in *Group Dynamics: Research and Theory*, ed. by D. Cartwright and A. Zander, Elmsford, New York: Row, Peterson & Co., 2nd Ed., 1960.

[2] *Ibid.*

[3] R. O. Blood and D. M. Wolfe, *Husbands and Wives*, Glencoe: Free Press, 1960.

[4] David M. Heer, "The Measurement and Bases of Family Power: An Overview," *Marriage and Family Living*, 25 (1963), pp. 133–139.

[5] French and Raven, *op. cit.*

[6] Reuben Hill and Howard Becker, eds., *Family, Marriage and Parenthood*, Boston: D. C. Heath, 1955, p. 790.

[7] French and Raven, *op. cit.*

[8] Blood and Wolfe, *op. cit.*

[9] Heer, *op. cit.*

[10] *Ibid.*

[11] *Ibid.*

[12] Willard Waller, *The Family*, rev. by Reuben Hill, New York: Dryden Press, 1951.

[13] Blood and Wolfe, *op. cit.*, p. 44.

[14] French and Raven, *op. cit.*

[15] Hill and Becker, *op. cit.*

[16] French and Raven, *op. cit.*

[17] Hill, *op. cit.*

[18] Waller, *op. cit.*

[19] French and Raven, *op. cit.*

[20] Nathan Hurvitz, "The Measurement of Marital Strain," *American Journal of Sociology*, 65 (1960), pp. 610–615; Sally Kotlar, "Measured Middle-Class Marital

Roles by Interpersonal Check List and 'Role Attitude Survey,'" unpublished Ph.D. dissertation, 1961; Robert S. Ort, "A Study of Role-Conflicts as Related to Happiness in Marriage," *Journal of Abnormal and Social Psychology*, 45 (1950), pp. 691–699.

[21] Carl J. Couch, "The Use of the Concept 'Role' and its Derivatives in a Study of Marriage," *Marriage and Family Living*, 20 (1958), pp. 353–357; Hurvitz, *op. cit.*; Kotlar, *op. cit.*; Ort, *op. cit.*

[22] Betty Friedan, *The Feminine Mystique*, New York: Dell Publishing Co., 1964.

[23] Alice S. Rossi, "The Case Against Full-Time Motherhood," *Redbook*, March, 1965.

[24] French and Raven, *op. cit.*

[25] *Ibid.*

[26] Milton Rokeach, *The Open and Closed Mind*, New York: Basic Books, 1960.

Role Perception and Marital Satisfaction—A Configurational Approach

ROBERT P. STUCKERT

The roles of husband and wife, like any set of culturally related roles, carry a complex pattern of expectations of the responses which are to come from the other. Adjustment to either role is influenced by the consistency with which the other responds by making the responses called for by the role pattern. Inconsistency in the responses of the other to the individual increases the insecurity of the person in either role since it makes him uncertain of the validity of his own role concept. This is particularly true when an individual first moves into a marital role. In this case, not only has he had no opportunity to test the validity of his role concept, it is also necessary for the other person in the role situation to make the changes in his responses and expectations called for by the new role.

Whether or not a marital partner responds consistently with the expectations of the other depends on his own preformed concept of his role, his own expectations regarding the reciprocal role of his spouse, his perception of his mate's expectations of him, and the degree of correspondence between the two sets of role concepts and expectations. If these role concepts are similar, communication is easier and the relationship existing between the marriage partners is more satisfactory to both. If role perception is accurate, each partner is better able to anticipate the other's feelings and gear his own responses to the expectations of the other.

Previous studies of the relationship between role perception and marital satisfaction indicate there are at least four significant components of perception. The first is the degree of similarity between the role concepts and expectations of one partner and the other's own role concepts and expectations. The second is the degree of similarity between the way a person perceives the role expectations of his marital partner and the partner's actual role expectations. The third is the degree of congruence between his concept of the marital role in general and his

Reprinted from the *Journal of Marriage and the Family,* Vol. 25 (1963). Figures and tables have been renumbered.

concept of his specific role, i.e., does he view his marriage as being similar to or different from most marriages? The fourth is the degree of similarity between a person's role expectations' and his perception of the expectations of his spouse.[1]

The results of these studies have not been in complete agreement as to the relationship between modes of perception and marital satisfaction. In some, congruent perception was found to be associated with marital success; in others, the relationship was not evident. One of the latest reported that ". . . satisfaction in marriage was related significantly to the congruency of the husband's self-concept and that held of him by his wife, but was found unrelated to the agreement of the concepts the wife holds of herself and that which her husband holds of her."[2]

The key to this may lie in an idea which everyone mentions but is seldom tested directly. Marital adjustment is not a function of any single component of perception or even of several taken independently. The major hypothesis of this study is that marital satisfaction is a function of the mutual interaction of these components. The way in which any one of these components is related to marital satisfaction may depend on the specific relationship of the others with this criterion.

SAMPLE

In order to study the effects of discrepancies in role expectations and perception on marital adjustment before other familial factors come into operation, a sample of newly married couples was used. The population consisted of all couples between the ages of 19 and 26 who were listed in the Milwaukee newspapers as having applied for marriage licenses during July and August, 1959. A random sample of 100 couples were selected. Locating these couples at the time of the study was a problem because the addresses given in the newspapers were those prior to marriage. To reduce the variability of the sample, only white, native-born persons were included. In addition, any couple with a child at the time of the interview was eliminated. The final sample consisted of 50 couples who had been married nine months or less. There was only one refusal.

PROCEDURE

Role concepts and expectations were determined by means of a set of 30 questions incorporated into an interview schedule. These questions involved the relative importance to the individual of selected personality factors in the husband and wife roles. The ten personality needs most frequently listed in a study of marital choice by Anselm Strauss were used in modified form.[3] These are:

1. Importance of love in marriage
2. Being able to confide in one's spouse
3. Showing affection
4. Respecting one's ideals
5. Appreciating the achievements of the other
6. Understanding the other's moods
7. Helping in making important decisions
8. Stimulating the other's ambition
9. Showing respect for the other
10. Giving self-confidence in relations with other people

During the interview, the respondent was asked to evaluate the relative importance of these factors in three different ways:

1. Their importance in marriage in general
2. Their importance in his own marriage
3. Their importance from the point of view of his spouse

In every case, the respondent was asked about his expectations with respect to both his role and the role of the other. The ten factors were rank-ordered on the basis of the respondent's evaluation of their relative importance. Husband and wife were interviewed separately.

Three sets of rankings were obtained from the husband and three from the wife: a total of six for each couple. The three rankings for the husband were designated H_G, H_S, and H_O respectively; the wife's rankings W_G, W_S, and W_O respectively.[4] A series of measures were obtained by correlating various pairs of rankings using the Spearman rank-order correlation coefficient. These are given in Table 1.

Each of these measures was dichotomized into "High" and "Low" categories. For the first three, the median was used as the cutting point. Because $H_G H_S$ and $W_G W_S$ were both negatively skewed, a rho = .55 was used as the cutting point. This value approximates the value of rho at the .05 level of significance using a one-tailed test.

TABLE 1

Role Measures

Correlation Between		Measure of
H_S	W_S	Similarity between marital role concepts and expectations of husband and wife
H_O	W_S	Accuracy with which husband perceives the role expectations of his wife
W_O	H_S	Accuracy with which wife perceives the role expectations of her husband
H_G	H_S	Degree to which husband views his marriage as being similar to most marriages
W_G	W_S	Degree to which wife views her marriage as being similar to most marriages

The individual's own evaluation of his marriage was used as the criterion of marital satisfaction. The criterion measure was based on the times of Schedule 3 of the Burgess and Wallin marital adjustment questionnaire concerning the general marital satisfaction of the self and the self's conception of the mate's general satisfaction.[5] Eighteen of the Burgess-Wallin items and two new items were included. The modal response category of each item was selected as an indicator of marital satisfaction. For all of the items that were clearly statements of either extreme satisfaction or dissatisfaction, the modal response was the one that would logically be expected from a person satisfied with his marriage. For this reason, the modal response categories were selected as indicators of satisfaction for the marginal items as well. The correlation between an individual's responses and the modal response pattern was computed using the phi coefficient and used as the measure of satisfaction. The respondents were divided into "Satisfied" and "Dissatisfied" categories according to their scores. Since the distribution of scores among the husbands was bimodal, it was cut at the point separating the two modes (phi = .35). The same cutting value was used for the wives although their distribution was unimodal. The range of scores was −.13 to .83.

RESULTS

A configurational approach was used in analyzing the data. In this approach, a sample is divided into relatively homogeneous subsamples according to factors related to the dependent variable (marital satisfaction). These factors are selected so that the probability of a given outcome occurring exceeds an arbitrary value.[6] The data were analyzed in two steps. First the correlation of each of the factors with marital satisfaction was computed. Table 2 presents the phi coefficients.

It can be seen that the correlation of these factors with marital satisfaction differs for the wives and husbands. The accuracy with which

TABLE 2

Phi Coefficients of Role Measures and Marital Satisfaction

Role Measure	Marital Satisfaction	
	Husband	Wife
Role similarity ($H_S W_S$)	.45*	.35
Accuracy of husband's perception ($H_o W_S$)	−.08	−.08
Accuracy of wife's perception ($W_o H_S$)	.08	.45*
Husband's generality view ($H_o H_S$)	−.12	.22
Wife's generality view ($W_o W_S$)	.03	.22

* Significant at .01 level.

the wife perceives the marital expectations of her husband is related to her marital satisfaction. The accuracy of her husband's perception of his wife's views is not associated with satisfaction in this early period of marriage. The degree of similarity between the views of husband and wife is related to the marital satisfaction of the husband but not to that of the wife. None of these five variables is correlated with any of the others.

Second, the total sample was divided into subsamples to develop a set of marital types. A set of factors was used to identify a distinct type if over 80 per cent of the cases included were similar with respect to the criterion of marital satisfaction. The variable most highly correlated with satisfaction was used as the starting point for both husbands and wives. The procedure resulted in three husband types and three wife types.[7]

FIGURE 1. Percentage of Husbands and Wives Expressing Marital Satisfaction, by Configurational Type

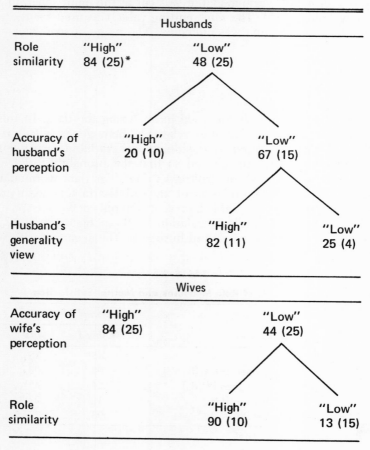

Husbands

| Role similarity | "High" 84 (25)* | "Low" 48 (25) |

| Accuracy of husband's perception | "High" 20 (10) | "Low" 67 (15) |

| Husband's generality view | "High" 82 (11) | "Low" 25 (4) |

Wives

| Accuracy of wife's perception | "High" 84 (25) | "Low" 44 (25) |

| Role similarity | "High" 90 (10) | "Low" 13 (15) |

(See Figure 1.) There was also a residual group of husbands who could not be classified.

Type H1 is defined by a single characteristic. He shares a common view of marriage with his wife. When other factors are examined, an interesting pattern emerges. On the one hand, there is no relationship bteween the accuracy with which he perceives his wife's role expectations and his marital satisfaction. Husbands in this category are about evenly divided between those who perceived their wives expectations accurately (56 per cent) and those who did not (44 per cent).[8] On the other hand, this is the only one of the three husband types in which the majority of the wives perceive their husbands' role expectations accurately. (See Table 3.)

Type H2, as defined by two characteristics, is a dissatisfied type. His view of marriage is different from that held by his wife. He also perceives his wife's expectations correctly. In this case, accuracy of perception is inversely related to marital satisfaction. This is the only group in which the husband and wife differ as to whether or not they view their marriage as being typical of marriages in general. The wife tends to view their marriage as being typical; the husband views it as being different. The wives of these men tend to be dissatisfied with the marriage as well.

Although the role expectations of Type H3 are different from those of his wife, he does not perceive her expectations accurately. He defines his marriage as being typical of marriages in general. In these two characteristics, he is similar to his wife. This types of husband was the only one that stated in the interview that things did not run smoothly and that he was often unsure of himself when family decisions had to be made. This may be due to his not perceiving his wife's differing marital expectations accurately. Since he may define this as being characteristic of marriage, this type of husband is generally satisfied with his marriage.

TABLE 3

Percentage of Husbands and Wives in "High" Category of Each Role Measure, by Configurational Type

Role Measure	Husband Type			Wife Type		
	H1	H2	H3	W1	W2	W3
Number of cases in type	25	10	11	25	10	15
Role similarity	*	*	*	.64	*	*
Accuracy of husband's perception	.56	*	*	.48	.80	.33
Accuracy of wife's perception	.72	.30	.36	*	*	*
Husband's generality view	.76	.40	*	.72	1.00	.60
Wife's generality view	.76	.60	.82	.72	.90	.67

* These measures were used in defining the configurational type.

Type W1 is the perceptive wife. She sees her husband's role expectations as he defines them himself. Apparently this is sufficient because 84 per cent of the 25 wives in this category have a "Satisfied" rating. It is interesting to note that these wives are not appreciably high on any of the other factors including similarity of the actual role expectations of the two marriage partners.

Although Type W2 does not perceive her husband's role expectations accurately, her expectations of both her own role and his are similar to those he has of the two roles. Her marital satisfaction score is also high. The husband may be the crucial factor because this is the only group of wives with husbands who perceive their wives' expectations accurately. Almost every one of these couples view their marriage as typical of marriages in general. Type W3, the dissatisfied category, not only has dissimilar views of marriage from her husband but also does not perceive her husband's views of the marital roles accurately.

CONCLUSIONS

This study reveals that the relation between the accuracy with which a recently married person perceives the role expectations of his spouse and marital satisfaction is not a simple one. For the wives in the sample, the extent to which their perception of their husband's expectations correlates with the husband's actual expectations is the dominant factor associated with marital satisfaction. In the case of the husbands, however, the actual similarity between their own role concepts and expectations and those of their wives is the most important single factor. Furthermore, in one-half of the cases studied, whether or not accuracy of perception is related to marital satisfaction depends on a configuration of factors of which it is a part.

The other factors included in the definitions of these configurations in this study are the individual's view of his marriage and the expectations each marriage partner has of the spouse. On the one hand, accurate perception may detract from marital satisfaction if the two marriage partners have widely differing expectations of the roles of husband and wife. On the other hand, inaccurate perception may not result in dissatisfaction if the person defines his marriage as being typical of marriages in general.

The data in this study support the thesis that the husband's role definitions and expectations may be more important to the early success of a marriage than the wife's. Family adjustment may be greatly affected by the extent to which the husband and wife are oriented toward both actual and potential role changes. Since American cultural patterns still generally define the husband as the dominant spouse, he may have a greater part in establishing the general structure of the new family.[9] A greater proportion of a woman's life is family-related. Her interests and activities tend to be family-centered to a greater extent than her husband's. Since our culture tends to define her role as centering around her family, there may be greater pressure on her to develop an accomodative pattern in relation to other members of the family. As Eleanor Luckey points out, if it is the wife who must make the greater adjustment in marriage, "it is to the benefit of the relationship if she knows what she's adjusting to! If she sees the husband as he sees himself, she is better able to make adjustments which bring more satisfaction to the marriage.[10]

NOTES

[1] Leland H. Stott, "The Problem of Evaluating Family Success," *Marriage and Family Living*, 13 (Fall, 1951), pp. 149–153; M. G. Preston and others, "Impressions of Personality as a Function of Marital Conflict," *Journal of Abnormal and Social Psychology*, 47 (April, 1952), pp. 326–336; Orville Brim and Nancy Wood, "Self and Other Conceptions in Courtship and Marriage Pairs," *Marriage and Family Living*, 18 (August, 1956), pp. 243–248; A. R. Mangus, "Family Impacts on Mental Health," *Marriage and Family Living*, 19 (August, 1957), pp. 256–262; Eleanor B. Luckey, "Marital Satisfaction and Congruent Self-Spouse Concepts," *Social Forces*, 39 (December, 1960), pp. 153–157; Nathan Hurvitz, "The Measurement of Marital Strain," *American Journal of Sociology*, 65 (May, 1960), pp. 610–615.

[2] Luckey, *op. cit.*, p. 153.

[3] Anselm Strauss, "Personality Needs and Marital Choice," *Social Forces*, 25 (March, 1947), pp. 332–335.

[4] After all of the interviews were completed, all of the husbands' evaluations of the importance of these factors in their own marriages were combined to form a general male ranking. The same was done for the wives' ratings to form a general female ranking. The general male ranking and the general female ranking were highly correlated (rho = .75). A few differences were evident. Husbands attributed greater importance to having a wife who appreciates her husband's achievements and who stimulated his ambition. Wives gave greater weight to showing affection in marriage and receiving help in making decisions.

[5] Ernest Burgess and Paul Wallin, *Engagement and Marriage*, Chicago: J. B. Lippincott, 1953, pp. 488–489. Eight items of Schedule 3 were not used since all respondents answered them in exactly the same way.

[6] The methodological assumptions and detailed procedures of the configurational approach are discussed in Robert P. Stuckert, "A Configurational Approach to Prediction," *Sociometry*, 21 (September, 1958), pp. 225–237.

[7] None of these types was related to either religious affiliation or occupational status of the husband.

[8] The terms used in the following paragraphs including "accuracy of perception" are defined in Figure 2.

[9] John Sirjamaki, "Cultural Configurations in the American Family," *American Journal of Sociology*, 53 (May, 1948), pp. 464–470.

[10] Luckey, *op. cit.*, pp. 156–157.

Transition to Parenthood: A Reassessment*

ARTHUR P. JACOBY

The study of the impact of the firstborn on each of the parents and on their marriage covers somewhat more than a decade. Unfortunately, the sociologist knows little more today about possible changes in attitude and behavior that come with parenthood than he knew in the middle 1950s when the first of several "parenthood as a "crisis" studies was undertaken. The relevance of most of this research to the broader framework of sociological theory has been minimal, and findings have been highly contradictory. This is, of course, not unexpected in exploratory research. The purpose of this paper is to suggest fresh theoretical, conceptual, and methodological perspectives for research on the transition to parenthood.

PRESENT STATE OF ACCESSION TO PARENTHOOD RESEARCH

A Brief Review

Four reports of empirical research on early parenthood as a crisis situation have appeared in the professional literature. The research of LeMasters, based on a non-probability sample of 46 middle-class couples whose first child had been born within the previous five years, indicated that this birth had precipitated an extensive or severe crisis for 83 percent (38 couples).[1] The extent to which a crisis had been experienced was determined by means of a discussion among the husband, wife, and the researcher.[2] The data, gathered over a four-year period, suggested that neither the quality of the marriage[3] nor the degree to which the child was planned was related to the amount of crisis experienced.

Dyer's data from much the same kind of sample (32 middle-class couples whose firstborn was not over two years old) led to similar conclusions.[4] Fifty-three percent experienced extensive or severe crisis with

Reprinted from *Journal of Marriage and the Family*, November 1969, 720–27.

the birth of the first child; another 38 percent were classified in the moderate crisis category. An attempt was made to develop a Likert-type scale to measure the crisis dimension. Significant negative relationships were observed between degree of crisis and (1) marital adjustment, (2) number of years married, and (3) having planned for parenthood. The university-educated husbands were significantly more likely to have reported difficulties than those with less education.

Using a probability sample taken from public birth records, Hobbs investigated the postpartum experiences of 53 couples who were first-time parents.[5] All social classes from lower-lower to upper-middle were represented. Babies were between three and 18 weeks old. In their responses to a 23-item check list, not one couple indicated that they had been greatly "bothered" by the arrival of their first child. Eighty-seven percent indicated that they had been slightly "bothered." There was no correlation between scores of husband and wife. The older the child (up to six months), the more problems admitted by the father (but not the mother). None of the variables which Dyer had found to be associated with difficulties in assuming the parental role was confirmed by this study.

Twenty-seven similar couples were later used by Hobbs to replicate and extend this study.[6] In addition to a check list, a relatively unstructured interview was used. The interviews were tape recorded and assessed later by judges. While the interview ratings provided a considerably broader range of scores, moderate but significant correlation coefficients were found between the scores obtained on the two instruments. The substantive findings of this replication were similar to those of Hobbs's original study.[7]

In an unpublished report Beauchamp compared the highly structured and loosely structured methods of measuring accession-type crisis.[8] Data were reported for 37 married student couples. In all cases the father was a student, the marriage was unbroken, the parents of the husband and wife respondents had middle-class occupations, and the firstborn was between five months and six years of age (mean age was two years, four months).

The extent to which the arrival of the first child created problems for Beauchamp's respondents was determined in two ways: (1) a semistructured interview jointly with both parents (approximating LeMaster's approach); (2) a structured questionnaire of 36 items administered to husband and wife separately (duplicating Hobbs's and Dyer's approach).[9] Eighteen couples were interviewed, and the questionnaire was administered to 9 couples. In view of the major discrepancy in crisis ratings between LeMasters and Hobbs, Beauchamp was surprised to find that roughly similar results (in a position between the two extremes) were yielded by these different techniques. Table 1 compares his results with those of previously published studies.

Other reports regarding the transition to parenthood are few and

TABLE 1

Percentage of Crisis by Category as Reported by Four Investigators

			Investigators			
Crisis Category[a]	LeMasters N = 46	Dyer N = 32	Hobbs (1965) N = 53	Hobbs (1968) N = 27	Beauchamp (interview) N = 18	Beauchamp (questionnaire) N = 19
None	} 17	0	0.0	0.0	5.5	10.5
Slight		9	86.8	85.2	38.3	57.9
Moderate		38	13.2	14.8	33.0	10.5
Extensive	} 83	28	0.0	b	11.1	5.3
Severe		25	0.0	0.0	11.1	15.8

[a] These categories are only roughly comparable.
[b] Only four categories were used in this study.
Source: Hobbs (A Replication), op. cit., p. 415 and Beauchamp, op. cit., p. 14

scattered. Feldman found that, although the initial reaction of new parents was positive, numerous problems developed after four to six weeks.[10] Meyerowitz indicated that parents reported more difficulties when the firstborn was five to six months old than during pregnancy or at age five weeks.[11] Christensen reported lower marital adjustment scores for parents of one or two children than for those with no children or three children (statistically significant differences were found for the wife's scores only).[12] An unpublished study by Belle Tutave, showing that the birth of the first child represented a major psychological turning point for the parents, was cited by Gavron.[13]

Conceptual Problems

In retrospect it seems unfortunate that an overwhelming emphasis has been put in these works on the concept of "crisis." In a recent article Rossi has suggested that the transition to parenthood is accomplished by most of us, more or less successfully, and with various adjustments required.[14] She views the assumption of the parental role as a stage through which most married persons pass. Each developmental stage of the life span has its unique tasks, problems of adjustment, and rewards.

It seems likely that any accession research oriented around "crisis" will provide the investigator with only a partial picture of the adjustments required by the parenthood role. An interest in the positive gratifications associated with the arrival of a child would seem equally appropriate to sociological research focusing on parenthood as a developmental stage. Empirical investigations of the rewards of parenthood are few.[15]

Previous research has failed to differentiate between a behavioral change or adjustment and the (possibly negative) attitude taken toward this required change by the parents. It seems likely that some persons may view even minor role alterations as highly problematical, while others who are experiencing major changes accept them with equanimity. For example, many new mothers report having to quit a job with the arrival of the baby. Although this accommodation to parenthood probably represents a major change for the married couple, the change is likely to be viewed negatively by some, in a neutral way by others, and positively by still others. It would seem that "parenthood as a crisis" research has allowed little opportunity or stimulus for the reporting of affectively positive or neutral attitudes toward the adjustments required by parenthood.

Methodological Problems

The lack of a standardized method of reporting "crisis scores" makes interpretation of the five studies reported above (see Table 1) both difficult and hazardous.[16] For example, is the absence of severe or extensive crisis scores in the two studies by Hobbs attributable to (1) an absence of any major problems in the early weeks of parenthood on the part of the respondents or (2) the specific items included in his check list and the scoring procedure adopted? The assignment of scale scores seems to have been arbitrary: presumably a different scoring procedure could have resulted in some respondents being placed in the "none," "extensive," and "severe" crisis categories.

Although there are good reasons for expecting that the impact of parenthood will be different for the father than for the mother, it has been common practice to report a combined score for both. All the scores found in Table 1 represent averages for husband and wife combined. Hobbs reported husband-wife mean scores in spite of a significant (.05 level) difference between them. The correlation coefficient between these scores was not significant.

Of the investigations of new parenthood reported to date, only Hobbs has employed samples that are representative of a larger population. LeMasters, Dyer, and Beauchamp used nonprobability samples of middle-class, urban, mostly college-educated Americans. The largest sample consisted of only 53 couples. Clearly, studies with larger and more representative samples of the North American population are needed if significant generalizations concerning the transition to parenthood are to be forthcoming.

THEORETICAL BASIS OF ACCESSION RESEARCH

Most writers on the transition to parenthood have used Simmel's thoughts on differences between dyads and triads as a theoretical base point.[17] These hold that the affection and intimacy often found to be characteristic of the dyad are greatly diminished or restricted to a sub-part in the triad.[18] Coalition theory and research have shown that, in situations where power is unevenly distributed within a triad (as in the father-mother-child system), the weakest member of the triad always becomes part of any coalition.[19] This would necessarily ally the child with one parent against the other.

The assumption common to most writings on coalition theory is that "other factors are equal." The father-mother-child triad is far removed from the typically artificial triad of the small group laboratory both because of the strong normative element imposed from without (the extended family, the community, and the state) and because of a unique and necessary structure. For example, Gavron has suggested that the usual delay between marriage and parenthood provides the basis for a strong coalition between the prospective parents before the third member of the triad makes his appearance.[20] Rossi has suggested that most small group theory is not directly applicable to the nuclear family because of the great disparity in status between the parents and children.[21] Caplow recently expressed his belief that the mother-father-small infant group is not a true triad, because the small infant "is not a social actor."[22] Indeed, three years before the first of the "parenthood as crisis" articles appeared, Strodtbeck warned against the direct application of Simmel's propositions to the family.[23]

Freilich's notion of the "natural triad" seems to have been neglected by writers in the field of family crisis.[24] Since the "natural triad" concept incorporates normative and structural assumptions that usually hold for the nuclear family, it may prove useful to the family theorist.

The natural triad is characterized by these conditions: (1) it is a three-position system with one position of distinctly lower status than the other two; (2) the relationship between one high-status position and the lower-status position is characterized by the exercise of legitimate authority and by negative affect; (3) the other high-status position and the position of lower status are related in a friendly manner characterized by positive sentiment. The three positions in this triad are labeled "high status authority" (HSA), "high status friend" (HSF), and "lower status subordinate" (LSS).[25]

Freilich has suggested that this traidic relationship is so commonly found among humans that it might be considered characteristic of human systems.[26] The authority relationship of negative sentiment between HSA and LSS meets the instrumental needs of the system and/or the group of which this triadic system is a part. The HSF-LSS relationship performs an expressive function. In psychological terms HSA creates tension within the system, while HSF acts so as to reduce tension.[27]

A case has been made for the existence of the natural triad in the Western nuclear family and the nuclear families of most other societies.[28] As noted below, the concept of the natural triad may provide a useful point of departure for the sociologist interested in the transition to parenthood.

In a more obvious way, there are good reasons to expect the transition to parenthood to be at least as difficult as, and probably more difficult than, many of the more frequently studied role changes typical of our society (e.g., the shift from a single to a marital state, or the change from student to "member of the work force"). In a recent analysis Rossi developed this theme in considerable detail. She listed the following reasons for expecting the transition to parenthood to be particularly difficult:[29]

1) The need of the newborn child for the mother is absolute. The mother must shoulder this entire burden almost immediately after birth. This is something like shifting from graduate student to full professor almost overnight.

2) Neither formal nor informal preparation for parenthood is available to most young people today. Few new mothers have experienced more than sporadic baby-sitting, possibly occasional care of a sibling, and perhaps a course in child psychology. Fathers are likely to be even less experienced. The learning opportunities for either prospective parent during pregnancy are limited.

3) The cultural pressure to become parents is great enough that a couple may plan to bear children in spite of a latent desire to the contrary. For the female the pressure to become a mother may be the equivalent of the cultural insistence that the male assume a productive occupational role.

4) Conception often occurs in spite of efforts to prevent it. There must be many more unwanted pregnancies than unwanted marriages.

5) Most role transitions are revocable. Parenthood usually is not.

6) Definitive and noncontroversial guidelines as to how the parental role should be enacted are not available. Many are the disagreements among authorities on the best way of bringing up children.

A NEXT STEP IN ACCESSION RESEARCH

Objective Aspect

There seems to be little doubt but that parenthood marks a major transition point for most Americans and for most marriages. An overwhelming majority of respondents in previous studies indicated that the arrival of the first child called for changes in their lives. LeMasters, Dyer, Hobbs, and Beauchamp have taken the first steps toward the development of an inventory of the major adjustments that husbands and wives make in assuming the status "parent." Variations almost certainly exist. Probably the arrival of a baby changes the life of the mother more than that of the father, although there seems to be no empirical confirmation of this. Variations in the objective impact of the child may well be found with regard to such variables as length of time married, age of the baby, whether the child was planned, social class, urban or rural residence, and others.

Subjective Aspect

How difficult do Americans find this transition to parenthood? Are the adjustments and accommodations required by this new status eagerly welcomed? Do they represent major difficulties or very minor hurdles? The evidence appears to be contradictory. As noted in Table 1, LeMasters and Dyer showed the first years of parenthood to be a period of considerable difficulty, whereas Hobbs found that few new parents were more than slightly "bothered" by the demands of parenthood. Beauchamp's data fall between these extremes. A contrast of this magnitude begs to be explained. Several possibilities suggest themselves:

1. The difference may be artificial. As noted above, the crisis scores reported by these four researchers are not directly comparable. It seems possible, but not likely, that, had LeMasters and Hobbs used the same scoring procedures, they would have produced similar crisis scores.

2. The difference may be a function of the method employed to obtain crisis data. Both Hobbs and Beauchamp have suggested that the interview method provides higher crisis scores than the check-list method. Their data provide only limited confirmation of this view.[30] The contrast between the LeMasters and Hobbs scores seems too great to be completely explained in this way. Furthermore, Dyer used a technique similar to Hobbs's (a Likert-type scale) and achieved rather high crisis scores.

3. The age of the child may be a significant variable. Several writers have suggested that the number of difficulties reported by the parents may depend on the age of the child at the time of the study. The babies in Hobbs's research were all under one year old: low crisis scores were reported. The children represented in LeMasters's work were up to five years old: very high crisis scores were reported. The other studies fall neatly into place when the relationship between crisis score and child's age is plotted.

Thus, some evidence exists to support the notion of a "baby honeymoon," although the nature of the relationship between age of the child and the extent to which he creates a problem situation for the parents (i.e., whether this relationship is linear or curvilinear, whether threshold points occur at certain ages, etc.) cannot be specified. It is noteworthy that the three studies which address themselves to this question present contradictory results; Dyer reported a significant negative correlation, Hobbs's first investigation resulted in a significant positive correlation (for the father's crisis score only) and his replication showed no relationship at all.[31]

4. This discrepancy in results may be partly explained on the basis of the samples employed. Studies limited to middle-class respondents (LeMasters, Dyer, Beauchamp) have classified between 20 and 80 percent of the parents in the severe or extensive crisis categories, whereas Hobbs's more representative samples (made up in large part of working-class parents) contained no case of severe or extensive crisis. Thus, it seems likely that much of the difference in degree of crisis reported may be explainable in terms of the social-class composition of the samples used.

This evidence strongly suggests social class as a significant variable. Since the middle-class samples (LeMasters, Dyer and Beauchamp) showed many more accession-type problems than the two predominantly working-class samples (Hobbs), it seems reasonable to consider the possibility that the transition to parenthood is more difficult for middle-class parents than for working-class parents.[32] The literature on social-class variations in family life provides ample theoretical justification for this expectation. Possible reasons are listed below.

Middle-class standards may be higher. In a discussion of why couples at various class levels bear children, Winch suggested that middle-class couples suffer the greatest penalties for parenthood.[33] Upper-class expectations, in terms of childbearing practices and personal advancement, are high but so is money income. Problems exist in the middle class, because income is inadequate to meet the demands of high expectations. Children create less of a problem for lower-class parents because both expectations and income are low.

Without doubt, the duties and responsibilities of parenthood are viewed very differently in the two classes.[34] Prospective working-class parents may see themselves as required to make fewer adjustments on becoming parents. Or, perhaps the accommodations they do make are not as readily perceived and reported as problems. Also, it may be that the perceived responsibilities of parenthood are just taken less seriously in the working class.

Kohn stated that most middle-class parents regard child-rearing as more problematic than do working-class parents.[35] Gavron concluded that most of the middle-class mothers she interviewed, in contrast to working-class mothers, felt psychologically tied to their young children and felt themselves compelled to stay at home regardless of their personal desires. One inexperienced and obviously middle-class mother is quoted:

> I felt such a failure as a mother, not knowing whether the baby was warm enough, or fed enough, or why it was crying. I began to doubt that I could ever do anything properly again.[36]

The working-class woman places a greater intrinsic valuation on having children.[37] Gavron indicated that in the working class there is little place for the unattached woman; this may also be true for the woman without children. To marry and to have children is the only way the working-class woman can acquire the outward signs of adulthood, in contrast to the middle-class woman who may be able to validate her status more easily via the occupational structure.

That working-class couples place a greater intrinsic valuation on children has been shown by Meyerowitz. When asked to rate the importance of having children to a satisfying marital relationship, the blue-collar respondents scored highest and the professional couples lowest.[38]

The principal sources of gratification for the working-class woman are located within the family rather than outside. Several studies have confirmed the expectation of the working-class wife that her main satisfaction will come from within the family. To become a mother is high on her list of priorities. The middle-class wife, however, thinks of herself as an independent person having an existence outside the family context: the presence of young children may be viewed as a frustration of, rather than as a fulfillment of, her role.[39]

The indices of external orientation on the part of middle-class couples are many. Gavron found a major difference between working-class and middle-class couples in the number of friends outside the family and the amount of evening entertaining.[40] Almost all of her middle-class female respondents went out without their husbands at least occasionally, whereas about one-half of her sample of working-class wives never went out without the husband.[41] Only 17 percent of the middle-class wives reported watching television each day; the figure for working-class wives was 79 percent.[42] Gavron concluded that, for the working class, leisure is essentially home-centered. There is less effort than in the middle class to keep up contacts in the outside world.[43]

The Newsons also have provided evidence for the extrafamilial orientation of the middle-class wife.[44] Meyerowitz indicated that professional couples agreed most often, and blue-collar couples least often, to the statements, "Care of the baby limits the recreational activities we can do," and "A baby's needs sometimes conflict with our own desires."[45]

Parenthood is far more likely to interfere with career aspirations for middle-class mothers. One middle-class mother put her dilemma this way:

> I didn't have time to finish my training and make a career for myself. I would like to have either married much later or much earlier so I could have finished things before having my children.[46]

This child-career conflict has been documented by many writers.[47] It is felt by both parents. Both Thompson and Gavron found that middle-class husbands are more likely to want the spouse to work than working-class husbands.[48] Working-class mothers are more likely to want to work for financial reasons, whereas middle-class women more frequently seek psychic satisfactions.[49]

Working-class respondents may be less honest in their responses. The social desirability factor presents the researcher in problems of accession with a major problem. Quite possibly it operates differentially according to social-class level. It seems reasonable to assume that middle-class respondents, presumably with a greater understanding of and sympathy for the goals of social science research, may be more inclined to admit to being bothered by one or more items related to the role of parent. Furthermore, to the extent that to have troubles with the parental role is seen as failing in that role, the lower-class respondent may more often fail to admit troubles because his self-esteem is more fully dependent on successful performance of the parenthood role than is the case for the middle-class respondent.

Middle-class mothers are less experienced in the care of children. Since middle-class women come from significantly smaller families, they might be expected to have had, on the average, less experience with babies. Eighty-one percent of Gavron's middle-class respondents reported absolutely no experience in caring for infants at the time of the first child as compared to 63 percent of her working-class respondents.[50]

The middle-class husband-wife relationship is more strongly established as affectively positive at the time of birth. Even casual reading of the literature on marriage in the lower class indicates a weaker and less affectionate conjugal tie than in the middle class.[51] The arrival of a child represents less of a threat to the marital relationship because there is less to threaten. For many mothers, particularly, the establishment of a relationship with the baby may provide some relief from an unhappy marital bond.

The middle-class couple exists as a dyad for a longer period, typically, than the working-class couple: 19 percent of Gavron's middle-class respondents had the first child within 18 months of marriage, compared to one-third of her working-class respondents.[52] Meyerowitz's data showed college student and professional couples to be rated higher in marital adjustment than white- or blue-collar workers.[53]

Heider's theory of sentimental balance within the natural triad seems to call for an affectively negative marital relationship. The marital dyad, which is likely to be more affectively positive in the middle class than in the working class, becomes, with the arrival of the firstborn, what Freilich has called a "natural triad."[54] The affectively negative relationship between HSA and LSS in this triadic system produces tension and is necessary for the performance of instrumental functions. Expressive needs of the system are met by a positive, tension-absorbing relationship between HSF and LSS.

The theory of sentimental balance calls for one negative relationship in a triadic system (HSA-LSS) to be balanced by another negative relationship. Since the HSF-LSS relationship is of great value to the system for its tension-absorbing function, pressure is put on the HSA-HSF (husband-wife) relationship to become negative. If this does not happen, there are two alternatives (assuming that all systems strive toward balance): (1) the HSA-LSS becomes positive and the system becomes less able to perform instrumental aspects of its functions; or (2) the HSF-LSS tie becomes negative and the system loses its expressive element.[55]

Since the typical working-class conjugal bond is less likely to involve a high degree of affection, the arrival of a child might easily push this HSA-HSF tie to one of negative sentiment, balancing the HSA-LSS negative tie with the child.[56] The pressure toward sentimental balance in the middle-class system creates problems, however. A strong and positive bond is more likely to exist between husband and wife at the time the child arrives. Sentimental balance can be achieved only if this relationship sours or if the system gives up, in large part, its ability to perform instrumental or expressive functions. It seems likely that middle-class parents will feel these pressures, even if they cannot verbally identify them. Thus, middle-class couples may well be more upset by the arrival of a child than working-class couples.

Some countervailing arguments. Although most arguments seem to favor the notion that the firstborn creates more problems for middle-class than for working-class parents, there are reasons for expecting the opposite. The most powerful pertains to the more pervasive use of birth control in the middle class.[57] Almost certainly there are more unplanned children in the working class than in the middle class. It seems reasonable that the births of unplanned (and possibly unwanted) children would create more than their share of problems, although, of the LeMasters, Dyer, and Hobbs studies, only Dyer found a significant negative relationship between the planning of children and number of reported difficulties.[58]

Since early marriage occurs more frequently in the working class than in the middle class, and since the first child comes sooner after marriage to the working-class couple, one might suspect that this working-class child would bring many problems to the parents. Presumably the parents have a lower income than they hope to have later, and they may be emotionally less mature. Possibly, as suggested above, objective factors are less important in determining the number of problems the parents perceive than are subjective elements.

Empirical findings concerning social class and transition to parenthood. The available evidence is slim and inconclusive. Hobbs found a significant negative relationship between income and degree of crisis experienced by the father. However, only 13 of the fathers in this sample had a college education or higher.[59] A more powerful argument against our suggestion of a positive relationship between class and problems of accession is Gavron's comment.

The general impression gained during the interviewing indicated that the impact of the first child had a more detrimental effect on the working class than the middle class
mother.[60]

Supporting the notion of a positive relationship between social
class and difficulties with the arrival of the firstborn are data from Dyer
(university-educated husbands reporting more crises)[61] and from Meyerowitz.[62] As compared to blue-collar couples, the latter indicated that professional couples were (1) less likely to anticipate an increase in satisfaction in the period ranging from pregnancy to the first month after
birth, (2) more likely to look forward eagerly to the return of the marital
dyad after the children were grown, (3) less likely to feel that the
child would make a great contribution to their marriage, and (4) more
able to see the possibility of the child as a rival to the husband.

SUMMARY

Although marital adjustment has been widely studied, the adjustment
of the parent to the child has received little significant attention.[63] The
research reported to date leaves no doubt but that most parents find
that the arrival of a child calls for major behavioral changes. However,
reports are contradictory regarding the attitudes of new parents toward
these role changes.

It would seem that requirements for future accession research include the following:

1. A clear differentiation between the changes and adjustments required
   by parenthood and the perception of these changes as affectively positive, neutral, or negative on the part of the parents.
2. The development of a standard, reliable, and valid method of measuring the gratifications and difficulties involved in the transition to
   parenthood.
3. Samples that are both larger and more representative of the general
   population than most of those that have been employed to date.
4. An effort to discover the structural variables related to differences in
   perceived difficulty in assuming the parenthood role.

NOTES

* I wish to express my thanks to Elaine Hess and Nicholas Babchuk for their
comments and criticisms of an earlier draft of this paper.
1 E. E. LeMasters, "Parenthood as Crisis," *Marriage and Family Living*, 19
(1957), pp. 352–355.

[2] LeMasters used Hill's definition of crisis: "any sharp or decisive change for which old patterns are inadequate." See Reuben Hill, *Families Under Stress,* New York: Harper and Brothers, 1949, p. 51.

[3] A self-rating scale was used.

[4] Everett D. Dyer, "Parenthood as Crisis: A Re-Study," *Marriage and Family Living,* 25 (1963), pp. 196–201.

[5] Daniel F. Hobbs, Jr., "Parenthood as Crisis: A Third Study," *Journal of Marriage and the Family,* 27 (1965), pp. 367–372.

[6] Daniel F. Hobbs, Jr., "Transition to Parenthood: A Replication and an Extension," *Journal of Marriage and the Family,* 30 (1968), pp. 413–417.

[7] In this research neither the father's nor the mother's crisis score correlated significantly with the baby's age.

[8] This work seems to have been carried out simultaneously with and independently of the replication by Hobbs. See David Beauchamp, "Parenthood as Crisis: An Additional Study," unpublished independent study paper, University of North Dakota, 1968.

[9] Forty-seven items were developed from earlier reports of crisis research, especially that of Hobbs. Initial testing reduced these to 36.

[10] As reported in Hobbs, "Parenthood as Crisis," *op. cit.,* p. 371.

[11] Joseph H. Meyerowitz, "Transition to Parenthood: Socio-Economic Variation," unpublished paper.

[12] Harold T. Christensen and Robert E. Philbrick, "Family Size as a Factor in the Marital Adjustment of College Couples," *American Sociological Review,* 17:3 (June, 1952), p. 308.

[13] Hannah Gavron, *The Captive Wife,* London: Routledge and Kegan Paul, 1966, p. 60.

[14] What follows is partly built on and owes much to the recent insightful analysis of accession research by Alice Rossi, "Transition to Parenthood," *Journal of Marriage and the Family,* 30:1 (February, 1968), p. 33.

[15] Robert Winch, *The Modern Family,* New York: Holt, Rinehart and Winston, 1963, p. 298.

[16] Although each researcher has noted this lack of uniformity, the temptation is strong for the reader to treat these scale scores as comparable.

[17] LeMasters, *op. cit.,* p. 354; Hobbs, "Parenthood as Crisis," *op. cit.,* p. 367.

[18] Theodore Mills, "Some Hypotheses on Small Groups from Simmel," *American Journal of Sociology,* 63:6 (May, 1958), p. 647.

[19] Morris Freilich, "The Natural Triad in Kinship and Complex Systems," *American Sociological Review,* 29:4 (August, 1964), p. 532.

[20] Mentioned by Rossi, *op. cit.,* p. 33.

[21] *Ibid.*

[22] Theodore Caplow, *Two Against One,* Englewood Cliffs, New Jersey: Prentice-Hall, 1968, p. 63.

[23] Fred Strodtbeck, "The Family as a Three-Person Group," *American Sociological Review,* 19 (1954), pp. 23–29.

[24] Freilich, *op. cit.*

[25] *Ibid.,* p. 531.

[26] *Ibid.,* p. 530.

[27] *Ibid.,* pp. 532–533.

[28] *Ibid.,* p. 535.

[29] The ideas and much of the phraseology following are Rossi's, *op. cit.*

[30] See Table 1 for the Beauchamp comparison; and Hobbs, "Transition to Parenthood," *op. cit.,* p. 416.

[31] Dyer, *op. cit.,* p. 199; Hobbs, "Parenthood as Crisis," *op. cit.,* p. 370; Hobbs, "Transition to Parenthood," *op. cit.,* p. 416.

[32] Not to be overlooked is the possibility that the differences noted here stem from the obvious difficulties involved in having children while maintaining the

status of "student." Not only were the respondents in the former samples solidly middle class, but most parents were college-educated. One is probably safe in assuming that the childbearing process often began while one parent, at least, was still in school. This was definitely the case with Beauchamp's sample.

[33] Robert Winch, *The Modern Family,* New York: Henry Holt and Co., 1952, pp. 194–197.

[34] Evelyn Duvall, "Conceptions of Parenthood," *American Journal of Sociology,* 52: (1946), pp. 193–203.

[35] Melvin L. Kohn, "Social Class and Parent-Child Relationships: An Interpretation," *American Journal of Sociology,* 68:4 (January, 1963), p. 463.

[36] Gavron, *op. cit.,* pp. 60–69.

[37] *Ibid.,* p. 53.

[38] Meyerowitz, *op. cit.,* p. 10.

[39] Suggested by J. Newson and E. Newson, *Infant Care in an Urban Community,* London: George Allen & Unwin, 1963, as quoted in Gavron, *op. cit.,* p. 72. Gavron's research confirmed this finding.

[40] Gavron, *op. cit.,* pp. 97–98.

[41] *Ibid.,* p. 104.

[42] *Ibid.,* pp. 102 and 105.

[43] *Ibid.,* p. 106.

[44] Suggested by Newson and Newson, *op. cit.,* as quoted in Gavron, *op. cit.,* p. 100.

[45] Meyerowitz, *op. cit.,* p. 12.

[46] Gavron, *op. cit.,* p. 56.

[47] Newson and Newson, *op. cit.;* Gavron, *op. cit.;* Rossi, *op. cit.*

[48] B. Thompson and A. Finlayson, "Married Women Who Work in Early Motherhood," *British Journal of Sociology,* 14:2 (1963), as quoted in Gavron, *op. cit.,* p. 122.

[49] Gavron, *op. cit.,* p. 121.

[50] *Ibid.,* pp. 60 and 71.

[51] See especially Lee Rainwater, Richard P. Coleman, and Gerald Handel, *Workingman's Wife,* New York: Oceana Publications, 1959; and Lee Rainwater, *And the Poor Get Children,* Chicago: Quadrangle Books, 1960.

[52] Gavron, *op. cit.,* p. 71.

[53] Meyerowitz, *op. cit.,* p. 6.

[54] See description above.

[55] The assumptions of this theory of sentimental balance and its application to the family triad are more fully explained in Freilich, *op. cit.,* pp. 536–537.

[56] Freilich has claimed that in the lower-class family the father plays the role of HSA toward boys and the mother toward girls, while the middle-class family includes both parents playing alternately in this role regardless of the sex of the child.

[57] One of many references might be Gavron, *op. cit.,* p. 71.

[58] LeMasters, *op. cit.,* p. 353; Dyer, *op. cit.,* p. 199; Hobbs, "Parenthood as Crisis," *op. cit.,* p. 369.

[59] Hobbs, "Parenthood as Crisis," *op. cit.,* pp. 369–370.

[60] Gavron, *op. cit.,* p. 61.

[61] Dyer, *op. cit.*

[62] Meyerowitz, *op. cit.,* pp. 9 and 18–23.

[63] This is true despite the publicly manifested concern of physicians, social workers, and clergymen over pathological symptoms that seem to be related to difficulties of couples in adjusting to the parental role. The "battered-baby syndrome" is often mentioned in this respect. There are also reports of mental illness and marital disruption caused by the arrival of a child.

Occupational Status and Husband-Wife Social Participation*

BERT N. ADAMS
JAMES E. BUTLER

These are days of husband-wife "togetherness" in the popular family magazines, and in much other family literature as well. They are days of the barbecue, the weekend at the lake, and the joint organizational membership. In view of the much-lamented impersonality of urban existence, husbands and wives are instructed to face life together, to enter the neighborhood, community, and society together. The assumed prevalence of the practice of couple mutuality has caused one author to caution about the dangers inherent in couples overdoing mutual recreational involvement.[1]

To what extent are the generalizations or admonitions regarding "togetherness" empirically correct? Which elements of urban populations do engage in activities together as couples, and in what activities do they participate? What, in fact, is the relation between occupational level and couple involvement? The answers to these and other questions regarding husband-wife leisure participation form the subject matter of the present paper.

There has been substantial recent research on social activity, but it is largely concerned with the individual rather than with the joint activity of husbands and wives. Nevertheless, a review of the literature on individual participation may serve as an appropriate point of departure for our discussion.

The most intensive and thorough analysis of social involvement refers to voluntary associations. This research has established the positive association between class, as measured by various indicators, and participation in both formal and informal organizations. This was reported by the Lynds more than a generation ago, and it has been documented in numerous subsequent studies.[2] A voluntary association of particular salience to family groups is the church or religious body. A majority of studies of this institution show a positive linear association between social class and membership and attendance.[3] Some simply indicate that

"Occupational status and Husband-Wife Social Participation," by Bert N. Adams and James E. Butler is reprinted from *Social Forces*, Vol. 45, No. 4 (June 1967), with permission of the University of North Carolina Press.

the middle classes attend church more frequently than the working classes.[4] Exceptions to the generalization regarding class and religious participation are of two types. A few researchers have found a slightly curvilinear relationship, with the middle classes attending more regularly than the upper classes, but both of these being more frequent in attendance than the lower or working classes.[5] The other exception is reported in Berger's study of the suburbs, where he finds church attendance negatively related both to education and to type of residence.[6] Of course, the findings of these studies are not truly contradictory, since many samples do not even include the upper classes, thereby overlooking the possibility of the sort of curvilinearity documented by Warner and Lunt, and Berger's work is focused on the middle range of the status distribution. It should be kept in mind, finally, that none of the above studies is concerned with the family unit, but with the individual.

A second area of participation that has received some attention is commercial recreation. Berger finds movie attendance and husbands and wives "going out" to be positively related to education level.[7] Rainwater *et al.* characterize the working-class wife as not sharing in her husband's recreational activities because she is absorbed in domestic activities and because her husband has no desire for her to participate.[8] Clarke, on the other hand, discovers in his investigation of leisure uses that commercial recreation appears to occupy a more important place in the lives of lower status persons.[9] In comparing Clarke with Berger and Rainwater, it is quite likely that individual versus couple involvement explains their divergent results.

Family recreation, including home entertaining, card playing, picnics, and so on, is referred to only in passing in the literature. However, Berger and Clarke do observe frequency of home entertaining to be positively related to social class.[10]

Several studies, both in England and in the United States, demonstrate the importance of kin-visiting as a leisure activity among the urban working classes.[11] Rainwater *et al.*, comparing middle-class and working-class wives, note the visiting of relatives to be more important in the working classes than the middle classes.[12] In kinship, therefore, we have a reported instance of a clearly inverse association between social class and participation which is apt to hold for couples as well as for individuals.

A fifth aspect of husband-wife interaction, which may be indicative of the mutuality or non-mutuality of economic concerns, is shopping together. It would be reasonable to assume, on the basis of research by Olsen on division of family responsibilities, that middle-class husbands and wives are more likely to shop together.[13] Yet the exploratory nature of our inquiry into couple shopping compels us to suspend judgment.

This, then, is the state of research in the five areas of husband-wife participation with which we shall be concerned. In any study of this nature, i.e., relating occupational status to some form of behavior, one becomes involved in the question of class boundaries or status continuum. Are status categories, particularly the manual–nonmanual dichotomy, meaningful, or is the stratification system of U.S. communities best explained in terms of minute gradations between the individual family units? Much early research established the notion of strata.[14] Recently, Ellis has supported the idea of classes as a valid distinction.[15] Lenski and others, however, caution against reifying social strata, explaining that such divisions are in actuality the result of somewhat arbitrary cutting points on the status continuum.[16] One of the newer developments in the stratum–continuum discussion has been the introduction of the "middle-mass" concept. This sees the American stratification system as becoming more and more composed, in terms of style of life, of a large, undifferentiated middle mass, separated from the upper or "elite" class, and with less distinct divisions from the upper-middles and the lower or unskilled working class.[17] Besides investigating husband-wife interaction, we also hope to increase our understanding of the strata, continuum, and middle-mass concepts in the process of analyzing social participation.

SAMPLE AND METHODOLOGY

Data for this study were collected by interviews administered during the summers of 1963 and 1964. The sample selection was by means of the random block technique, with the following restrictions upon inclusion: all respondents are white, married, have been married only once, and for 20 years or less. Greensboro, North Carolina, a city of approximately 150,000 population, was chosen for the study, and the total sample consists of 467 females and 332 males.[18] The median age of the males is 34.5, of the females is 32.3, and the median length of marriage is between ten and 11 years. For this paper the 11 respondents who were students or who for some other reason failed to report their (or their husband's) occupation are eliminated. This reduces our working sample to 788 cases.

In order to ascertain husband-wife activity patterns, the respondents were asked how frequently within the past two years they had engaged in commercial recreation (with examples given); home recreation (also with examples); attendance at religious services; visiting any relative, or shopping, with their spouse. Possible answers included never, once or twice in two years, from three times up to monthly, and monthly or more.

Measurement of occupational status is by utilizing the occupational portion of Hollingshead's Index of Status Position.[19] The seven major classifications are as follows: (1) top professionals, managers, and corporation owners; (2) lesser professionals, branch managers, and owners of medium-sized businesses; (3) semiprofessionals, administrators and agents, and small business men; (4) sales clerks, clerical, and technicians; (5) skilled craftsmen and foremen; (6) assembly line and other semiskilled workers; (7) unskilled laborers. Thus, four white-collar and three blue-collar categories will be utilized in the presentation of our results.

RESULTS

In Table 1 are shown the percentages of the various occupational categories engaging in the five types of activities with their spouses monthly or more and at least once within the past two years, as well as the total sample percentages.

Commercial Recreation

The results are consistent with the literature quoted above. Beginning with the lesser professionals and branch managerial category, whom we shall designate as upper-middles, there is a negative linear association between occupational stratum and couple participation in commercial leisure pursuits. Of especial note are the smaller percentages of top occupational status couples engaging in frequent commercial recreation and the extremely small number of unskilled families participating together in such activity at all. This latter result may be due both to the general role separation between couples in this occupational category and to the financial bind within which they live.

Family Recreation

Precisely the same association appears here as in commercial recreation. That is, the upper-middles are extremely likely to entertain friends, have picnics, perhaps play cards, etc., at least once a month, with percentages diminishing as we move down the occupational scale and as we compare the top managers and professionals. The differences are primarily a matter of frequency, for, as one would expect, over 90 percent of the sample indicate that they have had some form of family recreation at least once in the past two years. Even the lower-working-class families tend to report *some* occurrences of family activity within the two-year period.

Church Attendance

For a third time the same pattern of stratum—participation associations emerges. Our results agree generally with those of Warner and Lunt. That is, the upper-middles are both the most frequent attenders and most likely to attend at some time or another. The unskilled couples are as likely to be monthly attenders as are the semiskilled, but are more apt to be nonattenders than any other category. The two lowest categories are significantly less likely to be regular or frequent church attenders than are the five occupational strata above them. The question regarding religious attendance does not discriminate between Protestants, Catholics, and Jews, but it should be recalled that Greensboro is a southern, and therefore primarily a Protestant, city. More specifically, it is a Baptist and Methodist city, with smaller contingents of Presbyterians and Episcopalians in the upper strata and Pentecostal groups in the lower strata.

Kin-Visiting

As the literature would lead us to anticipate, there is a negative association between stratum and monthly or more frequent kin-visiting. The pattern, nevertheless, is not a continuum, but two clusters, one comprising the top three white-collar categories and the other the clerical-sales-technical along with the blue-collar couples. Of course, frequent kin-visiting is basically a function of proximity, and it is significant that these lowest white-collar couples have a history of residential stability rather than the mobility which characterizes the first three white-collar groups. Predominantly wage workers, the clerical-technical group, like the working classes, are apparently able to find jobs without the sort of residential movement which the occupational orientations of the other white-collar groups often demands. These lower-white-collar families, then, resemble the middle classes in certain values and types of social participation, while resembling the working classes in residential stability and thus in proximity to their kin networks.

Two other aspects of kin-visiting deserve comment. First is the widespread distribution of monthly visiting among the higher-white-collar categories. While there is a significant difference between the top three and bottom four strata, it is not as great as might have been expected. This illustrates as others have done that the residential mobility of managers and professionals has sometimes been overdrawn, and also that mobility may be *to* a community where kin are located as well as *away* from it. It also indicates that middle-class couples are ordinarily quite positively oriented toward their close kin, for many of them cover considerable distances to be with them. Further, the relatively small disparity between white-collar and blue-collar kin-visiting is indicative of the greater likelihood of working-class persons visiting their own kin apart from their marriage partners. The final noteworthy aspect of kin-visiting is its universality. Only 27 out of 788 respondents state that they have seen no kin within the past two years; stratum differences disappear completely when kin-visiting *at all* is observed.

Shopping

The association between stratum and couples shopping together frequently is somewhat curvilinear. The lower-white-collar couples stand out in this regard, with the skilled and semiskilled next. How may this finding be explained? Three factors would seem to encourage more shopping together among lower stratum couples. First is the shorter work

TABLE 1

Engagement by Young Married Greensboro Couples in Various Types of Social Participation in the Past Two Years, According to Their Occupations

Occupational Category	Number of Respondents	Commercial Rec. (% Mo.+)	Family Rec. (% Mo.+)	Church Attendance (% Mo.+)	Kin-Visiting (% Mo.+)	Shopping (% Mo.+)
Top Pro's and Mgrs.	(73)	51	60	63	55	25
Upper-Middles	(124)	65*	73*	78*	52	30
Middles	(206)	64	59*	68	52	28
Clerical-Technical	(83)	57	57	65	¯66*	49*
Skilled	(174)	45*	47	60	68	39
Semiskilled	(97)	38	40	45*	70	40
Unskilled	(31)	16*	13*	45	61	23*
Total Percentages	(788)	53	54	63	60	34
		(% at All)	(% at All)	(% at All)	(% at All)	(% at All)
Top Pro's and Mgrs.	(73)	90	97	89	97	78
Upper-Middles	(124)	92	98	95	97	79
Middles	(206)	87	95	84	96	71
Clerical-Technical	(83)	89	93	86	98	82
Skilled	(174)	86	86	80	95	74
Semiskilled	(97)	60*	85	72	97	70
Unskilled	(31)	35*	71*	61*	100	55*
Total Percentages	(788)	84	91	83	96	74

* Differences between contiguous strata which are significant according to the difference-of-proportions test beyond the .05 level.

week for the wage earner as compared to those whose income is by fee or salary. Second is the need for those with less financial resources to be more careful in purchasing, which may cause husbands in modestly financed families to take more interest in purchases. Third is the greater likelihood that upper status families will have two cars, freeing the wife to shop while the husband is at work. No one of these factors, however, should explain more than a fraction of the stratum variation. A countervailing factor is the tendency of higher status couples to do more things together generally. The curvilinearity perceptible in frequent couple shopping may be due to the interplay of such cross-influences.

Stratum Comparisons

Dotson, Rainwater, and others have referred to the manner in which kin-visiting dominates the leisure time of the working classes. Comparing the percentages engaging in the various activity types monthly or at all, we find nothing which would disprove or alter this generalization. We were unprepared, though, for the manner in which kin-visiting and churchgoing dominate the social participation of lower-white-collar couples. In many ways these lower-middle-class families keep the status continuum from breaking into a nice, neat white-collar–blue-collar division. The middle- and upper-middle classes are characterized by church, family recreation, and commercial recreation, and many of them by frequent kin contact as well. In Greensboro the top managerial and professional couples demonstrate a less widespread engagement than the upper-middles in every type of activity except kin-visiting. This may perhaps indicate the sort of occupational dominance over familism which has put them at the top of the status distribution.[20] Thus, a "flip-over" in dominant activity types does occur when the middles and upper-middles are compared with the working classes, but the highest and lowest white-collar categories keep the status comparisons from being either a smooth continuum or a simple white-collar–blue-collar dichotomy.

CONCLUSIONS

Husbands and wives have often been studied in their decision-making, their family problems, and their sexual life, but not in their common activity. In the course of our investigation of this latter aspect of couple relations, occupational status as a behavioral indicator has also received attention. A summary of the conclusions and their implications follows.

1. Church attendance and kin-visiting dominate the couple activity of the young married in Greensboro, with family and commercial recreation also quite widespread. Whether this is a function of Greenboro's

southern character can only be surmised until communities in other regions are compared. The authors feel, however, that this city, industrializing and having more than doubled in population since 1950, is hardly an example of that frequently overdrawn, kin-oriented, "Old South" city, and that the results in other urban places might not diverge greatly.

2. Upper-middle-class professional and managerial couples approximate most closely the notion of "togetherness" found in popular family literature. Frequent churchgoing, family recreation and entertaining, and various mutual commercial recreations are extremely prevalent among these persons. Such togetherness is less as one moves either direction in the occupational status continuum. Of course, the mass media are primarily in upper-middle-class hands, which may explain the widespread popular preaching of the doctrines of togetherness as these persons seek to promulgate their family values.

3. Working-class couples find most of their mutual social involvement in kin-visiting, although this is decreasingly true toward the upper or skilled end of the blue-collar occupational continuum. It is not that the skilled and semiskilled couples spend less time with kin than the unskilled, but that they incorporate a wider range of activities similar to those which characterize the togetherness of the middle-class couples as well.

4. Occupational position appears in this study to be a valuable indicator of diverse couple behaviors. In certain activities the distributions resemble quite closely a continuum, especially churchgoing, commercial recreation, and family recreation. Within-stratum comparisons, however, point up the basic dichotomy, still apparent in the urban United States today, between working-class and middle-class life situations and behaviors. There is thus considerable value in viewing occupations both as a continuum and as a dichotomy. It must further be concluded that the "undifferentiated middle mass" designation seems inappropriate to the interpretation of our data, even were we to restrict analysis to the three middle categories, i.e., skilled manual, clerical and sales, and agents and semiprofessionals.

While the continuum and dichotomy conceptions are useful, it should be repeated that the highest and lowest white-collar categories are difficult to fit neatly into either of these. The highest stratum couples manifest a statistically significant break from the remainder of the continuum in three of the five activity types, but their percentages are in fact lower, causing them to be similar to the middles and lower-middles in these respects. Also, the clerical-technical couples are characterized by much togetherness and by a history of residential stability and kin proximity, causing them to resemble in some ways both the middle and working classes.

Occupational orientation, family values and perception of husband-wife roles, and residential history all go into the interpretation of occupational stratum comparisons. Perhaps expansion of these results requires further subdivision of occupations using the notion of occupational situs, or horizontal equation and comparison of occupations, before the significance of occupation as a behavioral indicator can be better understood.[21] At any rate, both extension, e.g., looking at length of marriage or breaking down recreation into types, and replication are necessary in order to progress beyond the present characterization of husband-wife social participation in the various occupational strata.

NOTES

* The investigation was supported by Public Health Service fellowship (MH-15,571) from the National Institute of Mental Health, awarded to the senior author.

[1] T. R. Young, "Recreation and Family Stress: An Essay in Institutional Conflicts," *Journal of Marriage and the Family,* 26 (February 1964), pp. 95–96.

[2] Robert Lynd and Helen Lynd, *Middletown* (New York: Harcourt, Brace & Co., 1929), pp. 413–495; William G. Mather, "Income and Social Participation," *American Sociological Review,* 6 (June 1941), pp. 380–383; Mirra Komarovsky, "The Voluntary Associations of Urban Dwellers," *American Sociological Review,* 11 (December 1946), pp. 686–698; Frederick A. Bushee, "Social Organizations in a Small City," *American Journal of Sociology,* 51 (November 1945), pp. 217–226; W. A. Anderson, "Family Social Participation and Social Status Self-Ratings," *American Sociological Review,* 11 (April 1946), pp. 253–258; Leonard Reissman, "Class, Leisure, and Social Participation," *American Sociological Review,* 19 (February 1954), pp. 76–84.

[3] Louis Bultena, "Church Membership and Church Attendance in Madison, Wisconsin," *American Sociological Review,* 14 (June 1949), pp. 384–389; Komarovsky, *op. cit.;* Mather, *op. cit.;* Reissman, *op. cit.;* N. J. Demerath, III, *Social Class in American Protestantism* (Chicago: Rand McNally & Co., 1965), pp. 83–104, 205–208. In keeping with recent developments, we are tempted to perceive churchgoing more as simply a typical "family" voluntary association than as indicative of couple religiosity. On this viewpoint, see the Demerath reference and especially Erich Goode, "Social Class and Church Participation," *American Journal of Sociology,* 72 (July 1966), pp. 102–111.

[4] Richard F. Curtis, "Occupational Mobility and Church Participation," *Social Forces,* 38 (May 1960), pp. 315–319; Bernard Lazerwitz, "Some Factors Associated with Variations in Church Attendance," *Social Forces,* 39 (May 1961), pp. 301–309.

[5] W. Lloyd Warner and Paul S. Lunt, *The Social Life of a Modern Community* (New Haven: Yale University Press, Yankee City Series, Vol. I, 1941), pp. 356–359, 422–450; Lynd and Lynd, *op. cit.,* pp. 315–412.

[6] Bennett M. Berger, *Working-Class Suburb* (Berkeley and Los Angeles: University of California Press, 1960), p. 113.

[7] *Ibid.,* pp. 117–118.

[8] Lee Rainwater, Richard P. Coleman, and Gerald Handel, *Workingman's Wife* (New York: Oceana Publications, 1959), p. 76.

[9] Alfred C. Clarke, "The Use of Leisure and Its Relation to Levels of Occupational Prestige," *American Sociological Review,* 21 (June 1956), p. 304.

[10] Berger, *op. cit.,* p. 116; Clarke, *loc. cit.*

[11] Floyd Dotson, "Patterns of Voluntary Association Among Urban Working-Class Families," *American Sociological Review,* 16 (December 1951), pp. 687–693; Michael Young and Peter Willmott, *Family and Kinship in East London* (Baltimore: Penguin Books, 1964).

[12] Rainwater, Coleman, and Handel, *op. cit.,* p. 103.

[13] Melvin E. Olsen, "Distribution of Family Responsibilities and Social Stratification," *Marriage and Family Living,* 22 (February 1960), pp. 60–65.

[14] Lynd and Lynd, *op. cit.;* Warner and Lunt, *op. cit.*

[15] Robert A. Ellis, "Social Stratification and Social Relations: An Empirical Test of the Disjunctiveness of Social Classes," *American Sociological Review,* 22 (August 1957), pp. 570–578.

[16] Gerhard E. Lenski, "American Social Classes: Statistical Strata or Social Classes?" *American Journal of Sociology,* 58 (September 1952), pp. 139–145; John F. Cuber and William F. Kenkel, *Social Stratification in the United States* (New York: Appleton-Century-Crofts, 1954), pp. 23–28, 303–309; Bernard Barber, *Social Stratification* (New York: Harcourt, Brace & World, 1957), pp. 77–80; John L. Haer, "Predictive Utility of Five Indices of Social Stratification," *American Sociological Review,* 22 (August 1957), pp. 541–546.

[17] Werner Landecker, "Class Boundaries," *American Sociological Review,* 25 (December 1960), pp. 868–877; Berger, *op. cit.,* p. 96; Richard F. Curtis, "Differential Association and the Stratification of the Urban Community," *Social Forces,* 42 (October 1963), p. 72; Albert K. Cohen and Harold M. Hodges, Jr., "Characteristics of the Lower-Blue-Collar-Class," *Social Problems,* 10 (Spring 1963), pp. 309–314.

[18] Males and females are not separated in the analysis which follows, since we are discussing empirical relations between couples which should be identical regardless of which member of the couple was interviewed.

[19] For a brief explanation of the Index of Occupational Status, see August B. Hollingshead and Frederick C. Redlich, *Social Class and Mental Illness* (New York: John Wiley & Sons, 1958), pp. 387–397.

[20] See *Time Magazine,* 86, 23 (December 3, 1965), pp. 91–92, in reference to the small amount of time which wealthy men spend on family, religion, and friends. While our top category does not represent the nation's wealthiest families, we may be seeing in our upper echelon the trend in that direction which culminates in the life orientation of the wealthy.

[21] On situs, see Richard T. Morris and Raymond J. Murphy, "The Situs Dimension in Occupational Structure," *American Sociological Review,* 24 (April 1959), pp. 231–239; that situs can be useful is evidenced in Joel Gerstl, "Leisure, Taste, and Occupational Milieu," *Social Problems,* 9 (Summer 1961), pp. 56–68.

VI

The Family and Other Systems

Family units do not exist in a vacuum; they are related in many ways to the larger society of which they are a part. Families vary greatly in the extent to which they are embedded in a network of kin and friends, in the way in which they employ the educational and religious institutions in socializing their offspring, and in the amount of economic and political power which they provide. The readings in this part illustrate but four of the possible relations between the family and other systems which might be explored.

The excerpt from David Schneider's book on *American Kinship* concerns the determination of who is considered a realtive. Crucial to this determination is the perception of the individual himself, not the preconceived categories of the sociologist. This perception varies from one individual to the next because of the lack of commonly accepted rules governing kinship behavior and attitudes in the United States. Even the notion of kin distance, as Schneider points out so well, can have at least three different meanings in U.S. kinship. Are the boundaries of kin networks in the United States so fuzzy because kin are unimportant, or because kin are increasingly like friends, being cultivated or ignored at the will of the individual? Schneider's analysis introduces these and other issues regarding American kinship for the reader to ponder, and the subsequent paper by Adams focusses on kinship and friendship. Beginning with a characterization of kinship as based upon "positive concern" and of friendship as based upon "consensus," Adams notes that in terms of their dominant characteristics some friendships have in fact the character of kin relations, while some kin relations are found to resemble the typical friendship. What, the reader might ask, is it that turns a kin relation, such as that with a brother or cousin, into a "friendly" relation? And what does it require for a friend to become "like a brother?" Many of the unanswered questions regarding Adams' interpretation concern the subcategories of American society. Are the typical kinship and friendship relation the same in the various racial, religious, ethnic, and socioeconomic categories of the U.S. population? If they are not the same, how might they differ?

This final question brings us to Leichter and Mitchell's discussion of the interplay between family and business in the Jewish community of New York City. Family and kinship are not always neatly separated off from other systems in American society. In the case of Leichter and Mitchell's Jewish respondents, many of them were either currently, or had at some time in the past been, in a business relationship involving kin. Based upon the author's account, do the advantages of mixing business and family seem to outweigh the disadvantages, or not? Another study has found that those few kin who are in business together tend not to socialize together, so that the kin tie is subordinated or forfeited to the economic. Leichter and Mitchell's respondents do not seem to be able to effect such a separation, but in fact tend to have intense social involvements with those with whom they work. What does the inability to subordinate kinship to business say about the strength of kin ties within this particular ethnic subcategory of U.S. society?

Parsons' discussion of the family and religion in American society refers to the analogy between them, rather than their interplay. Both are "presocietal," in the sense that they impinge upon the individual prior to his involvement in the economic and other systems of society, and they are intermediate systems between the individual and the polity and economy. The educational institutions link religion and family to the economy and polity. Furthermore, the family and religion are what Parsons calls "boundary systems," being separated from each other and from the larger society more than they used to be in the days of which Ariès was writing in Part I of this reader. How useful is Parsons' analogy of family and religion for understanding these two institutions today? To what extent, in the light of Leichter and Mitchell's excerpt and Aldous' paper in Section Five, is he correct regarding the separation between these institutions and the larger society in the contemporary United States?

These are but a few of the intriguing questions regarding the relations between the family and other institutions of American society. Other issues you might wish to discuss would include the learning of political attitudes and behaviors within the family, whether family values determine the character of the school system or the school system is a source of change in family values, and whether there are certain powerful kinship groups through which economic and political power are passed along in American society.

A Relative Is a Person

DAVID SCHNEIDER

One of the first things that anyone who works with American genealogies notices is that the system is quite clear as long as one takes Ego
as the point of reference and does not venture far from there. As one goes
out from Ego—in any direction—things get more and more fuzzy. This
boundary fuzziness, or fadeout, is seen in a number of different ways.
Most fundamental, of course, is the fact that there is no formal, clear,
categorical limit to the range of kinsmen. Or, to put it in another way,
the decision as to whether a particular person is or is not to be counted
as a relative is not given in any simple categorical sense. One cannot say
that all second cousins are relatives, but all third cousins are not. An
American can, if he wishes, count a third cousin as a kinsman while a
second cousin is actually alive but unknown, or known to be alive but
nevertheless not counted as a relative.

The fadeout is also seen in the increasing uncertainty over names,
ages, occupations, and places of residence the farther out the relatives
are from Ego.

There is one particularly interesting way in which boundary fuzziness
is expressed; this is through the Famous Relative. During the course of
the field work we not infrequently encountered the statement that So-
and-So, a famous personage, was a relative. Sometimes the relationship
was traceable, sometimes not. When it was traceable, it could clearly be
seen that this was the only relative of such distance on the genealogy,
whereas closer relatives were unknown and unheard of.[1]

Yet another observation that is part of this picture is what I have
called the "Christmas-tree effect." American genealogies are often not
more than three or four generations deep; they take the form of a squat
Christmas tree or pyramid. At the top, there is often the Ancestor, sometimes in the form of a couple, like the star on a Christmas tree. As generations get closer to Ego, each sib-set somehow gets larger, so that the
whole thing seems to stand on a very firm, broad base. But if one looks
closely below the base one can see the trunk of the Christmas tree; Ego's
line, his children and grandchildren, who continue to move away from
Ego generation by generation. The Ancestor may or may not have had
siblings, but if he did, they are either not mentioned or they are forgotten. Sib-sets of the Ancestor's children are larger, while the sib-sets and

the collateral lines of cousins give the zero generation a considerable collateral spread of both cousins and siblings.

The squat Christmas tree consists in a network of blood relatives. This consanguineal network is adorned with spouses, like the decorations on a Christmas tree. But the adorning spouses only occasionally have siblings or parents, and the occasional spouses' parents only rarely have siblings.

One can take a genealogy in a wholly nondirective way by simply asking for a list of relatives and then asking if there are any more. Or one can take a very systematic genealogy using probes of the utmost specificity such as: "And has he any brothers? sisters? mother? father? sons? daughters? wife? (or husband)." In the first instance, the tree is rather skimpy. In the second, the tree is quite bushy and about one-third more persons are usually added to the genealogy. However, the basic shape remains very much the same, because informants don't remember if great-grandfather had any brothers or sisters; if he had, who they married; and if they married, how many children they had. As far as great-grandfather's wife is concerned, if she is remembered at all, informants imagine that she must have had a father and mother, but they do not know their names, or if she had any brothers or sisters, or what their names might have been.

There are two important points to note about the Christmas-tree effect in American genealogies. The first is that they are pyramids of greater or lesser range, but they include far fewer kinsmen than the definition of a relative as anyone related by blood or marriage would lead one to expect.

The second point is that they are fundamentally consanguineal networks to which spouses are added. In-laws are not common; in fact, they are notable by their absence. In genealogies, informants normally list their own spouse and the spouses of their blood relatives, but they do not often spontaneously list the parents or siblings of any of the spouses they list, and often not even the parents and siblings of their own spouse. There were a number of exceptions. In one extreme case, a man listed his mother's sister's husband's brother and sisters and their husbands and wives and children. These were the only brothers and sisters of the spouses of blood relatives that he listed spontaneously, although it turned out that he knew others and could easily name them. Asked if he considered these to be relatives, he affirmed that he did.

Closely related to this point is another of some relevance. Of the two theoretically possible ways of increasing the number of kinsmen actively engaged in a particular network, it is those who are related by marriage who constitute a major source of additional numbers rather than the wider spread which would be obtained by tracing back farther and then out to more widely placed collateral lines. It is by the addition of the consanguineals of spouses rather than by the increase in the number of more distant collateral lines of consanguineal kinsmen that the size of networks tends to be augmented in America.

Nevertheless, when the situation warrants, the net can be spread very widely indeed, as the cousins clubs and family circles reported by Mitchell[2] show. When the net is spread this widely, there is again a choice among kinds of links, so some organizations require blood connection through a founding ancestor while others permit the addition of members *through* spouses as well as *to* spouses.

The decision as to who is a relative is made by and about a person. Sometimes the decision which a person makes about another person is common and usual, and informants agree that it is the "right" decision. But sometimes, although the decision "makes sense" to informants, some may regard it as eccentric or even as "wrong." Such decisions, right or wrong, are nevertheless illuminating because they reveal the crucial elements which are involved.

The dead are a case in point.

The only standardized question asked of informants in Chicago was the first question of the very first interview. This was, "List for me all the people whom you consider to be your relatives."

All informants would start listing people, but some of them would suddenly interrupt the recitation with the question, "Do you want the dead ones too?" Or they would say, "What about those who are dead?" Or, "That's all, except for the dead ones, of course. . . ." It sometimes took the form: ". . . and Uncle Jim—but he's dead. . . ." But with almost every informant there was always something special about the dead ones, some remark, some comment, and almost invariably, if the person being listed was dead, this fact was spontaneously stated. Further there seemed to be a clear tendency for the dead to be omitted entirely in the very early phases of the collection of the genealogy, and only to come to light during later enquiry, often in another connection.

Another example is in the categories used to describe the fuzzy, faded area containing distant relatives. One of these is the term "shirt-tail relations," another is "wakes-and-weddings relatives," and the third is "kissin' kin" or "kissin' cousins." Wakes-and-weddings relatives are easily defined—they are, quite expectably, relatives who are only seen at wakes and weddings. Usually there is no direct contact, or even indirect contact, and some informants describe them as "relatives of relatives." Informants sometimes associate the term with Catholics, since in their view wakes are primarily a Catholic practice. Shirt-tail relations are very much the same, except that instead of specifying where certain relatives are seen (wakes and weddings), these are described as being "brought in on somebody's shirt-tail"; that is, they are seen as related through intermediaries and their main significance is that they are relatives' relatives. The terms "kissin' kin" or "kissin' cousins" are said to be primarily southern, though many Chicago informants knew the term even when they did not use it themselves. Here the kiss is the sign that no matter how distant, such persons are nevertheless relatives and therefore are entitled to that sign of being relative, the kiss.[3]

Yet another example is one I have already mentioned, that of the Famous Relative.

Two examples of the understandable, but perhaps eccentric decisions on who is counted as a relative are the following: One woman firmly asserted that her sister was not a relative because she had not seen her or spoken to her for some years now. I did not have great confidence in this informant, and in other ways she proved difficult to work with. Since this statement seemed in plain conflict with the fact that a blood relative always remains a blood relative, I at first dismissed her statement as absurd. I was wrong to do this, of course.

A young lady attending college raised the opposite problem; she affirmed, and could not be dissuaded from the position, that her roommate was a relative even though she claimed no connection of blood or marriage between them.

Why should the dead constitute a problem? In discussing the question of whether it is possible to terminate a blood relationship, some informants said that it is, in fact, possible to do. Some Jewish informants described a modified mourning ceremony which could be performed, according to certain religious and ritual prescriptions, by a parent to terminate the relationship to a child. This ritual could be performed only by a parent, not by a child. After this ritual the child was as if dead, and did not exist for the parent. So, these informants said, it was really possible, after all, for there to be an ex-child just as there can be an ex-spouse. The fact that this ritual is very rarely performed makes no difference. For informants who were not Jewish, the same situation could obtain, but it had neither ritual nor religious setting. A parent might simply terminate his relationship to the child, and act as if the child were dead by never seeing it again, and never speaking of it or with it. In this case the initiative could be taken by the child—since there is no formal rite—and the child could leave home and never speak to the parent again, acting as if the parent were dead.

When a Jewish parent holds a mourning ceremony for a live child (or a dead child), what is terminated is the *relationship* between them, but the child, as a child, is not "taken back" or made never to have existed. The Jewish parent, so moved as to have to hold a mourning ceremony for a child, is the object of special sympathy and pity, for the greatest tragedy of all has befallen him—his child, who need not have died, must now be treated as dead! This parent has lost a child. But he *had* a child, and the child is "there" and remains there.

It is perhaps obvious now why informants listing relatives stop and give the dead a special place: "Do you want me to list the dead ones too?"—for death terminates a relationship but does not undo or erase what is and was a fact. A dead person remains person enough to be located on a genealogy; person enough to be counted as an ascendant or descendant; person enough to be remembered if there is some reason to do so. Marriage is ". . . until death do us part." The *person* was and is; the *relationship* is no longer. Hence the half-status which is implied by the question, "Do you want the dead ones too?" An anthropologist asking politely, "Well, what do you think? Do you count them as relatives?" would be answered variously, "Oh, yes, of course," or "Well, yes, I guess so. But it's been so long now . . . ," or "No, not really."

The lady who said that her sister was not a relative because she had not seen her for so long was making the same point. She no longer had a relationship with her sister, and in this sense the sister failed to meet one of the defining criteria of a relative. For this woman the most important criterion was exactly the same as in the case of the other young lady, who valued a relationship above all things and so bestowed a kinsman's status on her roommate, even though the roommate lacked any other qualifications.

The Famous Relative is important because he stands out clearly against a fading groundwork of disappearing kinsmen. The blood connection can be traced to him, or is presumed to obtain. But no relationship can be maintained. Since no relationship is maintained with relatives of even closer genealogical distance, they are largely or wholly forgotten. Their names are forgotten, the names of their spouses, where they may be living, what their occupations are. They are, simply, not remembered because there is no good reason to remember them. But the Famous Relative is remembered—not because he is a relative, but because his fame makes his being a relative of some small value.

Shirt-tail relations, wakes-and-weddings relatives, and kissin' kin are so far out that they are neither here nor there. If one says that anyone related by blood or marriage is a relative, then they are relatives. But if one says that a relative is someone with whom a relationship obtains, then it is hard to count them, since they are seen so rarely, and then mainly on formal, ceremonial, or special occasions, and since the next occasion may or may not ever arrive.

There is, in sum, a tendency to forget distant collaterals and distant ascendants, but the boundary in either the past or the present is fuzzy and there are interstitial areas which are so faded at any given moment as to be barely visible. The distant ascendants are dead and no relationship obtains with them. Without a relationship, there can be no reason to retain them . . . unless, of course, they are famous, in which case they may be remembered though their descendants along collateral lines, lacking fame, will not be known. The distant collaterals "are too far away." They become shirt-tail relations, wakes-and-weddings relatives, and kissin' kin if they are known at all, or they may be one of the chief constituents of the large summer family picnic or reunion.

Americans say explicitly that relatives are persons related by blood or marriage. Yet when it comes to naming and describing concrete persons, the crucial question is whether or not a relationship obtains.

What, then, determines whether a relationship will exist or not? Why is there a relationship with one person but not with another on a given genealogy?

The reason Americans give is that one is "close" and the other is "too far away."

Distance, then, is said to be the deciding factor, given that a relationship of blood or marriage can be traced between Ego and some other person.

But what is distance?

Distance means three things in American kinship. One meaning is simple physical distance; that is, it means living in the same house, or the number of miles between houses, or the hours it takes to travel from one place to another. So one hears it said: "We never see them. They're too far away." "Too far away?" "Yes, it takes almost an hour to get there."

A second meaning of distance is a complex composite of what might be called socio-emotional distance. This in turn can mean anything from a mystical feeling of identity or difference, a feeling of emotional warmth and understanding—or the lack of it—to the fact that certain important prestige symbols are either similar (hence close) or different (hence distant). Thus it may be said, "We never see them. They're pretty far off. That part of town has gone way downhill in the last few years and we don't have much in common with them any more." Another informant put it this way: ". . . no one has had much to do with them either. It's a matter of the kind of life and education—hardly any of the people in her or Harry's family have been to college and that sort of thing."

The third meaning of distance can be called genealogical distance. This may be roughly measured by how many intervening categories of relatives there are, or how many generations back one must go before a common ancestor is found. It may be said, for instance, "They're pretty distant relatives. My great-grandfather's brother had a son, and he had a son—that's a pretty distant relationship, isn't it?"

These three different meanings of distance need not all apply in the same way or at the same time. A person who is genealogically close may be physically distant and neutral on the socio-emotional dimension. Or a person may be close socioemotionally and physically but distant genealogically.

If Ego is the point of reference, and we pose the direct question of whether, in real life, this person or that one is or is not a relative, then mother, father, brother, sister, son, and daughter, along with husband and wife, are all genealogically close relatives and are socio-emotionally close even when they may be physically distant. Uncle, aunt, nephew, niece, grandfather, grandmother, grandson, granddaughter, and cousin are also genealogically close relatives and are counted as relatives if they are alive, even if the relationship is so thin as to be barely perceptible.

But if we go out from Ego to his second or third cousins, many possibilities present themselves. Ego may say that he counts these persons as relatives simply because they are related by blood. Or he may say with equal propriety that they are too distant, so distant in fact that he does not even know how to count them. He may then ask, "What is a second cousin, anyway? And what does 'removed' mean?" Or he may affirm that anyone past first cousin is no relative of his since he does not count past first cousins.[4] Even if he claims them as relatives on the score of being related by blood, he still may not maintain interpersonal ties with them and therefore he may say that he does not "really count them as relatives." Or, unwilling to go so far as *not* to count them as relatives, and so perhaps hurt people's feelings, he may assign them to that limbo called wakes-and-weddings relatives, shirt-tail relations, or kissin' kin.

By one definition there is no option: those related by blood or marriage are relatives. But in fact, the decision as to who is a relative is made on grounds that are by no means purely matters of kinship. The number of miles between houses or the number of hours it takes to go from one place to another are not in themselves matters of kinship. Neither do they stand for kinship in the sense that physical distance might be used to express genealogical distance. Physical distance *could* stand for genealogical distance, but it does not in American culture. It stands for socioemotional distance. It is not polite for people to say that others are beneath them socially, so they say that they live far away, or they are stamped with the rank of the neighborhood they live in. By the same token, it is not always easy to explain that one's relatives are socially superior and so one may tactfully say that it's a terrible trip across town, all that distance, just to see them. But this is not genealogical distance.

One of our informants explained that she knew that her grandfather's brother had three sons. Two of them were farmers in Nebraska and she did not know their names, if they were married or not, or if they had any children. But the third son, she said, became a lawyer and went to Washington, D.C., where he married and had two boys and a girl. The girl, she said, was about her own age. The two boys were named Robert and John, the girl named Mary. Yes, she does consider them her relatives. They are related by blood, aren't they? she asked. Why, then, did she know all about one brother but not about the other two? She was unable to answer that question.

Another informant put it even more simply, saying:

> I frankly prefer not to be related to them. He is a river rat and she is a hillbilly, and they have five kids to prove it. Not that I'm saying one has to be successful and well off to be considered a relative, but goodness. . . .

In sum, the fuzzy boundary, the Famous Relative, the ambiguous notion of distance, and so on are all phenomena of American kinship which derive in part from the fact that at one level the relative is a person and the person of the relative is compounded of elements from a variety of different domains, only one of which is kinship. Hence whether a particular person is counted as a relative or not depends on how the general rule—a person is a relative if he is related by blood or by marriage—is applied. Because the decision as to who is and who is not a relative is made by and about a person, and because the rule governing who is and who is not a relative is so precisely ambiguous, the application of the rule leads to just such empirical regularities as I have here reviewed—a very fuzzy boundary to genealogies; what seem to be logical inconsistencies, such as the marvelous manipulation of the different meanings of words like "relationship" and distance"; and that peculiar ambiguity which marks the dead—those relatives without relationships.

NOTES

[1] Compare M. Young and H. Geertz, "Old Age in London and San Francisco: Some Families Compared," *British Journal of Sociology*, XII (1961), 124–41.

[2] W. E. Mitchell, "Descent Groups Among the New York City Jews," *Jewish Journal of Sociology*, 3 (1961), 121–28.

[3] Some informants say that the term is also used in another, and obviously closely related sense. If a person is seen with a stranger in a compromising position—perhaps they are seen kissing—one may offer the explanation that the other is a kissin' cousin. That is, though he is not recognized as being a relative by the observer, the kiss is explained as being one of kinship and not to be otherwise interpreted.

[4] There are three ways of counting cousins. The first is not to count them. The second combines degrees of collateral distance with generation removal, so that my father's father's brother's son is my first cousin once removed. The third adds degrees of collateral distance and generational removal together, so that my father's father's brother's son is my second cousin and the word "removed" is not used. I did not find any ways of counting cousins other than these three.

Interaction Theory and the Social Network[*]

BERT N. ADAMS

In urban, industrial society who interacts with whom and why? This twofold question has in the past decades been productive of two strands of sociological thinking and work. The question "why" has been couched in several theoretical postulates which have at times been subjected to empirical testing. Answers to the question "who" ordinarily appear categorically, friendship milieus and various degrees of kinship being distinguished, with frequency of interaction as the primary indicator of involvement. We shall begin the present paper by reviewing the social psychological and categorical aspects of social network investigation in order to explicate some of the problems inherent in each approach in isolation from the other. Subsequently, a componential theory will be proposed to interpret the social categories, and to empirically define the primary relationship.

SOCIAL INTERACTION THEORY

The individual's social network consists of those persons with whom he maintains contact and has some form of social bonds. Theories of interaction-involvement usually begin with a posited relation between affection and interaction. Synonyms for affection found in the literature include liking, positive sentiment, and attraction.[1] Much discussion has revolved about the temporal priority of liking or interaction. Their relation is probably symmetrical, or mutually reinforcing, and regardless of causation there is little doubt that liking or affectional closeness and interaction are closely related in the social network.[2]

A second social psychological attribute of social relations which has received considerable research attention is consensus, or the sharing of common values, interests, and attitudes. Several researchers have noted the influence of consensus upon liking, or interaction, or both.[3] These relationships also appear to be symmetrical. Fritz Heider affirms this in noting both attraction between those with similar attitudes and the attempt to persuade those to whom one is attracted but whose attitudes

Reprinted from *Sociometry*, Vol 30, No. 1 (March 1967).

are divergent from one's own.[4] In various social and experimental settings, Secord and Backman, Precker, and Byrne and Blaylock have reported tendencies to be attracted to those with attitudes similar to one's own, or to distort modest similarity in the direction of greater congruence when there is a strong affectional bond.[5] In summary, then, there appears to be a significant linkage between consensus, affection, and interaction in social relations.

The relations between consensus, liking, and interaction, while authentic and important, do not fully explain the social relationships found in the real world. Homans recognizes that there may be frequent interaction without liking. "What makes the difference is whether or not a man is free to break off interaction with another whose behavior he finds punishing" or unrewarding.[6] An important interpersonal attachment which the individual is likely to perceive as involuntary, but which nevertheless is an aspect of his social network, is the obligatory relationship. Alvin Gouldner has specified the manner in which social stability is furthered by the norm of reciprocity, by what he calls the continuation of the social debt.[7] There is, Berkowitz and Daniels comment, a "social responsibility norm" which becomes salient when specific help has been received in the past.[8] Obligation, or the reciprocity-responsibility norm, is thus an additional factor which is of value in understanding the social network.

Another approach to the concepts of consensus and reciprocity or obligation is found in the distinctions between *Gemeinschaft* and *Gesellschaft,* or between mechanical and organic solidarity as bases for societal integration.[9] Edward Gross, following Durkheim, labels these two types of interpersonal integration principles "symbiosis" and "consensus." Symbiosis, Gross asserts, is a relation of interdependence, a relation based upon common need. As long as need persists, the symbiotic tie remains.[10] A consensual tie is based upon agreement, upon common values, upon Durkheim's norms and bonds. A disharmony will break up a consensual group, and Gross might have added that a change in attitude, so that consensus is lessened, likewise weakens such relationships.

Thus far we have delineated what appear to be two distinct constellations accounting for much interaction in the social network. Affection and consensus in values and interests comprise one set of factors, while the other involves social necessity, based upon need or symbiosis and obligation. The general impression in the literature is that these two clusters operate in relative independence, and that the latter is in fact a constraining or alienating force.

The major contention of this paper is that consensus does not account for all positive or attractional social relations, with obligation-symbiosis as an additional, but constraining, factor. Rather, we would affirm that obligation and need, when coupled with long-term involvement and continuing interest, evolves into a positive or affectional force, which we shall label "positive concern." This positive concern, or interest-need-obligation with affection, may work in conjunction with or independently of consensus in the social network. To this thesis we shall return following a brief review of the dimensions of the social network.

SOCIAL NETWORK CATEGORIES

The two basic structural divisions of the social network are, very simply, kin and non-kin. The importance of the two axes of this kin-friend network in urban life has been the topic of much recent research. Greer and Kube report the frequency with which relatives and friends are visited by a Los Angeles sample, while Bell and Boat, and Axelrod, find that relatives are the most frequent informal social contacts in the urban United States populations which they studied.[11]

These and other students of the social network have further subdivided kin according to degree of relationship and friends according to the milieus in which they are located. Thus, parents, children, and siblings, are distinguished from other relatives, such as aunts, cousins, and grandparents.[12] Frequency of interaction and sometimes mutual aid are investigated with respect to these kin categories, the general conclusion being that the closer the kin relationship, the more likely is substantial interactional and mutual aid involvement.[13]

Greer and Kube, in their Los Angeles study, distinguish between friendship and neighboring, Bell and Boat between co-workers and neighbors, and Axelrod between friends, co-workers, and neighbors.[14] While there are definitional difficulties inherent in the attempt to differentiate among these categories, it is apparent that these authors are seeking to understand the complexities of urban milieus, and to locate friends within them.

Besides the structural categories of kin and friends, intensity categories are described by Raymond Firth and William Goode which cut across the above structural divisions. Firth speaks of intimate, effective, and nominal kin as the basic intensity distinctions. The intimate are precisely that; they include only those kin with whom contact is frequent, attachment is strong, and communication is open. Contact is maintained with the effective kin, but attachment and communication are relatively shallow. The nominal kin are other relatives who are known to exist but with whom contact and involvement are minimal or non-existent.[15] In his article on norm commitment in social relations, Goode speaks of close and mild friendships, the distinction being, as in the case of kin, in intimacy and emotional intensity.[16]

It is not the purpose of the present paper to review the numerous findings of previous studies regarding frequency of interaction with the various kin-friend categories. Suffice it to say that both kin and friends ordinarily form significant portions of the social network, and we are therefore confronted with the task of advancing a theory of social interaction which will deal with these two social categories, their similarities and differences.

KINSHIP, FRIENDSHIP, AND INTERACTION THEORY

Two dominant constellations of social psychological factors and two basic categories of social relations have thus far been distinguished. In relating the concepts or factors to the empirical network a first step might be to associate each of the theoretical constellations with one of the basic categories. Consensus and affection might tentatively be considered the essence of close friendship, with affectional or positive concern the dominant characteristic of intimate kinship. There are social relations which are apparently constrained or weakened by feelings of obligation, but we suggest that such feelings frequently combine with a basic desire to maintain contact and mutual aid potential (willingness to help when needed) to comprise an affectional factor. In order to account for kin bonds we therefore postulate a form of interpersonal attraction based upon positive concern, or the interest of one individual in the well-being and activities of another. This attractional factor, we repeat, explains much affection and contact in the social network, particularly with kin, apart from either consensus or sheer necessity.

Both concern and consensus are apt to be found in the empirical social world in the form of continua. Concern ranges from a vague sentiment that a modicum of contact ought to be maintained with an individual, in which case attraction is relatively mild, to a combination of mutual aid potential and desire for frequent contact, which indicates intense emotional involvement and affectional closeness. Consensus, on the other hand, ranges from one or a few shared activities, in which case involvement is once again mild, to a basic similarity of values or attitudes and interests, which would seem to provide for considerable interpersonal attraction. Furthermore, consensus and positive concern are not empirically mutually exclusive, but are found in differing degrees in the same social relationship. The closest social relations would therefore likely be those in which both consensus and concern are strong, as, for example, relations between children and parents.

The two attractional variables are more than analytic conceptualizations, but are identifiable components of social relations, identifiable in terms of their attitudinal and interactional indicators and effects. Some of the interrelations between consensus and positive concern, and the friendship and kinship relations which embody them, go considerably beyond the facile linkage of consensus with friendship and concern with kinship, and are made explicit in the following series of propositions. These propositions, which are more suggestive than exhaustive, form the bases for much of the ensuing discussion.

PROPOSITIONS

While varying proportions of consensus and positive concern characterize different social relations, (1) *consensus is likely to be modal in friendship and positive concern in kinship relations.* The consensus-affection-interaction pattern of involvement, drawn from hypotheses of Homans, Newcomb, and others, is more typical of friendship than it is of kinship in our society. The additional factor in kinship must be pieced together from several sources. Paul Reiss reports an expressed obligation to keep in touch with kin.[17] Muir and Weinstein note that all of their 120 housewife respondents understand and consider social debts, particularly to relatives, important.[18] Moreover, studies by Sussman and White, Bell and Boat, and others indicate that kin are more likely to be appealed to than friends in time of need.[19] The friend, then, might be epitomized as the social companion, the kinsman as the object of continuing interest.

In one chapter of his book *Political Power and Social Theory*, Barrington Moore discusses the future of the family. He contends that "one of the most obviously obsolete features of the family is the obligation to give affection (or attention) as a duty to a particular set of persons on account of an accident of birth. This is a true relic of barbarism."[20] Popular consciousness, Moore asserts, is at least dimly aware of the barbarism in this. In a society which focuses upon achievement rather than ascription, when obligation is central to a particular social relationship, that relationship tends to be less than satisfactory.[21] We have proposed that consensus is modal in friendship and positive concern in kinship, and have noted that concern and consensus are in reality continua, with less attraction as a relationship is characterized by simple obligation and/or simple activity. Our second proposition, based upon these two observations is that (2) *in general, interaction is likely to be desired with friends in preference to kin, due to the consensual component of friendship and the absence of strong obligatory feelings toward friends.* In actuality, this proposition compares the extremities of the kin and friend networks, indicating that mild friendships are preferable to mild kin relations.

According to Gross the symbiotic tie is more powerful than the consensual tie. Subsuming symbiosis under the conception of positive concern, and rephrasing in terms of our theory of attraction in the social network, the third proposition is that (3) *positive concern is more likely to lend to relationship persistence than is consensus.* Persistence may be defined as the continuation of some form of involvement despite the passage of time, or spatial separation, or occupational mobility. It is well to remind ourselves at this juncture that the social network includes all those with whom one maintains contact and emotional attachment. This may involve communication as well as interaction. In urban, industrial society the social network is simply not a regionally limited phenomenon. The least persistent relationship is apt to be the one in which concern is minimal and in which the primary activity occurs without a basic value consensus. The most persistent relation is the one characterized by strong feelings of positive concern.

The concomitants of positive concern may include greater intimacy as well as persistence. The relationship based upon moderate consensus may not extend below those surface characteristics which the two parties hold in common. Thus, Goode speaks of the type of mild friendship which certain elements of the population consider to be the ideal working relationship: "friendliness permits enough close observation of others to check on their behavior, but its shallowness prevents any real probe into the intensity of emotions felt by others."[22] Such a relationship may actually provide insulation against more intense interpersonal involvement. Our fourth proposition is that (4) *the relationship based upon positive concern is more likely than the consensual relationship to have as an element intimate communication.*

A fifth and final proposition concerns the componential and cross-categorical range of social relations. Briefly stated, it is that (5) *the consensual and concern components of social relations demonstrate a substantial overlap between the various structural categories of individuals frequently considered as "givens" in descriptive interactional studies.* This proposition is a necessary complement to the modal characterization by categories presented in proposition (1). There are empirical friendship relations in which positive concern is the prime component, and kin relations in which the primary characteristic is consensus. It is important to be aware of possible social psychological and interactional similarities if we are to understand the significance of specific social relationships. Some of the conditions for such cross-categorical overlap will be explicated in the discussion which follows.

The foregoing propositions are a means for inaugurating discussion of the social network in terms of the two major components of attraction. Though we shall not pretend to test them directly, one source for our observations is a series of interviews completed in Greensboro, North Carolina, a city of 150,000 population, during 1963–64. A random block procedure was used to sample households, with the following restrictions upon inclusion in the sample: all respondents are white, are married, have been married only once, and for twenty years or less. Included are 467 females and 332 males, with a median length of marriage of 10.4 years, and a median age of 34.8 years. More than eighty per cent of the sample are between 25 and 45 years of age. Of the 799 respondents, 737 identify some person as their best friend, 724 have at least one parent living, and 697 have one or more siblings. These latter respondents were requested to describe their relationship with the sibling closest to them in age. Interaction and attitude data regarding best friend, parents, and sibling may help us to illustrate the social psychological propositions drawn from our theory of attraction in the social network.

DISCUSSION

The first proposition is that consensus is modal in friendship and positive concern in kinship. While this cannot be measured directly with the Greensboro data, expressions of affectional closeness, general value consensus, and feelings of obligation may offer an indirect indication of the propositional distinction. In Table 1 may be observed several suggestive differences in relations with best friend, parents or living parent, and the age-near sibling. A greater proportion of the young adults express affectional closeness than express value consensus with parents and the sibling, while in the case of the best friend consensus is more prevalent than affectional closeness.[23] This would appear to signify the presence of some other variable besides consensus which increases affectional closeness to those kin. In best friend relations, on the other hand, there is evidence that perceived consensus is not necessarily a sufficient condition for affectional closeness. Consensus may, of course, be perceived in relationships which are relatively uninvolved or non-salient to the individual.

Obligation is clearly an additional factor which is more characteristic of the two kinship relations. However, our definition of positive concern includes mutual aid potential and contact desire as well as overt obligatory feelings, and consensus includes common interests or activities as well as values. Therefore it is important to note interactional manifestations of the distinction between concern and consensus in the kin-friend network. In Table 2 special occasions and social activities are consistent with the postulated modal distinction between kinship and friendship, while mutual aid is a bit misleading in that it is based upon actual occurrence rather than potential. Thus, mutual aid between best friends is primarily an exchange of baby-sitting by young adult females, while the majority express a willingness to help their sibling if the need should arise.

Combining the results of Tables 1 and 2, obligation, special occasions, and social activities lend support to proposition (1), and mutual

TABLE 1

Expression of Affectional Closeness, Value Consensus, and Feelings of Obligation Toward Best Friend, Parent(s), and Sibling, Among Young Married Adults

Social Category	Number Respondents	Pct. Quite or Extremely Close Affectionately	Pct. High in Value Consensus	Pct. Seeing Obligation as a Contact Motive
Best Friend	(737)	61	75	28
Parent(s)	(724)	75	65	73
Age-Near Sibling	(697)	48	45	59

TABLE 2

Any Special Occasions, Social Activities, or Mutual Aid Shared With Best Friend, Parent(s), and Sibling in the Past Two Years*

Social Category	Number of Respondents	Pct. Any Interaction on Special Occasions	Pct. Any Mutual Aid	Pct. Any Social Activities
Best Friend	(737)	20	43	74
Parent(s)	(724)	88	88	43
Age-Near Sibling	(697)	73	18	48

* Special occasions include birthdays, Christmas, holidays, and vacations; mutual aid includes tangible aid and services; social activities include commercial and outdoor recreation, shopping, and miscellaneous activities.

aid and value consensus demonstrate that positive concern and consensus are not mutually exclusive alternatives in empirical social relations. Such evidence is basically consistent with proposition (1), i.e., there are differing attractional variables dominant in kinship and friendship, but the componential overlap which is the subject of proposition (5) has also become perceptible.

It will be noted that sex, occupational stratum, and other possible sample divisions are not presented in Tables 1 and 2. This is not because there are no differences according to these variables, for females do manifest higher percentages on consensus and affection in parental and sibling relations than do males. However, the argument for not differentiating in the present paper is strengthened by the fact that when the sample is divided into white- and blue-collar males and females the percentage *patterns* or comparisons within each of these four categories are quite similar. Thus, for example, within each category obligation is a dominant factor in parental relations and a negligible factor in friendship, affectional closeness is more likely than is value consensus to be expressed in parental relations, while the inverse is true between best friends, and mutual aid and special occasions dominate parental interaction, while social activities dominate friendship. Further categorical comparisons will be reserved for a more direct test of the propositions and theory than is possible with the Greensboro data.

Proposition (2) requires only brief comment. When the question of preference for kin or friends is asked in general terms, 43 per cent of the 799 young Greensboro adults assert that they favor contact with friends, 27 per cent favor kin, and 30 per cent would like to equalize time spent with the two categories. The categorical proposition is therefore supported, though hardly overwhelmingly. It is intriguing to hypothesize that had we asked whether they would prefer to interact with secondary kin (aunts, cousins, etc.) or friendly acquaintances the response in favor of friends might have been more clear-cut than when the more salient kin and friends were included in their thinking and responses.

General inferences may be drawn from the Greensboro data in conjunction with other sociological literature regarding relationship persistence. When friends separate residentially, primary relations may die or be suspended, assert Babchuk and Bates.[24] However, in a day of high speed transportation, postal service, and the telephone, kinship or friendship relations need not *necessarily* be interrupted by the distance factor, by residential mobility. Instead, there may simply be a change from face-to-face interaction to communication as the dominant form of contact. Taking into account the residential mobility of both respondents and friends, a considerable turnover in friendships is apparent in the Greensboro data. With parents and siblings, on the other hand, distance is mitigated by frequent communication, i.e., telephoning and letter writing, and in the case of parents even by periodic tangible aid sent through the mails.[25]

Occupational mobility has a disruptive effect upon the social relationship in which consensus is central, since mobility itself is apt to be correlated with an increasing divergence of basic values and interests. The dropping and cultivating of friendships by those moving along the occupational ladder is generally believed to be part of the mobility process. However, there has been substantial disagreement concerning the effects of occupational mobility upon kin relations in urban, industrial society. Some have felt that mobility weakens kin ties,[26] while others have reported significant kin involvement despite occupational disparity.[27] The primary difficulty and the reason for such disagreement has been the attempt to generalize about all kin. Certain researchers, observing the viability of young adult—parent relations despite mobility, assert that kin relations are not adversely affected. Other writers, noting the tendency of mobility to weaken secondary kin ties, thus reducing the number of effective kin, have generalized that it is basically detrimental to kinship. Elizabeth Bott's partial solution to the problem is simply that the more distant the relative, the more objective differences receive consideration and determine involvement.[28] In the words of our theory, the premise of this conclusion is that the weakening effect of occupational disparity upon kinship increases as the positive concern component of the relation is found to be less.

We therefore find in Greensboro and in the literature on communication and mobility some justification for claiming that those social relationships in which the positive concern component is strong are most likely to persist in spite of complications of time, space, or social position. Since this component is frequently strongest in relations with members of one's family of orientation, particularly parents, it is these social relations which manifest the greatest persistence.

In the course of the interviews a few Greensboroites commented that they and their best friend are very close and talk freely to each other about everything. As a rule, however, a clear distinction was drawn between close friends, whom they enjoy, and certain kin, whom they can "count on" and confide in. Seeking advice from and confiding in parents is an accepted practice among these young adults, but most are unwilling to include intimate communication as a feature of close friendship. Such a discussion of proposition (4) is based on an overall impression received from the interviews. Yet the impression is unmistakable: intimate kinsfolk, more than any other social category, are considered available for open communication.[29] This, we feel, is in turn an aspect of the intense mutual feelings of positive concern which characterizes these kin relations.

The final proposition is an attempt to break down componentially the various kin-friend categories which have been the primary foci of empirical studies of urban social interaction. It is not enough to speak categorically of differences between friendship milieus or degrees of kin relation, for we find not only categorical differences but frequent similarity across categories in both the social psychological and interactional characteristics of social relationships. Thus, a sibling might be described as an individual of one's own generation, with whom he has been acquainted all or most of his life, in whom he has a continuing interest, and with whom he may or may not share common values and interests. Such a description might fit as well the "old friend," or childhood companion. In either case, when adult relations persist it is likely to be due more to concern than to consensus. Therefore, intentionally and attitudinally the old friend and the sibling may bear much resemblance. The statement regarding a close friend that "he is like a brother to me" may signify more in terms of relationship components than has heretofore been recognized. The implication is very probably that this is no ordinary friendship based narrowly upon values and interests, but includes an element of concern and intimacy which is ordinarily reserved for family ties. Similarly, one's brother or cousin may develop through the years into an activity companion rather than into merely an object of continuing interest. In the course of conversation one may remark: "I don't really think of John as a cousin; he is a good friend." The interpretation is that John is not just the object of the usual weak obligation to secondary kin; he is a sharer of common activities and perhaps basic values. Awareness and utilization of cross-categorical similarities as well as differences may make possible a significant step forward in understanding the traditional kin-friend categories of the social network.

The foregoing theoretical position regarding consensus and positive concern, and the propositions drawn therefrom, is of course not a complete theory of social contact, for there are compulsory and competitive aspects of social relations, and secondary or impersonal contacts as well. This is a theory of positive social relations, of attraction in the social network, of the primary relationship. Given such a theory of primary relations, we may be in a position to resolve some of the discrepancies in recent discussions. Babchuk and Bates, in their papers on the social network, define primary relations as those sharing a wide range of activities and characterized by strong positive affect.[30] Recently, S. C. Lee has argued against such redefinition of Cooley's "primary relationship" concept to fit modern society. Instead, he says, let us hold our definition and observe, if we must, the loss of primariness in urban, industrial society.[31] The present theoretical venture, with its attention to indicators of consensus and concern, brings us to the threshhold of quantifying primary relations. Not just Babchuk and Bates' activities and affection, but some combination of consensus and/or positive concern and affectional closeness is the essence of the primary relationship. Utilizing help potential, contact obligation, and perhaps ritual interaction, as indices of concern, and value similarity, attitudes, and social activities as indices of consensus, and some measure of attraction, makes conceivable the empirical quantification of primariness.

Previous attempts to cross categorical lines in defining social relationship intensity include Goode's distinction between close and mild friendship and Firth's references to intimate, effective, and nominal kin. Presenting the elements of positive social relations as we have done results in the virtual equating of intimate kin and close friends with our primary relations, defining them interactionally and attitudinally by consensus and/or concern and attraction.

Until now we have occupied ourselves with setting forth the components of social attraction, applying them in the most general manner to kinship and friendship relations. It seems apparent, however, that the utility of a theory of social network attraction or primary relationships may be extended in several directions. First, *conditions and indicators* merit further examination. There is need to specify the conditions for the growth of positive concern beyond Berkowitz and Daniels' notion of "past help." Childhood companionship, gratitude for help, sharing in the same life crises, family name and experience: these and other factors may be instrumental in developing feelings of positive concern in interpersonal relations. Such prior conditions are one internal extension which could increase our understanding of consensus and concern. Another internal extension involves the indicators. It is conceivable that a property-space model, based upon both interactional and attitudinal measures, might be devised to plot consensus and concern in social relations.[32] Ranging from mild enjoyment of a single interest and mild contact obligation to consensus on basic values and perhaps intimate communication, such a model would permit the empirical determination of primariness within "property-space."

A second extension entails the introduction of sex, social class, and *other variables* resulting in possible differences in social relationship components. Several hypotheses might include the greater likelihood of kin primariness among females than males, the likelihood of fewer primary consensual friends outside the kin network among working-class persons, and a more restricted primary network among working-class individuals generally.

A third extension of the empirical exploration of consensus, positive concern, and attraction as indices of primariness would be *cross-cultural*. It is too late to observe or test, with Lee, the loss or decline of primariness as a consequence of urbanization in our society. Yet it is not impossible to effect cross-cultural comparisons regarding the prevalence of primary relations in less industrialized, rapidly changing, and highly industrialized societies. The indicators of consensus and positive concern which we have suggested may be found to be cross-culturally applicable without substantial alteration.

A fourth extension of the theory of attraction in the social network would be into *other substantive areas* where it could increase understanding of phenomena. One example is the study of the family in America. Changes in the American family since Colonial days include the loss of family functions to other societal institutions and the greater likelihood of the dissolution of any given family today than formerly. Viewed in the light of the greater persistence of the concern relation, as a basis for interpersonal attraction, we would affirm the consistency of decreasing family stability with decreasing symbiotic bonds between husbands and wives. Another example would be the study of immigrant assimilation into the dominant society. The first stage is the extension and intensification of positive concern in the minority group kin networks in the face of major discrimination. However, a second generation is likely to experience both a weakening consensus, as the dominant culture impinges upon them, and a transformation of positive concern into a basic obligation. The result is, of course, ambivalence on the part of the offspring. These are but two possible adaptations of our componential theory to diverse sociological issues.

We have attempted to synthesize the questions "who" and "why" in social network analysis. Categories and components of social relations must be brought together, and the concern component—as a positive attribute—be incorporated into interaction theory along with consensus and liking, if such theory is to comprehend social network involvement. It is hoped that this theoretical position will be put to the empirical test in a variety of situations, and that its indicators and preconditions will be refined in subsequent research. If this occurs, its purpose will have been achieved.

NOTES

* The data utilized in this paper were collected with the support of Public Health Service fellowship (MH-15,571) from the National Institute of Mental Health.

[1] George C. Homans, *The Human Group,* New York: Harcourt, Brace, and World, Inc., 1950, uses the term "liking," primarily; Alan P. Bates and Nicholas Babchuk, "The Primary Group: A Reappraisal," *Sociological Quarterly,* 2 (July, 1961), pp. 181–191, speaks of "positive affect or sentiment"; Theodore Newcomb, *The Acquaintanceship Process,* New York: Holt, Rinehart, and Winston, 1961, refers to "attraction."

[2] On this, see especially Homans, *The Human Group,* p. 111; Maria Rogers, "The Human Group: a Critical Review with Suggestions for Some Alternative Hypotheses," *Sociometry,* 14 (February, 1951), p. 24; Muzafer and Carolyn W. Sherif, *Groups in Harmony and Tension,* New York: Harper and Brothers, 1953.

[3] Newcomb, "The Prediction of Interpersonal Attraction," *The American Psychologist,* 11 (November, 1956), p. 579; Homans, *Social Behavior: Its Elementary Forms,* New York: Harcourt, Brace, and World, Inc., 1961, p. 215.

[4] Fritz Heider, *The Psychology of Interpersonal Relations,* New York: John Wiley and Sons, Inc., 1958.

[5] Paul F. Secord and Carl W. Backman, "Interpersonal Congruency, Perceived Similarity, and Friendship," *Sociometry,* 27 (June, 1964), pp. 115–127; Joseph A. Precker, "Similarity of Valuings as a Factor in Selection of Peers and Near-Authority Figures," *Journal of Abnormal and Social Psychology,* 47 (April, 1952), pp. 406–414; Donn Byrne and Barbara Blaylock, "Similarity and Assumed Similarity of Attitudes Between Husbands and Wives," *Journal of Abnormal and Social Psychology,* 67 (June, 1963), pp. 636–640.

[6] Homans, *Social Behavior: Its Elementary Forms,* p. 187.

[7] Alvin Gouldner, "The Norm of Reciprocity: a Preliminary Statement," *American Sociological Review,* 25 (April, 1960), p. 175.

[8] Leonard Berkowitz and Louise R. Daniels, "Affecting the Salience of the Social Responsibility Norm: Effects of Past Help on the Response to Dependency Relationships," *Journal of Abnormal and Social Psychology,* 68 (March, 1964), pp. 275–281.

[9] Emile Durkheim, *The Division of Labor in Society,* Glencoe: The Free Press, 1933.

[10] Edward Gross, "Symbiosis and Consensus as Integrative Factors in Small Groups," *American Sociological Review,* 21 (April, 1956), p. 179.

[11] Scott Greer and Ella Kube, "Urbanism and Social Structure: A Los Angeles Study," in M. Sussman (Ed.), *Community Structure and Analysis,* New York: Thomas Y. Crowell Co., 1959, pp. 93–112; Wendell Bell and Marion D. Boat, "Urban Neighborhoods and Informal Social Relations," *American Journal of Sociology,* 62 (January, 1957), p. 395; Morris Axelrod, "Urban Structure and Social Participation," *American Sociological Review,* 21 (February, 1956), p. 17.

[12] Talcott Parsons, "The Kinship System of the Contemporary United States," *American Anthropologist,* 45 (January-March, 1943), p. 25; Bert N. Adams, *Urban Kin Relations,* unpublished monograph.

[13] Paul J. Reiss, "The Extended Kinship System: Correlates of and Attitudes on Frequency of Interaction," *Marriage and Family Living,* 24 (November, 1962), p. 334; Marvin Sussman, "The Isolated Nuclear Family: Fact or Fiction?," *Social Problems,* 6 (Spring, 1959), pp. 333–340.

[14] Greer and Kube, *op. cit.,* pp. 109–110; Bell and Boat, *loc. cit.;* Axelrod, *loc. cit.*

[15] Raymond Firth and J. Djamour, "Kinship in South Borough," in R. Firth (Ed.), *Two Studies of Kinship in London,* London: London School of Economics Monographs on Social Anthropology, No. 15, 1956, p. 45.

[16] William J. Goode, "Norm Commitment and Conformity to Role-Status Obligations," *American Journal of Sociology,* 66 (November, 1960), p. 258.

[17] Reiss, *op. cit.*, p. 336.

[18] Donald E. Muir and Eugene A. Weinstein, "The Social Debt: an Investigation of Lower-Class and Middle-Class Norms of Social Obligation," *American Sociological Review*, 27 (August, 1962), p. 537.

[19] Sussman and R. Clyde White, *Hough, Cleveland, Ohio: a Study of Social Life and Change*, Cleveland: Western Reserve University Press, 1959, pp. 76–77; Bell and Boat, *op. cit.*, p. 396.

[20] Barrington Moore, Jr., *Political Power and Social Theory*, Cambridge: Harvard University Press, 1958, p. 163.

[21] In this regard, see Peter Marris, *Widows and Their Families*, London: Routledge and Kegan Paul, 1958, p. 49; Bert N. Adams, "The Young Married Adult and the Widowed Mother," unpublished paper.

[22] Goode, *loc. cit.*

[23] The question regarding closeness reads as follows: "How close would you say you feel to your . . . ?" Answers of "quite close" or "extremely close" are combined, as are answers of "fairly close," "somewhat close," and "not too close." Value consensus is ascertained in response to the question: "Do you and your . . . agree in your ideas and opinions about the things *you* consider really important in life?" Responses of "completely" or "to a great extent" demonstrate high consensus, while "to some extent" and "very little" indicate considerable dissensus. Obligation is determined by answers to the question: "How important a reason for keeping in touch with . . . is the feeling that you ought to, or have an obligation to, keep in touch?" Answers of "somewhat important" or "very important" are combined as indicating at least some overt feeling of contact obligation.

[24] Babchuk and Bates, "The Primary Relations of Middle-Class Couples: a Study in Male Dominance," *American Sociological Review*, 28 (June, 1963), p. 384.

[25] Adams, *Urban Kin Relations*.

[26] David M. Schneider and George C. Homans, "Kinship Terminology and the American Kinship System," *American Anthropologist*, 57 (December, 1955), p. 1207; Robert P. Stuckert, "Occupational Mobility and Family Relationships," *Social Forces*, 41 (March, 1963), pp. 301–307.

[27] Michael Young and Peter Willmott, *Family and Kinship in East London*, Baltimore: Penguin Books, 1964, pp. 78–84; Eugene Litwak, "Occupational Mobility and Extended Family Cohesion," *American Sociological Review*, 25 (February, 1960), pp. 9–21.

[28] Elizabeth Bott, *Family and Social Network*, London: Tavistock Publications, Ltd., 1957, p. 147.

[29] See Bernard Farber, *Family: Organization and Interaction*, San Francisco: Chandler Publishing Co., 1964, pp. 196f.

[30] Babchuk and Bates, "The Primary Group . . . ," *op. cit.*, p. 185.

[31] S. C. Lee, "The Primary Group as Cooley Defines It," *Sociological Quarterly*, 5 (Winter, 1964), p. 34.

[32] For the application of this methodology, see Allen H. Barton, "The Concept of Property-Space in Social Research," in P. F. Lazarsfeld and M. Rosenberg (Eds.), *The Language of Social Research*, New York: The Free Press of Glencoe, 1955, pp. 40–62.

Family–Kin Businesses

HOPE JENSEN LEICHTER and WILLIAM E. MITCHELL

Like ad hoc kin assemblages, family-kin businesses can be examined from the point of view of their organization as a social system, as well as from the perspective of the client family. Family-kin businesses are significant because in them, occupational and kinship roles overlap. Many theorists consider the economy one of the major factors affecting family organization. If one wishes, for example, to understand the effect that participation in a family-kin business will have on a family, it is necessary to understand how the business itself functions. The functioning of a business is, in turn, affected by relationships among kin and may affect kin relationships as well. Both the functioning of the business and the relationships with kin that it supports will, in turn, have consequences for the family. Thus one is inevitably drawn outside the family to an examination of the social units that impinge upon it.

Family-kin businesses were found to exist at present, or to have existed in the past, in a relatively large proportion of client families. Of the husbands who responded to this item in the questionnaire, 30 per cent indicated that they were presently or had at some time been involved in a business with kin outside their present nuclear family. In most of these cases the husbands were no longer associated with the business. Here, as with other areas of kin activity, the importance of systematic examination of stages of the family life cycle is evident. Business involvement with kin is less frequent in the client group than other kinds of kin relationships. However, since these business activities constitute an overlap of kinship and occupational roles in an urban industrial economy, they would be theoretically crucial for an understanding of family and kinship, even if they occurred less frequently than they actually do.

A series of interviews examined the types of relationships with kin that are fostered in family-kin businesses, the ways in which joint business activity influences kin ties, and the influences of family-kin businesses upon the client family. Data were obtained in these interviews on the organization and operation of the business, on relationships with kin, and on roles and functions within the client family.

Reprinted from pp. 135–45 of Chapter 5, "Kin Groups and Assemblages" in *Kinship and Casework* by Hope Jensen Leichter and William E. Mitchell, with the collaboration of Candace Rogers and Judith Lieb, © 1967 by Russell Sage Foundation, Publishers, New York.

Interviews covered a variety of types of family-kin business: optical, diamond, drygoods, picture-framing, manufacturing elastic braid, fur trade, retail bathroom utilities, butchering, luggage manufacture, textiles, luggage-cover manufacture, poultry sale, garage, bowling alley, luncheonette, juke box distribution, grocery store, dry cleaning, burglar alarm, candy store, contracting, and air freight. In the 63 cases on which questionnaire data were obtained, roughly a third were in retail business, nearly as many were in manufacturing and service occupations. A smaller proportion were in wholesale businesses. Most of these businesses were small regardless of the type of activity. Twenty-seven per cent employed only one or two persons; 58 per cent, fewer than five; 76 per cent, ten or fewer. Someone other than the client husband was the head of the business more often than the client was, but in roughly a third of the businesses the client husband was head or joint head. Most often these were single-generation businesses headed by a member of the husband's own generation. Where they were cross-generational, they almost always included the generation above that of the husband; descendants were almost never involved.

BUSINESS FUNCTIONING AND KINSHIP STRUCTURE

It is difficult to evaluate the influences of kinship on a business, in part because there are no satisfactory criteria for the successful functioning of the business. Moreover, even where the business was clearly seen as unsatisfactory by its members; for example, where it was dissolved, a variety of factors other than kinship may have affected its failure. Small businesses, in general, are often precarious. In addition, these data are seen from the perspective of one or two participants, and their views may not correspond with those of other members of the business. Nevertheless, from interview data it is possible to obtain insights into the effects of kinship on business functioning.

As perceived by participants, family businesses are often fraught with problems and are usually not outstanding successes. The frequent change from one business to another reported in interviews is one indication of the difficulties that arise in some family-kin businesses. The essential problem in some businesses seems to have been the inability to go out of business when circumstances required, but frequently there were reports of a series of shifts of business ventures with various kin, and frequent shifts from one business to another.

The great majority of husbands indicated in answers to questions in the questionnaire that the business was not going well financially; only a few felt that it was doing all right financially. Most felt that there was a lot of tension and conflict. Conflicts among kin were frequent in businesses that were not doing well financially, but were reported in a few cases even in those that were successful. In any case, a conjunction of financial problems with tension and conflict among kin is frequent.

Most husbands reported negative feelings about the experience of working with kin. From write-in answers to the question, "From your experience, what are your feelings about working with relatives?" a preponderance of negative feelings was evident. The material was coded in terms of whether the response was generally "negative," "positive," "mixed," "neutral," or "contingent." In the majority of cases, 33 out of 56 comments were definitely negative with no positive statements at all. In only 11 cases were the comments entirely positive. Cases that were categorized either as mixed or contingent involved some negative statement either direct or implied, and thus in 42 out of 56 cases, or 75 per cent, there was some indication of negative feelings about working in business with kin.

Many vivid descriptions were given of the problems of these businesses. The following is a not uncommon statement of feelings about business problems:

> My business is atrocious. Sometimes I can't convey how bad it is. It's deteriorating like wagon wheels, like horses and buggies. It's a dying industry . . . dying. See, you got yourself an old Persian coat and made a lining out of it . . . but you're not going to buy again. It's the style and mode of fashion . . . it was time to throw it out twenty years ago. It's like if I were to keep a car for 400 years. It's a dying industry, and I bemoan, and bemoan, and bemoan.

Negative feelings of this sort do not characterize all family-kin businesses but they are typical of many. These negative feelings may be a reflection of the fact that this is a client group, many of whom have more pervasive individual and family problems. However, business problems may affect individual and family problems, as well as the reverse.

Lest the feelings of frustration and conflict that characterize many of those who have at sometime been in business with kin give an unduly pessimistic picture, it is worth noting that business families do not differ greatly from other client families in social status, as indicated by income and education. In fact, they were in somewhat better positions than most other clients.

The frustrations found in many family-kin businesses also do not appear to reflect major differences in life style between business and nonbusiness families. More husbands in business families than nonbusiness families indicated that they had moderate or few social activities. But this did not hold true for wives. Both husbands and wives in business families were somewhat less likely to list friends of the opposite sex than in nonbusiness families, but these differences were small. In all other areas of friendship, business and nonbusiness families did not differ. The parents in business families did not differ appreciably in religious orientation, as indicated by identification as Orthodox, Conservative, Reform, or "just Jewish," or as indicated by whether their present style of cooking was kosher or Jewish style, from those in non-business families.

Despite these general similarities in style of life and the indication that, if anything, business families may be slightly less disadvantaged than other clients; there may well be problems of business organization that derive specifically from its being conducted with kin.

Interviews indicated that in a variety of ways the diffuse obligations among kin and the problems of separating occupational and kinship status do affect the functioning of business, sometimes in ways that create problems for the business. Kin relationships do sometimes make it difficult to assign positions within the business on an objective basis; kinship sometimes clouds the objectivity of the hiring process and the setting up of salary and other benefit conditions; obligations of kinship sometimes limit the flexibility of the business, making it difficult to terminate employment when this is required in view of external conditions. The hierarchy of kinship positions that individuals have in relation to each other sometimes carries over into the business hierarchy, making it more difficult to maintain the business hierarchy if it does not correspond to that of kinship. In general, therefore, there are problems of segregating business from other kin relationships.

The assignment of statuses within the business is, in fact, often influenced by the kinship positions of those involved. In this respect, there is a tendency toward informality of procedures, which may typify small businesses generally, not merely those involving kin. Frequently, for example, financial records were handled informally. In 41 per cent of the businesses, records were handled by the participants themselves or did not exist at all. One woman described a situation of this sort, saying there was "nothing on paper . . . whatever was left at the end of the week they split up. It was all on a cash basis."

This lack of formal organizational procedure opens the way for the influence of kinship in filling positions originally and in assigning tasks within the business. Hiring was sometimes definitely on the basis of a kinship obligation. One man explained that his father wanted him to go into the business of his brother, but that there was no "special reason why he should want me . . . except for the fact that he is doing me a favor." Obligations among kin may also be used as pressures to recruit. For example, in one case a man was pushed to go into business with his family because of illness on the part of some of his kin. Here, his obligation to kin in time of illness was stressed in an effort to pressure him into entering the business.

The nonspecific, noncontractual character of many business relationships is clear in the descriptions given by one husband and wife of the husband's business dealings with his family:

WIFE: When we became engaged, he was earning the fabulous sum of $60 a week. . . . We felt that as the business grew, so would his salary . . . he was putting in 16 to 18 hours per day. And then the business did grow, and it did prosper . . . and his salary didn't grow. . . .

HUSBAND: Sometimes I didn't even get paid. . . .

WIFE: Before we were married, let me not neglect this, she [husband's mother] merely took $50 a week out of his $60 to buy him clothing, and this went on for months. . . . This $50 per week that she took for his clothing resulted in a half-dozen undershorts—seconds, faded—that I threw out, a magnificent bathrobe that I later discovered cost $2.00 at Klein's . . . a half-dozen shirts.

HUSBAND: They were broadcloth. . . .

WIFE: When he says broadcloth, he's being nice. This does not even lie near broadcloth. She didn't even spend $40 on all his junk.

At a later point, this noncontractual business arrangement was suggested again by the husband's family in an effort to get him to return to the business.

WIFE: And my mother-in-law came to me and said to me, "We're willing to take him into the business." . . . and I said, "What will the salary be?" And she said, "Your mother would feed you and the baby, and we would feed Abe [husband]." And with a great deal of self-control, I said, "What about rent?" And she said, "Oh, that we'll see about."

Feelings of exploitation were particularly strong in this case, but similar statements were repeated in interviews with other families. As one man wrote in his questionnaire, "A relative expects more from you than any other employer, and gives in return less."

Obligations of kinship not only affect the hiring process, they also affect termination of businesses. Size of business, competitive situation, technological changes, and many other factors were cited as problems for family-kin businesses. At best it is difficult to predict business conditions and know when to change an enterprise. When kinship obligations are involved, however, this may reduce the flexibility of the organization because it makes it more difficult to discharge employees or to leave the business. One man explained, for example, that he stayed for two and a half years in his uncle's business although he hated the job "because I didn't want to insult my uncle and disappoint my father."

Thus there is a potential merging of business and outside obligations among kin. These external obligations contribute to the difficulty of maintaining objectivity and strictly contractual relations within the business. As one man explained, when you work with kin "you are more or less obligated to defend and protect them. You overlook errors and avoid arguments."

These obligations may give an individual a certain assurance and freedom in business. Since kinship ties are conceived of as lifelong, and in many respects unbreakable, behavior may be tolerated from kin that would be intolerable from nonkin. One man explained about working with a relative that "if he were not related, I don't think he would take me." He went on to explain that he was always "complaining and bitching and crying and sobbing" and that his relative "certainly takes a lot of this nagging abuse that I give him." However, the emotional support derived from strong ties of kinship may not necessarily be beneficial for the overall operation of the business.

The hierarchy of kinship positions may also color the business hierarchy, making it more difficult to maintain the latter, particularly when the two hierarchies do not correspond. Relationships between generations, that is, father-son relationships, appear to have a particularly strong carryover into business dealings. One man described his brother's problem in standing up for his rights in business when working with his father:

> One of his troubles was that he worked under my father, because my father is an older person, and he gets quite irritable, and he does things that are wrong in business, harmful, or wasteful. . . . And my brother, well, he wouldn't talk fresh to my father, so he kept on bottling it up. . . . [With another boss] he could tell him off, or something. But you have to have respect for your father. You don't do that. So, it was a difficult situation.

This man might also have had difficulties in dealing with another boss, that is, a father figure, but with an actual father who reacts to the individual as a son, not merely as an employee, there are added pressures, making it difficult to segregate business relationships from other levels of involvement.

Birth-order distinctions among siblings may also carry over into business positions, affecting authority and decision-making. Sometimes it was considered difficult when a younger brother was in a business position senior to an older brother, or when a younger brother had no hope of achieving partnership with his older brothers.

The carryover of kinship statuses into the business hierarchies may not always produce problems. However, it is extremely difficult to disregard the fact that one has a different status with the same people in another relationship. When business and kin relationships involve the same individuals, business dealings are frequently inescapably pervasive in social life. As one woman explained, "When there's an argument, it's a family affair, and everybody has to know about it." Or as another woman claimed, "Things are brought back into the family, and this side's story is told and the other one's story."

This is a two-way process; the entanglement of kin and business statuses has consequences for relationships among kin as well as for the business. From the point of view of business functioning, it means that kin who are not directly involved in the business are told of the business affairs, and consequently apply sanctions to those in the business. In one case, a woman's husband had received financial backing from her mother for a business venture. Her mother felt that she had been exploited, and the wife, in turn, heard of this through her sister. Here, communication among kin meant that the mother's reaction was reported to the wife and had an effect upon the functioning of the business.

This feedback of the sanctions of kin to business activity, and the lack of separation of business and other relationships with kin, adds to the difficulties of making organizational changes. In one case the husband left his wife's father's business, and as a result, generally strained relationships pervaded the family social life:

> WIFE: The end was [a] very difficult period of time . . . very strained relations. We just felt bad . . . my mother said that time would . . . she thought it would get better. But there was lots of bitterness. My father was quite bitter also, and they had feelings or hopes that Joe would come back. They really never gave up the idea till they saw that it was a sure thing, the break . . . socially it was difficult. I mean we couldn't go places together . . . we would be there at the same time, but we couldn't go in the same car. It was a bad time.

The repercussions of business for kin relationships and the sanctions from kin for business activity may continue indefinitely in social life outside the business. One woman explained that her husband and his brothers had been in business with their father. After the father's retirement, the brothers had difficulty with the business, which eventually failed. The father claimed, and still claims, that the sons ruined the business. They continued to receive sanctions for this at almost every kin gathering; for example, one time when "he blamed them outright in front of everyone, and it was very embarrassing." In this case, because of the lack of separation of business and kinship, the business failure was with them at all times. As the wife explained about her mother-in-law, "She never let him forget it." It is clear that it is extremely difficult to segregate business and kinship relationships when these involve the same individuals. This connection may be a source of support for the business but it also often introduces problems for business functioning.

FAMILY–KIN BUSINESSES AND KIN RELATIONSHIPS

The lack of segregation of kinship statuses from business positions not only affects the business but also other areas of relationships with kin. Despite frequent comments that business dealings with kin are a sure way of making enemies, there are indications that business activity with kin tends to lend general support to obligations of kinship and involvement with kin. By definition, those who are in business with kin see each other daily and thus have much kin interaction. Moreover, business dealings often require financial assistance so that one would expect these families to have received assistance from kin. There are indications, moreover, that this involvement of kin in the business carried over into nonbusiness relationships among these kin as well as other kin outside the business.

A crucial factor is reciprocity. Even those families who are not in business with kin have extensive economic and service relationships with their kin, and the values of kinship give strong support for binding obligations of reciprocity. Thus when business ventures entail assistance from kin, as they often do, this assistance creates an obligation for reciprocity and for continuing involvement.

Reciprocity may be in the business itself or in other kinds of assistance or service. One woman described how, when her father retired, he "gave" his store to his brother and sister. A gift of this magnitude presumably involves reciprocity on the part of the kin at some later date.

Husbands who had at some time been in business with kin not only claim to have received financial assistance from relatives outside the business slightly more frequently than nonbusiness husbands, but they also claim to have given assistance of all kinds to kin somewhat more often. The differences are slight but, nevertheless, in view of general attitudes about reciprocity, it is clear that business activity that requires the assistance of kin tends to further the bind of reciprocal obligation.

Reports of conflict pervade many of the interviews with both business and nonbusiness families. The sources of kin conflict are innumerable. Nevertheless, those in business with kin often report that business dealings had been a specific source of conflict among kin. As one wife explained, when her husband went into business with his brother, "We almost lost a brother-in-law on account of it." Business activity may therefore increase not only kin contacts and obligations but also conflicts. It must be noted, however, that any small business, whether with kin or not, by intensifying contacts may provide many opportunities for conflict.

The conjunction of occupational and kinship statuses may affect the extent to which it is possible to express emotion within the family concerning occupational activities. Ordinarily the husband can express within his family the tensions that develop in his work. But when, as in one case, his boss is also his wife's father, it is not surprising that this complicates the possibility of an outlet at home for emotions built up on the job. In this case, the wife felt that she was in the middle, as a go-between, for her husband and her father. Although she was not formally involved in the business, she was drawn into the relationship between her husband and her father; as a result, there was a minimum segregation of business and family.

The wife frequently heard criticism of her husband from his boss, her father. The open channels of kinship communication were used to discuss the business. Such direct criticism of the husband's job performance to his wife can hardly help having implications for the marital relationship; here it was considered an important factor in the couple's marital problems:

> WIFE: My parents couldn't communicate with Joe. . . . They couldn't reach him, and they went to reach him through me. . . . I was between them, and they were talking to me to get to him, and he talked to me to get to them. Yes, I was in the middle.
> HUSBAND: She was the "intercom" wife.
> WIFE: So I heard now and then that he is a good worker and all the qualities that he did have, but they felt that he was not taking enough of an interest in the business. . . . My father felt that he was not interested enough to really break his head over it.

In this instance, the overlap between business, kinship statuses, and the nuclear family did not necessarily reduce the expression of feelings about the business in the home; on the contrary, it may have actually increased the amount of such expression. But it made it difficult for the wife to take an impartial position. Her position derived, in part, from her handling of the situation, but the structuring of kin and business relationships contributed significantly. The wife could not have been pressured into an intermediary role in the same way by a boss of the husband's who was not also her own father. Moreover, because business and family relationships overlap in the home of her parents as well, not only her father but also her mother was involved in discussions of the business.

Family-kin businesses are another area in which many families living in an urban industrial environment are deeply involved. with kin. Certain problems for the functioning of these businesses appear to derive from their kinship structure. The general inability to segregate kinship and occupational roles when these involve the same people means that there is likely to be a great deal of carryover from one area of relationships to another. Even though business activity is a source of considerable conflict among kin, this conflict does not appear to produce complete ruptures in kinship ties. Rather, since business frequently entails the financial or other assistance of kin, it reinforces obligations of reciprocity and tends to strengthen the momentum of kin interaction. The overlap of kinship and business roles affects both business functioning and kin relationships, and both of these, in turn, have consequences for the family.

Family and Church as "Boundary" Structures

TALCOTT PARSONS

It has been suggested that however fragmented in particular cases, a religious tradition is inherently part of a culture and that this in turn is in the first instance integrated with a society rather than the personality of an individual. With reference to the theme of values, it is closest to the level of value-commitment which is institutionalized in the society—it is the highest level in the general scale of "ultimacy."

Given this very fundamental difference between the involvement of values in the personality of the individual in the genetic sequence on the one hand, in the culture and from it the society on the other, can there be said to be any analogy between the duality of involvement in the individual in two families, and his involvement in religious organization? I should like to suggest that there is, but that the sense in which this is the case must be very carefully formulated.

There is a critical sense in which the pre-oedipal child is not yet "in the society"; he is in his family. The family is the borderline structure between the roots of the personality of the individual and his beginning participation in the society. As an adult he is a full participant in the society, but through his family of procreation he still participates in this "presocietal soil" of his being as a human personality. There is an analogous sense in which, in all the higher religions, but notably Christianity, the religious collectivity is not fully "in the society." It is in an important sense "set apart," a field of participation which, to use the old phrase, is "in the world but not of it." The way in which this is the case may of course vary immensely, but I should like to postulate an essential element of constancy in this respect.

In the case of a church or denomination in the modern sense, however, its typical member is, in his other roles, very much a member of society. But the church is a partially segregated area where the concerns of secular life can, within limits, be held in abeyance. This would seem to be an important aspect of the more general phenomenon of the "set-apartness" of the realm of the sacred.

Churches, in their symbolic and ritualistic traditions, utilize a set of references of meaning which are particularly "set apart" even from intelligibility in the context of secular life. My general hypothesis here is that these references are to what may be called metaphorically the "childhood of the culture." They do not refer primarily to stages in the life history of the individual, but to the "foundations" on which the present stage of religious commitment, particularly with reference to "the world," have been built up. In the Christian case, this reference is to the basic constitution of the early Christian church. There are four basic references, involved in all Christian ritual from this point of view, to God the Father as the transcendental reference of the ultimate ground of meaning; to the Christ figure as the mediator between Divinity and humanity and hence as the symbolic head of the church; to the church itself as the brotherhood of Christians imbued with the Holy Spirit, and to the individual Christian as participant in the church and, through it, in Divine grace.

From the point of view of adequate adjustment to and involvement in a society of the modern type, the early church was clearly "archaic." It was quite literally not "of" this world, particularly a modern world. Modern churches are the product of a complex process of evolution from the early church, but they of course still perpetuate this same fundamental complex of belief and symbolism and make it the focus not only of their ritualistic practices but in some sense of their organization as collectivities. In the "middle" period of this evolution the church became a very elaborate organization, which in a sense commanded jurisdiction over something approaching a half of life in society. Since the Reformation there has been a process of social differentiation in the course of which the church has become a more specialized agency to the point where, in the modern Protestant denomination, it has become predominantly a private association which has "lost" many of the functions of the earlier, particularly the mediaeval, church, notably with respect to jurisdiction over secular culture, education, and family life, whereas the political and economic spheres had earlier been predominantly institutionalized in secular terms. The pattern of the denomination has, particularly in the United States, profoundly influenced the religious organization of Judaism, and even considerably that of the Catholic church in that through its minority position and the separation of church and state the religious collectivity is deprived of many of the prerogatives it had traditionally enjoyed and still does where it is the established church.

The most important point for present purposes is that churches as social organizations constitute only a small fraction of the framework of organization of a complex modern society while the rest of the society is specifically categorized as secular. There is a certain parallelism to the fact that the family has, in the course of recent social evolution, also become a more differentiated, specialized agency, less diffusely embedded in larger social structures, such as the nexuses of extended kinship and local community.

This differentiation does not, as it is often contended, imply that either or both have lost most of their "importance" in modern society. It means that the influence they do exert is not through organizational jurisdiction over certain spheres of life now structurally differentiated from them, but through the value-commitments and motivational commitments of individuals. In spheres outside their families and their churches, then, individuals have come to be by and large free of organizational control and in this sense to act *autonomously*, on their own responsibility. But this is by no means to say that their behavior in these "external" spheres is uninfluenced by their participation in the family and the church respectively.

In modern society, then, the family and the church are "boundary-structures" vis-à-vis, respectively, the motivational and the value components of the individual personality. Let us try to sum up how these are related to each other. The axis on which I have tried to relate them is that defined on the one hand by the series of steps in the specification of orientation of value, from the highest religiously grounded level, down through the value system institutionalized in the society, to the levels which can become meaningful in the orientation of the particular individual, faced with a particular life situation within the society. The other series is grounded in the most general exigencies of the organization of the motivational system of the personality, starting in the earliest attachment to the mother, going up through the oedipal stage, through latency and adolescence to adulthood.

The latter series may, from one point of view, be regarded as a series of internalizations of value-patterns, of their "combination" with motivational components. But it starts with highly specific values, and only gradually works up to more and more generalized levels. Conversely the "religious" series is in the first instance one of the specification of values. It, however, starts at the *most* general level and must work "down" from there. Moreover, this process also, to be effective in conduct, must include the *institutionalization* of the values, and one major component of this process of institutionalization is the motivational commitment of individual personalities to them.[1] The church or churches have been the primary social agencies of this process of *institutionalization*.

For the given individual there must of course be a process by which the religious values are internalized in his personality; various aspects of religious education are involved here, but we cannot take space to go into them. Once internalized, however, their reinforcement and maintenance operate through mechanisms which are analogous to those operating in the family of procreation. This is universally the process of religious observance and teaching, perhaps notably observance, on the ritualistic level. The most important point is that in both cases the stabilization functions operate mainly through institutionalized mechanisms which do not require any elaborately specific attention to the problems of the particular individual. It is rather that he normally participates in a nexus of social relationships and the attendant activities, and this participation normally regulates his pattern of commitments.

Now we may raise the question of where and how these two series meet in the structure of the society and the life-pattern of the individual. Looking at the problem from the life-cycle point of view the evidence seems to be that a specially crucial point is adolescence. There are certainly normally what we would call religious components in the orientations internalized throughout the life cycle, and certainly in the pre-oedipal and latency periods. But it is in adolescence that the child first comes to play a more highly differentiated set of roles in a variety of different contexts of participation. Furthermore it is here that he first, in a sense implying real commitment, faces the formation of the basic pattern of his adult life, notably with respect to choice of occupation and of marriage partner. Late adolescence brings both these commitments and also the first formal admission to participation in community responsibility, in modern societies especially symbolized by the right to vote. Finally, most modern religious groups institutionalize full religious participation through ceremonies such as confirmation sometime during this period.[2]

We may thus say that it is typically in adolescence that the individual enters into full participation in his society; that he becomes a contributor through occupational performance to its functioning, and thereby economically self-supporting; that he assumes his share of collective responsibility; and that he begins to participate in the socialization function through marriage. Here for the first time he is really confronted with the problem of the nature and extent of his value-commitments as an adult member of the society.[3]

We have emphasized that this extent and nature of societal commitment is in the nature of the case problematical on cultural—that is, eventually religious—levels. Somehow societal interests must be balanced against others, notably those of the individual's own personality itself, and the balance grounded in some orientation defining the meaning of *his* life.

Our very broad conclusion is that the problems of the groundwork of the motivational structure of the personality come to a head in relation to the oedipal stage of personality development, and to the relation between the individual's participation in his family of procreation, as spouse and parent, as an adult. The problems of value-commitment and its grounding in the individual's relation to the deeper layers of the cultural tradition of his society come to a head in his life history in adolescence, and in principle in terms of the current social structure, in his relation to the organized religion in which he was brought up or toward which he may be drawn.

SOCIAL DIFFERENTIATION AS AFFECTING THE STATUSES OF FAMILY AND CHURCH

Let us now attempt to look at the problem from the point of view of the social structure. Here the salient fact about modern society is the high development of structural differentiation, and the rapidity with which processes of structural change at the requisite levels have gone on. It has already been noted how the family has become a substantially more specialized agency, more fully differentiated from other agencies. By virtue of this fact its members are placed in a position of far greater autonomy in their relations outside the family, and these spheres constitute an increasingly large share of their life-interests. For the child of course this increasing autonomy centers in his schooling, and the relations to his age peers which are closely associated with the school, but are also in important respects independent of it.

At the other end of our scale, the church in the denominational pattern has also become a more specialized agency and by virtue of this fact has lost many of its former functions. Its organizational involvement in the "things of this world" has in one important sense steadily receded. It has certainly lost notably in political power, relative to the situation in which established churches existed. It takes far less of a role in the control of economic production, and most notably perhaps it has renounced much of its formal jurisdiction over secular culture and education, and over family relations. By the same token as the family, it has tended to come to exert influence increasingly through its "moral" hold on individuals rather than through the more "massive" societal means of exerting influence.

Like marriage for the adult, church affiliation has become a voluntary matter. This is closely associated with the system of religious toleration, separation of church and state, and denominational pluralism. Religious adherence has become "privatized."

The fact that both institutional complexes have been so involved in the process of differentiation means that a gap has been created between them, which did not previously exist to the same extent. The "wedge" which symbolizes and has in part created this gap is, above all, secular education—in the United States, the public school system. But it is also clearly signalized by the tendency to deny to *organized* religion even directly moral, to say nothing of legal, jurisdiction over marriage and divorce and many of the problems of private morality, particularly those associated with the family.

It is in our opinion this process of structural differentiation in the society which underlies the emerging salience of the problem with which the discussion of this paper started. Our general thesis here is that the problems of mental health and illness root in the motivational organization of the personality of the individual. This in turn genetically is primarily concerned with the process of socialization down through the oedipal period, and in terms of the problem of adjustment of the individual, in the first instance with his roles in marriage and cognate relations and his role as a parent. Since mental illness ramifies into the personality as a whole, it affects all the behavioral contexts in which he is involved, but its structural core rests in the areas designated.

What has been referred to above as "spiritual malaise" is empirically often associated with psychopathology, but must be considered to be analytically independent of it. It concerns above all the individual's commitments to the values of his society and the various subsectors of it with which he is or potentially might be associated, and, from this point of departure, his involvements in problems of meaning. This is in turn genetically associated with his experience in the religious groups with which he and his parents and associates have been affiliated, an experience the personal significance of which has very generally come to a head in adolescence. It leads over into acute problems of the meaning of his life commitments.

Both sets of problems are closely related to strains which are inherent in the structure of a rapidly developing and differentiating society. The family itself has been rapidly changing its character. It is furthermore an important "residual legatee" of strains generated in other parts of the society and hence may often become disorganized under the impact of these strains. On the other side of the picture the religious organization is necessarily deeply involved in the structure of the society as a whole. Hence any major changes of the latter have a strong impact on organized religion. For these reasons, attitudes toward organized religion and its symbol-systems understandably play a major part in the impact on personalities of all the strains which are operative in a changing society.

Perhaps the most generalized formulation of the common factor in these two problem areas which is current in sociological thinking is the concept of *anomie*. This may be said to be the disturbance of the state of internalized expectations of persons occasioned by the processes of change in the normative components of the institutionalized culture, and hence in the definition of what can legitimately be expected of individuals and classes of them. The most essential point is that in the process of such change, what is expected often over wide areas becomes seriously indeterminate. Anomic components of the situation may, we feel, be propagated in both directions. On the one hand, they may raise questions on the more religiously based level of meaning. Where the normative structure involves serious anomic elements in particular, the balances between performance and sanction, between what is felt to be earned and the actual available rewards in fact forthcoming, will be upset. (The upset, it may be noted, may result from excessive as well as from inadequate reward.) In the other direction, looking to the motivation of the personality, life simply becomes more complex and there are problems of how far individuals are capable of "taking it" from the point of view of their own characters, particularly with respect to their "tolerance of ambiguity" and their capacity to handle risks.

This discussion has stressed the differentiation between the personality and religious contexts, between family and church. Before closing this structural analysis something should be said about one very important context of connection between them. Both the problem of mental health and that of religious commitment involve matters of intimate personal significance to individuals, what in a certain sense are highly "private" affairs. It is not fortuitous, therefore, that both center in the life of the local residential community and that by and large it is as family members that people are associated in churches. Both are hence somewhat withdrawn from the larger economic and political affairs of the society, and are associated together in this withdrawal. This situation has much to do with the sense in which the church has tended to maintain, and even develop further, a set of functions as a diffuse center of association at the first level beyond the household. It is a kind of substitute for the undifferentiated neighborhood, a place where "like-minded" people can get to know each other and be made to "feel at home" in contexts not specifically connected with religion.

It is not uncommon to suggest that this set of functions has in fact become primary, that modern churchgoers are "not really" religious at all, but are only interested in sociability. In my opinion this is a misinterpretation. This associational aspect of the modern denominational parish is a predictable feature of the general pattern of the development of modern society when the fact is taken into account that family and church have such intimate intrinsic relations to each other. The sociability pattern is the primary mechanism by which family and church are brought together with each other. Each, in its own specialized way, involves the "whole person." Unless they are to be, not merely differentiated, but *dissociated*, there must be some adequate mechanism of linkage. My hypothesis is that the church as a "social center" provides this mechanism, and that, as a result of the structural differentiation of modern society, this has become more rather than less important.

NOTES

[1] On the general nature of this process, see "Christianity and Modern Industrial Society," by Talcott Parsons, in *Sociological Theory, Values, and Sociocultural Change*, Edward A. Tiryakian, ed., New York: The Free Press of Glencoe, 1963.

[2] Particularly illuminating observations on the significance of adolescence for the religious orientations of the individual are presented in Robert N. Bellah, "The Place of Religion in Human Action," *Review of Religion*, March, 1958.

[3] An important, relatively new factor seems to have entered into this situation, the implications of which are far from clear. This is the increasing participation of the population in higher education even beyond the college level through advanced professional training. Just what are the limits of adolescence is a moot question, but certainly the middle twenties are beyond them. Anyway the effect is to postpone the full assumption of occupational roles and the attendant responsibilities and rewards to a much later point that has been typical of most of the population for most periods. It may well be that this is an important factor in the ferment about problems of meaning in our own time, since there is a certain conflict between the general emphasis on early independence and responsibility on the one hand, and the kind of tutelage in which persons in the system of formal education generally, and of professional training in particular, tend to be kept. One possible tendency may be to treat the higher commitments of meaning as even more tentative than before, since only the fully "mature" person should enter into them. But if this is the tendency, one would expect much conflict in the process of the working out of the new pattern, and that certain groups should feel a particularly urgent need to have firm "answers" almost immediately.

VII

Family Crisis, Disorganization, and Dissolution

A marriage is consummated, and during the next few years role relations are developed and decision-making patterns are evolved. This is not, however, the beginning of a permanent equilibrium, but is the first of many transitions and adjustments that will confront the couple. Some married couples never effect satisfactory role adjustments (recall Stuckert's paper), and burgeoning conflict eventually gives rise to divorce. Other couples must face the birth and raising of a handicapped child, or a severe economic setback, or the inclusion of an aged parent in their household. Even if the marriage escapes such adjustments and conflicts, it will eventually be confronted with the challenge of old age and the spectre of death. In this section we review the worst of events and conditions which give rise to crises and disorganization or to readjustments within the family.

Are all families with a father absent disorganized? Can all non-middle-class families be considered deviant? Is every divorce a result of deviance and a sign of disorganization? It is possible in the literature on "family problems" to find answers to these questions ranging from "absolutely" to "of course not." Thus, Jetse Sprey, in the first selection, takes upon himself the task of distinguishing between deviance, disorganization, unorganization, and conflict, as these relate to the family institution. A family with role conflicts, based on inadequate perceptions of expectations (recall Stuckert), would be considered disorganized without being deviant—the family members are living by their definitions of norms, however inadequate. Divorce may be due to deviance, but in and of itself it is neither deviant nor a sign of disorganization (recall O'Neil's discussion). The reader will benefit from reading Sprey's article, with its many conceptual distinctions, at the outset. Then, after completing the other papers, he should review the ways in which Sprey's analysis can be used to clarify alcoholism, divorce, old age, and death as they relate to the family.

Many crisis-provoking events confront families in the course of their existence. Mental illness, mental retardation, natural disaster, economic setback—the list of stimuli and processes that may require family adjustments is long and varied. In the second paper Joan Jackson analyzes the effect of alcoholism on the children and spouse of the alcoholic. A pre-alcoholic, or one with alcoholic tendencies, she feels, may choose a certain type of spouse. Or perhaps a certain type of spouse drives the pre-alcoholic toward alcoholism. Besides such hypotheses regarding the interplay between mate choice and alcoholism, and the issue of the effect of the alcoholic upon the spouse and children, Sprey asks a third important question. Using Sprey's terminology, we might phrase it thus: How might the family with an alcoholic (a deviant) avoid disorganization? The stages of crisis and reorganization are, according to Jackson, as follows: denial——→attempts to eliminate——→ disorganization——→reorganization. When coupled with Sprey's conceptual distinctions, how might Jackson's crisis stages be used to better understand other possible crisis events, including divorce and death?

The third and fourth articles in Part VII should be read together and with reference to O'Neill's historical account in Part I. Freed and Foster, reviewing the legal aspects of divorce, note the prevalence of divorce and the fact that the official grounds for divorce seldom match the actual reasons. Cruelty, including mental cruelty, has increasingly become the dominant legal basis for divorce in the United States. Now California has defined mutual desire as a legal grounds, which may be a step toward nonfault divorces, perhaps based upon the simple cessation of love. Freed and Foster, however, note the conservative bias of most legislatures, which slows down the process of reform in divorce laws. Alexander Plateris' government pamphlet, a portion of which is reprinted here, presents the most recent statistics on the prevalence of divorce according to several qualifying variables. Noteworthy among his findings are: (1) The divorce rate, as seen in the next-to-last column of Table 3, is low in depression and high in wartime; during periods of prosperity, people can afford financially to change their life commitments, and this includes both marriages and divorces. (2) Most divorces still occur within the first two or three years of marriage (see Figure 3), and they become decreasingly prevalent after that time. (3) More and more divorces involve couples who have children, and this is one of the more recent developments manifested by divorce statistics. This seems to bespeak the lesser holding power of children, and perhaps the perception on the parents' part that a conflict-filled marriage may actually be worse than a broken home, not only for the couple but for the offspring. The interested reader may want to relate Plateris' statistics to the longer time span provided in Paul Jacobson's book, *American Marriage and Divorce*. In addition, he should ponder whether Plateris' statistics, when coupled with the increasing leniency of divorce laws, still fit O'Neil's model of divorce as a safety valve for the family system, or whether they are gradual but perceptible signs of the disintegration of the U.S. family system.

Two brief excerpts from the excellent study of *Old People in Three*

Industrial Societies, by Ethel Shanas, comprise the fifth selection of this part. Her findings include the fact that most adults have several kin who are proximate enough for contact, and that very few aged are isolated from close kinship and friendship. Loss of a spouse leads to loneliness more often than does lack of social companions and activities. The aged, she finds, have disengaged from the major life roles of parenthood and occupation, but they have not withdrawn from personal relationships and are not passively awaiting death. Though Shanas presents a relatively optimistic picture of the social involvements of the aged, one might wonder how adequate their psychological adjustment is likely to be in a society which glorifies youthfulness and defines the aged as useless.

At the end of the family life cycle comes the death of the couple members. The excerpt from Waller's book focuses on family reorganization following death, referring to the desolation (Shanas) and readjustment through which families pass. Waller notes that remarriage, while increasingly likely, is still difficult for the female with children to effect. One is led to wonder whether the premature death of a spouse, which is much less prevalent than formerly, may actually lead to greater desolation and bereavement now than in the days when more families were broken by premature death than by divorce.

These are but a few of the issues that may alter the equilibrium of the family. The literature on various crisis events is plentiful, and can give the reader a clear sense of the family not as a finished product of role decisions, but as an evolving and ever adjusting response to internal and external challenges.

Family Disorganization: Toward a Conceptual Clarification*

JETSE SPREY

The history of the family disorganization concept is a long one. Moreover, despite repeated attempts at clarification, its present definition is still far from clear. Because a complete coverage of the past and present literature lies beyond the scope of this paper, a number of representative illustrations must suffice.

In Mowrer's early treatment,[1] the concept of family disorganization is defined as a "relative differentiation of interests and aims of its members in terms of another or other family groups." Elliot and Merrill,[2] in a text on social disorganization, simply classify every conceivable family problem under the heading of disorganization, while in a similar work Faris[3] used the term to deal with inadequate family functioning and dissolution. Three of the more recent definitions are by Goode, Winch, and Kirkpatrick. The latter[4] distinguishes between disorganization and disintegration while also separating the family and marital contexts of the two phenomena. Winch[5] defines disorganization as a process of change in the family system, manifested in one of three types: loss of consensus among members, reduction in the number of positions in the structure, and finally a loss of functionality. The choice of criteria seems arbitrary and logically far from clear. One wonders, for instance, why a reduction rather than an increase in the number of family positions is singled out for attention, unless this represents an attempt to define all incomplete families as disorganized. The accent on incompleteness is also reflected in the frequently quoted formulation by Goode:[6] "the breakup of a family unit, the dissolution or fracture of a structure of social roles when one or more members fail to perform adequately their role obligations." This definition is so broad as to include all broken families, while the designation "fracture of a structure of social roles" is so vague as to be practically meaningless.

Despite differences—semantic as well as analytical—the above formulations share certain characteristics. The most important common denominator is the usage of the disorganization concept as a normative one. Martindale's comments on the prevalence of normative rather than empirical theory in the general area of social disorganization seem to

Reprinted from *Journal of Marriage and the Family*, November 1966, 398–406.

hold equally well for the more specific treatment of disorder in the family institution.[7] Theory construction or attempts in that direction traditionally have been focused on desirable versus undesirable situations and the analysis of potential aids in the elimination of the latter. Thus, the term *family disorganization* tends to serve as a catchall category for family undesirables, such as divorce, adultery, illegitimacy, etc. Family dissolution, for example, whatever its actual cause or degree of permanence, is always to be found in the disorganization category. This is neither logically valid nor empirically true but a reflection of the judgment that families should contain two parents.

Implied in the above usage of the disorganization concept is its all too frequent equation with terms denoting other related family problems, such as deviations of various nature, marital maladjustment, and disintegration. Finally, the normative approach tends to lead to research centered around the presumed "badness" of specific kinds or symptoms of postulated family disorganization. The controversy about the effects of divorce upon children is a example. Recent findings indicate that children in homes broken by divorce may, as a category, be better off than those in complete but severely maladjusted families. However, apart from showing that divorce is not as bad as it was assumed to be, this type of study contributes neither to the explanation of the disorganization process nor to the understanding of its symptoms and manifestations. It merely suggests the replacement of one normative judgment by another. A similar comment can be made about much of the published materials on the topic of the working mother.

The aim of this paper is to formulate an objective definition of the concept of family disorganization. A clear distinction between this concept and related ones must be made to render the use of each of these analytical tools more specific and precise. If the concept of family disorganization cannot serve such a purpose it should be eliminated and replaced by others. This raises the issue of appropriate techniques for concept formulation and validation. In brief, the general adequacy of a concept is judged on the basis of its usefulness for the theoretical system of which it is designed to be a part. This thinking can be illustrated by a quote from Rudner's treatment of conceptualization in the social sciences.

> Both definitional and analytical conceptual schemata . . . are presumably destined for ultimate inclusion within some social-science theory. With respect to the context of validation or justification in science, their function within theories will be to assist deductive elaboration—and hence to assist in affecting the confirmation or disconfirmation of the theories of which they come to form a part. Similarly, their inclusion assists the predictive and explanatory uses of such theories.[8]

In the absence of a valid theory of family disorganization, it is assumed that the explanation of family disorders must occur within the framework of a general theory of social disorganization. The idea of a special theory designed to deal with family phenomena—of whatever nature—is rejected here. Such a theory will by definition be unrealistic and irrelevant. In view of the need for a general theory, two closely related conceptual formulations of social disorganization, those by Cohen and Merton,[9] will be discussed and applied to the family situation and family process.

SOCIAL DISORGANIZATION

Cohen has provided a meaningful analytical distinction between the concepts of deviant behavior and social disorganization. Borrowing Garfinkel's game analogy,[10] social disorganization is defined as a breach in the "constitutive order of events—an order conforming to the constitutive rules—of the game." If action terminates within the framework of the rules, no disorganization is postulated; the game is merely over. Deviant behavior is seen as the violation of institutionalized expectations, that is, those which are shared and recognized as legitimate within a social system.[11] In the game analogy, deviant behavior thus constitutes any violation of the rules. The above conceptualization is a structural one; given the game situation, in the case of disorganization something happens to disrupt or disturb its ongoing process. For the application of this analytic scheme to subsystems of society—in this case, the family—a further elaboration is essential. The state of the surrounding social network along the organization-disorganization dimension and the degree and nature of the interdependency of the family structures with it are of crucial importance. Conceptual tools must be powerful enough to allow the incorporation of such factors into the ultimate analysis.

Merton's more recent discussion of disorganization may serve as a further elaboration of Cohen's views. "Social disorganization refers to inadequacies or failures in a social system of interrelated statuses and roles," or, more briefly, it consists of "instrumental or technical flaws in the social system."[12] Deviant behavior and social disorganization are treated as major analytical categories of social problems, which are defined as "substantial unwanted discrepancies between what is . . . and what a functionally significant collectivity within that society . . . desires to be in it."[13] This formulation is a normative one, because the judgment of whether or not a given segment of the population lives under a condition of disorganization depends upon the evaluation by a "functionally significant collectivity." Of course, this may be so in the context of practical politics, but it does not furnish a valid framework for scientific analysis. By using the game analogy, Cohen avoids a normative definition. This analogy will be used, therefore, in combination with Merton's instrumental specifications. Before such a conceptual scheme is applied to the institution of the family, it should be further clarified.

ORGANIZATION, UN–ORGANIZATION, AND DISORGANIZATION

Cohen correctly maintains that disorganization must be analyzed along the dimension of organization. As such he postulates two logically necessary preconditions for the proper functioning of the organizational process.

> First, it presupposes . . . that, at any stage or phase of the system the situations that the participants confront and the alternative possibilities of action can be defined by the rules. Secondly, it presupposes that the participants are motivated to "play the game"—that is, to assume the perspectives provided by the rules and to select their actions from the constitutive possibilities designated by the rules.[14]

Disorganization is postulated to occur when one or both of the above conditions are not met.

Cohen's statement indicates that both preconditions are necessary for the process of organization, that is, the elimination of one or both is bound to result in some degree of disorder. This does not mean, however, that the absence of either or both is a necessary cause of disorganization, which can result from many other factors. Most of Cohen's examples describe events of an external and disruptive nature. As a matter of fact, in the causal explanation of family disorganization it seems that the sufficiency rather than the necessity criterion is of crucial importance. For example, it is clear that the elimination of one parent is not a necessary cause for family disorganization. Rather, the question is whether it is a sufficient cause.

Furthermore, the above preconditions should not be limited to disorder arising after the onset of the "game." Antecedent states of disorganization may become formalized, for various reasons, into structures. The practice of forced marriage due to premarital pregnancy would fit into this category. Cohen's treatment, reflected in his illustrations, suggests a hypothetical state of organizational "normalcy," which then deteriorates into one of disorganization. In view of the available data in the area of family disorder, it is this state of normalcy which would require an explanation, not the observed disorganization. To pursue the game analogy a bit further, it seems worthwhile to remember that people do not necessarily understand the rules of the games in which they participate. Thus, the question of why people would wish to participate in meaningless, ritualistic games arises; it requires a closer look at the second precondition and especially the meaning of the term "motivation." Sociologically put, the question is what motivates people to participate in social institutions—habit, force, ignorance, indifference, lack of alternatives, or combinations of these factors. Moreover, what exactly can one infer from the fact that some people or groups actually live under more or less permanent conditions of social disorganization—their motivation or lack of it? Applied to human participation in institutions, the explanation of motivation easily becomes tautological. People who are observed to live in disorganized families can be accused of not being motivated to live in "good" homes or of being motivated to live in "bad" ones. Either explanation will suffice, depending on the bias of the observer. This is not to say that the condition of the "willingness to play the game" is not important. It must be rephrased, however, to read: What are the rewards people associate with their decisions to participate in given institutions?

Merton's discussion is pertinent to the above-suggested alternative of a preexisting state of disorganization. He formulates the term *un-organization* and defines it as follows:

> Seen from a proper time perspective some recurrent social situations might better be described as involving a lack of organization than as being instances of disorganization. They are cases of un-organization, in which a system of social relations has not yet taken shape, rather than cases of disorganization in which an acute disruption has occurred in a once more or less effective system of social relations.[15]

Here again is the assumption that disorganization must be preceded by a state of organization. Merton thus offers a means of dealing with situations in which disorganization has been present from the beginning; structures of this nature are not disorganized but merely unorganized. Doubtless, there are social situations from which structure is absent. It could be argued which term would be more suitable for this kind of condition, *un-organization* or *non-institutionalization,* but this question is not relevant here. Important to consider, though, is the fact that in concrete cases of disorder—problem families, for example—no basis for distinction exists between disorganization and Merton's notion of un-organization, except for the time of its inception. No analytical purpose is served by this distinction; on the contrary, it eliminates one basic avenue of explanation, the existence of a state of disorder before the onset of the game. Merton's conception of un-organization therefore will be incorporated into the definition of disorganization formulated in this paper.

One final aspect of the game must be considered. Certain people may refuse to play a given game and instead devise their own versions. Within the context of the study of deviant behavior, this raises the question of distinguishing between nonconformist and deviant behavior. Both Cohen and Merton have treated this point analytically;[16] however, the present concern is with family disorganization rather than deviancy. How is the new game judged—by the rules of the old one or by its own? In relation to the social institution of the family, it seems unlikely that a simple sequence of events—traditional structure, change, new structure —will occur. A number of structures are likely to coexist, each with its own constitutive order of process. Under these conditions, judgments concerning the existence of disorganization within given families or categories of families must be formulated with a great deal of objectivity. This does not mean that an evaluation about the existence or nonexistence of disorganization cannot be made. Merton's statement about social disorganization can be applied equally well to the family situation, in that disorganization of the family results in a lesser realization of the collective purposes and individual objectives of its members than would be the case in an alternative workable system.[17] In other words, one game can be judged less meaningful to its participants and less functional in its social consequences than another.

MARITAL AND FAMILY DISORGANIZATION

Before focusing upon the conceptualization of family disorganization, one must make a clear distinction between this and marital disorganization. The difference between these two related concepts must reflect the essential distinction between the institutions of marriage and the family. The latter is defined as a small kinship group whose key function is nurturant socialization of the newborn.[18] Marriage is a socially sanctioned relationship between two or more members of opposite sex for the purpose of reproduction. Its major function is to provide the children with a set of legitimate parents. It is relevant to underline Goode's observation that marriage tends to bestow legitimacy on parenthood more than on sex.[19] It can be suggested that sexual behavior as an end in itself, rather than a means of reproduction, is becoming independently institutionalized outside the marital context. This implies, among other things, that judgments about the degree and nature of possible sexual disorganization should no longer be made exclusively within the "game" of marriage.

Marital disorganization thus can be defined as a state of disorder within the institutionalized pattern of human reproduction. Therefore, illegitimacy, rather than divorce, is one indication of this type of disorganization. Within this frame of reference, the distinction between marital maladjustment and disorganization also becomes apparent. The former refers to interpersonal difficulties within the marital dyad, with a marital dissolution through divorce, separation, or desertion as a possible outcome. This formulation implies that the phenomenon of marital maladjustment is essentially a social-psychological, rather than a sociological one, and should be studied as such. The sociological categories of disorganization and deviance within families must be treated as conditions rather than causes in the explanation of the interpersonal processes in marital dyads and family groups.

Family disorganization can be seen as a process or a resulting situation. It can thus be defined either way. In the first instance, the concept denotes a state of disorder in the constitutive pattern of family process; in the second, a condition of inadequacy within the structure of interrelated status-roles that constitute a family system. The latter definition differs from the previously cited one by Goode on two points. First, no dissolution or fracture of the family structure is postulated as a necessary component. Second, the inadequacy of the structure is defined, instead of deviant or inadqeuate role performance of its members. Goode's definition blurs the basic distinction between disorganization and the violation of family role prescriptions.

THE NATURE OF FAMILY ROLE BEHAVIOR

Family role behavior differs significantly from most other categories of behavior in this society. People spend most of their time outside the family situation participating in fairly large, formally organized social structures. As March and Simon put it,[20] "In our society, preschool children and nonworking housewives are the only large groups of persons whose behavior is not substantially 'organizational.'" In such formally organized structures, role prescriptions are specific, positions ranked, and communication channels clearly defined. Membership status is primarily achieved. In contrast, family role obligations are particularistic and diffuse. Family status is ascribed or, in the case of the spouse, reflects a quality rather than performance. Finally, the family process occurs most frequently within the setting of a small group. It will thus be well to remember that a breach or disturbance in the constitutive order of family process is something quite different from disorganization in a bureaucratic structure. Merton's criterion of instrumentality can almost serve as an operational definition of disorder within a highly formal structure, but it cannot so serve for the family. The so frequently suggested precondition for family disorganization, elimination of one parent, makes more sense in a small bureaucratic structure than in the family. After all, was the family "designed" to contain two parents? Unlike most formal organizations families, to their members, are primarily ends in themselves, a condition which should be taken into account in any realistic analysis of family functioning.

The categorization of family roles along the dimensions of task versus emotional specialization is relevant in the above context. A differentiation between family disorganization and deviancy in combination with the analytical distinction between expressive and instrumental role performance allows for the formulation of 16 logically possible categories, 15 of which contain at least one element of disorganization or deviance. A classification of this kind will most often be unnecessary and cumbersome; however, it will provide a scheme in which all logically possible alternative interpretations of a given set of findings can be covered.

FAMILY DISORGANIZATION AND DEVIANCE

The analysis of family behavior within a field delimited by the dimensions of organization-disorganization and conformity-deviance leads to the formulation of four categories. The chart below shows the various combinations; for the sake of simplicity each dimension has been dichotomized.

	Well-Organized	Disorganized
Conforming to family roles	A "normal"	C
Violation of family roles	B	D "multi-problem"

Within the frame of reference of this paper, the types B through D warrant further discussion.

Type B represents a situation in which disorganization is absent, but where one or more family members more or less consistently violate their roles. For the husband, for example, violations of this nature may range from occasional adultery to the refusal to support his dependents. Serious as such violations may be—each can be sufficient to destroy a family—they fall within the framework of the rules of the game. In the context of the family system, even divorce is a game event. This implies that, given a smooth divorce procedure and a high rate of remarriage, even a fairly high divorce rate cannot be considered an indication of family disorganization. In summary, violations of family roles do not necessarily disrupt the order of family process nor its functioning. For example, a wife may tacitly ignore her husband's infidelity and thus maintain the family as a functioning unit.

Type C is characterized by disorganization but without the presence of a significant degree of deviance. The empirical importance of this category depends on the exact definition of deviancy. Some authors limit it to the motivated violation of norms; others include violations due to ignorance, lack of skills, and other types of incapacity. This paper adheres to the latter definition. Category C thus contains families in which the members conform as best they can to inadequately defined, poorly understood, or incompatible role prescriptions.

Finally, *type D* contains those cases that are often impressionistically described as multiproblem families. Here both disorganization and deviancy are present. The notoriety achieved by this kind of family in the popular press and among family workers may well be largely responsible for the indiscriminate and frequent equation of the phenomena of disorganization and deviancy in families. The study of this kind of family situation especially requires a rigid conceptual distinction to prevent erroneous conclusions.

This simple classification scheme is designed only to serve as an analytical tool. Although in concrete situations most families will fall into one or two cells, this paper separately conceptualizes family disorganization, violation of family roles, and marital maladjustment. Each of these, in the investigation of concrete situations, can and should be treated as an independent factor relative to the analysis of each of the others. Only in this manner will it be possible to investigate and explain potential causal relationships. For example, will a situation of more or less permanent violation of family obligations by one or both marital partners necessarily lead to disorganization? Does disorganization always lead to violation of family roles, and, if so, which ones? Can one assume that if a family dissolves through divorce, disorganization was a necessary precondition? These hypotheses cannot be accepted without empirical validation, but none of them could have been formulated without the clear conceptual distinctions defined above.

The conclusions presented in a fairly recent research study further illustrate the need for conceptual clarity. Geismar and associates close their report of a study of impaired family functioning as follows:

> The corresponding hypotheses might read as follows: Family disorganization is a process that has its origin in problems in the area of intra-family relationships and proceeds over time to affect relationships beyond the family system and social functioning of a predominantly instrumental nature.[21]

The hypothesis in question reflects the finding that interpersonal relations in so-called problem families appeared more frequently impaired than strictly instrumental types of family behavior.

Unfortunately, however, no clear distinction was made between family disorganization, marital maladjustment, and violation of family obligations. Deviant acts were used as a "measure" of family disorganization. Because of this lack of conceptual clarity, Geismar's hypothesis becomes quite ambiguous. A hypothetical state of organization is implied, which, as a result of "problems in the area of intra-family relationships," subsequently develops into a state of disorganization, then affecting "social functioning of a predominantly instrumental nature." This is not one hypothesis, but a series of them. They are so loosely formulated that some will be verified by almost any kind of data for sheer lack of clearly defined alternative explanations. The original data reflecting a possible interdependence between emotional and instrumental role behavior in families are interesting and relevant to the explanation of the potential causal relationships between disorganization, maladjustment, and deviancy within the family system, but this explanation will not be possible without a great degree of conceptual clarity.

DEVIANT FAMILY BEHAVIOR

The relationship between the concepts of family disorder and deviance is so intricate that some of the essential aspects of deviant family role behavior must be further clarified before a final discussion of the phenomenon of disorganization is warranted. Deviancy has been defined previously as the violation of family role obligations. This definition is sufficient to draw a basic distinction between deviancy and disorganization but is too broad to allow a meaningful study of family behavior. In view of this consideration, a number of additional specifications must be incorporated into the framework formulated in this paper.

In the first place, Lemert's distinction between primary and secondary deviance is pertinent here.[22] He defines primary deviance as the occasional violation of the obligations associated with normal socially accepted roles, while in the secondary type a new and socially deviant role is created. Thus, in the family situation the occasionally philandering husband falls into the category of primary deviance, while roles such as those of the prostitute and the concubine are clearly of a secondary nature. In concrete cases the difference between these two types of deviance is hard to draw. When, for instance, does a perpetually adulterous husband become identified with the role of the philanderer? Lemert is aware of this difficulty and deals with it at some length:

> The deviations remain primary deviations . . . as long as they are rationalized or otherwise dealt with as functions of a socially acceptable role. Under such conditions normal and pathological behaviors remain strange and somewhat tensional bedfellows in the same person. Just how far and for how long a person may go in dissociating his sociopathic tendencies so that they are mere troublesome adjuncts of normally conceived roles is not known. Perhaps it depends upon the number of alternative definitions of the same overt behavior that he can develop. . . . However, if the deviant acts are repetitive and

have a high visibility, and if there is a severe societal reaction, the probability is greatly increased that reorganization based upon a new role or roles will occur.[23]

The above quote raises two relevant issues: (1) the distinction between deviancy and nonconformity and (2) the reaction of others to instances of deviancy.

Some people deviate from role obligations but take pains to avoid detection of their violations. Merton[24] calls this behavior aberrant, in contrast to the type of deviancy in which existing rules are openly challenged and rejected. Merton's notions combined with Lemert's make it appear that nonconformity must by necessity be secondary deviance but that the reverse is not true. It becomes equally clear that much, if not most, of the deviant role performance in families is of the deviant role performance in families is of a primary and aberrant type. Parenthetically, this may well be the reason that sociologists have paid so little attention to this sort of deviant behavior, especially in so-called normal families. Lemert, among others, makes it quite clear that secondary deviancy—that which leads to the formation of deviant roles— is of major interest to the sociologist. Only after it has resulted in divorce or other forms of dissolution does primary family deviancy receive (post facto) attention. Moreover, it is this kind of aberrant and primary deviancy which is most frequently equated with or taken for family disorganization. Nonconformist behavior is as a rule clearly visible and defined by both participants and observers as a separate category. It appears overtly far from "disorganized." The same can be said for secondary deviancy in the family area, while nonconformist and secondary deviant behavior are not mutually exclusive.

In addition to the above considerations, a more precise understanding of the response of other family members to deviance is essential. Both Merton and Lemert stress the importance of visibility as a factor in the final social judgment of deviant acts and the subsequent effect of the latter upon the deviant himself. Unlike many organizations and groups, however, the family can, to a great extent, reduce the visibility of its members' deviance. Cohen stresses the fact that in no system of social control can the response to deviance be left unregulated. "Whose business it is to intervene, at what point, and what he may or may not do is defined by a normatively established division of labor."[25] However, within the family the initial response to role violation by a member is very much left to the others. For example, the situation of a philandering husband depends to a large extent on the response of his wife. She can take him to court, ignore the situation, or even react in kind and thus deviate herself. Cuber's recently published study of upper-middle-class marriages provides a good illustration of the various ways in which families in this class deal with the latter kind of primary deviance.[26]

Finally, unlike disorganization, the deviant performance of family roles cannot be analyzed within the framework of family functioning. In other words, the violation of family role obligations may be an important independent variable in the explanation of impaired family functioning, but the reverse is not necessarily true. A family containing an alcoholic husband may or may not be capable of fulfilling its social functions, but whether it does or does not sheds little light on the question of why the man drinks. In short, deviant role performance in families should be analyzed within the framework of a theory of deviant behavior and social control. One of the major consequences of such an approach will be the necessity to formulate concepts that will by their nature tie in the family with its surrounding social network rather then isolate it in an unrealistic and theoretically sterile corner of its own.

THE NATURE OF FAMILY DISORGANIZATION

The concept of family disorganization now has been defined and analytically separated from closely related notions, especially that of deviancy. It must still be shown that the concept in question will allow one to come to grips with a set of crucial aspects of problematic family behavior. For this purpose, the implications of the preceding definition of disorder in families will be outlined.

First, the concept of family disorganization—unlike deviancy of marital maladjustment—can refer to the disorder of the family institution as well as that occurring in individual family units. The former is a more abstract and analytically relevant usage. The second application cannot be discarded, however, for even in the study of concrete family problems, the concept of disorganization is a meaningful analytical tool. Disorganization on the system level may or may not be associated with its occurrence in individual families. The exact nature of this relationship is a crucial topic for investigation.

In the case of disorganization on the system level, the norms and values that form the structure of a social institution fail to provide a meaningful setting for the actions of its participants. To paraphrase Blumer,[27] such an institution has lost its orientation. The so-called lower-class urban Negro family may serve as an example of this type of disorganization. This does not mean that all families in that category show disorder or deviance, but that the kind of disorder found goes beyond occurrences of an incidental nature. The definition of disorganization on the institutional level does not imply any specific type of causal explanation; it merely allows for analysis. Explanations must, by necessity, be on the societal level and must adapt theoretical propositions of a general nature to the specific conditions of the family system. Turner's attempt to account for social disorganization primarily as a conflict of values[28] would fall into this category, as would an application of Merton's conception of anomie.

It must be added that explanations on a societal level necessarily presume neither a one-way causality nor a "functional interdependence" in which everything is finally related to everything else. As was stressed earlier, disorganization must be analyzed within the general context of organization. It is thus logical to postulate that under certain conditions order in the family system may be a contributing cause to disorder in the surrounding social network or community. Banfield's discussion of the "society of amoral familists" [29]—those limiting morality to their nuclear family—furnishes an interesting example of such a situation.

Disorganized families may be a symptom of disorder of the social institution. In this case the explanation must be sought mainly on the institutional level. Actually it is the well-organized family in a larger disorganized institutional network that requires an explanation. For the sake of clarity, the logical relationship between the two categories is presented in the chart below:

The Family Institution

	Well-Organized	Disorganized
Organized families	I "normal"	II "exceptional"
Disorganized families	III "exceptional"	IV "symptomatic"

The categories II and III are exceptional in that they contain those cases that deviate from the institutional pattern. The categories I and IV are self-explanatory.

Category III requires some additional discussion. Here are families in which the so frequently hypothesized state of organization preceding the onset of disorder occurs at a later stage. It is here also that the category of external disruptive factors, such as death in the family, chronic illness, etc., is most meaningful as one potential source of explanation. Something goes wrong in a family that presumably started out right. However, in many concrete instances the concept of disorganization is not suited to this type of family problem. The notions of marital maladjustment and deviancy will suffice. As was indicated earlier, unhappy families, or those in which one or more members violate their obligations, are not necessarily disorganized. Disorganization may result from deviancy and vice versa, but neither is a necessary condition for the other. In further clarification of what exactly is meant by disorder, two brief illustrations follow:

The study child, a nine year old boy, shows in his interview that he cannot differentiate the ages and role statuses of the family members. In giving the composition of the family, he lists siblings ahead of the mother.[30]

In the majority of the families, while the relationship to the relatives especially to the mother's mother is always important . . . it carries little meaning of shared family goals or recognition and satisfaction of the needs of individual family members. Indeed, in the poorest functioning families, it seems to be only an extension of the mother's and children's clinging together in a dependent fashion. The fact that the study mother clings so dependently to a continuing relationship with her own mother does not mean that she is turning back to a relationship she found helpful or sustaining. In most instances it means she is turning desperately to a relationship she phantasizes much about, but from which in reality she receives little.[31]

Both quotes come from a recently published study of 40 young AFDC families in New York. They reflect disorganized families, a disorganized kinship system, and a disorganized family system as well. To revert to the game analogy once again, one can say that the rules of the game have deteriorated to a poorly understood ritual to which people seem to adhere for sheer lack of any other meaningful alternatives. Unlike many game situations, participation in one's family of orientation is not a voluntary matter. The little boy referred to above is literally participating in a meaningless game. Yet it is a game, because he and his fellow participants have no choice but to define it as such. Under these conditions, one's subsequent decisions about his family of procreation also become a conditioned response to an ongoing process of disorder. The nature of the relationships described in the second quotation clearly illustrate this.

The examples cited above deal with an extreme situation, one that could be called the non-family. It is a setting in which, even if its members try to conform to their role obligations as they perceive them, a state of continuous disorder is the rule. Disorganization which occurs after a preceding state of order and which does not result from observable external factors, may well be difficult to measure. Goode's "empty shell family"[32] may serve as an illustration and can be seen as a middle-class counterpart of the lower-class multi-problem family. In other words, sufficient funds may make it possible in families which have stopped functioning as meaningful entities for members to pursue their instrumental tasks. Good illustrative material can be found in Cuber's earlier-mentioned study.

This leads to a final consideration, that of the measurement and evaluation of the consequences of family disorganization for both the surrounding community and the family members themselves. As shown by the "empty shell family," the nature of these consequences will depend very much on the external conditions which characterize the families or system under survey. Conclusions which do not incorporate such external conditions will be theoretically meaningless.

CONCLUSION

This paper has presented a conceptual treatment only. No hypotheses or other statements of a theoretical nature about family disorganization have been formulated except those occasionally used for illustrative and heuristic purposes. In the formulation of the concept of family disorganization, a systematic analytical distinction was made between the violation of family role obligations and a state of disorder in the family's structure. The validity of the presented conceptualization can be judged on the basis of the arguments set forth in this paper. Its empirical fruitfulness, however, will have to be decided upon the basis of research in the field.

NOTES

* Revision of a paper read at the April, 1966, meetings of the Ohio Valley Sociological Society.

[1] Ernest R. Mowrer, *Family Disorganization*, Chicago, Illinois: University of Chicago Press, 1927, p. 131.

[2] Mabel A. Elliot and Francis E. Merrill, *Social Disorganization*, New York: Harper and Brothers, fourth ed., 1961, p. 339.

[3] Robert E. L. Faris, *Social Disorganization*, New York: Ronald Press, second ed., 1955, pp. 383–435.

[4] Clifford Kirkpatrick, *The Family*, New York: Ronald Press, second ed., 1963, pp. 563–568.

[5] Robert F. Winch, *The Modern Family*, New York: Holt, Rinehart and Winston, Inc., rev. ed., 1963, p. 742.

[6] William J. Goode, "Family Disorganization," in *Contemporary Social Problems*, ed. by Robert K. Merton and Robert A. Nisbet, New York: Harcourt Brace, 1961, p. 390.

[7] Don Martindale, "Social Disorganization: The Conflict of Normative and Empirical Approaches," in *Modern Sociological Theory*, ed. by Howard Becker and Alvin Boskoff, New York: Dryden Press, 1957, p. 341.

[8] Richard S. Rudner, *Philosophy of Social Science*, Englewood Cliffs, New Jersey: Prentice-Hall, Inc., 1966, pp. 31–32.

[9] Albert K. Cohen, "The Study of Social Disorganization and Deviant Behavior," in *Sociology Today*, ed. by Robert K. Merton, Leonard Broom, and Leonard S. Cottrell, Jr., New York: Basic Books, 1959, pp. 461–484; Robert K. Merton, "Social Problems and Sociological Theory," in Merton and Nisbet, eds., *op. cit.*, pp. 718–735.

[10] From Harold Garfinkel, "Trust as a Condition of Stable Concerted Action,"

paper read at the annual meetings of the American Sociological Society, 1957, as quoted by Cohen, *op. cit.*

[11] Cohen, *op. cit.,* p. 476.

[12] Merton, *op. cit.,* p. 720.

[13] *Ibid.,* p. 718.

[14] Cohen, *op. cit.,* p. 480.

[15] Merton, *op. cit.,* p. 723.

[16] Albert K. Cohen, "The Sociology of the Deviant Act: Anomie Theory and Beyond," *American Sociological Review,* 30:1 (February, 1965), p. 12; Merton, *op. cit.,* p. 725.

[17] Merton, *op. cit.,* p. 720.

[18] For the source of this definition see Ira L. Reiss, "The Universality of the Family: A Conceptual Analysis," *Journal of Marriage and the Family,* 27:4 (November, 1965), p. 449.

[19] William J. Goode, *The Family,* Englewood Cliffs, New Jersey: Prentice-Hall, 1964, p. 21.

[20] James G. March and Herbert A. Simon, *Organizations,* Pittsburgh: Carnegie Press, 1958, p. 2.

[21] L. L. Geismar, Michael A. LaSorte, and Beverly Ayres, "Measuring Family Disorganization," *Marriage and Family Living,* 24:1 (February, 1962), p. 56.

[22] Edwin M. Lemert, *Social Pathology,* New York: McGraw-Hill, 1951, pp. 75–76.

[23] *Ibid.,* p. 75.

[24] Merton, *op. cit.,* p. 275.

[25] Cohen, "The Sociology of the Deviant Act: Anomie Theory and Beyond," *op. cit.,* p. 9.

[26] John F. Cuber, *The Significant Americans,* New York: Appleton, Century, Crofts, 1966.

[27] Herbert Blumer, "Social Disorganization and Individual Disorganization," in *Mass Society in Crisis,* ed. by Bernard Rosenberg, Israel Gerver, and F. William Howton, New York: Macmillan Co., 1964, p. 60.

[28] Ralph H. Turner, "Value-Conflict in Social Disorganization," *Sociology and Social Research,* 38 (1954), pp. 301–308.

[29] Edward C. Banfield, *The Moral Basis of a Backward Society,* Glencoe, Illinois: Free Press, 1964, Chapter V.

[30] Alice R. McCabe, *Forty Forgotten Families,* New York: Community Service Society of New York, August, 1965, p. 82.

[31] *Ibid.,* p. 60.

[32] Goode, "Family Disorganization," *op. cit.,* p. 391.

Alcoholism and the Family

JOAN K. JACKSON

Until recently it was possible to think of alcoholism as if it involved the alcoholic only. Most of the alcoholics studied were inmates of publicly supported institutions: jails, mental hospitals, and public general hospitals. These ill people appeared to be homeless and tieless. As the public became more aware of the extent and nature of alcoholism and that treatment possibilities existed, alcoholics who were still integral parts of the community appeared at clinics. The definition of "the problems of alcoholism" has had to be broadened to include all those with whom the alcoholic is or has been in close and continuing contact.

At present we do not know how many nonalcoholics are affected directly by alcoholism. However, an estimate can be derived from the available statistics on the marital histories of alcoholics. The recurrently arrested alcoholic seems to affect the fewest nonalcoholics. Reports range from 19 per cent to 51 per cent who have never married [1]—that is, from slightly more than the expected number of single men to three to four times the expected rate. The vast majority who had married are now separated from their families. Alcoholics who voluntarily seek treatment at clinics affect the lives of more people than jailed alcoholics. While the number of broken marriages is still excessive, approximately the expected number of voluntary patients have been married.[2] Any estimate of nonalcoholics affected must take into consideration not only the present marital status of alcoholics, but also the past marital history. About one-third of the alcoholics have been married more than once. Jailed alcoholics had multiple marriages less frequently than clinic alcoholics.

There has been no enumeration of the children and other relatives influenced by alcoholism. From the author's studies it can be estimated that for each alcoholic there are at least two people in the immediate family who are affected. Approximately two-thirds of the married alcoholics have children, thus averaging two apiece. Family studies indicate that a minimum of one other relative is also directly involved. The importance of understanding the problems faced by the families of alcoholics is obvious from these figures. To date, little is known about the nature of the effects of living with or having lived with an

Reprinted from the *Annals of the American Academy of Political and Social Science*, 1958, with permission of the Academy.

alcoholic. However, there is considerable evidence that it has disturbing effects on the personalities of family members.

Once attention had been focussed on the families of alcoholics, it became obvious that the relationship between the alcoholic and his family is not a one-way relationship. The family also affects the alcoholic and his illness. The very existence of family ties appears to be related to recovery from alcoholism. Some families are successful in helping their alcoholic member to recognize his need for help and are supportive of treatment efforts. Yet other types of families may discourage the patient from seeking treatment and may actually encourage the persistence of alcoholism. It is now believed that the most successful treatment of alcoholism involves helping both the alcoholic and those members of his family who are directly involved in his drinking behavior.[3]

THE ALCOHOLIC AND HIS CHILDREN

The children are affected by living with an alcoholic more than any other family member. Personalities are formed in a social milieu which is markedly unstable, torn with dissension, culturally deviant, and socially disapproved. The children must model themselves on adults who play their roles in a distorted fashion. The alcoholic shows little adequate adult behavior. The nonalcoholic parent attempts to play the roles of both father and mother, often failing to do either well.

The child of an alcoholic is bound to have problems in learning who he is, what is expected of him, and what he can expect from others. Almost inevitably his parents behave inconsistently towards him. His self-conception evolves in a situation in which the way others act towards him has more to do with the current events in the family than with the child's nature. His alcoholic parent feels one way about him when he is sober, another when drunk, and yet another during the hangover stage.

What the child can expect from his parents will also depend on the phase of the drinking cycle as well as on where he stands in relation to each parent at any given time. Only two frequently he is used in the battle between them. The wives of alcoholics find themselves disliking, punishing, or depriving the children preferred by the father and those who resemble him. Similarly, the child who is preferred by, or resembles the mother is often hurt by the father. If the child tries to stay close to both parents he is caught in an impossible situation. Each parent resents the affection the other receives while demanding that the child show affection to both.

The children do not understand what is happening. The very young ones do not know that their families are different from other families. When they become aware of the differences, the children are torn between their own loyalty and the views of their parents that others hold. When neighbors ostracize them, the children are bewildered about what *they* did to bring about this result. Even those who are not ostracized become isolated. They hesitate to bring their friends to a home where their parent is likely to be drunk.

The behavior of the alcoholic parent is unpredictable and unintelligible to the child. The tendency of the child to look for the reasons in his own behavior very often is reinforced inadvertently by his mother. When father is leading up to a drinking episode, the children are put on their best behavior. When the drinking episode occurs, it is not surprising that the children feel that they have somehow done something to precipitate it.

Newell [4] states that the children of alcoholics are placed in a situation very similar to that of the experimental animals who are tempted towards rewards and that continually frustrated, whose environment changes constantly in a manner over which they have no control. Under such circumstances experimental animals have convulsions or "nervous breakdowns." Unfortunately, we still know very little about what happens to the children or about the duration of the effects.

Yet some of the children appear undisturbed. The personality damage appears to be least when the nonalcoholic parent is aware of the problems they face, gives them emotional support, keeps from using them against the alcoholic, tries to be consistent, and has insight into her own problems with the alcoholic. It also appears to mitigate some of the child's confusion if alcoholism is explained to him by a parent who accepts alcoholism as an illness.

THE ALCOHOLIC AND HIS WIFE

The wives of alcoholics have received considerably more attention than the children. The focus tends to be on how they affect the alcoholic and his alcoholism, rather than on how alcoholism and the alcoholic affect them. Most writers seem to feel that the wives of alcoholics are drawn from the ranks of emotionally disturbed women who seek out spouses who are not threatening to them, spouses who can be manipulated to meet their own personality needs. According to this theory, the wife has a vested interest in the persistence of the alcoholism of her spouse. Her own emotional stability depends upon it. Should the husband become sober, the wives are in danger of decompensating and showing marked neurotic disturbances.[5]

A complementary theory suggests that prealcoholic or alcoholic males tend to select certain types of women as wives. The most commonly reported type is a dominating, maternal woman who uses her maternal role as a defense against inadequate femininity.

Any attempt to assess the general applicability of this theory to *all* the wives of alcoholics runs into difficulties. First, the only wives who can be studied by researchers are those who have stayed with their husbands until alcoholism was well under way. The high divorce rate among alcoholics suggests that these wives are the exception rather than the rule. The majority of women who find themselves married to alcoholics appear to divorce them. Second, if a high rate of emotional disturbance is found among women still living with alcoholics, it is difficult to determine whether the personality difficulties antedated or postdated the alcoholism, whether they were partly causal or whether they emerged during the recurrent crises and the cumulative stresses of living with an alcoholic. Third, the wives who were studied were women who were actively blocking the treatment of their husbands, who had entered mental hospitals after their husbands' sobriety, who were themselves seeking psychiatric care, or who were in the process of manipulating social agencies to provide services. It is of interest that neither of the studies which deal with women who were taking an active part in their husbands' recovery process comment upon any similarities in the personality structures of the wives.[6]

It is likely that the final test of the hypotheses about the role of the wives' personalities in their husbands' alcoholism will have to await the accumulation of considerably more information. No alcoholic personality type has been found on psychological tests; no tests have been given to the wives of alcoholics. Until we know more about the etiology of alcoholism and its remedy, the role of the wives' personalities in its onset, in its persistence, and in its alleviation will remain in the realm of speculation.

No one denies that the wives of active alcoholics are emotionally disturbed. In nonthreatening situations, the wives are the first to admit their own concerns about "their sanity." Of over one hundred women who attended a discussion group at one time or another during the past six years, there was not one who failed to talk about her concerns about her own emotional health. All of the women worry about the part which their attitudes and behavior play in the persistence of the drinking and in their families' disturbances. Although no uniform personality types are discernible, they do share feelings of confusion and anxiety. Most feel ambivalent about their husbands. However, this group is composed of women who are oriented towards changing themselves and the situation rather than escaping from it.

THE IMPACT OF ALCOHOLISM ON THE FAMILY

When two or more persons live together over a period of time, patterns of relating to one another evolve. In a family, a division of functions occurs and roles interlock. For the family to function smoothly, each person must play his roles in a predictable manner and according to the expectations of others in the family. When the family as a whole is functioning smoothly, individual members of the family also tend to function well. Everyone is aware of where he fits, what he is expected to do, and what he can expect from others in the family. When this organization is disrupted, repercussions are felt by each family member. A crisis is under way.

Family crises tend to follow a similar pattern, regardless of the nature of the precipitant. Usually there is an initial denial that a problem exists. The family tries to continue in its usual behavior patterns until it is obvious that these patterns are no longer effective. At this point there is a downward slump in organization. Roles are played with less enthusiasm and there is an increase in tensions and strained relationships. Finally an improvement occurs as some adjustive technique is successful. Family organization becomes stabilized at a new level. At each stage of the crisis there is a reshuffling of roles among family members, changes in status and prestige, changes in "self" and "other" images, shifts in family solidarity and self-sufficiency and in the visibility of the crisis to outsiders. In the process of the crisis, considerable mental conflict is engendered in all family members, and personality distortion occurs.[7] These are the elements which are uniform regardless of the type of family crisis. The phases vary in length and intensity depending on the nature of the crisis and the nature of the individuals involved in it.

When one of the adults in a family becomes an alcoholic, the overall pattern of the crisis takes a form similar to that of other family crises. However there are usually recurrent subsidiary crises which complicate the over-all situation and the attempts at its resolution. Shame, unemployment, impoverishment, desertion and return, nonsupport, infidelity, imprisonment, illness and progressive dissension also occur. For other types of family crises, there are cultural prescriptions for socially appropriate behavior and for procedures which will terminate the crisis. But this is not so in the case of alcoholism. The cultural view is that alcoholism is shameful and should not occur. Thus, when facing alcoholism, the family is in a socially unstructured situation and must find the techniques for handling the crisis through trial and error behavior and without social support. In many respects, there are marked similarities between the type of crisis precipitated by alcoholism and those precipitated by mental illness.

ATTEMPTS TO DENY THE PROBLEM

Alcoholism rarely emerges full-blown overnight. It is usually heralded by widely spaced incidents of excessive drinking, each of which sets off a small family crisis. Both spouses try to account for the episode and then to avoid the family situations which appear to have caused the drinking. In their search for explanations, they try to define the situation as controllable, understandable, and "perfectly normal." Between drinking episodes, both feel guilty about their behavior and about their impact on each other. Each tries to be an "ideal spouse" to the other. Gradually not only the drinking problem, but also the other problems in the marriage are denied or sidestepped.

It takes some time before the wife realizes that the drinking is neither normal nor controllable behavior. It takes the alcoholic considerably longer to come to the same conclusion. The cultural view that alcoholics are Skid Row bums who are constantly inebriated also serves to keep the situation clouded. Friends compound the confusion. If the wife compares her husband with them, some show parallels to his behavior and others are in marked contrast. She wavers between defining his behavior as "normal" and "not normal." If she consults friends, they tend to discount her concern, thus facilitating her tendency to deny that a problem exists and adding to her guilt about thinking disloyal thoughts about her husband.

During this stage the family is very concerned about the social visibility of the drinking behavior. They feel that they would surely be ostracized if the extent of the drinking were known. To protect themselves against discovery, the family begins to cut down on their social activities and to withdraw into the home.

ATTEMPTS TO ELIMINATE THE PROBLEM

The second stage begins when the family defines the alcoholic's drinking behavior as "not normal." At this point frantic efforts are made to eliminate the problem. Lacking clear-cut cultural prescriptions for what to do in a situation like this, the efforts are of the trial and error variety. In rapid succession, the wife threatens to leave the husband, babies him during hangovers, drinks with him, hides or empties his bottles, curtails money, tries to understand his problem, keeps his liquor handy for him, and nags at him. However, all efforts to change the situation fail. Gradually the family becomes so preoccupied with the problem of discovering how to keep father sober that all long-term family goals recede into the background.

At the same time isolation of the family reaches its peak intensity. The extreme isolation magnifies the importance of all intrafamily interactions and events. Almost all thought becomes drinking-centered. Drinking comes to symbolize all conflicts between the spouses, and even mother-child conflicts are regarded as indirect derivatives of the drinking behavior. Attempts to keep the social visibility of the behavior at the lowest possible level increase.

The husband-wife alienation also accelerates. Each feels resentful of the other. Each feels misunderstood and unable to understand. Both search frantically for the reasons for the drinking, believing that if the reason could be discovered, all family members could gear their behavior in a way to make the drinking unnecessary.

The wife feels increasingly inadequate as a wife, mother, woman, and person. She feels she has failed to make a happy and united home for her husband and children. Her husband's frequent comments to the effect that her behavior causes his drinking and her own concerns that this may be true intensify the process of self-devaluation.

DISORGANIZATION

This is a stage which could also be entitled "What's the use?" Nothing seems effective in stabilizing the alcoholic. Efforts to change the situation become, at best, sporadic. Behavior is geared to relieve tensions rather than to achieve goals. The family gives up trying to understand the alcoholic. They do not care if the neighbors know about the drinking. The children are told that their father is a drunk. They are no longer required to show him affection or respect. The myth that father still has an important status in the family is dropped when he no longer supports them, is imprisoned, caught in infidelity, or disappears for long periods of time. The family ceases to care about its self-sufficiency and begins to resort to public agencies for help, thereby losing self-respect.

The wife becomes very concerned about her sanity. She finds herself engaging in tension-relieving behavior which she knows is goalless. She is aware that she feels tense, anxious, and hostile. She regards her precrisis self as "the real me" and becomes very frightened at how she has changed.

ATTEMPTS TO REORGANIZE IN SPITE OF THE PROBLEM

When some major or minor subsidiary crisis occurs, the family is forced to take survival action. At this point many wives leave their husbands.

The major characteristic of this stage is that the wife takes over. The alcoholic is ignored or is assigned the status of the most recalcitrant child. When the wife's obligations to her husband conflict with those to her children, she decides in favor of the children. Family ranks are closed progressively and the father excluded.

As a result of the changed family organization, father's behavior constitutes less of a problem. Hostility towards him diminishes as the family no longer expects him to change. Feelings of pity, exasperation. and protectiveness arise.

The reorganization has a stabilizing effect on the children. They find their environment and their mother more consistent. Their relationship to their father is more clearly defined. Guilt and anxiety diminish as they come to accept their mother's view that drinking is not caused by any behavior of family members.

Long-term family goals and planning begin again. Help from public agencies is accepted as necessary and no longer impairs family self-respect. With the taking over of family control, the wife gradually regains her sense of worth. Her concerns about her emotional health decrease.

Despite the greater stabilization, subsidiary crises multiply. The alcoholic is violent or withdraws more often; income becomes more uncertain; imprisonments and hospitalizations occur more frequently. Each crisis is temporarily disruptive to the new family organization. The symbolization of these events as being caused by alcoholism, however, prevents the complete disruption of the family.

The most disruptive type of crisis occurs if the husband recognizes that he has a drinking problem and makes an effort to get help. Hope is mobilized. The family attempts to open its ranks again in order to give him the maximum chance for recovery. Roles are partially reshuffled and attempts at attitude change are made, only to be disrupted again if treatment is unsuccessful.

EFFORTS TO ESCAPE THE PROBLEM

The problems involved in separating from the alcoholic are similar to the problems involved in separation for any other reason. However, some of the problems are more intense. The wife, who could count on some support from her husband in earlier stages, even though it was a manipulative move on his part, can no longer be sure of any support. The mental conflict about deserting a sick man must be resolved as well as the wife's feelings of responsibility for his alcoholism. The family which has experienced violence from the alcoholic is concerned that separation may intensify the violence. When the decision is made to separate because of the drinking, the alcoholic often gives up drinking for a while, thereby removing what is apparently the major reason for the separation.

Some other events, however, have made separation possible. The wife has learned that the family can run smoothly without her husband. Taking over control has bolstered her self-confidence. Her orientation has shifted from inaction to action. The wife also has familiarity with public agencies which can provide help, and she has overcome her shame about using them.

REORGANIZATION OF THE FAMILY

Without the father, the family tends to reorganize rather smoothly. They have already closed ranks against him and now they feel free of the minor disruptions he still created in the family. Reorganizations is impeded if the alcoholic continues to attempt reconciliation or feels he must "get even" with the family for deserting him.

The whole family becomes united when the husband achieves sobriety, whether or not separation has preceded. For the wife and husband facing a sober marriage after many years of an alcoholic marriage, the expectations for marriage without alcoholism are unrealistic and idealistic.

Many problems arise. The wife has managed the family for years. Now her husband wishes to be reinstated as head of the house. Usually the first role he re-establishes is that of breadwinner. With the resumption of this role, he feels that the family should reinstate him immediately in all his former roles. Difficulties inevitably follow. For example, the children are often unable to accept his resumption of the father role. Their mother has been mother and father to them for so long that it takes time to get used to consulting their father. Often the father tries to manage this change overnight, and the very pressure he puts on the children towards this end defeats him.

The wife, who finds it difficult to believe that her husband is sober permanently, is often unwilling to relinquish her control of family affairs even though she knows that this is necessary to her husband's sobriety. She remembers when his failures to handle responsibility were catastrophic to the family. Used to avoiding any issues which might upset him, the wife often has difficulty discussing problems openly. If she permits him to resume his father role, she often feels resentful of his intrusion into territory she has come to regard as her own. If he makes any decisions which are detrimental to the family, her former feelings of superiority may be mobilized and affect her relationship with him.

Gradually the difficulties related to alcoholism recede into the past and family adjustment at some level is achieved. The drinking problem shows up only sporadically—when the time comes for a decision about permitting the children to drink or when pressure is put on the husband to drink at a party.

PERSONALITY DISTURBANCES IN FAMILY MEMBERS

Each stage in the crisis of alcoholism has distinctive characteristics. The types of problems faced, the extent to which the situation is structured, the amount of emotional support received by individual family members, and the rewards vary as to the stage of the crisis. Some stages "fit" the personalities of the individuals involved better than others.

Although each stage of the crisis appears to give rise to some similar patterns of response, there is considerable variation from family to family. The wife whose original personality fits comfortably into denying the existence of the problem will probably take longer to get past this phase of the crisis than the wife who finds dominating more congenial. The latter will probably prolong the stage of attempting to eliminate the problem. Some families make an adjustment at one level of the crisis and never seem to go on to the next phase.

With the transition from one stage to another, there is the danger of marked personality disturbance in family members. Some become their most disturbed when drinking first becomes a problem; others become most disturbed when the alcoholic becomes sober. In the experience of the author, there has been little uniformity within families or between families in this respect. However, after two or three years of sobriety, the alcoholics' family members appear to resemble a cross section of people anywhere. Any uniformities which were obvious earlier seem to have disappeared.

THERAPY AND THE FAMILY

The major goal of the families of most alcoholics is to find some way of bringing about a change in father's drinking. When the alcoholic seeks treatment, the family members usually have very mixed feelings towards the treatment agency. Hope that father may recover is remobilized and if sobriety ensues for any length of time, they are grateful. At the same time, they often feel resentment that an outside agency can accomplish what they have tried to do for years. They may also resent the emotional support which the alcoholic receives from the treatment agency, while they are left to cope with still another change in their relationship to him without support.

Most families have little awareness of what treatment involves and are forced to rely on the alcoholic patient for their information. The patient frequently passes on a distorted picture in order to manipulate the family situation for his own ends. What information is given is perceived by the family against a background of their attitudes towards the alcoholic at that point in time. The actions they take are also influenced by their estimate of the probability that treatment will be successful. The result is often a family which works at cross purposes with therapy.

Recently there has been a growing recognition that the family of the alcoholic also requires help if the alcoholic is to be treated successfully. An experiment was tried at the Henry Phipps Psychiatric Clinic of Johns Hopkins Hospital. Alcoholics and their wives were treated in concurrent group therapy sessions. The Al-Anon Family Groups provide the same type of situation for the families of AA members and have the additional asset of helping the families of alcoholics who are still not interested in receiving help for themselves. Joint treatment of alcoholics and the members of their family aims at getting a better understanding of the underlying emotional disturbance, of the relationship between the alcoholic and the person who is most frequently the object and stimulus of the drinking behavior, and of the treatment process.[8]

Joint treatment of the alcoholic and his family has other assets, as Gliedman and his co-workers point out.[9] Joint therapy emphasizes the marriage. In addition, with both spouses coming for help, there is less likelihood that undertaking treatment will be construed as an admission of guilt or that therapy will be used as a weapon by one against the other. The wife's entrance into therapy is a tacit admission of her need to change too. It represents a hopeful attitude on the part of both the alcoholic and his wife that recovery is possible and creates an orientation towards working things out together as a family unit.

The members of an Al-Anon group with which the author is familiar receive understanding of their problems and their feelings from one another, emotional support which facilitates change in attitudes and behavior, basic information about solutions to common problems, and information about the treatment process and about the nature of alcoholism as an illness. Shame is alleviated and hope engendered. The nonalcoholic spouses gain perspective on what has happened to their families and on the possibilities of changing towards greater stability. Anxiety diminishes in an almost visible fashion. As they gain perspective on the situation, behavior tends to become more realistic and rewarding. By no means the least important effect derived from membership in the group is a structuring of what has seemed to be a completely unstructured situation and the feelings of security which this engenders.

NOTES

[1] J. K. Jackson, "The Problem of the Alcoholic Tuberculous Patient," in P. J. Sparer (Ed.), *Personality, Stress and Tuberculosis* (New York: International Universities Press, 1956), pp. 504–38; R. Straus and S. D. Bacon, "Alcoholism and Social Stability: A Study of Occupational Integration in 2,023 Male Clinic Patients," *Quarterly Journal of Studies on Alcohol*, Vol. 12, June 1951, pp. 231–60.

[2] *Ibid.*; E. P. Walcott and R. Straus, "Use of a Hospital Facility in Conjunction with Outpatient Treatment of Alcoholics," *Quarterly Journal of Studies on Alcohol*, Vol. 13, March 1952, pp. 60–77; F. E. Feeny, D. F. Mindlen, V. H. Minear, E. E. Short, "The Challenge of the Skid Row Alcoholic: A Social, Psychological and Psychiatric Comparison of Chronically Jailed Alcoholics and Cooperative Clinic Patients," *Quarterly Journal of Studies on Alcohol*, Vol. 16, December 1955, pp. 645–67.

[3] D. J. Myerson, "An Active Therapeutic Method of Interrupting the Dependency Relationship of Certain Male Alcoholics," *Quarterly Journal of Studies on Alcohol,* Vol. 14, September 1953, pp. 419–26; L. H. Gliedman, D. Rosenthal, J. Frank, H. T. Nash, "Group Therapy of Alcoholics with Concurrent Group Meetings of Their Wives," *Quarterly Journal of Studies on Alcohol,* Vol. 17, December 1956, pp. 655–70.

[4] N. Newell, "Alcoholism and the Father Image," *Quarterly Journal of Studies on Alcohol,* Vol. 11, March 1950, pp. 92–96.

[5] D. E. MacDonald, "Mental Disorders in Wives of Alcoholics," *Quarterly Journal of Studies on Alcohol,* Vol. 17, June 1956, pp. 282–87; M. Wellman, "Toward an Etiology of Alcoholism: Why Young Men Drink Too Much," *Canadian Medical Association Journal,* Vol. 73, November 1, 1955, pp. 717–25; S. Futterman, "Personality Trends in Wives of Alcoholics," *Journal of Psychiatric Social Work,* Vol. 23, 1953, pp. 37–41.

[6] J. K. Jackson, "The Adjustment of the Family to the Crisis of Alcoholism," *Quarterly Journal of Studies on Alcohol,* Vol. 15, December 1954, pp. 562–86; Gliedman, Rosenthal, Frank, Nash, *op. cit.* (note 3 *supra*).

[7] W. Waller (Revised by Reuben Hill), *The Family: A Dynamic Interpretation* (New York: Dryden Press, 1951), pp. 453–61.

[8] Gliedman, Rosenthal, Frank, and Nash, *op. cit.* (note 3 *supra*).

[9] *Ibid.*

The Passive Fifties and Swinging Sixties

DORIS J. FREED and HENRY H. FOSTER, JR.

The basic ground rules regarding migratory divorce and interstate recognition were set by the *Williams* cases and *Sherrer v. Sherrer*. When both parties wanted a divorce and submitted to jurisdiction by appearing in person, or in the case of the defendant, through counsel, even if, in fact, the proceedings were uncontested, their divorce decree was relatively immune from attack. They could lift themselves by their bootstraps. In addition, one party, by actually moving to another state, might procure a divorce which was entitled to recognition everywhere. Finally, regardless of the legal rules, most invalid divorce decrees were never challenged, frequently because the defendant did not care to bother about it or received a financial settlement.[1]

Not all states were willing to accept the full faith and credit mandate of the Supreme Court. Beginning in 1948, a law was passed in some ten states authorizing nonrecognition of divorce decrees where domiciliary jurisdiction was lacking, but state courts construed such statutes so as to conform with the Supreme Court decisions.[2] Moreover, most states, despite occasional grumblings, gave effect to the letter and the spirit of the federal law.

The social change which had produced federal intervention and control of interstate divorce also affected the local administration of divorce laws. Since over 90 percent of American divorce cases were uncontested, the vast majority of them were routine, and proof was according to formula. In effect, the crucial issues, including alimony and custody matters, were settled by law-office negotiation, and were not litigated. Tragically, the contested case, more often than not, involved a spouse who was recalcitrant, spiteful, or too greedy, rather than one who was fighting to save a marriage. It became increasingly obvious that the fraud, hypocrisy, and intolerance that had characterized our divorce law for more than a century had now grown to such dimensions that it threatened to undermine public confidence in the administration of justice. Earlier generations, because of their moral fervor, had refused to recognize the facts, but in the 1950's church leaders, as well as lawyers and sociologists, began to acknowledge the realities of the divorce dilemma and to demand reform.

Reprinted from "Divorce, American Style," in the *Annals of the Academy of Political and Social Sciences*, May 1969, with permission of the Academy. Footnotes have been renumbered.

The general public during this period was constantly reminded about the high divorce rate in America, and as concern about family stability became widespread, reformers first turned towards counseling as an answer to the problem. Judge Paul W. Alexander in Toledo and Judge Louis Burke in Los Angeles presided over two types of family courts which offered counseling services in the court setting. The Toledo court became a social agency of which the court was a part, and all divorce petitioners with children under fourteen were forced to consult with court counselors. Los Angeles, on the other hand, assumed jurisdiction in its Conciliation Court only upon the petition of one or both parties, and its technique was to promote entry into a husband-wife agreement which set the ground rules for the marriage. The Toledo court provided long-term counseling and therapy; the Los Angeles service referred to outside agencies those couples needing professional help. Both courts claimed substantial success and a high reconciliation rate, and that their reconciliations endured. The Los Angeles court received a great deal of publicity, and its procedures were adopted in several western cities and states.[3]

Perhaps the most extreme example of the family court emerged in Wisconsin, where all parties to divorce must appear before a judge or counselor in order at least to explore the possibility of reconciliation. In addition, guardians may be appointed to represent the interests of children of the divorcing parties, and the court has authority to grant only a legal separation even when an absolute divorce is requested and grounds are established.[4] In theory, the New York Divorce Reform Law of 1966 adopted the Wisconsin system, but, in practice, conciliation procedures are not imposed upon unwilling couples.

The idea of a family court with comprehensive jurisdiction over all legal matters pertaining to the family makes sense and has a wide appeal.[5] The difficulty lies in its implementation within an archaic and patronage-ridden court system. Moreover, it may be difficult to get competent personnel to man the staffs of such courts, and to get the plant and resources that are needed for effective operation. It is the familiar problem of public parsimony, which has been so tragic with reference to our juvenile courts in most states. Without adequate resources and personnel, a socialized court tends to become a monster, providing bad services and making poor law. Only an exceptional judge can command or commandeer the needed resources for effective social and legal work, and usually he will be at the mercy of budget-cutters and philosophical opponents in the legislative or executive branches of government. Such are the facts of political life, even if it is logical and correct to insist that family problems and problem families cannot be helped on a piecemeal basis and that there must be a comprehensive and integrated jurisdiction lodged in one court.

In addition to conciliation and counseling in the court setting, there was an expansion of community counseling services during the period in question. Marriage counseling and social work both came to be recognized as professions. Family-service agencies were created by public, religious, and private groups. Pastoral counseling was undertaken by many churches. Divorce lawyers became more perceptive in regard to the emotional difficulties of clients, and frequently they referred clients to psychiatrists or marriage counselors before initiating or settling matrimonial disputes.[6] Ethical lawyers assumed that their professional responsibility required them to inquire into the possibility of reconciliation if there was a chance to save the marriage and it would not be dangerous or ill-advised to do so. The cynics of the legal profession, however, continued to process divorce cases without regard to the real needs or desires of their clients.

It will be noted that cruelty is the ground alleged in at least 70 percent of American divorce cases. Adultery is the alleged ground in less than 3 percent, and after cruelty, desertion is the most common ground. Before the Civil War, cruelty was a ground in only 12.9 percent of divorce cases, but at the turn of the century it had risen to 21.8 percent, in 1932 it accounted for 42.7 percent, and in 1949, it had reached 66.9 percent.[7] In the 46 states having cruelty as a ground, only South Carolina requires a finding of actual personal violence. Twenty-six states will grant a divorce upon the purely subjective evidence of mental distress, have "mental suffering" as a part of their cruelty statute, or comparable grounds such as "indignities" or "incompatibility." The remaining eighteen states require the injured party to show, by objective means or medical evidence, that cruel treatment impaired the health of the plaintiff, or, if allowed to continue, could have such an effect.[8]

Although it is obvious that, in most states, cruelty as a divorce ground has been expanded by judicial interpretation to include the more common types of family warfare, there still is some social stigma attached to the finding, especially where the phrase is "cruel and inhuman treatment." Alaska, Nevada (since 1967), New Mexico, Oklahoma, the Virgin Islands, and, most important, the state of Chihuahua (Juarez), Mexico, avoid the stigma by making incompatibility a ground for divorce.

Social scientists have repeatedly pointed out that there is little, if any, relation between statutory grounds for divorce and the causes of marriage breakdown. Most often advanced as reasons for marital failure are such factors as emotional immaturity, the romantic concept of marriage, personality differences, irresponsibility, mother-in-law trouble, drunkenness, social mobility, urban anonymity, the decline of religious influences, industrialization, financial difficulties, and a whole host of other contributing factors. In short, all of the stresses, strains, traumas, and circumstances of urban living combine to affect the quality of family life and emotional health. There are a multitude of factors which are a threat to marriage stability, and, as distinguished from past generations, modern man is committed to the proposition that he has a moral right to pursue marital happiness. In most states, the principles and rules relative to divorce have been adjusted so as to convert that moral right into a legal right. Considering all the circumstances, the amazing thing is that most marriages endure and are reasonably happy. The modern marriage, when successful, is an almost unprecedented relationship, for it must be remembered that the romantic concept of marriage is peculiar to our times, insofar as the mass of people are concerned, and that the independence of the modern woman is unparalleled in history.

Current efforts to reform our divorce laws, in addition to the family-court movement previously discussed, take the form of recommending either the abolition of all grounds and substituting a finding of irreparable breakdown of the marriage, or the addition of non-fault-grounds to existing fault-grounds for divorce. The first approach was endorsed by the report of the Governor's Commission of California in 1966, and was considered, but rejected, in England and Canada. The addition of non-fault-grounds was New York's expedient decision or compromise in its Divorce Reform Law in 1966.

Substitution of marital breakdown for the fault issue has logic and a great deal of sociological data on its side, but there are practical and political difficulties which inhibit the selection of that alternative. The notion that a cuckolded husband or wife is entitled to divorce as a matter of right is strongly entrenched in both popular and judicial attitudes.[9] That feeling is not diminished by sophisticated arguments that adultery is a symptom of family breakdown rather than a cause of it. Much the same emotional reaction is engendered by desertion or by cruel and inhuman treatment which exceeds the bounds of ordinary family warfare. Even if judges and lawyers are convinced, for the most part, that marital fault is a difficult, if not impossible, thing to assess, legislators are most apt to be committed to the fault-concept. In other words, the breakdown theory is a radical departure from prior law, and is not likely to appeal to most state legislatures.

Addition of non-fault-grounds, however, is a more acceptable method of achieving substantial divorce reform. Kentucky in 1850, Wisconsin in 1866, Rhode Island in 1893, and eventually a total of some 28 states, adopted some form of separation or living apart as a non-fault-ground for divorce.[10] Most countries in Europe provide that separation, usually for two or more years, is a ground for divorce, and the same is true in Australia and New Zealand. The usual objective of such provisions is to grant legal authority to terminate dead marriages, whatever the causes of the demise, and the fact of living apart due to marital difficulties is deemed to be objective proof that the marriage is defunct. The various statutes differ as to details, including the stipulated length of separation, which is one year in the District of Columbia but ten years in Rhode Island. A substantial number of states (Alabama, Arizona, Idaho, Kentucky, Louisiana, Nevada, North Carolina, Rhode

Island, Texas, Virginia, Washington, and Puerto Rico) make separation a ground for divorce, regardless of who was to blame for the original separation. Delaware, the District of Columbia, Maryland, and Wisconsin, however, require that the separation be consensual, and Vermont, that the noncohabitation must have been without the fault of the plaintiff. Wyoming has a similar limitation. The Divorce Reform Law of New York is unique in that it requires that the two or more years of separation must be pursuant to a separation agreement or court decree.

There are some thirteen jurisdictions where judicial separation may be converted into absolute divorce after a stipulated period. These jurisdictions are Alabama, Colorado, Connecticut, District of Columbia, Hawaii, Louisiana, Minnesota, New York, North Dakota, Tennessee, Utah, Virginia and Wisconsin. In each instance, either the plaintiff or the defendant in the judicial separation action may convert the decree into a final divorce, except that only the innocent party may do so in the District of Columbia and Hawaii. Moreover, in some states, such as North Dakota, the conversion is discretionary with the court, and in New York it must be shown that the petitioner has substantially complied with all prior court orders. The conversion ground has some appeal because it discourages bed-and-board divorce, an unnatural status which Chancellor Kent described as placing the parties "in the undefined and dangerous character of a wife without a husband and a husband without a wife" and as a hazard to morals.[11]

Both types of separation grounds have the advantages of being relatively honest grounds for divorce and of eliminating the need for washing dirty linen in public, and there is assurance that, in fact, the marriage is dead. However, if the required period of separation is too long, such grounds will not be used with any frequency. Any period over two years seems too long, and perhaps the period of one year or more, established by Congress for the District of Columbia, is preferable. There are certain tax advantages that flow from the shorter period, and a year's estrangement due to marital difficulties is long enough to assure that the marriage no longer is viable.

In the last third of this century, many legislatures will choose between reformation of divorce laws by adding non-fault-grounds or by the breakdown theory.[12] The chances are that the former will have greater legislative appeal because, with 28 states and many foreign countries already adopting such measures, it is an established ground for divorce. The irreparable breakdown theory is a more radical departure from familiar divorce law, but it may be possible to relate it to prior law by treating certain marital sins, which formerly were grounds, as evidence that a breakdown in fact has occurred. It is the latter factor of proving breakdown that has troubled those who have considered making breakdown the exclusive basis for divorce. Moreover, unless there is a competent professional staff to process all cases, the fact-finding as to breakdown may be most uncertain. In the background, also, is controversy over socializing the courts and assigning them tasks that might better be left to behavioral scientists.[13]

CONCLUSION

Family law is responding, although slowly, to the social changes of our times. The law of divorce is being reevaluated, and substantial reforms are in prospect. Just what form reforms will take is uncertain, but the traditional ambivalence of the public regarding divorce, which accounts in some measure for the hypocrisy of tolerating strict laws in theory and lax administration in practice, is being dissipated and replaced by an insistence that divorce law be modernized.

In the past, divorce law has been almost wholly negative and pre-occupied with the Puritan concept of fault. A modern law must be constructive and offer affirmative help to families in trouble and help them to plan sensibly for the future. Perhaps children of divorcing parents should have independent representation in divorce proceedings. In any event, rather than inflaming the parties, and further embittering them, the law should provide counseling and conciliation so that adjustment to life after divorce is not unduly traumatic. The bonds of acrimony should be severed upon divorce, and the objective should be a restoration of the parties to a meaningful and worth-while life. Once a helpful and therapeutic approach is adopted concerning the problem of broken families, it becomes clear that greater emphasis should be given to education and preparation for marriage. Students and young couples should be encouraged to take practical courses, provided by church or state, so that, in advance, there will be a better understanding of the adjustments and concessions that marriage requires.

There is no ideal law of divorce, but progress may be made in human and marital relations if there is a pragmatic concern about consequences and the emphasis is on problem-solving rather than the assessment of blame. From the husband's point of view, the Todas of southern India may have devised the most sensible divorce law, for it was their rule that a husband may divorce his wife either because (1) she is a fool, or (2) she will not work. That would seem to cover about everything, although some might want to add another ground, recognized in ancient China, that talkativeness warranted divorce. From the modern wife's point of view, the Zuni Indian custom which permitted the squaw to divorce by putting her husband's belongings outside the tepee, or the ancient Celtic law which permitted her to obtain a divorce if she was not able to receive a satisfaction of her desires in the community of marriage, might seem ideal. In any event, the perennial problem of divorce is summed up in an oriental fable. It is said that the following inscription was written in large characters over the principal gate of the City of Agra in Hindustan:

In the first year of the reign of King Julief, two thousand married couples were separated, by the magistrates, with their own consent. The emperor was so indignant, on learning these particulars, that he abolished the privilege of divorce. In the course of the following year, the number of marriages in Agra was less than before by three thousand; the number of adulteries was greater by seven thousand; three hundred women were burned alive for poisoning their husbands; seventy-five men were burned for the murder of their wives; and the quantity of furniture broken and destroyed, in the interior of private families, amounted to the value of three millions of rupees. The emperor re-established the privilege of divorce.[14]

NOTES

[1] Student research disclosed that there were only 88 cases between 1945 and 1960 where collateral attacks were made on a sister-state's *ex parte* divorce. In 56 cases the *ex parte* decree was denied recognition, and in 32 it was held valid. During this same period, Nevada alone was grinding out an average of more than 10,000 divorces a year, most of them for migratory New Yorkers.

[2] The Uniform Divorce Recognition Act was enacted in California, Nebraska, New Hampshire, Rhode Island, Washington, and Wisconsin in 1949; in North Dakota in 1951; in Louisiana in 1952, but repealed in 1954; in Montana in 1963; and, in part, in New York in 1966. For a discussion of judicial construction of the act, see Note, 1616 *Hastings L. J.* 121 (1965).

[3] For a discussion of family courts and conciliation services, see H. Foster, "Conciliation and Counseling in the Courts in Family Law Cases," 41 *N.Y.U. L. Rev.* 353 (1966). For an account of a failure of conciliation procedures, see Bodenheimer, "The Utah Marriage Counseling Experiment: An Account of Changes in Divorce Law and Procedure," 7 *Utah L. Rev.* 443 (1961).

[4] For a report on Wisconsin law, see Hansen, "The Role and Rights of Children in Divorce Actions," 6 *J. Family Law* 1 (1966).

[5] See Gellhorn, *Children and Families in the Courts of New York City* (1954).

[6] FREEMAN, *Legal Interviewing and Counseling* (1964), is designed for law students and practitioners. The National Council on Legal Clinics, *Professional Responsibility Problems in Family Law* (1963) may be obtained from the American Bar Center, Chicago, Illinois.

[7] JACOBS & GOEBEL, *Domestic Relations* 428 (4th ed., 1961).

[8] FOSTER & FREED, *Commentary on the Divorce Reform Law* (Lawyers Co-operative Publication Company Pamphlet, 1967).

[9] See Public Lecture by Sir Leslie Scarman (entitled "Family Law and Law Reform,"), University of Bristol, March 18, 1966. See also LAW COMMISSION, *Report on Reform of the Grounds of Divorce: The Field of Choice* (1966).

[10] For discussions of the "living apart" ground, see Wadlington, *Divorce without Fault without Perjury*, 52 Va. L. Rev. 32 (1966); and Foster & Freed, *Living Apart as a Ground for Divorce*, 153 N.Y.L.J. Nos. 94–96. May 17, 18, 19, 1965, reprinted in a monograph distributed by Family Law Section, American Bar Association.

[11] 2 KENT, *Commentaries on American Law*, § 128 (Lacy ed., 1889).

[12] The Commission on Uniform State Laws is currently studying a complete revision of marriage and divorce law, with the objective of preparing a model law on the subject that will be recommended for adoption by state legislatures.

[13] For a criticism of counseling in the court setting, see Seidelson, "Systematic Marriage Investigation," 36 Geo. Wash. L. Rev. 60 (1967).

[14] Printed in 28 Niles Register 229, June 11, 1825, and reported by Blake, *The Road to Reno* 80–81 (1962).

The Statistics of Divorce

ALEXANDER A. PLATERIS

INTRODUCTION

Family Formation and Dissolution

During the year 1963, 428,000 divorces and annulments were granted in the United States (2.3 per 1000 total population, or 9.6 per 1000 married women 15 years of age and over). Because some families were disrupted by the death of one spouse, these figures represent only a part of all family dissolutions that took place during the year. The total number of all family dissolutions due to death was 850,112 in 1963 —597,814 by the death of the husband and 252,298 by the death of the wife (Table 1). Thus out of a total of 1,278,112 family dissolutions that occurred in 1963, 46.8 percent were due to the death of the husband, 33.5 percent to a judicial decree, and 19.7 percent to the death of the wife.

As shown in Figure 1, the total number of family dissolutions during 1963 (1,278,112) was smaller than that of new families established during the same period of time (1,654,000). This represents an increase of 375,888 in the total number of married couples. These figures are limited to family formation and dissolution that occurred within the United States and do not include couples that migrated to the United States; hence, the total increase in married couples was larger than 375,888. . . .

Measures of Family Formation and Dissolution

A set of comparable rates, all based on the same population and presenting a much clearer picture of the incidence of family formation and dissolution than rates computed using different populations, are shown in Table 2. Inasmuch as accurate data are not available for the population at risk—the population of all married couples—the estimated numbers of married women were used as approximations.[1] (National divorce rates per 1000 married women 15 years and over, which have been computed routinely, are shown in Table 3 for the years 1920 through 1963.)

Excerpted from *Divorce Statistics Analysis* (*United States—1963*), Vital and Health Statistics Series 21, No. 13, October 1967. Tables and figures have been renumbered.

TABLE 1

Family Formation and Dissolution: United States, 1940, 1959–51, and 1959–63.

Year of Occurrence	Marriages	Family Dissolution					Net Increase in Married Couples
		Total	All Deaths	Husbands	Wives	Divorces and Annulments	
				Deaths of Married Persons			
1963	1,654,000	1,278,112	850,112	597,814	252,298	428,000	375,888
1962	1,577,000	1,235,099	822,099	576,277	245,822	413,000	341,901
1961	1,548,000	1,210,533	796,533	559,038	237,495	414,000	337,467
1960	1,523,000	1,190,769	797,769	558,801	238,968	393,000	332,231
1959	1,494,000	1,164,218	769,218	536,671	232,547	395,000	329,782
1951	1,594,694	1,066,800	685,800	464,105	221,695	381,000	527,894
1950	1,667,231	1,058,615	673,471	453,656	219,815	385,144	608,616
1949	1,579,798	1,059,987	662,987	443,573	219,414	397,000	519,811
1940	1,595,879	900,465	636,465	406,240	230,225	264,000	695,414

Data refer only to events occurring within the United States. Data on international migration are not included. Deaths of married persons include numbers published in sources listed in the appendix that have been adjusted by distributing proportionally the deaths of persons with marital status not stated.

Figure 1. Family Formation and Dissolution.

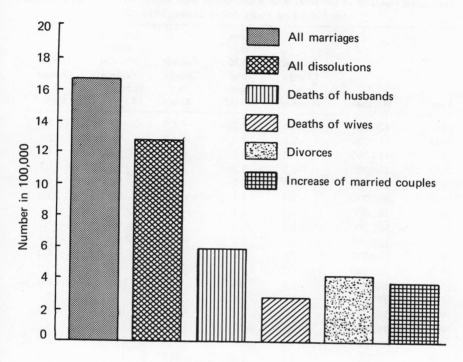

TABLE 2

Rates of Family Formation and Dissolution Per 1000 Married Men and Women: United States, 1963.

Type of Rate	Rate per 1000 Married Persons	
	Men	Women
Marriage rate—rate of gross increase of married population	38.0	37.3
Total dissolution rate	29.2	28.6
Death rate of married population	19.4	19.0
Of husbands	13.6	13.3
Of wives	5.8	5.7
Divorce rate	9.8	9.6
Rate of growth of the married population	8.8	8.6

Data refer only to events occurring within the United States.

TABLE 3

Estimated Number of Divorces and Annulments and Rates, with Percent Changes from Preceding Year: United States, 1920–63.

Year	Number	Percent Change in Number	Rate per 1000 Total Population*	Percent Change in Rate	Rate per 1000 Married Female Population 15 + yrs.†	Percent Change in Rate
1963	428,000	+3.6	2.3	+4.5	9.6	+2.1
1962	413,000	−0.2	2.2	−4.3	9.4	−2.1
1961	414,000	+5.3	2.3	+4.5	9.6	+4.3
1960	393,000	−0.5	2.2	...	9.2	−1.1
1959	395,000	+7.3	2.2	+4.8	9.3	+4.5
1958	368,000	−3.4	2.1	−4.5	8.9	−3.3
1957	381,000	−0.3	2.2	−4·3	9.2	−2.1
1956	382,000	+1.3	2.3	...	9.4	+1.1
1955	377,000	−0.5	2.3	−4.2	9.3	−2.1
1954	379,000	−2.8	2.4	−4.0	9.5	−4.0
1953	390,000	−0.5	2.5	...	9.9	−2.0
1952	392,000	+2.9	2.5	...	10.1	+2.0
1951	381,000	−1.1	2.5	−3.8	9.9	−3.9
1950	385,144	−3.0	2.6	−3.7	10.3	−2.8
1949	397,000	−2.7	2.7	−3.6	10.6	−5.4
1948	408,000	−15.5	2.8	−17.6	11.2	−17.6
1947	483,000	−20.8	3.4	−20.9	13.6	−24.0
1946	610,000	+25.8	4.3	+22.9	17.9	+24.3
1945	485,000	+21.3	3.5	+20.7	14.4	+20.0
1944	400,000	+11.4	2.9	+11.5	12.0	+9.1
1943	359,000	+11.8	2.6	+8.3	11.0	+8.9
1942	321,000	+9.6	2.4	+9.1	10.1	+7.4
1941	293,000	+11.0	2.2	+10.0	9.4	+6.8
1940	264,000	+5.2	2.0	+5.3	8.8	+3.5
1939	251,000	+2.9	1.9	...	8.5	+1.2
1938	244,000	−2.0	1.9	...	8.4	−3.4
1937	249,000	+5.5	1.9	+5.6	8.7	+4.8
1936	236,000	+8.3	1.8	+5.9	8.3	+6.4
1935	218,000	+6.9	1.7	+6.3	7.8	+4.0
1934	204,000	+23.6	1.6	+23.1	7.5	+23.0
1933	165,000	+0.6	1.3	...	6.1	...
1932	164,241	−12.6	1.3	−13.3	6.1	−14.1
1931	188,003	−4.1	1.5	−6.2	7.1	−5.3
1930	195,961	−4.8	1.6	−5.9	7.5	−6.2
1929	205,876	+2.8	1.7	...	8.0	+2.6
1928	200,176	+2.0	1.7	+6.3	7.8	...
1927	196,292	+6.3	1.6	...	7.8	+4.0

TABLE 3 *(Continued)*

Estimated Number of Divorces and Annulments and Rates, with Percent Changes from Preceding Year: United States, 1920–63.

Year	Number	Percent Change in Number	Rate per 1000 Total Population*	Percent Change in Rate	Rate per 1000 Married Female Population 15 + yrs.†	Percent Change in Rate
1926	184,678	+5.3	1.6	+6.7	7.5	+4.2
1925	175,449	+2.6	1.5	...	7.2	...
1924	170,952	+3.5	1.5	..	7.2	+1.4
1923	165,096	+10.9	1.5	+7.1	7.1	+7.6
1922	148,815	−6.7	1.4	−6.7	6.6	−8.3
1921	159,580	−6.4	1.5	−6.2	7.2	−10.0
1920	170,505	+20.5	1.6	+23.1	8.0	...

* Population enumerated as of April 1 for 1940, 1950, and 1960 and estimated as of July 1 for all other years; includes armed forces abroad for 1941–46.

† Population enumerated as of July 1 for 1920 and as of April 1 for 1930, 1940, 1950, and 1960 and estimated as of July 1 for all other years.

Data refer only to events occurring within the United States. Includes Alaska beginning 1959, and Hawaii, 1960.

TOTALS AND RATES

The National Divorce Trend

The national divorce total of 428,000 for 1963 was the highest annual number ever observed, except for the years 1945–47 when the post-World War II divorce peak occurred. The 1963 total represents an increase of 3.6 percent over the figure for 1962 and an increase of 8.9 percent over that for 1960. The 1963 divorce rate of 2.3 per 1000 population was much lower than that for the early postwar years, when the maximum rate of 4.3 was observed in 1946. The 1963 rate is close to the levels observed since 1955.

The trend of the divorce rate since 1867, the first year for which this rate was computed, showed a long-term increase that lasted 80 years, reaching a record peak in 1946. During this period, the rate increased from 0.3 to 4.3 per 1000 total population. The trend was accelerated by wars and reversed by economic depressions. During the 44 years shown in Table 3 and Figure 2, the rate first declined from the slight post-World War I peak, then resumed its upward trend (which was interrupted by the great depression), and almost doubled during the war and early postwar years—from 2.2 in 1941 to 4.3 in 1946. It declined rapidly afterwards, going back to 2.2 in 1957; since then it has

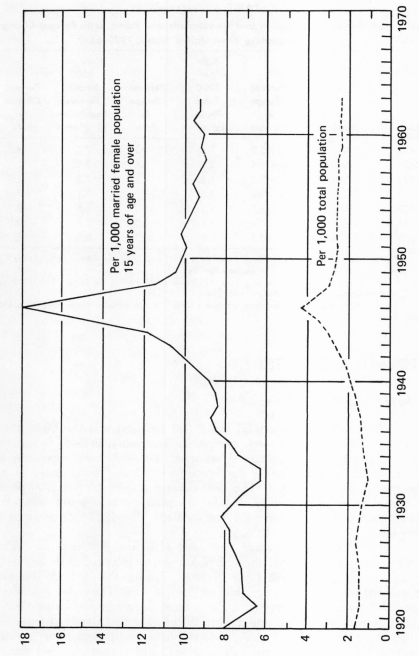

Figure 2. Divorce Rate: United States, 1920-1963.

remained approximately at the same level. At the present moment it is too early to say whether the slight increases of the rate found in 1961 and 1963 indicate the beginning of a new period of growth, but the provisional estimates of the national divorce totals for 1964 and 1965 (445,000 and 481,000, respectively, or 2.3 and 2.5 per 1000 population) suggest that the upward trend may have resumed.

The crude divorce rate, computed for the total population, depends in part on the proportion of married persons in the population, as married persons in the population, as married persons only are subject to the risk of divorce. Therefore the divorce rate per 1000 married women is a more refined measure of the incidence of divorce. The divorce rate per 1000 married women was 9.6 in 1963—slightly higher than the 1962 rate of 9.4, equal to the 1961 rate, and higher than the rates for all years from 1954 to 1960. These differences indicate that the increase in the number of divorces was partially due to reasons other than the growth of the married population. This statement can also be illustrated by ratios of the population to divorce: in 1963 a divorce was granted to one of every 104 married women, in 1962 to one of every 106, and in 1960 to one of every 109.

Inasmuch as the number of persons divorced is twice the number of divorces granted, 856,000 persons were divorced in 1963. In addition, 583,000 children of divorced couples were involved in divorce cases. This brings the total number of persons involved in divorce to 1,439,000. The involvement rate was 7.6 per 1000 population. Analogous figures for other years are shown in Table 4.

TABLE 4

Number of Husbands, Wives, and Children Involved in Divorce and Rates Per 1000 Total Population, with Percent Change from Preceding Year: United States, 1953–63.

Year	Total Involved	Percent Change	Rate
1963	1,439,000	+5.6	7.6
1962	1,363,000	+2.6	7.3
1961	1,329,000	+6.4	7.3
1960	1,249,000	−0.7	7.0
1959	1,258,000	+10.9	7.1
1958	1,134,000	−0.6	6.5
1957	1,141,000	+1.4	6.7
1956	1,125,000	+2.2	6.7
1955	1,101,000	+0.2	6.7
1954	1,099,000	−1.0	6.8
1953	1,110,000	. . .	7.0

Divorces by Region, Division, and State

Variation in the incidence of divorce was more pronounced within the United States than among the other countries. In 1963 the rate for the United States (2.3 per 1000 population) was about nine times as high as the lowest rate (0.25 for Venezuela), but in the same year the rate for Nevada was 62 times as high as that for New York. The differences between the states were due in part to variations in the permissiveness of the divorce laws and to the concentration of migratory divorces (those granted to persons who came to the state solely for the purpose of obtaining a divorce decree rapidly). However, comparatively high divorce rates were also found in states where few if any migratory divorces occurred. It was observed before the beginning of this century that the divorce rate tended to increase from East to West; this generalization still holds. In 1963 the divorce rate was 0.9 for the Northeast; 2.2 for the North Central, 2.8 for the South, and 3.6 for the West. The rate for the West was approximately four times as high as that for the Northeast. . . .[2]

Migratory Divorces

Migratory divorces are divorce decrees obtained outside the usual state of residence of the parties in places where divorce laws are particularly permissive and/or judges interpret these laws to the advantage of the seekers of speedy divorce. Such places are often referred to as "divorce mills." Typically, the plaintiff moves to a divorce-mill state for the minimum period of time required to establish legal residence and to come under the jurisdiction of courts of that state, then leaves as soon as the decree is rendered, and, presumably, returns to his or her earlier state of residence.

Migratory divorces should be distinguished from divorces of migrants, i.e., divorces of people who migrate and obtain a decree in their new place of permanent residence. In the case of migratory divorce, the residence established in the divorce-mill state is a legal fiction necessary for taking advantage of the permissive divorce laws, while in the case of divorcing migrants, the plaintiffs honestly intend to live indefinitely in their new state of residence.

Migratory divorces should also be distinguished from those obtained outside the county of usual residence of the plaintiff but in his state of residence. Some persons may wish to be divorced where they are not known or may have other reasons for filing the divorce petition in another county. Such moves may result in the concentration of divorces in particular counties. These divorces are not considered migratory as long as the plaintiff does not cross a state line in order to obtain the decree.

The opinion is often expressed that low divorce rates in many Eastern states with strict divorce laws are due to large numbers of East-erners obtaining divorces in divorce mills and that variations among state rates would be much less pronounced if rates were computed by usual residence rather than by place of occurrence. In order to explore such possibilities, estimates of the numbers of migratory divorces have been prepared.

These estimates were based on variations among county divorce rates in states where the existence of divorce mills seemed likely. These states are characterized by permissive legal grounds for divorce, by short periods required to establish legal residence, and by the avail-ability of various services useful to the divorce seekers. County rates were computed for states that possessed these characteristics, and one entire state and 26 counties in four other states were identified as proba-ble divorce mills. Then divorces of the permanent residents of these areas were estimated and subtracted from the totals. . . . Because the method [of estimation] is based on divorce rates by counties, estimates were prepared only for 1960, a year for which county population figures were available from the census enumeration.

Altogether, 19,000 migratory divorces were estimated to have oc-curred in the United States in 1960. This is 4.8 percent of the national divorce total, or 0.1 per 1000 population (Table 5). Even if it were assumed that migratory divorces are underestimated by 100 percent, their number would be less than ten percent of the national total. How-ever, there is no reason to believe that they have been substantially underestimated, particularly in view of the inclusion of several mar-ginal counties among the presumptive divorce mills. Some migratory divorces are granted to Americans in Mexico and in other foreign coun-tries. These were not included in the estimate.

The comparative insignificance of the number of migratory di-vorces granted in the United States in 1960 can best be visualized when compared with divorces occurring in states from which, presumably, large numbers of divorce seekers come. If it is assumed that all migra-tory divorces that were granted in 1960 were exclusively to residents of New York, then the crude resident divorce rate for that state would have increased to 1.6 and still would have been considerably below the national rate of 2.2. Since many migratory divorces were granted to residents of states other than New York, the resident divorce rate for that state had to be much lower than 1.6. On the other hand, if it is assumed that all migratory divorces granted in Nevada were obtained exclusively by residents of California, then the resident rate for that state would have been 3.6 as compared with the observed rate of 3.1. Hence, the resident divorce rate for California, though above 3.1, was considerably below 3.6.

These figures indicate that the incidence of migratory divorce in 1960 was not as large as it is widely believed to be. Migratory divorces may have declined since 1960, as the state authorities and the Bar

TABLE 5
Total, Resident, and Migratory Divorces and Rates: United States and Five Selected States, 1960.

Area	Population	All Divorces		Estimated Resident Divorce		Estimated Migratory Divorce	
		Number	Rate	Number	Rate*	Number	Rate
United States	179,323,175	393,000	2.2	374,000	2.1	19,000	0.1
Percentages	...	100.0	...	95.2	...	4.8	...
Total	1,338,740	23,307	17.4	4,082	3.0	19,225	14.4
Alabama, 8 counties	255,124	9,122	35.8	689	2.7	8,433	33.1
Arkansas, 8 counties	472,303	2,533	5.4	1,275	2.7	1,258	2.7
Florida, 7 counties	259,869	2,532	9.7	936	3.6	1,596	6.1
Idaho, 3 counties	66,166	665	10.1	212	3.2	453	6.9
Nevada, the state	285,278	8,455	29.6	970	3.4	7,485	26.2

* Estimated rates for resident divorces are rates for combined counties outside the divorce-mill areas for Alabama, Arkansas, Florida, and Idaho, and rate for the West region for Nevada.

Rates are per 1000 total population in area. For estimating methods, see appendix.

Association of Alabama took action against unconstitutional granting of migratory divorce in that state. Following this action, the total number of divorces granted in Alabama declined from 17,320 in 1960 to 12,566 in 1963, a decline of 4,754 (or 27.4 percent), and the annual divorce rate declined from 5.3 to 3.7. However, it should be pointed out that the number of divorces in other states with divorce mills increased during the same period, but no information is available as to whether the increases were largely among migratory divorces.

Annulments

Divorce statistics shown in this report refer to absolute divorces and to annulments and exclude various limited matrimonial decrees such as divorces from bed and board, limited divorces, legal separations, decrees of separate maintenance, and others. The national total for 1963 included 12,701 reported annulments, which was 3.0 percent of the absolute divorces and annulments combined. These figures were incomplete because Idaho, Massachusetts, and Missouri failed to report divorces and annulments separately. The number of annulments granted in these three states is usually small; it was 229 in 1962 and 204 in 1961. In addition, for a small number of decrees reported by other states, it was not stated whether they were absolute divorces or whether they were annulments.

The number of annulments granted in most states was small—0 in Vermont, less than 100 in 31 states and the District of Columbia, and between 100 and 1000 in 13 states. California and New York were the only two states that reported more than 1000 annulments.

The 1963 annulment total for California was 6134 as compared with 5984 in 1962 and 5643 in 1961. The figure for 1963 represented 10.9 percent of all divorces and annulments granted in the state and almost one-half of all annulments reported in the United States. For New York 2284 annulments were estimated, 36.2 percent of the combined annual total of divorces and annulments for that state and 18.0 percent of the national annulment total. The annulment figures reported for past years from New York were 2331 in 1962 and 2310 in 1961. As in prior years, about two-thirds of all annulments reported for 1963 were granted in California and New York.

DURATION OF MARRIAGE

Reporting and Definition

The duration of marriage at time of decree was computed by subtracting month and year of marriage from month and year of divorce. When only the year of marriage was given on the divorce record it was assumed that the marriage occurred at the midpoint of the year. Information about the time of marriage is required in all registration states and is almost always reported. For the DRA information about duration of marriage was available for 97.1 percent of divorces granted in 1963, and this percentage was below 85 in two states only.

The time that elapses between marriage and divorce comprises three distinct periods: (1) period between marriage and final separation of the couple (there may have been earlier separations followed by reconciliations, but the important date is that when husband and wife ceased for the last time to live in the same household); (2) the time between separation and filing the petition for divorce, and (3) the time between filing the petition and the decree. The family functions as a social unit only during the first period, and, therefore, the date of the last separation is of great interest for the study of family disruption. . . .

The duration of the second period, that between the separation and the filing of the divorce petition, depends partly on the decision of the parties to start divorce proceedings and partly on laws that specify the time that must elapse in order for a certain legal ground for divorce to arise, e.g., desertion, voluntary separation, or insanity. The duration of the third period depends almost exclusively on laws. Thus it can be seen that the three periods into which the duration of marriage to decree is divided have different characteristics, and their length is caused by different factors. All of these factors affect the duration of marriage to decree.

Distribution of Divorces by Duration of Marriage

Data for the divorce-registration area indicated that the modal number of divorces occurred when the marriage had lasted more than one year but less than two years. Almost the same proportion of divorces took place when the marriage had lasted between one and three years, 8.6 and 8.4 percent, respectively. The number of divorces declined consistently with each additional year of duration (Figure 3); and when the marriage had lasted nine years (the last single year of duration for which data are available) the proportion had declined to 3.7 percent. . . .

The group of divorces that had a very short duration, less than one year, included 5.2 percent of all decrees granted in the DRA. As this duration included the time the case was pending in court, the divorced couples had an extremely short period of married life before separation. The percentages of divorces after less than one year of married life showed very marked variation from state to state—from 0.4 percent in Virginia to 10.5 in Idaho. The regional factor is pronounced; all registration states in the Northeast region, in the northeastern part of the South region, and in the East North Central division of the North Central region had low proportions of divorces granted within less than one

Figure 3. Percent of Divorces and Annulments, by Duration of Marriage to Time of Decree, Divorce-Registration Area, 1963.

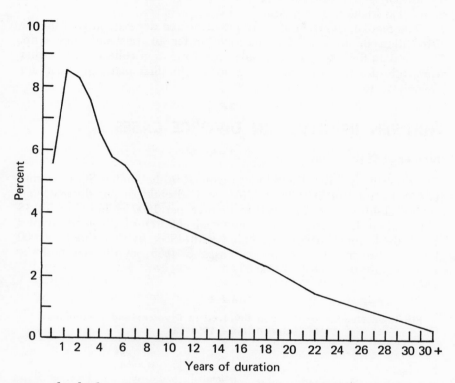

year—the highest percent being 4.3 in Ohio—while states in the remaining part of the country (including the West, the remainder of the North Central region, and the remainder of the South) had much higher percentages—the lowest being 6.0 percent in Hawaii. Thus all seven states in the first area had percentages lower than that for the DRA, and all states in the second area had higher percentages.

At the other extreme, 3.0 percent of divorced couples had a duration of marriage of 30 years or more, and this percentage ranged from 1.2 in Alaska to 4.9 in Alabama. Altogether 6.5 percent of the divorced couples had reached their silver wedding anniversary. Many of the states that had very low percentages of divorces after marriages with durations of less than one year had comparatively high percentages of those divorces after marriages with durations of 25 years or more and vice versa; the range was between 3.6 in Utah and 8.9 in Virginia. The regional distribution was also pronounced, with high percentages found in the Northeast and in the South between 6.3 and 8.9 percent), median percentages in the North Central (between 5.1 and 6.7), and low percentages in the West (between 3.8 and 5.2). . . .

The median duration of marriage at divorce was 7.5 years for the registration states combined; the figures for individual states ranged from 5.0 in Idaho to 10.3 in Maryland. . . .

The median duration of marriage at decree depends in part on the distribution of divorces by marriage order of husband and wife. Though data for 1963 are not available, information collected for earlier years indicates that the duration is longer for first marriages than for remarriages for all age categories. . . .

CHILDREN INVOLVED IN DIVORCE CASES

Number of Children Involved

It is estimated that the couples divorced in the United States during 1963 had a total of 583,000 children, or 1.36 children per divorce, and that 8.5 children were involved in divorce per 1000 children under 18 in the nation. Estimates of the number of children of divorced couples are available for 11 years, beginning with 1953. At that time, 330,000 children were involved in divorce cases, or 0.85 per divorce, and the involvement rate was 6.4 (Table 6).

TABLE 6

Estimated Number of Children Involved in Divorces and Annulments: United States, 1953–63.

Year	All Divorces and Annulments	Estimated Number of Children Involved	Average Number of Children per Decree	Rate per 1000 Children under 18
1963	428,000	583,000	1.36	8.5
1962	413,000	537,000	1.30	8.0
1961	414,000	501,000	1.21	7.6
1960	393,000	463,000	1.18	7.2
1959	395,000	463,000	1.18	7.5
1958	368,000	398,000	1.08	6.5
1957	381,000	379,000	0.99	6.4
1956	382,000	361,000	0.95	6.3
1955	377,000	347,000	0.92	6.3
1954	379,000	341,000	0.90	6.4
1953	390,000	330,000	0.85	6.4

Refers only to events occurring within the United States. Figures for 1960–63 estimated from frequencies based on sample; those for other years estimating from total counts.

TABLE 7

Proportion of Divorces and Annulments with Children Involved: Total Reporting States, 1953–63.

Year	Number of Reporting States	Percent of Decrees with Children Involved	Ratio of Children per Decree with Children
1963	22	61.6	2.16
1962	21	60.2	2.14
1961	20	60.3	2.06
1960	50	56.7	2.08
1959	16	59.1	2.00
1958	12	55.1	1.96
1957	23	50.9	1.95
1956	22	48.9	1.93
1955	22	48.1	1.92
1954	22	47.8	1.88
1953	22	45.5	1.86

Figures for 1960–63 based on sample data; those for 1953–59 based on total counts.

Between 1953 and 1963, the number of divorce decrees granted annually increased by 9.7 percent, but the number of children involved increased by 76.7 percent; from 1962 to 1963 these increases were 3.6 and 8.6 percent, respectively. . . .

Some factors that contributed to the growth of the number of children involved in divorce cases are shown in Table 7. The proportion of divorces with children involved increased in the reporting states from' 45.5 to 61.6 percent, while the number of children per divorce with children involved increased from 1.86 to 2.16. The increase in the proportion of divorced couples reporting children (or conversely, the decline in the proportion of childless couples in divorce courts) was 35.4 percent, while the increase of the ratio of children per divorce with children was 16.1 percent. This indicates that the decline in the proportion of couples who reported no children contributed most to the increase in the number of children involved in divorce.

. . . Almost two-thirds of all couples divorced in 1963 reported children, and only 38.4 percent had no children under 18. The latter included couples that had no children because they were only recently married, couples to whom no children have been born irrespective of the length of marriage, and couples that had been married for many years and had grownup children. Because of the composite character of the childless group, there are many factors that may have affected its decline during the last decade. The proportion of couples reporting no children varied considerably among the states, from less than one-fourth (24.5 percent in Rhode Island) to almost one-half (45.2 percent in Missouri). In no state did the divorces of childless couples comprise more than one-half of all divorces. In 1956 and earlier years, however, in the reporting states combined this proportion was more than 50 percent. This indicates a rapid decline of the proportion of childless divorced couples.

NOTES

[1] Population bases given in Table 1 of U.S. Bureau of the Census. "Marital Status and Family Status, March 1964 and 1963," *Current Population Reports*, Series P-20, No. 135, Washington, D.C., April, 1965.

[2] Wilcox, Walter F. *The Divorce Problem* (New York: Columbia University Press, 1897), 37–38, 42.

The Process of Aging

PETER TOWNSEND

THE STRUCTURE OF THE FAMILY

The main theme of this chapter is that family structure is a crucial analytic variable in understanding social organization and relationships and therefore individual processes of aging.

First, the structural characteristics of the families of old people in the three countries can be described. Nearly half the elderly population in Denmark and the United States, and just over half in Britain, are single or widowed. Nearly a fifth in the former countries, and nearly a quarter in the latter country, have no surviving children. Rather more old people in the United States than in Denmark or Britain have six or more children but in each of the countries from two-fifths to a half of those with children have only one or two. One of the interesting features of family structure is the large proportion who have children of one sex only. Apart from the fifth to a quarter of the elderly who have one son only or one daughter only, around another fifth have two or more sons or two or more daughters only. The vast majority of those with children have grandchildren, and more than a fifth in Denmark and Britain and more than two-fifths in the United States have great-grandchildren. The fact that the four-generation family is already a common phenomenon in industrialized societies is one of the more surprising results to emerge from the cross-national survey.

Nearly four-fifths of the elderly population have surviving brothers or sisters; a large minority have five or more. Some people can depend on their siblings for companionship and help if they have no children, so it is useful to consolidate the information about children, grandchildren, and siblings. It emerges that from a half to three-fifths of the elderly in the three countries belong to an immediate family structure of three or four generations and also have more than one surviving child. They might be said to have good potential family resources for help in old age. Another fifth have resources in depth over two, three, or four generations, but either they have only one child or, if they have two or more children, they have no grandchildren. The remaining persons, amounting to rather less than a fifth in Denmark and the United States,

Reprinted from Ethel Shanas, Peter Townsend, Dorothy Weidenburn, Henning Friis, Poul Milhoj, and Jan Stehouwer, *Old People in Three Industrial Societies,* by permission of the publishers, Atherton Press, Inc. Copyright © 1968 **Atherton Press,** Inc., New York. All rights reserved.

but nearly a quarter in Britain, have no direct descendants alive. A minority of from 2 to 4 per cent are childless, are single or widowed, *and* have no siblings. (At the other extreme there is a similar minority with five or more children *and* five or more siblings.)

One important feature of structure is the difference in years between the generations. In all three countries the trends towards earlier marriage, earlier childbirth, and fewer large families inevitably contribute towards a narrowing of the average span in years between successive generations. In Britain the difference in age between old people and their eldest children was 26.4 years for women and 29.0 for men, and between old people and their first grandchildren about 54 years for women and 57 for men. But the range is extremely wide, with some old people having young dependent children and others having middle-aged grandchildren.

As age increases the structure of the family changes—at least from the viewpoint of the individual. Old people experience the loss of family members. For example, at the age of 65 to 66 over half the women in all three countries have a husband alive, whereas over the age of 80 from only a tenth to a fifth of the women have a husband alive. Again, in the late 60's six in seven women have a sibling alive, but after the age of 75 only two in three old people have siblings alive. But just as old family members are discharged by death, new ones are recruited by birth. For example, by the age of 80 and over, nearly half the old people with children in Britain, over half in Denmark, and over two-thirds in the United States have great-grandchildren. With increasing age old people tend to find themselves nearer one of two extremes—experiencing the seclusion of the spinster or widow without children and surviving brothers and sisters, or pushed towards the pinnacle of a pyramidal family structure of four generations.

Second, having outlined the structural characteristics of the families of old people in the three countries, some of the consequences for family organization and interaction can be described. The composition of the rest of the household is affected by whether or not old people have a spouse or are single or widowed, and is further affected by the number and sex of old peoples' children. Compared with widowed old persons, for example, married persons more often maintain households independent of their married children and less often share them with other relatives. Single persons are more likely than widowed persons—even than widowed persons who lack children—to share households with siblings. A widowed person is in fact less likely in all three countries to live with a child than a single person is to live with a sibling. Widowed persons with sons only are more likely to be living alone than widowed persons with daughters only. Divorced persons are less likely to live with their children than widowed persons.

Findings such as these imply various conclusions about family organization. They suggest a structural explanation for existing patterns of household composition, given certain social norms. The integrity of marriage is respected, partly by recognizing the right of a married couple to live in an independent household. Social distance between the adult generations in the family is also observed. Preferment is given in family organization and management to relations with daughters over relations with sons. Preferment is given to relations with children over relations with siblings, but if people do not marry, or if they marry and do not have children, then relations with siblings can be maintained throughout life—especially with other childless or single siblings. Once weakened, family relationships are difficult to renew or repair; they need to be regularly reinforced—like conditioned reflexes.

Family structure also affects the geographical distribution of family members. Fewer widowed than married old persons live at considerable distances from their children. Again, it is more common for widowed persons to be living with a child than near him but it is more common for married persons to be living near a child than with him. The chances of living farther than thirty minutes journey from the nearest child are greater the smaller is the number of children, though children in the small families tend to compensate: proportionately *more* of them live with or near their parents. Although married daughters more often live with old people than married sons, they are not in general more likely to live near old people. On a broad cross-national basis, then, there is no evidence of marked matrilocal family organization.

One important finding about family organization is the working of a principle of compensation or substitution. More widowed than married old people of comparable age live with unmarried children. It is hypothesized that children sometimes postpone marriage if a father or mother, particularly a father, dies during their adolescence or early adulthood. There are other examples of such compensation. A child in a small family tends to "make good" the inadequacy of numbers; in other words, he tends to live closer and see more of his elderly parents than a comparable "average" child in a large family. Again, a person without children will often share a household with a sibling, or see more of his siblings than a person with both children and siblings.

Finally, family structure affects individual relationships. The shortest period since an old person saw a child was taken as one simple measure which would reveal this. In the 1962 cross-national survey more of the widowed than the married, more of those with several children than one child only, and more of those with daughters than with sons only, had seen a child the same or the previous day. Broadly speaking, fewer in these categories had not seen a child within the previous month. Even when living at comparable distances daughters tended to have been seen more recently than sons. Nevertheless, in all three countries contacts between old persons and their sons were frequent.

Two interesting conclusions emerged about the elderly in individual countries. First, slightly more of the elderly in most types of family in

Britain, defined according to sex and number of children, had frequent contacts with their children. Second, relationships in Denmark between old people and their children tended to be more loose-knit than in the other two countries (for example, fewer shared a household) and were also bilateral (for example, relations with sons were nearly as frequent as those with daughters). In Britain and the United States there was greater emphasis on the mother-daughter relationship. Three times as many widowed persons lived with married daughters as with married sons, and in tracing the four possible relationships of widow/married daughter, widower/married daughter, widow/married son, and widower/married son, the proportion seeing a child on the same or the previous day tended to decrease and the proportion not seeing a child in the last month tended to increase.

Both these conclusions, however, tended to be overshadowed by the broad similarity in pattern of family contacts. Since more of the elderly in Britain than in the United States had only one or two children and had sons only, the over-all difference between the elderly populations in patterns of contacts with children were relatively small. Over three-fifths in each of the three countries had seen a child the same or the previous day and another fifth within the previous week. The surprising conclusion for many readers will be that despite structural variations the over-all patterns are so similar.

ISOLATION, DESOLATION, AND LONELINESS

In this chapter we have pursued the twin themes of *isolation* and *desolation*. We began by distinguishing different types of isolation and showing how difficult it is to get a rational measure of social interaction. One important meaning of social *isolation* is to have little contact or relationship, by comparison with persons of the same age, with family, local community, and society. In all three countries only a very small minority (4 per cent or fewer) of old people were found to be living in extreme isolation in the sense that a week or even a day could pass without human contact. Few people were without meaningful everyday relationships and social activities. A larger proportion (a quarter in each country) said they were often alone. Relatively more women than men said they were often alone, and this tended to correspond with the larger proportion of women who were found to be widowed and living alone.

Those who were isolated were generally persons who were living alone, older than average, single or widowed, lacking children and other relatives living nearby, retired, and infirm. Three or more of these factors acting together were more likely to produce social isolation than was any single factor.

Desolation, a special form of isolation related to a previous individual situation, is typified by the loss (by death, hospitalization, or migration) of a social intimate, usually someone who is loved, such as a spouse or another close relative. The proportion of old people who have experienced the recent loss of a spouse, close relative, or friend is high— and seems to be higher still at the advanced ages. Desolation and peer-contrasted isolation overlap but do not coincide.

The data tended to support the hypothesis that desolation rather than peer-contrasted isolation is the causal antecedent of loneliness (defined as the unwelcome feeling of lack or loss of companionship) and may also be more important than isolation in explaining the propensity to suicide in old age. But we also found that the feelings of some of those who have experienced severe social loss are relieved by remaining or substitute contacts and relationships, particularly with members of their families. Companionship may thus prevent or mitigate loneliness, although lack of companionship does not appear to be a strong causal antecedent of loneliness.

Finally, we considered whether people disengage from society in advanced old age. We found that in all three countries substantially more persons in their 80's than in their late 60's are living alone and say they are often alone. But the trend towards isolation with age is not steep, and on none of our measures are more than two-fifths of those in their 80's "isolated" or alone. The small minority of extreme isolates increases marginally in Britain and the United States, and rather more sharply in Denmark, but still only to 6 per cent. Moreover, there is some evidence that when people become widowed or infirm they move to join their children.

The great majority of those living alone have a number of daily social activities and relationships and, although there is some falling off with increasing age, the fall is not marked and much of it is attributable to the higher prevalence of infirmity. While the data do not allow more sophisticated handling they do not suggest that, independent of growing infirmity, social disengagement is a widespread phenomenon. Bereavement is perhaps the most important isolating experience in old age and yet even this, as at other ages, draws a chain of "reintegrating" responses from family and community. Once he overcomes his initial grief, the old person himself often finds that compensating relationships provided by his family and friends may gradually mitigate his sense of loneliness.

Bereavement and the Family

WILLARD W. WALLER

CHANGES IN FAMILY CONFIGURATION

Numerous adjustments of the configuration of the family attitudes are involved in the social processes initiated by bereavement. The sociological structure of the group has been altered; although the original pattern may seem to continue to exist for a time, the fundamental pattern of the dyad or triad later establishes itself; it is at first an all-but-one configuration, and later the absent member is out of the picture entirely. For the group which is left, the loss of a member may nonetheless be a sentimental asset; it happens sometimes that parents are woven more closely together by the loss of a child, or that the whole family is given a rallying point by the loss of a central member. As we have seen, the life of the departed is always idealized; we may say that the family loses a member but gains a collective representation."

Every one-to-one relationship within the family is altered by the loss of a member from the configuration; this is a generalization which seems to hold for almost every case. Affects generated by the loss of a family member or set free from their habitual objects are now projected upon the screen of other family members or on an outside object. It would be possible to cite an endless number of familiar examples of this process. The widow turns to her son and perhaps wrecks him with her emotional demands. The relationship of a widower and his son, once a rivalry for the mother's affection, is greatly improved by the decease of the woman who was the cause of discord. The mother, bereft of one child, turns to another. In a typical case, a woman was called upon to make a number of such shifts in a period of ten years; when her daughter died, she turned to her eldest son; this son died within a few years, and she transferred her principal interest to her husband; the husband dying within the year, she was left with one remaining son, with whom her relations became increasingly embittered because she insisted upon regulating his life completely. Not infrequently affects are transferred to religious interests which may produce any number of effects upon the family configuration.

From chapter 22, *The Family: A Dynamic Interpretation*, by Willard Waller. Revised by Reuben Hill. Copyright 1938, 1951, by Holt, Rinehart & Winston, Inc. Reprinted by permission of Holt, Rinehart & Winston, Inc.

SUCCESSION OF ROLES

When a squad of soldiers has lost a member, the remaining members alter their positions so that the essential points in the configuration of the squad will always be occupied. In an exactly similar way, certain shifts of position in the family, not necessarily conscious or intended, bring it about that all the essential family roles are perpetuated. This is termed "the closing of ranks" and has been observed in adjustment to other crises of dismemberment, particularly war separation.[1] We turn to Marcel Proust for a description of a shift of roles in his own family. In the passage quoted below,[2] he describes and attempts to account for certain changes which took place in his mother after the death of her mother:

> But, what struck me most of all, when I saw her cloak of crape, was—what had never occurred to me in Paris—that it was no longer my mother that I saw before me, but my grand-mother. As, in royal and princely families, upon the death of the head of the house his son takes his title and from being Duc d'Orléans, Prince de Tarente or Prince des Laumes, becomes King of France, Duc de la Trémoille, Duc de Guermantes, so by an accession of a different order and more remote origin, the dead man takes possession of the living who becomes his image and successor, and carries on his interrupted life. Perhaps the great sorrow that follows, in a daughter such as Mamma, the death of her mother only makes the chrysalis break open a little sooner, hastens the metamorphosis and the appearance of the person whom we carry within us and who, but for this crisis which annihilates time and space, would have come gradually to the surface. Perhaps, in our regret for her who is no more, there is a sort of auto-suggestion which ends by bringing out on our features resemblances which potentially we already bore and above all a cessation of our most characteristically personal activity (in my mother, her common sense, the sarcastic gaiety that she inherited from her father) which she did not shrink, so long as the beloved was alive, from exercising, even at her expense, and which counterbalanced the traits that we derived exclusively from her. Once she is dead, we should hesitate to be different, we begin to admire only what she was, what we ourselves already were only blended with something else, and what in future we are to be exclusively. It is in this sense (and not in that other, so vague, so false, in which the phrase is generally used) that we may say that death is not in vain, that the dead man continues to react upon us. He reacts even more than a living man because, true reality being discoverable only by the mind, being the object of a spiritual operation, we acquire a true knowledge only of things that we are obliged to create anew

by thought, things that are hidden from us in everyday life.
. . . Lastly, in our mourning for our dead we pay an idolatrous
worship to the things that they liked. Not only could not my
mother bear to be parted from my grandmother's bag, become
more precious than if it had been studded with sapphires and
diamonds, from her muff, from all those garments which
served to enhance their personal resemblance, but even from
the volumes of Mme. de Sévigné which my grandmother took
with her everywhere, copies which my mother would not have
exchanged for the original manuscript of the letters. She had
often teased my grandmother who could never write to her
without quoting some phrase of Mme. de Sévigné or Mme. de
Beausergent. In each of the three letters that I received from
Mamma before her arrival at Balbec, she quoted Mme. de
Sévigné to me, as though those three letters had been written
not by her to me but by my grandmother and to her. She must
at once go out upon the front to see the beach of which my
grandmother had spoken to her every day in her letters. Carrying her mother's sunshade, I saw her from my window advance, a sable figure, with timid, pious steps, over the sands
that beloved feet had trodden before her, and she looked as
though she were going down to find a corpse which the waves
would cast up at her feet. . . . Daily, after this, my mother
went down and sat upon the beach, so as to do exactly what
her mother had done, and read her mother's two favorite
books, the *Memoirs* of Madame de Beausergent and the
Letters of Madame de Sévigné. . . . But when, in reading the
Letters, she came upon the words, 'My daughter,' she seemed
to be listening to her mother's voice.

Proust has shown clearly how certain roles, here that of the matri-
arch, are resident in culture, and how when the bearer of such a role
passes from the scene another succeeds to it. He has also described the
internal compulsion of love and sorrow which causes the individual to
react like the parent after the parent is dead and to make profound
alterations in his own personality in the interest of his new role.

These concessions which we make to the wishes of persons who can
no longer wish anything are curious; we find people eating the meals
which the dead person liked, planting flowers as he planted them, and
painting the house and barn the colors which he preferred—strange behavior, coming often enough from persons who were not particularly
tender to those wishes when the person was alive. More might be said
concerning the psychological basis of the imitation of the parent which is
delayed until after the parent's death. We should realize that this is no
random transition, but the fulfillment of the pattern of life in which one
has been trained from childhood. Complete fulfillment of the parent's
role has been prevented by the very presence of the parent, which has
imposed the filial role as a limiting factor. When the presence of the

parent no longer compels the child to play the role of the son, when the child is at length acted upon by precisely the same situation which the father once faced, the son becomes wholly the father. This is the delayed identification with the parent which has been previously discussed.

NEW ROLES IN THE COMMUNITY

The widow or widower must find a new role in the community. A number of adjustments are necessitated by the fact that in our culture the marriage pair joins in many social activities as a group, and now the surviving member of the pair must go alone. Some adjustments on the fringes of one's social group must always follow the death of the person who was the relative or particular friend of those concerned; if a socially active wife dies, the husband's circle of contacts narrows somewhat. The widower, unless of quite advanced age, probably changes the composition of his social world considerably, for after a time his interests have regressed toward those of his bachelor days and he takes less satisfaction in his married friends. The role of the widow is rather precisely defined, it seems that the widow usually keeps her friends of her married days, but plays the role of the widow.

Particularly in rural groups, the stereotype of the widow seems to carry some rather definite implications. According to the stereotype, the widow clings to her sorrow; when the young people are singing she comes into the room and asks them to sing once more the hymns that were sung at her husband's funeral. It is considered somewhat admirable for her to prolong her period of mourning and to put aside the thought of remarriage. The widow is excused from some community duties, is greatly respected if she takes up the burden of support of her children, but is not pardoned for sexuality. The term *widow* has certain emotional connotations which enable us to verbalize her role; she is an object of pity, of special concern, of admiration if she is virtuous. It is probable that our emotional attitudes toward the widow are derived from Hebraic sources, for the widow was in ancient Hebrew society a person without a place in the world, far more justifiably an object of special concern than in our own life.

REMARRIAGE

The difference between the widow and the widower is worthy of note with regard to remarriage. Remarriage for the widower is the respectable and even the expected thing. Twice as many widowed men as widows remarry during the first five years after widowhood, and the same ratio maintains for the first fourteen years after the spouse's death.[3] Whether this is due to the greater opportunity of the aging male to contract a marriage or to a fundamental difference between the sexes would be difficult to say. Certainly there is no strong taboo upon the remarriage of a widow, and it seems that something of the old colonial attitude, that it is a good thing to marry a widow, may have persisted to the present day. But there is a certain difference in the attitude of the community, else the saying credited to Oscar Wilde, "When a man remarries, it is because he loved his first wife; when a woman remarries, it is because she hated her first husband," could not have such wide acceptance. In our culture we pity and venerate the widow and grant her the privilege of remaining alone.

In the urban middle classes, the status of the widow is changing rapidly. In such groups it is taken for granted that a young widow will remarry, probably rather quickly, and her friends relieve themselves of the pain of sympathy by saying, "Oh, well, she'll get somebody else. She won't stay single long." The entry of women into the professions makes it possible for the widow to make a satisfactory economic adjustment and also for her to work off some of her emotional tensions in her career. Even the taboo upon sex behavior has relaxed greatly.

One change in the status of the widow in some subgroups is probably a handicap to her emotional adjustment. A generation which grew up in the era of A Farewell to Arms and The Sun Also Rises did not permit itself to grieve too long. It was so impressed by the elemental tragedy of being alive—a sorrow which all must share—that it would not permit, or at least did not encourage, any individual to add to the sorrows of another by asking that another feel sorry for him. Because of the mores of such subgroups, the "emancipated" widow often failed to mourn adequately.

Dickinson and Beam[4] have supplied some much needed information concerning the adjustment of the widow to her state. Severe sexual tension seems to be characteristic. There is intense reliving of the marriage. Dickinson and Beam speak somewhat eloquently of the mental conflict of the widow: "The single woman's conflict is with imagination; the married woman's conflict is with reality; this third conflict is that mingling of imagination and reality which mourns the dead." Dickinson and Beam hint very strongly at the conclusion that the postmarriage idealization of sex life in marriage has led this group of women to picture their marriages in terms of impossible perfection. The investigators also believe that idealization of the first mate is an important factor in preventing remarriage.

The fact is that in spite of powerful and continuing sex interests, many widows do not remarry. Obviously, idealization of the first mate or, more accurately, a continued involvement of her emotions, of which the idealization is a part, is a factor of importance, but we must try in each case to separate cause from effect, for it must often be true that persistent preoccupation with the dead husband is a result of failure to establish relations with the living. We may, nevertheless, suppose that the idealized image of the dead mate, an image to which no living man could measure up, is an important deterrent to remarriage.

Possibly a number of other factors are also involved. The widow's image of her husband is not merely idealized; usually it is also obsolete. Our image of the person we love seems to stabilize at an early age period in the association. The widow tends to think of her deceased husband as young and virile, and her own spontaneous love interests are likely to go out strongly to men of this type; this interferes seriously with remarriage. The young minister is often the recipient of the attentions of the aging widow.

We need also to think of our widow in terms of our bargaining process of courtship. Since she made her first love choice, the widow has suffered a sad decline in her bargaining power, and it is difficult for her to adjust her standards to her own changed status. In addition, there are community attitudes to consider, and these do not always approve of remarriage of the widow. If there are children beyond a certain age, they may usually be counted upon to disapprove of their mother's remarriage.

Most of these factors are different in the case of the widower. The idealization of the first mate is quite as great, perhaps greater, for the male possibly has greater capacity to idealize. The idealization of the dead is not quantitatively less in the man, but the tendency to idealize the living—the overvaluation of the sex object—is quantitatively greater; any feeling of the man that the new woman does not measure up to the former wife is more easily overcome by the urgency of present desire. And if the widower thinks of his dead wife as of the time when he first met her and has a predilection for younger women, he can often gratify his desire, for no strong taboo opposes marriage with a woman a decade or so younger than himself. The widower has lost something of his courtship bargaining power, but age, at least, counts less strongly against a man than against a woman. If he has mature children, and also property, the widower must reckon with the opposition of the children to his marriage.[5]

It is probable that continued attachment to the first mate is a factor of importance in the second marriage of either the widow or the widower; we usually speak of this merely as idealization of the first mate. It would be impossible to say whether the constant comparison of the first wife with the second is a factor which generally makes for discord in such marriages. Where friction exists, this factor often gives it a characteristic form. The man, perhaps never completely freed of his attachment to his first wife and his first marriage, encounters certain frustrations in his life with the second; he immediately reactivates his fantasies concerning his first wife and his first marriage, is perhaps unfortunate enough to make some of his comparisons verbal, and the peace of his home is shattered; his wife thereafter feels insecure, unloved, perhaps, and inflicts further frustrations upon the husband.

We postpone certain remarks on the process of reconstruction in general until after we have considered divorce and readjustment after divorce.

NOTES

[1] Reuben Hill, *Families Under Stress*, Harper, 1949, pp. 315–317.

[2] M. Proust, *Cities of the Plain*, 1930, pp. 236–238. By permission of Random House.

[3] Actual figures for 1948 are supplied by Paul C. Glick, "First Marriages and Remarriages," *American Sociological Review*, 14 (Dec. 1949), 726–734. He reports that approximately one half of the men and one quarter of the women who had lost their spouses during the five years preceding the survey had remarried; of those losing their spouses by death between 6 and 14 years before the survey, about two thirds of the men and one third of the women had remarried. In assessing the role of dependent children in remarriage, he writes, "In fact, it is possible that there is a selective tendency for widowed or divorced women with children to remarry *more quickly or not at all* [italic ours] than those with no children." The editors of the *Statistical Bulletin* (Jan. 1949) in an article entitled "The Frequency of Remarriage," calculate ". . . the presence of dependent children reduces by more than one eighth the chances of remarriage for women past the reproductive ages." In comparison with 1910 they and both widowed and divorced were more likely to remarry in 1940, especially in the younger age groups. The proportion remarrying in the age group 25 to 34 years, for example, increased from 50 percent in 1910 to 60 percent in 1940.

[4] Robert Latou Dickinson and Lura Beam, *A Thousand Marriages, A Medical Study of Sex Adjustment*, Williams and Wilkins, 1931, pp. 270–287.

[5] A case which is perhaps not too atypical to mention points this out. The daughter, strongly fixated on her father, was extremely jealous of the mother, whom she was nevertheless unable to replace in her father's affections. She developed an obsessive fear that the mother would die (death wish) and that the father would remarry and give the daughter's inheritance to the second wife.

SELECTED READINGS

BECKER, HOWARD. "The Sorrow of Bereavement," *Journal of Abnormal and Social Psychology*, XXVII, 391–410.

CAVAN, RUTH S., *The Family*, Crowell, 1942, Chapter 10.

COCHRANE, A. L., "A Little Widow Is a Dangerous Thing," *International Journal of Psycho-Analysis*, XVII, 494–509.

ELIOT, THOMAS D., "The Adjustive Behavior of Bereaved Families, A New Field of Research," *Social Forces*, VIII, 543–549.

——, "The Bereaved Family," *Annals of the American Academy of Political and Social Science*, 160, 184–190.

————, "Bereavement: Inevitable but Not Insurmountable" in Howard Becker and Reuben Hill (eds.), *Family, Marriage and Parenthood,* Heath, 1948.

FRITZ, MARY A., "A Study of Widowhood," *Sociology and Social Research,* XIV, 553–561.

MACK, R. J., "A Dream from an Eleventh Century Japanese Novel," *International Journal of Psycho-Analysis,* VIII, 402–403.

RADO, SANDOR, "The Problem of Melancholia," *International Journal of Psycho-Analysis,* IX, 420–438.

SHAND, A. F., *The Foundations of Character,* Macmillan, 1914.

SPIEGELMAN, MORTIMER, "The Broken Family—Widowhood and Orphanhood." *Annals of the American Academy of Political and Social Science,* 188, 117–130.

TAYLOR, M. P., "A Father Pleads for the Death of His Son," *International Journal of Psycho-Analysis,* VIII, 53–55.

VIII

The Family's Future

Where is the American family headed? Is it tumbling toward the breakup predicted by the conservatives and desired by the radicals? Is it moving toward the greater personal freedom and fulfillment in role choices, socialization, and mate selection that liberals perceive? Or is it merely retrenching itself as a result of the propaganda of the mass media and the employment of safety valves for the maladjusted. Four papers are presented in this final part to introduce the reader to the various possibilities that lie in the future for the American family.

Dennis Wrong's article on the family's "breakup" is one of the oldest pieces in this book of readings. It states well, however, the optimistic-liberal position regarding the significance of twentieth century changes in the U.S. family. The family, Wrong asserts, is not breaking up. All the dilemmas that confront the family member are a result not of disintegration but of the greater range of choices which confront him in his family experience. All these options seem to the author to foreshadow the opportunity for greater individual fulfillment, as the family is molded around the personalities of its members, instead of the members being molded to some traditional version of what the family should be. Wrong's discussion might well be compared with more recent analyses such as that of Krech in Part V. Perhaps there is greater freedom than formerly to choose from a range of options, but two decades after Wrong's article first appeared the patriarchal flavor of the U.S. family is still apparent and many role options still appear closed—such as the female working and the male staying home. While Wrong argues clearly and persuasively against the conservative view that recent changes presage the family's destruction, one should note with caution those points at which his analysis appears to be found by the time period when he was writing. Coming at the close of the period when the U.S. divorce rate was at an all-time high, Wrong notes, for example, that the desirability of marriage is being questioned "today," meaning 1950. Yet O'Neil and Parke and Glick find that marriage is more popular today (1960's) than ever before in American history.

The statistical analysis of Parke and Glick is based upon census figures, and is an attempt to project current trends into the future. Noting the decline in the proportion of the American population that never marry, the decline in the rate of teen-age marriages, the tendency for families to maintain their own households, and the likelihood that the divorce rate may decline, the authors base their predictions upon the continuation of such trends. While insightful in their use of statistics, an important question raised by such projection is whether things ever remain the same. This question should be posed again regarding Parke and Glick's analysis once the reader has completed Nimkoff's discussion of the effect of technological developments upon the family.

Presented as the Burgess award lecture for 1969 at the National Council on Family Relations meetings, Robert Winch's speculative statement regarding the future of the American family is quite thought-provoking. Winch notes that the family may continue to lose or give up functions to the larger society, and that even the reproductive function may be reduced to a minimum as families have fewer and fewer children. He does not, however, see the possibility that reproduction might be *entirely* removed from the family, and at this point Nimkoff's speculations in the succeeding article again become pertinent. And what about sex outside marriage? It is possible that extramarital sex can become legitimated in such a way as not to affect the marriage, or are sex and marriage too closely intertwined?

Alongside the statistical projections and functional speculations of the preceeding two papers, the reader should now place the technological possibilities reviewed in Nimkoff's paper. The family, many functionalists feel, has always existed for the purpose of reproduction and early socialization, and therefore it will continue to exist to perform those functions. But suppose incubator birth became a reality, and it were found that by keeping the fetus outside the human body all birth and pregnancy defects could be avoided; would people's values ever espouse such a development as "good" and "right?" Nimkoff's analysis raises this and other issues concerning the possible effects on the family of the many technological advances which are either now being made or are just around the corner.

A final type of paper not included in this part is the radical action proposal for the destruction of the family as we know it. Based either on the Freudian position that the family is the instrument for the development of "corporate neuroses," or on the Marxian assertion that the nuclear family is the basic capitalist unit for the "domestic slavery of the wife," these writings claim that the family "ought" to be destroyed. The final question the reader should ponder is this: Is the combination of technological possibilities and radical criticism likely to result in the replacing of the nuclear family with communal or other forms of primary group life, or are the familistic values of the United States and other industrial societies so strong as to withstand indefinitely the onslaughts of technology and criticism?

The "Break-Up" of the American Family

DENNIS H. WRONG

The "break-up" of the family has become a perennial theme of American sociologists. It is one with which they are sure to enlist the interest of laymen, harried as everyone is by the problems of relations with the opposite sex, marriage and divorce, and having and raising children. For the last two decades at least, they have warned us that the family is "losing its functions," and that the home is becoming little more than a hotel for its members. They have accumulated the statistics on divorce, bastardy, marital misery, and juvenile delinquency, and they habitually use such drastic terms as "disappearance," "disintegration," and "degeneration" to characterize the condition of the family today. Projects for restoring and "revitalizing" family life are legion among sociologists.

The family whose break-up is thus heralded is the traditional monogamous and patriarchal family of Western civilization. Sociologists point out that this family, developed for the most part in a rural environment, had economic, educational, and recreational functions which it has now relinquished to large business enterprises, schools, and the mass entertainment industries. In just about all the historical civilizations and primitive societies with which we are acquainted, the family has been both the basic economic unit and the major educational agency for its youth. Having lost these functions, what will hold it together?

The modern urban family, the standard sociological critique continues, is held together only by the individual needs of its members. Our socio-economic order does not depend to the extent it once did on the stability and solidarity of the family, and consequently exercises less control over people's domestic lives. The pressures of economic necessity and communal censure no longer play much role in binding the individual to the family group. Sex, marriage, and bearing and raising children are becoming private affairs to be settled by individual decisions at individual convenience rather than by the institutional regulations of law and religion or by the "unwritten law" of accepted codes and mores.

This critique is now to be found in the discussions of marriage and the family in most of the better textbooks, as well as in the sociological

Reprinted from *Commentary,* by permission; copyright © 1950 by the American Jewish Committee.

works written specifically on the subject. In such texts we will generally find a historical account of the family in pre-industrial Western society and ethnological data on the kinship systems of primitive peoples—and there may be an effort to classify the modern family according to its formal institutional attributes as monogamous, conjugal, patronymic, multilineal, patrilocal, etc. We will also find typologies constructed to indicate the main distinctions between the modern family and earlier forms. Thus, Carle Zimmerman (*The Family of Tomorrow,* Harper, 1949) discerns three basic family types and contrasts the "atomistic" modern family with the "trustee" and "domestic" families of the past. It is clear what *he* thinks of the modern family. Ernest Burgess and H. J. Locke, the authors of the most widely used text on marriage and the family (*The Family,* American Book, 1945), use a more neutral terminology, and distinguish between the "institutional" family of the past, "with family behavior controlled by the mores, public opinion, and law," and the "companionship" family of the present, in which "behavior is determined by the affection and consensus of its members."

This analysis has led rather naturally to an emphasis on empirical studies of "success and failure" in marriage—undertaken with teh explicit and implicit hope that they would give guidance to efforts to help stem the tide of disintegration. These studies have involved elaborate statistical investigations of given samples of married couples to find out which type gets divorced ("failure") and which type stays married ("success"), and they reach such conclusions as: marriages have a better chance of success when the bride is virgin and fifteen pounds underweight, when the groom lives in the suburbs, when both are devoutly religious, and when neither is particularly interested in politics. The results of these studies generally lend themselves easily to use by textbook writers and advice-to-the-lovelorn columnists as authoritative scientific evidence to back up their warnings against violating traditional precepts.

Of late, however, this main line of sociological writing and thinking on the American family has been under attack by sociologists who have taken to heart the more recent developments in anthropology and psychiatry. For one thing, these critics object that to use such terms as "disintegration" and "disappearance" in speaking of the modern family only indicates a nostalgic and unscientific preference for one type of family—the family of our rural past, which in any case cannot be restored in modern industrial society. More radical critics have also suggested that it is equally nostalgic and unscientific to consider divorce a sign of "social pathology" and the continuance of marriage a sign of "social health": we must consider the functions and meanings of marriage and divorce in different social contexts. Because the family pattern of today is different from that of an earlier day is no evidence, *per se,* that it is worse; it may be better, if it works better for its members and society in terms of present needs and considerations. Conceivably a society can be perfectly happy and adjusted with a very high rate of divorce.

These critics are also unimpressed by the typologies constructed by the sociologists of the family: these, they suggest, too often give the illusion of analytic depth to what is merely low-grade description blended with inadequate conceptions of causal relationship; their evaluative overtones give away the fact that it is prejudgments that are operating, rather than an objective effort to trace basic connections. For example, Burgess and Locke list just about every conceivable influence on sexual behavior in the last twenty years, from the automobile and avant-garde literature to urbanization, and assert that the decline of Puritan taboos is the result of the "combination of all these converging factors." But what was responsible for this miraculous "convergence"? How can one blithely mix causes on all levels of abstraction? Does such a proliferation of causes indicate real grasp or lead to better understanding?

In short, the critics of the classic American sociology of the family object to the failure to face the fundamental relation between developments in the family and developments in the rest of the society, a failure covered up by the manufacture of terminologies and the accumulation of hosts of "factors" and "causes."

This is the position of the "functional sociologists": the school of sociological thinking led by Talcott Parsons of Harvard and Robert Merton of Columbia. Their ideological orientation derives from the leading ideas of the fathers of sociology—Durkheim, Pareto, Weber—modified somewhat by an interest in contemporary anthropology and psychoanalytic psychiatry. The "functional" in the name of their school refers to their emphasis on the *function* of any social institution—the role it plays in the larger society, rather than its conformity to some earlier pattern or traditional social or moral value. Thus, they would be very chary of speaking of divorce as a sign of social pathology; rather, they would point out that divorce locks in with these social and these emotional problems in our present-day society, permits the release of these tensions, and so on: leaving us with the unstated conclusion that if we reduce divorce, something else (which moralists may find equally unpleasant) will take its place.

From anthropology—particularly from the "functional" anthropology of Malinowski, pursued in this country by such well-known writers as Ruth Benedict and Margaret Mead—they take the point of view of seeing any problem against the background of possible behaviors in all societies, including primitive societies; and a strong awareness of what is possible supports their effort to free themselves from value judgments. (So, for example, knowing that some societies allow premarital sexual freedom, some post-marital sexual freedom, some both, and some neither, G. P. Murdock, an anthropologist from Yale, finds it easy to suggest an active effort to eliminate our sexual taboos.) From psycho-analytic psychiatry and psychology the functional sociologists take the emphasis on the subtle interrelationship of a variety of life-history factors in producing some psychological result, and this, too, supports their opposition to the listing of unintegrated causes.

Functional sociology does not yet have the impressive list of works —texts, studies, and popular writings—on marriage and the family that the older approach to the sociology of the family has piled up. But when we look at such a volume as *The Family: Its Function and Destiny* (edited by Ruth Nanda Anshen, Harper, 1949) we see that the functional sociologists, with their anthropological and psychiatric allies, have almost completely crowded out the older writers on the sociology of the family, and are given sizable scope in which to develop their distinctive point of view.

Let us look first at the lengthy and impressive article in which Professor Parsons tries to show how the family is integrated with the larger social structures of American society. Professor Parsons takes certain formal features of the American family, particularly the fact that one is allowed a free choice of a marriage partner and that there are no kinship regulations closely tying members of the immediate conjugal family with relatives outside it, and shows how they conform to the requirements of our occupational system and class structure. For example, the absence of large and cohesive kin groups like the primitive clan or the Chinese ancestral line permits individuals to be highly mobile occupationally; their background and their family loyalty do not hold them back. And our loose kinship ties also check the possibility of nepotism, which would violate the impersonal evaluation of individual merit on which the more efficient and more democratic occupational system of the United States rests.

Professor Parsons thus ingeniously demonstrates the "functional interdependence" of the family and the other major institutions of American society. However, in order to present his picture of a highly articulated and systematically inter-related network of institutions, he is forced to assume that the units he is relating to one another are fairly stable. For example, he makes much of the difference between the male role as jobholder and economic provider and the female role as house-wife and mother, taking her status from her husband. But he must concede that "there are strong tendencies in the United States towards identical treatment of the sexes." However, ignoring the broad impli-cations of this admission, he then says that the difference in roles is *necessary* in order to preserve the solidarity of the family, because if husband and wife both worked, their job statuses might differ and this would impose serious competitive strains on the marriage relationship. This argument rather neatly links sex roles to the occupational system, but, even if its far-fetched character is ignored, it completely overlooks the fact that married women *do* work, and in increasing numbers. Married women, in all classes, now make up a considerable percentage of the total labor force, and there is clearly other evidence as well that sex roles in America are changing. How then can it be "necessary," if the whole system is to keep on working, that women should *not* work?

Professor Parsons' failure to stress present-day changes in sex roles leads to the main point that can be made against the newer, anthropologically influenced efforts to understand the American family: their concentration on efforts to detect in Americans' behavior the patterns and norms of an "American" culture, parallel to the culture of a primitive tribe, is misplaced. It seems to me that the urbanization and mechanization of American life, now in the process of steamrolling traditional values and modes of conduct out of existence, make it impossible to speak with real precision any more of static "culture patterns" or "social norms" governing the sphere of family life. There is no question that the older patterns and norms are severely shaken; but I doubt whether many new ones have emerged in any crystallized fashion, and certainly no total overall system, worthy of being called a culture, is as yet apparent.

If we look at a few of the subjects sociologists regularly deal with in their discussions of the family, we will see that the difficulties involved in pinning down present-day norms and patterns of family behavior are, by comparison with primitive societies, enormous.

Courtship: The term itself evokes anachronistic images of the chaperons, horsehair sofas, stammering proposals, and chaste first kisses after betrothal that were at one time required by a clearly formulated code. We do not need Kinsey to tell us that it is no longer followed by most people, although, with minor modifications, it remains the "official morality" promulgated by the organs of mass communication, upheld by Dorothy Dix, and transmitted by most middle-class parents to their children. Here the voice of Puritanism, the Victorian era, and the rural farm family—not to mention Catholic and Jewish education—still speaks. Its growing irrelevance to actual behavior gives it the status of an "ideal pattern" rather than a "real pattern," to use the language of the anthropologists.

The relaxed censorship standards of Hollywood and the publishing industry, the popularity of such books as the Kinsey report, and the spread of popular psychiatry with its promotion of "sexual adjustment" as an ideal plus the idea that "sexual frustration" is unhealthy, indicate that values are changing. The most marked trend in sexual behavior within the last generation unearthed by the Kinsey statistics is the growing sexual independence of unmarried women. At the very least, there seems to be an increasing acceptance of pre-marital sex relations and a more general awareness of almost universal participation in the erotic life.

Looking at the middle class alone, we see that the majority still probably adhere to a secularized Puritanism which uneasily co-exists with the "having-a-good-time" attitude nurtured by the entertainment industries. Some groups countenance pre-marital sex relations, but only after betrothal; to others the "affair" is an accepted type of pre-marital relationship (and often extra-marital as well); and there are still those who regard a "Bohemian revolt" demanding virtual promiscuity as the essence of modernity. Everything from sheer "having fun" to the orgiastic philosophy of Wilhelm Reich is invoked to justify this variety of behavior. Only in the educated, "liberal" sector of the metropolitan middle class do we find that new values are systematized to any degree. It is here that psychiatry becomes the basis for a new ethic governing sexual conduct (and not infrequently *all* conduct).

The individual often is caught in this confusion and profusion of values, and must fall back upon himself for canons of personal conduct. Who is so lonely as the adolescent girl wondering if she has become a "loose" woman by submitting to her lover, and finding no unanimous community opinion to answer her either negatively or affirmatively? Or the boy responding to the value placed by his male companions on "having an affair" while remaining deeply unconvinced of his right to make sexual demands on girls of his own social status? No wonder attempts to establish an ethic based solely on analysis of the biological and psychological nature of the individual are so popular. A great deal of the intense interest which Americans have in psychoanalysis is due simply to its revelation of what Lionel Trilling has called "a community of sexuality."

The sociologists are hardly consistent with one another in their efforts to extract generalizations from this chaos of shifting standards. Carle Zimmerman, a belligerent traditionalist, thunderously denounces America's "Voice of the Turtle sexual ethics," while those influenced by psychoanalysis continue to speak as if they were engaged in storming the last bastion of Puritanism in the modern world. And these conflicting positions are supported by empirical studies of different segments of American social reality. These writers may accurately characterize certain groups; but they fail to stress the significance of the existence side by side of so many *different* norms of sexual conduct. The demonstration that widely different norms do exist is certainly one of the most significant findings of the Kinsey report. For it is this bewildering diversity of values which is primary to the situation confronted by middle-class Americans growing up in the larger cities today. Not only do they face a variety of possible patterns in their own world, but in social mobility and migration they become aware of new ranges of patterns characteristic of different classes. Surely it is an instance of what

Durkheim called "anomie," of the breakdown of norms, that condition which under the more familiar label of "alienation" is recognized as oppressing all of us.

The sociologists would seem to have overworked the concept of "culture." Modern life cannot be fitted into the frames of uniform "culture patterns," and the attempt to force a fit often results in neglect of basic features of *social structure*—the objective realities, such as the need to make a living in a certain social system, which enforce a certain type of behavior regardless of pre-existing norms, values, and social rituals. One of the outstanding characteristics of the modern world is, in fact, the destruction of culture by sweeping changes in social structure. The adjustment to modern industry and modern cities wrecks the complicated and varied cultural patterns built up in the American rural hinterland, or in European villages. Edward Sapir, the late Yale anthropologist, suggested this a long time ago when he distinguished between the "genuine" culture of older societies and the "spurious" culture of an industrialized world.

Marriage: We have already pointed out that a major focus of empirical study has been the "causes" of marital unhappiness. I believe that an inquiry into *why people get married at all* might prove far more revealing than these usually banal undertakings, but since all writers on the family assume the desirability, or at least the permanence, of the institution of monogamous marriage, no one has posed this question for systematic investigation. It is taken for granted that romantic love, and the desire for emotional security or for sanctioned sexual gratification, induce most people to marry.

These motives seem so self-evident that the radical change in the meaning of marriage which they imply is easily overlooked. For marriage was formerly both an economic necessity and a moral obligation, rather than simply a means of satisfying individual psychological needs. Today marriage no longer confers of itself added standing in the community. It no longer symbolizes the achievement of full status as adult and citizen as it did in rural society. While a vague stigma still clings to the middle-aged bachelor, it does not affect his occupational career and perhaps is based on suspicion of homosexuality rather than on an echo of the conviction that failure to marry constitutes unnatural and immoral shirking of responsibility. The spinster, of course, remains an object of contempt and pity, but this attitude will presumably disappear as differences in sex roles continue to diminish. Indeed, no one takes this attitude even today towards an unmarried woman who has achieved some type of distinction. Again, a variety of possible roles is offered to people where one stood before.

It is asserted by both laymen and sociologists that romantic love is the prime basis for marriage in America. To many it is as uniquely American as baseball or hot dogs. Now romance is linked with youth;

it is, as a matter of fact, a primary feature of the American "youth culture." However, the boundaries of this youth culture are being steadily expanded downward to a youthful age level where marriage is quite impossible economically. Originally centered on the college campus, it has diffused, with the creation of high school Greek-letter fraternities modeled on those of the colleges, to late and middle adolescents. And now twelve- and thirteen-year-old "bobby-soxers" are also being brought within its orbit. While the age at which one enters the romance market drops, the age at which one marries has been rising, and, with college education becoming more and more a matter of course, will rise further. The trend towards greater pre-marital sexual freedom also encourages the postponement of marriage and destroys a strong psychological support of romantic love—sexual frustration.

If, as Denis de Rougemont asserts in another essay in the Anshen volume, "it is the very essence of romance to thrive on obstacles, delays, separations, and dreams," it may be that the romantic dramas of the future will be mainly enacted by youngsters in their early teens facing the economic impossibility of marriage, the jeers of older adolescents who have become confirmed sexual realists, and the indifference of adults who have "settled down" to marriage in a matter-of-fact, utilitarian way. Marriage is already looked on by many as "settling down" rather than as full achievement of adult status or as the blissful climax of romance. Perhaps marriage is becoming an escape from romance— from the emotional wear-and-tear of a succession of bouts with love followed by disillusionment, although the high divorce rate would seem to indicate that it is not a very successful escape.

In any case, the reasons why people marry are problematical and may become even more so. Their problematical character is ignored by the sociologists, who concentrate on the reasons why marriages break up. "To marry or not to marry?" is a real question for many people. Or, more accurately, it becomes "whether to marry now or later?" John Levy and Ruth Monroe, in their book *The Happy Family*, point out that people frequently rationalize a deep-seated reluctance to marry by finding fault with all prospective partners who present themselves. Freely expressed concern over *whom* to marry conceals the more fundamental doubts about *when* to marry. This would have applied to very few Americans of fifty years ago; indeed, there have been few periods in world history in which the desirability of marriage has been as widely questioned as it is today—though the questioning is as yet indirectly revealed in people's behavior and emotions, rather than in thought and speech.

The 1940 census shows that about 10 per cent of each sex remained unmarried at the age of 45. This figure undoubtedly represents an increase in the number of unmarried people over earlier years; yet it is perhaps equally significant to note that 90 per cent of the population still gets married before early middle age.

Children: The wish for an heir to perpetuate one's name and status was the strongest male incentive to marriage in aristocratic society; later, children were needed as workers on the farm and in the small business when these were predominantly family enterprises; and motherhood has always been considered woman's crowning achievement in her traditional feminine role. Today it is obvious that emphasis on success as a major life goal, the perils of child-raising stressed by popular psychiatry, the uncertainty of the future, and, finally, the availability of birth-control methods, lessen the meaning and value once associated with the creation of one's own image in the person of an offspring. The ambivalence which middle-class parents, both male and female, have towards raising a family has been fully and ably described by Arnold Green in his article "The Middle Class Male Child and Neurosis" (*American Sociological Review*, February 1946). Having children, like sexual conduct and marriage, is increasingly taken out of the realm of "mores" and "culture patterns" and becomes a matter of individual option.

Child-rearing must inevitably become a focal point for the tensions of social change, for parents can scarcely fail to recognize that the world faced by their children differs considerably from that in which they themselves grew up. Margaret Mead and Geoffrey Gorer both attribute the absence of stable patterns for raising children in the United States to historical causes: the influx into the country of immigrants who were of necessity forced to reject much of their Old World culture in adjusting to life in alien America. They contend that the anxiety felt by immigrant parents bringing up children in a strange country, and the inevitable rejection by the young of their parents' way of life, have somehow been universalized and now characterize even families whose forefathers have lived in America for generations.

But large-scale immigration has ended and a third and a fourth generation of descendants of the immigrants are now growing up. Are we to infer that the attitudes of the immigrant population have "diffused" through the rest of society and mysteriously become part of a unitary American "ethos"? The almost exclusive concern with cultural concepts—in this case the "acculturation" of the foreign-born—leads Mead and Gorer to ignore contemporary socio-economic changes which obliterate traditional values and drive as wide a gap between the second and third generations as that created by immigration between the first and second. Everyone, old American and third-generation immigrant alike, is victimized by this process. There is no need to refer to immigration to explain it. Surely suburban living, commuters' trains, and unglamorous office jobs, leading to the father's absence from home most of the day, have as much to do with the decline of paternal authority as a "pattern" of rejecting fathers ostensibly inherited from the children of the foreign-born. Perhaps second-generation immigrants did originate the pattern, but it has not simply persisted just so: it must have been strengthened by these social trends unrelated to immigration. And in the long run it is more valuable to understand the significance of such trends than the particular historical situation of the immigrant family.

Big city urbanism provides the setting in which child-rearing is viewed as an enterprise fraught with danger, and recourse to the "expert" becomes an almost compulsive response. But science, and particularly a new and undeveloped branch of it, is an unstable authority on which to depend, and it has produced a rapid succession of verdicts on child-rearing over the last two decades. John B. Watson told the mother to sterilize herself emotionally before approaching her child in order to "condition its reflexes" as impersonally as possible. Or better still she shouldn't approach the child at all, but should surrender this archaic privilege to the behavioral psychologist. Today Watson is a back number, and the Freudians tell us that the child must have the demonstrative love of the mother. Approved methods of feeding and toilet training have changed even more rapidly. You pick your pediatrician and you get your technique for rearing children.

These trends in sexual behavior, marriage, and child-bearing and rearing all move in the direction of greater freedom of individual choice. Modern life has broken through the rigidity of traditionally prescribed patterns of conduct. Man's emancipation from the last of the trinity of institutions, Church, State, and Family, which dominated him before the Industrial Revolution, is now well under way.

Bourgeois society had guaranteed religious freedom and created the limited, *laissez-faire* state, but as Max Horkheimer, another contributor to the Anshen volume, points out, *families* rather than individuals were liberated from authoritarian institutions. In fact, the Victorian era, the peak of bourgeois liberalism, has come to symbolize familial control and oppression—the domination of woman by man, of children by parents, and of all by a Puritanical moral code. Professor Horkheimer writes:

> Man, liberated from serfdom in alien households, became the master in his own. Children, however, for whom the world had been a penitentiary throughout the Middle Ages, continued to be slaves well into the 19th century. When the separation of state and society, of political and private life, was completed, direct personal dependence survived in the home.

Despite the emphasis on democratic living to be found in contemporary sociology, hardly any American student of the family views it as Professor Horkheimer does, from the perspective of the history of human freedom. Seen in this perspective, most of the current negative evaluations become positive. We can, if we wish, see the variety and uncertainty of behavior in "courtship," marriage, and child-raising as indications of the breakdown and disintegration of the family, as in a sense they are. But we can also see these trends as inevitable *expansions of the area of the personal freedom of the individual.* Of course increased freedom means more uncertainty concerning desirable sexual conduct and more divorce, certainly at first and probably forever: but then we must stop hedging and decide what we really mean by individual freedom and how much of it we want.

And even our failure to discover "patterns," "norms," and "rules," equivalent to those described from primitive societies, and earlier stages of Western culture, can be seen positively: it means that the individual is not faced with one or a few fixed courses of development, but has to create a life for himself that combines the old patterns and desires with new possibilities. This is more difficult, emotionally, and creates a confused situation, socially and morally: but what else can freedom mean?

The study of the family can lead us directly to the consideration of the most important questions of freedom and individuality: perhaps the functional sociologists will yet arrive at the discussion of those questions on a high level.

Meanwhile, it should be clear that none of the trends we have described points in any way to the disappearance of the family, nor even to changes in its formal structure. Although by 1945 roughly one in every three marriages ended in divorce, it is estimated that as high as 70 or 80 per cent of the divorcees remarry, which, to say the least, does not indicate a loss of faith in marriage. And in spite of our much publicized falling birth rate, people continue to have children and raise them in the time-honored and traditional place for such functions, the family. In our mass society the ties of marriage and kinship are almost the only stable framework for close personal relationships.

Indeed, the family we have today, with its freedom from extended kinship bonds and from excessive ceremonial, may be considered as better meeting the needs and more appropriately reflecting the spirit of a free, mobile, and individualistic society; Professor Parsons in his essay is well aware of this.

By one of those ironies of history, this accelerating freedom from the authoritarian family comes at a time when totalitarianism menaces freedom in all areas of life. And as Professor Horkheimer shows, this threat is not unrelated to the family: for on the one hand, totalitarianism restores the authority of the family as a means of raising the birth rate and enhancing national power; but on the other, this is a false restoration, for in reality the totalitarian state demands loyalty only to itself, and it destroys all other loyalties, including those that develop within the family. This would seem to be one more piece of evidence that the freer society and the freer family are closely interrelated and interdependent.

Prospective Changes in Marriage and the Family*

ROBERT PARKE, JR., and PAUL C. GLICK

TRENDS IN MARRIAGE AND STABILITY OF MARRIAGE

Consideration of prospective changes in American families can begin with no more appropriate issue than what is happening to the age at marriage. This subject is of interest in its own right, partly because of concern over the number of teen-age marriages. In addition, the age at marriage significantly influences events in the middle and late stages of the family life cycle; it determines, in part, the age at which the wife's responsibilities for child-care have declined to the point where she is free to seek full-time employment and the probability that she and her husband will survive to enjoy life together after the husband retires.

Increasing Similarity of Marriage Ages

For several years Americans have married at an exceptionally young average age for an industrial society. Furthermore, American women marry men who are more nearly their own ages than is generally true elsewhere.[1]

One of the striking features of recent trends in American marriage is the extent to which marriage patterns are becoming standardized.

First, nearly everyone gets married nowadays. The projections shown in Table 1 suggest that as few as three per cent of the men and women now in their late twenties may enter middle age without having married. These proportions are one-third of the corresponding proportions actually experienced by persons who are now in late middle age.

Second, to a greater extent than before, young persons are getting married at about the same age. The reduction in the age at marriage has been accompanied by a compressing of marriages into a narrower age range than before. This is shown in Figure 1 and Table 2. Among the ever-married men now in late middle age, about eight years elapsed

Reprinted from *Journal of Marriage and the Family*, Vol. 29 (1967). Tables have been renumbered.

TABLE 1

Percent of All Persons Who First Married Before Specified Age, by Age in 1966 and Sex, for the United States: March, 1966*

Age in 1966 and Sex	Percent of All Persons in Age Group Who First Married Before Age —						
	18	20	22	25	30	35	45†
Male							
18 and 19 years	2.9	—	—	—	—	—	—
20 to 24 years	3.9	18.4	—	—	—	—	94.7
25 to 29 years	4.4	18.5	42.5	72.2	—	—	96.7
30 to 34 years	4.1	17.9	38.1	65.4	84.0	—	95.3
35 to 39 years	3.6	13.8	34.3	59.3	81.1	88.7	93.6
40 to 44 years	3.3	12.0	29.9	58.3	81.3	88.3	93.1
45 to 49 years	2.2	8.8	23.3	49.5	79.7	89.5	94.1
50 to 54 years	2.5	8.4	19.7	43.5	71.1	83.9	90.7
55 to 64 years	2.6	9.6	22.5	42.6	67.1	80.1	89.1
65 to 74 years	2.1	8.7	20.1	41.8	69.0	78.8	87.8
Female							
18 and 19 years	14.7	—	—	—	—	—	—
20 to 24 years	19.1	45.6	—	—	—	—	95.5
25 to 29 years	20.3	48.8	69.1	85.2	—	—	97.2
30 to 34 years	22.9	46.7	67.2	84.0	92.8	—	97.1
35 to 39 years	17.1	42.9	63.4	80.3	90.5	93.7	95.9
40 to 44 years	15.0	33.0	53.1	76.1	87.8	91.6	95.0
45 to 49 years	12.8	27.8	46.4	68.3	85.4	91.0	94.1
50 to 54 years	15.6	30.1	44.0	63.6	81.2	88.7	93.0
55 to 64 years	15.4	31.7	46.3	62.2	77.6	84.8	90.7
65 to 74 years	13.5	28.8	45.3	64.2	80.7	85.8	89.6

* Source: Based on answers to March 1966 Current Population Survey question on data of first marriage. The data cover the population of the United States, except for members of the armed forces living in barracks and similar quarters, who are not included in the survey.

† For persons under 45 years old in 1966, the percent first married by age 45 was projected on the assumption that the rate of first marriage per 1,000 single persons between the current age and age 45 will be the same as observed between corresponding ages among persons 45 to 49 years old in 1936. See John Hajnal, "Age of Marriage and Proportions Marrying," Population Studies, 7:2 (November, 1953), p. 115, for method of calculation.

between the age by which the first one-fourth of the men had married and the age by which three-fourths had married. For men who are now in their late twenties, the corresponding figure is expected to be about five years. That is to say, even after the younger group of men have been exposed to another two decades of first marriage experience, the inter-quartile range of age at first marriage for this group is expected to be only about two-thirds of that for the older men. A corresponding trend has occurred among women. The interquartile range of age at first marriage experienced by the women who are now in late middle age was about seven years. This is expected to contract to about four years by the time the women who are now in their late twenties reach middle age.

Third, women are marrying men who are closer to their own ages. This observation is suggested by the declining difference between the median ages at first marriage for men and women shown in Table 1 and is confirmed by data from the 1960 Census, which showed the median difference between the age of the husband and the age of the wife for married couples in which both partners were married only once. Husbands over 55 years old in 1960 were 3.6 years older than their wives on the average; while husbands under 35 were only 1.9 years older on the average. Forty-two percent of the older husbands were at least five years older than their wives, as compared with only 17 percent of the younger husbands.[2]

Marriage Age and Joint Survival

The lessening of the difference between the ages of the husband and wife causes a significant improvement in the chances of joint survival of the married couple. Under mortality conditions prevailing in 1960, a woman who was married at age 20 to a man four years her senior ran a 42-percent chance of being widowed before age 65, assuming that she survived to that age. If she married a man only two years older than herself, her chances of widowhood before reaching 65 would be only 37 percent, and, if her husband were the same age as she, her chances of widowhood would be only 33 percent.

The joint survival of a married couple depends, of course, on a number of factors besides the difference between their ages. The fore-going figures assume no divorce, a fact which would not affect the in-terpretation if there is no fundamental change in the trend of the divorce rate; and the foregoing figures assume constant mortality conditions, whereas mortality conditions will likely change somewhat though prob-ably not enough to negate the points being made. Nor do they take into account the effect of separation and desertion on the population of married couples; but, as indicated below, there seems actually to be a real likelihood that desertions will diminish, assuming that the edu-cational and economic levels of the population improve over time.

Figure 1. Median and Quartile Ages at First Marriage, by Age in 1966 and Sex

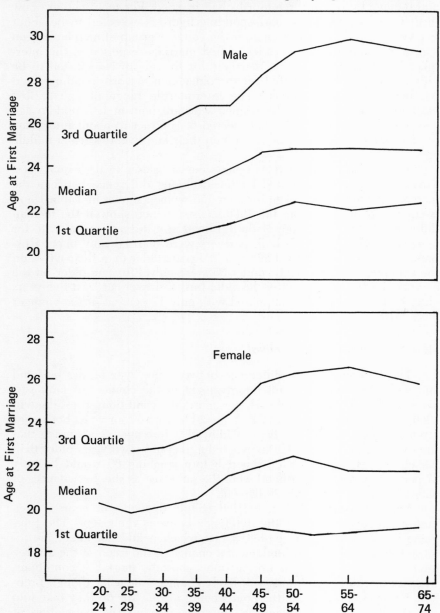

Source: Table 1   Age Group in 1966

TABLE 2

Median and Quartile Ages at First Marriage, by Age in 1966 and Sex, for the United States: March, 1966*

Age in 1966	Male				Female			
	First quartile	Second quartile (median)	Third quartile	Inter-quartile range (years)	First quartile	Second quartile (median)	Third quartile	Inter-quartile range (years)
20 to 24	20.4†	—	—	—	18.4	20.2†	—	—
25 to 29	20.5	22.5	25.1‡	4.6	18.3	20.0	22.5	4.2
30 to 34	20.6	22.9	26.1	5.5	18.1	20.4	22.7	4.6
35 to 39	21.0	23.3	26.8	5.8	18.5	20.4	23.2	4.7
40 to 44	21.4	23.7	26.8	5.4	19.0	21.5	24.3	5.3
45 to 49	22.0	24.7	28.2	6.2	19.5	22.1	25.5	6.0
50 to 54	22.4	25.2	29.3	7.4	19.1	22.4	26.2	7.1
55 to 64	22.0	25.3	29.3	7.9	19.1	21.9	26.5	7.4
65 to 74	22.3	25.3	29.3	7.0	19.2	21.9	25.7	6.5

* Note: Based on data by single years of age at first marriage. Percent ultimately marrying used to calculate these values is percent first married before age 45 shown in Table 2. Source: Based on answers to March 1966 Current Population Survey question on data of first marriage. The data cover the population of the United States, except for members of the armed forces living in barracks and similar quarters, who are not included in the survey.

† Experience during age 20 based on data for persons 21 to 24 years old in 1966.

‡ Experience during age 25 based on data for persons 26 to 29 years old in 1966.

However, the net effect of these factors over the past ten years has been such as to suggest substantial future increases in the proportion of persons living with their spouses in late middle age and in old age. For example, 64 percent of all women 55 to 64 years old were married and living with their (first or subsequent) husbands in 1965. According to experimental projections, the corresponding figure may increase eight points to 72 percent by 1985. The smaller increase of about three points that is projected for women over 65 nonetheless represents a substantial relative improvement over the current level of 34 percent in this age range.

Decline in Teen-Age Marriages

The public concern over the number of teen-age marriages has arisen because of the notorious instability of these marriages. The 1960 Census showed that, among the men who first married at age 18 during the period five to 15 years prior to the census, the first marriage was not intact at the time of the census in about 21 percent of the cases. This was twice as high as the proportion of not intact first marriages among men who first married at ages 23 to 24. A similar relationship was evident in the data for females.[3] (Nearly all such persons with first marriage not intact were divorced, separated, or remarried at the time of the census.)

Actually, however, figures that have recently become available (shown in Figure 2 and Table 2) show that the marriage rate among very young women reached a peak perhaps ten to 15 years ago and is now on the decline. Twenty-three percent of all the women who are currently 30 to 34 years old married before age 18. The rate of early teen-age marriages is successively smaller for each younger group of women. Only 15 percent of all the women who are currently 18 and 19 years old married before age 18.

Extremely young age at marriage has never been very widespread among men. Thus, the proportion of men who married before age 18 appears to have been no greater than four percent for any of the age groups shown. Even so, the percent of very young marriages among men who are now in their late twenties was twice as high as it was among men now in their forties, and there is evidence of a recent downturn in this percent among men who are now in their late teens.

This may or may not portend a downturn in the percent of all men who marry under age 20, which rose in recent years from nine percent for the men who are now in their late forties to a stable level of around 18 percent for the men who are now under 35.

The recent downward trend in teen-age marriages among women may be in part a response to the changing ratio of males to females in the marriageable ages. If so, this has interesting implications for the pattern of age at marriage in the next few years.

The "Marriage Squeeze"

Because of past changes in the annual number of births and because women marry men who are two or three years their senior, on the average, there has been, in the past few years, a drop in the number of males per 100 females in the main marrying ages. By the main marrying ages, the authors mean those between the first and third quartile ages at first marriage according to recent experience, or approximately ages 18 to 22 for females and 20 to 24 for males.

In the early 1950's there were, in the average year, about 104 males per 100 females in the main marrying ages. In the late 1950's this ratio had dropped to 99 per 100, and in the early 1960's it was only 94. In the latter half of the 1960's, it will average only about 93 and will subsequently return to 99 per 100 in the early 1970's.[4]

These figures describe, in broad terms, the "marriage squeeze" that has resulted from the fact that the girls born in the postwar baby boom have come of age (for purposes of marriage) sooner than the boys.

Generally speaking, the squeeze can be resolved in any or all of several ways: by the boys marrying for the first time at younger ages or by the girls marrying for the first time at older ages or marrying older widowed and divorced men or older single men who might not otherwise have married. Or it is possible that more girls will ultimately not marry at all.

Any of these ways out of the squeeze involves a sequence of changes in age at marriage and in the difference between the ages of the husband and wife. The evidence so far available suggests that, in the first half of the 1960's, the marriage squeeze was resolved in large part by changes in the marriage patterns of the women and not by alteration of the trend of ages at first marriage for men. The data in Figures 1 and 2 show no acceleration in the downward trend of male ages at first marriage. This fact may be construed as implying that, up to now, the young men have been successfully warding off any pressure from the mounting numbers of marriageable young women.

The marriage squeeze will continue for perhaps a decade. If the pattern of ages for men at marriage from 1965 to 1975 is like that observed in the first half of the 1960's, then about a million women will have to postpone getting married (Table 3). This figure represents the difference between (a) the number of women who would get married if marriages followed the rates observed for females from 1959 to 1964 and (b) the number who would marry if the number of marriages were governed by the observed marriage rates for males. If such a postponement occurred, it would force the lifetime age at first marriage up about one-third of a year for the women who enter the marriage ages during this period. Such an increase would represent a continuation of the rise in the female age at first marriage that has been observed since the late 1950's.[5]

Figure 2. Percent of All Persons Who First Married Before Specified Age, by Age in 1966 and Sex

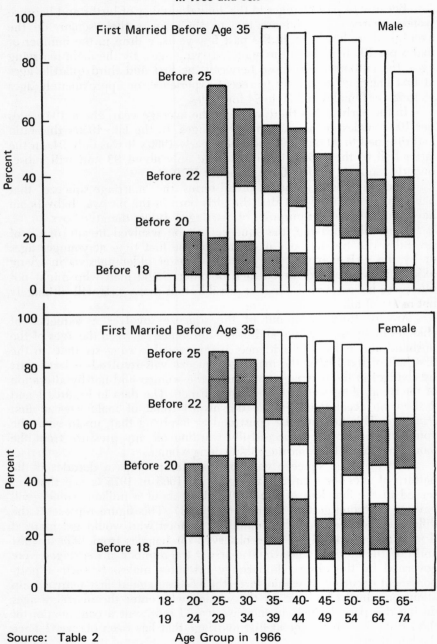

Source: Table 2   Age Group in 1966

TABLE 3

Test Projections of Marriages in the United States: 1965 to 1985*
(in Millions)

Period (Beginning and Ending July 1)	Total Marriages in Period, Assuming Continuation of 1959 to 1964 Rates for:		Difference
	Males	Females	
1965 to 1970	9.3	9.9	.6
1970 to 1975	10.7	11.2	.5
1975 to 1980	11.9	12.3	.4
1980 to 1985	12.6	12.7	.1

* Source: See text.

Of course, in the next few years the tide may turn so that the women, rather than the men, will have their way. Thus, if the girls persuade the boys to marry prematurely, by the standards of recent years, there will be more marriages and more young husbands than otherwise.

More Marriages Remaining Intact

The preceding discussion already suggested the extent to which marital dissolution due to widowhood will be reduced by recent reductions in the difference between the ages of the husband and wife. Additional changes toward more marriages remaining intact may be expected as a natural result of the anticipated continuation in the upgrading of the population with respect to income inasmuch as separation and divorce are less extensive among the affluent than among the poor.[6]

Hollywood to the contrary notwithstanding, statistics from the 1960 Census provide further confirmation of the fact that stability of marriage is a condition that is shared less by the lower-status segments of the population than by the rest.

The special reports of the 1960 Census on *Marital Status* and *Age at First Marriage* devoted much attention to social and economic analysis of the patterns of marriage and dissolution of marriage among men 45 to 54 years old, a group that has reached its peak earning capacity and among whom few additional first marriages will occur. There were one and a half million ever-married white men in this age group with incomes of less than $3,000, and more than two million with incomes of $10,000 or more. Fully 29 percent of the poor men, but only 16 percent of the affluent men, were no longer living with their first wives at the time of the census. The corresponding relationship was even more striking among nonwhites than it was for whites.[7] These differences are too great to be attributed solely to socioeconomic differences in the proportion of men whose wives have died. It follows that these differences reflect, in part, socioeconomic differences in divorce and separation.[8] Barring a rise in the divorce rate or major changes in the pattern of divorce and separation by socioeconomic status, the reduction of poverty should result in a substantial long-term improvement in the average stability of marriages.

This expectation is expressed with slight reservations in view of the increases over the past few years in the percent of the population who are divorced. A recent Census Bureau report shows the following age-standardized percentages of divorced persons in the population 14 years old and over:[9]

Year	Male	Female
1966	2.2	3.1
1965	2.2	2.9
1960	1.9	2.6
1955	1.8	2.3

However, these increases do not necessarily imply the existence of a rising divorce rate, nor is there independent evidence of such. A stable divorce rate may produce an increasing accumulation of divorced persons in the population unless remarriage is universal and instantaneous. This it is not, although remarriage rates for divorced persons are high. Glick estimated that about three-fourths of the persons who were divorced from 1943 to 1948 had remarried by 1948.[10]

FAMILY SIZE AND LIVING ARRANGEMENTS

Reference has been made to estimated future marriages and changes in the marital status of the population. These projections, and the ones to follow, are test calculations that have been produced in the course of work at the Bureau of the Census toward the preparation of a new set of household and family projections. These projections have been prepared in order to examine the effect of various assumptions on estimates for the future. They do not constitute official projections of the Bureau of the Census. They do represent a few among a variety of plausible or instructive ways of expressing the implications that recent trends may have for the future.

The family structure of the future is studied here by means of statistics on anticipated trends in the living arrangements of the population. In these figures, marriages have been projected by assuming that the marriage rates of 1959 to 1964 will continue and by imposing the condition that the number of marriages will be the average of the number projected separately for men and women. It is assumed further that the living arrangements of the population (as measured by percent living in families, percent maintaining their own households, etc.) will continue to change at the same rate at which they changed from 1957 to 1964. The population assumed in these projections is the Census Bureau's Series B. The results of one set of such assumptions are set forth in Tables 4 and 5.

TABLE 4

Persons per Household and Family in the United States, 1940 to 1966, and Test Projections for 1985*

Year	Persons per Household			Persons per Family		
	All Ages	Under 18	18 and Over	All Ages	Under 18	18 and Over
1940	3.7	1.1	2.5	3.8	1.2	2.5
1950	3.4	1.1	2.3	3.5	1.2	2.4
1960	3.3	1.2	2.1	3.7	1.4	2.3
1966	3.3	1.2	2.1	3.7	1.4	2.3
1985	3.1	1.1	1.9	3.5	1.4	2.2

* Source: See text.

TABLE 5

Percent of Married Couples and Individuals with Their Own Households, for the United States, 1965, and Test Projections for 1985*

Type of Unit and Year	Percent with Own Household		
	Total, age 20 and over	20 to 64	65 and over
Married couples and individuals			
1965	78	78	79
1985	86	84	90
Married couples			
1965	98	98	98
1985	99	99	99
Individuals†			
1965	51	45	66
1985	64	56	84

* Source: See text.
† All persons except married with spouse present, and inmates of institutions.

Adults Per Household Declining

These results indicate a continued decline in the average number of adults per household and family and little change in the average number of children.[11] The figures express the average size of households and families in terms of the number of persons living together at any one point in time. The 1966 figures on children, for instance, refer to the average number now living in the household or family and not to the number born. Furthermore, the numbers of households and families include those with no children as well as those with children.

The 1985 estimate of 2.2 adults per family is very close to a minimum average. It is subject to substantial further reduction only by further reducing the number of offspring over the age of 17 who live with their parents. The average number of adults per family cannot fall much below two, since nearly nine out of ten families include a husband and wife.

The average size of household declines a small amount in the test projections; however, the relative decline is slightly greater than that for the average family size. The average size of household is smaller to begin with because it takes into account persons who live alone and maintain their own home. This average is subject to greater potential decline than the average family size, because there are still many people who potentially might set up housekeeping by themselves who have not yet done so. Moreover, there is a strong prospect for further household formation from this source if the projections in Table 5 prove to be well founded.

Increasing Headship Among Individuals

In 1965 about 78 percent of the married couples and individuals who might have maintained their own household were actually doing so. An *individual* who might maintain his own household is defined, for present purposes, as anyone 20 years old and over who is not "married with spouse present" and is not an inmate of an institution. The category includes heads of broken families, persons living alone, adult children and relatives in the home, lodgers, and other persons who live with a relative or share the living accommodations of someone else, and persons in rooming houses and other group quarters.

No substantial increase in the number of separate households can result from an increase in the propensity of married couples to maintain their own households, since 98 percent already do so. However, only half the eligible individuals were maintaining their own households in 1965. Recent trends suggest that this figure may rise to two-thirds of the eligible individuals by 1985. The increase anticipated among individuals at age 65 and over is fairly striking, rising as it does from 66 to 84 percent of the eligibles. Medicare and other social programs may cause this to rise even further by making it possible for higher proportions of aged relatives who now share the homes of children to be self-sustaining or to remove themselves from the population of eligibles, as here defined, by entering a nursing home.

CONCLUSION

A review of recent trends in marriage and family statistics provides a basis for the following expectations, if one keeps in mind the foregoing qualifications:

1. Persons now in their late twenties and their early thirties are more likely to marry at some time in their lives than any other group on record.

2. The rate of teen-age marriage, which is now on the decline, will continue to go down for a while, then level off.

3. The relative oversupply of young women will tend to produce a further rise in the next ten years in the age at which women marry for the first time.

4. The compression of marriages into a narrow age range will cause marriage and household formation to be somewhat more responsive than before to changes in the number of past births from which the marrying population comes.

5. Over and above any general decline in mortality, the declines in the difference between the ages of the husband and wife will reduce the frequency of widowhood and increase the proportion of couples who survive jointly to retirement age.

6. Declines in the relative frequency of divorce and separation should result to the extent that there are reductions in poverty and general improvements in the socioeconomic status of the population.

7. The small average size of American families (in terms of related persons sharing the same living quarters) will not change very much, but the average number of adult members may come very close to a minimum size. Greater changes are likely to develop only if there are major changes in the average number of children in the home.

8. Nearly all married couples now maintain their own households. In addition, there is a good prospect that within the next 20 years five out of every six aged individuals not in institutions will keep house on their own, and more than half the adult individuals of other ages will do so.

In closing, it is acknowledged that here and there the observations presented have gone a step or two beyond the projections. Furthermore, the future patterns could actually veer off in new directions not anticipated in the projections. However, there is reason to expect that further development of the program for preparing marriage and family projections, and improvements in the data available, will make it possible to reduce the area of uncertainty and to provide prompt corrections of future readings so as to bring them in line with current developments.

NOTES

* This is a slightly revised version of a paper prepared for presentation to the annual meetings of the American Sociological Association, Miami Beach, Florida, August 29 to September 1, 1966. Tabulation of part of the data in this paper was made possible by funds provided by the U.S. Public Health Service (Research Grant CH-00075, formerly GM-08262) to the American Public Health Association for a series of monographs on vital and health statistics.

This paper focuses on data for the total population; marriage patterns by race were the subject of a companion paper, entitled "Marital Status of the Nonwhite Population in 1970," by Daniel O. Price, in the same session of the 1966 A.S.A. meetings.

1 Based on comparisons of average age at first marriage for males and females. Except as noted, "marriage" in this paper refers to first marriage; in recent years about four-fifths of all marriages in the United States have been first marriages. For comparative data on the United States and selected European countries see John Hajnal, "Age at Marriage and Proportions Marrying," *Population Studies*, 7:2 (November, 1953), pp. 119 and 120, Tables 5 and 6. In addition, several recent volumes of United Nations *Demographic Yearbook* have included comparative statistics on marital status and on number of marriages, by age.

2 See *1960 Census of Population*, Final Report PC(2)-4E, *Marital Status*, Table 9, p. 151. To be sure, the younger men have had less opportunity than the older men to marry women who are five or more years younger than themselves. This is true even though the foregoing figures exclude second and later marriages. The biasing effect of this fact on the foregoing comparison is, however, probably compensated in large part by the fact that, by the time of the census, the marriages of the older men had been subject to years of selective attrition through divorce and widowhood with the result that the proportion of the older couples in which the husband was much older than the wife would have been much smaller than it was in the marriages of the original cohort. The facts in the paragraph following illustrate the faster than normal attrition by death of those couples in which the husband is considerably older than the wife. For evidence of a similar effect attributable to divorce, see Thomas P. Monahan, "Does Age at Marriage Matter in Divorce?" *Social Forces*, 32:1 (October, 1953), pp. 81–87.

3 See *1960 Census of Population*, Final Report PC(2)-4D, *Age at First Marriage*, Table 10.

4 Data for 1950 to 1964 were based on U.S. Bureau of the Census, *Current Population Reports*, Series P-25, Nos. 311 and 314. Data for 1965 to 1974 were derived, on the assumption of no mortality or net immigration, from population estimates by single years of age for 1965 shown in Series P-25, No. 286.

5 The difference between the figures in the first two columns of Table 3 continues to 1974–1980, even though the sex ratio in the main ages at marriage returns to near balance in the early 1970's. This is in part because the ratio of men to women in selected ages does not adequately describe the relative availability of marriageable men and women of all ages and, in part, because marriage patterns over a period of years affect the proportions of single persons in ways that are not taken account of in ratios that include all persons regardless of marital status. However, the apparent discrepancy is being made the subject of further study.

6 Furthermore, to the extent that poverty and unfavorable health conditions are deterrents to initial marriage or remarriage, the reduction of poverty and the improvement of health conditions in the future should increase the proportion who marry and the proportion who remarry. Available statistics on the relationship between socioeconomic status, health, and marriage are discussed in a monograph in preparation by Hugh Carter and Paul C. Glick, *Marriage and Divorce: A Social and Economic Study*, forthcoming.

[7] The data are set forth in *1960 Census of Population,* Final Report PC(2)-4B, *op. cit.,* Table 6.

[8] To assert the contrary is to imply extraordinary socioeconomic differences in the mortality of the wives. Suppose that 4.6 percent of the affluent white men were widowed. (This is an average figure based on white female mortality between ages 22 and 47 as given in the 1950 life tables.) Subtracting this figure from the 16.2 percent who were not living with their first wives leaves 11.6 percent as the estimate of unstable marriages. If it be asserted that the same rate of instability characterized the marriages of the poor men, then the implied widowhood rate among these men is given by $28.7 - 11.6 = 17.1$ fhere 28.7 is the percent of ever-married poor men not living with their first wives. The implied mortality of the poor wives is therefore, nearly four times that assumed for the affluent wives. The present writers know of no reason to believe such a figure. The ratio of death rates among wives of the poor to those among wives of the affluent is more likely to be on the order of two to one according to the findings of Hauser and Kitagawa as reported in the *Washington Post,* July 10, 1966, page M3.

[9] *Current Population Reports,* Series P-20, No. 159.

[10] Paul C. Glick, "First Marriages and Remarriages," *American Sociological Review,* 14:6 (December, 1949), p. 733.

[11] A household is all the occupants of a housing unit and may consist of one person living alone, a family and any lodgers, a few persons sharing an apartment, etc. A family consists of two or more related persons living in the same household.

Some Speculations as to the Family's Future

ROBERT F. WINCH

In my family textbook I have presented an analysis of the family as a social system within the larger societal system. According to this analysis the major function that the family fulfills for the society is to replace human beings lost through death, i.e., the function of replacement. Some call it the reproductive function. In most societies, of course, the family carries out other functions that are corollaries of its function and structure. Because of its function of replacement the family usually fulfills what I call the socializing-educational function and also the position-conferring function. The first of these is quite obvious. The second refers to the fact that the family ascribes to each member a position in the society *because* of his membership in the family. Some speak of this as the status-conferring function. Because of its structure as a primary group, moreover, the family has also the function of providing emotional gratification and security.

As we try to see what is happening to the family it is in order to keep these functions in mind, i.e., the functions of replacement, of socialization and education, of position-conferring, and of emotional gratification.

Now what changes can we observe? One of the more interesting is the variation that takes place with respect to the family's prime function —replacement. The index is, of course, the birth rate. Here we are dealing with a phenomenon that fortunately is measurable. What we know is that there has been a long-run decline from say, 1800 to the middle 1930's, a gradual rise to the end of World War II, a sharper rise to 1950, a sizable but less marked rise to the latter 1950's, and then a very considerable decline so that the crude birth rate today is about back to depression levels. I understand from the demographers that it is too early to interpret the meaning of these data. The decline of the birth rate may merely represent a shift in age at first marriage and a shift in interval between marriage and first birth. On the other hand, it may mean something more significant, such as fewer births to ever-

Excerpted from Robert F. Winch, "Permanence and Change in the History of the American Family and Some Speculations as to Its Future," in *Journal of Marriage and the Family,* February 1970. Footnotes have been renumbered.

married women, lower marriage rates, and an increase in the proportion of childless women.

To the extent that it may augur more childless women and fewer marriages, the datum has profound significance for the future of the family, for it would seem to foreshadow an increase in what Carle Zimmerman has called the "atomistic" family, which he saw as the precursor to the fall of the civilizations of ancient Greece and Rome and also of the West.[1]

Related to the birth rate is another trend that seems to have import for the future of the family. This is the development of ever more efficient means of contraception. To be sure, there is evidence that some of the most widely used contraceptives today may have serious side-effects, but the prospect of a completely efficient, easy means without any side-effects seems likely to be a matter of no more than another decade or so. Such a contraceptive will probably be effective for at least a fortnight or perhaps a month, and in any case will eliminate the need for application at the time of the sex act. Then we shall have arrived at the point where sexual activity may be readily classified into procreation and recreation.

There seems to be a disposition on the part of some sociologists and demographers to think of contraception—no matter how efficient it may be—as constituting a variable of merely instrumental or intervening significance—as compared, say, with the level and mode of subsistence—and hence not very important for sociological analysis. To me, however, it seems that the prospect of an easy, efficient, readily accessible, inexpensive, and safe contraceptive—especially if used by the woman—is a development of critical significance for it truly provides a basis for distinguishing between procreational and recreational sex. Let us assume that such a procedure is developed in the next few years. What would follow?

The rational basis for a society's prohibition of heterosexual intercourse outside marriage has to do with the consequences of such intercourse because many societies—probably most societies—do not have suitable provisions for raising children born out of wedlock. As unwanted pregnancies would become rare to non-existent, the society would lose the basis of its interest in trying to control such behavior. Then—with some cultural lag—the strength of legal and moral sanctions against extra-marital intercourse would weaken. Such a change in norms seems to be happening now. Although moral sanctions have not disappeared, it does seem correct to say that they have loosened in the past century. And we hear that the younger generation is critical of the cultural lag and speaks of the remaining moral sanctions as hypocrisy. The first consequence of the development of an efficient contraceptive and widespread access to it, then, would seem to be a disappearance of moral and legal sanctions against extra-marital sex.

It would appear that there should be four other consequences.

First, there should be some decline in the marriage rate. In part this decline would come from those who would no longer enter marriage primarily to have a socially acceptable sexual liaison, and in part the decline in the marriage rate would come from those who would no longer get married to give respectability to an unintended pregnancy and to legitimize the issue thereof. Second, there should be some decline in the birth rate for unwanted pregnancies would virtually cease to exist.[2] Although the first two of these consequences are negative, the other two are positive. The third consequence I foresee is that those who get married would be doing so for more exclusively positive reasons— because of the strength of the man-woman relationship and/or the desire to raise children. And the fourth consequence would be that there would be far fewer children who are rejected even before they are born. (Given the costs and frustrations of parenthood and the feelings such considerations may generate, perhaps it would be more correct to say only that virtually all children would be wanted at the moment of conception.)

Another trend that seems nearly as clear-cut as trends in the birth rate has to do with the degree of differentiation of sex-roles. Elsewhere I have proposed that there are at least two conditions that tend to maximize the degree of differentiation of sex-roles. These have to do with the importance of the society of activities that require: (1) strenuous physical exertion and strength, and/or (2) absence from home and spatial mobility. Since we are a "high-energy" society and are becoming more so all the time, the importance of masculine strength has diminished greatly. This is of course implied in the high proportion of our labor force engaged in white-collar occupations. Since we have highly developed transportation systems (except for the purpose of getting into and out of our major cities), the importance of spatial mobility as leading to protracted absence has been reduced. From these considerations it follows that we have been minimizing the conditions that I believe generate a high degree of sex-role differentiation.

Although it is still possible to classify most of this audience by gender at a glance—or at least it appears so from the platform—we are all aware of the disposition among our youth to play down features of sexual differentiation in their self-presentations. This disposition has been captured in the expression of "unisex" to refer to some current styles of dress.

What has this drift toward de-emphasizing the difference between the sexes to tell us about the future of the family? One element is that women are continuing to enter the occupational system in an increasing proportion. If the falling birth rate and the rising divorce rate do presage real rather than merely apparent trends, the decrease in differentiation of sex-roles is undoubtedly desirable for it would then appear that an ever increasing proportion of women would be called upon to support themselves.

What does the reduction of sex-role differentiation mean for the organization of the household? Does it mean that an increasing proportion of husbands will be complaining of dishwater hands? Or of back-strain from bending over to place dirty dishes in the electric dishwasher? It is uncertain whether or not the experience of Communist urban populations constitutes an enlightening precedent, but to the extent that it does, the answer would appear to be "no." The impression one gets from articles on the urban family in the eastern European countries is that there is an expectation that women who are wives and mothers will be employed, that these women have thought that their employment outside the home would result in an increase in the participation of their husbands in domestic chores, and that these women appear disappointed and grossly overworked when the husbands refused to do so.[3]

The kibbutzim of Israel seem also to offer some hints here. As you know, kibbutzim such as the one described by Spiro were founded on the philosophy that women should be freed from the chains of the family. Accordingly, the women were assigned jobs along with the men; and cooking, dishwashing, driving tractors, and digging in the fields were initially assigned to members of the kibbutzim without regard to sex.[4] Gradually, however, there seems to have been some reversion to a more traditional sex-linked division of labor.[5]

Of course there is a hazard in basing predictions about the American family on either of these examples because our conditions are quite different, but both of these examples do suggest that we may be in a swing of the pendulum from which we shall presently be returned toward a norm that will give increasing emphasis to the differences between the sexes.

What has been happening to the function of socializing and educating the young? The most conspicuous trend has been toward an increase in the degree of responsibility assumed by government at all levels. To the degree that it becomes a tenet of national policy to try to create equality of opportunity for all, it seems evident that this tendency will continue. Public support seems likely to embrace more nursery schools and day-care nurseries. Given the sky-rocketing cost of private institutions of higher learning, moreover, it seems likely that the state will begin to provide relief for middle-income parents of college students. As the state does this—or if the state does this—there is of course an implication for the position-conferring function of the family. In their study of the American occupational system Blau and Duncan point out that the prime importance of the family with respect to the position-conferring function is that the socioeconomic level of the family has so much to do with the amount of education that the offspring receives, and of course the level of the offspring's education has much to do ultimately with the kind of job the offspring holds and the amount of income he receives.[6] Hence to the degree that the state succeeds in equalizing educational opportunities, it will thereby reduce the importance of the family in conferring position on its children. It should be noted also that to the degree that women do pursue their own careers, they become less dependent upon their husbands for socioeconomic status. At this point, then, the statuses of all family members—husband, wife, and offspring—cease to be ascribed by the family and become achieved, first in the educational arena and ultimately in the occupational system.

I have deferred until last, consideration of the function of emotional gratification because its destiny seems more derivative and hence more problematic than seems true of the other functions. As you may have noted from the foregoing remarks, this analysis sees the likelihood of change only in the direction of reduction with respect to the familial functions of replacement, position-conferring, and socialization-education. This presents a situation similar to that commented upon by Ogburn some forty years ago—the decline of the other functions and at least *a relative* increase in the importance of affection, or of emotional gratification.[7] It is not a logical necessity that even the relative importance of emotional gratification must increase when the others decline since it is conceivable that this too could be fulfilled in increasing degree in other relationships outside the family. But if the importance of the other functions *is* to continue to decrease, then it seems inescapable that if the nuclear family is to maintain its present strength, the importance of emotional gratification will have to increase, absolutely as well as relatively.

Unfortunately the quality of familial love, which is the basis of emotional gratification, is a most elusive phenomenon. I am aware of no longitudinal data on this matter. The widespread view that the "generation gap" has never been wider is relevant, for it suggests that many dissident adolescents are getting their emotional gratification from extrafamilial relationships. But we have no quantitative data to inform us as to the proportion of the adolescent generation of which this is true.

With respect to the marital relationship it seems to me that there is one important question that bears on the future of the function of emotional gratification in the family. I have remarked that easy and efficient contraception makes feasible the distinction between procreational and recreational sex, and that such conditions reduce the society's interest in the sex act *per se*. It follows that there should be a relaxation of sanctions against, and an increasing acceptance of, sexual relations outside marriage. And of course this is apparently happening. To my knowledge there has been no study of the consequences of this for the marital relationship. The uncertainty I see in trying to make a prediction here has to do with the degree to which we continue to believe that sexual attraction culminating in sexual intercourse is integrally and indissolubly linked to marital love. If we interpret the conditions mentioned as becoming increasingly permissive with respect to extra-marital sex and if the sex = love conviction continues, then it seems clear that an increasing proportion of marriages will be ruptured because of jealousy and feelings of rejection. On the other hand, if the belief develops that sex is separable, then sex is, to be sure, somewhat downgraded, and an increase in extra-marital sex has less bearing on the stability of marriages.

This has been a far-reaching if sketchy survey of the family—from hunting and gathering societies to urban-industrial America, from early American families to contemporary familial types and even to some speculations about the near future of the family in this country. Let me try to summarize.

From the studies of Goode and of Nimkoff and Middleton we have hypothesized that very low and very high levels of societal complexity tend to foster small-family organization. Settled agriculture, collectively owned land, and the use of the family as the unit of labor tend to foster large-family organization.

We know that American families have lived under a great variety of circumstances—freedom and slavery; frontier, ranch, farm, village, city, ghetto, and suburb; in poverty, comfort, and riches; in sacred ethos and secular ethos. Ethnographic studies give us cues that familial structures have also varied, but precise information is elusive. From historical statistics we can only reconstruct measures of central tendency. From such measures it would appear that the average American domestic family has always been nuclear. The major change to be learned has to do with the number of children in households at any one time, which seems to have shrunk by about two over the 170 or so years covered by the records.

We undertook to identify contemporary structural types of American families by means of two dimensions of analysis: completeness versus incompleteness of the nuclear family, and isolation of the nuclear family versus extended familism. As a result we found a majority pattern of the embedded nuclear family, and two minority patterns—the isolated nuclear family, and the mother-child family, sometimes with matrilineal extension.

Scrutiny of the functions of the contemporary American family suggests that it is reducing the level of its reproductive function, and that the various levels of government will probably continue to take over more and more of the function of socializing and educating the young. This, plus the entry of more married women into the labor force as the differentiation of sex-roles diminishes, seems to suggest a reduction of the family's position-conferring function.

And I have ventured an interpretation that our increasingly permissive attitude to sex outside marriage is related to increasingly accessible and efficient contraception, and that consequences of this trend will probably be reductions in the rates of marriage, birth, and conceivably of divorce, and that there will be an increase in the proportion of those who make an affirmative and voluntary undertaking of marriage and of parenthood.

NOTES

[1] Carle C. Zimmerman, *Family and Civilization* (New York: Harper & Row, 1947).

[2] According to data from the National Fertility Study—based on interviews in 1960–1965 with about 4,800 married women under 45 in the United States—one-sixth of all births and nearly one-third of black births were reported as unwanted by both spouses; one-fifth of all births and two-fifths of black births were reported as unwanted by at least one spouse. Larry Bumpass and Charles F. Westoff, "The Perfect Contraceptive Population: Extent and Implications of Unwanted Fertility in the United States," unpublished manuscript, 1970.

[3] H. Kent Geiger, *The Family in Soviet Russia* (Cambridge: Harvard University Press, 1968), pp. 55–60.

[4] Melford E. Spiro, *Kibbutz: Venture in Utopia* (Cambridge: Harvard University Press, 1956).

[5] Yonina Talmon, "The Family in a Revolutionary Movement—The Case of the Kibbutz in Israel," in M. F. Nimkoff (ed.), *Comparative Family Systems* (Boston: Houghton Mifflin, 1965), pp. 259–286, espy. pp. 272–273.

[6] Peter M. Blau and Otis Dudley Duncan, *The American Occupational Structure* (New York: Wiley, 1967), chap. 9.

[7] *Cf.* 2 supra.

Biological Discoveries and the Future of the Family: A Reappraisal*

M. F. NIMKOFF

A little over a decade ago, I advanced the thesis that discoveries in human biology are potentially more significant for the social psychological aspects of family life than are technological developments.[1] Biological discoveries are more proximate or direct in their influence on the family because they change the internal environment of man—that is, man's constitution. Technological innovations change the external environment and only indirectly affect the internal environment.

This fact notwithstanding, social scientists have paid more attention to technological changes. They have done so in part presumably because technological changes are more visible, and up to now, have been more extensive than biological discoveries. But an additional reason is that, because of occupational bias, sociologists are not so familiar with developments in human biology and tend to overlook or underestimate the internal environment of man.

When, in 1950, I advanced the thesis I have stated, I took an inventory of several promising lines of development in the biochemistry of sex and reproduction. Now, a little over a decade later, it seems appropriate and worthwhile to take another inventory, to see what progress has been made and what we can learn about factors in social change, with special reference to the family.

In 1950, there was considerable interest in the prospect for a physiological means of contraception. In that year James Conant, former President of Harvard University, in an address before the American Chemical Society, predicted that in ten years an effective contraceptive would be developed which could be taken as a supplement to the diet. This prediction was accurate, and the contraceptive pill is now a reality. We can see now that this prophecy was based on accurate knowledge of two factors: the cultural base and the social demand. Conant correctly saw that there was a sufficient base of existing knowledge of the reproductive process to warrant optimism regarding the additional discovery that had to be made; and he correctly estimated

Reprinted from M. F. Nimkoff, "Biological Discoveries and the Future of the Family: A Reappraisal," *Social Forces*, Vol. 41, No. 2 (December 1962), with permission of the University of North Carolina Press.

the social demand for such a discovery. Absence of demand for an innovation is a retarding factor, as is the lack of a sufficient body of accumulated knowledge.

As to the demand for a more effective contraceptive, the social climate in recent decades has become more favorable because of the sexual revolution resulting from such influences as the increasing emancipation of women and the impact of the work of Freud and Kinsey and their followers. It is a far cry from the early days of stubborn opposition to birth control in the United States, highlighted by the arrest and jailing of Margaret Sanger, to the Planned Parenthood Clinics that now dot our land, the current widespread discussion of birth control in mass circulation journals, and the availability on our news stands of authoritative pocket books on birth control.

For some time, government in the United States has supported birth control, especially in the South at the state level although not yet at the federal level. But the national governments of other lands are backing such a program: Scandinavia for some time, England and Japan more recently, and India and Pakistan more recently still. The impetus in the Far East is the so-called population explosion, and in Europe, the extension of the democratic principle.

Also it may be surmised that the opposition from religious sources has been diminishing, not at the formal level but at the informal. The doctrines of the Roman Catholic Church regarding contraception may not change but there is evidence of diffusion of contraceptive practices among Catholics. It is perhaps symbolic that a prominent figure in the development of the steroid pill, Enovid, was Dr. John Rock, a Catholic.

The steroid pill is not the last word in physiological control of conception but only the first word. The reproduction cycle is complex and may be amenable to control at a number of stages of the cycle. An extensive program of research is underway, under such notable auspices as the Population Council. A realistic possibility in the future is a contraceptive vaccine which would provide immunity for an extended period of time. The immunity must, however, be reversible.

As to the social effects of the innovations in contraceptives, it may be noted that the improvements in contraception are mainly a matter of degree of control, safety, convenience, and economy. There are other choices open to potential users, some rooted in hoary tradition. Indeed, there is evidence that the reduction in the birth rate in Sweden in the 1930's was accomplished by the use of folk methods, without benefit of modern contraceptives. The import of these remarks is to indicate that where innovations are matters of degree of improvement, they will not —all things equal—have as much social impact or significance as where innovations introduce entirely new elements, where the choice is between all or nothing. Immunization against conception is in this regard vastly different from immunization against typhoid. It is important to note also that a variation in degree of control can have significant social consequences. An inexpensive, reversible contraceptive vaccine would of course greatly facilitate the attack of certain nations on their population problem. It would also not be without influence on marital relations.

Potentially more revolutionary in its social effects than an improved contraceptive would be the knowledge of how to control the sex of the child, for at present we have no substitute for such knowledge. As to demand for it, we have in many cultures a strong preference for males. One of my graduate students, from Iraq, tells me that in his country the displeasure over the birth of girls may be reflected in the names they are given, such as Unwanted One and Allah's Displeasure. So strong is the preference for males in some cultures that when the family lacks a male child, the problem is solved by adoption. Only a male heir can say the prayers for the departed, and such prayers are necessary for salvation. In the United States, parents may prefer boys, in part because boys —and not girls—preserve the family name, in which there may be pride. Margaret Mead[2] believes most American parents would like a balanced family of boys and girls but probably prefer that the first born be a boy. If so, they would welcome control over the sex of the child, if it could be had.

Even so, there is considerably less demand for sex control than for birth control, and this difference in demand is reflected in the appreciably small effort which scientists are making in the field of sex control. A decade ago a promising advance in our knowledge in this field was provided by Newton Harvey with his discovery of the fact that the X and Y chromosomes differed in the size and density. It has long been favored theory that the sex of the child depends on these chromosomes, a combination of X's producing a female and a combination of X and Y a male. Since the female sex cell consists only of X chromosomes, the sex of the child is determined by the father on the basis of chance, depending on whether an X or Y chromosome of the spermatazoa combines with the X chromosome of the ovum. Harvey's discovery of a difference in size and density of the X and Y chromosomes led him to speculate that the two types of spermatazoa might be separated by a special centrifuge, roughly in the way in which cream is separated from milk. I checked with Professor Harvey some years later and learned that he had not continued his interest in this problem but had turned his attentions to a very different field, luminescence. Professor Harvey has since died and recent word from his widow, who is also a scientist of note, is to the effect that neither he nor she ever did anything more with the problem of sex control.

Since Harvey's studies, the X chromosome has been found to be three times larger than Y. Thus the human female cell is about 4 percent greater than the male in chromosome volume.[3] The female cell has a substantially richer genetical capacity than the male, and one may speculate as to whether this contributes to the female's greater longevity. The fact that the female generally outlives the male is an important reason why there are many more widows than widowers, with serious consequences for family life.

Some work has gone forward in this field on the part of persons interested in animal husbandry, where the demand for sex control has an economic or pecuniary value and where there are no mores to worry about. Knowledge gained in connection with experimental animals often has value for human beings. A promising technique of separating X and Y sperms, reported since my inventory of 1950, involves electrical charge. The control of sex ratio in rabbits by electrophoresis is based on the fact that Y sperms will migrate to the cathode and X sperms to the anode with approximately 80 percent accuracy, as determined from the sex of offspring. This process requires artificial insemination.[4] The same researcher comments on the work of others in which the migration of human sperm was noted under elertrophoresis, but without progeny testing, for obvious practical reasons. Another process of separating X and Y chromosomes is counter steaming centrifugation. Used with the spermatozoa of bulls, it has led to an alteration in bovine sex ratio, apparently resulting from the differential destruction of X-bearing sperm in the process of centrifugation.[5]

The most exciting new report regarding control of human sex is that of Dr. Landrum Shettles, Columbia Presbyterian Medical Center, New York. He has discriminated two morphologically distinct groups of human spermatazoa, about equal in number, using a phase-contrast microscope. The differences, which include a contrast of smaller rounded heads and larger oval ones, are clearly discernible in a color photograph in the citation given below.[6] Although it is not yet possible to assign X and Y status to the sperm groups and thus identify them for artificial insemination, this seems a likely development in the near future.

When the identification and separation of X and Y spermatazoa is accomplished, artificial insemination will have to be utilized if sex control is to be achieved. This will pose a problem for the mores. Artifical insemination, a rather simple technical process, is now employed without objection in certain cases of sterility. But considerable opposition to artificial insemination exists where donors are involved. The moral problems in sex control are different from those in insemination with donors, and it will take time to work them out. Developments in biological science are often ahead of the mores. The period during which the moral issues are raised, debated, and settled, may be a rather lengthy period. Lacking a specific societal directive, the scientists may take the matter into their own hands and utilize the new skills if they are convinced that these procedures contribute to the health and happiness of their patients. Doctors tend to take an instrumental rather than an ethical view of scientific advances. This probably accounts for the number of inseminations utilizing donors—a number thought to be considerable although no accurate figure is available.

A decade ago, beginnings had been made in the preservation of human spermatazoa by freezing. Possible developments here are in the nature of the case limited, but improvements have been made in the decade in the conditions of preservation which increase the percentage of viable cells. A decade ago, physicians reported that they had inseminated three women using stored spermatazoa. Now, the same physicians report 20 such cases and indicate that no genetic defects have been detected in any of the cases, nor any health problems which can be ascribed to the inseminations.[7]

The knowledge of how to store human male sperm cells bring somewhat closer to realization the dreams of the eugenists—somewhat closer, but not much. Still lacking is the knowledge of how to collect and preserve ova, a much more difficult problem. Even more important, we still do not know much about human heredity, what traits are desirable, and how they are carried and transmitted. If all the technical knowledge were available, there would still remain the question whether men and women in a democratic society would look with favor on relinquishing individual control over the process of reproduction in the interest of eugenic ideals.

The eugenic ideal may be remote, but the knowledge of how to preserve male spermatazoa, presumably indefinitely, has some immediate societal utility. It provides a safeguard where the sterilization of the male is practiced, should the couple at a later date wish to have children. In a nuclear age it offers insurance against the effects of irradiation, particularly in the case of men whose work exposes them to special risk.

No review of the biochemistry of sex and reproduction is complete without reference to the sex hormones. A decade ago it was possible to report a substantial body of knowledge in this field. A great deal of success was reported in modifying the secondary sexual characteristics of males and females. The increase in knowledge in this field has continued although no major break-through seems to have occurred. Doctors now recommend that steroid support be given when the individual reaches the climacteric.[8] This is not a panacea but is often beneficial. The administration of androgenic steroid to aged men has resulted in some restoration of muscle tone.[9] Female sex hormones, given to a group of women 75 years old, led to improvements in intellectual functions.[10] In another group, oral androgen improved memory on some tests.[11] On the negative side, treating pregnant women with progestins led to harmful masculinizing effects on 18 female babies. The experimenters recommend that such treatment be abandoned.[12]

The relative lack of major developments in the area of sex hormones, at least so far as hormonal therapy or practical aspects are concerned, is not perhaps so much the result of diminished attention to the problems of this field as it is to a scientific impasse. If I may digress, such impasses are not uncommon in natural science where many workers may labor hard and long on a problem without much success until someone comes up with a serendipitous discovery which opens up new possibilities. The phenomenon of the impasse is not to be confused with the problem of discontinuity which is also a common factor affecting the pace of discovery. There are discontinuities as well as impasses in natural science, as I have shown in connection with the problem of controlling the sex of the child. But it is my impression that impasses are more common than discontinuities in natural science, and that discontinuities are more common than impasses in sociology. I am very much impressed by the discontinuities in research in the field of the family. I am struck by the fact that since the pioneer work of Burgess-Cottrell and Burgess-Wallin, there have been, except for Burgess' own continuing work, no major follow-up studies; so far as I can determine, no one else but E. Lowell Kelly has administered prediction schedules and then followed them through to see the extent to which the test actually did predict marital adjustment. Much the same thing has happened to Winch's theory of complementary needs in mate selection; that a little has been done with it since his research was published although it is a promising and intriguing theory. Why there should be so much discontinuity in sociological research compared to biological research is an interesting question.

The final area of biological research to be reassessed pertains to geriatrics. Anyone reviewing this field must be impressed by the prodigious growth of interest in it. The literature in the decade is voluminous, and the amount of researches committed is very large. It is estimated that in 1960 the expenditure of over 16 billion dollars was administered by the Federal Government alone in providing services and benefits for older people.[13] Most of the amount involves income maintenance programs (old-age and survivors insurance, retirement systems, veterans compensation, and the like), requiring 19 of every 20 dollars. Such services are not the concern of this paper, but the scope of the economic programs is an indication of the social demand. Expenditures for health and medical care in the United States in 1958–59 mounted to 25.2 billion dollars, of which less than 5 percent was spent for research.[14] The fact that there is available an estimate of 16 billion dollars as the amount administered by the Federal Government in behalf of older people in 1960 is interesting in itself, for on inquiry to the Children's Bureau and the Women's Bureau I learned that no comparable estimates have been made as to federal expenditures for children and women. On April 9, 1962 the Children's Bureau celebrated its fiftieth birthday. The Women's Bureau was established later, in 1920. There is at present no comparable autonomous, independent bureau for the aged, but bills have been introduced in Congress to establish one. The aged are riding the wave of the future. If Ellen Key was right in calling the first half of the twentieth century the Children's Century, it may turn out to be appropriate to call the second half the Century of the Aged.

Why the increased accent on the health needs of the aged? For one thing, they constitute an increased proportion of our population. In 1940, there were 9 million persons in the United States 65 years old and over, comprising 6.9 percent of the total population. In 1960, the number exceeded 16.5 million, or 9.2 percent of the total. Incidentally, the average age of the aged population has increased. So also has the percentage of women among the aged, the figure being 55 in 1960. More important from the standpoint of political influence, the aged as a proportion of the voting population (21 years old and over) has increased from 10.7 in 1940 to 15.4 in 1960. This is a significant point when considering the shift in national interest from children to old people, for the aged are voters and the children are not.

Also affecting the shift in demand is the fact that the medical needs of the aged are paramount. The diseases of old age are many but the principal ones are the so-called degenerative diseases, mainly cancer, degeneration of the blood vessels, arthritis, and nervous and mental disorders. There are 900,000 deaths a year in the United States caused by cardiovascular disease; 260,000 deaths from cancer. Arthritis and rheumatism afflict 11 million, including an estimated 97 percent of persons over 60.[15] It is difficult, of course, to delimit the diseases of old age, for they extend downward into the earlier years and even into childhood.

The progress in the last decade in dealing with degenerative diseases has not been impressive. There have been biological-medical advances pertaining to all stages of the life span, but the most notable progress has been made in coping with infections and nutritional disorders, having the greatest impact on the earlier years of life. Some saving of life of cancer patients has resulted from early detection and treatment, but there has not been a major break-through in the last decade comparable to the conquest of poliomyelitis. An extraordinarily comprehensive study of six years duration has demonstrated that blood lipid elevation does precede heart attacks rather than the reverse. The association between serum cholesterol and the incidence of atherosclerosis has thus been established. But whether diet is a factor in control has not been established and is a medical policy taken on faith.[16] As to the third major disease of old age, steroid drugs reduce the pain of rheumatoid arthritis but offer no cure.

Although the biological gains in terms of specific cures have not been spectacular in the decade, the progress in other terms is not inconsiderable. For one thing, in general old people today are in better health than in the immediate past, which means they are more capable of being useful and are not so long an economic burden.[17] For another thing, the progress that is occurring in the biochemistry of man is at a basic, theoretical level which may not pay off in control immediately, or very soon, but offers great prospect for success in the future. The greatest achievement in scientific medicine in 1959 is said to have been made in the chemistry of genetics, pertaining to such discoveries as the synthesis of

DNA and RNA.[18] DNA is the substance that controls vital activities in all living cells. It is found in the nuclei of cells and acts as a blueprint for making enzymes and other proteins. The DNA molecule consists of two long strands of atoms twisted together, resembling a spiral staircase. Between the strands, like steps in a staircase, are hundreds of smaller groups called bases. Only four types of bases have been found and their particular arrangement along the DNA molecule is believed to be the code containing the information on heredity. When a cell divides, DNA is duplicated so that both new cells receive a complete "set of instructions."[19] For the first time, in 1960, the exact spot affected by a mutation, or change in heredity, was pinpointed. The discovery was made in the tobacco mosaic virus, and the mutations were identified as tiny loops in molecules of DNA.[20]

The growing knowledge of the chemistry of the DNA, and the knowledge of the location of the genes that are involved in inherited disease combine to give an optimistic picture of the future of research in human heredity. With our current interest in man's chromosomes, mutations, and genes, a leading student of medical genetics has predicted that progress in that field will occur at a much faster rate than that at which the medicine of communicable diseases has advanced. To reach our present position in preventive medicine where many diseases are virtually controlled, it has taken about one hundred years. According to Professor Kloepfer, it will take much less time before we reach a comparable position in the control of genetic disease.[21]

To conclude, our review of developments in the biochemistry of man during approximately the last decade shows great progress in birth control, promising although much slower achievement in sex control, an intermediate degree of control of sex characteristics in hormonal therapy and of the biological problems of aging. In all these fields, there is no major problem of opposition from the mores, rather, American society is favorable to more biological research. The uneven progress in the several areas is partly the result of uneven difficulty in coping with the problems involved and partly the result of uneven demand. The simplest scientific problem is that of birth control; somewhat more difficult from a theoretical standpoint is the problem of the control of the sex of the child; and much more complex are the problems of the control of aging and of sexual characteristics. As to social demand, that for control over the process of aging is probably greatest; that for an improved contraceptive is considerable; that for increased control over sex characteristics is less; and that for control over the sex of the child is least. The greatest control, then, has been achieved in contraception where the scientific problems are the simplest and the demand is great. For the long pull, however, the greater promise lies in fundamental research. It is intriguing to speculate upon what another review a decade hence may show as to the nature of the living cell and the location of the genes which control the constitution of man.

NOTES

* Presidential Address, Southern Sociological Society, April 13, 1962, Louisville, Kentucky.

[1] M. F. Nimkoff, "Biological Discoveries and the Future of the Family," *American Journal of Sociology*, 58 (1951), pp. 20–26. Presidential Address, Eastern Sociological Society, Boston, April 12, 1950.

[2] *Male and Female* (New York: William Morrow, 1949), p. 264.

[3] J. H. Tjio and T. T. Puck, "The Somatic Chromosomes of Man," *Proceedings of the National Academy of Sciences* (December 1958), p. 1229.

[4] M. J. Gordon, "Control of Sex Ratio in Rabbits by Electrophoresis of Spermatazoa," *Proceedings of the National Academy of Sciences*, 43 (1957), pp. 414–18.

[5] P. E. Lindahl, "Separation of Bull Spermatazoa Carrying X- and Y-Chromosomes by Counter Steaming Centrifugation," *Nature*, 181 (1958) p. 784.

[6] Robert Demarest, "Sperm Shape and Sex of Offspring," *What's New* (a trade journal of Abbott Laboratories, North Chicago, Illinois), number 225 (August–September 1961), pp. 2–3.

[7] In correspondence of the writer with R. G. Bune, M.D., University Hospitals, University of Iowa, November 27, 1961.

[8] William H. Masters (Washington U. School of Medicine, St. Louis, Mo.) and John W. Balles, "The Third Sex," *Geriatrics*, 10 (1955), pp. 1–4.

[9] The work of Dr. Gregory Pincus, Worcester Foundation for Experimental Biology, Shrewbury, Mass., reported in *Science News Letter* (January 9, 1960), p. 19.

[10] Bettye McDonald Caldwell, "An Evaluation of Psychological Effects of Sex Hormone Administration in Aged Women. II: Results of Therapy after Eighteen Months," *Journal of Gerontology*, 9 (1954), pp. 168–174.

[11] V. A. Kral and B. T. Wigdor, "Andreas Effect on Senescent Memory Function," *Geriatrics*, 14 (July 1959), pp. 450–456.

[12] Melvin M. Grumbach, Jacques R. Duchanan and Ralph E. Moloshok, "On the Fetal Masculinizing Action of Certain Oral Progestins," *Journal of Clinical Endocrinology & Metabolism*, 19, pp. 1369–1380.

[13] *Programs for Older People* (1960 Report to the President, Federal Council on Aging), p. 67.

[14] Union Calendar No. 103. 87th Congress, 1st Session. House Report no. 321, pp. 2–3.

[15] *Research in Gerontology: Biological and Medical.* Reports and Guidelines from the White House Conference on Aging. Series Number 10. U.S. Department of Health, Education, and Welfare, Special Staff on Aging, Washington 25, D.C., August, 1961, p. 119.

[16] *Ibid.*, p. 30, 90.

[17] *Ibid.*, p. 20.

[18] *Science News Letter* (January 16, 1960), p. 38.

[19] *Science News Letter* (April 30, 1960).

[20] *Science News Letter* (December 17, 1960), p. 407.

[21] Dr. H. Warner Kloepfer, Professor of Medical Genetics, Tulane University Medical School reported in *Science News Letter* (June 27, 1959), p. 403.